Comparing Prison Systems

INTERNATIONAL STUDIES IN GLOBAL CHANGE

Edited by **Tom R. Burns**, Uppsala University, Sweden
Thomas Dietz, George Mason University, Fairfax, Virginia, USA

This book series is devoted to investigations of human ecology, technology and management and their interrelations. It will include theoretical and methodological contributions to the analysis of social systems and their transformation, technology, risk, environmental problems, energy and natural resources, population growth, public health, and global economic and societal developments.

This book is part of a series. The publisher will accept continuation orders which may be cancelled at any time and which provide for automatic billing and shipping of each title in the series upon publication. Please write for details.

Comparing Prison Systems

Toward a Comparative and International Penology

Edited by

Robert P. Weiss

State University of New York at Plattsburgh

and

Nigel South

University of Essex, England

Gordon and Breach Publishers

Australia Canada China France Germany India Japan
Luxembourg Malaysia The Netherlands Russia
Singapore Switzerland Thailand

Amsteldijk 166
1st Floor
1079 LH Amsterdam
The Netherlands

Cover art by Craig Alan Johnson.

British Library Cataloguing in Publication Data
.
Comparing prison systems : toward a comparative and
  international penology. – (International studies in global
  change ; v. 8)
  1. Prisons – Cross-cultural studies   2. Imprisonment –
  Cross-cultural studies
  I. Weiss, Robert P.   II. South, Nigel
  365

  ISBN   90-5700-511-5

To

the memory of my mother and father
Maria and *Rudolf Weiss Sr.*

—RPW

my mother *Lily South*
and the memory of my father *Geoffrey South*

—NS

I have been studying how I may compare
This prison where I live unto the world

—Shakespeare, *King Richard II, V.v.1*

CONTENTS

INTRODUCTION TO THE SERIES

This series brings together under one banner works by scholars of many disciplines. All of these researchers have distinguished themselves in their specialities. But here they have ventured beyond the frontiers of traditional disciplines and have developed new, innovative approaches to the study of social systems and social change.

Why? What has prompted this foray into unchartered territory? What is the reason for broadening theoretical perspectives and developing new methodologies? The impetus comes from the world we seek to understand. Scholars have traditionally made "boundary" assumptions that limited their scope of inquiry to the concerns of a discipline. Such limitations facilitate concentration, though they have always been artificial. The interpenetration of social, economic and environmental phenomena, and the precipitous pace of change in the late twentieth century make it clear that such convenient intellectual boundaries are not only unrealistic, they are untenable.

How complex waves of change sweep through the contemporary world, altering the natural environment, technology, the economy and social systems; the interaction of these forces, their impact on nations, communities, families and individuals; and the response to them by individuals and collectivities—this is the focus of the research to be presented in this series. The scholars writing in the series are themselves engaged in social change—the restructuring of our way of thinking about the world.

In this pioneering work, Weiss and South bring together the world's leading experts to provide the first truly global and comparative examination of prison systems. The book provides systematic analysis with a breadth and depth never before available. It demonstrates that prisons are being shaped by both globalization

and by the persistent influence of national culture and institutions.
Further, the editors provide an important theoretical synthesis of
current understanding that is sure to guide future debate and
inquiry. This volume will define future comparative work on
imprisonment, and we are very proud to include it in our series.

Tom R. Burns
Thomas Dietz

ACKNOWLEDGMENTS

The editors wish to give special thanks to Rita M. Latour, Sociology Department secretary at SUNY – Plattsburgh, for her expert word processing, skilled manuscript management, and formidable patience—especially at the final stages of production. We also thank editor Carol Hollander and associate editor Janell E. Robisch for their enthusiastic support, even during the most frustrating moments.

Robert Weiss is grateful to Anne E. Rowland for her help in editing several manuscripts and for her encouragement throughout the project. Marek Lyzwinski of the Institute for International Business Education Research and Training, SUNY – Plattsburgh, graciously reinserted Polish diacritics.

Nigel South acknowledges the financial assistance of the Jessie Fuller Bequest Fund, Department of Sociology, University of Essex.

ABOUT THE CONTRIBUTORS

DAVID BROWN teaches criminal law and criminal justice at the University of New South Wales in Sydney, Australia. He has published widely in the fields of criminal law, criminal justice, criminology and penology. His books include (with George Zdenkowski) *The Prison Struggle* (1982); (with David Farrier, David Neal and David Weisbroth) *Criminal Laws* (1990) and (1996); and the co-edited *Judgments of Justice Lionel Murphy* (1986) and *Death in the Hands of the State* (1988). He also has been active in criminal justice social movements and campaigns.

ROSA DEL OLMO received her BA in sociology from the University of Wisconsin, an MA in criminology from the University of Cambridge, and PhD in social sciences from Universidad Central de Venezuela. Currently, she is research advisor, Juridical Sciences Institute, Universidad Catolica, Caracas. Professor del Olmo is also president of Fundacion Jose Felix Ribas, an organization fighting drug abuse problems in Venezuela. Author of 16 books, 21 book chapters, and over 60 scholarly articles, Professor del Olmo was awarded the American Sociological Association's 1984 Latin American Scholar.

DAVID DOWNES is professor of social administration at the London School of Economics, where he is a member of the Mannheim Centre for Criminology. He was editor of the *British Journal of Criminology* from 1985–1990. His books include *The Delinquent Solution* (1966); (with others) *Gambling, Work and Leisure* (1976); (with Paul Rock) *Understanding Deviance* (1982, latest ed. 1995); and *Contrasts in Tolerance* (1988), a comparative study of English and Dutch penal policy.

MICHAEL DUTTON is a senior lecturer in the Department of Political Science, University of Melbourne. He is the author of *Policing and Punishment in China: From Patriarchy to "The People"* (Cambridge, 1992) and is currently working on a history of policing in China.

JOHANNES FEEST studied law in Austria and Germany, graduating from the University of Munich. Professor Feest also holds an MA in sociology from the University of California, Berkeley. He has been professor, Faculty of Law, University of Bremen, since 1974. Dr. Feest's main areas of teaching are criminal procedure, penitentiary law and sociology of law. His empirical research has been on courts, police, prisons and industrial tribunals. Dr. Feest is director of the International Institute for the Sociology of Law, Oñati, Spain (1995–1997).

BOB GAUCHER is an associate professor of criminology at the University of Ottawa in Ontario. He has been involved in prisoners' struggles in Canada for the past 30 years. Currently an editor of the *Journal of Prisoners on Prisons*, Professor Gaucher is developing a "prisoners" standpoint.

ELMER H. JOHNSON received his PhD (1950) from the University of Wisconsin, and taught at North Carolina State University (1949–1966) and Southern Illinois University at Carbondale (1966–1987). He retired in 1987 as Distinguished Professor. Of his numerous articles and several books, his most recent are *Japanese Corrections: Managing Convicted Offenders in an Orderly Society* (1996) and *Criminalization and Prisoners in Japan: Six Contrary Cohorts* (1997).

MARK G. LETTIERE is a PhD candidate in sociology at the University of California at Davis and a researcher with the Center for Inner-City Ethnography at the San Francisco Urban Institute. His research focuses on the criminalization of homelessness and the relationship between imprisonment, homelessness and urban street culture. He is currently teaching sociology at San Quentin Prison.

JOHN LOWMAN is professor of criminology at Simon Fraser University in British Columbia. He has authored or co-authored numerous research reports and essays on prostitution, several articles on punishment and social control, and has co-edited four books. Currently he is an editor of the *Journal of Prisoners on Prisons*.

DARIO MELOSSI, after a long sojourn at the University of California, is now back in Europe. He is based at the School of Law of the University of Bologna, where he teaches sociology of deviance. Professor Melossi is working on the current relationships of "crime" and "punishment" to social exclusion and social control in Europe, in a cross-cultural and historical-comparative mode.

J. MICHAEL OLIVERO received his PhD from Southern Illinois University in 1989. He is currently serving as chair of the Department of Law and Justice at Central Washington University, and he also serves as a consultant to Centro Mexicano Internacional. Dr. Olivero has published several monographs of his research on the Mexican criminal justice system.

MONIKA PŁATEK is on the Law Faculty of Warsaw University. Her research is in the areas of comparative criminal policy, criminology and gender studies. Professor Płatek was a Fulbright Scholar in 1992–1994 and a visiting professor at the Department of Criminal Justice at the University of Illinois at Chicago (1994). She was a Jean-Monnet Scholar (1996).

VINCENZO RUGGIERO received his PhD at the University of Bologna, Italy. He is now based at Middlesex University in London, UK. He has published three books on prisons and has also worked on illicit drugs and the crimes of the powerful. His most recent book is *Organized and Corporate Crime in Europe: Offers That Can't Be Refused* (Dartmouth, 1996).

MICK RYAN is professor of penal politics at the University of Greenwich, London. His most recent book, *Lobbying from Below: INQUEST in Defence of Civil Liberties* (UCL Press, 1996), is an investigation into deaths in prison and police custody. He jointly edited *Western European Penal Systems: A Critical Anatomy* (Sage, 1995).

JOE SIM is professor of criminology in the School of Social Science, Liverpool John Moores University, England. He has authored and edited a number of texts including *Medical Power in Prisons; British Prisons* (with Mike Fitzgerald); *Prisons Under Protest* (with Phil Scraton and Paula Skidmore); and *Western European Penal Systems* (co-edited with Vincenzo Ruggiero and Mick Ryan).

NIGEL SOUTH is reader in sociology and a member of the management committee of the Human Rights Centre at the University of Essex, England. He has published widely on privatization and criminal justice and on drug issues. His current interests include developments in European criminology and arguments for a "green criminology."

DIRK VAN ZYL SMIT is professor of criminology in the Department of Criminal and Procedural Law at the University of Cape Town. He is the author of *South African Prison Law and Practice* (Butterworths, Durban, 1992) and the editor with Frieder Dünkel of *Imprisonment Today and Tomorrow: International Perspectives on Prisoners' Rights and Prison Conditions* (Kluwer, Deventer, 1991). He is currently working on life imprisonment issues and advising the South African government on the rewriting of South African prison legislation in light of the new South African Constitution with its entrenched bill of fundamental rights.

HARTMUT-MICHAEL WEBER studied psychology, graduating from the University of Bonn, and worked several years as a prison psychologist. He has been a professor in the Department of Social Studies, Fachhochschule Fulda since 1977. His teaching areas are criminal justice policy and criminology. He has researched pressure groups, marginalization and criminalization, treatment of prisoners, prediction of dangerousness, life imprisonment and prisoners' rights. Professor Weber is chairperson of the European Committee for the Abolition of Life Sentences.

ROBERT P. WEISS is a professor and former chair of the Sociology Department at SUNY–Plattsburgh. He has published on penal history and the origin and development of private policing organizations. Dr. Weiss has also taught and helped to administer prison education programs in a number of states since 1969.

XU ZHANGRUN is an associate professor of criminal and penal law at the China Political Science and Law University in Beijing. He is one of China's most distinguished scholars in the field of penology, having written widely on the topic, including *Penology* (China Public Security University Press, 1991).

INTRODUCTION

Crime, Punishment and the "State of Prisons" in a Changing World

Nigel South and Robert P. Weiss

> It is necessary to distinguish a trivial from a nontrivial sense of comparative analysis. The latter is concerned with the formulation of unrealized historical possibilities and alternative realities (Schluchter, 1984: xiii).

In his Foreword to Reinhard Bendix's essays on comparative sociology, *Force, Fate, and Freedom* (1984), Wolfgang Schluchter recounts Bendix's professional and personal (as a Jew exiled from his native Germany) concern for historical awareness and action. Overcoming determinism and ethnocentrism in social analysis, according to Bendix, requires that we contrast our realities with other realities through structural-historical analysis. Such an analysis focuses on not only social, economic and political conditions, but also examines cultural forces (what Bendix termed "historical legacies").

From Bendix's perspective, Schluchter (1994: xiii) continues, a "comparative sociology must also begin with universal questions, such as the problem of domination, and with such diachronic schemata as the juxtaposition of tradition and modernity." Bendix's first great comparative study was an examination of work and authority in Russia and the West since the Industrial Revolution. *Comparing Prison Systems* is much less ambitious, but the prison is a useful object of comparison—a fruitful way to get at the universal problem of domination. *Comparing Prison Systems* provides the sociological literature with the basis for comparison of a wide range of differing prison systems over a 20-year period—roughly from around 1975 to 1993–96, the years during which this collection was brought together. If we add in a few years to allow for speculation on trends to the year 2000, then we can describe this collection of essays as providing an international perspective on imprisonment in the last quarter of the 20th century.

The turn of the millennium coincides with profound social, political and economic changes, many of them interconnected, that have had a great impact on imprisonment everywhere. Powerful traditions are in the process of being displaced, most notably in China, Eastern Europe, Latin America and South Africa, where, nevertheless, historical legacies persist. The editors asked 18 scholars of law and social science to provide us with structural and cultural analyses of recent penal change in countries and regions around the world. The chapters in this volume address the features of their respective prison systems in an analytical fashion: They provide rich description, empirical data and also work within some version of a theoretically-informed framework. But no single perspective was proposed or endorsed by the editors, other than asking contributors to approach their task in such a critical and analytical fashion.

In our volume, five great developments bear on the state of imprisonment: (1) the rise of neoconservative politics and neoliberal economics in North America and Western Europe, and the concomitant economic decline, class polarization and fiscal crisis affecting most Western nations; (2) the introduction of a market economy in China; (3) the collapse of the Soviet Union and associated communist regimes of Central and Eastern Europe; (4) a return to civilian rule in most of Latin America, as well as a renewed push by elected officials toward privatization and other neoliberal economic prescriptions for the region, and (5) the fall of the apartheid regime in South Africa.

These macro socio-economic and political events have generated new patterns of crime, protest and repression. Fiscal cutbacks and joblessness in the West have increased youth alienation, giving rise to skinheads, street gangs and neo-Nazi terrorism against minorities in Germany. In South Africa, continuing unemployment and poverty intensify street crime and drug gang activity, presenting a formidable challenge to this new democracy. Growing inequality in Eastern Europe, along with the void left by the breakup of police state apparatuses and ill-defined lines between legitimate capitalist activity and theft and fraud have led to an increase in organized criminal activity. In China, market initiatives have created rural unemployment, value conflict, and an increase in crime everywhere. Intensified suffering in Latin America brought on by privatization and fiscal restraint has provoked agrarian rebellion and a rise in crime. Illegal drug production and marketing activities have become the object of a world-wide drug war. Paradoxically, greater political and economic freedoms have not demonstrably lessened the use of imprisonment nor improved prison conditions. These events have increased the use of law enforcement for political repression by right- and left-wing dictatorships (and democracies) throughout the world, much of it justified as a war against drugs.

In most Western nations, the benign, communitarian bases for informal control, such as family, school and community networks have been eroded by forces of commercialization, privatization and withdrawal of state financial support. Politicians may call for the strengthening of informal controls by invoking nostalgic visions, but they pursue the very kinds of repressive measures of crime control and punishment that undermine the bonds of informal control. They embrace populist "get tough" remedies over good sense and expert advice, and self-servingly court the "law and order" vote. Sometimes they justify crime control as the only road "back to better times." In such a climate of political posturing, repressive measures continue to gain popularity, especially in the West, but also in parts of Eastern Europe and Russia. Yet, harsher criminal legislation, expanded police forces and burgeoning prison populations have done little to change the reality of crime or victimization in any country.

While the focus of criminal justice systems continues to be on the young, the poor and minorities (increasingly termed the "underclass" in Western discourse), white collar and corporate offenses often go unpunished. In most Western criminal justice systems, blacks and other minorities are clearly disproportionately

represented. This is why imprisonment has lost its moral ground-
ing, an irony in an age when politicians of both the right and the
left throughout the West constantly call for the reinforcement of
moral principles in societies. In a recent influential article, Feely and
Simon (1992: 455) suggest that the US is in a transitional period of
penal rationales. The emergence of new discourses, objectives and
techniques they call "the new penology" is neither about punishing
nor about rehabilitating individuals: "It is about identifying and
managing unruly groups...". The authors contrast this "language of
management"—part of an ideology based on technique rather than
values—with other discourses characterizing penal policies, such as
Sweden's language of therapy and rehabilitation and Japan's
emphasis on moral responsibility. But these rationales are under
stress. And, not only in the industrialized world is there uncertainty
of moral compass; the penal systems of South Africa, China, Latin
America and Central and Eastern Europe are all in transition.

SURVEYING OTHER INTERNATIONAL AND
COMPARATIVE STUDIES

The last two decades have seen the appearance of various penal
studies employing different perspectives: cultural, historical, philosophical and sociological. This development is admirable, but as
Norval Morris comments, we still face "an extraordinary need for
research; serious research that provides new knowledge in the area
of incarceration is very scant." The most serious shortcoming is that
we have little cross-cultural knowledge, and the few comparative
studies are regional or ahistorical.

The scholarly and comprehensive bibliography in *Comparative
Criminology* compiled by Beirne and Hill (1991: 101–17) provides 85
annotated references under the heading "Criminal Justice and
Penal Policies." The majority of these studies, however, concern
policing and social control broadly. Only 12 studies appear to be
international or comparative works on prisons and prison systems:
Akers (1977); Bensinger (1984); Bureau of Justice Statistics (1987);
Cooper (1972); Doleschal (1977); Doleschal and Newton (1979);
Downes (1988); Iacovetta (1981); Lynch (1988); Marnell (1972);
Sandhu (1972), and Wicks and Cooper (1979). As is evident from
the small number and the dates of these studies, *comparative* penology remains undeveloped. Where comparative work has recently

begun to expand modestly, it has been through the comparison of regional neighbors. Hence, we see that of the few international collections on prison systems that have recently been published, several have focused on Western Europe (Ruggiero, Ryan and Sim, 1995; Vagg, 1994; Muncie and Sparks, 1991; Downes, 1988) or on countries of Latin America (Salvatore and Aguirre, 1996; Hernández-Cuevas, et al., 1994).

Volumes on European penology by Muncie and Sparks (1991) and accountability among Western European prison systems by Vagg (1994) make arguments for the validity of attempting comparative work, but express caution about generalizing. They then pursue similar agendas for investigation: What is the state of European prisons today? What is the changing nature of accountability? How will the new managerialism affect prison systems? What are the implications of recent political changes, such as East-West reintegration and European enlargement?

A collection edited by Whitfield (1991) on behalf of The Howard League for Penal Reform contains contributions that reflect on the conditions and functioning of individual prisons in England, India, Poland, South Africa, The Netherlands, Nicaragua, Sweden, Mexico, Germany and the US. Published as a tribute to John Howard's social surveys of European prisons, *The State of the Prisons* (1777), these studies are insufficiently critical and non-sociological. Although Non-Governmental Organizations (NGOs) such as Amnesty International, Human Rights Watch and the Howard League for Penal Reform, regularly produce international and national reports examining prison conditions in different countries and political contexts, their work is largely descriptive. This methodology is, of course, the most appropriate for the purposes of the NGOs: to reveal and condemn ill-treatment and torture.

In a comparative effort that attempts to provide a social context in which to place a comparative penology, King and Maguire (1994) have edited *Prisons in Context*, a collection of essays that survey recent developments in a small number of diverse nations (Italy, Russia and the US) alongside international trends such as privatization, increasing racial disproportion and growing numbers of female prisoners. Another essay addresses questions about the comparability of the national and international data. *Western European Penal Systems: A Critical Anatomy*, edited by Ruggiero, Ryan and Sim (1995), is a critical study of the penal systems of eight European countries. The editors highlight several common trends in Western European penal policy and strategy, connecting these commonalities to wider social and political processes.

The most recent approximation of a global study of prisons is *Prisons 2000: An International Perspective on the Current State and Future of Imprisonment* (1996), edited by Roger Matthews and Peter Francis. It provides broad analyses of punishment in the US, Poland and Russia, while other essays focus on ethnic minorities in the UK and foreign detainees in Greece. Key issues of concern to developed nations are taken up in chapters on privatization, less eligibility and women's imprisonment in the UK. Broader in scope than others readers, *Prisons 2000* raises important comparative issues, but still falls short of our aim for a global volume.

Those comparative studies with non-sociological or otherwise restricted orientations include Kaiser (1984) on prison systems and penal laws in Europe, the US and Japan; Hood (1989), which is important but narrowly focused on the death penalty in worldwide perspective and van Zyl Smit and Dünkel (1991), with a particular focus on prisoners' rights and prison conditions. Other globally comparative volumes (Pease and Hukkila, 1990; Johnson, 1983; Clinard and Abbott, 1973) are concerned with comparative crime patterns or international criminology. All of these foci are valuable, but they are not the whole picture. While our volume cannot present "the whole picture" either, we hope that its coverage and the issues it addresses will at least provide a broader portrait of penal systems than has been available heretofore.

TOWARD AN INTERNATIONAL AND COMPARATIVE PENOLOGY

Our effort to create an internationally comparative penology draws on Jon Vagg's (1993) article, which outlines four main approaches taken by recent contributions to comparative work in criminology. Let us briefly review these approaches to locate the approach taken by *Comparing Prison Systems*. Vagg first identifies approaches that attempt "to *link crime trends or problems to common social, economic, or political denominators,* either across a very wide range of countries or within, for example, the third world" (1993: 541–2). If, for "crime trends" we substitute *prison* trends, and add our interest in *dissimilar* as well as common socio-economic, political or cultural denominators, then our collection fits this model. The resulting definition, however, would be rather wide.

The second approach outlined by Vagg, "where the focus is *directly comparative in relation to a particular question and two or three countries,*" as with, for example, Downes (1988), does not apply to our volume. The aims and breadth of this comparative project are simply much larger. The third approach "consists of attempts to *produce broad generalizations and policy recommendations*" (1993: 544). Such studies may, to paraphrase Vagg, have a tendency toward "extraordinary feats of generalization and vague qualification," perhaps "coupled with observations to the effect that the policy problem is much more complex than was originally supposed." Our contributors do not shy away from analysis and critique of policy, and several offer prescriptions for policy change and practice reform. No one, however, is in any doubt about the complexity of penal systems in any context. The concluding chapter of this volume attempts a synthesis and theoretical critique that pulls together the collection, but takes pains to avoid the pitfalls of the third approach that Vagg identifies.

This volume also shares Vagg's fourth model of comparisons based on "*particular regional developments*" like the EU, but, for the most part, we have sacrificed a regional focus for the opportunity to provide a global picture of policy decisions and consequences. Our volume, then, falls across modified versions of Vagg's first, third and fourth categories of comparative endeavor.

The Approach and Scope of Comparing Prison Systems

Working with Vagg's general approaches, our specific aims for this collection were: first, to help identify both common and distinctive problems among penal systems in order to facilitate comparisons among the variety of penal responses; second, to ask "How have changes in social structure affected the theory and practice of penology in particular settings?" A third objective was to allow contributors to explore the future, based on the trends they identify in the present. In other words, we are interested not only in what is, but in what *could* be—a theme echoing our opening quote from Bendix. Briefly, this project invited scholars in various significant sociocultural contexts to produce "state of the art" analyses of their penal systems and patterns of crisis and change.

Ours is a truly international volume, with chapters that cover a total of 16 countries. Some contributors write about their country of residence; others have worked in and written about another

country. Some contributors have the challenge of discussing different penal systems within a single nation-state (e.g., where there are
federal and provincial or state systems). Yet others discuss several
nations within a region. The nations covered are selected from a
variety of major geographic regions. It would be surprising if such a
selection could satisfy everybody and, indeed, there are some countries and areas that we would have liked to include, particularly
Russia and countries within the Middle East. Other countries were
excluded for technical, definitional reasons. The absolute technical
reason for many omissions is, of course, that we simply could not
include all countries. The chapter selection for *Comparing Prison
Systems*, therefore, was partly strategic, partly theoretical, partly
contingent, and it is in the nature of such an endeavor that the editors could not include everything.

To provide a meaningful basis for comparison, we chose to focus
upon the prison systems of societies that could be defined broadly
as "industrial." This is to some extent an argument for a degree of
similarity among countries selected, for it requires a sufficient
degree of "development" to establish and maintain a major prison
system supported by some kind of guiding penology, bureaucracy
of prison administration, law enforcement establishment, judicial
system and explicit politics of penal discourse. This excludes, therefore, certain African nations where prisons may serve less as institutions of a developed criminal justice system and more as
detention camps, often employed for political and tribal ends in
cases of civil war or suppression of opponents, and involving gross
violations of human rights. This nonetheless leaves some regions
on a definitional edge. In the case of Latin America, individual
nations fall in various positions along the continuum of development. To exclude the whole region would have been a serious omis-
sion. Rosa del Olmo provides a particularly useful comparative
chapter in her examination of Colombia, Ecuador, Peru and
Venezuela. China and India are also clearly of immense interest as
advancing and rapidly developing economies, yet they may not be
easily comparable with other nations, either East or West. Hence,
there could be grounds for arguing for their inclusion or their
exclusion in a collection such as this. Our resolution of this problem
again had to be pragmatic—not every nation can be included and
we were able to engage experienced analysts to provide a chapter
on China whereas we could not for India.

The contemporary global significance of the Pacific Rim region
must also find some representation in a collection such as this.

Whatever the relationships between society, culture, economics and penality found in the West, it is important to ask about the nature of such relationships in the countries of change and development in the Pacific Rim. The Pacific Rim includes countries of potentially great interest, on a spectrum including harsh, illiberal regimes and reformist democracies. For those who are interested in the history of colonial subjugation of peoples, the accompanying systems of control and recent post-colonial developments, David Brown's essay on Australia is of great value. Here Australia occupies an interesting position as a southern hemisphere "Western" nation that is also a part of developments in the Pacific Rim. For contrast, we have chosen Elmer Johnson's chapter on Japan to represent the Asian Pacific.

Within our limits of space, we have tried in this collection to incorporate examples of great difference between, and of close similarity among, nations and regions. Of course, even within the range of "similar" nations there will be profound differences and these are interesting also. For example, as post-colonial nations which inherited similar principles in their legal systems, what differences are there between Australia and Canada, with their federal, provincial and state systems?

On Human Rights and Cultural Relativism

One rationale for seeking diversity in our selection (as opposed to seeking roughly similar countries) was to obtain a sample of prison systems across the political continuum, from liberal to authoritarian. Human rights violations may be seen as one index of authoritarianism. As Cohen (1993) has recently observed, human rights issues have been neglected by criminology for far too long. This is a curious situation given that such matters have been central to the study of prisons since the days of John Howard and his contemporary reformers. Nonetheless, poor conditions, ill treatment and unjustifiable regimes have received less prominence or clear identification as matters of human rights violation until recent decades.

Only with the promulgation of international standards, laws and courts of judgment could a body of human rights reference points emerge (Turner, 1993). Even then, cultural and other factors make the deciding of *absolute* standards a difficult task. Morgan and Evans (1994: 141) observe in their review of the structure of the "international mechanisms and inspection agencies" that promote standards for the treatment of prisoners: "In the same way that what is to count as acceptable conditions changes over time in relation to standards and expectations of life in the community at large, so cultural and economic differences between jurisdictions make it especially difficult to agree to common standards and set reform priorities."

In practice, it might be hard to clearly demonstrate the bases for positioning nations across a continuum of repressiveness. For example, The Netherlands, a remarkably liberal country in most respects, has been criticized for the regime adopted in some of its institutions, while South Africa, previously a rigidly authoritarian, segregated society, is moving toward a liberalized penal regime supported by a constitution which is more progressive (at least in intent) toward the rights of the accused and convicted than that of the United States, whose penal regime (along with that of the UK) has moved sharply toward the authoritarian pole in recent penal history. The Japanese prison system superficially seems merely austere, yet once examined beneath the surface, appears to be guilty of various human rights offenses (Human Rights Watch, 1993). In the case of Japan, new difficulties may face the comparative exercise. Without denying the strategic importance and practical desirability of universal standards for human rights, we must also note (even if we do not accept) the significance of cultural relativism, which may make problematic any judgments based solely on Western perceptions of what constitutes undesirable penal practice (Morgan and Evans, 1994).

In his chapter on Japan, there are very good reasons why Elmer H. Johnson takes great pains to emphasize the importance of cultural understanding in approaching Japanese society and institutions. When comparing human rights abuses in prison, how easily does "authoritarian" Japan, which resorts to imprisonment sparingly (relatively speaking), then compare with "liberal" US, which is "among the world leaders" in use of imprisonment (Human Rights Watch, 1993: 247)? Both systems may be unsatisfactory from the vantage point of "universal" standards and expectations concerning human rights, but in practical comparative terms, it is not always easy to compare and contrast on the basis of an abstract notion of authoritarianism.

Even in the former communist states of Eastern Europe and in contemporary China, the ideological and policy purposes of defining prison labor as "rehabilitation" as well as punishment are more complex than sometimes perceived in Western accounts (on Poland, see Płatek; on China, see Dutton and Xu). This is not, of course, by any means intended as an apologist justification for the Gulags (Solzhenitsyn, 1973; Wu, 1992; Wu and Wakeman, 1994; Christie,

1993). It is simply to note that a comparative enterprise can only be misleading if it does not try to understand the internal features of prison systems and the societies that produce them before attempting an external comparison.

Clearly, the study of prisons and punishment must be situated within the contexts of culture and politics. As Morris and Rothman (1995) have argued, the prison reflects the society, and can throw into relief many other institutions and features of the host society. This observation finds renewed expression in a number of recent influential commentaries. Appropriately, then, contributors to *Comparing Prison Systems* have not assumed a mere technical frame of reference (penology). Instead, their chapters relate prison systems to variations in social structure and culture. As Johnson (1983: 9–10) pointed out some years ago:

...comparative studies, regardless of the particular theoretical orientation, test the limits of principles assumed to be of universal validity. Since criminological phenomena are subject to cultural and structural variations, comparative criminology must seek generalizations that fall between universal propositions (applicable as stated to all situations, times, and places) and propositions that hold true under specified conditions (applicable only to specified situations, times, and places that exhibit those conditions).

Thus, the comparative enterprise is not simply, as often perceived, the "positive" exercise of identifying and "ticking off" boxes in a survey of what are the common features of different situations. Rather, it is also a "negative" exercise, illuminating that which is *not*—for various reasons of history, economy, culture or society—at all meaningfully comparable. There is, of course, no international uniformity of prison systems just as there is no uniformity of nations. Some methods of comparison, principally statistical analysis of incarceration rates, attempt to address this problem. The more sophisticated studies can control for many characteristics of prison and criminal justice systems, by manipulating and weighting data on sentencing and admissions, and also factoring in data on crime rates, prosecutions, convictions, and so on, to produce comparable, underlying rates (Lynch, 1988). These can be related to, for example, unemployment rates, political and economic swings, etc. (Box and Hale, 1982; Hale, 1989; Inverarity and McCarthy, 1988). However, such an exercise requires extensive data from a country, usually only available for the more advanced industrialized nations. The scope of our project here is too broad to support such comparative statistical exercises. Instead, our contributors, and the final chapter, aim to tease out and amplify discernible patterns and variations within and across jurisdictions. The conclusion places these patterns and variations within a theoretical comparative framework of economic globalization, with the hope that we have avoided the pitfalls of reductionism and sweeping generalization, and the fallacy of retrospective determinism.

CONCLUSION

The spread of nations that are examined in *Comparing Prison Systems* provides a portrait of prisons and imprisonment on a truly international scale. Given the task of assessing the state of imprisonment in their countries, contributors were asked to put policy developments within the context of recent socio-political events, and to analyze the extent to which ideas about punishment and prisons in the official and unofficial discourses of other countries have affected their penal policy. Finally, contributors were asked to provide "visions of the future."

Emerging Similarities and Dissimilarities Across Nations

We do not wish to anticipate too much further here the contributions that follow, and we also leave the task of synthesis and analysis to the concluding chapter. Nonetheless, it may be useful if we signpost some of the similarities and differences that we see emerging among nations and their penal systems.

Emergent themes based on similarities include: The first and most salient theme in most advanced nations is the politicization of crime, which has led to a hardening line of penal control supported by a "just deserts" philosophy. Nonetheless, we note that the mediating influences of changes in economic success and cuts in welfare services and expenditure are not necessarily clear-cut across our sampled nations. Further, it is no longer simply the political parties of the right who are supporting increased penal austerity and "get tough" sentencing, but now also the middle-ground, left-leaning parties (e.g., the Democrats in the US, the Labour Party in the UK).

A second theme relates closely to the significance that labor market conditions might hold as a domestic barometer of social satisfaction and dissatisfaction, as well as to another great historical rationale for the use of imprisonment, fear of "the Other"—the unwelcome and the marginal on whom labor market dissatisfaction can be blamed. In other words, if there are no jobs, let's blame the "foreigners," the "unentitled," the "unwanted," who "steal our jobs," "our welfare," "our culture," and so on. The question raised here is: How far does recession push nations toward xenophobic and nationalistic appeals to "law and order" and policies of "inclusion" and "exclusion"?

A third theme concerns the use of labor *within* the prison. Some form of work—or its absence—is a key issue in prison systems of every nation, reflecting debates on the purposes of the prison and interpretations of rehabilitation and useful punishment. Variations are, of course, enormous, from the case of China, through the changes in Poland, to new debates about the use of labor in The Netherlands' system. There are also external factors in operation: labor markets, economic impact of subsidized labor, and the penological welfare problem of "less eligibility" as a continuing feature of the punitive and moral discourse about the state and its responsibilities regarding the incarcerated.

A fourth discernible commonality is the growth of managerialism within several systems. Reflecting trends in Western social control aimed at the management of problem populations (Spitzer, 1975; Cohen, 1987) and refined in the late 20th century as the "new penology" of managerialism identified by Feely and Simon (1992), this approach to auditing prison populations and actuarially assessing risk, to better identify and control unruly groups, seems ascendant in the US and UK as well as other jurisdictions.

Fifth, in several European nations there has developed a dual policy in regard to imprisonment, with only the most "severe" felony cases going to prison, but for a longer sentences. This trend in "selective incapacitation" naturally has variations and exceptions, notably in the US.

Sixth, there is a proliferation of maximum security units and establishments. This phenomenon, noted by most contributors to this volume, clearly signals a trend in the globalized "hardening" of penal philosophy, and translates in practice into the toughening of penal regimes.

Finally, among the most advanced capitalist countries—especially the UK, US, Australia—the relentless commodification of neoliberalism has led to greater prison privatization. This is combining with managerialism to produce high technology units that more effectively segregate staff from prisoners, a move designed to reduce staff costs and avoid conflict and diminish legal liability (Weiss, 1989).

***

While the list of similar developments is substantial and depressing, our study does not suggest historical fatalism. Some nations find themselves in the repressive mainstream largely as the result of unintended consequences—victims of history that is not only a matter of reason and will, but also of preexisting conditions. *Comparing Prison Systems* reveals hopeful signs of more enlightened penal policy. Contributors report *differences among nations* in regard to penal repression. While a few nations have long liberal traditions and are managing to hold out against the global wave of neoliberal punitiveness (The Netherlands), other nations have only recently been liberated from repressive regimes (Eastern Europe and South Africa), and are struggling to resist the temptations of strong repressive legacies. Even in the hard-line law-and-order countries, the future of repression is not certain. Exceptionally brave individuals, organizations and governmental officials are struggling to bridle the most draconian tendencies.

Whether their penal regimes are liberal or authoritarian, various contributors underscore the importance of a strong and independent judiciary in penal policy and sentencing. A diminution of judicial authority and discretion is reported in the Andean region, Poland, Italy and the US. But there is also judicial resistance. In Britain, senior judges have challenged the Government over prison conditions and sentencing changes; in the US, several senior federal judges have resigned over mandated sentencing for drug crimes; in The Netherlands, the judiciary and influential academics still fight tenaciously for leniency. Human rights groups in China, Japan, the Andean region are pressing for justice and moderation. Also important, several of our contributors argue, is the effort to enshrine democratic ideals in constitutions and other legal documents as a way to heighten the contradictions of authoritarian practice.

The editors and contributors of *Comparing Prison Systems* hope that this volume will encourage "the formulation of unrealized historical possibilities and alternative realities," the comparative perspective advocated by Reinhard Bendix, the astute student of authority, domination and the problem of legitimation in society, who ardently believed in the possibility of free action and economic and political progress through social knowledge.

References

Akers, R., Hayner, N. and Gruninger, W. (1977) "Prisonization in five countries: type of prison and inmate characteristics." *Criminology*, 14, 4: 527–554.

Bendix, R. (1984) *Force, Fate, and Freedom*. Berkeley: University of California Press.

Bendix, R. (1965) "Concepts and Generalizations in Comparative Sociological Studies." *American Sociological Review*, 28 (August): 535–538.

Beirne, P. and Hill, J. (1991) *Comparative criminology: an annotated bibliography*. New York: Greenwood Press.

Bensinger, G. (1984) "Corrections in Israel and the United States: a comparative analysis." *International Journal of Comparative and Applied Criminal Justice*, 8, 1: 55–62.

Box, Steven and Hale, Chris. (1982) "Economic Crisis and the Rising Prisoner Population in England and Wales." *Crime and Social Justice*, Vol. 17.

Bureau of Justice Statistics. (1987) *Imprisonment in Four Countries*. Washington DC: US Department of Justice.

Christie, N. (1993) *Crime Control as Industry*. London: Sage.

Clinard, M.B. and Abbott D.J. (1973) *Crime in Developing Countries: A Comparative Perspective*. New York: Wiley and Sons.

Cohen, S. (1987) *Visions of Social Control*. Cambridge: Polity Press.

Cohen, S. (1988) *Against Criminology*. New Brunswick, New Jersey: Transaction Books.

Cohen, S. (1993) "Human Rights and Crimes of the State: The Culture of Denial." *Australian and New Zealand Journal of Criminology*, 26: 97–115.

Cooper, H. (1972) "Prison problems in the USA and Peru." *International Journal of Offender Therapy and Comparative Criminology*, 16, 1: 25–31.

Doleschal, E. (1977) "Rate and length of imprisonment: How does the United States compare with the Netherlands, Denmark and Sweden?" *Crime and Delinquency*, 23, 1: 51–56.

Doleschal, E. and Newton, A. (1979) *International Rates of Imprisonment*. Hackensack, New Jersey: National Council on Crime and Delinquency. (5 pp)

Downes, D. (1988) *Contrasts in Tolerance: Post-war Penal Policy in the Netherlands and England and Wales*. New York: Clarendon Press.

Feely, M. and Simon, J. (1992) "The New Penology: Notes on The Emerging Strategy of Corrections and Its Implications." *Criminology*, 30, 4 (November): 449–474.

Garland, D. (1990) *Punishment and Modern Society*. Oxford: Oxford University Press.

Gerber, J. and Weeks, S. (1992) "Some Reflections on Doing Cros-scultural Research: Interviewing Japanese Inmates." *The Criminologist*, 17: 6.

Hale, C. (1989) "Economy, Punishment and Imprisonment." *Contemporary Crises*, 13, 4: 327–349.

Hernández-Cuevas, J., Cesar-Kala, J., Marquez-Haro H. and Torricellas-Rodríguez, M. (1994) *Prisiones: Estudio Prospectivo de su Realidad Nacional*. México City: Programa Nacional de Capcitación Penitenciaria.

Hood, R. (1989) *The Death Penalty: A World-wide Perspective*. Oxford: Oxford University Press.

Howard, J. (1777) *The State of the Prisons in England and Wales*. Warrington: William Eyres; 2nd edition reprinted, 2 vols., 1973. Montclair, New Jersey: Patterson, Smith.

Human Rights Watch. (1993) *The Human Rights Watch Global Report on Prisons*. New York: Human Rights Watch.

Iacovetta, R. (1981) "Research problems and issues in comparative corrections." *International Journal of Comparative and Applied Criminal Justice*, 5, 2: 205–211.

Johnson, E.H. (1983) *International Handbook of Contemporary Developments in Criminology: General Issues and The Americas*. Westport, Connecticut: Greenwood Press.

Kaiser, G. (1984) *Prison Systems and Correctional Laws: Europe, the United States and Japan, a Comparative Analysis*. Dobbs Ferry, New York: Transnational Publishers.

King, R. (1994) "Russian prisons after *perestroika:* End of the Gulag?" in R. King and M. Maguire (eds.), *Prisons In Context*. Oxford: Clarendon Press.

King, R. (1996) "Prisons in Eastern Europe: Some Reflections on Prison Reform in Romania." *The Howard Journal*, 35: 3.

King, R. and Maguire, M. (eds.) (1994) *Prison In Context*. Oxford: Oxford University Press.

Lynch, J. (1988) "A comparison of prison use in England, Canada, West Germany and the United States: a limited test of the punitive hypothesis." *Journal of Criminal Law and Criminology*, 79, 1: 180–217.

Marnell, G. (1972) "Comparative correctional systems: United States and Sweden." *Criminal Law Bulletin*, 8, 9: 748–760.

Mathiesen, T. (1990) *Prisons on Trial*. London: Sage.

Matthews, R. and Francis, P. (1996) *Prisons 2000*. London: Macmillan.

Melossi, D. (1989) "An introduction: Fifty years later, *Punishment and Social Structure* in comparative analysis," in D. Melossi (ed.) *Contemporary Crises*, 13, 4, (December): 311–326.

Morgan, R. and Evans, M. (1994) "Inspecting prisons: the view from Strasbourg." *British Journal of Criminology*, 34: 141–59.

Morris, N. and Rothman, D. (1995) *The Oxford History of Prisons*. Oxford: Oxford University Press.

Muncie, J. and Sparks, R. (1991) *Imprisonment: European Perspectives*. Hemel Hempstead: Harvester Wheatsheaf.

Pease, K. (1994) "Cross-National Imprisonment Rates" in R. King and M. Maguire (eds.) (1994) *The Oxford History of Prisons*. Oxford: Oxford University Press.

Pease, K. and Hukkila, K. (1990) *Criminal justice systems in Europe and North America: report of the ad hoc expert group on a cross-national study of trends in crime prevention in Europe and North America*. Helsinki: Institute for Crime Prevention and Control.

Prowse, R., Weber, H.-M., and Wilson, C. (1992) "Rights and prisons in Germany: Blueprint for Britain?" *International Journal of the Sociology of Law*, 20: 111–34.

Ruggiero, V., Ryan, M. and Sim, J. (1995) *Western European Penal Systems: A Critical Anatomy*. London: Sage.

Sandhu, H. (1972) "Perceptions of prison guards: a cross national study of India and Canada." *International Review of Modern Sociology*, 2: 26–32.

Schlesinger, S.R. (1987) "Imprisonment in Four Countries." Bureau of Justice Statistics: Special Report, US Department of Justice.

Schluchter, W. (1984) "Foreword" to Bendix, R. (1984) *Force, Fate, and Freedom: On Historical Sociology*. Berkeley: University of California Press.

Shelley, L.I. (1981) *Readings in Comparative Criminology*. Carbondale, Illinois: Southern Illinois University Press.

Solzhenitsyn, Aleksandr I. (1973) *The Gulag Archipelago.* New York: Harper & Row.

Sparks, R. (1994) "Can prisons be legitimate? Penal politics, privatization, and the timeliness of an old idea." *British Journal of Criminology,* 34: 14–28.

Spierenburg, P. (1991) *The Prison Experience.* New Brunswick, New Jersey: Rutgers University Press.

Spitzer, Steven. (1975) "Toward a Marxian Theory of Deviance." *Social Problems,* 22: 638–51.

Terrill, R.J. (1992) *World Criminal Justice Systems: A Survey.* 2nd ed. Cincinnati, Ohio: Anderson.

Turner, B. (1993) "Outline of a Theory of Human Rights." *Sociology,* 27, 3: 489–512.

Vagg, J. (1993) "Context and Linkage: Research and 'Internationalism' in Criminology." *British Journal of Criminology,* 33, 4: 541–553.

Vagg, J. (1994) *Prison Systems: A Comparative Study of Accountability in England, France, Germany and the Netherlands.* Oxford: Clarendon Press.

van Zyl Smit, D. and Dunkel, F. (1991) *Imprisonment Today and Tomorrow: International Perspectives on Prisoners' Rights and Prison Conditions.* Deventer: Kluwer.

Weiss, R.P. (1991) "Introduction: The 'Bitter Lessons' Forgotten?" *Social Justice,* 18, 3: 1–12. Special Attica Issue.

Weiss, R.P. (1987) "Humanitarianism, Labour Exploitation, or Social Control? A Critical Survey of Theory Research on the Origin and Development of Prisons." *Social History,* 12, 3, (October): 331–350.

Whitfield, D. (ed.). (1991) *The State of The Prisons—200 Years On.* London: Routledge.

Wicks, R. and Cooper, H. (eds.). (1979) *International Corrections.* Lexington: Lexington Books.

Wilkins, L.T. (1991) *Punishment, Crime and Market Forces.* Aldershot: Dartmouth.

Wu, Harry. (1992) *Laogai: The Chinese Gulag.* Westview Press.

Wu, Harry and Wakeman, C. (1994) *Bitter Winds: A Memoir of My Years in China's Gulag.* New York: Wiley.

Young, Warren. (1986) "Influences upon the Use of Imprisonment: A Review of the Literature." *The Howard Journal,* 25, 2: 125–136.

I
The Americas

Chapter ONE

Punishment in the American Democracy: The Paradoxes of Good Intentions

Dario Melossi and Mark Lettiere

When Gustave de Beaumont and Alexis de Tocqueville were sailing toward the coasts of North America in the early May of 1831, in order to prepare a report for the French government about the state of the penitentiaries in the United States, the prison system of this country, albeit quite young, was already famous.

About one century before Independence, in 1682, William Penn had spearheaded a penal reform which had abolished the death penalty for many crimes and had tried to introduce a new punitive institution shaped after the Dutch workhouse (Sellin, 1944), an institution that seemed to embody the ideals of the Quaker community more fully. Even if Penn's project in the end was abandoned and the traditional British penal ways brought back, his project marked the importance of Quaker thinking on penality, a specificity which would not disappear in the centuries to come and that was to shape the American experience of penality.

It would be only after Independence that the now autonomous colonies would be free to impress their mark on the question of punishment—a mark greatly shaped by the moral and religious thinking of the Protestant sects (Weber, 1906). Around the time of Independence and then in the decades immediately following, in the most important centers of the Atlantic coast, the traditional problems linked to industrialization and urbanization, which were already plaguing parts of Europe, began to appear also in the United States.

In spite of the "natural" extension of land toward the West—that all throughout the 19th-century would constitute the destiny of so much of the immigrant population coming from Europe—the cities of New York, Philadelphia, Boston, were already large enough to know the scourges of pauperism, alcoholism, and abandoned children. The model of the workhouse, the institution structured around a forced discipline of labor, was therefore rediscovered and became the basis for the new *penitentiary* institution.

PUNISHMENT IN THE NEW REPUBLIC

In 1787, the "Philadelphia Society for Alleviating the Miseries of Public Prisons" was created, so that "such degrees and modes of punishment may be discovered and suggested, as may, instead of continuing habits of vice, become the means of restoring our fellow creatures to virtue and happiness" (Barnes, 1930: 127). It was under the leadership of the Society that, in the garden of the old Walnut Street Jail, a cellular prison was created, the main organizing principle of which was to be solitary confinement (Takagi, 1975; Sellin, 1953).

The new institution reflected other famous European institutions and projects belonging in the new atmosphere of the Enlightenment, like Ghent's *Maison de Force*, completely rebuilt in 1775, and Jeremy Bentham's *Panopticon* (1787). The main inspiring principle of all these institutions was separation: isolation of the sinner from his fellow creatures and relations only with the representatives of divine and secular authority. The model was that of penance, first developed in the medieval monasteries of Europe for the crimes and sins of the monks (Treiber and Steinert, 1980). This system was now secularized and extended to all the members of God's flock, in this representing a true embodiment of Protestant

Reformation, especially in its more radical variants. The reformed believer, in fact, could not find solace in the intermediation of the Church. That the rich had been paying their way into salvation, was the accusation that had been directed against the corrupt, power-eager and fundamentally skeptical Church of Rome, whose *indulgence* was seen more as a means to secure temporal power than as true compassion for the weakness of the flesh. The Philadelphia inmate had no resort other than gazing at the depth of his fall in the solitary confinement of his cell. No pagan delusion could save him from staring at the terrible spectacle of God's rage. No wonder that the new system soon appeared to be connected to an impressive rise of suicides—as in uncanny forewarning of a theory that the French sociologist Émile Durkheim would spell out only at the end of the century (1897).

The system worked fine in the sense that it did certainly make an impression on the poor souls that happened to be punished in this new, modern and rational way. However, there was a problem. In a society eager for work—work skills, work discipline and work *tout court*—the Philadelphian system seemed to represent a waste of precious human energy, and what from one perspective seemed to be quite successful, from another perspective appeared to be a waste.

These considerations allowed for the rise in the State of New York, in Auburn, of the great competitor of the Philadelphian system, the Auburn system, based on separation at night and work in common during the day—a situation that allowed the introduction of real work discipline and of actual industrial production inside the penitentiary. The fundamental principle of separation among the inmates was to be preserved through a rigid rule of silence. This of course represented a problem, because the temptation to talk to one's neighbor was high, and corporal punishment had to be administered generously in order to enforce the rule. It was somewhat of a step back from the spiritual life of the Philadelphian inmate, but a step forward toward the more material interests of a energetic young capitalism already characterized, no doubt, by "rugged individualism!"

The competition between these "two systems," that was soon won in the materialist (i.e., characterized by a scarce offer of labor) United States, by the Auburn system, for almost a century fascinated the European governments that were attracted by the idea that one could find the promise of the end of crime and domestic turmoil in a technical "quick fix!" In spiritual Europe (i.e., characterized by an overabundant supply of labor), the Philadelphia system was instead victorious (Rusche and Kirchheimer, 1939: 127–37).

It cannot escape the eye of the keen observer, however, that it would seem incongruent that the American Republic, praised then and later as the most direct vessel to ferry peoples and intellects from the Land of the Social Contract to that of Democracy, would at the same time be the harboring place of an institution, the prison, that however wisely revised, is usually identified with pain, suffering and oppression. It is this, probably, a not irrelevant development of what Horkheimer and Adorno would call the *Dialectic of Enlightenment* (1947). Indeed they wrote:

> Since de Tocqueville the bourgeois republics have attacked man's soul, whereas the monarchies attacked his body; similarly, the penalties inflicted in these republics also attack man's soul. The new martyrs do not die a slow death in the torture chamber but instead waste away spiritually as invisible victims in the great prison buildings which differ in little but names from madhouses (1947: 228).

This is *in nuce*, almost 30 years earlier, the central topic of what would then be the focus of Michel Foucault's *Discipline and Punish* (1975)—even if the punctilious observer might note that the same argument had been made by Marx about one century earlier, where he addressed the transition from Catholicism to Protestantism in one of his early papers (1844: 138).

In any event, it was quite a coincidence that the French aristocrat who had arrived in 1831 to write of penitentiaries would find himself not only deserting his original topic (Sellin, 1964), but producing instead one of the most important and lasting contributions to the theory of democracy, *Democracy in America* (Tocqueville, 1835–40). Could it be that the two topics had so much in common? Or was this just an idiosyncratic joke that fate had played with Alexis de Tocqueville? According to American political theorist Thomas Dumm, the "right" answer to the question is the former, because:

> I argue... the emergence of the penitentiary in the United States was a project *constitutive* of liberal democracy. That is, the penitentiary system formed the epistemological project of liberal democracy, creating conditions of knowledge of self and other that were to shape the political subject required for liberal and democratic values to be realized in practice. The American project, a system of self-rule, involved not only the establishment of representative government with an extensive suffrage, but also the establishment of institutions

which would encourage the internalization of liberal democratic values, the creation of individuals who would learn how to rule their
selves (Dumm, 1987: 6).

The crucial term here is—indeed following Foucault's lesson—*self-
government*, literally the government of the self. We could in a sense
say that the American penitentiary was erected by the Founding
Fathers of the Nation as an imposing and monumental Gateway to
the Republic. And indeed the Quaker philanthropist and reformer
Benjamin Rush had described them as producing *Republican
machines* (Dumm, 1987: 88), human beings, that is, that were supposed to turn from men who were uncivilized, or who had lost
their civilization, into good workers and citizens, able to be introduced into a conversation with their fellow men—the very prerequisite for democracy.

As Mexican writer Octavio Paz has in fact observed in a sharp
essay comparing the political–cultural history of the United States
and that of Mexico (1978), a major prerequisite of the Republican
social contract is the *identity* of the parties to the contract, their basic
commonality of civilization. They were to be part of a rational discourse. They could not simply be *peones* at the base of the social
pyramid, as could happen in the Catholic, authoritarian structure of
the Spanish Conquest. The colonists of North America were too
ambitious about the greatness and goodness of the institutions they
were building to allow uncivilized men and women to become part
of it simply as labor power.

Indeed, as Horkheimer and Adorno wrote, their souls had to be
conquered. That is, they had to enter into a conversation with the
other members of the American covenant. The natural consequence
of such lofty ambitions therefore—Paz observes with chilling
logic—was the extermination of those whose souls (if they indeed
had been endowed with one!) could not be reached, such as the
native inhabitants of North America. Those who, in other words,
were perceived as unable, or unwilling, to enter into an enlightened, Republican, democratic dialogue.

For those lucky ones instead who, in spite of their being uncivilized or having lost their civilization, were still perceived as similar
enough to the members of the religious covenant to be accepted at
least as potential members, then it was necessary to arrange those
instruments that would lead them to democracy. Of the two "races
which inhabit the territory of the United States," whose destiny
deeply moved the observation of Tocqueville in *Democracy in*

America (1835: 393–456), one, the Native American, was too *different* to be conducted through such narrow passage. The second one instead, "the colored," once free, would have been generously exposed to the philanthropy of the new penitentiary institutions.

For a long time the "two races" were treated in an exclusionary mode, for Native Americans to the extent of genocide (Fitzpatrick, 1995). "Indians," considered as foreign nationals, were continuously pushed forward toward the West, until their land was almost completely taken over by white colonists (Takaki, 1979: 80–107). As Ronald Takaki notices, citing Tocqueville, what particularly amazed the French nobleman was,

> the ability of white society to deprive the Indians of their rights and exterminate them 'with singular felicity, tranquilly, legally, philanthropically... It is impossible to destroy men with more respect for the laws of humanity' (Takaki, 1979: 81 citing Tocqueville, 1835: 352–3, 364).

There was no place, in fact, at the time, for Native Americans in the white men's penitentiaries exactly because the penitentiary was deeply connected to an inclusionist ideology. It was intended to be the entrance into a social contract that one had voluntarily or involuntarily ignored.

At the dawn of the Republic, the same exclusionist policies applied generally to all the "black or tawny" races (Franklin, 1751), a label that Benjamin Franklin applied to practically all non-English settlers (in fact the occasion of this essay by Franklin was his preoccupation with the increasing numbers of Germans in Pennsylvania (Takaki, 1979: 14; Cohn-Bendit and Schmid, 1993: 96)). It is no big surprise then if that same founding father, psychiatrist, educator, reformer and philanthropist who had advocated penitentiaries able to produce "Republican machines," Benjamin Rush, was to present an essay at the 1792 meeting of the American Philosophical Society entitled "Observations intended to favor a supposition that the black Color (as it is called) of the Negro is derived from the LEPROSY," that the black color was in other words a disease of the skin that could be cured with "[d]epletion, whether by bleeding, purging, or abstinence [which] has been often observed to lessen the black color in negroes." In the meanwhile, however, the separation between the two races had to be maintained also for medical reasons (Takaki, 1979: 28–35).

Still in 1850, blacks were largely concentrated in the South, of course as slaves. In the South, their special status made it so that they could not be admitted to the honors of the penitentiary, their discipline "of choice" being *domestic* discipline (Sellin 1976: 133–44). And in fact their incarceration rate in the South in 1850 was less than half that of whites: 8.34 (per 100,000) against 18.62 (notice anyway how, at that time, the incarceration rate was extremely low by contemporary standards). The opposite was true in the North where, despite their small number, their condition of *free* men and women opened them the gates of penitentiaries: 289.81 per 100,000 blacks vs. 26.23 per 100,000 whites, a disproportionality which is even higher than the contemporary one (Sabol, 1989: 408–09). In fact, already Beaumont and Tocqueville had noticed in their Report on the penitentiary system that:

> A young society, exempt from political embarrassments, rich both by its soil and its industry, should be supposed to furnish less criminals than a country where the ground is disputed foot by foot, and where the cries produced by political divisions tend to increase the number of offenses, because they increase misery by disturbing industry.
>
> Yet if the statistical documents which we possess of Pennsylvania, should be applied to the rest of the Union, there are in this country more crimes committed than in France, in proportion to the population. Various causes of another nature explain this result: on the one hand, the colored population, which forms the sixth part of the inhabitants of the United States, and which composes half of the inmates of the prisons; and on the other hand, the foreigners pouring in every year from Europe, and who form the fifth and sometimes even the fourth part of the number of convicts (Beaumont and Tocqueville, 1833: 99).

In the North, therefore, the freed colored population and the immigrants had to go through the gateway to the Republic, prisons. This would start happening also in the South, after the Civil War, when many of the "freed" blacks would again be reduced into servitude, this time penal servitude, through the convict lease system that flourished in the Southern states after the Civil War, and the clients of which were largely blacks (Sellin, 1976: 409).

So, already in 1870 in the South, black incarceration rate was the triple of whites (120.35 vs. 42.56) and almost 15 times what had been twenty years earlier, before the Civil War and their "liberation" (Sabol, 1989: 408). However, the disproportionality rate in the South remained lower than in the North (Sabol, 1989: 409) because in the North it accompanied the process of migration of blacks from the rural South to the northern cities, such as Chicago.

If in fact the prison system represented the gateway to democracy, migrants were and are the system's candidates of choice: domestic migrants as in the case of blacks, foreign immigrants as with Europeans until the 1920s, later on Asians and Spanish-speaking immigrants from Central and South America.

From the very origins of the American prison system, then, Americans' love for punishment was tightly connected to their love for democracy. Democracy is the expression of the will of the people. Who counters that will, which expresses itself into the law, has to be punished. In the Protestant New England mold of American culture—a mold which still has a firm grip over the essentials of American culture, *pace* the current fads of post-modernism and multiculturalism—there is no place for the fuzzy, authoritarian and deeply conservative indulgence of Catholicism. Right or wrong, black or white: who is (or is perceived to be) on the wrong side of the law, shall be punished. But, alas, as with everything else in society, who breaks the law and is powerful (economically, politically, ethnically, racially, culturally and in regard to gender, and so on and so forth) can afford a full use of the safeguards that a developed legal system provides them with. For the others, tough luck.

All in all, this policy, however weak on the side of social justice, is "useful," because an economic system based on competition cannot work without a system of punishments and rewards. Who is at the bottom of the social pyramid is perceived as being tempted to break the law more often: less to lose and more to gain. Isn't it therefore only fair that the law pay more attention to their behavior? As, once again, Beaumont and Tocqueville noted,

> If we should deduct from the total number of crimes, those committed by negroes and foreigners, we should undoubtedly find that the white American population commits less crimes than ours. But proceeding this, we should fall into another error; in fact, to separate the negroes from the whole population of the United States, would be equal to deducting the poorer classes of the community with us [in France], *that is to say, those who commit the crimes* (Beaumont and Tocqueville, 1833: 99; our emphasis).

PUNISHMENT AND REFORM IN THE POST-BELLUM ERA

As the Post-Bellum era developed, with its rapid industrial growth and its attendant broad social problems, so too did a new era of imprisonment emerge. Calls for penal reform were being heard as the Auburn and Pennsylvania systems were assailed for their inhumane treatment of prisoners. Soon gone was the role of the penal visionaries in the Quaker tradition, and their principled purpose of moral salvation and penal penitence. In their place, substituting for the simple vision of punishment as a mechanism of individual redemption and strict social conformity, was the emergence of a new class of professional penologists.

This group, bent on grasping institutional power and respect, combined reformist ideals with an increased focus on centralization, bureaucratic efficiency, managerialism, routinization and professional status. They helped shape the course of penal developments in the United States for the next hundred years. Names like Brockway, Wines, Wright, Sanbourn and Howe became synonymous with penal reform, the introduction of State Boards of Charity, Conferences on Penal Reform and the National Association of Prisons. These reform organizations took their lead from the post-Civil War reorganization of the federal government to deal with the "penal question" in states throughout the country (McKelvey, 1977; Rothman, 1980; Irwin, 1970; Friedman, 1993).

The two-pronged evolution of increased centralization and state administration of the prison, and reform-minded enthusiasm created conflicts in many regions of the country, especially as many southern states and local jurisdictions attempted to hold control over "their prisons," rejecting many of the humanistic advances of the new penal reformers and the turning over of local powers to centralized control.

In particular, the Confederate defeat in April 1865, signaled the end of slavery for black Americans but, as we have seen, did little to change the attitudes of white property owners toward blacks in the South. However, it did force a reconceptualization of the place of black southerners in the "newly democratized" South. With the Emancipation Proclamation of 1863 and the ratification of the Thirteenth Amendment in December 1865, black ex-slaves were now subject to the same penal laws that whites from the *master class* had been subject to, prior to the abolition of slavery. This created a lamentable situation for white southerners who had established a system of industrial penitentiaries for whites, not unlike themselves, and were now faced with "the rapidly growing criminality of poor, unskilled, bewildered ex-slaves cast into a freedom for which few of them were prepared" (Sellin, 1976).

As Sellin notes, the South, forced to rebuild a shattered economy after the war, and consigned to the entrenched ideal that convicts should, by their work, both compensate for their cost and provide profits for the state while imprisoned, resulted in a renewed emphasis on penal serfdom as many black and some poor white prisoners were entered into a convict lease system in which their labor was leased to private interests for years or even decades (Sellin, 1976: 146–47). States like Mississippi, Georgia, Arkansas, North and South Carolina, Tennessee and Florida leased prisoners to provide labor to agricultural, mining, railroad and timber interests. The practice of leasing prison labor remained a pillar of the penal system in the South well into the 20th century, regardless of the reforms underway in other regions of the country. This prompted Sellin to conclude that the convict lease system was "a form of chattel slavery even worse than that from which blacks had been freed. It began, grew, and flourished only because almost all who suffered under it were ex-slaves whom the master class still thought of as belonging to an inferior race" (Sellin, 1976: 162).

The question of penal labor was also one that plagued both reformers and industrial workers in the North. The industrialization of the prison saw the emergence of private contractors setting up machinery to produce everything from shoes to furniture to wagons. The "labor problem" in the North was brought to the forefront of political debate as a developing labor movement, with organizations like the National Labor Party and the Knights of Labor, sought relief from the rivalry of prison sweat. By the 1880s the demand for, and agitation by, organized labor, as well as by companies competing with prison contractors, resulted in legislative protection from prison competition, and in many states the implementation of anticontract laws, forbidding the use of contracted prison labor.

However, the issue was not so easily remedied, as reformers like Brockway warned against the evils of prison indolence and the cost of housing prisoners without any economic offset provided by their labor. The import of work for rehabilitation was not to be abandoned. In 1870, Brockway's *The Declaration of Principles* still held to the notion that crime was a moral affliction and that its cure was to be found in the dual principles of work and education (Friedman, 1993: 160–61). The Jacksonian precepts of lock step marching and silent solitude were seen as counter-productive to the restoration of individual civic responsibility. Inmates' dignity and self respect could only be restored through labor and education.

In 1883, Brockway proposed a solution to the contract labor issue in the way of a piece-rate work and state accounting system, which moved the control of inmate labor out of the hands of the contractors and into the control of prison wardens (McKelvey, 1977: 118–119). Clearly, the reform of the prison and the prisoner was to take place from within the prison, rather than from without. Reform through incarceration was still the motto, and it was firmly believed that to reform the convict, the *proper* amount of time in prison should be spent. This was one of the decrees with which Brockway would mold the new reformatory, Elmira, in New York. Brockway's recommendations were met with mixed responses, but in 1889 other states, like Pennsylvania, New Jersey and Massachusetts, adopted the principles of the Brockway system which differentiated the prison population into segregation based on perceived behavior and classes of laborers (McKelvey, 1977; Friedman, 1993: 161). Regarding this move, McKelvey notes,

> [t]he convicts were to be divided into three classes: those with good prospects of reformation were to be instructed in trade schools and employed at these trades with no idea of state profit; the repeaters who were at least good prisoners and possibly reformable were to be assigned to industries at which they could find a living after discharge and in the meantime earn their keep; the desperate criminals were to be rewarded with all the drudgery and menial labor rather than the choice jobs which their long terms and professional standing had formerly secured them. In addition, a wage not to exceed onetenth of the earnings was to be paid to meritorious prisoners (McKelvey, 1936: 99).

This group differentiation was key in the development of indeterminate sentencing, and the promise that through work and education the prisoner would reform *himself* and return to the ranks of citizenry. As Brockway stated "[i]t is only by these means that every avenue of hope for release from imprisonment, save the one of personal fitness for future liberty, can be closed to the prisoner…and his mind be turned…to the matter of preparing himself for restoration to citizenship" (Rothman, 1980: 33). Again, the goal of the new reform movement was the reintegration of the prisoner into the social and political body.

The advent of prison commissions and committees, and their ability to influence legislative reform, signaled an end to the reign of localized decision-making and began the systematization of hierarchical chains of command whose centralized decision-making lent uniformity to institutionalized modes of incarceration. Reformatory penology found its impetus in the influence of increased scientific knowledge and expertise, in part brought about by a newly found positivistic criminology (Rafter, 1992), as well as by the expansion of a socially mindful professional class fresh from college and medical school seeking to administer rehabilitation, rather than punishment. The development of indeterminate sentencing, parole, probation, juvenile courts, the separation of women and of the insane were all products of this new climate. As Rothman suggests, by the time of the Progressive Era reformatory penology had forged a "major divide in attitudes and practices toward the deviant, creating new ideas and procedures to combat crime, delinquency, and mental illness" (Rothman, 1980: 43). Progressive precedents were to be found in the work of Brockway and others, and in reformatories like Elmira.

PROGRESSIVE PENALITY

By the turn of the 20th century Progressive reforms were in full tilt. The focus on ameliorating deviant behavior and the corrupt conditions of the growing urban industrial centers like Boston, New York and Chicago would merge with the robust Progressive movement of the 1900–1915. "Reformatories" were created in order to deal with various groups of those who would later be called *deviants*, in highly differentiated way. This was specifically true for women and children as the emergence of a welfare ideology provided a framework for the moral entrepreneurs of the early 1900s whose focus was on saving individuals, especially the "weak" members of society, from lives of vice and delinquency.

This has led some to suggest that the Progressive Era witnessed "the invention of delinquency" (Platt, 1969). The advent of the juvenile court, first established in Chicago in 1899, radically changed the way in which juvenile offenders were processed by the judicial system. As Platt notes, the treatment of children at this time was about saving them from a future of crime and the model of reform was one of "juridical therapy" in which the child would enter into a doctor–patient relationship with the newly emerging juvenile court judge. The focus on individualized, case-by-case investigations was a hallmark of the Progressive Era and gave rise to a focus on social work, psychology and psychiatry as part of the criminal–legal apparatus (see also Sutton, 1989).

For women, the reformatory movement during the Progressive Era saw the construction of 17 state reformatories for women between 1900 and 1935 (Rafter, 1985). As Rafter notes, the focus was on rescue and reform; that is, women had to be rescued from men's prisons in order to be reformed. Led by middle-class women and groups like the all-female Committee on Delinquent Women in Connecticut, many states did in fact construct women's reformatories, but this was also done under the auspices of preventing society from the particular scourge applied to women, namely prostitution and venereal disease. The focus on women's hygiene saw that women would be treated for their sexual promiscuity and immorality behind the walls of the reformatory.

This is an important difference, for while much of the Progressive movement was a search for alternatives to prison and long incarceration for men, this was not the case for women and girls. As Rafter notes:

> Social purity concerns…were expressed in terms of anxiety about sexual immorality. [T]he Progressive period was one of considerable apprehension about changing gender roles—a period when, it seemed, girls and young women, especially those of the working class, were growing indifferent to the older concepts of womanliness. Conservatives mobilized to establish institutions that would "correct" deviations from traditional roles. [T]he public response to female delinquency…formed part of a larger cultural reaction, an attempt to revitalize Victorian morality and to punish women—prostitutes and sexually precocious girls alike—who impeded attainment of that goal (Rafter, 1985: 61).

The potential for long stays in the reformatory for the act of having sex was not uncommon. In Arkansas during World War I, between four and five hundred women were convicted of "immorality" and held for treatment of venereal disease (Rafter, 1985: 58). The treatment of black women was also far worse in prison. As Rafter shows, during this period, the higher the incarceration rate of black women in a prison, the lower the standard of treatment. Reformatories were first reserved for white women only, whereas black women were treated much more "like men" to the point of being sent, in some Southern states, to join the chain gangs (Rafter, 1985: 152–156).

For men during the Progressive era things were much different. The widespread adoption of parole and indeterminate sentencing laws throughout the country revolutionized the treatment of

inmates, although not without opposition by the public, as numerous stories of released prisoners committing heinous crimes were
made public. Yet, the Progressive impulse won out early in the century and parole maintained its place in the reform schema.

The most discerning quality of Progressivism was the underlying
confidence in the state's power of benevolence and ability to do
good. As David Rothman has pointed out, "[t]he state was not the
enemy of liberty but the friend of equality—and to expand its
domain and increase its power was to be in harmony with the spirit
of the age" (Rothman, 1980: 60). The state was seen as the compas-
sionate agent of reform for the offender who had lost his or her
way. Therefore, policies which called for the state to administer care
to the individual were generally met with enthusiasm. The state
was seen as the promoter of the general welfare of the citizenry and
the individual welfare of the offender. The use of probation, parole
and indeterminate sentencing were tools of the state in curing the
ills of the individual and therefore necessary as the penal/juridical
system continued to flourish. This, of course, meant a dramatic
expansion and routinization in the prison system. As David
Garland suggests more generally:

> ...[t]he rationalization and bureaucratization of the penal process has
> undoubtedly been the most important development to have taken
> place in penality in the nineteenth and twentieth centuries...the
> localized, *ad hoc*, and frequently makeshift penal arrangements of
> previous periods have given way to a professionalized, administra-
> tive infrastructure which commands significant tax-funded budgets,
> large numbers of career personnel, an extensive network of institu-
> tions and agencies, and a range of technical knowledges and social
> scientific discourses (Garland, 1990: 180).

The increased rationalization of the prison reflected social developments outside, as governmental expansion and societal embrace of
increased bureaucratized organization, modes of efficiency and
professional ideologies grew. Yet, as the "Roaring Twenties" rolled
in, uncertainties about the very nature of crime and the criminal in
the United States were calling the rehabilitative model into question. Increases in crime statistics, prison populations and a budding
understanding of the concept of recidivism had some calling for a
return to earlier modes of punishment and a renewed interest in
Lombrosian understandings of the "nature" of crime (McKelvey,
1977: 267–68).

THE BIG HOUSE AND BEYOND

As the prison population continued to grow, a new phase in American imprisonment appeared in the construction of the "Big House." The Big House came into existence between the two World Wars to signify a shift away from the reformatories of the early century. It became the symbol of imprisonment in the United States for many, as it was characterized time and again in film and literature. From Sing Sing and Attica in the East, to Stateville and Joliet in the Midwest, to San Quentin, Alcatraz and Folsom in the West, the Big House evokes images of the "total institution," as Erving Goffman would later call it. Its architecture was foreboding, as tiers of massive concrete and steel cells and other features like the wall and the yard, told of the Big House's fortress-like quality.

Several classic studies of the Big House gave a sense of its tremendous scope and scale, as well as of the prison culture which developed within its walls. Clemmer's (1940) now classic study of Menard in Illinois in the late 1930s overstated the impenetrability of the prisoners' world, but nevertheless gave a vivid description of the culture within the Big House. Systems of domination and hierarchical cliques maintained control and fueled what Clemmer described as a process of *prisonization*, in which inmates recoiled from any attempts of rehabilitation. Later sociological studies of imprisonment would serve as correctives to this overdetermined account of the Big House, but Clemmer brought us into the prison community and detailed the group dynamics within the walls of Menard.

After World War II, a "correctionalism" developed which gradually replaced the Big House by returning to the reformist ideals of the early century (Irwin, 1980). Correctionalism reflected a resurgence in the reform spirit, as well as in the detached scientism of the positivistic criminology and penology of the early century. Perhaps there is no better example of this shift away from authoritarianism and towards a more legalistic and rational social control than in Jacobs' (1977) analysis of Stateville Prison in Illinois. Here the demise of the "Big House" and its authoritarian image gradually gave rise throughout the middle of the century not only to increased bureaucratic efficiency and professional prison management, but also to a growing sense of prisoners' rights and political citizenry.

This shift in prisoners' understandings of broader political developments and social conditions was also articulated in Gresham

Sykes' (1958) *Society of Captives*. Sykes' analysis showed how New Jersey prison culture reflexively articulated broader social environmental changes. As Sykes argued:

> The prison is not an autonomous system of power; rather, it is an instrument of the State, shaped by its social environment, and we must keep this simple truth in mind if we are to understand the prison... . The prison as a social system, does not exist in isolation any more than the criminal within the prison exists in isolation as an individual; and the institution and its settings are inextricably mixed despite the definite boundary of the wall (1958: 8).

While writing in the long shadow of Parsonian functionalism and the hegemony of system-based approaches, Sykes nonetheless hinted to the prison as inextricably bounded within more complex social events (Sparks, Bottoms and Hay, 1996: 32–96). The prison as a permeable institution is key to understanding many penal developments throughout the early and middle parts of the century. Inmate populations came to recognize the disjuncture between the reform philosophies and policies of the time and the often deplorable conditions within the prison (Useem and Kimball, 1990). In fact, the prison riots of 1952–53 were a result of the disparity in prison material conditions, a growing political identity among inmates and their expectations to be treated in ways articulated by well-intentioned penal reformers. The awareness of a political identity would increasingly become a focal point throughout the 1960s, as prisoners both coalesced and balkanized around the social issues of the time including social class, race and ethnicity, the war in Vietnam and democratic freedom movements (Carroll, 1974; Irwin, 1970).

CRISIS IN AMERICAN SOCIETY AND CRISIS IN CORRECTIONALISM

In the early 1970s, American traditional leadership—C. Wright Mills' (1956) "power elite," or Dwight D. Eisenhower's "military-industrial complex"—was faced with the task of reestablishing social order after a season of deep social unrest. The erosion of profit margins was—as we will see—only an element of a larger picture that was defined at the time as one of crisis. The 1960s had been marked by the rise of a number of social movements, from the civil rights struggle of larger and larger segments of African Americans

and of "peoples of color" in general, to the movement against the
Vietnam war, from the "counterculture," to the turmoil on college
campuses (Gitlin, 1987). The problem of *discipline* therefore was on
the agenda and appeared, especially to conservatives, as inextricably linked with a thorough-going restoration of the type of ethic
which had presided to the constitution of America: hard work,
responsibility, individualism.

One of the major problems that appeared in the 1960s was
"crime." Deep, protracted social change of the kind Americans
were exposed to between the late 1950s and the 1970s, almost a
"cultural revolution," was bound to be productive of deep anxieties,
because one's place in society, one's destiny in life, one's roles as
worker, son, father or citizen, was deeply and fundamentally questioned.

As Durkheim had insightfully noted in his sociological commentary on modernity, social change breeds anomie. The result of such
a situation of anomie is usually two-pronged. On the one hand,
ceteris paribus, there will probably be an increase in deviant activities (or at least in those activities defined as deviant from the perspective of the old order that is being shattered). On the other hand,
there will be an effort by the elites attached to the cultural values
and to the material advantages of the old order, to defend it by
reestablishing their legitimacy through the use of all available
means of social control. Because in a situation of social change and
conflict, consensual social control is gone by definition, what the
old elites are left with usually is coercion, while at the same time
the most enlightened sections among them are busy trying to
rebuild a *new* consensus.

The kind of reactions that may happen to be rationally chosen
and evaluated at the level of intellectual and moral elites, are con-
fusedly and emotionally felt at the level of the public, especially in
an age in which the greatest part of the process of social communication is handled though so-called mass-media. In the type of situation, therefore, that developed in the United States and in other
countries in the 1960s, there was a "natural" reflex by elites to turn
themselves toward coercive measures and punishment to try and
control cultural change, and there was a "natural" reflex in the public to "buy" such choice in a situation of deep emotional anxiety
caused by the uncertainty that was penetrating their lives. "Crime"
became a master-metaphor to designate what was wrong with
American society, with the criminals certainly, but also with work

absenteeism, students taking over campuses, pot-smokers, free-sex lovers, rebellious minorities, "liberated" women and so on and so forth. At the same time, "punishment," and the connected concept of "individual responsibility," increasingly became a master-metaphor of what "the cure" ought to be.

This backlash, however, was slow to come about and was symmetrical to the fact that part and parcel of the cultural revolution of the 1960s had been a rejection of punitiveness. One has only to mention the anti-institutional critiques of authors like Erving Goffman (1961). Whereas such criticism was directed particularly against mental institutions, it was clear, as we have seen, that many of the same arguments applied also to imprisonment and had been already developed in Clemmer's (1940) and Sykes' (1958) work. One of the results of this critique—within the more general public mood of anti-authoritarianism, cultural change and experimentation—was that, in the early 1970s, opposition to imprisonment as the solution to crime problems had reached a climax. In 1973, the *Task Force Report on Corrections* of the National Advisory Commission on Criminal Justice Standards and Goals could state that, "no new institutions for adults should be built and existing institutions for juveniles should be closed," and that "[t]he prison, the reformatory and the jail have achieved only a shocking record of failure [...] these institutions create crime rather than prevent it" (1973: 358, 597, quoted in Zimring and Hawkins, 1991: 65–66). And the National Council on Crime and Delinquency would add that "only a small percentage of offenders in penal institutions today" would really need incarceration, so that "[i]n any state no more than one hundred persons would have to be confined in a single maximum security institution" (NCCD 1973: 456, quoted in Zimring and Hawkins, 1991: 87).

Between 1969 and 1973 in Massachusetts the Department of Youth Services, under the leadership of Commissioner Jerome G. Miller, closed all the confining juvenile institutions and replaced them with community care. Whereas the measure was limited to juvenile offenders, the ethos that inspired the reformers implied an option for "deinstitutionalization" that, as it has often happened with juvenile reform, could have been extended to adult offenders (Bakal, 1973).

Such a situation of historical transition was somehow reflected upon in a number of revisionist accounts of the history and origins of punishment, of which the most famous is certainly Michel

Foucault's *Discipline and Punish* (1975), that soon became very popular also in the United States (published there in 1977) but that was only one among many (Garland, 1985; Ignatieff, 1978; Melossi and Pavarini, 1977; Rafter, 1985; Rothman, 1971 and 1980; Rusche and Kirchheimer, 1939 reissued in 1968). Indeed, in 1977 Andrew Scull published his *Decarceration*, assuming that the reductionist, if not abolitionist, premises were winning. Scull's argument based itself on the kind of reasoning that had been first advanced in James O'Connor's *Fiscal Crisis of the State* (1973). Institutional social control was too costly for a welfare state taken between the increasing opposite and contrasting demands of legitimation and repression. Because community care as an alternative was no more than lip service rhetoric, the closing down of total institutions would have saved the American economy precious resources. It was far from the imagination of those authors to predict that, in spite of the fiscal crisis, an increasingly conservative America would have made the choice of diverting even more resources from health and education to locking people up!

Jankovic (1977) and Melossi (1980) gave similar accounts of what was going on but in more Marxist-orthodox versions: Because capitalism was entering its post-industrial phase and the prison had been shaped on the model of industrial factories (Melossi and Pavarini, 1977), then the obsolescence of the factory had to extend to the prison system. If anything, the control system of the future would have been in the community, i.e. through such systems as probation, parole, etc. Actually Scull, Jankovic and Melossi were correct in identifying "treatment" in the community as the fastest growing area of corrections, given that probation has been increasing even faster than imprisonment in 1973–1996. What they were unable to predict, however, was that the *total* amount of correctional control would increase so much, that probation would grow even more than imprisonment in spite of the fact that imprisonment would have *quadrupled* its size between 1970 and 1994!

Note that, as it often happens, at first the conservative positions developed almost from within the more liberal positions (Greenberg and Humphries 1980). At the time, everybody was a critic of treatment or, as Ian Taylor, Paul Walton and Jock Young put it in their very topical *The New Criminology* (1973), of "correctionalism." Robert Martinson's famous article "What Works?" (1974) contributed to steering penal and criminal policies away from rehabilitation and toward "just deserts." Martinson surveyed a number of studies that were critical of rehabilitative programs, and concluded that there were no signs that the emphasis on correction and rehabilitation worked.

These critiques were shared by progressives. In an article based on a survey that had been commissioned by the Committee for the Study of Incarceration—whose final report would yield Andrew von Hirsch's famous reductionist proposal of *just deserts* (1976)—David Greenberg concluded:

> This survey indicates that many correctional dispositions are failing to reduce recidivism, and it thus confirms the general thrust of the Lipton, Martinson, and Wilks survey, which ended in 1967 (Lipton et al., 1975; Martinson, 1974). Much of what is now done in the name of "corrections" may serve other functions, but the prevention of return to crime is not one of them... The blanket assertion that "nothing works" is an exaggeration, but not by very much (Greenberg, 1977: 140–41).

In the same way in which American liberals and European social-democrats at the time were under the fire from both left- and right-wing radicals, so "mainstream" correctionalism was defined as "bankrupt" and in need to be replaced, either by "tearing down the walls" of the prisons, or by "locking them up and throwing away the key." If some of the responses were first coming from the left, as in a pamphlet by the AFSC Working Party (1971), expressing a concern for the defendants' civil liberties and the dignity of the inmates, soon the situation turned toward a mere emphasis on the principle of individual responsibility and certainty of punishment.

So, if there was a comeback of the "classical" school of criminology, represented especially by David Matza's critique of determinism in the sociological tradition, that had failed in respecting the human dignity of the offender (Matza, 1969), soon years and years of prison terms were piled up on defendants in recognition of a renewed sense of their individual responsibility.

This "post-sociological" criminology revamped, therefore, the traditional neo-classical and neo-positivist approaches that had occupied the field of North American criminology before the emergence of sociological hegemony, from Gary Becker (1968) to Ernest van den Haag (1975), and from James Q. Wilson and R. Herrnstein (1985), to Michael R. Gottfredson and Travis Hirschi (1990).

THE CONSERVATIVE TURN AND THE
RETURN OF IMPRISONMENT

The media reflected and at the same time oriented the neo-punitive move in a very important way. Ronald Reagan's victory in 1980 was crucial for such a change, even if it should not be forgotten that the cultural turn goes back at least to 1973 or 1974. The changed rhetoric about crime, however, was part and parcel of a more general change in political rhetoric. As a *Time* magazine article put it, in 1982, an "imprisonment spree" ran across America:

> ...the public wants to 'get tough' with criminals, and legislators, prosecutors and judges are obeying that diffuse mandate by sending more people away for longer stretches [...] U.S. citizens [have] reached a critical level of panic and anger at what they feel is a constantly lurking threat (Anderson, 1982: 38, 40, quoted in Zimring and Hawkins, 1991: 128–29).

The increasing degree of propensity to punishment among the American public in this period can be gauged by the rising percentage of Americans answering "yes" to the question "Do you favor the death penalty for a person convicted of murder?" asked by Gallup every year since 1936. This percentage rose to an all-time-high of 72% in 1985, having reached an all-time low of 42% in 1966 (Zeisel and Gallup, 1989).

Imprisonment rates changed accordingly. Since 1870, American imprisonment rates had oscillated between 61 per 100,000 (in 1880) and 131 (in 1940). The relative stability, if not decline, of imprisonment rates in the 1950s and 1960s, until the low mark of 96 per 100,000 in 1970, was followed, after 1973, by "a long and uninterrupted ascent" (Zimring and Hawkins, 1991: 121). In 1994, for the first time one million people were locked up in United States and state prisons (excluding jails), or 387 per 100,000, up from 139 in 1980 and 96 in 1970—the rate, that is, quadrupled in 25 years!

To this, one should add another half a million in jail and about 3.5 million on probation or parole, reaching the astonishing count of 2.6% (in 1993) of United States resident population 18 years or older being under some kind of correctional care or supervision—that means almost 5% of males and almost 10% of the African-American population! In 1993, there were 2,920 black males in prison (without counting the jails) per 100,000 African Americans—in contrast with 398 white males, a ratio about seven times higher. Jerome Miller, Director of the National Center on Institutions and

Alternatives, stated that, if present trends continue, by 2010, "we will have the absolute majority of all African-American males between age 18 and 40 in prisons and camps" (Butterfield, 1995; see also Mauer, 1992; Tonry, 1995 and Miller, 1996).

It is quite interesting to note that even the rate for *female* black inmates was 165 per 100,000, a rate that is substantially higher than the *general* rate in all European countries—an interesting commentary on the fact that, whatever the reasons for such deep differences based on culture and race, they seem to be even stronger than gender. These rates were the highest in American history, and at the same time the highest in the world, leading South Africa (311/100,000) and the former Soviet Union (268/100,000 in 1989; even if not everybody agrees with this "low" estimate of imprisonment rates in the last year of the Soviet Union: According to Nils Christie the right number of Soviet inmates was between 353 and 392 per 100,000 (Christie, 1993: 30). Western European countries and Japan trail far behind with 40–120/100,000.

In other words, one could say that the United States seems to have been conducting a gigantic experiment. It is almost as if the American people had decided to take punishment seriously, and had tried to see whether, by increasing the rate of punishment indefinitely, something would happen to crime rates. Given, however, the very problematic nature of the impact on crime rates (see below), it seems that, under a criminal and punitive vocabulary, one can find the spearhead of a moral crusade that has the objective of bringing back America to the old and true values, as they were spelled out clearly in Ronald Reagan's 1981 inaugural address, which indicated the direction to the right-wing of the 1980s and 1990s.

Were this not the case, one would not understand the great emphasis on "fighting drugs," an emphasis that has been working as a terrible crime-multiplier in so far as there is no crime that is of a complete construction by law-makers and law-enforcers as much as drug crime. "In 1980, 19 people of every 1,000 who were arrested for narcotics violation were sent to prison. By 1992, 104 people were being imprisoned for every 1,000 arrested for drug offenses" (Holmes, 1994). As a result, between 1980 and 1993 the percentage of drug offenders among state and federal inmates rose from 8% to 26% (violent offenders fell from 57% to 45%, property offenders fell from 30% to 22% and public-order offenders rose from 5% to 7% (Beck and Gilliard, 1995: 10). Such results were connected to a "drug scare" triggered by the supposed "crack epidemic" that swept through the country in the second half of the 1980s (Reinarman and Levine, 1989; Bourgois, 1995).

Many were, however, the "crime waves" that punctuated the period between the mid-1970s and the present, from the campaign against driving under the influence (Gusfield, 1981), to the construction of the "missing children's crisis" (Joe, 1991), from the efforts to again penalize reproductive rights to calls for an intensification of punishment about such issues as domestic violence, censorship, pornography and rape (Daly, 1992; Lacombe, 1994; Pitch, 1990). Ironically, recent moral panics have shifted from children as victims to children as villains, as the concern around "youth crimes" has prompted the development of labels such as "super predators" (Cockburn, 1996).

As police "productivity" went up so did the judges' tendency (sometimes mandated by state and federal laws against their expressed uneasiness) to sentence defendants to prison terms. For instance, after the new sentencing guidelines were introduced with the United States Sentencing Reform Act that took effect on November 1, 1987, analyses showed that, whereas the average term indicated in the sentence was lower after the guidelines were passed, actually the average sentence *served* was longer than before the guidelines (analysis by the Administrative Office of the United States Courts (Margolick, 1992)). Furthermore, parole was severely limited and this became one of the main reasons for the increasing imprisonment rates, for instance in California (Berk et al., 1983). At the same time, the changes in the composition of the Supreme Court and the general conservative shift in the country made sure that, even where laws were not changed, the social, judicial and political environment would emphasize severity versus leniency at each decisional juncture in the criminal justice system. This very impressive increase in punishment accompanied through the 1980s a corresponding increase in crime that abated only in the first half of the 1980s, to start again after 1984, especially for violent crime.

The *results* of this impressive surge in imprisonment do not seem too impressive, therefore, except apparently for the years of the first Reagan presidency. However, many years earlier the unsuspectable James Q. Wilson had declared that he would have loved to be an adviser on crime to whoever was going to be elected president in 1980 (Wattenberg, 1983). He would have advised him to declare war on crime and after a few years to declare victory. This was mainly for demographic reasons. In fact, Darrell Steffensmeier and

Miles D. Harer (1991) have shown that the drop in the Uniform
Crime Reports and the National Crime Surveys in the period
1980–1988 (the Reagan period) was greatly responsive to changes
in the age structure of the population, which saw a decline of the
young males and an increase of its aging part. Accordingly, the idea
that "deterrence works" has been defined by James Austin and
John Irwin as "voodoo criminology" because:

> [F]or many young males, especially African Americans and Hispanics,
> the threat of going to prison or jail is no threat but rather an expected
> or accepted part of one's life. Most minority males will be punished
> by the criminal justice system during their lifetime. Deterrence and
> punishment are effective only when the act of punishment will actu-
> ally worsen your lifestyle. For millions of males, imprisonment poses
> no such threat (Austin and Irwin, 1993).

Probably also for this reason, the turn toward greater severity of the
last 20 years has been increasingly accompanied by all kind of ways
in which imprisonment can be made into an even harsher reality
than mere deprivation of liberty, from cutting TV watching and
sport activities in prison (Nossiter, 1994) to making prisoners pay
their own health costs, room and board and other bills (Schmitt,
1995), from reintroducing striped uniforms and chain gangs (Bragg,
1995) to creating "maximum security" nightmares such as Pelican
Bay State Prison in California (Rosenfeld, 1993; Cooper, 1995) and
the Federal Penitentiary under construction in Florence, Colorado
(Clines, 1994). Of course, increasing levels of violence have been
accompanying this overall worsening of the situation (Holmes,
1995; Purdy, 1995).

LESS ELIGIBILITY IN "THE CRISIS DECADES"

This *de facto* harshening of conditions of life in prisons—accompanied, as usual in the history of the institution, by an increasing
"overcrowding"—calls attention to a lasting trait of prison policies,
the idea, that is, of "less eligibility." Less eligibility is the penal
maxim by which the standard of living within prisons should
always be set at a lower level than the standard of living of the lowest "free" social stratum outside, in order to preserve the deterrence
of imprisonment as a punishment (Rusche and Kirchheimer, 1939).
     The very drastic penal turn that developed around 1974 coin-
cided almost exactly with the watershed year of 1973, the year of

the oil crisis and the start of "the crisis decades" (Hobsbawm, 1994: 403–32). After 1973, and for a good 20 years, all over the world but especially in the United States a global retrenchment from industrial production and from a factory-based economy took place: the beginning of so-called post-Fordist era.

At the same time, we have been witnessing an intensified international competition, which was particularly dramatic for the United States, a country that, for many years after World War II, had enjoyed the very special privilege of being almost the only really developed industrial nation. In 1960 the United States' standard of living was more than twice that of the other industrial countries; in 1992 it was only in the ninth place (Anonymous, 1992). There was a corresponding increase in poverty and inequality, with the return of social situations that many believed disappeared for ever, at least during "normal" times, such as homelessness.

This deterioration of economic and social conditions has triggered a general climate of resentment that, as Svend Ranulf showed in 1938, is often associated with calls for heightened punitiveness. When competition intensifies, then also social pressure to perform intensifies, together with the spread in social inequality (it is a common observation among economists that in good times the spread in income distribution reduces; the opposite happens in bad times).

In bad times, indulgence, generosity, experimentation tend to be shunned away and the social structure of rewards and punishment is again emphasized, both monetarily and, for those at the bottom of the social pyramid, penally. Accordingly, both in the United States and in Europe (even if much less in Europe), imprisonment increased.

In fact, in spite of the rhetoric associated with the "Reagan prosperity years," scholars have pointed out that, starting in the early 1970s through the early 1990s recession, the American economy has known a veritable "Silent Depression" during which, "abruptly after 1973 the rate of growth in *real* weekly earnings dropped... . [F]rom a 1973 peak of $327.45 in constant (1982–84) dollars, *real* weekly earnings [fell] to $264.76 in 1990 [...] the real weekly income of a worker in 1990 was 19.1 percent *below* the level reached in 1973!" (Peterson, 1991: 30).

In spite of the myth of consumerist 1980s, the so-called "me decade," only the richer 20% of the population spent appreciably more (Hall, 1990). Median family incomes in constant dollars stayed about the same during this period because more and more women entered the work-force and so more work outside the home made up for decreasing individual earnings. The result has been an unprecedented and unique increase in the time worked by Americans and especially by American women, both individually and as a whole. Juliet B. Schor has documented this increase in working hours since the end of the war and especially since the late 1960s, which has brought American workers, and especially American working women, to work an average of about two months a year longer than their European counterparts (1991: 2), and about a month a year more than they would have done some 20 years earlier (Schor, 1991: 29).

For the great majority of Americans, therefore, the last 20 years have meant working increasingly more for less and less real earnings. Correspondingly, inequality has increased and so has the poverty rate, which has been on a steady increase since 1974 (when it reached only 11.2%) and particularly since 1979, approximating the very high mark of 15% in 1991. This is particularly true for inner-city areas. In 1992, at the time of the South Los Angeles "rioting," the poverty rate, 30.3%, was even higher than at the time of the Watts riots of 1965, when it was 27% (Hubler and Ramos, 1992). That this area has become a terrain of contest between the ethnic gangs and the Los Angeles Police Department should therefore surprise nobody (Davis, 1990: 221–322).

One could very well consider the 1980s and the 1990s as an attempt by the United States' economic and political elites to restore class inequality and economic profitability to pre-1960s levels, given that, during the 1960s, profits had been declining and wage differentials had been reduced especially in favor of the poor and the minorities (Boddy and Crotty, 1975: 4–5, 9; Heap, 1980; Bowles and Gintis, 1982).

As Ronald Reagan promised in his famous speech on "America's New Beginning" (1981), this new beginning was supposed to take America back to the good old days before the New Deal—a mix of propaganda and wishful thinking certainly, but enough to cause at least a social redistribution of income and send everybody employed back to work harder! This is in fact all too apparent in the huge declines in the unionization rate (from 25.5% of the work force unionized in 1975 to 12.1% in 1990) and in the number of strikes, counted in the few hundreds in the early 1970s and in the few tens in 1990 (Hall, 1991).

The use of fear of crime for political and ideological purposes was crucial to such developments. It probably reached its climax with the presidential campaign of 1988 and the Willie Horton Story—the threatening black murderer who escaped from a prison furlough in Massachusetts to commit new crimes. George Bush's campaign used Horton's image *ad nauseam* to attack his opponent Michael Dukakis, who had been Massachusetts' Governor and who was then made to appear responsible for the furlough (Anderson, 1995). A sort of penal obsession—a penal obsession that ultimately gave rise to a veritable "crime industry" (Christie, 1993)—came to dominate American public life in the 1980s to reach its climax, in the early 1990s, with the "three-strikes-you-are-out" provisions (see below) and the new federal death penalty proposals.

Both George Bush and Bill Clinton, even if the latter had been elected on a somewhat moderately liberal platform, put forward crime bills that reflected this obsession. In fact Bill Clinton's crime bill, held hostage to a vocal "anti-crime" Republican majority in both houses, received backhanded praise from the right-wing. An editorial of *The Wall Street Journal* of January 26, 1994, wrote, under the title "Dick Tracy wins":

> We are writing these words just a few hours before a liberal President is to go before the nation in his State of the Union address and [...] call for: putting 100,000 police on the streets, putting three-time felons in prison forever and putting bad boys in boot camps. It looks like we're all Dick Tracy's now. An awful lot of innocent Americans have had to be robbed, beaten, stabbed, raped, tortured and murdered to arrive at the point where a Bill Clinton could feel compelled to get tough on crime. The good news is that the American system, most of the time, is able to bring off a mid-course correction before the train goes over the cliff (Anonymous, 1994).

Alongside, an opinion by Professor John J. Dilulio Jr. figured prominently, under the telling title "Let 'em Rot":

> ...solid majorities of Americans... believe that criminals who assault, rape, rob, burglarize, deal drugs or murder should be arrested, prosecuted and punished in a swift and certain fashion... Among the liberal elite, however, only gun control is politically correct; criminal control isn't... . By every measure, the anti-incarceration elite has been winning its tug-of-war with the public on crime (Dilulio, 1994).

These statements are particularly surprising because, as we have seen above, they were expressed at the end of 20 years of increasing

emphasis on the importance of certainty and severity of punishment in political and criminological discourse, and correspondingly
of rapidly increasing imprisonment rates. Crime rates on the other
hand had somehow stabilized or increased much less rapidly in the
1980s and 1990s than in the 1960s and 1970s (we have seen above
that the debate is open between conservatives and liberals whether
this was because of incapacitation and deterrence or because of the
demographic decline).

A hypothesis could be advanced that the fear of crime that fuels
the ongoing harshening of penality in the United States may be
more related to the intensity of media presentations of crime rather
than to the intensity of crime itself (Heath and Gilbert, 1996). It has
been shown, for instance, that between 1992 and 1993, the increase
in public preoccupation with crime was correlated much more
closely with the intensity of crime news coverage in the media than
with the intensity of criminal events. In a March 11, 1994 *San
Francisco Chronicle* article entitled: "Networks Boost Crime News"
the writer notes that:

> ...although government tallies found no substantial increase in crime
> or violent crime rates in 1993, the number of crime stories doubled
> last year on the ABC, CBS and NBC evening news shows. After
> monitoring all 13,474 stories on those broadcast, researchers at
> Washington's Center for Media and Public Affairs found that from
> 1992 to 1993, the number of crime stories was up from 830 to 1,698;
> broadcast reports of murder tripled, from 104 to 329. From May to
> February 1993, six times as many Americans rated crime as the coun-
> try's most important problem (up from 5 percent to 30 percent).

BOOMING IMPRISONMENT AND POST-FORDISM:
THE CASE OF CALIFORNIA'S "THREE STRIKES" LAW

Perhaps the most glaring example of the type of social processes we
are writing about occurred in California in 1994. As stated, over the
span of the past two decades California has shared with many other
North American states in an exponential growth in imprisonment,
heretofore virtually unseen. While most states have shown stag-
gering rates of increase, California has led the way in the scope and
scale of imprisoning. Between 1980 and 1994 the number of adult
individuals imprisoned in California increased fourfold, raising the
state's present prison population to just over 120,000, doubling the
rate of most other states (Zimring and Hawkins, 1994; Christie,

1993). By way of comparison, California's enormous prison population is now equivalent to the combined prison population of three European countries with a much greater general population than California: England, Germany, and Italy (Zimring and Hawkins, 1994). Yet, as grand as these numbers may appear, recent legal developments suggest California, along with several other states, has only just embarked on its imprisonment voyage.

On November 4, 1994, California's electorate joined 15 other states by voting into law its own version of one of the "toughest" pieces of penal legislation in recent history. California's proposition 184, more commonly referred to as the "three strikes and you're out" law (also known in other states as a habitual offender law), promised to redefine the way repeat felons are treated in the state. In an official title and summary prepared by the California State Attorney General, proposition 184 proposed to:

1. Increase sentences for defendants convicted of *any* felony who have prior convictions for violent or serious felonies such as rape, robbery, or burglary [emphasis added].
2. Convicted felons with one such prior conviction would receive twice the normal sentence for the new offense. Convicted felons with two or more such prior convictions would receive a sentence with a minimum term three times the normal sentence or 25 years, whichever is greater.
3. Includes as prior convictions certain felonies committed by juveniles 16 years of age or older.
4. Reduces sentence reduction credit which may be earned by these convicted felons.

Conservative estimates suggested that implementation of "three strikes" would result in tripling the state's prison population in 20 years, raising the prison population to over 350,000 (Greenwood, 1994). To date, over 12,000 "second" and "third strike" admissions have been exacted in just over two years.

As expected, given the considerable increase in imprisonment figures, the economic impact of the law was also predicted to be monumental. A summary of a legislative analyst's estimate of net state and local government fiscal impact of proposition 184 noted that the law would cost hundreds of millions of dollars annually, reaching about $3 billion in 2003 and about $6 billion annually by 2026. The bill would also ensure increased state prison construction costs by about $20 billion (California Ballot Pamphlet, 1994).

Albeit hints of possible economic savings due to potential reductions in crime associated with increased imprisonment were part of the pro "three strikes" discourse, in fact, most economic analysts argued quite the opposite. As with the above analysis, most provisions of increased funds necessary to house and feed California's post "three strikes" prison population hovered in the billions annually (Esparza, 1995).

The development and subsequent passage of "three strikes" occurred in the midst of a well documented, long-term, deep fiscal crisis which has rendered California, once considered an economic giant, an economic disaster. California's protracted economic woes were highlighted by a 1994 state fiscal deficit of over five billion dollars. As a result of the enormity of cost associated with the new law, analysts pointed to "three strikes" as a catalyst for ruin with several indicators suggesting that by the turn of the century, as "three strikes" gains momentum, one in every five tax dollars in California will go toward imprisonment.

In addition to confounding orthodox economic logic, the passage of "three strikes" defied conventional processes of law-making which tend to require lengthy public hearings, committee formation and debate as well as some period of partisan wrangling (Calavita, 1992). In contrast, California's "three strikes," in its present incarnation, was quickly pushed forth by a self-proclaimed fiscally conservative governor, and signed with barely a whisper of resistance among the state's political elite, including both ideological liberals and fiscal conservatives.

Some explanations for the development of the "three strikes" law have unconvincingly pointed to dramatic increases in crime. "Three strikes" is argued to be a rational, retributivist response to the rapidly growing and increasingly violent crime rate in California. The crime wave claim has been offered by both criminologists and politicians who contend that recidivist felons are the main culprits fueling the state's supposed recent crime wave. This argument, however, proves to be highly tendentious, as almost all state crime indicators show no significant rise in crime in California over the past decade. In fact, most indices point to a slight to moderate decrease in California's overall crime rate over the past few years. As Zimring and Hawkins note with regard to California's imprisonment "explosion":

> Whatever may have caused the explosive growth in prison population, crime trends in California...are not significantly related to the

imprisonment boom. Crime rates decreased during the first half of the 1980s in California and that pattern holds whether the subject is total reported crime, index felony offenses, or violent offenses (Zimring and Hawkins, 1994).

In addition to effects of election year "law and order" politicking, the development of California's "three strikes" law was influenced by the dramatic growth in the power of California's prison guards union. The CCPOA (California Correction Peace Officers Association) has become one of the most potent lobbying groups in the state. In fact, in both the 1992 and 1994 election campaigns, the CCPOA gave the second largest amount of PAC contributions in the state; in excess of one million dollars (Johnson, 1993). California now has nearly 23,000 prison guards, up from 7,000 only a decade ago.

The enormous growth in California prisons (now at 28 up from 12 a decade ago with an estimated 41 more prisons, at a construction cost of $10.2 billion, needed to house all of the inmate population attributed to "three strikes") has resulted in pro-prison legislators being the beneficiaries of CCPOA monies, and ensuring that pro-prison legislation continues. The imprisonment boom has also resulted in communities now competing for the monetary honor of being the home to one of California's fastest growing industries, the prison (Davis, 1995).

CONCLUSIONS

It is hard to believe that a society and a criminal science that are not able to go much beyond the very questionable goal of "incapacitating" criminals (forgetting both the replaceability of individuals in the criminal structure and the high rate of crime *inside* prisons) may still be able to conceive of prisons as gateways to democracy, able to produce "Republican machines," as in Benjamin Rush's apt image. The current aim of imprisonment seems to consist at most in *warehousing* criminals (Cohen, 1985). Maybe after the deep crisis of the 1970s, when penal institutions were deeply questioned at their very foundations, current penal systems have almost reconciled themselves with, and therefore accepted, their "demise," a demise, as Foucault indicated, that has always been functional to *using* the penal and prison systems to transform a potentially dangerous "illegalism" in a useful "delinquency" (Foucault, 1975: 257–92; Melossi, 1994).

The American prison system seems to be taken between an actual practice informed by this skeptical viewpoint and an almost desperate effort at incapacitation and deterrence, an experiment that is throwing into jail larger and larger sections of its citizenry and that, in the case of urban African American males, is approximating social if not biological genocide. Will such policies bring about an actual reduction in crime rates (independent of demographic change), or the "umpteenth" declaration of a failure in the war on crime, this time, however, after having devastated whole generations of Americans?

The fact is that, in spite of the often generous efforts of so many working in the prison industry, the situation seems today to have gone back to the days when the ends of imprisonment were at most custodial, and the institution had no loftier ambitions than keeping the officially defined bad apples from contaminating the others.

We could probably only conclude that in the same way in which, in the 18th-century, imprisonment was conceived as part of a more general moral and political program, a program that in North America was summarized under the banner of Republicanism, so today our attitudes toward officially defined deviance cannot be separated from the possible emergence, on the horizon of our societies, of new ideals and solutions, fitting the dawn of the new millennium. What such ideals and solutions might be is a matter that luckily escapes criminological imagination, and rests instead with the political and moral strivings of generations to come.

References

AFSC Working Party. (1971) *Struggle for Justice*. New York: Hill and Wang.

Anderson, Kurt. (1982) "What Are Prisons For?" *Time*, September 13: 38–41.

Anderson, David C. (1995) *Crime and the Politics of Hysteria*. New York: Random House.

Anonymous. (1994) "Dick Tracy Wins." *Wall Street Journal*, January 26: A14.

Anonymous. (1992) "Can America Succeed?" *San Francisco Chronicle*, May 26.

Austin, James and Irwin John. (1993) *Does Imprisonment Reduce Crime? A Critique of "Voodoo" Criminology*. San Francisco: National Council on Crime and Delinquency.

Bakal, Yitzhak (ed.). (1973) *Closing Correctional Institutions*. Lexington, Massachusetts: Lexington Books.

Barnes, Harry E. (1930) *The Story of Punishment*. Boston: The Stratford Company.

Beaumont, Gustave de and Tocqueville, Alexis de. (1833) *On the Penitentiary System of the United States and Its Application in France*. Philadelphia: Carey, Lea and Blanchard.

Beck, Allen J. and Gilliard, Darrell K. (1995) *Prisoners in 1994*. Bureau of Justice Statistics Bulletin. Washington, DC: US Department of Justice.

Becker, Gary. (1968) "Crime and Punishment: An Economic Approach." *Journal of Political Economy*, 76: 169–217.

Bentham, Jeremy. (1787) *Panopticon*, in *The Works of Jeremy Bentham*. (1971) New York: Russell and Russell. pp. 37–66.

Berk, Richard A., Messinger, Sheldon L., Rauma, David and Berecochea, John E. (1983) "Prisons as Self-Regulating Systems: A Comparison of Historical Patterns in California for Male and Female Offenders," *Law and Society Review*, 17(4) Fall: 547–586.

Boddy, Raford and Crotty, James. (1975) "Class Conflict and Macro Policy: The Political Business Cycle." *The Review of Radical Political Economics*, 7: 1–19.

Bourgois, Philippe. (1995) *In Search of Respect: Selling Crack in El Barrio*. Cambridge: Cambridge University Press.

Bowles, Samuel and Gintis, Herbert. (1982) "The Crisis of Liberal Democratic Capitalism: The Case of the United States." *Politics and Society*, 11: 51–93.

Bragg, Rick. (1995) "Chain Gangs to Return to Roads of Alabama." *New York Times*, March 26.

Brockway, Z. R. (1969) *Fifty Years of Prison Service; An Autobiography*. Montclair, New Jersey: Patterson Smith.

Butterfield, Fox. (1995) "More in U.S. Are in Prison, Report Says." *New York Times*, August 10: A14.

California Ballot Pamphlet. (1994) Election Ballot for State General Election. Sacramento, California.

Calavita, Kitty. (1992) *Inside the State: The Bracero Program, Immigration, and the I.N.S.* New York: Routledge.

Carroll, Leo. (1974) *Hacks, Blacks, and Cons: Race Relations in a Maximum Security Prison*. Lexington, MA: P.C. Heath.

Christie, Nils. (1993) *Crime Control as Industry*. London: Routledge.

Clemmer, Donald. (1940) *The Prison Community*. New York: Rinehart & Co.

Clines, Francis X. (1994) "A Futuristic Prison Awaits the Hard-Core 400." *New York Times*, October 17: A1.

Cockburn, Alexander. (1996) "The War on Kids." *The Nation*, June 3.

Cohen, Stanley. (1985) *Visions of Social Control*. Cambridge: Polity Press.

Cohn-Bendit, Daniel and Schmid, Thomas. (1993) *Patria Babilonia: La sfida della democrazia multiculturale*. Roma: Theoria, 1994.

Cooper, Claire. (1995) "Judge Orders Changes at Pelican Bay State Prison." *Sacramento Bee*, January 12: A1.

Daly, Kathleen. (1992) Comments in Plenary Session on "The Legal Construction of Social Identity: The Hill/Thomas Hearings." Law and Society Annual Meeting, Philadelphia.

Davis, Mike. (1995) "Hell Factories in the Field." *The Nation*, February 20.

————. (1990) *City of Quartz: Excavating the Future in Los Angeles*. London: Verso.

Dilulio, John J. (1994) "Let 'em Rot." *Wall Street Journal*, January 26: A1.

Dumm, Thomas L. (1987) *Democracy and Punishment: Disciplinary Origins of the United States*. Madison: The University of Wisconsin Press.

Durkheim, Emile. (1897) *Suicide*. Glencoe: Free Press, 1951.

Esparza, David. (1995) *The "Three Strikes and You're Out" Law: A Preliminary Assessment*. Sacramento: Legislative Analyst's Office.

Fitzpatrick, Peter. (1995) "The Constitution of The Excluded— Indians and Others," in Ian Loveland (ed.) *A Special Relationship? American Influences on Public Law in the United Kingdom*. Oxford: Clarendon Press. pp. 191–212.

Foucault, Michel. (1975) *Discipline and Punish*. New York: Pantheon, 1977.

Franklin, Benjamin. (1751) "Observations Concerning the Increase of Mankind," in *The Papers of Benjamin Franklin*, Vol. 4. New Haven, Connecticut. pp. 234.

Friedman, Lawrence M. (1993) *Crime and Punishment in American History*. New York: Basic Books.

Garland, David. (1990) *Punishment and Modern Society: A Study in Social Theory*. Chicago: The University of Chicago Press.

————. (1985) *Punishment and Welfare: A History of Penal Strategies*. Aldershot: Gower.

Gitlin, Todd. (1987) *The Sixties*. New York: Bantam Books.

Goffman, Erving. (1961) *Asylums*. New York: Anchor Books.

Gottfredson, Michael R. and Hirschi, Travis. (1990) *A General Theory of Crime*. Stanford: Stanford University Press.

Greenberg, David F. (1977) "The Correctional Effects of Corrections: A Survey of Evaluations," in D.F. Greenberg (ed.), *Corrections and Punishment*. Beverly Hills: Sage. pp. 111–48.

Greenberg, David F. and Humphries, Drew. (1980) "The Cooptation of Fixed Sentencing Reform." *Crime and Delinquency*, 26: 206–25.

Greenwood, Peter W. (1994) *Three Strikes and You're Out: Estimated Benefits and Costs of California's New Mandatory Sentencing Law*. Santa Monica: Rand.

Gusfield, Joseph. (1981) *The Culture of Public Problems. Drinking-Driving and the Symbolic Order*. Chicago: University of Chicago Press.

Hall, Carl T. (1991) "Hard Times for American Unions." *San Francisco Chronicle*, February 11: D1.

————. (1990) "1980s Wasn't a Decade Of Spending, Study Says." *San Francisco Chronicle*, April 17: C1.

Heap, Shanu H. (1980) "World Profitability Crisis in the 1970s: Some 1981 Empirical Evidence." *Capital and Class*, 12: 66–84.

Heath, Linda and Gilbert, Kevin. (1996) "Mass Media and Fear of Crime." *American Behavioral Scientist*, 39: 379–86.

Hobsbawm, Eric. (1994) *Age of Extremes: The Short Twentieth Century 1914–1991*. London: Michael Joseph.

Holmes, Steven A. (1995) "Inmate Violence Is On Rise As Federal Prisons Change." *New York Times*, February 9. p. A1: 5.

————. (1994) "Ranks of Inmates Reach One Million in a 2-Decade Rise." *New York Times*, October 28. p. A1: 1.

Horkheimer, Max and Adorno, Theodor W. (1947) *Dialectic of Enlightenment*. New York: Herder & Herder, 1972.

Hubler, Shawn and George Ramos. (1992b) "South L.A.'s Poverty Rate Worse Than 65." *Los Angeles Times*, May 11. A1: 6.

Ignatieff, Michael. (1978) *A Just Measure of Pain: The Penitentiary in the Industrial Revolution 1750–1850*. London: Macmillan.

Irwin, John. (1970) *The Felon*. Englewood Cliffs, New Jersey: Prentice-Hall Inc.

————. (1980) *Prisons in Turmoil*. Chicago: Little, Brown and Co.

Jacobs, James B. (1977) *Stateville: The Penitentiary in Mass Society*. Chicago: The University of Chicago Press.

Jankovic, Ivan. (1977) "Labor Market and Imprisonment." *Crime and Social Justice*, 8: 17–31.

Joe, Karen A. (1991) *Milk Carton Madness: The Heart of the Missing Children's Crisis*. Ph.D. Thesis in Sociology, University of California, Davis.

Johnson, Tom. (1993) "Prison Powerbrokers: The Rise of California's Correctional Officers Union." *Sacramento News and Review*, March 11.

Lacombe, Dany. (1994) *Blue Politics: Pornography and the Law in the Age of Feminism*. Toronto: University of Toronto Press.

Lipton, D., Martinson, Robert and Wilks, J. (1975) *The Effectiveness of Correctional Treatment: A Survey of Treatment Evaluation Studies*. New York: Praeger.

Margolick, David. (1992) "Chorus of Judicial Critics Assail Sentencing Guides." *New York Times*, April 12: 1.

Martinson, Robert. (1974) "What Works? Questions and Answers About Prison Reform." *The Public Interest* 35: 22–54.

Marx, Karl. (1844) "Contribution to the Critique of Hegel's Philosophy of Right. Introduction," in K. Marx, *Early Writings*. New York: McGraw-Hill, 1964: 41–60.

Matza, David. (1969) *Becoming Deviant*. Englewood Cliffs, New Jersey: Prentice-Hall.

Mauer, Marc. (1992) *American Behind Bars: One Year Later*. Report by The Sentencing Project, Washington DC.

Mckelvey, Blake. (1977) *American Prisons: A History of Good Intentions*. Montclair, New Jersey: Patterson Smith.

————. (1936) *American Prisons: A Study in American Social History Prior to 1915*. Chicago: University of Chicago Press.

Melossi, Dario. (1994) "The 'Economy' of Illegalities: Normal Crimes, Elites, and Social Control in Comparative Analysis." in D. Nelken (ed.) *Futures of Criminology*. London: Sage. pp. 202–19.

————. (1980) "Strategies of Social Control in Capitalism: A Comment on Recent Work." *Contemporary Crises*, 4: 381–402.

Melossi, Dario and Pavarini, Massimo. (1977) *The Prison and the Factory: Origins of the Penitentiary System*. London: Macmillan, 1981.

Miller, Jerome G. (1996) *Search and Destroy: African American Males in the Criminal Justice System*. New York: Cambridge University Press.

Mills, C. Wright. (1956) *The Power Elite*. New York: Oxford University.

National Advisory Commission On Criminal Justice Standards And Goals. (1973) *Task Force Report on Corrections*. Washington, DC: Government Printing Office.

National Council On Crime And Delinquency. (1973) "The Non-dangerous Offender Should Not Be Imprisoned," *Crime and Delinquency*, 19: 449–56.

Nelken, David. (ed.) (1994) *The Futures of Criminology*. London: Sage.

Nossiter, Adam. (1994) "Making Hard Time Harder, States Cut Jail TV and Sports." *New York Times*, September 17: 1.

O'Connor, James. (1973) *The Fiscal Crisis of the State*. New York: St. Martin's Press.

Paz, Octavio. (1978) "Mexico and the United States." In O. Paz, *The Labyrinth of Solitude*. London: Penguin Books.

Peterson, Wallace C. (1991) "The Silent Depression." *Challenge* 34/4: 29–34.

Pitch, Tamar. (1990) "From Oppressed to Victims: Collective Actors and the Symbolic Use of the Criminal Justice System." *Studies in Law, Politics and Society* 10: 103–17.

Purdy, Matthew. (1995) "Even at a Time of Relative Calm, Rikers Stands on the Razor's Edge." *New York Times*, May 15. A1: 4.

Rafter, Nicole H. (1992) "Criminal Anthropology in the United States." *Criminology*, 30: 525–45.

————. (1985) *Partial Justice: Women in State Prisons, 1800–1935*. Boston: Northeastern University Press.

Ranulf, Svend. (1938) *Moral Indignation and Middle Class Psychology*. Copenhagen: Levin and Munskgaard.

Reagan, Ronald. (1981) "America's New Beginning: Program for Economic Recovery." Address Before the Congress, February 18.

Reinerman, Craig and Levine, Harry G. (1989) "Crack in Context: Politics and Media in the Making of a Drug Scare." *Contemporary Drug Problems*, 16: 535–77.

Rosenfeld, Seth. (1993) "Inmates Sue Prison for Cruelty." *San Francisco Chronicle*, September 12. B1: 13.

Rothman, David J. (1980) *Conscience and Convenience: The Asylum and its Alternatives in Progressive America*. Boston: Little, Brown and Co.

————. (1971) *The Discovery of the Asylum: Social Order and Disorder in the New Republic*. Boston: Little, Brown and Co.

Rusche, Georg and Kirchheimer, Otto. (1939) *Punishment and Social Structure*. New York: Russell & Russell, 1969.

Sabol, William J. (1989) "Racially disproportionate prison population in the United States." *Contemporary Crises*, 13: 405–32.

Schmitt, Richard B. (1995) "Debt to Society: More and More Jails Are Charging Inmates For Their Incarceration." *Wall Street Journal*, March 3. A1: 1.

Schor, Juliet B. (1991) *The Overworked American*. New York: Basic Books.

Scull, Andrew T. (1977) *Decarceration: Community Treatment and the Deviant A Radical View*. Englewood Cliffs, New Jersey: Prentice-Hall.

Sellin, J. Thorsten. (1976) *Slavery and the Penal System*. New York: Elsevier.

————. (1964) "Tocqueville and Beaumont and Prison Reform in France," in De Beaumont and De Tocqueville (1833). pp. xv–xl.

————. (1953) "Philadelphia Prisons of the Eighteenth Century." *Transactions of the American Philosophical Society*. New Series, 43, Part I, pp. 326–30.

————. (1944) *Pioneering in Penology*. Philadelphia: University of Pennsylvania Press.

Sparks, Richard, Bottoms, Anthony E. and Hay, Will. (1996) *Prisons and the Problem of Order*. Oxford: Clarendon Press.

Steffensmeier, Darrell and Harer, Miles D. (1991) "Did Crime Rise or Fall During the Reagan Presidency? The effects of an 'aging' U.S. population on the nation's crime rate." *Journal of Research in Crime and Delinquency*, 28: 330–59.

Sutton, John. (1989) *Stubborn Children: Controlling Delinquency in the USA, 1640–1981.* Berkeley: University of California Press.

Sykes, Gresham M. (1958) *The Society of Captives: A study of a maximum security prison.* Princeton: Princeton University Press.

Takagi, Paul. (1975) "The Walnut Street Jail: A Penal Reform to Centralize the Powers of the State." *Federal Probation* (December).

Takaki, Ronald. (1979) *Iron Cages: Race and Culture in 19th-Century America.* New York: Knopf.

Taylor, Ian, Walton, Paul and Young, Jock. (1973) *The New Criminology.* London: Routledge.

Tocqueville, Alexis de. (1835–40) *Democracy in America.* Two volumes. New York: Schocken, 1961.

Tonry, Michael H. (1995) *Malign Neglect: Race, Crime and Punishment in America.* New York: Oxford University Press.

Treiber, H. and Steinert, Heinz. (1980) *Die Fabrikation des zuverlässigen Menschen.* Munich: Moos.

Useem, Bert and Kimball, Peter. (1991) *States of Siege: U.S. Prison Riots 1971–1986.* New York: Oxford University Press.

Van Den Haag, Ernest. (1975) *Punishing Criminals.* New York: Basic Books.

Von Hirsch, Andrew. (1976) *Doing Justice.* New York: Hill and Wang.

Wattenberg, Ben. (1983) "The Crime Nightmare Could Be Over." *Los Angeles Times,* July 20: II–5.

Weber, Max. (1906) "The Protestant Sects and the Spirit of Capitalism," in H.H. Gerth and C. Wright Mills (eds.) *From Max Weber: Essays in Sociology.* New York: Oxford University Press, 1946: 302–22.

Wilson, James Q. and Herrnstein, R. (1985) *Crime and Human Nature.* New York: Touchstone.

Zeisel, Hans and Gallup, Alec M. (1989) "Death Penalty Sentiment in the United States." *Journal of Quantitative Criminology,* 5: 285–96.

Zimring, Franklin E. and Hawkins, Gordon. (1994) "The Growth of Imprisonment in California." *British Journal of Criminology,* 34: 83–96.

————. (1991) *The Scale of Imprisonment.* Chicago: The University of Chicago Press.

Chapter
TWO

Canadian Prisons[1]

Bob Gaucher and John Lowman

In memory of Clare Culhane, prison activist

The Correctional Service of Canada, as part of the criminal justice system, contributes to the protection of society by actively encouraging and assisting offenders to become law abiding citizens, while exercising reasonable, safe, secure and humane control.

> Correctional Service of Canada, *Mission Statement* (1989).

Boredom, blood, tears, futility, that is what prison is all about. How uncanny that this description echoes words often spoken of life in the trenches of war.

> Jo-Anne Mayhew (1988), prisoner at Kingston Penitentiary for Women

Ever since Kingston Penitentiary opened in 1835, the Canadian prison system has been the subject of numerous commissions and inquiries, beginning in 1849 with the Brown Commission. Through the years, these reports have offered everything from supportive criticism to scathing condemnation of the prison system. While they have differed in the way they justify future use of prisons, and they all do, they nearly all share the same disillusionment: the realization that the punitive and reformative purposes of imprisonment cannot easily be reconciled. One could go to just about any period over the past 150 years in Canada to find a pithy quote to summarize this, the most abiding dilemma of Western prisons. Because in this paper we focus on developments during the past 20 years, here is one from a recent edition of *Maclean's*, a national weekly news magazine. In this case, the opinion is that of a prison guard with some 20 years' experience at Collin's Bay, a maximum security penitentiary in Ontario:

> If you want to make a bomb, you take a hard outer casing, you put a fuse on it, and you pack it with all kinds of volatile material...In our prisons you have a hard outer casing, which is the fence, and you put all sorts of volatile people inside and they're all bouncing off each other trying to get along. There's drugs and tension and violence. (Jenish, et al., 1996: 46)

It's difficult to see how one might make more law abiding people by putting them in a "world where horror is routine, and cruelty commonplace" (Marron, 1996: 4), and indeed, the guard continues, "When inmates come out, they need to shed the survival skills they've learned inside" if they want to stay on the street. The idea that imprisonment as we know it is, itself, criminogenic, is hardly new. But it seems to be completely ignored by those people who are currently lobbying for longer sentences and more restrictive parole.

Another feature of prison held out to be an impediment to its reformatory goal is the nature of the relationship between the turnkey and the prisoner. It is difficult for "guards," or whatever we call them, not to see their work as the imposition of punishment on offenders for crime they have committed. Euphemisms from the past, like "correctional officer" and "living unit officer" (Gamberg and Thomson, 1984), or the "case management teams" of contemporary parlance do not change the resentment that any human being is likely to feel when someone else locks him or her up. Regardless of what management rhetoric might say about the service component of the job, for the turnkey, the custodial function tends to be paramount. Through the years, many observers of Canadian prisons (notably the reports by Ouimet, 1969; MacGuigan, 1977; and Arbour, 1996) have recognized that custodial and reformatory efforts tend to contradict each other. But more than this, some critics have questioned the very idea that the state can reintegrate someone into society by separating him or her from it.

And yet, because of a new emphasis on public safety and concern for victims' rights through the 1980s and '90s, Canadian imprisonment rates are climbing, sentences for certain offenses are getting longer and parole eligibility rules have been tightened. In 1989, the Correctional Service of Canada (CSC) published a *Mission Statement* that signaled key changes in the philosophy guiding the operation of the prison system. Then, in 1992, the legislation governing prisons and parole was completely overhauled when the *Correctional and Conditional Release Act* (CCRA) replaced the *Penitentiary Act* and the *Parole Act*.

In this paper we describe trends in prison practice, and changes in the formal rhetoric guiding the Canadian prison system, particularly as identified in the *Mission Statement* and the *CCRA*, and identify some of the forces producing those changes. However, while the *Mission Statement* and new *Act* have been heralded as ushering in a new era of "corrections"—or, at least, a new era in terms of how system managers represent what they are doing—when outsiders have looked inside prisons, they have told a very different story about change.

We review two accounts published in the Spring of 1996 that indicate how practice and rhetoric diverge. The first is the report by Madam Justice Arbour of her *Commission of Inquiry into Certain Events at the Prison for Women in Kingston*. Arbour did not restrict her comments to certain shocking law violations by CSC staff at the women's prison known as "P4W," but attacked the very way the prison service is run.

The second is journalist Kevin Marron's book, *The Slammer: The Crisis in Canada's Penitentiary System*. Aided by a grant from the Canada Council, Marron traveled Canada from coast to coast interviewing prisoners, guards, administrators, members of the parole board and prison activists about the state of Canada's prisons. The picture he paints of prison is of a cruel and degrading environment plagued by the very problems it is supposed to protect citizens from.

We build on these and other accounts, such as Melnitzer's (1995) prisoner ethnography and the recent report by the Federal Sentencing and Corrections Review Group (1996), to outline some of the issues facing Canada's prison system.

POLITICAL CULTURE AND IMPRISONMENT:
GETTING TOUGH ON CRIME

Canadian penal policy has been strongly influenced by the USA from the outset, and still is today. Kingston, the first penitentiary in Upper Canada (opened in 1835), was modeled after the Auburn system in New York State. The Youth Reformatory at Elmira, New York, had a major influence on penological discourse at the beginning of the 20th century, and from the late 1930s through the 1970s, the treatment of youth and the liberal reform model in Canada were strongly influenced by the US discourse on rehabilitation fashioned by the social scientists involved in penological matters. Since the 1970s, the US literature pronouncing the demise of rehabilitation has had an on-going influence in Canada, and here in the 1980s and 90s, as in the US, there has been a shift to the right in both political rhetoric and fiscal policy.

In Canada, since the election of the Conservative Mulroney government in 1984, there has been a distinct shift away from the policies of the liberal interventionist state, and a rejection of the philosophy of Keynesian economics in favor of the monetarist policies of the Reagan/Bush and Thatcher/Major regimes (Chernomas and Black, 1996). Various US-originated innovations in policing and surveillance (e.g. Crime Stoppers, Neighborhood Watch) are emulated in Canada. And US law and order rhetoric, as reported through reactionary US media which have a pervasive influence in Canada (most cities have as many or more US TV stations than they do Canadian ones), has come to the fore in a model of criminal justice that stresses incapacitation of offenders in the name of social defense. This "creeping conservatism" (Young, 1996) is prominent in the policies of the right-wing Reform Party of Canada, which is now lobbying for a Bill of Victims' Rights and longer sentences for persons convicted of all indictable offenses. Also, it is prominent among the network of police organizations, such as the National Police Association, and citizens groups allied with them (e.g. Victims of Violence and CAVEAT) who lobby for a more punitive approach to crime in the name of public safety. There is widespread public support for the return of the death penalty, but so far Canada's politicians of both liberal and conservative stripe have declined to take this step backwards. The main targets of these influential victims' rights lobby groups have been the *Young Offenders' Act*, sentence lengths for violent offenders, capital punishment, parole and judicial review legislation applying to life sentences, the release of sex offenders who have served their time and several high profile multiple murder "monsters" who occasion vast amounts of publicity (Olson, Bernardo). Victim rights lobbying focused around several high profile murders committed in the late 1980s by offenders on temporary absence permits (Gingras, Stanton) or parole (Fredericks), and helped to bring about wholesale changes to the policy, practice and membership of the Parole Board.

A new federal bill was recently tabled that, if passed, will keep violent offenders in prison for longer, and allow electronic monitoring of individuals deemed to be potentially violent, even if they have not been charged with a crime (*Maclean's*, 1996). The bill would create the new category of "long term offender," this designation applying mainly to "sexual predators." Such offenders would be supervised for at least ten years after release. Also the bill would allow indefinite sentences for persons adjudicated to be "dangerous offenders."

In Ontario, almost immediately after the right wing Harris government was elected in 1995, rehabilitation programs in the provincial prison system were gutted. Provincial halfway houses were closed down, and the head of the Provincial Parole Board and many members were replaced. There were major reductions in the funding of Legal Aid. Defense lawyers in Toronto and Ottawa demonstrated against the cuts; some lawyers now refuse to handle legal aid cases, and others are threatening to. There may be more legal aid budget cuts to come, including cutting of aid to repeat offenders, except in homicide cases. The Harris government is also considering privatization of traffic control on highways (Canadian Press, 1996d).

None of this is to say that Canadian trends can simply be "read off" developments in the US, or that the neoconservative incursion is quite as complete as some authors (e.g. Chernomas and Black, 1996) imply. For one thing, conservative parties have recently suffered some resounding defeats in Canada, as was the case with the "Progressive Conservatives" (an oxymoron, if there ever was one) at the federal level in 1993, and the "Social Credit" Party in British Columbia, which, with one four-year exception in the 1970s, held power continuously from 1945 until 1992, when it was reduced to six seats, and subsequently to no seats in the 1996 election. Also, there are major differences in the political colors of the Canadian provincial governments. In British Columbia, the NDP, a left-leaning

social democratic party, has now held power since 1992, and also in
Quebec the political current is very different from the conservative
tide that has swept Ontario, and from the long-standing conservatism of Alberta. The social-democratic philosophy of the Parti
Québécois and Bloc Québécois has produced increasingly liberal
views on prisons. This has resulted in the closing of four provincial
prisons with more closures to come. Many Quebec politicians are
still in the business of supporting the welfare state. Sovereignty
association is held out to be one way of defending it from the right
wing policies of other Canadian parties, particularly the fledgling
Reform Party, which now represents the main right wing political
party in Canada following the massive defeat of the Progressive
Conservatives in 1993.

In Canada, the neoconservative discourse on crime and punishment has not been so overwhelming as to drown out all other
voices. For example, in June 1996 the Canadian Broadcasting
Corporation program "Ideas" aired ten one-hour evening segments
on *Prison and Its Alternatives* examining penal theory and practice in
North America, Europe and Japan (Doran, 1996). The series included
interviews with many of the prison's most noted critics, including
Nils Christie and Louk Hulsman. Also, the *Prison News Service* and
Journal of Prisoners on Prisons provide forums for prisoners and ex-
prisoners to write about their experiences.[2]

At a more general level, there are many differences between
Canada and the US in terms of the material, political and cultural
contexts of the two countries. The growth of imprisonment in
Canada described below pales in comparison to the great exclusion
that has recently taken place in the US, where the number of people
imprisoned at any one time rose from just over 200,000 in 1974 to
1.5 million in 1994.

One important difference between the two countries is the "bifurcation" that is occurring in the Canadian punishment system. While
there has been increasing pressure put on government to get tough
with serious crime, so there has been a countervailing movement by
senior justice system officials and both provincial and federal politicians to push for decarceration of less serious property offenders.

Growth and Composition of the Prison Population

The major expansion of federal penal institutions commenced in the
late 1950s. In 1958 there were nine federal penitentiaries in Canada

operating on a budget of $19 million. By 1993 there were 60 federal institutions[3] operating on a budget of $959.2 million. In 1992–93 federal and provincial governments combined spent about two billion dollars on corrections, a 28% increase from five years earlier.[4] The growth of federal prison populations has kept pace with the expansion of prison capacity over the past two decades. In 1993–94 there were 32,500 prisoners on average in federal and provincial institutions (Bronskill, 1995), and in 1994 the Canadian Center for Justice Statistics reported that the peak daily average reached 33,900 (*Ottawa Citizen*, 1996a). In 1981 the average was 22,800 (Solicitor General, 1982).

The change in federal prison populations reflects the growth of the number of life and other long term sentence prisoners, including sex offenders and drug traffickers. For example, in 1993–94 the median sentence for new federal prisoners was 46.3 months, up 6.7% from the previous year. In 1984, sex offenders comprised 7% of the federal prison population. By 1994, that proportion was 17% (Marron, 1996: 194–197). Because of the introduction of mandatory minimum parole eligibility periods for first and second degree murder, the number of prisoners serving life sentences has increased. Also, since the death penalty was formally abolished in 1976, there has been a shift in charging practices and jury adjudications. With the death penalty gone, there has been a greater willingness to charge and convict people for first degree murder, as opposed to second degree murder or manslaughter.[5] For example, in 1977 when there were 711 homicides, 202 (28.4%) involved first degree murder charges. In 1985, the proportion of first degree murder had risen to 48% (Statistics Canada, 1987), and in 1994 when there were 596 homicides, it was 50.5% (Statistics Canada, 1995). The relative increase in length of sentences created by the increased proportion of first degree murder charges occurred during a period when the actual homicide rate declined.

Fewer prisoners are receiving early release (Federal Sentencing and Corrections Review Group, 1995). There has been a decline in the parole granting rate over the past 20 years ranging from a high of 39% in 1983–84 to a low of 29% in 1988–89 (Federal Sentencing and Corrections Review Group, 1995). From 1993 to 1995 the number of day and full parole cases fell by nearly 20%. The rate of day paroles granted fell from 65% to 58%, and the number of full paroles from 34% to 19%, prompting the Executive Director of the Ontario John Howard Society to comment, "the parole board has abolished parole... It's become a lock up system" (Jenish, et al., 1996: 45).

Also, there is evidence of further "proliferation" of control, the process by which new classifications of control and treatment require new sets of rules and codes, the violations of which are sanctioned (Lowman and MacLean, 1992). Technical violations (missing a curfew, drinking, etc.) are now more likely to result in parole revocation.[6] For example, in March 1996 parolees were notified by a letter from the National Parole Service that if they were convicted of any offense, no matter how minor, their parole would be revoked immediately, and they would have to re-apply from inside the prison. Lifers and long term parolees who had been on parole long enough to reduce contact with their parole officer to once a year, or if they were moving, etc., have been told they must start again reporting to police and to their parole officer monthly.

At the same time there has been an expansion of imprisonment, the debt problems of the Canadian state have worsened. More punishment at the hard end of the system must be achieved for less money overall. The solution now being proposed is to reduce the flow of prisoners by following through the argument that dates back to the Ouimet Committee of 1969: Use prison only as a last resort, decarcerate the less serious offenders.

Bifurcation

In his discussion of decarceration and the economy of penal reform, Matthews (1979) suggested that criminal justice net widening involves three inter-related processes: "expansion" (the growth of the prison population, growth of staff numbers and building of new facilities), "acceleration" (the process whereby people who are classified into the lower security levels of the system make a more and more rapid progression through the lower levels to the point at which they are discharged), and "bifurcation" (the tendency for every new classification of lesser severity to be accompanied by the development of one of greater severity). In Canada over the past 20 years, we have seen all these processes at work, plus the "proliferation" noted above. Over the past five or so years, a form of bifurcation has emerged to lessen the fiscal strain that get tough policies engender.

The counterpoint to the get tough policy with violent offenders, sex offenders and recidivists is the initiative to reduce prison intake of non-violent offenders. This initiative has occurred in several provinces and at the Federal level. For example, in Alberta, "Up to 15 percent of the 2,700 criminals in Alberta's jails could be kept out of prison under a new provincial plan to get tough on violent offenders. The new strategy...would see harsher sentences for serious and violent offenders while keeping minor criminals out of jail" (Southam Newspapers, 1996). In New Brunswick, plans are under way to reduce adult provincial prison space by 25% and shift five million dollars of expenditures to community-based rehabilitation programs (Cox, 1996). In Quebec, there are plans to close six provincial facilities, creating a saving of sixteen million dollars (Seguin, 1996). And recently Ontario announced sweeping restructuring of its justice system to reduce the number of crimes being formally processed through court. A three tier system is being proposed, with "serious" crime (violence, sexual offenses and drugs) in the top tier, impaired driving in the second, and all other offenses (break-ins, fraud, business theft, mischief, embezzlement etc.) in the third. Under this plan, the majority of offenders will only go to court if there is a "substantial likelihood" of conviction. The new focus on taking only "sure winners" and the most serious crimes through court is proposed in the name of cutting costs by about 60 million dollars a year (Canadian Press, 1996b; Branswell, 1996).

Then there is the federal Bill C-41 which "will give judges the right to sentence non-violent crooks to 'conditional' jail terms to be served at home while abiding by other court ordered conditions, including taking drug and alcohol counseling, refraining from their addictions, doing community work service and providing for their families" (Clark, 1996). The explicit purpose of the new style of proposed sentence is to reduce overcrowding in the provincial prison system.

The Bill presumably got some of its stimulus from the report of the Federal Sentencing and Corrections Review Group, which came to light only after a journalist obtained it under the *Access to Information Act* (Bronskill, 1995). The working group comprised some of Canada's top criminal justice officials including the Commissioner of the Correctional Service of Canada (CSC), the Chair of the National Parole Board and the deputy ministers of the Departments of Justice and the Solicitor General. The working group concluded that the growing prison population—Canada now has the second highest imprisonment rate among Western democracies—will produce a financial and social crisis: "Canada's criminal justice system is at a crossroads...We face a crisis in the medium term if governments do not act now to create an effective and sustainable system of policing, sentencing, corrections and parole." Like its provincial counterparts, the Committee recommended a two-pronged approach: heavy penalties for violent offenders, and new cheaper alternatives for offenders who pose little risk to public safety. The group is said to have little faith in the highly punitive approach in the US, which has led to "more prisons, more inmates, minimal programming and less effective corrections" (Bronskill, 1995).

 · Of course, it is important to recognize that the philosophy of decarceration at the soft end of the system fits different political manifestos. In Quebec, it is geared to treating convicts with greater compassion and humanity, in a liberalism that self-consciously resists the conservative trend sweeping across North America. But decarceration also fits the fiscal agenda of neoconservatives in provinces like Alberta, because one effect of longer sentences is that the federal government has to pay for them (recall that the provinces pay to house prisoners serving less than two years, while the federal government pays for the rest: see endnote 4). With longer sentences at one end, and more community programs at the other, the provinces can save money at both ends of the prison system for which they are responsible.

And while Canadians may distance themselves from the punitiveness of the US system which imprisons people at more than three times the Canadian rate, one Yukon Judge has said that in Canada one in three young people who go to court end up in custody as compared to one in six in the US (Doran, 1996). The rate at which Canadian young offenders have been sentenced to closed custody has steadily risen over the past five years. And yet, for some victims' rights groups, this is not enough. They are still calling for an overhauling of the *Young Offenders Act*, and for an increase in the maximum three year sentence currently available, even though under the current legislation youths can be raised to adult court where they are subject to the same sentences as adults.

Another aspect of Canadian developments that has gone largely unnoticed is that drug trafficking and importation offenders continue to be ranked as "dangerous" in institutional and parole decisions. In all the talk about decarcerating less serious offenders, there is no indication that drug charges will be treated any more leniently than they are now. In other words, there is every indication that the Canadian state intends to continue to treat drug use and abuse as a criminal rather than a health problem, which is one reason why there are more illicit drug users in Canadian prisons than there are in treatment centers (Marron, 1996: 76).

CONTROL TALK: PRISON SYSTEM RHETORIC

In order to describe the rhetoric of imprisonment prevailing in Canada today, we focus on the Correctional Service of Canada (CSC) *Mission Statement* first published in 1989, and the *Corrections and Conditional Release Act* (*CCRA*) enacted in 1992, because they spell out the principles that are supposed to guide the operation of the contemporary penitentiary system.

The *CCRA* has been interpreted as marking a fundamental break from the rehabilitation principle that guided Canadian control talk from the 1938 Archambault report on because its first operating principle is that, "the protection of society be the paramount consideration in the corrections process" (for example, see Ratner, 1992; Griffiths and Verdun-Jones, 1994). However, it does not abandon the rhetoric of rehabilitation, and is consistent with the *Mission Statement*. And while Canadian prisons are moving more and more to a warehousing model in practice, there is an important rights discourse in their rhetoric.

The issuing of the *Mission Statement* is partly a reflection of the growing pressure for public institutions to be more accountable. Also, there has been an increasing corporatization of corrections over the past ten years, and the refinement of a "management" approach (Ekstedt and Jackson, 1997). One indication of this growing pressure for accountability is that neither the *Corrections Act* nor the *Parole Act*, which the *CCRA* replaced, made any statement about the principles or purposes of imprisonment or parole, which were taken as being self-evident. As of 1985, there are references to custody, treatment, training, employment and discipline in the *Penitentiary Act* (see the "interpretation" of "penitentiary" under section 2, and regulation 37(1)(b), but the term "rehabilitation" was not used. Similarly, the *Parole Act* as it stood in 1985 said nothing about the philosophy and purpose of parole. Instead, the two acts read like manuals describing the "how to" and "by what authority" of corrections.

Alongside the general pressure for government institutions to become more accountable are the specific issues that have been

raised by the observers and critics of Canada's prisons, be they sit-
ting on government commissions (e.g. MacGuigan Commission,
1977; Task Force on Federally Sentenced Women, 1990; etc.) or
working independently (e.g. Culhane, 1980; 1985; 1991; Jackson,
1983). Many key issues have been fought out in the language of
prisoners' rights, and the results can be seen in the new legislation.
Of course, how the rhetoric plays out in practice is a different story,
an issue we take up in the second half of this paper.

The CSC Mission Statement and Corporate Operation Plan

There is a substantial prison service literature describing the role of
the service. We focus on two documents, the CSC *Mission Statement
(1989)* and the Corporate Operational Plan (1994, in Ekstedt and
Jackson, 1997) to describe the most important dimensions of the
prison mission and the values guiding it.
According to the *Mission Statement*:

> The Correctional Service of Canada, as part of the criminal justice
> system, contributes to the protection of society by actively encourag-
> ing and assisting offenders to become law abiding citizens, while
> exercising reasonable, safe, secure and humane control.

The "core values" guiding the mission are as follows:

1) We respect the dignity of individuals, the rights of all members
   of society, and the potential for human growth and development.

2) We recognize that the offender has the potential to live as a law
   abiding citizen.

3) We believe that our strength and our major resource in achieving
   our objectives is our staff and that the human relationships are
   the cornerstone of our endeavour.

4) We believe that the sharing of ideas, knowledge, values and
   experience, nationally and internationally, is essential to the
   achievement of our Mission.

5) We believe in managing the service with openness and integrity
   and we are accountable to the Solicitor General.

Although "protection of society" is usually associated with conservative arguments about deterrence, retribution and incapacitation,
there is an important liberal rights discourse contained in the core

values. The *Statement* makes it clear that the power of the turnkey must be accountable, that grievance procedures must be available and that the dignity and rights of all individuals should be respected.

The *Correctional Strategy* (1994), includes a "Corporate Operational Plan" that has eight objectives:

1. enhance the Service's contribution to the protection of society by safely reintegrating a significantly larger number of offenders as law abiding citizens while reducing the relative use of incarceration as a major correctional intervention;
2. reduce recidivism of specific groups of offenders whose unique needs or problems require attention through the development and implementation of those programs tailored to those unique needs or problems;
3. reduce the number of incidents involving violent behaviour in institutions;
4. enhance correctional programs and the management of the Service through increased research and development;
5. increase public understanding, acceptance of, and participation in corrections through effective internal and external communications emphasizing open dialogue with the Canadian public and within the Service;
6. be a Correctional Service that is people-oriented, well-managed, professional, and visibly committed to delivering high quality service to the public;
7. establish a personnel management framework which includes retirement, employment equity, training, developmental opportunities and quality of work life programs which will provide competent and motivated staff representing the cultural composition of Canadian society;
8. contribute to a healthy environment.

Again, in the *Correctional Strategy*, the emphasis on rehabilitation is clear enough.

Corrections and Conditional Release Act, 1992

The *CCRA* consolidated the principle already set out in the *Mission Statement* that "the Correctional Service of Canada, as part of the criminal justice system, contributes to the protection of society...".

According to the *Act*, the purpose of the Correctional Service of Canada is:

"(a) carrying out sentences imposed by courts through safe and humane custody and supervision of offenders; and (b) assisting the rehabilitation of offenders and their reintegration into the community as law-abiding citizens through the provision of programs in penitentiaries and in the community."

Ten principles are supposed to guide the service. While protection of society is the paramount consideration, a rights discourse is enshrined in the *Act*: "Offenders retain the rights and privileges of all members of society, except those rights and privileges that are necessarily removed or restricted as a consequence of the sentence." Furthermore, correctional decisions shall "be made in a forthright and fair manner, with access by the offender to an effective grievance procedure." Other principles relate to circumstances of staff, enhancing effectiveness and openness by exchanging information with other criminal justice institutions and the public, and involving members of the public in matters relating to operation of the service.

The Risk Management Model of Prison and Parole

A reading of the *CCRA*, the *Mission Statement* and other literature emanating from CSC (see, for example, Baylis and Porporino, 1993) reveals that the rehabilitation ideal is not dead, although it has been reworked from the "treatment" models of earlier regimes. The treatment model as such was first articulated in the Archambault report (1938), but was not implemented until after the Second World War (in particular, see the Fauteux Committee of 1956) and held sway until the late 1960s, when critiques of total institutions and the medical model began to appear. In Canada, the Ouimet Committee (1969) embraced this critique, thereby paving the way for the community corrections "reintegration model" which was based on the premise that it was difficult to reintegrate people into society by removing them from it. In this scheme of things, prison was to be used only as a last resort.

In one of the most scathing attacks on the Canadian penitentiary system, the MacGuigan Committee of 1977 is said to have developed a new concept of rehabilitation for prisons. Ekstedt and Griffiths (1988: 76) term this the "opportunities model." Based on the premise that rehabilitation cannot be imposed, the role of the prison authorities in this model is to provide opportunities for reformation. It is up to the prisoner to choose to participate. Programs emphasize education and job training. In shifting the emphasis to the prisoner, however, the administration did not necessarily provide the opportunities that the prisoner was supposed to take advantage of.

The 1989 *Mission Statement* retains certain aspects of the opportunity model. It emphasizes the prisoner's responsibility to become law abiding, but through a variety of devices, it operates with a new concept of rehabilitation. It aims to provide prisoners with the tools necessary to help them avoid falling back into their "crime cycle." In this system, the classification of prisoners and parole decision-making are based on various kinds of risk assessment. Prisoner classification and programs for prisoners are geared to reducing risk, hence our calling this the *risk management model*.

CSC has adopted what it calls a cognitive skills/social learning model for prisoner programs. This model purports to instill the power of positive thinking by teaching problem solving and decision-making skills. Current programs include living skills, literacy, substance abuse treatment, special needs treatment (women, natives, violent offenders, sex offenders), social development (family, life and parenting skills, violence and anger management) and community-based programs (Ekstedt and Jackson, 1997, ch. 5). Community supervision is geared to prevent the parolees from relapsing into their "crime cycle."

Both inside the prison through the use of "case management teams"—which we prefer to call "risk management teams"—and outside it by use of intrusive supervision techniques, the intent is to create a highly structured program of control. All of this is done in the name of protection of society.

> According to the *Correctional Strategy*, the "criminogenic needs" of offenders, as determined by corrections research, should guide programs. The goal is to ensure that offenders receive the most effective programming at the appropriate time in their sentences to allow them to serve the greatest proportion of their sentences in the community with the lowest risk of recidivism.

Or, at least, that is how the rhetoric goes.

MEANWHILE, BACK IN THE CELL BLOCK: PRISON SYSTEM PRACTICES

In holding up the rhetoric of the CSC *Mission Statement* and the *CCRA* to the mirror of practice, we first examine the recent report on events at the Kingston Prison for Women and their implications for the prison system as a whole, and then move on to a series of other issues, some of which are generic, while others pertain mainly to men's prisons.

The Arbour Inquiry into Certain Events at the Kingston Prison for Women (P4W)

Because the special powers conferred on us by law impact on individual liberty and security of the person, we have a special obligation to treat offenders humanely. ...It is therefore essential that we make every effort to respect the spirit of the Charter of Rights and Freedoms in all our actions. (*CSC Mission Statement*, 1989: 6)

The projected image of a criminal justice system whose personnel promote the utmost respect for the law by modelling a humane and just exercise of power is a stark contrast to the image that has emerged throughout both phases of the Commission of Inquiry. The experiences of women prisoners has exposed too many profoundly disturbing examples of oppression and abuse of power, as well as arbitrary decision making. In our view, the Correctional Service of Canada has repeatedly exhibited callous indifference to prisoners, flagrant disregard for its own policies, and disrespect for the legislation pursuant to which it operates. (Kim Pate, Executive Director of the CAEFS[7], 1996: 49)

Obviously the degree to which the Canadian Correctional Service measures up to the goals of its own rhetoric cannot be judged only on the basis of what happened in one prison. But it is not so much the specific incident at P4W that interests us here, shocking though that is. Rather, what we find most revealing about the report is what it says about the corporate culture of the Correctional Service of Canada. Nevertheless, the details of the incidents at P4W are required to set the stage for a discussion of the inquiries that followed.

To understand events at P4W in April 1994, one needs some understanding of the long history of resistance to the deplorable conditions at the prison, particularly the segregation unit. Up to

1934, when P4W opened, female prisoners were held in men's prisons. Like the first men's prison in Kingston, P4W was the subject of
inquiry and condemnation soon after it opened, and several times
since. It was designed as a maximum security prison, with two tiers
of cage-cells, an arrangement that has been described as entirely
unnecessary for women. There has never been adequate exercise
space. In what is now an often quoted line, the 1977 MacGuigan
Committee reported that it was "unfit for bears, much less
women." Between 1989 and 1991, suicides of five incarcerated
Native women drew further attention to the deplorable conditions
at P4W.

Creating Choices: The Report of the Task Force on Federally Sentenced Women

In 1990, the Federal Task Force on Federally Sentenced Women provided another stinging indictment not just of P4W, but of the whole
approach to the punishment of women. Among other things, the
Task Force concluded that P4W was over-secure, erroneously based
on a male model of corrections, unfair because it housed federally
sentenced women in a single location far removed from the families
of most prisoners and it did not provide programs catering to the
needs of lifers, or aboriginal and francophone women. Building on
the recommendations of earlier inquiries, it recommended that
P4W be replaced by five regional prisons designed specifically for
women, including an aboriginal healing lodge, in which a woman-
centered correctional philosophy would prevail, based on principles of empowerment, responsibility, meaningful choices and
respect for the dignity of women prisoners.

As a result of the report P4W will soon close, two new prisons,
including the healing lodge, are already open, two more are about
to open, and another facility has been converted.

The "Incidents" in April 1994

The incidents leading to the Inquiry began on evening of April 22,
1994. There was a short violent confrontation between six women
prisoners and guards. The six were immediately segregated, and
criminal charges laid against them. Five of the six subsequently
pleaded guilty to these charges. Two days later, there was a hostage

taking, a slashing and an attempted suicide by other prisoners in segregation not involved in the first incident.

In the morning of April 26, guards demonstrated outside the prison demanding transfer of the six women from the prison. That evening, the Warden called in the all male Emergency Response Team from Kingston Penitentiary for men to forcibly "extract" eight women from their cells and strip search them. In order to show that the guards acted properly, the extraction was videotaped.

In January 1995 the Correctional Service of Canada released the report of its own Board of Investigation of the April 1994 incidents. This internal report made much of the dangerousness of the six prisoners and the effect they were having on guard morale, but said little about the incident involving the male Emergency Response Team.

A month after the internal CSC report was released, the Solicitor General tabled a second report in the House of Commons, this one by the Correctional Investigator, an independent ombudsperson. The Investigator's report was sharply critical of the Board of Investigation report, pointing out its many serious errors and omissions, and its failure to adequately scrutinize the activities of the Correctional Service itself.

The same night the Correctional Investigator's report was released, parts of the videotape of the forcible extraction of women from their cells was televised nationwide on the Canadian Broadcasting Corporation's *Fifth Estate*. The visual images played into the nation's living rooms were every bit as gripping as the video of the beating of Rodney King by LA Police, and a rare opportunity for Canadians to witness something that most of them probably did not believe could happen in their own country. The authorities did not attempt to negotiate with the prisoners. Instead, the all-male emergency response team dressed in black combat suits, gas masks on, visors down and batons drawn, entered the segregation tier to "extract" the female prisoners, and help carry out a strip search. The response team was accompanied by female guards. In the first instance, one of the team slammed a clear plastic shield against the bars of the cell to intimidate the potentially recalcitrant occupant. Then two others entered the cell, subdued the woman, cut her clothes off and then shackled her, while the remaining members of the emergency team encircled her, batons at the ready and mace cans drawn. Other women were prodded with batons, but were allowed to remove their own clothes. The women were then forced to stand naked, each covered only by a small bib or ill-fitting gown, with the men looking on. Added to the stark one-sidedness of the encounter was the raw display of gender power. The experience revictimized women who had long-suffered at the hands of men. One of the prisoners said she relived a group rape as she was being searched by guards. The video conjured up vivid images of "political atrocities, pornography and extreme sexual abuse" (Marron, 1996: 124).

The women were kept virtually naked overnight in stripped down cells, and then held in segregation for lengthy periods afterwards. They were denied timely access to legal counsel. In the furor following the screening of the video, Madame Justice Louise Arbour was appointed to investigate events leading up to the incident, and the treatment of prisoners in the months following.

The Injustice of Justice

Thumbing through the reports of the numerous inquiries into Canadian penitentiaries over the past 150 years reveals numerous references to the lawlessness of guards and prison administrations. So it was with the Brown Commission of 1849 investigating circumstances at Kingston, Canada's first penitentiary. Over 100 years later we find the MacGuigan Commission (1977) reporting: "There is a great deal of irony in the fact that imprisonment... the ultimate product of our system of justice itself epitomizes injustice." In the 20 years that have passed since this report was released, apparently little has changed.

Madame Justice Arbour's "Public Caning"[8] of CSC

The prison service supposedly operates according to a hierarchy of rules and directives under the umbrella of the *Corrections and Conditional Release Act*. However, Madame Justice Arbour found serious noncompliance at every level, and showed that prisoners were systematically denied the rights enshrined in the *CCRA*.

The strip search of women by male guards goes against the spirit of many CSC directives about honoring human dignity and prohibiting inhumane and degrading punishment, not to mention violating a CSC Standing Order that forbids cross-gender strip searches. After the incident, even though the *CCRA* guarantees segregated prisoners the right to legal counsel, they were denied it. Indeed, according to Arbour (43), this and other *CCRA* requirements were unknown to many of those administering it. Mandated daily exercise was withheld from segregated prisoners for one month. Prisoners were sometimes even denied water. The protocol for processing grievances was ignored, as were the regulations governing prison transfers. Regardless of how prisoners acted— behavior that Arbour attributed mainly to the environment in the segregation unit—she concluded that the treatment of prisoners was cruel, inhumane and degrading.

CSC Corporate Culture

According to Arbour, events at P4W are a reflection not of the fallibility of the individuals involved, but of a prison service culture that does not value individual rights (xiii) and is characterized by "a disturbing lack of commitment to ideals of justice" (198). Her interaction with the higher ranks of CSC management led Arbour to conclude that "the lack of observance of individual rights is not an isolated factor applicable only to the Prison for Women, but is probably very much part of CSC's corporate culture" as a whole (57). Similarly, the Correctional Investigator has long been critical of inadequacies of the CSC grievance policy, the Board of Investigation process and CSC's failure to follow law and policy with respect to use of physical force on prisoners and prisoners' access to daily visits (Arbour: 168).

Arbour's Recommendations

Arbour recommended that, in the future: prisoners should be allowed to apply for early release if they are mistreated; male riot squads should never again be deployed in women's prisons; a separate deputy minister of female corrections should be appointed; at least one female prison should have no male guards;[9] an effective prisoner grievance procedure be established; guards be better trained, especially with respect to prisoner rights; use of segregation be limited; and the women who were strip-searched and kept in prolonged segregation be compensated. Shortly after the release of her report, the Commissioner of Corrections resigned, and the Solicitor General publicly apologized to the eight women who had been forcibly extracted from their cells.

AND ELSEWHERE

With the public placing more demands on the prison system and becoming more unforgiving of its mistakes, it is a system that feels itself under siege from the outside, while the mounting tensions within are reaching a crisis that threatens to erupt into anarchic violence. (Marron, 1996: 291)

At about the same time Louise Arbour was concluding her Inquiry, journalist Kevin Marron published *The Slammer: The Crisis in Canada's Prison System*. Prompted by the belief that Canadians have "lost faith" in the prison system, Marron spent a year interviewing penitentiary staff, parole supervisors and federal prisoners about what has gone so badly wrong. His work is useful for our purposes because of its description of the attitudes and opinions of prisoners and staff. In the remainder of this paper, we use Marron's work as a platform for talking about issues facing Canada's prison system. We begin with the argument that imprisonment defeats two of its main purposes.

Imprisonment Is Self-Defeating

What is the main impact of imprisonment, Marron asks? It is to harden the prisoner's attitude, and acculturate him to the value system (the "con-code") of male prison subculture, including the mechanisms of violent conflict resolution that lie at the core of prison social order. This value system is particularly attractive to certain young disadvantaged men, because it gives them an identity, a way of being, and a camaraderie that they did not find outside the prison. Prisoners who are prepared to resort to violence to exert their will tend to be the dominant influence. In large part the value system represents a group adaptation to the privation of imprisonment, one that is shaped by a particular expression of masculinity that operates both inside and outside the prison. Guard subculture embodies a similar set of values. Indeed, prisons encourage the worst aspects of traditional Western male cultures, and encourages its reproduction in both prisoners and guards.

People who want a more punitive response to crime ignore the fundamental conundrum that prisons pose. The experience of imprisonment tends to acculturate both prisoners and guards to a value system that puts a premium on dealing with other people in aggressive and manipulative ways.

The response of the Correctional Service of Canada has been to try to change both prisoner and guard subcultures. The response to guards has been "professionalization," including the tactic of calling guards something other than "guards" (such as "correctional officers," "living unit officers" or "case management teams"). The response to prisoners has been to deliberately try to break down prison subculture, the existence of which has been recognized from the Archambault Report (1938) on through the Ouimet (1969) and MacGuigan (1977) reports. There have been two mechanisms for doing this: (a) the long-time network of CSC informers who operate throughout the prison system; and (b) more recently, the "case management system."

If a prisoner wants to descend the "cascading" levels of security classification and subsequently win a favorable parole recommendation, he has to strike a rapport with members of his case management team. The idea is that, this way, the prisoner will begin to identify with the values of the case management team rather than those of other prisoners. The process involves individualizing the prisoner through the rhetoric and coercive practice of rehabilitation. This incentive to change is reinforced by CSC's network of informers who create a destabilizing influence by interfering with the operation of the prison's illicit economy, which involves the bartering and sale of various kinds of contraband, from kitchen supplies to drugs. Nevertheless, despite the attempt to break it down, the values of prison culture are still pervasive in both federal and provincial prisons. The culture survives, partly because, in their day-to-day life, prisoners generally have to answer as much to each other as they do to guards, and partly because the culture represents a group adaptation to the privations of prison life.

Drugs in Prisons: A Double Edged Sword

Aside from the prisoner code, the other main problem identified by the CSC officials Marron interviewed is "drug distribution," which they say has invaded and corrupted every aspect of prison life. Indeed, we would argue that the effect is much broader than this: The development of illicit global drug economies has profoundly changed the nature of crime in general.

When it comes to illicit drugs in prisons, many prisoners and staff believe that trying to stem the flow would do more harm than good. Both illegal and prescription drugs play an important role in the prison underground economy. And they are an important component of social control in prisons. Because drug distributors want a peaceful environment to facilitate their economic activity, and because the administration similarly wants a peaceful institution, prisoners and guards manipulate each other in the process of negotiating social order (for examples, see Lowman, 1986). Guards may ignore drug consumption, and even facilitate drug distribution in order to maintain, or not disrupt, order in the prison. No doubt most guards would rather deal with prisoners stoned on marijuana than blitzed on home brew. And short of locking them up 24 hours a day, there is virtually nothing that can be done to stop prisoners from fermenting alcohol.

Double Bunking

For Marron, one of the biggest problems facing Canadian penitentiaries is overcrowding. As things stand, 25% of federal prisoners are double bunked, with the highest proportion being housed in medium security prisons.

If the prison population continues to expand at its current rate, overcrowding will get worse. For the past two decades, the average growth of federal prison population has been 2–3% per year. In the fiscal years 1992–3, 1993–4, 1994–5, the rate of increase rose to 5%, 8.5% and 5.5% respectively. If the federal prison population were to continue to grow at a rate of 4% per annum, it would reach approximately 18,000 by the year 2000. The rate of increase may be greater than this, as CSC anticipates increases in the flow of prisoners because of pending changes in the *Young Offenders Act*, new convictions made possible by DNA analysis, new firearms and high risk offender legislation and longer sentences for certain offenses. CSC's accommodation plan calls for an increase of 2113 beds during the fiscal years 1996–97 through 1998–9. This will be accomplished by constructing a new 400-cell medium security institution near Gravenhurst, Ontario, a new medium-security institution for male aboriginal prisoners in Hobbema Alberta, and by expanding Saskatchewan Penitentiary and Drumheller in Alberta. CSC has also acquired the Grand Cache facility from the provincial government of Alberta (Theoret, 1996). This expansion will increase the total number of cells to 14,516 by the end of the 1999 fiscal year, potentially leaving at least the same proportion of prisoners being double bunked as at present.

There are relatively few studies of the effects of overcrowding in the Western literature on prisons. These are written from an administrative point of view, examining the effects of overcrowding on prisoner violence (Eklund-Olsen et al., 1983) and prisoner health (e.g. Wener and Keys, 1988; Gaes, 1994). In Canada, apart from Marron's (1996) work, there has been little attention paid to the effects of overcrowding from the prisoner's perspective. CSC downplays the issue. At least one CSC official (Theoret, 1996) has claimed that Canadian prisons comply with or exceed *The UN Minimum Standard Rules for Treatment of Prisoners* (1984), which would prohibit double bunking in individual cells, except under temporary conditions. But it is difficult to see how in Canada, double bunking can be called "temporary."

Prisoners offer a very different view of the impact of overcrowding than the CSC party line. Concern about the effects of privacy deprivation figure prominently in prisoner accounts of life inside. The following two statements from a Survey of Federal Prisoners (Inmate Advocacy Program, 1996) capture well the general prisoner perception of double-bunking:

> It is hard to feel safe and at ease, because you really don't know what mental stability (and lack thereof) that person (cell mate) possesses, or to what lengths they will go to achieve their means. Being stabbed to death or sodomized while you try to sleep is a very disturbing thought to anyone, not just a prisoner...We are social beings of course, but we also need our 'private' space to relax and unwind. Some turn to drugs, some to home brews, some to other unsavory activities as the nature of the beast which lays inside them bubbles to the surface.
>
> I can honestly say that I was never close to or never violent when I was young and had never been imprisoned. But it now seems the longer I am (imprisoned) I am worse and worse. This has all been because of stupid things like double-bunking, being told to live with rapists and rats.

From the prisoner's point of view, overcrowding is a fundamental problem. And even if not all prisoners are double bunked, they are all affected by the problems created by overcrowding when it comes to provision of programs, counseling and general medical and dental services.

Medical Issues

Because of the close proximity in which prisoners live, they are potentially breeding grounds for various diseases. There is a high incidence of TB in some penitentiaries. Of 468 prisoners recently tested in Kingston, 100 had been infected. Fortunately, the TB turned out not to be one of the new drug resistant strains. In December 1994, out of roughly 14,000 federal prisoners, approximately 120 were known to be HIV infected (Marron, 1996: 98). There are probably many more infected prisoners, with some estimates suggesting that 1 in 20 inmates are HIV positive. Indeed, a 1996 report by the Canadian AIDS Society and the Canadian HIV/AIDS Legal Network reported that 160 prisoners across Canada have AIDS, that HIV infection in federal prisons is 10 times the rate of the general population, and that between 28% and 40% of prisoners are infected with hepatitis C (Fayerman, 1996). The report attributed the increased number of HIV and hepatitis C infections to lack of government intervention (*Ottawa Citizen*, 1996b).

Of 110 P4W women tested for HIV in 1994, only one was positive; however, 48 of them had contracted some form of hepatitis. The prison authorities will not contemplate needle exchange (although in British Columbia, they distribute bleach for needle cleaning, and in special circumstances allow methadone maintenance), but Marron reports that they do distribute condoms and dental dams even though officially CSC does not condone consensual sex among prisoners.

The other pressing health issue is the large proportion of mentally disordered persons who are finding their way into prisons as a consequence of deinstitutionalization of mental hospitals. It is difficult to conceive of how to set up a therapeutic caring environment for such persons in a prison, especially when many of them, for their own protection, have to be segregated from the general population.

Ethnicity

There is a great ethnic diversity of prisoners. Many visible minorities form gang-like affiliations as a way of coping with imprisonment. Such affiliations sometimes lead to turf wars. Visible minorities make up 19% of the federal prison population. Aboriginals, who comprise just 3% of the Canadian population, comprise 12% of the male and 17% of the female federal prison population (Marron, 1996: 110). In the Prairie provinces, where the Native population is 5% of the total, it comprises 32% of the Prairie Region Federal prison population, with proportion much higher than this in certain prisons. CSC has determined that tests used in assessing new prisoners are not relevant to the cultural backgrounds of Native people, and both the *Mission Statement* and *CCRA* commit CSC to providing special programming for Native prisoners. But while both Marron and Arbour acknowledge that CSC is beginning to recognize the value of Native culture for rehabilitation purposes, the lot of most Native prisoners is still particularly grim. This may change as the Native prison population is becoming increasingly politicized.

Making Programs Meaningful

There is no doubt that prisoners could benefit from all manner of programs, including very basic education. For example, data from intake assessments show that about 65% of prisoners are functionally illiterate when they enter the federal system. Programs can help, and many prisoners say as much. But programs all too easily lose their value in a prison setting: "Often distrustful and contemptuous of the instructors, inmates tend to be cynical about the programs and regard them merely as hoops through which they have to jump in order to satisfy the requirements of their case management officers and the parole board" (172). The problem is made worse, Marron says, by many guards because they do not take the programs or the instructors' assessments of prisoners seriously.

Most of the available programs are relatively short, thus making it difficult for prisoners to pursue long term goals. Since on-site university programs were axed, the only post-secondary education available is through correspondence courses.

Marron suggests that the "Offender Management System"—a tracking system providing a potentially huge dossier on each prisoner—further undermines the usefulness of many programs. Because the assessment of risk a prisoner poses is based on how he or she compares to certain statistical profiles, prisoners come to feel trapped by their records. If they fit a certain aggregate risk profile, it does not matter how they perform in various programs because they are already damned by the profile. Prisoners also realize the injustice of the file information system that may contain unsubstantiated reports by informers, police and prison staff. Prisoners often do not know about the existence of these reports, and even when they do, they do not have the right to challenge them. This suspension of the normal rules of due process provides one more powerful incentive for prisoners to orient to each other rather than to the values of a prison administration which they perceive to be unjust.

Work in Prisons

There is very little meaningful work available for Canadian prisoners, because it is difficult to make meaningful jobs in an isolated and dysfunctional environment. CORCAN is a semi-independent entity which employs 1800 prisoners in 32 federal institutions. It endeavors to finance its own operations through revenue generated from prison industry. Most of the produce is sold to CSC or other government agencies. Most of the work is menial, and does little to prepare prisoners for life on the outside (for discussion, see Culhane, 1991).

The Dilemmas Created by Longer Sentences and Stricter Parole

Marron suggests that, under the current system, it is inevitable that some people on parole will reoffend. About a quarter of parolees commit another crime or otherwise violate parole and are re-admitted to prison. There are about 10,000 people on parole or statutory release at any one time. Between 110 and 160 each year are charged with committing a violent crime. Over one eleven-year period 130 murders were committed by persons on parole or statutory release, but Marron points out that this accounts for just two percent of the 7838 homicides during that period. The only way to prevent these murders would have been to deny parole to 52,482 offenders released during that period. But, then, all that denying them parole would have done was to postpone some of the offenses until after the offenders had been released anyway (249–50).

Ironically, the highest risk offenders, because they are denied statutory release, are thrown out into the community at the end of their sentence with no supervision, no preparation and few or no possibilities for earning a living.

Future of the "Faint Hope" Clause

The emotive content of arguments about parole is perhaps best exemplified by attempts of victims' rights groups and police organizations to do away with the so-called "faint hope clause" of the *Canadian Criminal Code*. Although first degree murderers are sentenced to serve 25 years before being eligible for parole, under *Criminal Code* Section 745 they can apply after 15 years for a judicial review of their eligibility period, with an eye to reducing it. The purpose of the so-called "faint hope" clause is to give lifers a glimmer of hope in what might otherwise seem like an impossibly bleak situation. The judicial review is held before a jury comprising people from the community in which the offense occurred. The jury considers various factors, including an applicant's character, his or her conduct in prison, and the nature of the offense. A two-thirds majority of the jury can reduce the period a person has to serve to be eligible for parole.

Backed by victims' rights groups across the country, one member of parliament has introduced three private members' bills seeking repeal of the faint hope clause. Critics of the bill have said that there could be uproar in prisons if the clause is removed since it would take away the incentive for lifers to behave (Canadian Press, 1996b). The Minister of Justice, Alan Rock, is not prepared to dispense with the Section altogether. In a speech to the Canadian Association of Chiefs of Police, he said that:

> Making the streets safer has as much to do with literacy as it does with law. It has as much to do with the strength of families as it has to do with the length of sentences. It has as much to do with early intervention as it does with mandatory supervision. (quoted in Graham, 1996)

Nevertheless, the Minister has introduced amendments that would make it more difficult for most murderers to get parole, despite the actual risk of reoffending that murderers pose. Marron points out that between 1975 and 1986, 457 murderers were released from Canadian prisons, of whom 9% committed another offense, including only two murders (unfortunately, Marron does not report how many murderers were not released).

Not only do opponents of the faint hope clause neglect statistics like these, they also fail to acknowledge that the provision merely gives the applicant the right to petition to apply for parole prior to serving 25 years. The petition might not be successful, and even if it is, parole might not be granted. Thus opponents of the clause need not worry that the fabled monsters, like child killer Clifford Olson, will ever be released. Consequently, even commentators like former member of the National Parole Board Lisa Hobbs Birnie, who believes that victims' rights groups "are one of the best things that has happened to the criminal justice system in years," says that lobbying for repeal of the faint hope clause reduces a complex problem to "fear driven simplicity" for political effect, thereby "insulting a lot of hard-working people in the criminal justice system in the process" (Hobbs Birnie, 1996).

Segregation as Punishment

It is now 13 years since the publication of Michael Jackson's *Prisoners of Isolation*, a stinging and wide ranging indictment of the practice of solitary confinement in Canada. While more strict criteria are now supposed to govern the use of "segregation," it is still a principle component of the disciplinary system used to control prisoners.

While many CSC officials interpreted events at the P4W segregation unit in April 1994 as evidence of the dangerousness of some female prisoners, and reason in and of itself for their segregation, Louise Arbour interpreted the prisoners' behavior as a reflection of the situation in which they found themselves. Despite the supposedly strict criteria governing use of segregation, the eight women involved in the April 1994 incidents were segregated from the main population for many months afterwards. In October 1994 prison psychologists warned, "If the current situation continues it will ultimately lead to some kind of crisis, including violence, suicide and self-injury. [The prisoners] will become desperate enough to use any means to assert some form of control of their lives" (Arbour, 1996: 140). It was clear to Arbour that CSC used segregation punitively, not administratively in the way that the *Corrections and Conditional Release Act* requires. And yet, according to the Executive Director of the Correctional Investigator, most prisoners currently in segregation are not there on grounds defined by the *CCRA* (Arbour, 1996: 187).

While there is some debate about the effects of solitary confinement, it is difficult to conceive how long-term segregation might have any rehabilitative value. But there is every reason to believe it is quite harmful and, by any reasonable standard, inhumane. Consequently, we concur with Arbour that we must break the mindset which assumes the inevitability of segregation.

Policing the Guards

Numerous Commissions of Inquiry in Canada, and most recently Louise Arbour, have concluded that one of the greatest impediments to rehabilitation is the punitive attitudes of guards. The most recent example of this attitude comes from the British Columbia prison system in an incident involving a tactical squad drill at the Vancouver pre-trial center (Hunter, 1996). Tactical team leaders decided it would be useful for trainees to experience a simulated emergency situation. Squad members were told that an officer needed help in one of the jail's living units. But they were not told the exercise was a simulation. In the ensuing lock down, four inmates were injured by baton strikes. In the subsequent investigation, inmate and staff accounts were "at odds" when it came to how much force was used. The British Columbia Attorney General has assured the public that "heads will likely roll" as a result of the way the squad dealt with inmates (Hunter, 1996).

The usual recommendation flowing from criticisms of guards is for greater professionalization and better and more comprehensive training. But it is open to question whether better training can overcome the problems created by the fundamentally adversarial nature of the guard-prisoner relationship. While there are potentially many dimensions to this relationship, its defining characteristic is that one party has not only the power, but also the obligation to lock the other up. When suppression occurs for a long period, revolt is to be expected.

These kinds of incidents emphasize the need to realize effective grievance procedures at all levels of the Canadian prison system in order to make administrators accountable. While the CCRA does contain a grievance procedure, both Arbour and the Correctional Investigator have shown that it is far from effective. Indeed, on the basis of the track record of CSC to date, Arbour concluded that it would be unwise to leave the adjudication of grievances in the hands of prison authorities.

Prisons for Women: Can a Woman-Centered Approach Survive?

One of the most alarming aspects of events at the Prison for Women in April 1994 is that many prison insiders saw nothing wrong with male guards "extracting" female prisoners from their cells and strip searching them. To its opponents, the events at P4W provided conclusive evidence of the prison's failure. But for CSC investigators and many other insiders, the events provided conclusive proof of how dangerous some women can be. The insiders predict "tragedies" in the "cottage-like" environment of the new prisons for women (Marron, 1996: 143). Needless to say, there was a quick chorus of "we told you so" when trouble surfaced at one of the newly opened prisons.

Within weeks of the "model" Edmonton prison for women opening, there was a suicide, an attack on staff and several self-slashings. Then three women escaped. Critics of the new regime charged that the prison system was "spinning out of control," and called for the Warden's resignation. But the Warden held her ground, reasoning that problems must be expected in the process of trying to introduce an entirely new correctional philosophy. Another CSC official commented that such incidents are not surprising given the often abuse- and violence-filled lives of the women prisoners (Weber, 1996). He also pointed out that similar problems had not arisen at the other two new prisons for women.

It remains to be seen whether these more progressive attitudes will be able to survive in the midst of the control-oriented male standpoint that dominates the prison service at both federal and provincial levels.

Federal Prison Cigarette Smoking Ban to Commence in 1998

Prisoners in all federal prisons will have to quit smoking by 1998 as part of a 1989 Treasury Board policy to prohibit smoking in all federal buildings (News Services, 1995). Nicotine is a highly addictive drug, and a large majority of prisoners smoke. Tobacco and other drugs form the principle currencies of the illicit economy of the prison. It is not difficult to think through the ramifications of a tobacco ban for life on the inside. There would be widespread and prolonged mayhem if thousands of already frustrated men were to be subjected to compulsory nicotine withdrawal. Imagine what would happen if the ban were to be long-lived. In addition to all the other strains they experience at the point of losing their liberty, newly admitted cons who smoke would be forced to go cold turkey.

One can only hope that the architects of the proposed ban think through its implications and, in the interest of the safety of guards and prisoners alike, make an exception to the no-smoking rule in federal buildings.

CONCLUSIONS

In keeping with the typically dichotomous mode of Western thinking, all too often we are presented with either-or choices that leave
no room for "and." So it is in the contemporary discourse on crime
which portrays victim rights and prisoner rights as mutually exclusive domains, with the latter inevitably infringing on the former.
The idea that someone concerned about the treatment of law break-
ers might be equally concerned about crime victims has no room in
this piebald world of good and evil. We need to make room.

During the past 20 years in Canada victim rights advocates have
focused media attention on the most extreme end of the crime continuum. In the process, they have succeeded in hardening the
response to crime. However, no one calling for more prisons and
longer sentences seems to consider Marron's argument that more
prisons are likely to make us less safe. If the purpose of prison is to
punish—i.e. to deliberately inflict pain—it succeeds. And, for the
period the prisoner is incarcerated, s/he most certainly is incapacitated. But in learning how to live inside, prisoners tend to forget
how to live in society.

By focusing on deterrence, neoconservatives promulgate a thor-
oughly individualized analysis of low-level predatory street crime.
Totally ignored in this emotive analysis are the social forces—
including labor market conditions, lack of adequate housing, inadequate social support services for families living in poverty,
etc.—that produce street crime, and the central role of prisons in
reproducing the culture of male violence that accompanies it.

By way of conclusion, take as an example of the issues at stake
the story of the "riot" at Headingly jail in Manitoba during which
seven guards were beaten. Some Manitoba guards have refused to
work claiming prisons are unsafe (Oostrom, 1996). This "incident,"
and the discourse surrounding it, highlights the issues that ultimately lie at the heart of all debates about crime and punishment.
Commentators on the right have attributed the riot to the "cold-
blooded gangbangers" in Headingly, just one more reason we need
to get tough on crime (Canadian Press, 1996c). But the description
attributing the incident to rival gangs fighting ignores the *process*
that leads to the "don't give a damn" attitude displayed by prisoners, which guards and other commentators find so alarming. To
understand the forlorn subjectivity of young men who are prepared
to cut each others' fingers off, to give but one example of the rather

nasty things that are said to have happened, one needs to understand the conditions in this Depression-era jail, and the youth
poverty, racism, family problems and unemployment that helped
put the prisoners there in the first place.

No amount of punishment will solve the problems that led these
young men to abandon hope.

Notes

1. Thanks to Karlene Faith and John Ekstedt for providing key material
   that otherwise would not have been available to us at the time of
   writing.
2. The *Prison News Service* offers news analysis and commentary from
   prisons in the US and Canada, and is written mainly by prisoners for
   prisoners, and their friends, family and supporters (for more information, contact website: http://www.igc.apc.org/justice/prisons/pubs/
   pns/). The purpose of the *Journal of Prisoners on Prison* is to encourage
   research on a wide range of issues related to crime, justice and punishment (for more information, contact website: http://www.synapse.
   net/ ~arrakis/jpp/jpp.html).
3. The roughly 14,500 federal men are housed in 44 institutions: two
   Special Handling Units, 12 maximum, 18 medium and 12 minimum
   prisons, and 13 community correctional centers. The Kingston Prison for
   Women is about to close, and is in the process of being replaced by five
   regional prisons for the approximately 320 federally sentenced women.
4. In Canada, the federal government is responsible for criminal law,
   while the prison system has federal and provincial tiers. Prisoners with
   two years or more are housed in federal penitentiaries, while prisoners
   with less than two years go to provincial prisons.
5. As a proportion of all homicide charges, manslaughter declined from
   21% in 1961 to 8% in 1974 (Statistics Canada, 1976), and has remained
   roughly the same since then.
6. In 1995–96, 10,534 prisoners were paroled. Of these, 3062 had their parole revoked. Over two-thirds (2078) of the revocations were for breaking parole rules; the other 984 were charged with a crime (Morris, 1996).
7. The Canadian Association of Elizabeth Fry Societies.
8. Hess (1996).
9. Although most of Arbour's report and her recommendations have
   been warmly welcomed by the critics of the women's prison system,
   this recommendation has not been well received—detractors say that
   there should be no male guards in women's prisons. For this and other
   supportive criticisms, see the Strength in Sisterhood (SIS) commentary
   (1996) on the Arbour recommendations (available from SIS, PO Box
   184, 3456 Dunbar St. Vancouver, Canada V6S 2C2).

References

Arbour, L. (1996) *Commission of Inquiry into Certain Events at the Prison for Women in Kingston.* Ottawa: Public Works and Government Services Canada.

Archambault, J. (Chair) (1938) *Report of the Royal Commission to Investigate the Penal System of Canada.* Ottawa: King's Printer.

Branswell, B. (1996) "Restructured court could handle fewer non-violent cases." *Ottawa Citizen*, May 13: C1.

Bronskill, J. (1995) "Crisis looms in Canada's prison system, report says." *The Vancouver Sun*, December 4: A3.

Brown Commission. (1849) *Report of the Royal Commission to Inquire and then Report upon the Conduct, Economy, Discipline and Management of the Provincial Penitentiary.* Ottawa: Journals of the Legislative Assembly.

Canadian Press. (1996a) "Uproar in prisons predicted if hope for early parole dies." *The Vancouver Sun*, February 17: A7.

Canadian Press. (1996b) "Ontario tries to cut trials for less serious offenders." *The Vancouver Sun*, May 13: A5.

Canadian Press. (1996c) "Cold-blooded kids behind jail riot." *The Vancouver Sun*, May 9: A3.

Canadian Press. (1996d) "Ontario mulls cheap cops for highway-patrol duties." *Montreal Gazette*, May 14: A11.

Chernomas, R. and Black, E. (1996) "What Kind of Capitalism? The Revival of Class Struggle in Canada." *Monthly Review*, 48:1: 23–34.

Clark, G. (1996) "New law could let criminals avoid jail." *The Province*, April 21: A4.

Clarkson, S. (1991) "Disjunctions: Free Trade and the Paradox of Canadian Development," in D. Drache and M.S. Gertler (eds.) *The New Era of Global Competition: State Policy and Market Power*, Montreal and Kingston: McGill-Queen's University Press.

Cox, K. (1996) "Penal reform draws little reaction in New Brunswick." *Globe and Mail*, June 10: A6.

Culhane, C. (1980) *Barred From Prison.* Vancouver: Pulp Press.

Culhane, C. (1985) *Still Barred From Prison.* Montreal: Black Rose Books.

Culhane, C. (1991) *No Longer Barred From Prison.* Montreal: Black Rose Books.

Doran, H. (1996) "CBC's Ideas gives voice to the ins and outs of prison life." *The Weekend Sun*, June 15: F9.

Ekstedt, J. and Griffiths, C.T. (1988) *Corrections in Canada: Policy and Practice*. (Second edition) Toronto: Butterworths.

Ekstedt, J. and Jackson, M. (1997) *The Keepers and the Kept: Correctional Practice in Canada*. Toronto: Nelson.

Ekland-Olson, S., Barrick, D.M. and Cohen, L.E. (1983) "Prison Overcrowding and Disciplinary Problems: An Analysis of the Texas Prison System." *The Journal of Applied Behavioural Science*, 19:2: 163–176.

Fayerman, P. (1996) "B.C. leads in protecting convicts against AIDS, report says." *Vancouver Sun*, September 17: B1.

Federal Sentencing and Corrections Review Group. (1995) *Rethinking Corrections*. Ottawa: Unpublished report.

Gaes, G.G. (1994) "Prison Crowding Research Reexamined." *The Prison Journal*, 74:3: 329–363.

Gamberg, H. and Thomson, A. (1984) *The Illusion of Prison Reform: Corrections in Canada*. New York: Peter Lang.

Gaucher, R. and Crow, M. (1994) "Judicial Review Hearings (Criminal Code S.745): A Preliminary Study of the First Forty Cases." *University of Ottawa Working Papers* # 9402C.

Graham, C. (1996) "Cutting down crime rate. Social programs must stay: Rock." *The Gazette, Montreal*, August 29: A10.

Griffiths, C.T. and Verdun-Jones, S.V.J. (1994) *Canadian Criminal Justice*. (Second edition) Toronto: Harcourt Brace and Company.

Hess, H. (1996) "Right groups urge quick action on prison report." *Globe and Mail*, April 3: A5.

Hobbs Birnie, L. (1996) "He'll never go free. One cannot imagine a jury giving this devil Olson another chance." *Vancouver Sun*, August 14: A15.

Hunter, J. (1996) "Jail drill guards erred." *Vancouver Sun*, July 20: A7.

Inmate Advocacy Program. (1996) "Survey of Federal Prisoners on Overcrowding." Unpublished manuscript, Office of the Honourable Chris Axworthy, MP, Ottawa.

Jackson, M. (1983) *Prisoners of Isolation: Solitary Confinement in Canada*. Toronto: University of Toronto Press.

Jenish, D.:Chisholm, Steele, S., D'Amour, M., Nemeth, M., and Harris, J. (1996) "Parole: Should convicted killers be allowed to rejoin society." *Maclean's*, March 25: 44–48.

Lowman, J. (1986) "Images of Discipline in Prison." in N. Boyd (ed.) *The Social Dimensions of Law*. Toronto: Prentice-Hall.

Lowman, J. and MacLean, B. (1991) "Prisons in Canada." *Social Justice*, 18: 130–154.

MacGuigan, M. (Chair). (1977) *The Sub-Committee on the Penitentiary System in Canada Report to Parliament*. Ottawa: Ministry of Supply and Services.

Maclean's. (1996) September 30: 29.

Marron, K. (1996) *The Slammer: The Crisis in Canada's Penitentiary System*. Toronto: Doubleday.

Matthews, R. (1979) "Decarceration and the Fiscal Crisis." In B. Fine, R. Kinsey, J. Lea, S. Picciotto, and J. Young (eds.) *Capitalism and the Rule of Law*. London: Hutchinson.

Mayhew, Jo-Anne (1988) "Corrections is a Male Enterprise." *Journal of Prisoners on Prisons*, 1:1: 11–21.

Melnitzer, J. (1995) *Maximum, Medium, Minimum: A Journey Through Canadian Prisons*. Toronto: Key Porter Books.

Morris, J. (1996) "10% of paroled prisoners face new charges." *Vancouver Sun*, July 19: A4.

News Services. (1995) "No butts for Canuck convicts." *The Province*, July 20: A17.

Oosterom, N. (1996) "Jail guards facing back-to-work threat." *Vancouver Sun*, May 7: A4.

Ottawa Citizen. (1996a) "Prison population reaches peak." January 25: A5.

Ottawa Citizen. (1996b) "Governments blamed for rise in jail AIDS cases." September 16: A13.

Ouimet, R., (Chair). (1969) *Report of the Canadian Committee on Corrections—Towards Unity: Criminal Justice and Corrections*. Ottawa: Information Canada.

Pate, K. (1996) "CSC and the 2 Percent Solution." *Journal of Prisoners on Prisons*, 6:2: 41–61.

Porporino, F.J. and Baylis, E. (1993) *Designing a Progressive Penology: The Evolution of Canadian Federal Corrections*. Ottawa: Correctional Service of Canada.

Ratner, R.S. (1992) "Bilateral legitimation: the parole pendulum," in K. McCormick and L. Visano (eds.) *Canadian Penology; Advanced Perspectives and Research*. Toronto: Canadian Scholar's Press.

Seguin, R. (1996) "Quebec launches prison reforms: Measures include six closings, fewer jailings of non-violent criminals." *Globe and Mail*, April 3: A1.

Statistics Canada. (1976) *Homicide in Canada: A Statistical Synopsis*. Ottawa: Queen's Printer.

Statistics Canada. (1987) *Homicide in Canada 1986: A Statistical Perspective*. Ottawa: Supply and Services Canada.

Statistics Canada. (1995) *Crime Statistics 1994*. Ottawa: Supply and Services Canada.

Strength in Sisterhood. (1996) "Commentary on the Summary of Recommendations." Mimeo, Vancouver.

Solicitor General. (1982) *Basic Facts About Correction*. Ottawa: Solicitor General.

Southam Newspapers. (1996) "Alberta wants emptier prisons."*The Province*, April 19: A30.

Task Force on Federally Sentenced Women. (1990) *Creating Choices: Report of the Task Force on Federally Sentenced Women*. Ottawa: Correctional Services Canada.

Theoret, L. (1996) "Reply to inquiry from Robert Bult of the office of MP Chris Axworthy." CSC National Headquarters correspondence, March 22.

United Nations. (1984) "Standard Minimum Rules for the Treatment of Prisoners, and Procedures for the Effective Implementation of the Rules." Department of Public Information, New York.

Weber, B. (1996) "Security problems plague new women's prison?" *Vancouver Sun*, April 16: A5.

Wener, R.E. and Keys, C. (1988) "The Effects of Changes in Jail Population Densities on Crowding, Sick Calls and Spatial Behaviour." *Journal of Applied Social Psychology*, 18:10: 852–866.

Young, M.G. (1996) "The Return to Punishment; Creeping Conservatism and Its Effect on Correctional Policy in Canada." Mimeo, Dept. of Sociology, University of Victoria.

Chapter
THREE

The Crisis in Mexican Prisons: The Impact of the United States

J. Michael Olivero

This chapter provides a glimpse into the organization and administration of prisons in Mexico. It begins with the historical development of the prison, and then attempts to bring the reader up to date as to the current state of affairs. We suggest that, as a third world country, the system suffers from a lack of adequate resources for associated social services, as well as political corruption, and that these problems are exacerbated by the United States' "War on Drugs."

HISTORY OF PRISONS IN MEXICO

Early Mexican prison history is similar to that of Europe and the US. As in Europe and other parts of the Americas, there were detention facilities in Mexico long before the 18th century, or even the Spanish Conquest. The Mayans and Aztecs, as well as other indigenous tribes or nations of the area, had buildings whose purpose it was to hold offenders (Galindo, 1979; Olivero, Mounce and Morgado, 1991).

Also as in Europe and North America, these facilities were used to hold offenders (criminals, prisoners of war, runaway slaves and adulterers), only *until* they could be punished. Eventually, Spain imported its penal system to Mexico following its conquest of the land and people, replacing tribal law. The Spanish introduced incarceration as a form of punishment, rather than detention until punishment (Galindo, 1979; Olivero, Mounce and Morgado, 1991).

Beginning in 1871, with President Benito Juárez, Mexico attempted to reform its prisons to conform with the goals of rehabilitation and humane treatment of prisoners. Unfortunately, this effort has been thwarted by a lack of resources. Almost a century later, reform of the prison system remained elusive. In 1966, Mexico became a signatory of the United Nations' minimum standards for the treatment of offenders.[1] The effort to comply with these standards ground to a halt in 1976, when Mexico suffered a devastating economic crisis, due to large foreign debt. A survey of Mexican federal prisons in 1979 revealed that only 35 percent had accomplished the progressive objectives and improvements called for in 1966 (Galindo, 1979; Olivero, Mounce and Morgado, 1991).

Presently, Mexico is experiencing yet another severe economic depression partially due to a large foreign debt incurred while attempting industrial development, and its prisons are suffering greatly. Due to economic constraints that prohibit expenditures on social service programs, and exacerbating factors outlined below, it would appear that the progress of the 1970s has been lost as well (Olivero, Mounce and Morgado, 1991).

ORGANIZATION AND ADMINISTRATION OF MEXICAN PRISONS

It is difficult to gain detailed information on Mexican prisons, in comparison with industrialized countries such as the US, Japan, etc. Part of this problem comes from a lack of centralized record keeping by Mexican prison officials. As is the case for criminal records, we found Mexican authorities had no computerized data base on prisons either on the federal or state level. Moreover, Mexican prison authorities are reluctant to allow researchers (Mexican researchers as well) into Mexican prisons or access to information, although human rights groups have found recent success (Americas Watch, 1990).[2]

The most up-to-date material available appears to have been prepared by Hernández-Cuevas, Cesar-Kala, Marquez-Haro and Torricellas-Rodríguez (1994), researchers for the Programa Nacional de Capacitación Penitenciaria de la Secretaria de Gobernación, published in 1994. Table 1 illustrates the number of correctional facilities in Mexico as of July 31, 1994. They also reported the population capacities at these facilities. This analysis is reflected in Table 2. Finally, they reported upon the number of persons held for years 1992 through 1994. Their analysis included both those who were preconviction detainees and those who had been sentenced. Table 3 depicts this analysis.

TABLE 1 Types and Frequency Distribution of Correctional Facilities in México, July 1994

Types of Prisons	Frequency
Centros de Readaptación Social	124
Penitenciarias	5
Reclusorios Preventivos	25
Cáraceles Municipales	177
Cáraceles Distritales	86
Cáraceles Regionales	26
Colonia Penal (on Marias Island)	1
Total	438

Source: Hernández-Cuevas, et al. (1994), p. 49.

TABLE 2 Number of Centers and Population Capacities, July 1994

Number of Centers	Population Capacities
253	1 to 50 persons
143	51 to 500 persons
14	501 to 1000 persons
34	+1000

Source: Hernández-Cuevas, et al. (1994), p. 51.

TABLE 3   Total Number of Persons Incarcerated for
Years 1992 through 1994 and Status

Year	Detainees	Convicted	Total
1992 (December)	42,194 (49.22%)	43,518 (50.77%)	85,712
1993 (December)	44,045 (48.20%)	47,319 (51.79%)	91,364
1994 (March)	43,562 (47.80%)	47,558 (52.19%)	91,120
1994 (July)	42,013 (47.08%)	47,221 (52.91%)	89,234

Source: Hernández-Cuevas, et al. (1994), p. 63.

Like the US, Mexico has state and federal correctional facilities. Mexico has 31 states and each state maintains a prison system. State prisons are called by the acronym of "CERESO," or Center for Social Readaptation (Centro Readaptación Social, Gobierno Del Estado). The CERESOs are a branch of each state's Department of Social Readaptation, overseen by the Governor's office (Olivero, Mounce and Morgado, 1991).

Administrative positions in the Department of Social Readaptation and the CERESOs are held by political appointees and members of the Institutional Revolutionary Party, also called the PRI. The PRI has dominated Mexican politics since 1929, and Mexico has stood until now as a single party government. These are patronage positions, rather than positions held as the result of professional credentials (Olivero, Mounce and Morgado, 1991).

In a similar fashion, prison guards are equally undereducated and untrained. Usually, they are paid very little and struggle to survive on meager wages. For example, at the CERESO in Matamoros (adjacent to the US border city of Brownsville, Texas), in the state of Tamaulipas, guards are paid $4 per day. They also work 24 hours to earn this, and then take 48 hours off. Many guards stay at the prison to obtain whatever extra money they can earn for additional work. Throughout Mexico, guards wear differing degrees of uniform, and in some prisons, especially those along the border, the visual distinction between prisoners and guards is difficult to make (Olivero, Mounce and Morgado, 1991).

Further, the staff-to-prisoner ratio is usually quite disparate. For example, the CERESO located at Reynosa, Tamaulipas, holds between 1,200 to 1,500 prisoners, with a guard staff of 90 personnel. Prison guards in the majority of prisons we have toured stand near the entrances of the prison or on top of the walls. They usually do not patrol the living areas (Olivero, Mounce and Morgado, 1991).[3]

PRISON LIFE

The organization of life within Mexican prisons is a mirror image of life in Mexican society.[4] That is to say that there are clear class and economic distinctions. Those who can afford the quality amenities of life can purchase them. Wealthy prisoners can serve their sentences in relative comfort, with the exception of poor sanitation and hygiene conditions brought on by overcrowded and decaying facilities (Olivero, Mounce and Morgado, 1991).[5]

Prisoners are virtually free to bring into the prisons almost anything, as long as prison administrators are paid or guards are given their share. Money and goods float freely through Mexican prisons and are not seen as contraband.[6] Paying off law enforcement officials is commonplace throughout Mexico, and is not readily seen as criminal in nature.[7] The common term for this practice is paying the "mordida," which means "the bite" (Americas Watch, 1990; 1991; Human Rights Committee, 1990; Oster, 1989; Shannon, 1989).[8] Housing, visiting privileges, food, medical care, access to the opposite sex, even drugs and alcohol, are purchased (Olivero, Mounce and Morgado, 1991).[9]

We have suggested that administrators pilfer supplies and funds, limiting what reaches prisoners (Olivero, Mounce and Morgado, 1991). Those prisoners who cannot afford to purchase amenities suffer. Clothing and bedding is not in ready supply from prison officials. Prisoners wear their own clothes brought in by family members or bought within the prison from other prisoners. Cells are purchased from guards ranging from air conditioned apartments, to sleeping on an open air soccer field, to standing under a ledge all night to stay out of the rain (Olivero, Mounce and Morgado, 1991).[10]

There is very little food provided by prison officials, and what food there is is of poor quality. Food is brought in by family members and cooked in makeshift kitchens. Prisoners who cannot afford to purchase food or have it brought in suffer the possibility of starvation. They beg or receive handouts, or sell their services (cleaning, cooking, laundry, etc.) to other inmates to earn food and money (Olivero, Mounce and Morgado, 1991).

Mexican prisons have medical staff, but they are few in number, with insufficient medical supplies and substandard equipment. Prisoners who can afford it have doctors come into the prison to examine them and prescribe treatment. Medication is then purchased and then brought into the prison.

There is little programming such as vocational education, etc. Prisoners seem to idle the time away on their own projects and industriously attempt to make goods or provide services for barter and money. The only classification system we have seen relates to disciplinary segregation, medical segregation for communicable diseases, and sometimes, but not always, separation based upon differences in gender. This means that the non-convicted (procesados),[11] the convicted (sentenciados), the violent, the nonviolent, murders, petty thieves, the young and the old, are all housed in the same cell blocks, depending upon their ability to pay (Olivero, Mounce and Morgado, 1991).

On the more positive side, Mexican prisons hold some features which have received acclaim from researchers. Conjugal visits are a universal practice in Mexico, independent of one's marital status. In some facilities, entire families are allowed to live for extended periods behind prison walls with their loved ones.[12] It is common for children to be seen running and playing throughout Mexican prisons. With the exception of noticeable instances due to their scarcity, there appears to be little violence. Throughout Mexico, we never found a prisoner who expressed concerns about unwanted sexual advances or sexual assault (Olivero, Mounce and Morgado, 1991).[13]

There has been some effort to assess the impact of AIDS infection among prisoners in Mexico. The number of prisoners infected with the AIDs virus in Mexico remains largely unknown. There are heroin addicts and intravenous drug users in Mexican prisons. At this point, it may be that Mexico will experience a pattern of infection among prisoners similar to that of the United States; i.e., AIDS infection among intravenous drug users. However, the spread of AIDS through homosexual activity may be reduced in Mexico by the presence of women and conjugal visits (Olivero, Clark, Morgado and Mounce, 1992).

THE IMPACT OF THE UNITED STATES ON PRISONS IN MEXICO: OVERCROWDING

The hallmark of Mexican prisons would appear to be overcrowding.[14] In Mexico's 460 state and federal prisons in 1991, there were 88,000 prisoners held in facilities with a capacity to hold 55,000 prisoners (Americas Watch, 1990; Olivero, 1991).[15] The problem is especially pronounced in facilities along the US-Mexican border. In

1987, there were 240 prisoners housed at the CERESO located in Reynosa, Tamaulipas, adjacent to the US city of McAllen, Texas (Wilkinson, 1990). In 1991, this had increased to 1,250 prisoners. The prison was designed to hold 150 prisoners (Olivero, 1991).

There appear to be three main causes of overcrowding that exacerbate efforts at reform and increase the costs of Mexico's criminal justice system: (1) lack of resources to build additional facilities; (2) the presence of family members living within prison walls as discussed above; (3) its placement next to a country harboring major drug problems, the United States, and the expediency of giving the appearance of participation in drug intervention in exchange for PRI diplomatic support.

THE US INSPIRED "WAR ON DRUGS" IN MEXICO

Mexico became the gateway for drugs into the US during the early 1970s, replacing European sources. In the case of marijuana and heroin, these drugs were grown and manufactured in Mexico, and then transported to the US ("Mexico Main Source," 1974, June 11). Mexico has replaced Europe as the main source of heroin traffic to the United States (Reuter, 1988).[16]

In 1971, United States President Richard M. Nixon declared a "War on Drugs" (Wiesheit, 1990). Part of this war was to interdict drugs from Mexico. Until the late 1980s and early 1990, the Mexican government was reluctant to cooperate in efforts to interdict drugs toward the United States. Mexico has no significant drug problem, nor has there been an increase in domestic drug use through the years (Franco, 1980; Reuter, 1988).[17] Further, there is every indication that Mexican officials, including high ranking PRI members and federal police, are involved in drug smuggling (Olivero, 1991).

The United States government has bullied the Mexican government into taking part in this war through economic sanctions or incentives. During the Nixon presidential administration in 1969, US Deputy Attorney General Richard Kleindienst reported that the Mexican government lacked the political will to take on drug smugglers. The US response was to stop every vehicle for a thorough search coming across the border from Mexico into the United States, causing massive delays. The Mexican government eventually capitulated and negotiated an end to the policy by agreeing to allow US agents into Mexico to conduct surveillance (Shannon, 1989).

In the fall of 1975, Mexico refused to use herbicides on its poppy fields (used to produce heroin), despite the insistence of the US that this was the most efficient method of elimination. Mexico would provide no indication as to why it would not use herbicides ("Mexico Bars Chemicals", 1975, November 17). By 1978, Mexico was harangued into the use of herbicides by threats of halting US economic aid ("US Stops Financing," 1979, October 1).[18]

Previous to 1985, no major drug figure had been arrested in Mexico for over eight years (Meislin, 1985, March 10). In 1986, a public furor ensued after US Customs Commissioner William van Rab (*Houston Post*, 5/18/86) and John Gavin, the former US Ambassador to Mexico, testified before Congress and complained about Mexico's lack of cooperation in interdicting drugs (Palomo, 8/15/86). In July of 1987, the US and Mexico signed a treaty pledging to cooperate in the War on Drugs. This included exchanges of information and evidence (Rohter, 1989, April 11).

By 1990, there were reports that US President George Bush and Mexican President Carlos Salinas de Gortari were in cooperation and supporting US drug interdiction efforts (Americas Watch, 1990). Salinas even went as far as to appoint an elite force of the Federal Judicial Police to lead anti-narcotic efforts (Olivero, 1991). Some have suggested that part of Salinas' willingness to cooperate stemmed from Bush's allowance of latitude on repayment on Mexico's development loans, as well as significant US aid to the Mexican military (Olivero, 1991).

The unintended consequence of interdiction cooperation has been overcrowding in Mexican prisons, especially along the border. For example, of the 1,300 to 1,500 people incarcerated at CERESO at Matamoros (the Mexican city adjacent to Brownsville, Texas), 90% were imprisoned for drug related offenses (Olivero, 1991). In fact, we have found that the majority of persons housed in Mexican prisons, whether or not along the US border, are incarcerated for drug trafficking.[19]

The disruptive influence of the United States and the crisis it produces in Mexican prisons can be best exemplified by the murderous riot at the CERESO in Matamoros on May 17, 1991, in which 18 prisoners were killed and around the same number seriously injured. The riot was the culmination of a struggle between Mexican drug lords selling drugs in the US. Oliverio Chávez was incarcerated at the CERESO in Matamoros for drug dealing, and was in competition with Juan García Abrego, wanted in both the US and Mexico following a nine-ton seizure of cocaine in Texas.

Associates of Abrego were kidnapped from an immigration office in Matamoros, by persons identifying themselves as members of the Mexican Federal Judicial Police. Their bodies and that of a Texas attorney were found dead from machine gun bullets in a rural area outside of Brownsville, Texas. The Chief of Police in Brownsville, Texas, publicly claimed that the Mexican Federal Judicial Police were involved in the murders and was upset by a lack of cooperation by Mexican authorities.

In response to the murders, Matamoros CERESO inmate German Yepez, associated with Abrego, shot Chávez twice in the chest and once in the face. Factions associated with Chávez and Abrego began a fight which included shooting with cuerno de chivos (AK-47 machine guns, given the slang name of "goat horn"), allegedly smuggled in by prison personnel. Guards and prison administrators abandoned the prison. Chávez supporters set fire to Abrego's section of the prison and shot down his associates as they fled the fire.

Three days later the prison was operating as usual, with noticeable exceptions. The Mexican army surrounded the prison to deter escapes. Prison authorities did not retake the prison for several months until after they negotiated a settlement with Chávez. The families of prisoners were allowed back into the facility immediately following the riot, even though there were no prison officials administrating the prison. Donald Wells, US Chief Consul at Matamoros, went into the prison three days after the riot and reported that there was nothing unusual in the prison and that it appeared to be running back to normal (Olivero and Mounce, 1991; Uhlig, 1991).

CONCLUSION

Mexican prisons can be characterized as having both positive and negative qualities. On the positive side are included the following: (1) The organization and activities within prison walls are a close approximation to life outside of prison walls, or Mexican society in general; (2) Prisoners have access to the opposite sex; and, (3) There exists a low level of violence. It is this researcher's conclusion that, in comparison to the US, these qualities of Mexican prisons are progressive. The problems of institutionalization and adjustment associated with prisons in the US are greatly reduced.

However, the situation inside Mexican prisons, like Mexican society in general, is greatly and negatively impacted by the presence of the US, and the US-inspired War on Drugs. High illicit drug consumption in the US has led to significant profits for drug manufacturing and smuggling in Mexico. These profits have led to corruption greatly influencing all aspects of prison life, including a lack of food, poor prison construction and hygiene, less than adequate medical care, lack of prison rehabilitation programs, nontrained guards and low staff-to-prisoner ratios.

For the last 20 years Mexico has been virtually ruled by a single political party, the PRI (the Institutionalized Revolutionary Party). Every modern presidential administration in Mexico has launched an anti-corruption campaign in the face of excessive graft by his predecessor administration. Recently, former president Juan Salinas fled Mexico a wanted man for involvement in drug smuggling and is in asylum in Ireland. The PRI appoints administrators in Mexican prisons, with graft from prison resources as one of the plums of office holding. In essence, a lack of funds for social services is joined with pilfering.

The US government cannot help but be aware of corruption within the PRI. However, the present situation is commensurate with policies followed by the US government in Latin America for at least the last 30 years; i.e. to support corrupt and oppressive governments who are friendly to the US. Some have suggested that there has been a trade-off between Mexico and the US for the free trade agreement. Mexico has supposedly agreed to take part in drug interdiction efforts in exchange for the agreement. Further, it has the over-crowded prisons to prove it. The US government has not spoken out on PRI abuses or corruption. In essence, then, it can be said that the US is responsible for both prison overcrowding and the inducements for corruption in Mexico.

Notes

1. Mexico sought to improve its correctional system by standardizing sentences, building appropriate facilities, selecting mechanisms and training of personnel and developing post-institutional supervision.
2. However, even with human rights groups there are problems of access. Americas Watch (1990) was denied access to the detention center at Campo Militar No. 1, where there are charges that people who have "disappeared" following political activity are being held.

3. In many prisons we have visited, there are prisoners who have been issued clubs, who serve to police other prisoners.
4. Stirewalt (1981: 46) a former inmate held in a prison in Tapachula, Chiapas, Mexico, stated that "Those entering prisons in Mexico immediately become a part of society very little different from the one they left."
5. For example, in one prison, we found that there were 10 showers and toilets to serve 1,250 prisoners. The sewage system was incredibly antiquated and would back up during significant rainfall, and raw sewage would flood the facility's main building (Olivero, 1991).
6. Price (1973) reported on the economic distribution of goods in a Mexican prison in 1968, and called it a "free market economy." As such, this facet of Mexican prison life may be a long term condition, rather than the result of recent overcrowding or other issues.
7. US citizens typically see this as a crime. In the 1970s family members of US citizens incarcerated in Mexican prisons complained to the US Congress about corruption and extortion by Mexican prison officials (US Congress House Committee on the Judiciary (U.S.C.H.C.J.) 1977), which led to a Congressional investigation (Narcotics Digest, 1975) and a prisoner exchange treaty between the US and Mexico (U.S.C.H.C.J., 1977).
8. See Wilkinson (1990) for a more in-depth discussion of "la mordida" practices. He found that while you could bribe officials, it was impossible to bribe one's way out of prison.
9. See Vega (1974) for a discussion of drug smuggling by correctional officers at Morelos State Prison.
10. Rafael Quintero, serving a sentence in the Reclusorio Norte in Mexico City for the torture slaying of a US drug enforcement agent, had accommodations which included a pool table, a Turkish bath, radio and video equipment, television and a telephone. Drug lord Oliverio Chávez at the CERESO at Matamoros had a cell with wall-to-wall carpeting, wood panels, a live-in cook with a kitchen, air conditioning, all of which took up the space normally used to hold 150 prisoners. While he slept in cool comfort, others slept out of doors.
11. Mexico's criminal justice system is based upon the Napoleonic Code, and individuals are seen as being guilty until proven guilty. People are sometimes placed in prison until they are found guilty and sentenced.
12. Americas Watch (1990) reported that prison officials encouraged family visits not only because family members brought in food and other essentials, but also because they serve as a stabilizing influence on the prison population. However, they also found that in some prisons, families were forced to pay for the privilege of visiting.
13. Viveros (1972) reported that prison officials at the Lecumberri and Santa Marta prisons found it necessary to segregate gay prisoners and that homosexuality was a major source of conflict and fighting within

the two prisons. He also reported that a prisoner was raped with a riot baton by a guard as punishment for sexually assaulting young male prisoners.

14. Americas Watch (1990) reported that the crowded conditions fall short of minimally acceptable levels of human decency.

15. In 1990, the government of Mexico anticipated that by the end of 1991, its prison system would be operating at double capacity, even after the construction of three new maximum security prisons (Americas Watch, 1990; Olivero, 1991).

16. At the same time, US citizens and others began to arrive in Mexico to share the drug culture. For example, Oaxaca came to be Mexico's version of the Haight-Ashbury section of San Francisco and young people from around the world gathered there to engage in drug use, etc. (Severo, 1973, March 31).

17. This does not mean that Mexico has no drug addicts, nor is there an absence of addicts in Mexico prisons. Price (1973) reported a growing population of addicts in the Tijuana prison that he observed. Vega (1974) reported on drug addiction. Teran et al. (1974) researched addicted female inmates in Mexico City. Finally, we recently reported the presence of addicts in Mexican prisons in relationship to the potential for a US paralleled AIDS epidemic (Olivero and Mounce, 1993).

18. Following this, the US government then requested that they discontinue the process due to the health hazard presented by sprayed drugs sold in the US. However, Mexico refused to stop spraying herbicides. The US attempted to stop the spraying by discontinuing funds to pay for spraying. Mexico continued to spray using their own resources ("US Stops Financing," 1979, October 1). Mexico continued into the 1980s to spray the herbicide paraquat on marijuana and poppy fields, stating that spraying would only halt if the harmful effects could be proven ("Paraquat," 1980, May 4).

19. Price (1973) reported that in 1968, La Mesa Penitenciaria, located in Tijuana, Mexico, adjacent to San Diego, California, the most frequently committed crime among US citizens incarcerated within the prison was possession of illegal drugs. He also found that among Mexican offenders in the facility, the most common felony was grand theft committed by drug addicts.

References

Americas Watch. (1990) *Prison Conditions in Mexico*. Los Angeles, California: Human Rights Watch.

Americas Watch. (1990) *Human Rights in Mexico: A Policy of Impunity*. Washington, DC: Americas Watch.

Americas Watch. (1991) *Unceasing Abuses: Human Rights in Mexico One Year After the Introduction of Reform.* Washington, DC: Americas Watch.

Franco, J. (1980) *El Sistema Penitenciaria del Estado de Nayarit.* México City: Artes Gráficas Independencia.

Galindo, A. (1979) "Present Situation Regarding Prisons in Mexico." As it appears in *International Corrections*, by R. Wicks and H. Cooper (eds). Lexington, Massachusetts: Lexington Books.

Houston Post. (1986) "Helms Says Mexican Government Tilted Elections." May 18: 16A.

Hernández-Cuevas, J., Cesar-Kala, J., Marquez-Haro, H. and Torricellas-Rodríguez, M. (1994) *Prisiones: Estudio Prospectivo de su Realidad Nacional.* México City, México: Programa Nacional de Capacitación Penitenciaria.

Human Rights Committee. (1990) *Paper Protection: Human Rights Violations and the Mexican Criminal Justice System.* Minneapolis, Minnesota: Minnesota Lawyers International Human Rights Committee.

Koulish, R. and Olivero, J. (1991) "Immigration and Naturalization Services (INS) Detention Center Conditions and the Mexican Federal Judicial Police: The Criminalization of the Victims of Political Persecution." Unpublished paper presented before the *Academy of Criminal Justice Sciences*, November 1991: San Francisco, California.

Meislin, R. (1985) "Killing in Mexico brings US anger into the open." *New York Times*, March 10: 5.

Narcotics Control Digest. (1975). "Torture Charges Leveled On Behalf of Mexican-jailed Americans." *Narcotics Control Digest*, 5 (No. 18) 4/10/89: 1.

New York Times. (1975) "Mexico bars chemicals to destroy poppy fields." November 17: 4.

New York Times. (1975) "Mexico has replaced Europe as main source of heroin traffic." June 11: 1.

New York Times. (1979) "US to stop financing of Mexican drug spray." October 1: 11.

Olivero, J. (1991) "A Recent Look at US Prisoners in Mexican Border Prisons." *International Journal of Comparative and Applied Criminal Justice.* Fall 1991, 15(2): 251–258.

Olivero, J., Clark, A., Morgado, A. and Mounce, G. (1992) "A Comparative View of AIDS in Prisons: Mexico and the United States." *International Criminal Justice Review*, Volume 2: 105–118.

Olivero, J., Mounce, G. and Morgado, A. (1991). "Corrections in Mexico." *American Jails*, September/October 1991: 130–137.

Olivero, J. (1991, October–November) "Americas Watch Produces Investigative Report on Prison Conditions." *CJ the Americas*, 4(5): 3.

Olivero, J. and Mounce, G. (1993) "Research Note: Acquired Immunity Deficiency Syndrome and Mexican Inmate Knowledge and Behavior." *Journal of Criminal Justice*, Vol. 21: 285–293.

Olivero, J. (1991) "US Prisoners in Border Prisons in Tamaulipas, Mexico." *Rio Bravo*, 1(1): 106–122.

Olivero, J., Mounce, G. and Morgado, A. (1991) "Corrections in Mexico." *American Jails*, V(4): 130–136.

Olivero, J. and Mounce, G. (1991) "Struggle Between Drug Lords Generates Riot at Matamoros." *CJ the Americas*. Vol. 4, Number 4, August–September, 1991: 3–4.

Oster, P. (1989) *The Mexicans: A Personal Portrait of a People*. New York: William Morrow and Company, Inc.

Palomo, J. (1986) "Attacks on Agent of Drug Initiative." *Houston Post*, August 15: 3A.

Price, J. (1973) "Private Enterprise in a Prison- The Free Market Economy of La Mesa Penitenciaria." *Crime and Delinquency*, 19 (No. 2) 4/73: 218–227.

Reuter, R. (1988) *Sealing the Border*. Santa Monica, California: The Rand Corporation.

Rohter, L. (1989) "Mexicans arrest top drug figure and 80 policemen." *New York Times*, April 11: 1.

Severo, R. (1973) "In Mexico's south, they are drugged with music too." *New York Times*, March 31: 8.

Shannon, E. (1989) *Desperados: Latin Drug Lords, U.S. Lawmen, and the War America Can't Win*. New York: Viking Press.

Stirewalt, W. (December 1981) "Mexico's Prisons Deserve Emulation." *Corrections Magazine* 7 (No. 6): 45–48.

Teran, C., Schnass, L., Vargas, G. and Belsasso, G. (1974) "Drug Abuse Among the Inmates of a Women's Prison in Mexico City." *Addictive Disease*, 1(2): 153–175.

Uhlig, M. (1991) "Standoff at Matamoros." *New York Times Magazine*. Sunday, October 6: 40–44, 47–48, 73.

US Congress House Committee on the Judiciary. (1977) "Providing Implementation of Treaties for Transfer of Offenders To or From Foreign Countries." *Report of the Committee on the Judiciary on S1682, October 19, 1977*. Washington, DC: US Congress.

Vega, E. (1974) *La Cárcel*. Mexico City: Cámara Nacional de la Industria Editorial.

Viveros, M. (1972) *Anatomia de una Prisión*. Mexico City: Cámara Nacional de la Industria Editorial.

Wilkinson, W. (1990) "An Exploration of the Mexican Criminal Justice System: Interviews with Incarcerated Inmates in a Mexican Prison." *International Journal of Comparative and Applied Criminal Justice* 14 (No. 1) Spring: 115–122.

Chapter
FOUR

The State of Prisons and Prisoners in Four Countries of the Andean Region

Rosa del Olmo

With the wide variety of histories and structural conditions, it is impossible in such a short chapter to approach the state of prisons and prisoners in all of Latin America. Perhaps some day the literature will make possible the use of Garland's (1991: 193) cultural analysis, but at this point only an overall picture of four countries will be presented, chosen for being all part of the Andean region and apparently similar and more useful to compare (Lynch, 1995: 12). But, as it will be shown, there also are striking differences among the countries chosen—Colombia, Ecuador, Peru and Venezuela.

In 1983, the United Nations Latin American Institute for Crime Prevention and the Treatment of Offenders (ILANUD) published *El Preso sin Condena en América Latina y el Caribe* (*The Prisoner Without Sentence in Latin America and the Caribbean*). That book presented the results of a comparative legal and statistical study done by the criminologist Elias Carranza and three other experts, following information received from 30 countries. One of the main findings of this research was the striking difference between code tradition and common law countries in the number of "prisoners without sentence," that is, those awaiting trial. In the code nations "prisoners without sentence" comprised 68.47%, while common law nations averaged 22.57% (Carranza et al., 1983: 49).

"PRISONERS WITHOUT SENTENCE"

The number of pretrial detainees in the Andean region is extremely high in comparison to other countries. Thus, the expression "prisoners without sentence" has become the symbol of Latin American penal systems, especially after *El Preso sin Condena en América Latina y el Caribe* was published. In the words of Carranza (1992: 19): "In Latin America, preventive imprisonment is the rule and prison as conviction the exception. Preventive imprisonment assumes retributive and repressive functions anticipating the execution of punishment." This says a great deal about the distinctive nature of punishment in Latin America. A high number of prisoners who remain long periods of time inside prisons are eventually discharged after having been found not guilty. Thus, detention in itself becomes a form of punishment, and what the law establishes as penal sanctions for different types of crime is no longer relevant.

Ten years after its first study, ILANUD financed a second one, also led by Elias Carranza, under the name *Sistemas Penitenciarios y Alternativas a la Prisión en América Latina y el Caribe* (*Penitentiary Systems and Alternatives to Prison in Latin America and the Caribbean*). When comparing these studies, we observe that Latin America's prison situation has gotten worse. It is true that common law countries continue their lower rates of "prisoners without sentence" but, along with code tradition countries, there is evidence of an unmanageable increase in prison population. What Young and Brown (1983: 42) point out regarding the relationship between higher prison populations and longer sentences, however, doesn't seem to apply here. In Latin American courts the explanation is more complicated. Anachronistic procedures, corruption and inefficiency play important roles, but so does the significant rate of drug-related offenders who are now punished very harshly by recent legislation. Prisoners now awaiting trial for an average of at least three years are the most serious problem.

At the same time, due to the collapse of the economies and high foreign debts, fiscal expenses have been reduced, affecting welfare sectors as well as the penal system (Carranza, 1992: 2). Today it is not only a matter of "prisoners without sentence" but of old and deteriorated establishments with a physical capacity incapable of handling such an excessive prison population. As a result, the separation of pretrial detainees from convicted offenders, mandated by the National Penitentiary Legislation and International Standards, is non-existent. This overcrowding situation is responsible for "the increasingly frequent report of mutinies, rebellions, deaths, inhumane feeding methods and widespread contamination by the AIDS virus, which constitute serious violations both in the UN Standard Minimum Rules for the Treatment of Prisoners and of Fundamental Human Rights" (Alves Costa, 1991: 21). Therefore, it is from a human rights perspective that the Latin American penal system should be tackled. Despite the fact that all Latin American countries have signed international agreements for the protection of prisoners, only rarely have they complied with their standards.

A few words about available data. In the countries studied, offenders under 18 are not counted in prison rates, nor are those in local jails. Only data on prisoners brought to court and who are registered at the Ministry of Justice of each country will be considered. Thus, data on the population of juvenile institutions, mental health facilities, local police jails and military institutions will not be included. Lastly, incomplete records, out-of-date and unreliable statistics, and inadequate libraries have made the study of the four Latin American countries a difficult one, compounded by the problem of writing about countries at a distance. In this respect, I have to acknowledge the support given to me by several colleagues, especially Jesús Antonio Muñoz and Patricia Ramos in Colombia, Alfonso Zambrano in Ecuador and María Gracia Guerrero in Venezuela.

PRELIMINARY COMPARATIVE GENERAL DATA

According to United Nations data, the 1995 estimated total population of the four countries studied was the following:

Colombia: 35.839 million inhabitants
Ecuador: 12.906 million inhabitants
Peru: 25.606 million inhabitants
Venezuela: 24.718 million inhabitants

The attempt to relate prison population totals and rates per 100,000 inhabitants every five years, from 1980 to 1990 (last date available), shows considerable variations between those years, as displayed in Table 1, below.[1] Venezuela had the highest rates in 1985 and 1990. In contrast, Ecuador and Peru show an apparent decline, after special legislation was sanctioned to free "prisoners without sentence" who had been incarcerated longer than they would have been had they been convicted and served average sentences.

Following the European tradition, penal practice in the four countries of our study is established in penal codes, which also define offenses and their respective penalties. Each country has specific penitentiary legislation, most of it following quite closely the UN Standard Rules (see Table 2). In the "Penitentiary Legal Frame" we see that Colombia has the 1993 Penitentiary and Prison Code. Ecuador has the 1982 Code of Sanctions Execution and Social Rehabilitation, Peru has the 1991 Penal Execution Code and Venezuela operates under the 1961 Penitentiary Regime Law. To implement these penal laws, each country has its Administrative Body as shown also in Table 2.

No reference is found to capital punishment because it was abolished many years ago, but maximum penalties vary among the four countries. Colombia's 1980 Penal Code establishes a maximum of 30 years' imprisonment, but recent special legislation increased it to 60 years for "public security offenses" which include terrorism, kidnapping, arms manufacture and trafficking and certain drug-related offenses. Ecuador's 1978 Penal Code refers to a maximum of 25 years as "special major imprisonment." Peru's 1991 Penal Code establishes two types of sentences according to the nature of the

TABLE 1   Prison Population Totals and Rates
(Per 100,000 Inhabitants)

	1980		1985		1990	
	Total	Rate	Total	Rate	Total	Rate
Colombia			28,467	98.5	32,354	100.2
Ecuador	4,773	59.5	6,822	72.5	7,679	59.4
Peru	17,368	100.4	20,936	106.1	17,859	79.3
Venezuela	12,623	83.8	27,218	147.4	29,370	136.4

Sources: Ministries of justice statistical reports.

TABLE 2 "State of Prisons"

	Penitentiary Legal Frame	Administrative Body	Number of Prisons	Prison Population (Over 18 Years Old)		
				Pre-Trial %	Sentenced %	Total
Colombia	Penitentiary and Prison Code (Law 65, 1993)	Penitentiary and Prison National Institute (IINPEC) (1992) Adscript to the Ministry of Justice	175 Prison Establishments (1994)	(1994) 52.3	47.7	29,548
Ecuador	Code of Sanctions Execution and Social Rehabilitation (1982) General Regulation of Application (1982)	National Council of Social Rehabilitation National Direction of Social Rehabilitation (1982)	36 "Social Rehabilitation Centers" (1993)	(1994) 69.3	30.7	8,860
Peru	Penal Execution Code (1991)	National Penitentiary Institute (1991)	93 "Penitentiary Establishments" (1994)	(1994) 72.5	27.5	20,124
Venezuela	Penitentiary Regime Law (1961) Regulation (1975)	Ministry of Justice Direction of Prisons (1955)	31 "Penitentiary Establishments" (1995)	(1994) 67.5	32.5	24,352

Sources: Ministries of justice statistical reports.

offenses: "temporal," with a maximum of 25 years, and life imprisonment. Homicide, for example, has a maximum penalty of 20 years' imprisonment (Article 106), while "whoever participates in money laundering from drug trafficking or narcoterrorism" gets life imprisonment (Article 296). Venezuela's 1964 Penal Code establishes a maximum penalty of 30 years' imprisonment, present also in 1993 anti-drug legislation. Aside from what the penal codes define as offenses, there is a recent tendency to produce "special legislation" whose effect on prisons has yet to be fully determined.

Regarding the Administrative Body in charge of prisons, there is a tendency lately to use members of the armed forces, rather than professionals, to manage prisons. For example, in Colombia the head of INPEC is a lieutenant-colonel. And in 1986, and again in 1992, Venezuela appointed a military General as Director of Prisons. In recent years, several prisons have been officially "militarized."

In the four countries under consideration, the discourse of therapy and rehabilitation prevails as the aim of penal policy. Colombia included it in its 1980 Penal Code, as a special article, with the following words: "Penalty has a retributive, preventive, protective and resocializing function. Security measures are aimed at healing, caring and rehabilitation" (Article 12). Curiously, Peru's 1991 Penal Code reproduces the same text in its Article IX. At the same time, and in contradiction with this discourse, a military model of discipline prevails in both countries, emphasizing the management of high risk groups, but defined in a different way than the "new penology" (Feeley and Simon, 1992: 449) in terms of "public security." In this regard, in practice the prison scene of the countries studied is dominated by the "less eligibility principle,"[2] but with a different connotation since it is not related to conviction in itself, but to a struggle for survival.

Prison populations are above the physical prison capacity, but Venezuela is the worst today. When comparing Colombia and Venezuela with closely similar prison populations, the difference in the number of prisons between these countries is surprising. As Table 3 displays, Colombia had in 1995, 175 prisons for an estimated 31,058 population, while Venezuela in 1992 (and also today), had 31 prisons for an estimated population of 28,870 inmates. Both suffer from overcrowding but Venezuela's is shocking, especially when comparing it with Ecuador's. These differences alone would require further research to explain its reasons and the possible connection with different patterns of prison violence in each country.

TABLE 3   Prison Overcrowding

Country	Number of Prisons	Total Capacity	Number of Prisoners (Yearly Average)	Difference
Colombia (1995)	175	26,395	31,058	−4.663
Ecuador (1993)	36	6,371	8,856	−2.485
Peru (1994)	93	16,965	20,124	−3.159
Venezuela (1992)	31	15,325	28,870	−13.545

Sources: Ministries of justice statistical reports.

Most of the prison overcrowding in the Andean region is a product of the large number of "prisoners without sentence," according to official reports. In 1973, the percentage was the following: Colombia, 79%; Ecuador, 64.8%; Peru, 70% and Venezuela, 79.0%. Examining the percentage in the last ten years (the only complete data available), as shown in Table 4, the situation remains basically the same, except perhaps in the case of Colombia.

Finally, it is important to include comparative data on offenses of the prison population, divided into three main groups, following the terminology used in the Penal Codes, as Property Offenses and Offenses against Persons,[3] and the special category of Drug-related Offenses, which has to do with recent legislation. Of the four countries, only Peru has included new drug legislation as part of the new Penal Code. When comparing these three groups, as displayed in Tables 5.1, 5.2, and 5.3, the only significant increase worth considering has to do with Drug-related Offenses, confirming its relationship with the recent increase in prison population. An exception has to be made regarding Peru, which, as it will be shown later, has also a very significant increase in terrorist prisoners as a result of State action against the Shining Path movement. Nevertheless, all four countries, with their own specificity, follow the pattern of the Latin American penal systems in general, where the priority of police, courts and prisons is on drug traffic control (Muñoz, 1993: 65)

TABLE 4 Pretrial Prisoners (Percentages)

Year	Country			
	Colombia	Ecuador	Peru	Venezuela
1985	64.5	69.2	74.5	76.8
1986	61.2	68.9	68.1	68.1
1987	59.7	67.7	70.3	65.9
1988	55.6	69.7	72.3	61.9
1989	53.7	69.2	76.3	67.2
1990	51.6	70.3	76.3	66.9
1991	48.1	69.9	75.6	61.5
1992	49.0	69.0	70.1	59.9
1993	57.2	67.7	68.2	61.3
1994	52.3	69.3	72.5	67.5

Sources: Ministries of justice statistical reports.

TABLE 5.1 Prison Population: Property Offenses
(Percentages)

	Colombia	Ecuador	Peru	Venezuela
1985	41.4	37.8	35.1	52.0
1986	47.4	33.3	37.8	50.1
1987	48.5	27.1	40.6	48.1
1988		26.9	37.3	47.7
1989	46.0	33.2	41.6	48.2
1990	38.7	32.3	37.8	49.4
1991	34.9	27.8	33.0	48.3
1992	32.7	29.1	37.8	45.7
1993	37.5	27.3	26.6	

to comply with US Government pressure. At the same time, the other type of offenses show a tendency to decline in the prison population in all four countries, despite the fact that, according to police and media information, there has been an increase in violent offenses, especially in the main cities. Venezuelan statistics, for example, reveal that there were a total of 2942 homicides known to the police in 1992, compared to 4271 in 1995. There were 22,262

TABLE 5.2   Prison Population: Offenses Against
Persons (Percentages)

	Colombia	Ecuador	Peru	Venezuela
1985	27.0	26.9	12.7	22.9
1986	26.6	26.7	15.6	22.7
1987	25.9	29.2	15.8	22.4
1988		29.5	14.6	22.5
1989	24.1	22.0	13.8	22.4
1990	27.4	22.7	12.6	22.6
1991	29.1	21.6	11.0	22.4
1992	29.0	20.1	12.9	23.5
1993	26.0	18.6	13.6	

TABLE 5.3   Prison Population: Drug-Related
Offenses (Percentages)

	Colombia	Ecuador	Peru	Venezuela
1985	15.6	19.2	31.4	11.5
1986	10.5	22.1	26.5	13.9
1987	10.4	28.1	24.0	16.5
1988		27.2	25.5	17.8
1989	16.3	30.0	25.0	18.2
1990	19.3	35.3	24.5	18.2
1991	15.2	37.4	28.0	19.2
1992	24.5	40.2	15.5	20.4
1993	21.2	39.3	24.6	

cases of robbery known to the police in 1992, compared to 34,628
cases in 1995. Melossi's (1989) discussion regarding the statistically
significant association between crime rates and imprisonment rates
would be pertinent analysis here.

On specific issues, such as prison health conditions and especially
the problem of AIDS, it is impossible to obtain data, except for individual references, although it is well known that the general health
situation inside the prisons as a whole is dramatically bad. The situation of women should require a special chapter. Table 6 presents

TABLE 6   Female Prison Population
(Percentages)

Year	Country			
	Colombia	Ecuador	Peru	Venezuela
1985	7.0	8.0	8.0	3.0
1986	6.6	—	6.5	3.4
1987	6.4	—	6.5	4.2
1988	7.3	—	7.0	4.6
1989	8.5	10.8	6.7	4.6
1990	—	10.4	7.7	4.9
1991	7.7	12.1	9.1	5.3
1992	7.5	12.7	9.0	5.7
1993	6.0	12.9	8.9	—
1994	5.9	12.1	8.2	6.1

the available data. Of the four countries studied, Ecuador has the highest increase and rate of female imprisonment: In 1985, females represented 8% of the total prison population, but in 1993 this increased to 12.9%. Venezuela also shows an increase from 3.0% in 1985 to 6.1% in 1994. However, what is significant here is the proportion of women imprisoned for drug-related offenses. For example, according to official statistics, in Ecuador, only 18.5% of all female prisoners in 1982 were incarcerated for drug-related offenses; but in 1990, the figure was 72.0% and in 1994, 73.6%. In Peru 74% of all women in prison in 1986 were incarcerated for drugs and terrorism and in 1988, 38.5% were for drugs only. In Venezuela in 1991 the figure was 73.4%. In Colombia, although no official data were obtained, studies show that it is also in first place (Martínez, 1996: 92).

Regarding political prisoners, only Colombia and Peru have a significant number. But it is not easy to obtain data since the issue is considered a matter of "national and public security."

BRIEF NATIONAL HISTORIES

Any attempt to cover more than one Latin American country in a comparative prison reader is a very daring enterprise when individual country histories are examined in depth. This complexity is evident when we examine briefly some of the main characteristics and differences of our four Andean nations.

Colombia

Colombia's penal system should be the subject of a special book, not a brief history. Although presenting the same general problems as the other three countries selected, Colombia is perhaps the most complex to analyze. At the same time, there is a vast official and academic literature available plus a permanent interest in holding congresses and seminars, attempting at least formally to find solutions to Colombia's penal problems. Also, for a long time universities have been concerned with the prisoner through a series of research projects, the results of which were often shared at official events.

The General Direction of Prisons was created in 1914 by Law No. 35, becoming the Department of the Ministry of Justice until 1992, when by Decree No. 2160 the National Penitentiary and Prison Institute (INPEC) was created as an administrative independent body ascribed to the Ministry of Justice, to take care of the country's 175 penitentiaries and prisons. That same year Law 24 was sanctioned, creating the institution of People's Defense (Defensoría del Pueblo), under the direction of the attorney general, to watch, promote and implement human rights. In 1993, a new Penitentiary and Prison Code was sanctioned as Law 65. These legal developments were considered an essential part of the State's modernization, in accordance with the 1991 new constitution.

These laws did indeed help transform Colombia's penal system. Decree 2160 gave priority to resocialization and a progressive system for treatment (but, at the same time, since its creation INPEC has been run by the military). Law 65 introduced maximum security establishments for offenders against public security (political prisoners and drug traffickers). These prisons have increased considerably in the last few years. Meanwhile, Law 24 has served as a watchdog of human rights in Colombia's penal establishments. In a few individual cases, authorities have even reinstituted rights by decisions of the Constitutional Court.

But Colombia's complexity—with an important presence of several guerrilla movements, and a series of entrepreneurs playing a key role in drug production and trafficking—has created a series of obstacles to the Constitution's objectives. Also, Colombia's previous legal situation is a factor: From January 1980 to May 1991, 138 penal norms were sanctioned (only 26 of them in 1989), most of them by the Executive as a result of the state of siege during that decade (Muñoz, 1991). The analysis of this legislation reveals the influence of the US Government's pressures against drug-trafficking. The new penal law has changed Colombia's European legal tradition into US law. This legal confusion has diminished public trust in the law of the State (Muñoz, 1993).

In the words of the Colombian criminologist Jesus Antonio Muñoz, "the 'exception justice' or 'public order justice' is becoming a permanent norm which permeates the entire penal procedure. Behind the emergency norms we find the conflicts with drug traffickers and the armed insurgency. And behind both, US pressures" (1993: 53). In other words, Colombia's law is negating Liberal Penal Law by the development of "emergency law," "faceless judges," "public order" justice and in general by the Executive's intervention in the Administration of Justice.

One of the last Executive decisions was President Gaviria's "submission to justice" policy in 1991 in connection with his proposal to build maximum security prisons to hold drug traffickers and guerrilla leaders. As a result, a double-standard penal system has been created. Great financial resources and foreign aid are dedicated to building these special prisons while the rest is abandoned. Also, despite the severe restrictions, those few who are sent to maximum security prisons are in better daily conditions regarding their main needs than the rest of the prison population, which continues suffering severe overcrowding, lack of work and study, minimum health conditions, etc. From this situation are not excluded the majority of drug-related offenders, a rate which keeps growing in Colombian prisons, despite the high number imprisoned in other countries, estimated at 25,000 according to Colombia's House of Representatives Commission of Foreign Relations (El Nuevo País, Caracas, June 7, 1995: 8).

In the same situation are those detained as suspected guerrilla members. For example, the 6,500 captured between 1991 and 1993 (Castro, 1995: 13) had to be sent to regular prisons, at least until convicted. According to INPEC's former director, a real problem is created by these prisoners because, if they are placed in special wings, they become a united and powerful force, and if they mix with other prisoners, they indoctrinate them (Muñoz, 1993: 58). In fact, guerrilla members have created inside the prisons Human Rights Committees, have gone on hunger strikes and have induced other prisoners to stand up for their rights (Comisión Andina de Juristas, 1995: 13).

As a result, Colombia's president has been obliged to sanction, on several occasions, decrees declaring the prisons and penitentiaries "in a state of emergency and internal commotion" and thus allow the authorities to rotate prisoners from one prison to another "due to a strong wave of violence, insecurity and alteration of the internal regime" (Pelaez Restrepo, 1995: 4). But the government also had to declare a judiciary emergency three times in two years to avoid the release of pretrial prisoners for not having gone to court in the 180 days mandated by law. Despite having the highest rate of violent deaths in Latin America, according to official sources, Colombia's prison deaths show a decreasing tendency, reporting 158 in 1990, 118 in 1991, 85 in 1992 and 59 in 1993.

Much more could be written about Colombia's penal system, but the 1993, 1994 and 1995 Annual Reports of the International Prison Observatory summarize some of the key issues in the following words: "Drugs, alcohol, guard indifference and prisoner idleness characterize Colombian prisons..." (1993: 21); "Militarization of penitentiary authorities has not solved the serious problems. Violence, corruption and arbitrariness prevail. Hygiene conditions are deplorable and overcrowding aggravates the situation" (1994: 56); "Since 1993, several new procedures have hardened the penitentiary system, affecting the rights of those in prison. Repression is worse for those suspected of drug-related offenses and terrorism" (1995: 45).

Ecuador

Of the four countries examined, Ecuador is the smallest in terms of inhabitants and prison population and in terms of prison violence. The Direction of Prisons was created as late as 1970 "to guarantee to society the rehabilitation and readaptation of offenders" (Rossero and Muñoz, 1989: 92). Before then, prisoners were in the hands of charitable establishments called "Patronatos de Cárceles y Trabajos Reglamentarios." In 1982, when the Code of Sanctions Execution and Social Rehabilitation was sanctioned, prisons and penitentiaries were renamed as "Social Rehabilitation Centers," subdivided into

Maximum, Medium and Minimal Security, following the impact that Italian positivist criminology had, and still has, in this country.

In this respect, the penal discourse emphasizes penal sanction as "rehabilitative sanction" rather than punishment and highlights the study of the offender's personality to determine his degree of "dangerousness" and the implementation of a biotypological classification to separate offenders in terms of "normal," "induced," "non-adapted," "hypoevolutive" and "psychopath" (Narváez S., 1984: 390). However, Ecuadorian specialists complain that since 1982 it has been impossible to implement this classification due to the lack of resources, overcrowding and the high number of pretrial detainees. Today, there are 36 Centers of Social Rehabilitation in abominable physical condition, where classification is applied only in terms of sex.

Ecuador does not have alternative measures to imprisonment, and thus a high proportion of the prison population is made up of petty thieves who often spend more time in prison awaiting trial than the time established by law for their offense. In this respect, a penal lawyer pointed out the following: "What violates most a State of Law is the excessive length of pretrial detention. For minor offenses, this violates the legal principle of presumed innocence and contradicts the traditional mild Ecuadorian penal law regarding the maximum penalty" (Raub, 1987: 241). Since 1985, annual penitentiary censuses are carried out to determine the state of "prisoners without sentence" and the length of pretrial detention. But no solutions seem to have been found to that problem.

In an attempt to solve the overcrowding problem, nevertheless, special legislation was sanctioned in 1992 as Law 04 and Decree 716, which freed prisoners awaiting trial more than the third of the time established by the Penal Code as the maximum sentence for the offense and, for those sanctioned, to diminish their penalty by good behavior. Some prisoners were able to leave as a result, but the prison population has not diminished. One possible explanation has to do with the continued increase in drug-related offenders, and in the fact that they were excluded from these special measures because, as pointed out by several penal lawyers, drug legislation segregates this type of prisoner in violation of the Ecuadorian Constitution (Narváez S., 1993; Zambrano P., 1992).

Of the four countries studied, Ecuador has the highest increase in drug-related offenders, although it is not the one with the greatest drug problem. Here, again, Melossi's (1989) discussion would be pertinent. In 1972, the proportion was 3.5%; in 1984, 27.1%; in 1993, 38.9%; and in 1994 it went up to 43%, becoming the first in frequency among the prison population. Most of those sentenced for drugs are unemployed drug couriers or minor street sellers. But also a proportion of foreigners, mainly Colombians, are involved. According to official records, in 1994, 18.9% of the 3814 prisoners for drug-related offenses were foreigners. Of the total 721 foreign prisoners, 600 were Colombians involved in drug offenses, which implied 83.2% of the total foreigners in Ecuadorian prisons (ILANUD, 1994).

Authorities are very concerned about the Colombian prisoners issue because of their high degree of organization in prison. They press their leadership within prisons to claim rights which might affect the Ecuadorian prison population, who traditionally have been more passive. Thus, the possibility of returning them to their native country is being discussed.

Regarding prison violence, and specifically deaths within prisons, Ecuador reports a total of 99 deaths from 1990 to 1993, of which 39 were from natural diseases and seven from firearms (Narváez S., 1993).

Peru

Detailed studies on Peru's prison system are difficult to obtain. It is important, nevertheless, to include in this chapter the data available to stress the striking differences among Latin American countries and, in particular, within the Andean region. According to official sources, the Peruvian prison population increased at a very fast rate, especially from 1981 to 1985 (Peru, 1987). Deteriorating conditions have precipitated prison mutinies, rebellions and mysterious deaths. For example, in 1982, 30 prisoners were killed in a single mutiny (Lamos P., 1989: 191). All through the 1980s, Peru's prisons had a history of mutinies, rebellions and deaths involving Shining Path members. Perhaps the most violent prison mutiny took place at the beginning of Alan Garcia's government, the night of June 18, 1986, at Lima's Lurigancho prison. That night 300 Shining Path prisoners, on trial for terrorism, were killed by the Armed Forces as they destroyed the entire prison (Lamos P., 1989: 191).

Peru has since 1980 been one of the most violent Latin American nations—first as a coca leaf producer, but especially as a consequence of the appearance and development of the Shining Path

guerrilla movement. Both developments had very important consequences for the penal system and in the Peruvian government's
penal practices. For example, in 1986, 74% of female prisoners were
sentenced for terrorism and drug-related offenses, and by 1990, 153
women were in prison for terrorism alone.

According to Coletta Youngers, a Washington Office on Latin
America expert on Peru, the situation today is worse. In this
respect, she says (1996: 4): "Peru's draconian antiterrorist legislation, implemented after the 1992 coup, has resulted in the imprisonment of hundreds...if not thousands... of innocent Peruvians who
face sentences ranging from 20 years to life in prison. The trial on
treason charges of US citizen Lori Berenson in a secret military tribunal has brought attention across the country to the lack of due
process and the rule of law in Peru today. The lack of democratic
accountability was starkly evident last June, when the Peruvian
Congress passed a sweeping amnesty law for state agents" (responsible for the killings in the 1986 Lurigancho prison mutiny).

Table 7 below indicates the rapidly growing percentage of prisoners incarcerated for "terrorist" activities. This data might explain in
part the apparent decrease in drug-related offenses in Peru (Table
5.3), since there is now the offense called "narcoterrorism." Many of
Peru's prisoners are foreigners: 32% of Lurigancho's 4700 prisoners

TABLE 7   Imprisonment for Terrorism
in Peru*

Year	Number of Prisoners	% From the Total Prison Population
1985	974	4.7
1986	432	2.9
1987	739	4.6
1988	716	4.4
1989	951	5.4
1990	1109	5.2
1991	1451	10.4
1992	2027	13.4
1993	2867	15.1
1994	3562	18.4

*Peru (1995).

in 1994 were foreigners imprisoned for drug-related offenses. Without family and support groups, they are especially prone to victimization.

New criminal policy was implemented in 1986, in the form of a depenalization law; the abolition of vagrancy law (Law No. 4891), and the introduction of penitentiary benefits which resulted in a decrease of the prison population. In 1987, however, the prison population increased again, with a high proportion of "prisoners without sentence." In 1989 the rate was 76.3% according to official figures. When President Fujimori took over, one of his aims was to reorganize the prison system made up of 108 deteriorated establishments. Up to May 9, 1992, when security forces violently stopped a new mutiny in Lima's Canto Grande prison, Peru's prisons were "academies of subversive indoctrination and especially in Lima's prisons, Shining Path prisoners had total control" (Valenzuela, 1993: 18). In Canto Grande for example, prison staff had not been able to enter in three years. On visiting days, prisoners set up a stage to play scenes where the armed forces were attacked by Shining Path members. In May, fire arms, grenades and communication tunnels between male and female pavilions were found (Peru, 1995). Today, there are special Maximum Security prisons for the increasing number of convicted terrorists.

Of the four countries studied, Peru shows on average the highest percentage of pretrial prisoners (see Table 4). Over the last decade, overcrowding and the inappropriate "mix" of prisoners (Sparks, 1994: 18) in inhuman conditions have been the norm. Thus, as several Peruvian penal lawyers have pointed out, a real treatment program has been impossible (Prado S., 1987; Lamos P., 1989; Pedraza S., 1991). In practice, the concept of prison population refers to "anyone who has lost his freedom, regardless of his legal situation" (Pedraza S., 1991: 471). Meanwhile, the resocialization discourse continues to predominate in legal texts as the aim of the prison system. According to the president of the National Penitentiary Council, today's 93 prisons have as a main objective "the re-education, rehabilitation and reincorporation of the prisoner to society adapting the Progressive Treatment System," following the 1991 Penal Execution Code (ILANUD, 1994). However, official sources speak of 72.5% pretrial prisoners for 1994 (Peru, 1995: 90). Peru's National Police control 70 prisons and the rest are in the hands of civil personnel from the National Penitentiary Institute.

An interesting aspect of Peru's penal policy which differs from the other countries is that the Peruvian government has given the same rights and benefits to prisoners sentenced for drug-related offenses (but not big traffickers) because it has become aware that there is a relationship between these offenses and hard socioeconomic conditions. In this respect, for example, one day of work or study is counted as two days' imprisonment (ILANUD, 1994).

Venezuela

Human Rights Watch America (HRWA) visited Venezuela the first week of March 1996 to examine the state of prisons and prisoners. The conclusion was that Venezuelan prisons are catastrophic, one of the worst in the American hemisphere, violating the Venezuelan State international obligations on human rights. Its most important characteristic is the "terrible overcrowding, intolerable violence among prisoners and from guards, very slow trial procedures, extreme physical deterioration of several establishments, lack of minimum medical requirements, lack of respect for the prisoners' families during visiting days, corruption of prison staff and idleness" (El Nacional, Caracas, March 23, 1996: D/7). The US State Department 1996 Human Rights Report states the following:

> Prison conditions are deplorable due to underfunding, poorly trained staff, corruption among prison staff and National Guard members and overcrowding so severe as to constitute inhuman and degrading treatment. Inadequate diet, minimal health care, a prisoner to guard ratio as high as 40 to 1 and physical abuse by guards and by other inmates led to many prison riots. Inmates often have to pay guards as well as each other to obtain necessities such as space in a cell, a bed and food. Guns, knives and illegal drugs are easily smuggled into most prisons, and violence between prisoners is very common (United States, 1996: 2).

In the 1993 Report, the International Observatory of Prisons (IPS) pointed out "the difficult detention conditions in Venezuela, the arbitrariness, the 250% overcrowding and violence between inmates or imposed by guards, the lack of hygiene and the deterioration of the establishments." The Report concluded: "A strange violence characterizes a good number of Venezuelan prisons. Impunity, staff corruption, overcrowding, the length of pretrial detention and the bad living conditions produce a state of permanent revolt" (Observatoire, 1993: 89). In its 1994 Report, the IPS observed: "An unusual violence prevails in Venezuelan prisons with the outcome of hundreds of dead" (Observatoire, 1994: 76). While there is widespread agreement regarding Venezuela's deplorable penal system, the causes of this outrageous situation are more complicated.

Of all the countries studied, Venezuela has the oldest Penitentiary Regime Law, although following closely the UN Standard Minimum rules and the resocialization and treatment discourse. It has had a Law of Vagrants and Rogues since 1956 which is applied to "dangerous behaviors," although it violates Venezuela's 1961 Constitution. Also, since 1980, it has had non-institutional treatment with the Ley de Sometimiento a Juicio y Suspensión Condicional de la Pena (a combination of probation and parole), modified in 1993 as Law of Benefits in the Penal Process. Today, however, this law is not implemented as it should be because of frequent corruption and because of the complicated procedure required (PROVEA, 1994: 95). From 1980 to 1995, a total of 120,148 offenders were placed on the equivalent of probation ("sometimiento a juicio") and 19,980 received parole ("suspensión condicional de la pena") (Guerrero, 1995: 4). In 1992, the Provisional Freedom under Bail Law was sanctioned also to reduce overcrowding, except for vagrants and rogues and drug-related offenders, but it is not applied today due to technical reasons.

The main characteristic of Venezuela's prison administration is its unsteadiness. From 1985 to 1993, nine Ministers of Justice were appointed, and between 1989 and 1993, eleven Directors of Prisons took charge, most of them without any knowledge or experience of penological matters. Official unstableness is a serious handicap for implementing a sound penal policy. Among the four nations studied, Venezuela is the country with the smallest number of prisons, despite having the second largest prison population, and consequently it has the greatest overcrowding. However, its official statistics are the least reliable and often the same source presents contradictory data. For example, there is no explanation for the prison population decrease from 28,870 in 1992 to 24,352 in 1994.

Today, Venezuela's Direction of Prisons does not know its exact prison population, nor the number of prisoners killed daily. However, human rights non-governmental organizations try to keep, as far as possible, a close record of the situation. For example, PROVEA's recent Annual Reports indicate the following situation:

• 1993: 195 dead and 387 wounded, plus 63 killed at Caracas Reten de Catia's massacre on November 27, during the "coup d' etat" (PROVEA, 1993: 87).

- 1994: 498 dead and 1127 wounded in violent acts. In one single mutiny in Maracaibo's prison in January approximately 100 inmates were killed (PROVEA, 1994: 101).
- 1995: From January 1 to November 5, 274 dead and 926 wounded (PROVEA, 1995: 104).

Thus, of all the countries studied, Venezuela has the greatest known number of prisoners killed as a result of prison violence. The number of dead recorded by PROVEA does not include those by natural disease, data which are not available.

Venezuela also shows a significant increase in drug-related offenders, as displayed in Table 5.3, who receive extremely harsh treatment and discrimination. An important proportion is made of Colombians, approximately 2000, making them the second largest number after those imprisoned in the United States. Several legal attempts have been made to return them to their country, but so far they have not been very successful. About Venezuela much more could be written, but in conclusion we can say that a climate of impunity permeates the entire system of Administration of Justice.

SUMMARY AND CONCLUSION
THE STATE OF HUMAN RIGHTS IN THE ANDEAN REGION

We have seen that the prison systems of the four countries studied present commonalities and differences. In all four nations, the discourse of therapy and rehabilitation is the aim of penal policy, despite the tendency for prisons to be run by the armed forces. Meanwhile, prison populations are well above the physical prison capacity because of the extremely high number of prisoners awaiting trial—"prisoners without sentence"—many of them for periods of time beyond what penal procedure law establishes.

Deprivation of liberty in itself becomes a punishment, independent of the time established by law for each offense, because preventive imprisonment assumes retributive and repressive functions anticipating the execution of punishment. Thus, the legal concept of sanction acquires a different meaning and loses its original function.

There is a close relationship between drug-related offenses and the recent increase in prison population. Colombia shows a minor increase because the main drug activity is done outside the country, which explains the high number of Colombians imprisoned in other countries. Also, the high proportion of women imprisoned for drugs and particularly their violent increase in the last years is striking. When trying to solve the overcrowding problem through special legislation, however, drug-related offenders are excluded from these benefits.

In the four countries there is a tendency to change the European legal tradition into US law. The extreme case today is Colombia, followed by Peru. At the same time, "special legislation" is sanctioned to take care of what is called "offenses against public security" such as drug trafficking and terrorism. Also, there is a tendency to build maximum security prisons to hold the most active drug traffickers and guerrilla leaders.

To establish the differences among the four countries much more research is needed. Nevertheless, it is evident that Colombia and Peru differ from Ecuador and Venezuela because of their persistent guerrilla movements, parts of which are today in prison. However, on several occasions in Peru, Shining Path prisoners have been killed in large numbers inside prisons, which has not been the case in Colombia. At the same time, Colombia is the only country which has the institution of People's Defense to watch, promote and implement human rights also within prisons.

Ecuador shows the smallest prison violence but the highest increase in drug-related offenders. It is the only country which does not have alternative measures to imprisonment. Venezuela has the highest overcrowding, prison violence, riots and the greatest known number of prisoners killed daily.

As stated above, all four countries have signed international agreements for the protection of prisoners, but only rarely have they complied with their standards. Thus, the best way to end this essay is to suggest the need to discuss the state of human rights in the prisons studied. When reviewing UN Standards and some of the recent handbooks produced by United Nations (1994) and Penal Reform International (1995), in relation to pretrial detention and good penal practice, and recalling the state of prisons and prisoners described here, the only possible conclusion is that those basic human rights do not correspond to that reality.

In our countries inmates face two types of punishment. The first one is established by law and often not applied. The second one is not found in legal texts nor applied by courts, but is established by the daily prison living and applied by other inmates or by guards in the form of rape, abuse, blackmail, robbery, torture or death (del Olmo, 1995). Thus, to defend the right to life and integrity of the person is the only human right which makes sense in the penal systems of this type of society. Survival is the priority.

Notes

1. The four countries have extremely high populations under 18, which should be considered to obtain more accurate information on the prison population totals and rates per 100,000 inhabitants. Unfortunately, it was impossible to gain access to this data.
2. I.e., "prisoners endure worse conditions than those of the poorest non-dependents...in terms of suffering and humiliation" (Pratt, 1993: 375).
3. It is important to point out here that we chose "offenses against persons" because this is commonly used in all Latin American countries, although Colombia's Penal Code speaks of "Offenses Against Life, the Body and the Health." All the Codes in this chapter include the following offenses: homicide, body injuries, abortion, abandonment of minors, calumny and injury. Peru adds genocide. None, however, includes rape, which is dealt with in the chapter, "Good Manners and Good Order of the Family" in Venezuela and Ecuador as "Offenses Against Freedom and Sexual Bashfulness" in Colombia and in Peru within "Offenses Against Freedom."

References

Alves Costa, Sidney. (1991) "The Penal System and alternatives to imprisonment in Latin America" in Penal Reform International: *The Alternative Target Community-oriented Prisons and Community Based Sanctions*, Report on an International Conference on Penal Reform held in The Hague, The Netherlands, September 12–15.

Castro Garcia, Lourdes. (1995) *Leyes, Cárceles y Derechos Humanos en Colombia*. San José de Costa Rica: MINGA.

Carranza, Elias; Houed, Mario; Mora, Luis P. and Zaffaroni, Eugenio Raul. (1983) *El Preso sin condena en América Latina y el Caribe*. San José de Costa Rica: ILANUD.

Carranza, Elias; Houed, Mario; Liverpool, Nicholas J.O.; Mora, Luis P. and Rodríguez Manzanera, Luis. (1992) *Sistemas Penitenciarios y alternativas a la prisión en América Latina y el Caribe*. Buenos Aires: Ediciones Depalma.

Comisión Andina de Juristas. (1995) *Informe Preliminar sobre Prisiones en Colombia*. Santafé de Bogotá, February.

Colombia. (1986) *Código Penal Decreto 100 de 1980*. Bogotá: Editorial Temis.

Colombia. (1994) *Memorias I Simposio Internacional de Criminologia y Asuntos Penitenciarios, 26 abril 1993*. Santafe de Bogota: INPEC.

del Olmo, Rosa. (1995) "La funcion de la pena y el Estado latinoamericano" en *La Experiencia del Penitenciarismo Contemporaneo: Aportes y Expectativas*. Mexico D.F.: Comision de Derechos Humanos.

Feeley, Malcom and Simon, Jonathan. (1992) "The New Penology: Notes on the Emerging Strategy of Corrections and its implications." *Criminology*, 30(4).

Garland, David. (1991) "Punishment and Culture: the Symbolic Dimensions of Criminal Justice." *Studies in Law, Politics and Society*, Vol. 11.

Guerrero, Maria G. (1995) "Venezuela: cambios legislativos." Caracas: Mimeo.

—————. (1995b) "Sistema Carcelario Venezolano: Problemas y Soluciones." XLV Convención Nacional de ASOVAC. Caracas: Mimeo.

ILANUD. (1994) *Primer Encuentro de Directores de Sistemas Penitenciarios Latinoamericanos*. Quito, November 30–December 2.

Lamos P., Luis. (1989) "El Sistema Penitenciario en el Peru." *Debate Penal*, No. 7–9, Lima.

Lynch, James. (1995) "Crime in International Perspective" in *Crime*, James Q. Wilson and Joan Petersilia (eds.) San Francisco, California: ICS Press.

Martinez S., Mauricio. (1996) *Justicia Penal y Derechos Fundamentales*. Santafe de Bogota: Ediciones Jurídicas Gustavo Ibañez.

Melossi, Dario. (1989) "An Introduction: fifty years later, *Punishment and Social Structure* in comparative analysis." *Contemporary Crises*, 13(4), (December): 311–326.

Muñoz, Jesus Antonio. (1991) "Normas penales creadas a partir de 1980." Santafe de Bogota: Mimeo.

Muñoz, Jesus Antonio. (1993) "Marginalidad y Violencia en el espacio urbano latinoamericano: el caso de Santafé de Bogotá." Santafé de Bogota: Mimeo.

Narváez S., Grimaneza. (1984) "Tratamiento Penitenciario." *Archivos de Criminología, Neuro-Psiquiatría y Disciplinas Conexas*, XXV(27), Quito.

—————. (1993) *Breve Estudio del Sistema Penitenciario Ecuatoriano Quinquenio 1989–1993*. Quito: Mimeo.

Observatoire International des Prisons. (1993) *Rapport*. Lyon: Plan Fixe.

Observatoire International des Prisons. (1994) *Rapport*. Lyon: Plan Fixe.

Observatoire International des Prisons. (1995) *Rapport*. Lyon: Plan Fixe.

Pedraza S., Wilfredo. (1991) "Evolución de la Población Penal entre 1977 y 1988" en Varios: *Derecho Penal, Homenaje al Dr. Raúl Peña Cabrera*. Lima: Ediciones Jurídicas.

Pelaez R., Norberto. (1995) "Gestion Penitenciaria INPEC Colombia." *I Congreso Internacional Iberoamericano sobre Administracion Penitenciaria*. Cartagena de Indias, 27 noviembre–1 diciembre.

Penal Reform International. (1995) *Making standards work: an international handbook on good prison practice*. The Hague, March.

Peru. (1986) *Censo Nacional Penitenciario*. Lima: Instituto Nacional Penitenciairo.

Peru. (1987) *Anuario Estadistico Penitenciario*. Lima: Instituto Nacional Penitenciario.

Peru. (1991) *Codigo Penal*. Decreto Legislativo No. 635. Lima.

Peru. (1995) *Informe Nacional al IX Congreso de la ONU sobre Prevención del Delito y Tratamiento del delincuente*. Lima: Ministerio de Justicia.

Peru. (1996) *Texto Ordenado del Nuevo Código Penal Decreto Legislativo No. 635 de 1991*. Lima: Ediciones Berrio.

Prado S., Victor. (1987) "Notas Críticas a la política criminal del Gobierno de todos los peruanos." *Debate Penal*, No. 1, Lima.

Pratt, John. (1993) "This is not a Prison: Foucault and the Panopticon and Pentonville." *Social and Legal Studies*, 2(4).

PROVEA. (1993) *Situacion de los derechos humanos en Venezuela*. Caracas: Edisil.

PROVEA. (1994) *Situacion actual de los derechos humanos en Venezuela*. Caracas: Edisil.

Raub, Nikolas. (1987) "Presentación de la obra Historia y Estado Actual de la Pena Privativa de Libertad en el Ecuador." *Archivos de Criminologia, Neuro-Psiquiatria y Disciplinas Conexas* XXVI(28).

Rossero, Hernando C. and Muñoz, Luis A. (1989) "Sistema de Reha-
bilitación Social Ecuatoriano." *Archivos de Criminología, Neuro-
Psiquiatría y Disciplinas Conexas* XXVII(29), Quito.

Sparks, Richard. (1994) "Can Prisons be Legitimate?" *British Journal
of Criminology*, Vol. 34, Special Issue.

United Nations. (1994) *Human Rights and Pre-trial Detention A
Handbook of International Standards relating Pre-trial Detention*.
New York and Geneva: United Nations.

United States State Department. (1996) "Human Rights in
Venezuela." Report. Washington DC: Mimeo.

Valenzuela, Cecilia. (1993) "Penales: Malas Maneras." *Caretas*, June.

Vega U., Victor; González Miño, M. and Rivadeireira S. (1987)
"Tendencias de la criminalidad en el Ecuador." *Archivos de
Criminología, Neuro-Psiquiatría y Disciplinas Conexas*, XXVI(28),
Quito.

Vega U., Victor and Narváez S., Grimaneza (1989) "La Justicia Penal
en el Ecuador y los Derechos Humanos." *Archivos de Criminología, Neuro-Psiquiatría y Disciplinas Conexas*, XXVII(29), Quito.

Venezuela. (1964) *Codigo Penal*. Gaceta Oficial No. 915, Caracas.

Young, Warren and Brown, Mark. (1993) "Cross-national Comparisons of Imprisonment," in M. Tonry (ed.) *Crime and Justice: An
Annual Review*. Chicago: University of Chicago Press. pp. 1–49.

Youngers, Coletta. (1996) "The Andean Quagmire: Rethinking US
Drug Control Efforts in the Andes." WOLA Briefing Series,
Washington DC: Washington Office on Latin America.

Zambrano P., Alfonso. (1992) "La Carcel: Utopia y Realidad."
Criminologia y Derecho Penal, No. 2, July–December.

II
Europe

Chapter
FIVE

The Buckling of the Shields: Dutch Penal Policy 1985–1995

David Downes

In the post-war period, Dutch penal policy came to symbolize relative sanity and humanity in an increasingly punitive world. As in the late 18th century to John Howard, so in the late 20th century to penal reformers in general, Dutch penal policy suggested that rationality could prevail in a field where emotions swamped the major lesson of the history of penology: that harsh punishments do not deter. If it were otherwise, the capital offense of pickpocketing would not have flourished at the scene of public executions and the death penalty would prove an effective antidote to murder. This is not to say that the Dutch drew the opposite conclusion, that offenders should be allowed to act with impunity. Such an inference, if acted upon, would force victims to "take the law into their own hands" to seek redress. The Dutch achievement was, for a few decades at least, to strike a new compromise between these extremes. First, the prison population, expressed as a rate per 100,000 of the population as a whole, was reduced to an unprecedented minimum of 25. Secondly, the prison system itself was radically overhauled to reduce the "pains of imprisonment" to an extent seldom achieved elsewhere.

Both achievements in tandem constituted a unique social experiment, whose significance is now being thrown into doubt and even somewhat devalued. In retrospect, the conditions which favored its accomplishment were perhaps themselves unique. They have now largely evaporated due to rapid social change and, in consequence of rising rates and changing patterns of crime, a new volatility in the politics of law and order. However, the basic facts of the Dutch experience remain that crime rates in The Netherlands are no worse than those of comparable societies, despite a resort to custody which, until now, has been for four decades markedly more sparing (see Graph 1). The question addressed here is how and why recarceration has succeeded decarceration so emphatically over the past ten years.

FROM TOLERANCE TO DISILLUSIONMENT, 1945–1985

The bare facts of this singular experiment in decarceration can be simply conveyed. In 1950, the daily average prison populations of The Netherlands and England and Wales were much the same in relation to the general population. Twenty-five years later, in 1975, the situation had been transformed. In The Netherlands, the prison population had been halved while that in England and Wales doubled, producing a ratio of 1:4 from rough parity (see Graph 2). It is, of course, the case that the daily prison population is but *one* indicator of the extent of imprisonment. As Steenhuis, Tigges and Essers (1983) have stressed, sentences to custody as a proportion of convictions tell a less dramatic story. However, the daily average prison population per 100,000 is arguably the best single indicator, because it is the *product* of annual admissions to prison and the length of detention combined. No indicator means much in isolation from the crime rate and other key variables, such as the clear-up and conviction rates. Taking these factors into account for 1980, it remained the case that two-thirds of the difference between the Dutch and English daily prison populations was attributable to sentencing variables, the use of custody and especially the length of sentence (Downes, 1988). The other third was due to differences in the crime rate, the clear-up rate and other factors. Comparative analysis of sentencing trends in relation to three serious offenses (burglary, rape and robbery) showed that the Dutch judiciary had

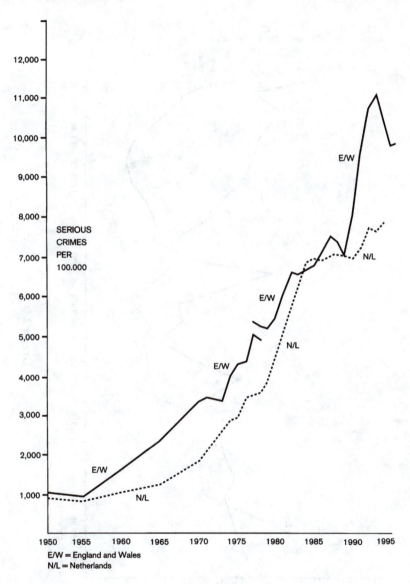

Graph 1

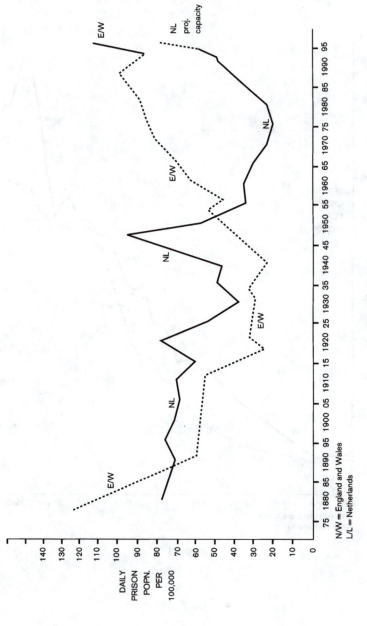

Graph 2

N/W = England and Wales
L/L = Netherlands

over time stepped up their resistance to both prosecution and to custodial sentencing. By contrast, in England and Wales the pattern was of little net change over the same period. This finding confirmed the view that judicial sentencing policy and practice are central to any explanation of trends in imprisonment.

How can this largely silent revolution, which mainly took place between 1945 and 1975, be explained? It stands in sharp contrast with experience not only in Britain but also in most comparable countries. Even Japan, which also progressively reduced its prison population after the war, did so in the context of a *falling* crime rate. Five reasons can plausibly be advanced.

First, the war and its aftermath gave penal reformers an exceptional experience and opportunity to effect long-germinated change. "After the war, prison experts were immediately struck with an almost revolutionary urge to reform. This had much to do with 'their own suffering in prison' of many members of the underground" (Franke, 1995: 245–6). Widespread pressures for reform led to the setting up of the Fick Committee, which in 1947 recommended sweeping changes to reorganize the prisons along associational lines, replacing solitary confinement with a mixture of cellular and communal regimes. The 1951 Prison Act substituted resocialization for retribution as the governing principle for prison life. The stage was set for dramatic changes to the character of penal confinement, and Franke emphasizes the extent to which the prisoners themselves actively engaged in moves towards self-emancipation within walls. What remains unclear is why similar experiences of imprisonment in other occupied countries did not generate pressures for comparable reforms.

A second development, even more peculiar to The Netherlands, was the pivotal role played in penal reform by a diverse group of criminal lawyers, criminologists and psychiatrists known as the "Utrecht School." In the 1950s in particular, "the Utrecht School set the standards for the penal climate in the decades to follow" (De Haan, 1990: 69). The group's influence helps explain why the impetus to reform regimes was both so sustained and so reductionist (Rutherford, 1986). What bound the group together both intellectually and morally was their deep aversion to imprisonment, particularly long-term imprisonment, and their profound belief that the offender must be treated as a thinking and feeling fellow human being, capable of responding to insights offered in the course of a dialogue (a concept freighted with complex philosophical meanings) with therapeutic agents. The principle of resocialization thus became animated with more than benevolent purpose. The single most influential book of the group was Rijksen's 1958 study of the damaging effects of long-term imprisonment as documented by the prisoners themselves. This book (Rijksen, 1958) influenced a critical mass of the judiciary, reinforcing what De Haan, following Langemeijer, termed their "bad conscience" (op.cit.: 68). Their acceptance of the need for *some* punishment, their lack of a wider radical aim, and their influence in all fields and at all levels of the criminal justice system gave the anti-penal impact of their work immense and lasting appeal, which persisted even when, after the mid-1960s, the momentum of resocialization started to wane. Their high point of influence was probably reached in the mid-1950s, when one-third of those institutionalized for criminal offenses were placed in special treatment centers rather than prisons; and when the Heads of the Prison, mental institutions and probation systems joined other experts at the Psychiatric Observation Clinic in Utrecht to discuss cases, sometimes with the prisoners concerned (Downes, 1988: 90–95). Though there was marked continuity between the "old" and the "new" Utrecht Schools, which took over the mantle of progressive reform in the 1970s, in the emphases on humane standards and minimal use of custody, the latter placed prisoners' rights and due process at the center of their concerns (see, for example, De Haan, op.cit.; Kelk, 1983; 1995; Peters, 1986). At the height of "progressivism," the views of such leading abolitionists as Louk Hulsman and Herman Bianchi, who favored alternative forms of mediation to the criminal justice system, were taken seriously; and the radically reformist Coornhert Liga, founded in 1971, was treated with respect.

   Third, a characteristically flexible strategy for protecting the prison system from the overcrowding endemic in other societies was evolved by the Dutch judiciary over this period. Waiving prosecution, "self-reporting" for a prison place, the development of home leave and interruptions to sentence, parole and pardons all made for a more efficient matching of numbers to capacity. What Andrew Rutherford termed the "shields" of the Dutch prison system were even more numerous if other, non-judicial, factors are invoked. For example, until the 1980s, the Dutch media were notably restrained in their reporting of crime news compared with the sensationalism endemic in Britain. The "politics of law and order" were relatively muted until the mid-1980s. There was a marked deference to expertise and, if the experts favored decarceration, few authoritative figures challenged policy directions. By the mid-1960s, the reductionist trend had been crystallized in policy terms by the Senior Prosecutors, so much so that in the early 1970s, prison closures were actually effected, despite a rising crime rate. Though the climax of decarceration was reached in 1974, with a prison population as low as 2200, 22 per 100,000, it remained strikingly low, despite a soaring crime rate, until the mid-1980s, a sign of the lengths to which the flexibility of the "shields" could be pushed (Fionda, 1995).

Fourth, the political context was unusually favorable to such developments being allowed to take their course, even if not—as some have argued (Hulsman, 1978; Johnson and Heijder, 1983)—actively propelling them. In Lijphart's celebrated phrase, the Dutch had evolved a "politics of accommodation" which turned to good advantage religious denominationalism which elsewhere, notably Northern Ireland, has provoked bitter sectarian conflict. The "pillars" of Dutch society, based on the Protestant and Catholic churches, and their secular counterparts, were topped by elites which negotiated political compromises reflecting their constituencies' own interests while yielding ground to other groups. This bargaining process was alleged to have involved trading off lenient penal policies from Left-liberal groups as part of coalition settlements in the 1950s and '60s. At the very least, this pillarization of Dutch society guaranteed a stable social order within which such policies could be fostered. The fifth pre-condition for such policies, a crime rate which rose until the 1970s less sharply than in England, was a result of such stability, further enhanced by extensive and comprehensive welfare rights, growing prosperity and full employment. Under such conditions, rapid social and economic change, mass tourism, and large-scale immigration were, on the whole, successfully absorbed. Signs of strain were, however, evident in the mid-1960s. Largely owing to generational conflict and squatting movements, enough patriarchal rules of Dutch tolerance were breached for Lijphart to augur the demise of the politics of accommodation (1975).

THE NEW MANAGERIALISM 1985–1995

Such was the situation until the mid-1970s. Twenty years on, dramatic changes have occurred on several fronts. The distinctively pillarized structure of Dutch society—which provided the basis for the educational system, labor unions, probation and social work and the mass media (where it still exists for TV, but is widely seen as on the way out even there)—is waning fast. Although the process may be traced back to the 1960s' revolts of the young against authority in the squatting and student movements, it only gathered pace in the 1970s and made its institutional impact in the 1980s. It is being replaced by a commercialized managerialism that is becoming somewhat standardized across industrial societies.

Insofar as pillarization provided the pre-conditions for the "politics of accommodation," which in turn formed the main basis for Dutch tolerance in social, political and cultural matters, these processes greatly strengthen the prospects for convergence with other EU countries in penal as well as other public policy respects. Hence, "de-pillarization" helps account both for the rise in crime (due to weakening informal social controls) and for the hardening of responses to it. Welfare has been pruned back, though it remains far more generous than in the UK. Most significantly, however, social integration is widely perceived as under threat, for the first time in the post-war period. In particular, second-generation Turks, Moroccan, Surinamese and Antillean minority groups are disproportionately excluded from employment and effective citizenship, on the one hand; and—arguably as a result—are disproportionately involved in street crime. The cast of Dutch tolerance, which is to accommodate levels and forms of deviance that other societies seek (usually in vain) to suppress, as long as the groups concerned accept "the rules of the game," is thus under siege. One very senior judge interviewed said he had "given up on" hopes that the younger generation of Moroccans could ever be integrated into Dutch society, whatever welfare measures were undertaken. So bleak a view from so pivotal a figure in the Dutch establishment is symptomatic of a new disillusionment about the scope for ameliorative policies to curtail social conflicts stemming from what he termed "the huge and growing gulf between rich and poor. The Netherlands has tried very hard with social policies but it doesn't help the 'underclass' group."

Such disillusion is widespread and feeds off the insecurities created by rapid social and economic changes that find a ready symbol in the fear of and resentment towards rising crime. The crime problem has, however, shown signs of being curbed by those very measures about which such disillusion is expressed. The steepest rise in the crime rate occurred between the late 1970s and 1984, after which it stabilized to a negligible rate of increase, ending up somewhat lower than that in England, for example, by the mid-1990s. Social crime prevention policies launched by the *Society and Crime* initiative of 1985 may have played some role in this slowdown in the rate of increase. However, the crime rate did not fall and, after 1985, a relatively steep increase still took place in some more serious offenses. "Up to 1985, the rise in crime was quantitative; after 1985, it was qualitative," as Bert Berghuis (Head of the Statistics Branch of the Ministry of Justice) put it in interview. In other words, the great upsurge in crime until 1985 was mainly in nuisance-value crime, burglary, theft and vandalism in particular. After 1985, the increase was more keenly experienced in drug-trafficking, armed robbery and complex frauds. How far the experience of the last ten years bears out the widespread view among the police and the media that organized crime has targeted The Netherlands as a base for operations would only become clear when a Commission of Inquiry, which includes four criminologists, reported on the subject in 1996. In essence, they argued that The Netherlands was a conduit, not a base, for organized crime (see below). But the perception fueled what critics of the hardening of penal policy (van Swaaningen, 1995; De Haan, n.d.) see as the ingredients for a "moral panic," "on the brink" of inducing unwarrantedly punitive measures.

Crime Trends

As we see in Table 1, the trends in crime as officially recorded by the police broadly confirm Berghuis's view. The total crime increase 1980–92 occurred mainly in the pre-1985 period. However, the rate of increase in the more serious crimes, except rape, occurred disproportionately after 1985, particularly in the case of robbery and hard drug-trafficking; and spectacularly in the case of firearms and economic offenses (which are mostly environmental, involving pollution). This pattern is held by Berghuis to account for the bulk (some 80%) of the rise in the prison population since 1985. The other 20% is to be accounted for by selective increases in sentencing but *not* by any significant increase in punitiveness (Berghuis, 1994). On the other hand, some academic criminologists (De Haan; Kelk; van Swaaningen) point to a hardening of crime categorization. Street bagsnatching, for example, was found in a case-by-case study, which compared samples from 1977 and 1989, to be defined in every case as robbery now for offenses which, two decades ago, would in

TABLE 1   Crime Trends 1980–92: % Changes (Official
Police Reports)

	1980–85	1985–90	1990–92	1980–92
Total crimes	+51	+0.5	+10	+69
Robbery	+84	+52	+30	+265
Rape	+52	+9	+2	+69
Burglary	+101	+13	+21	+175
Offenses against life	+16	+13	+31	+76
Opium Act (hard drugs)		+2	+64*	+68
Firearms Act		−17	+81*	+50
Economic Offenses	−34	+1204	+67	+1338

Source: Police-Numbers 1980–1992, Ministry of Justice, The Hague.
(*=1985–92 prosecution cases).

some instances have eventuated in a theft charge (Freeling, 1993).
Moreover, while in 1977 such cases were not always prosecuted for
policy reasons under the expediency rule, by 1989 this was no
longer the case. Also, sentences in 1977 were more lenient and often
conditional, whereas in 1989 they were harsher and usually unconditional. Though the critics do not seek to deny the reality of *some*
upward trend in robbery, armed robbery in particular, they see the
"up-tariffing" of less serious street crimes as feeding the "fear of
crime" which helps to justify tougher penalties. Moreover, De Haan
(1994) argues that the pool of predatory street offenders in one of
the two worst-hit areas in Amsterdam, the Bijlmer project, is much
smaller than the authorities claim; that the heaviest offenders are
mostly motivated by "survival" due to homelessness and drug
addiction; and that illegal immigration is "insignificant" compared
with these variables. A targeted social program would be a far more
appropriate response than penal measures as a result.

The case for a "moral panic" (Cohen, 1972),[1] having unduly influenced the course of penal policy in The Netherlands, takes other
forms. From the petty to the most serious types and levels of offending, the Dutch evidently feel under siege as never before. The
International Crime Survey of 1989, based on victim responses (Van
Dijk, Mayhew and Killias, 1990), in which The Netherlands emerged
as having the highest crime rate of the 14 countries surveyed,

including the USA, was widely reported as disturbing and jolting news. The fact that bicycle theft contributed heavily to that outcome hardly reassured "public opinion." A second, wider survey in 1992 found The Netherlands less crime-prone relative to several other societies, England included. But the damage to national self-confidence was done, and was now supplemented by additional fears that organized crime in the shape of the "Octopus"—a joint Latin American/Mafia cartel—had targeted Holland as its Western European base for drug-trafficking and money-laundering. These fears have fed through the political process to heighten concerns that tough action is needed to prevent The Netherlands being a "soft island" on the European map. The scope, nature and mediation of these fears illustrate the extent to which two shields crucial for the relatively sparing use of imprisonment by the Dutch judiciary have been dented: restrained media reportage and a muted "politics of law and order" are now things of the past.

Examples of these developments include the hardening of official rhetoric; "reality TV," enabling viewers to be visually present at police raids, arrests and scenes of violent crime; and a stream of surveys showing crime to be second only to unemployment as a social problem. While De Haan (1991) asserts that a "moral panic" did *not* result from such ingredients (and it is difficult, given the opacity of the concept, to be conclusive either way on this point), the moral climate was clearly tilted in a more punitive direction by such trends. "No left-wing politician can afford to be seen to be soft on law and order," said one criminologist. In these respects, the Dutch have now joined the club of societies whose governments are under perpetual and mounting pressure to "do something" about "law and order," even if being seen to be doing something is more important than doing anything effective.

That there is substance in reality to the view that crime over the past decade has increased qualitatively rather than quantitatively can hardly be denied, even if the worst fears of public, police and politicians may be unfounded. The recent report of the Parliamentary Inquiry by the Van Traa Commission included an analysis of organized crime in The Netherlands by four criminologists.[2] They concluded in essence that the country was an entrepot center for organized crime, drug-trafficking in particular, much as it is for conventional goods and business. There was thus no massive presence of organized crime in the sense of a powerful network threatening civil society, or a "mafia" constituting an alternative state.

Dutch criminals act as transporters and middlemen with foreign criminals there to do business, not become part of society. There was little infiltration of the "upper world," though some ethnic involvement occurs disproportionately. However, this still means marked changes in the political economy of crime. Some 6000 people are reportedly employed full-time in drugs networks (*Guardian*, Feb. 2, 1996). Gangsters throw their weight around in night-clubs, bringing a whiff of Chicago to old Amsterdam. The Dutch don't like it, and expect the authorities to act.

In the courts, the results of their labors, despite major blunders, are beginning to come through. In early 1995, major cases of a scale and complexity unknown several years ago preoccupied the Amsterdam Court of Appeal, particularly involving drugs but also money-laundering by respected banks and pensions groups; the large-scale dumping of garbage contrary to anti-pollution laws; the defrauding of the Revenue by a restaurant chain employing informal economy personnel; vice organizations; and arms and explosives trading. The sums involved run into hundreds of millions; the sentencing is correspondingly severe. As a result, "it is not true that judges punish more severely than five years ago: they have heavier cases to deal with" (Mr. J. Willems, Amsterdam Court of Appeal). For example, one huge case involved a cocaine cartel for which 16 offenders received the maximum sentence of 16 years. Overall, prison sentences of 3 years or more have risen from 287 in 1985 to 988 in 1994.

Trends in Criminal Justice Policy

Trends in criminal justice policy have reflected this hardening. Four sets of policy statements symbolized and reinforced the growing acceptance of a stiffening response to crime. First, in 1984, a working group recommended the expansion of penal capacity from some 3000 to 7000 by 1990, to match the projected rise in the custodial sentencing of drug-traffickers in particular. The case for the increase was reinforced by the *Society and Crime* report of 1985, which reviewed policy strategies for both petty and more serious crime trends (the former had been considered earlier by the Roethof Committee in 1984). Critics of *Society and Crime* overlooked one of its principal achievements: the setting of the explanation for rising crime in the context of "de-pillarization," thereby meeting one of the key arguments for more punitive penalties: that rising crime had somehow been caused by lenient penal policies. The weakening of informal community controls consequent on de-pillarization was seen as the key reason for rising trends in crime and provided its authors with a key policy solution: more coordinated and better-resourced community crime prevention. Indeed, a new Department of Crime Prevention was set up under the Directorship of Jan van Dijk, the principal author of the Report. Overall, however, bifurcation—a problem rather than a solution to the coiner of the concept, Tony Bottoms (1977)—was adopted as the main strategy. Community penalties and crime prevention were to be the antidote to petty crime, a stiffening of custodial penalties to drug-trafficking, violent and the more serious property offenses. Some increase in penal capacity was predictably required to meet the increasing resort to custody which, given the trends and the endorsement of the one-to-a-cell principle, meant careful forward planning to match capacity to numbers.

In any event, the 1985 Report proved a watershed rather than a holding operation, though its policies for petty crime prevention and avoiding prison overcrowding succeeded remarkably well. However, its legitimation of an all-round tightening-up, particularly in its curbs on the unconditional waiving of prosecution, fueled the strong secular tendency to replace a humane paternalism with managerial instrumentalism. A significant hardening was evident in the 1990 report *Law in Motion*, which "dictated a change in the whole philosophy of criminal policy. The focus has shifted away from the perpetrator of an offense and towards the victim and the law-abiding citizen, the protection of whose safety and rights is now targeted. The philosophy is to ensure that *something* is seen to be done in most reported cases of crime, although what actually happens seems to be less important" (Fionda, 1995: 120). Kelk goes further: The focus is now the case and not the person. As with bifurcation, "net-widening" (Cohen, 1979) is embraced as a solution rather than a problem. The use of the prosecutorial *transactie* is extended to moderately serious offenses with quite serious powers to fine. The restoration of credibility to the system of criminal justice, a state of affairs which the Report asserts rather than demonstrates as in crisis, is given top priority by measurable indices of effective intervention.

Law in Motion represented a signal break with the past. Unlike the 1985 *Society and Crime* report, it openly castigated "modern trends in criminology," for allegedly encouraging euphemisms about criminality and abolitionist views on the criminal law (15). Another shield against custodial sentencing was not so much dented as scrapped in the process: the catholicism of policy-making which took the views of radical and critical criminologists seriously. In short, its tone reflected the influence of Dato Steenhuis, the leading advocate of the "new managerialist" school (Rutherford, 1996, Ch. 3), rather than Jan van Dijk, who sought a compromise between the old and the new approaches. Also very influential was the Minister of Justice, Hirsch Ballin, who prioritized the war against "organized crime" and was driven ideologically by the need to re-moralize Dutch society. The "de-pillarization" thesis was ironically, in this regard, self-defeating, for while on the one hand it exoner-ated penal leniency from responsibility for rising crime, on the other hand it left the penal armory as the only weapon against it. If the premise of a social void opening up is accepted, a "heart of darkness" in Dutch society which threatens to envelop the most cherished values and beliefs, then the only logical response to this threat is a more disciplined, punitive society. In The Netherlands, as elsewhere in the affluent capitalist world, the other explanation for anomie—that it flourishes in response to the force-feeding of mate-rialist and hedonist aspirations—is the theory that dare not be allowed to hold sway.

The fourth report of symbolic as well as practical consequence is *Effective Detention* (1994). Its focus is on the character of prison regimes, which are defined as too ineffective in targeting resources on different types of prisoners. The main priority of this report is to increase the hours and yield of prison labor, an objective to be achieved by new work programs for all but 20% of prisoners, who have earned the right to special facilities. Reactions to this scheme, which is the outcome of perceived criticisms that the prisons, and not just the legal responses to crime, lack credibility, have been very criti-cal, both within the Prison Service and by penal reformers. The ethos of Dutch prisons is seen as liable to be damaged by the move from universal to selective provision. Moreover, the logistics of the new work programs are seen as tilting the system away from work that is geared to prisoners' needs to work that is primarily profit-making. More "workmasters" will be needed, a shift which, from fixed bud-gets, will reduce the resources available for security (ironically at a time when public concern centers on that very issue) as well as for social, educational and recreational facilities. What *Effective Detention* signals is that prisons must be seen to be toughening up, along with the rest of the criminal justice system, as part of the process of public reassurance that all possible measures are being taken in the control of crime.

Taken together, these measures should not be read as a wholesale repudiation of the humane character of Dutch penal policy as it has evolved since 1945. But they do add up to a progressive tightening-up which will severely test the system's capacity to preserve that objective in the context of a far more volatile politics of law and order.

Sentencing Trends

The trends in sentencing have not in general involved any significant abandonment of the relatively "low punitiveness" (Kommer, 1992) of Dutch judicial sentencing. Yet prison capacity is now planned to rise to 13,000 by the end of 1996—in effect, the second stage of the expansionist trend which brought capacity up to 7,000 by 1990: an increase from 44 to 78 prisoners per 100,000 population. The question that arises is why this second stage was felt to be required, on such a scale, when the main rise in crime, even much serious crime, had occurred *before* 1990. Critics such as Hans Tulkens and Rene van Swaaningen see the Ministry of Justice as pursuing a self-fulfilling prophecy, by extrapolating numbers from existing trends on assumptions which invite the judiciary to fill the places even if the crime problem abates—a familiar story in other countries, Britain included, but one which the Dutch had, in the past, seemed determined to avoid. There is a sense of repeating mistakes by not learning from failures elsewhere, no longer leading the way but adopting short-term solutions that don't solve problems.

While data on sentencing broadly bear out the view that it is the cumulative rise in the volume of the more serious offenses, rather than any marked increase in punitiveness, which accounts for the continuing rise in prison numbers since the late 1980s, some trends do not fit that pattern consistently, as we see in Table 2.

As these figures show, the contribution made by increases in custodial sentencing, in terms of both sentencing to imprisonment and mean sentence length, varies markedly by offense type. The results, however, do not always accord with the view that only the more serious offenses have attracted more punitive custodial sentences. The proportionate contribution to the increase in total months of imprisonment made by increased *length* of sentence (as distinct

TABLE 2 Sentencing for Serious Offenses in The Netherlands,
1983 and 1993

Offense	Year (excl. tech. waivers)	Total Cases	% Prison Sentence Duration (months)	Mean Waivers	% Policy Months	Total Custody
Hard Drugs	1983	4,059	32	13	55	16,885
	1993	7,719	29	12	35	26,862
Offs v Life	1983	568	44	27	41	6,750
	1993	1,029	54	34	9	18,904
Burglary	1983	14,586	21	3	49	9,189
	1993	12,654	24	6	16	18,221
Rape	1983	351	54	10	21	1,895
	1993	357	56	20	12	3,998
Robbery	1983	1,494	48	10	27	7,171
	1993	3,086	55	15	6	25,460

Sources: 1983: Downes, *Contrasts in Tolerance*: 42; 1993: Ministry of Justice, The
Hague: *Prosecution and Trial of Indictable Offenses in the Kingdom of The Netherlands*
(Facts and Figures of 1992 and 1993) Tables 6, 9, 10, 16, and 17. Figures have been
recalculated to yield percentages net of technical waivers.

from by any increase in the numbers for each offense, or the proportion sentenced to imprisonment) is: nil for hard drugs; 17% for
offenses against life, i.e. serious violence, including murder, etc.;
29% for robbery; 80% for burglary; and 96% for rape.

The trends for drug-trafficking, offenses against life and robbery
have led to roughly twice as many cases coming before the courts
in 1993 compared with 1983. Since sentences to custody were much
the same in both years for drug-trafficking, the entire increase in
total custody time stemmed from the increased number of cases.
For offenses against life, numbers doubled, the proportion sentenced to imprisonment rose by 23% (from 44 to 54%) and sentence
lengths rose by 25% (from 27 to 34 months). Some two-thirds of the
threefold rise in total time served stemmed from the increase in
numbers, with one-sixth due both to increases in the proportion
imprisoned and extra sentence length. In the case of robbery, numbers also contributed two-thirds to the increase in total custody
time, a near-quadrupling, but the 50% rise in mean sentence length

underlay almost one-third of the increase. Robbery thus soared to account for virtually the same amount of total custody time as drug-trafficking in 1993; in 1983, it had accounted for less than half. In the case of rape, numbers were unchanged, and virtually the whole doubling of total time served in custody was due to the doubling of sentence lengths. The doubling of custodial time in the case of burglary, where numbers before the court actually fell, is almost entirely due to the doubling of sentence lengths.

The picture, therefore, is highly varied, with sentence length increases a very important factor in some cases, not all of them among the most serious (such as burglary), but hardly at all in others. Most surprisingly, drug-trafficking—allegedly a main factor in the rise in penal capacity—is a less serious factor than robbery, where the strictures of De Haan and others apply most forcefully. In sum, the quantitative/qualitative distinction does not explain the trend at all consistently: There is some scope for the "moral panic" variable to be reinstated as accounting for at least part of the increase, one that might have been avoided but for the political context. On the other hand, the surprisingly high proportion of drug-trafficking cases that still attracted a policy waiver in 1993 (far higher in such cases than for other offenses) indicates a determination on the part of the judicial authorities to deal with any case that is not deemed serious as sparingly as possible. The fall in the number of burglary cases coming before the court may reflect a softening of definitions, on the one hand, so that only more serious cases now reach that stage compared with 1983; and the proliferation of diversionary schemes, such as the HALT projects for juveniles (Kruissink, 1990 and Gelsthorpe et al., 1995); and the Dordrecht project for persistent offenders (Bruinink and Langendijk, 1994). Only a comparative case study could test the reality of the basis in consistency for the doubling of sentences in burglary cases since 1983.

Other points worth noting are, firstly, that the stepping-up of conditional waivers does not seem to have led to any marked increase in the prison population. In 1986 and 1994, numbers imprisoned for breaches of non-custodial sentences were 3,209 and 4,179, with peaks of 6,078 and 6,624 in 1992 and 1993. As such prison terms were presumably very short, they cannot account for the marked increase in capacity planned for 1996. That increase flowed far more directly from a second variable, the numbers released from pre-trial detention due to cell shortages. In 1994, these numbered 5,316. Much adverse publicity had attached to the release of such detainees in the early 1990s, prompting prosecutors to press for the sharp upturn in capacity plans. However, over two-thirds of those released were Category B detainees, held for offenses attracting a maximum sentence of three to nine years, i.e. they would predictably include a large number of suspects for burglary and theft. Growing antipathy towards the bothersome and disquieting character of persistent, petty property crime is therefore a factor in the increased prison population, along with the rise of more serious offending.

Further Trends in Criminal Justice Policy

Trends in criminal justice policy have influenced the system as well as its outcomes. Since the mid-1980s, successive changes have been effected on the prosecutorial system and the police in particular. The need to overhaul the machinery of justice had begun to be argued in the early 1980s by those, such as Dato Steenhuis, who feared that its credibility was being undermined by constant improvisations to ease "bottlenecks" in the system. Greater powers and coordination were demanded from the *Openbaar Ministerie* (OM, the Dutch prosecution service) to enhance overall effectiveness, but the solutions led to counter-criticisms that "Due Process" was being eroded and the prosecutors becoming too powerful vis-à-vis the judges (Peters, 1988; Kelk, 1995; t'Hart, 1988). The key changes in the 1985 Report enhanced prosecutors' powers to impose *transactie* (a form of fine) as a condition for waiving prosecution, and to reduce the proportion of unconditional waivers by 50%. In cases of petty crime, this involved the payment of such penalties as small fines and could be defended as the extension of an existing principle. However, the 1990 Report and the Prosecution Policy Plan envisaged a much more extensive near-elimination of the unconditional waiver (down to 5% of cases) and the use of *transactie* in more serious cases. The dangers of "net-widening," already present in the 1985 Report, loomed far larger in that of 1990. In short, prosecutorial powers to improvise discretionary measures for reductionist ends were fast becoming bureaucratized to the point where due process seemed directly threatened, "net-widening" automatic, and—as unwanted side-effects—the prison population enlarged by those breaching the requirements of the diversionary conditions. The Dutch seem to have fallen into the same trap as the English in the 1970s and early 1980s, but with their eyes open or, at least, only semi-closed. As Fionda comments: "It seems appropriate to talk of recent Dutch prosecution policy in terms of a harsher philosophy; indeed, persons interviewed often used the words 'repression' and 'severity' to describe that new philosophy. This spirit of repression and severity..., which is clearly the foundation of the two recent policy plans, has also been present in the day-to-day practice of prosecutors... [Their] approach seems to have changed, and cases which would have been considered too trivial to warrant formal intervention are now being considered as serious" (op.cit.: 113).

Moreover, the prosecution service has been the site for a frenzy of organizational activity (leading to jokes about the "Samsonite circuit," a reference to expensive management consultants, brought in to report on practically every aspect of the system), so much so that in 1993 an Inquiry was commissioned into their organization and the exercise of their powers. The Donner Report (1994) was essentially about changing an old-fashioned apparatus, based on professional autonomy, into a more efficient, managerially-oriented organization. It concluded that the prosecutors were over-stepping their constitutional role, as was the Minister of Justice. Faced by the twin pressures of rising case-loads and new offenses (e.g., pollution), prosecutors mounted police inquiries which embarrassingly backfired: Evidence was gathered by inadmissible methods or lost; errors were made in documents which led to cases being dropped; and attempted cover-ups produced further entanglements. Though the recommendations of the Donner Report were widely criticized and largely rejected—they included the winding-up of the role of the five Senior Prosecutors in formulating policy—its analysis of the problems facing a very small and overworked group of prosecutors was sufficiently penetrating to fuel concern about the adequacy of the system to cope with rapid changes in organized crime in particular. One solution, the retention of the role of the five Senior Prosecutors, but the creation of a President to direct their activities, may not suffice to effect the reassertion of their somewhat shaken authority. At early 1996, the new Minister of Justice, herself a former Senior Prosecutor, is seen as both sympathetic to preserving their independence and keen to resist changes to their role and funding which might undermine it.

The problems of the OM are compounded by the pressures for their reorganization coinciding with an immense upheaval in the administrative framework of policing. Some 140 police areas have been amalgamated into 25, with a regional rather than a local authority base, a major and necessary achievement but one which has produced a host of transitional problems. Foremost among these is the so-called "democratic gap": The new force areas do not correspond with existing structures of accountability. The burgomasters of the smaller local authorities in a region have now lost their role in formulating policing policy. That role is now played by the head of the region's largest local authority, but they can speak only by proxy for the rest. The changes have also meant the loss of much specialized knowledge as local teams have been broken up and reassembled. One of the five inter-regional teams (the Utrecht/ North Holland IRT, based in Amsterdam), created to combat organized crime, was disbanded after several major cases were dropped on alleged grounds of illegally procured evidence—events which entailed such acrimonious exchanges as the threat by the Chief of Police to "pull the chain" on the Senior Prosecutor (whose more sinister interpretation was that he would be "run through the computer" until something was found on him). A flurry of official inquiries ensued. The Wierenga Commission (1994) focused on the hostility between the OM and the police in Amsterdam. The first Van Traa Commission (1994) reported on the operation and adequacy of police methods to deal with organized crime. The IRT affair had led to the resignations of the Ministers of Justice and Home Affairs. Given so critical a state of affairs, and anxious both to defuse criticism of the police and to reassert its powers, Parliament took the unusual step of setting up a Select Committee, led by Van Traa (1996), to report on police methods and organized crime by means of a Parliamentary Inquiry. Such an inquiry had exceptionally high visibility, involving witnesses under oath, public hearings and interviews with prominent police and judicial figures, including the Ministers of Justice and Home Affairs. The report, published on February 1, 1996, sought to allay the worst fears about organized crime as having penetrated Dutch civil society and politics, but was highly critical of major operational blunders in the strategy for its control. Its recommendations for new rules and structures to improve the targeting of drug-trafficking and manufacturing networks will be of signal importance for the future development of policing. The newly created national force for the combating of organized crime, a momentous development in a country whose suspicions of centralized policing have a long history borne of enemy occupations dating back to the war against Spain in the 17th century, will severely test the dual control over policing long exercised by the Ministries of Justice and Home Affairs.

THE IMPACT ON IMPRISONMENT

Dutch penal capacity is planned to grow to 13,000 cells by the end of 1996 (13,600 if places for compulsory admissions to an institution for mentally disturbed offenders are included—see Graph 2). This growth represents a trebling of capacity since the mid-1980s and a quintupling from the lowest point reached in 1974. The addition of 10,000 prison places since the late 1970s is much the same as the increase in England and Wales over the same period, a country with 3½ times the population of The Netherlands. The ratio of prisoners to total population in the two countries will thus narrow from 1:4 in the mid-1970s to 3:4 in 1996, 76 per 100,000 in The Netherlands compared with 100 per 100,000 in England and Wales. The Dutch are now on track to reach the European average custody ratio after three decades of standard bearing for its minimum use. A senior planner in the Ministry of Justice remarked that "without financial constraints, we would have built even more prisons." "We cannot afford to have lower prison capacity than other European countries around us, because we are very similar to them and there is now the lack of borders." The objective of convergence with other European countries is an "orientation point," partly rhetoric, but needed to get more resources out of central government. The "natural place to stop yet more increases" is at the point of near-convergence. However, the increases planned thus far were necessary because, without them, "we would have major problems now" (e.g., of over-crowding), and the sending away of very serious offenders, for lack of cell space, is politically a very sensitive issue (see below).

It is as well to stress the strong continuities in Dutch penal policy despite this relatively immense growth in the current and projected prison population. With significant exceptions, conditions in Dutch prisons remain relatively good. The very growth in capacity reflects the determination of prison staff and governors—as well as a critical mass of opinion in the Ministry of Justice—to maintain the one-to-a-cell policy widely seen as the pre-condition for humane and decent standards. Max Kommer, an experienced Ministry researcher, when pressed on whether the strength of official commitment to that policy remained, replied that, "Two-to-a-cell is *never* raised as a solution" in a Working Group on prison capacity on which he served. Despite strong political pressures to weaken the policy for budgetary reasons, and a change in the small number of exceptions to the rule which are permissible, the strong opposition of prison governors, staff and prisoners to any fundamental change should hold the line for the foreseeable future. Governors in particular now have increased autonomy to do so. Even so, the principle is constantly under siege, given the huge costs of prison building and operations.

In general, staff–prisoner relations, relations *among* prisoners, conditions, rights and the "quality of life" in Dutch prisons do not as yet seem to have suffered significant impairment as a result of expansion. The system of complaints, widely regarded as the best in Europe (see, for example, Vagg, 1995), is seen by Herman Franke as strengthened by the Prisons Bill currently before Parliament. However, there are clear signs that the system is on the brink of changes that will test its resilience to the hilt. The "tightening-up" of the criminal justice system in general is specifically formulated for prisons in the *Effective Detention* program. First, the rise in the proportion of prisoners who are foreigners, and who therefore lack the capacity to benefit to the full from the array of devices to enable prisoners to maintain links with the community by home leave, visits, etc., means that a critical mass of prisoners is more likely to withhold compliance. One remand prison governor expressed such concerns as follows: "Nowadays it's all about drugs, violence, foreigners and disturbed inmates. South American couriers aren't really a problem, they remain polite. But some of the people from Eastern Europe and from Marokko are really tough characters" (quoted in van der Vijver, van Dijk and Punch, 1995). The proportion of non-Dutch prisoners has risen steeply from 12% in 1981 to 26% in 1992 (*The Prison System*, 1993: 12). By contrast, in England and Wales, in 1992 some 6% of male and 20% of female prisoners were foreign nationals (Richards et al., 1995: 158–59). Secondly, a comparatively high, though diminishing, proportion of prisoners are convicted of Opium-act violations—20% in 1989 falling to 16% in 1994; by contrast, just under 10% of prisoners under sentence in England and Wales were convicted of drugs offenses in 1993 (NACRO, 1994: 23). Far higher proportions are drug-dependent, a state of affairs which has led to extensive urine-testing and allied control techniques. Thirdly, a high and growing proportion especially of the younger prisoners are from ethnic minorities, who are allegedly more disaffected both from society and the prison system than is traditionally the case for Dutch prisoners. Given these pressures, it is noteworthy that the system has broadly held up so well.

On at least two fronts, however, problems are distinctly heightened. First, *Effective Detention* in effect imports bifurcation into the prison system. A harsher climate is explicitly wrought to appease public opinion. The policy plan explicitly condemns the leniency of the past and invokes the need for more austere regimes, based on more work and fewer facilities in general, all within fixed budgets plus 3 percent savings in 1995–6. The 1994 White Paper proposes one standard regime—26 hours' work weekly, 6 hours of recreation, etc.—from which prisoners showing proper "motivation" can proceed to more specialized programs. But the proportion envisaged as so motivated is set at 20 percent. In this sense, critics, such as Constantijn Kelk, see the program as "a real step backwards." Their fears include the apprehension that a two-tier prison system will develop, setting the "motivated" against the rest, for whom opportunities will be *reduced*; that tests of "motivation" will be little more than superficial reports from the guards; that logistically, the programs will simply not be viable, both as regards selling the products and in relation to competing for limited markets with other socially handicapped groups; that the regimes overall will be of a lower standard, and will remove incentives for staff to provide enhanced regimes; and that even the greater legal protection upholding the right to complain will be adversely affected, since there will be far fewer grounds for complaint over reduced regime facilities. Prison governors were mixed in their reactions to the plan. Some saw it as workable: In many ways, the new plan is already practiced. But the central clash is between the "wishful thinking" involved in imposing the new standard regime on all prisons and on all prisoners (many of whom are just not capable of producing the higher quality work required, so that an austere work ethic will have to be imposed on those who *can* in order for the prison budget to break even) and the currently humane principles of the system.

What this means in practice is, for example, the confinement to cells of all those not willing to work, in the remand houses, for 26 hours more a week; fewer opportunities to engage in education, sport and recreation; and the substitution of work training personnel ("workmasters") for other staff, including guards, out of fixed budgets: "The new work programs will play havoc with guards' shifts," said one governor, by fragmenting their duties. Ironically, this could strain security just when public alarm about it has led to these changes. Four pilot schemes were devised as a compromise to assuage governors' unease about the plan, though some cynicism was expressed about this as two of the four pilot sites have very good work facilities already. Their main defense is that governors are allowed some autonomy in how to implement the proposals. However, autonomy in implementing a plan which makes such harsh choices inevitable is a mixed blessing. As one governor put it: "The real limit that must be preserved is time out of the cell, because the real strength of our system is staff–prisoner relations." Though small units have been preserved as the typical size in the expanded system, it is difficult to see how that limit can be upheld. In this context, as Boin (1995: 21, 27) comments, it is all too easy to perceive that "the introduction of a standardized regime, instead of a way to reduce inmate idleness, then becomes a concerted effort to re-establish control over organizational process ... (However,) the position of the warden is codified and expanded in the new Prison Act ... If the Justice Department seeks to alter prison regimes, officials are well informed [i.e. advised] to aim for co-operation instead of confrontation."

The second front on which conditions have clearly deteriorated is the development of new, heavy-end, top security units for prisoners who present serious escape risks (comparable to the most high-risk Category A prisoners in England). Between 1991 and 1993, several escapes occurred which involved hostage-taking, a sequence of events which threw into question the rationale on which the system had been run for at least two decades: that humane relations and decent conditions, combined with an extensive and legally under-written system of rights and complaints, would guarantee the smooth and relatively harmonious operation of the prisons. One policy change has been to inaugurate a "closed door" response to any act of hostage-taking, to signal that escapes will not be tolerated by such means. All exits will be sealed off the moment a hostage-taking incident occurs. Also, partly to reduce the chances of such threats to staff security, partly to avoid upgrading security to extreme lengths in the mainstream system, and partly to assuage an inflamed political and public opinion, the Prison Department created a temporary maximum security unit at Vught which, apart from the notorious cage at Peterhead prison in Scotland, operates constraints as yet unprecedented in Dutch and English jails. For the 20 prisoners held in the Unit, and in particular for four who are defined as extreme risks, the "depth of imprisonment" in The Netherlands has been precipitously increased. One conclusion seems inescapable: Very long sentences, especially of foreign prisoners, are a recipe for the motivation to risk such escapes. The four top risks included an Irish prisoner sentenced to 16 years for armed robbery and a Colombian drug-trafficker with a lesser but still lengthy sentence.

The regime at Vught gives top priority to maximum security, both for staff and to prevent escapes, by cellular confinement broken only by very limited periods of recreation and outside activity. All cells have "letter boxes," through which prisoners must be handcuffed before coming out. They are accompanied by three guards to the recreation room, in which no more than two other prisoners can be present at the same time; or to the exercise yard, a bleak cage made of razor-sharp wire, in whose roof are set snares to forestall escape by helicopter; or to meet visitors, in a room which is wired for sound and monitored by one-way glass. For visits, handcuffs are removed, then replaced for body searches after the visit. Visitors, who have been driven to the Unit in a sealed van, are also body-searched—the Irish prisoner had refused family visits to spare his family the indignity involved, but this only served to heighten his isolation. Cells are stiflingly devoid of decent light or ventilation, though this is explained as a result of the temporary nature of the unit, which is due to be replaced by a purpose-built block.

The oppressive nature of the regime is magnified by the lack of any possibility of progression within it. Treating prisoners as "dangerous objects" (Sparks, Bottoms and Hay, 1996) removes any scope for their earning credit for good behavior. Superhuman control is needed on their part to avoid even the slightest movement that might signal aggressive intent. Manacled outside the cell and confined for all but an hour or two per day within it, their situation is in stark contrast to the humanity displayed elsewhere in the Dutch system. To some, it is the price to be paid for those relatively decent standards elsewhere to be maintained. But even in other systems which practice "concentration" strategies for the worst risks, less draconian measures are used.

On a visit to The Netherlands in 1993, the Committee for the Prevention of Torture (CPT) predictably found little to criticize, and much to commend, about regimes and conditions for the average prisoner. Nevertheless, there were several areas of concern: For example, for the first six hours after arrest, suspects were effectively denied knowledge of their full legal rights. The main anxieties of the CPT team focused on the regimes for certain exceptional categories of prisoner held under conditions of maximum security in Demersluis 4A (part of the main Amsterdam prison) and in three Special Detention Units (EBIs). The very small proportion of the prison population classified as "dangerous" requires exceptional provisions if they are not to be subject to "a greater risk of inhumane treatment than is the case with the average prisoner" (CPT, 1993: 33). Within the severe confines of the EBI's, every effort should be made to provide a "relatively relaxed regime," "a good internal atmosphere" and a "satisfactory program of activities" (34). The CPT concluded: "It is quite clear that the situations encountered in the De Schie EBI and Unit 4A in Demersluis do not meet (these) criteria" (34). It was in Unit 4A also that a serious case of physical violence by several staff against a prisoner (who had punched an officer) was encountered, involving injuries that were not medically logged.

In their Response (1993) to the CPT Report, the Dutch government tended to brush such criticisms aside. Only the barest description was given of the alleged incident of staff violence against a prisoner, and no inquiry was instituted, as the CPT had recommended. On the other hand, the authorities clearly took the other recommendations seriously, implying that the staff concerned had been moved elsewhere (Ministry of Justice Response: 32) and replaced by staff "more qualified to work in this environment." Though the CPT's call for an inquiry into the operation of Unit 4A was not taken up, measures were introduced to create "a regime which answers in the broadest sense to the CPT's requirements." The replacement of the EBI's by the new, single, temporary EBI at Vught was regarded as meeting the CPT's call for improvements in their operation. However, as mentioned above, the Temporary EBI (TEBI) is far from equipped to conform to the criteria against which the EBI's had been found wanting.

Security is so over-riding a priority in the TEBI Unit that little is possible by way of social measures of education, recreational activities and skills training to alleviate the rigors of the regime. While staff have been specially trained to cope with high-risk prisoners, and interacted humanely with them insofar as the regime allowed, it remained the case that a total lack of trust ruled. It is as if the

Unit was designed with Hannibal Lector in mind. From the heli-copter snares and the razor sharp wire of the exercise cages to the poor quality air which eventually percolates into the cells through a thin slat of heavily protected metal, every single aspect of the regime—whose worst feature is the absence of any hope of pro-gression—is geared to security, surveillance and control. The Gov-ernor agreed with many of the prisoners' complaints about the Unit but commented that "the political climate rules." Vught is the end-product of a system which, shaken by the spate of hostage-taking escapes in the space of a few years (none have occurred since 1993), is all too vulnerable to the force of "populist punitive-ness" (Bottoms, 1995).

CONCLUSIONS

It would appear that the Dutch judiciary has decisively abandoned the policy of a minimal resort to imprisonment which lasted for three decades from the mid-1950s to the mid-1980s. This shift is, however, in part illusory: Most of the upward trend in prison num-bers can be accounted for by the rising rate of serious crimes which would have attracted heavier penalties in the earlier period. However, the hardening of crime categorization, the tightening-up of the system at every point from arrest to custody and the escala-tion of popular demands that politicians do something (anything) to curb the growth of serious crime, have led to tougher sentences even in some cases (such as burglary and "disorganized" robbery) where a more sparing use of custody would have occurred in the past. New fears (the lack of borders, the problems of integrating minorities); new offenses (armed robbery, pollution, major frauds, drug-trafficking and manufacture); and new offenders (Moroccan youth, "criminal tourists" and organized crime with international affiliations) all combine to generate a highly volatile politics of law and order. The notion of volatility, however, at least holds open the possibility of a return to a more tolerant climate, in which the conti-nuities in Dutch penal policy—the concern for humane standards, in particular—will reassert themselves. On the evidence of present trends, however, such an eventuality seems remote. Any impetus towards re-strengthening the "shields" awaits new policy initia-tives concerning the fears and realities of national and transnational crimes affecting The Netherlands.

Acknowledgments

Above all, I would like to thank Hans Tulkens and Herman Franke, who enabled me to make far better use of limited time in The Netherlands than seemed feasible in advance; and Maurice Punch, who supplied a rich stream of constructive criticism of the results. As well as on their advice and expertise, I also drew heavily on those of Willem de Haan, Constantijn Kelk, Arjen Boin, Geert de Vries and Rene van Swaaningen. At the Ministry of Justice, Bert Berghuis, Jan van Dijk, Max Kommer and Jos Verhaegen were generous providers of both data on and insights about criminal justice trends as, at the Bonger Institute of Criminology, were Marta Komter, Dirk Korf and Arte Meertens. I am extremely grateful to members of the prosecution service and courts in Amsterdam for making time for enlightening interviews in packed schedules; and to the governors, staff and prisoners who did so at Norderhaven, de Grittenborg, Westlinge, Amsterdam and Vught. Along the way, I gained much from talks with Frank Kuitenbrouwer, Theo de Roos, Juri Pen and Nico Keijzer, and from helpful material and comments by Rod Morgan, Paul Rock, Vincenzo Ruggiero and Andrew Rutherford on an earlier draft. Finally, I must express fervent thanks to Daphne Ahrendt and Hartsje van de Noort for timely translations of key articles.

Notes

1. According to one eminent authority, Professor Erhard Blenkenberg of the Free University, Amsterdam, this atmosphere of panic is now (at mid-1996) "at boiling point."
2. The four academic criminologists who reported on the extent and character of organized crime are Professors C. Fijnaut (Erasmus University, Rotterdam); F. Bovenkerk (State University of Utrecht); H. van der Bunt (Free University of Amsterdam and Head of the Research and Documentation Center, Ministry of Justice); and C.J.N. Bruinsma (University of Twente).

References

Berghuis, A.C. (1994) "Punitiviteitsfeiten" [Punitive facts], in M. Moerings (ed.) Hoe Punitief is Nederland? [How Punitive is The Netherlands?]. Arnhem: Gouda Quint. pp. 299–312.

Boin, A. (1995) "Organizational autonomy in times of institutional adversity: threats and opportunities for Dutch prison management." Paper presented at the 1995 Annual Meeting, Academy of Criminal Justice Sciences, March 7–11. Boston: forthcoming.

Bottoms, A.E. (1977) "Reflections on the renaissance of dangerousness." *Howard Journal of Penology and Crime Prevention*, 16: 70–96.

—————. (1995) "The philosophy and politics of punishment and sentencing," in C. Clarkson and R. Morgan (eds.) *The Politics of Sentencing Reform*. Oxford: Clarendon Press.

Bruinink, J.E. and Lagendijk, E.P. (1994) *Aanpak Stelselmatige Daders in Dordrecht: Een Stok Achten de Deur* [Dealing with Persistent Offenders in Dordrecht: A stick behind the door!]. Amsterdam: Van Dijk, Van Soomersen en Partners.

Cohen, S. (1972) *Folk Devils and Moral Panics*. Oxford: Blackwell.

—————. (1979) "The punitive city." *Contemporary Crises* 3: 339–63.

Council of Europe. (1993) *Report to the Dutch Government on the Visit to The Netherlands Carried Out by the European Committee for the Prevention of Torture and Inhuman or Degrading Treatment or Punishment (CPT) from 30 August to 8 September 1992*. Strasbourg.

—————. (1994) *Response of the Netherlands Government to the Report of the European Committee for the Prevention of Torture and Inhuman or Degrading Punishment (CPT) on its Visit to The Netherlands from 30 August to 8 September 1992*. Strasbourg [Report in Dutch publ. December 20, 1993; in English September 1, 1994].

Dijk, J.J.M.van, Mayhew, P. and Killias, M. (1990) *Experiences of Crime Across the World: Key Findings of the 1989 International Crime Survey*. Deventer: Kluwer.

Downes, D.M. (1988) *Contrasts in Tolerance: Postwar Penal Policy in The Netherlands and England and Wales*. Oxford: Clarendon Press.

Fionda, J. (1995) *Public Prosecutors and Discretion: A Comparative Study*. Oxford: Clarendon Press.

Franke, H. (1995) *The Emancipation of Prisoners: Two Centuries of Imprisonment in The Netherlands*. Edinburgh: University Press.

Freeling, W. (1993) "De straf op tasjesroof: hoe het strafklimaat strenger werd" [The sentencing of bag-snatching: how the sentencing climate is tougher]. *Proces*, 5: 76–82.

Gelsthorpe, L., Nellis M., Bruins, J. and Van Vliet, A. (1995) "Diversion in English and Dutch Juvenile Justice" in C. Harding et al. (eds.) *Criminal Justice in Europe*. Oxford: Clarendon Press.

Haan, W.J.M. de. (1990) *The Politics of Redress: Crime, Punishment and Penal Abolition*. London: Unwin Hyman.

————. (n.d.) "A moral panic on the brink: Moroccan gangs in the city of Amsterdam." Utrecht: Willem Pompe Institute.

————. (1994) "Counting muggers in a local area: a new statistical model for estimating the actual number of perpetrators." Utrecht: Willem Pompe Institute.

t'Hart, A.C. (1988) "Criminal law policy in The Netherlands," in J.J.M. van Dijk et al. (eds.) *Criminal Law in Action*. Deventer: Kluwer.

Hulsman, L.H.C., Beeling, H.W.R. and Van Dijk, E. (1978) "The Dutch criminal justice system from a comparative legal perspective" in D.C. Fokkema et al. (eds.) *Introduction to Dutch Law for Foreign Lawyers*. Deventer: Kluwer.

Johnson, E.H. and Heijder, A. (1983) "The Dutch deemphasize imprisonment: a sociocultural and structural explanation." *International Journal of Comparative and Applied Justice*, 7: 3–19.

Kelk, C. (1983) "The humanity of the Dutch prison system and the prisoners' consciousness of their legal rights." *Contemporary Crises* 7: 155–70.

————. (1995) "Criminal justice in The Netherlands," in P. Fennell et al. (eds.) *Criminal Justice in Europe: A Comparative Study*. Oxford: Clarendon Press.

Kommer, M. (1992) "Punitiveness in Europe—a comparison," *European Journal on Criminal Policy and Research*, 2, 1: 29–43.

Kruissink, M. (1990) *The HALT program: diversion of juvenile vandals*. The Hague: Research and Documentation Center.

Lijphart, A. (1975) *The Politics of Accommodation*. Berkeley: University of California Press.

NACRO. (1994) *Criminal Justice Digest*, 82 (October).

Netherlands, Ministry of Justice. (1985a) *Samenleving en Criminaliteit: Ein beleidsplan voor de komende jaren* [Society and Crime: A policy plan for the future]. The Hague: State publications.

————. (1985b) *Structuurplan Penitentiaire Capaciteit* [Plan for the Construction of Penal Capacity]. The Hague: State publications.

————. (1990) *Law in Motion: A policy plan for Justice in the years ahead*. The Hague: Information Dept.

————. (1993) *The Prison System*. The Hague: Information Dept.

————. (1994a) *Werkzame Detentie* [Effective Detention: Summary and Implementation Plan]. The Hague.

————. (1994b) *Prosecution and Trial of Indictable Offences in the Kingdom of The Netherlands: Facts and Figures of 1992 and 1993.* The Hague: CDWO/SIBa.

————. (1995) *Police-figures*: 1980–1994 The Hague: DB/SOA/BIA.

Netherlands, Commissie Openbaar Ministerie. (1994) *Het Functioneren van het Openbaar Ministerie Binnen de Rechtshandhaving* [The Functioning of the Public Prosecution Office within Law Enforcement][Donner Report]. The Hague.

Netherlands, Commissie Wierenga. (1994) *Rapport van de Bijzondere Onderzoekscommissie IRT* [Wierenga Committee: Report of the Special Investigative Committee on the IRT]. The Hague.

Netherlands, Werkgroep Van Traa. (1994) *Rapport van de Werkgroep vooronderzoek opsporingsmethoden* [Report of the working group for preliminary enquiry into (police) investigatory methods]. The Hague: Tweede Kamer der Staten-Generaal.

Netherlands, Commissie Van Traa. (1996) *Inzake Opsparing: Enquetecommissie Opsparingsmethoden* [Parliamentary Commission of Enquiry, chaired by M. van Traa, on organized crime, investigatory methods used by police and judicial authorities, and organization of investigation in The Netherlands]. SDU Uitgevers: The Hague.

Peters, A.A.G. (1988) "Main currents in criminal law theory," in J.J.M. van Dijk et al. (eds.) *Criminal Law in Action.* Deventer: Kluwer.

Richards, M., McWilliams, B., Batten, N., Cameron, C. and Cutler, J. (1995) "Foreign nationals in English prisons: I. Family ties and their maintenance." *Howard Journal of Criminal Justice*, 34, 2, 158–75.

Rijksen, R. (1958) *Meningen van Gedetineerden over de Strafrechtspleging* [Prisoners Speak Out]. Assen: van Gorcum.

Rutherford, A. (1986) *Prisons and the Process of Justice.* Oxford: Oxford University Press.

————. (1996) *Transforming Criminal Policy.* Winchester: Waterside Press.

Sparks, R. (1995) "Prison Control Issues." Paper delivered at Prison Service Research and Development Conference, Coventry, England, Sept. 18–19.

Steenhuis, D.W. (1988) "Coherence and co-ordination in the administration of criminal justice" in J.J.M. van Dijk et al. (eds.) op.cit.

————, Tigges, L.C.M. and Essers, J.J.A. (1983) "The penal climate in The Netherlands: Sunny or Cloudy ?" *British Journal of Criminology*, 23: 1–16.

Swaaningen, R. van and Jonge, G. de. (1995) "The Dutch prison system and penal policy in the 1990s: from humanitarian paternalism to penal business management," in V. Ruggiero, M. Ryan and J. Sim (eds.) *Western European Penal Systems: A Critical Anatomy*. London: Sage.

Vagg, J. (1994) *Prison Systems: A Comparative Study of Accountability in England, France, Germany and The Netherlands*. Oxford: Clarendon Press.

Vijver, C. van der, Dijk, N. van and Punch, M. (1995) *Toekomst Gezocht: Het functioneren van de politie ter discussie* [Looking for a Future: The functioning of the police under scrutiny]. Dordrecht: SMP [Dutch Police and Society Foundation].

Chapter
SIX

Power, Punishment and Prisons in England and Wales 1975–1996

Mick Ryan and Joe Sim

Things were good he reminded her: as measured by official standards, they had not often been better. This time only the poor were very poor, and the need for new prison cells was more urgent than the needs of the homeless: there were too many people who needed food, and there was too much food to be able to feed them profitably. What was wanted was more shortages, he added, with just a small smile. He did not volunteer that by now he was one more in the solid middle class who was not keen to have his taxes raised to ameliorate the miseries of those who paid none. He preferred more prisons. (Heller, 1995: 56).

On April 30, 1996, there were 53,974 males and females confined in the 133 prisons in England and Wales. This latest expansion in the numbers detained in the country's prisons had begun in the early 1990s and was propelled forward by a combination of three factors:

the significant rise in the proportionate use of custody by the courts, the increase in the length of sentences passed by judges and magistrates and the increasing length of time served by those on remand and in the sentenced population. This trend is expected to continue into the 21st century. By the year 2004, the average daily prison population is projected to increase to 59,900. The corresponding figures for 1994 and 1984 were 48,800 and 43,300 respectively (Home Office, 1996, Table 4).

The tightening of the penal screw has been fueled and legitimated in the speeches made by Michael Howard, an avowedly populist and retributive Home Secretary, whose every pronouncement excoriated liberal and radical views on the purposes and goals of imprisonment. In a series of speeches beginning at the Conservative Party's annual conference in October 1993, Howard articulated his view that penal policy should be built on programs based on disciplined austerity which would intervene into the lives of prisoners and those sentenced to non-custodial alternatives and confront the moral degradation and lack of responsibility which he and his Conservative Party colleagues argued lay at the root of criminal behavior.

The slogan "prison works" became Howard's political mantra and provided the ideological justification for locking up individuals in record numbers. This slogan was articulated against a background in which recorded levels of crime had spiraled to over five million in 1994 and where the corrosive impact of deep cuts in the social welfare budget was being felt by the poorest and most vulnerable whose behavior and lifestyle was also under sustained ideological attack by the equally populist Secretary of State for Social Security. "Welfare doesn't work" was the reverse side of the "prison works" coin. One indication of these trends lay in the number imprisoned for defaulting on fines imposed by the courts. Between 1990 and 1995 their number rose by over one-third. For women the increase was 68%. At the same time there had been a seven-fold increase in the numbers jailed for non-payment of poll tax or local rates, from 195 in 1990 to 1475 in 1994 (National Association for the Care and Resettlement of Offenders, 1995: 10). Initially, we wish to begin this chapter by situating these developments within a broader historical context and will focus in particular on the crisis which gripped the prison system in the 1970s. It was out of that crisis, and the state's response to it, that current events and future projections and strategies for the penal system in England and Wales can be understood and analyzed.

THE 1970s: GENERATING AND SUSTAINING THE CRISIS

The idea that the prison system was in crisis during the 1970s was commonplace (Fitzgerald and Sim, 1979, Ch. 1). While there has been much discussion about the exact nature of this crisis, few dispute that it had both ideological and practical components, some of which were clearly of the government's own making (Cavadino and Dignan, 1992, Ch. 1).

At the level of ideas, the potential of prisons to reform offenders was called into question. At first this critique was seen to be somewhat extravagant, the property of new abolitionist groups like Radical Alternatives to Prison (RAP), whose understanding of criminal behavior reflected the academic theories of the National Deviancy Conference and whose strategy owed much to the street politics of the counter culture. By the mid-1970s, however, other groups in the penal lobby who were arguably more plugged into the mainstream of the political process began to echo this message, arguing that for most offenders a sentence of imprisonment could be safely replaced by other, cheaper and equally effective punishments. The prison thus came to be perceived as an over-used, expensive anachronism, while its legitimacy was being challenged (Ryan, 1983).

This challenge was reinforced by the birth of a union for the Preservation of the Rights of Prisoners (PROP), formed in 1972 (Fitzgerald, 1977). This union was organized by ex-prisoners and was sufficiently strong to coordinate a series of sit down strikes in a number of prisons around the country. While PROP campaigned for more immediate reforms, it also adopted prison abolition as part of its Charter. However, arguably far more important than this formal commitment to abolition was PROP's critique of such practices as parole, its cataloging of demands around due process and its exposure as the 1970s progressed of increasingly repressive regimes driven forward by segregation, technology and medicine, all of which brutally exposed the hypocrisy behind the official discourse of reform.

The force of these arguments, which in their different ways questioned the effectiveness of imprisonment while searching for alternative sentences, was given added and weighty support in 1977 by the Government's own Advisory Committee on the Penal System in England and Wales which reported that:

> A steadily accumulating volume of research has shown that if conviction rates are used to measure the success or failure of sentencing

policy, there is certainly nothing to choose between the length of custodial sentences, different types of institutional regimes, and even
between custodial and non-custodial treatment (Home Office, 1977,
para. 8).

It is true that some of the more radical attacks on the utility of imprisonment displayed a certain willful naiveté. There were plenty
of sympathetic critics available to remind abolitionists that the purposes of imprisonment were many, including the recycling and control of marginal groups, and that these functions had always
been—and would continue to be—far more important than the
business of reforming prisoners which had never amounted to
much in the first place (Fitzgerald and Sim, 1979; Foucault, 1977;
Ignatieff, 1978). In this important sense prisons had worked, and
perhaps more to the point, *were* working, and working well.

Notwithstanding this important qualification, it remains true that
the force of the critique we have outlined made its mark. So much
so that when the May Committee, the government's official inquiry
into prison unrest, reported in October 1979, the pretense that
reform was possible had been dropped, and instead of training
offenders to lead a "good and useful life" on their release, all that
was on offer was the notion of "positive custody" (Home Office,
1979, para. 4.46; Maguire, Morgan and Reiner, 1994: 895).

The significance of this retreat is that the ostensibly liberal notion
of reform which had once been so strong at an ideological level, in
spite of the evidence of penal practice, and which had obfuscated
the wider purposes of imprisonment, was swept aside. It is not
insignificant that this displacement occurred at a time of growing
social and labor conflicts and the emergence of the New Right
which stressed individual responsibility and punishment rather
than reform. However, it is important to understand that the gene-
sis of the May inquiry was not academic or lobby speculation about
the alleged failures of the prison system, but rather a series of disturbances and disruptions which in quite contradictory ways had
challenged the capacity of the government to run the prison service.

SEGREGATION, MEDICALIZATION AND MILITARIZATION

The first serious disturbance took place at Hull prison in 1976. This
was a dispersal prison. There is no maximum security prison which
takes all the "hard cases" in England and Wales. Instead, all Category

A prisoners, those who, it is thought, would pose the most danger to the public if they were to escape, are held in a number of selected, dispersal prisons which are provided with special high security wings. At Hull it was rumored that a prisoner had been assaulted in the segregation unit. This set off a chain of events which led to a four day occupation of the prison, much of which was destroyed. However, what was at issue was the prisoners' allegations that once the disturbance was over they were subject to systematic beatings.

This is what PROP referred to as the second Hull riot. These accusations were strongly denied by the Prison Officers' Association (POA). Initially no action was taken against the staff involved, although in April 1979 eight prison officers were found guilty of conspiring with others to assault and beat prisoners and were given suspended prison sentences, one of which was overturned on appeal. Those prisoners who could be identified were given exemplary sentences by Hull's Board of Visitors, the body which then controlled disciplinary hearings. One prisoner lost 720 days' remission. To counter this injustice, PROP subsequently held its own public inquiry presided over by a well-known barrister. It was a result of this inquiry that the eight prison officers faced charges three years later (Ryan, 1983: 63).

The trouble in the segregation unit at Hull was not entirely unexpected and reflected the growing practice of segregating "difficult" prisoners. Always a weapon in the armory of the prison authorities, moves to segregate "identifiable trouble makers" were stepped up after PROP held its series of strikes in 1972. Control units were then introduced at Wakefield prison which involved total segregation split into different stages effectively involving sensory deprivation (Fitzgerald and Sim, 1979: 102–105). PROP marshaled a public campaign against these units which forced their closure, but the practice of segregation continued. This was largely justified by the fear that the growing number of "lifers" in the system, and the increasing number of those serving very long sentences, posed an intractable control problem because they had nothing to lose. It was taken as the logical outcome of official sentencing policies which encouraged a process of "bifurcation" in which those committing more serious offenses were to serve very long sentences while those committing less serious offenses were given alternative, community-based punishments.

The next serious prison disturbance occurred at Gartree prison in 1978. The reason behind this was the rumor that a prisoner had been improperly drugged. The growing use of the "liquid cosh" had become a high profile issue in the 1970s. Campaign groups like RAP and PROP came together with medical advisers to form the Medical Committee Against the Abuse of Prisoners by Drugging. Their main concern was the growing use of psychotropic drugs such as Largactil, particularly in women's prisons, most notably, Holloway. The government at first insisted that in cases where such drugs had been used, they had only been used for medical purposes. This always implausible defense was quickly breached, and the ethics of prison medicine became a public issue (Sim, 1990, Ch. 5).

Another concern was the growing militarization of the prison service. This is well illustrated by the official response to a peaceful sit down protest in the high security wing at Wormwood Scrubs in London in 1979. This had been prompted by the governor's proposal to reduce the privileges of all prisoners on the wing, privileges normally available to every prisoner in the dispersal system. The protest was ended by the intervention of the Minimum Use of Force Tactical Intervention (MUFTI) squad, officers specially trained and equipped to deal with riots. The existence of such a squad was unknown (even Parliament had not been informed) and their heavy-handedness led to injuries being sustained by over 50 prisoners. At first the government denied that any injuries had been sustained, and it was only due to the efforts of PROP that the truth was uncovered. Although there was prima facie evidence of criminal assaults on prisoners, no prison officers were disciplined. The only losers were again the prisoners; 120 were disciplined by the prison's Board of Visitors (Ryan, 1983: 64).

The government had been less able to hide the sequence of events at Albany two years before when a small group of Irish prisoners were involved in a pitched battle with prison officers who according to an independent report from Amnesty International, the National Council for Civil Liberties and the Howard League, acted in a way to make the incident far worse than it might have been. But again it was not the prison officers who suffered, only the prisoners. One lost 630 days' remission, another was sentenced to 19 weeks in solitary confinement (Ryan, 1983: 58). Irish prisoners, like black prisoners, were regularly singled out for abuse. Thomas and Pooley, for example have pointed out that after the Hull riot:

> many prisoners, in their evidence, observed how the IRA and black prisoners were specially humiliated. One of the former, for example,

was made to sing "God Save the Queen." He replied, "Go play with yourself, you puff [sic]. An officer then said, "Hold his legs open," and then "he put the boot in my testicles... . One of the black prisoners stated that he had been kept awake on the night of the surrender by officers switching on his light, kicking his door and shouting; "National Front rules, big black bastard"... another officer poured the contents of a chamber-pot over him (Quoted in Sim, 1991: 115–116).

The presence of Irish prisoners particularly, including those wrongly convicted of bomb explosions at Woolwich and Birmingham, was an added embarrassment to the British government which with one or two notable exceptions set itself against repatriation and refused to grant special status to prisoners, a policy which eventually led to the dirty protest and the deaths of 10 hunger strikers (Ryan, 1983: 59–61).

While the capacity of successive governments to manage the system was made more difficult by prisoners' resistance to the growing emphasis on segregation and discipline, medicalization and militarization, the system's troubles were compounded by the attitude of the POA which became more obstructive following the formation of PROP. The growth and extent of this opposition was well illustrated in 1978, a year when more than 60 POA branches became involved in over 100 disputes. Again prisoners were the losers. The POA refused to accept prisoners from overcrowded police cells, closed down workshops and confined prisoners without recreation, sometimes for 23 hours a day. Industrial relations became so bad that one observer has remarked that during the second half of the 1970s the POA was challenging the authority and management of the system at every level (Rutherford, 1986: 85–7).

OVERCROWDING

To what extent were these various disturbances and disruptions triggered by overcrowding? At one level this is an easier question to ask than to answer. Certainly there was overcrowding. The number of prisoners sharing two to a cell more than doubled between 1970 (4886) and 1977 (11,040), and even though the number of those sharing three to a cell had leveled off, it stood at around 5,000 in 1977 (Fitzgerald and Sim, 1979: 16). It is extremely important not to underestimate the frustrations that this caused, not least in local prisons which housed an increasing number of untried prisoners on remand, and where overcrowding was worst. And it is unlikely that overcrowding played *no* part in creating the climate of disenchantment and instability that characterized the prison system in the 1970s.

However, it is equally clear from a detailed investigation of the disturbances which occurred during these years that they had more to do with an organized resistance to increasingly repressive prison regimes, albeit a resistance which was organized by sometimes quite different sets of prisoners, each with a growing sense of its own situation and its own power. This awareness, combined with the ideological challenge to the legitimacy of the prison which transformed the POA and its members from careers into simple caretakers, produced a crisis that went beyond bread and butter issues about cell space, slopping out, or for that matter, of overtime rates.

In November 1978 in response to this perceived sense of crisis, the Labor government established a Committee of Inquiry under Mr. Justice May. However, wider political events were to overtake May's deliberations. The Labor government lost the general election in the spring of 1979 and was replaced by a right of center Conservative government. A new phase in the turbulent history of the prisons was about to begin.

RIGHTING PRISONS

The election of a free market Conservative government in May 1979, based around the apocalyptic zealotry of Margaret Thatcher's monetarist fundamentalism, was to have a profound effect on every social institution in British society, including what were euphemistically called "law and order services." From its first days in power, the government held out a conciliatory hand to those in these "services" who felt frustrated and alienated by the previous Labor government and who had supported the Tories' election call for a tougher law and order response to crime and punishment. For the police there was promise of more resources, better equipment and increased numbers. It was a promise that was delivered: Between 1979 and 1983 their number rose by over 11,000, pay rose by 86% and expenditure reached nearly 2.5 billion (McFadyean and Renn, 1984: 71). In delivering on its manifesto promises the Conservatives not only cemented the relationship between the new government and the police (something which was to prove mutually beneficial in the year-long coal dispute in 1984–5) but also in the feverish law and order climate of the late 1970s it articulated a stark and chilling message that it was prepared to clamp down ruthlessly on those whose subversive moral and political behavior had reduced the nation to the derogatory status of the "sick man" of Europe.

The government's relationship to the prison system was more complex for two significant reasons. First, the May inquiry which as we noted above had been established by the Labor government in October 1978 as a response to the crisis, had not yet reported. Second, like their Labor predecessors, the Conservatives were confronted by a group of state servants—prison officers—who themselves had been integral to the generation of the prison crisis in the 1970s. This powerful group based around rank-and-file officers was part of the problem rather than part of the solution to the crisis. When May reported in October 1979, his committee not only failed to deal with or indeed confront the key issue of the discretionary power of prison officers, but more generally offered little by way of policies for alleviating the crisis. As was noted at the time:

The May Report was an opportunity not simply to review but to change fundamentally the 100-year-old recipe of more prisons and more prisoners. In the event it passed up that opportunity, preferring like so many inquiries before it, to represent the recipe for prison crisis as recipe for prison salvation. It simply won't work (Fitzgerald and Sim, 1980: 84).

These words were to prove prophetic. Between 1979 and 1983, the period of the first Conservative administration, prisons remained in a state of crisis: Conditions deteriorated still further; the build up in the number of long-term prisoners was maintained; prison officers remained defiant; militarization intensified and demonstrations continued (State Research, 1982: 100–103). The re-election of the Conservatives for a second term in June 1983 introduced a new Home Secretary whose response to the crisis was to announce a set of policies at the party's annual conference in October which were designed not only to re-establish the legitimacy of the institution but also to reaffirm its centrality as a key element in what was increasingly being constructed as a war against the criminal and a broader "enemy within."

THE MOMENT OF BRITTAN

Leon Brittan's conference speech on October 11, 1983, delivered a package of measures which was overwhelmingly endorsed by his audience. They were designed not only to restore the legitimacy of the prison system through the introduction of a number of authoritarian penal policies but they also represented and symbolized an important moment in the Conservative's attempt to rationalize and professionalize what for Ministers and their party was a ramshackle, problematic criminal justice system which was prone to crises, disputes and conflict. Brittan's proposals were far reaching and included: minimum sentences for certain categories of crimes, introducing legislation to allow "over-lenient" sentences to be referred to the Court of Appeal and restricting parole for particular groups of prisoners such as drug traffickers sentenced to more than five years who were to be "treated with regard to parole in exactly the same way as serious violent offenders—they should not get it!" (Leon Brittan cited in Ryan and Sim, 1984: 6). As we noted above the Home Secretary was also clear about the strategy he wished to pursue on taking office:

> I decided that we needed a strategy that would enable us to pursue our priorities and objectives in a deliberate and coherent way. Such a strategy is now in place. It covers all the main areas of the Department's work, both general policies and specific legislative or administrative objectives. We shall be reviewing it regularly. Our principal preoccupation is, and I believe ought to be, the criminal justice system which incidentally I wish to see treated in all that we do as a system (Brittan cited in Home Office, 1984: Foreword).

Brittan's hard-line approach to penal policy mirrored developments in the criminal justice system in general as the party of law and order introduced a range of acts and bills which consolidated the power of a state whose authoritarian interventions into the lives of the powerless were paralleled by an equally ruthless disengagement from policing the activities of the powerful (Sim, 1987). However, the hegemony which the Conservatives attempted to assert over the prisons was fragile. At the level of policy, as Barbara Hudson (1993: 49) has indicated, it was "difficult to deduce any overall goal or ethos for the decade 1975 to 1985."

For Hudson developments in policy at this time can be characterized in terms of three dichotomies: continuum/bifurcation, informalism/formalism and corporatism/individualism (*Ibid*: 32–46). On the ground, the crisis inside remained unresolved. In particular, the demonstrations and disturbances which we discussed earlier and which had been central to the crisis in the 1970s intensified and became more widespread. From the mid-1980s disorder spread from long-term to short-term and remand prisons. This culminated in April 1990 with the seismic disturbance at Strangeways prison, Manchester, where prisoners not only destroyed a major part of the institution but held the prison for 25 days in a siege that was to become the longest and most sustained in the history of British prisons. The government's response was to appoint a senior judge, Lord Justice Woolf, to inquire into the cause of the disturbance at Strangeways and other prisons and to make recommendations. For many liberal commentators Woolf's report, which was published in February 1991, provided a set of policies which would not only alleviate the crisis inside but also offered a visionary blueprint for the future. For other more critical voices Woolf not only failed to address a number of fundamental issues affecting the penal system, but his liberal prognosis for progressive change was immediately undermined by the government's response to his report (Sim, 1994). This response was to be the start of the renewed emphasis on coercion, discipline and austerity which, as we noted at the beginning of this chapter, had become central to the policies of Michael Howard by the mid-1990s. Before considering this issue in depth we wish to focus on two other strands in the Conservative's penal policy, those of privatization and managerialism. These two intertwined discourses which had been virtually ignored in 1979 had become, by the early 1990s, central to the philosophy and politics of the Conservatives. As Hugo Young (1991: 605) put it: "Scarcely thought of in 1979, by 1991 privatising state businesses had become a practice constrained by financial, but no longer by political factors. It was widely thought to be quite normal... ." Like every other institution in the society, the penal system was not to be denied its chance to participate in a process which in the spirit of the free market was to transform prisoners into customers and managers into business executives.

PRIVATE PRISONS

During the second half of the 1980s the issue of private prisons slowly worked its way up the political agenda. It appealed to a small number of Conservative MPs and right wing think tanks like the Adam Smith Institute which had followed the debate in the US (Ryan and Ward, 1989: 44–47). At first it was discarded, largely for practical and political reasons.

In the first place, British prisons had been nationalized at a stroke in 1877 and thereafter run in a tightly controlled way from the center. Disentangling this was not going to be easy, and would almost certainly be fought every inch of the way by the powerful POA. Other more pressing, and arguably more profitable, privatizations were therefore given priority. Second, the hope that private prisons might help to relieve overcrowding, a claim made by their proponents in the US, was less compelling in Britain than it might have been towards the end of the 1980s when the prison population leveled off and the impact of the government's earlier prison building program began to be felt (Newburn, 1995: 32). Third, the release of market forces associated with the policies of the New Right had social costs which needed to be policed—the miners' strike and the inner city disturbances, to give two examples. The free market thus needed the strong regulatory state, and the advisability of passing over one of the major instruments of social discipline at this time to the private sector was therefore not without its risks.

While these factors delayed privatization, they could not prevent it. Within two years of arguing that he did not think that the responsibility for "keeping prisoners safe" belonged to anyone other than public servants, the Minister responsible for the penal system announced in Parliament that two new, government-financed remand prisons would be handed over to the private sector to manage on an experimental basis (Hansard, March 1, 1989, Col. 278).

Accounting for this change of direction is far from easy. Certainly the advocates of private prisons had strong supporters in government like Lord Windlesham who sought to bypass any perceived constitutional difficulties by stressing that privatization should be first tried in the remand sector where those involved were suspects and not offenders. The thorny issue of handing over public *punishment* to the private sector therefore did not apply, or at least that is what was argued. Concentrating on the remand population was seen to have other advantages. It was here that some of the worst overcrowding could be found (King and Morgan, 1976). If private prisons could relieve overcrowding here, aiming at those who were still technically innocent, surely this was desirable?

Pressing these arguments mostly took place behind closed doors, and it is only relatively recently as politicians have retired from public office that the extent of this lobby has been fully appreciated. Prime Minister Thatcher herself was approached and persuaded; think tanks addressed other Ministers and senior civil servants at privately organized seminars; MPs like Sir John Wheeler kept up the Parliamentary pressure, and perhaps above all, building contractors with close links to the Conservative Party moved in, linking up in the process with American contractors like the Corrections Corporation of America (Windlesham, 1993, Ch. 6).

Extent of Privatization

The experiment which started with the Wolds remand prison on Humberside, built by UK contractors Mowlem and McAlpine with technical assistance from the Corrections Corporation of America, was never in truth an experiment. Legislation was introduced to extend privatization to the mainstream prison system in 1991, well before any evaluation of the Wolds could reasonably have been completed.

By 1995 there were five private prisons operating in the UK. Blakenhurst came on stream after the Wolds and caters for both remand and sentenced prisoners. This is being managed by UKDS, a consortium led by the Corrections Corporation of America supported by Mowlem and McAlpine. Doncaster prison, managed by Premier Prisons as a joint venture between the British security firm Serco and Wackenhut (US), also holds remand and convicted prisoners, as does Buckley Hall, which like the Wolds is managed by the British security company Group 4. Finally, the former Strangeways prisons which was largely rebuilt following the major disturbance there in 1990 was the subject of a successful management buy-out.

The government is now in the process of market testing other state prisons in the hope of forcing more public sector workers into the private sector. By the millennium it hopes to have around 10 percent of the entire prison stock either owned/and or managed by the private sector, including six new prisons whose building costs are, for the first time in the UK, being met by the private sector. Two of these, at Fazakerley and Bridegend, are being tendered with contracts extending over 25 years (PRT, 1995a: 14).

The provision and management of secure units for very young offenders has likewise been offered to the private sector as has the building of new "borstals" for somewhat older children (Ryan, 1995: 240; Prison Reform Trust, 1993: 13). While all these developments are new, the government has for along time now permitted the private sector to manage immigration detention centers (Ryan and Ward, 1989: 67–68). Group 4 has secured some of these contracts. It is also involved with other companies like Securicor in escorting prisoners between both public and private prisons to the courts.

Performance

The performance of the private sector has been a matter of some controversy. Private operators claim that their prisons have been under greater scrutiny than those in the public sector. There is some truth in this. On the other hand, private sector operators and their supporters have greatly exaggerated their potential. To give just two examples: When moves to extend privatization to the mainstream of the prison system were being made, a British MP claimed that private sector prisons in the US and Australia had lower rates of recidivism—this at a time when Australia's first private prison at Borallon was hardly up and running (Ryan, 1995: 238). More recently at a sales pitch in Holland, Anthony Hopkins of UKDS told his audience that:

> First class security and an orderly community are obvious prerequisites for the maintenance of a safe environment for prisoners and staff and the public. [We believe] in dynamic security which only comes from the successful integration of all prison operations and programmes. Prisons with ample programmes, active prisoner cooperation and good communications between staff and prisoners rarely have serious security problems. Our staff have been trained and motivated...to prevent situations from occurring rather than reacting (Ryan, 1995b).

Not long after this boast Blakenhurst's trained and motivated staff were fined for losing control during a disturbance and one of its officers has been sentenced for conspiring to assault a prisoner (Prison Reform Trust, 1995a: 13).

At the Wolds the Chief Inspector of Prisons identified a serious drugs problem and one prisoner claimed to have been forcibly injected with heroin. Group 4's public image was further damaged when members of its prison escort service overlooked a prisoner who was later found dead after having been transported back and forth to prison. He had allegedly drunk large quantities of alcohol (Ryan, 1995: 245). A tribunal also found the company guilty of racism in its recruitment processes (Prison Reform Trust, 1995c: 5).

At Doncaster prison too there were problems, partly it would seem as result of economizing on staff. The Home Office intervened and extra staff were drafted in. On the question of cost effectiveness generally the jury is still out, partly because commercial confidentiality has meant that the data necessary to compare public and private prisons are unavailable, an impediment which has forced some opponents of privatization to turn to America where US companies are involved and where company disclosure and access are more open (Prison Reform Trust, 1995c).

This catalog of errors should not obscure the fact that some very positive features were identified at the Wolds and not all the news from Blakenhurst is bad either. Furthermore, it could be that some private sector prisons turn out to be cheaper to run in the long run and that the sometimes debilitating POA stranglehold over the prison service is now being weakened for the better. But having made these qualifications, it is equally clear that running prisons and prison escort services is a highly specialized business and that some of the promises made by the private sector were grossly exaggerated. Private operators can no more prevent disturbances, curtail drug taking or secure rehabilitation than their often maligned counterparts in the public sector. The rhetoric which claims otherwise is starting to look threadbare.

Perhaps the most objective, recent comment on this largely partisan debate is contained in a summary of the findings of a Home Office study which compared the performance of the Wolds and similar prisons in the public sector, and which concluded that comparable achievements were to be found in some public sector local prisons. There was, therefore, no evidence that the Wolds' achievements were necessarily related to its contracted-out status (Home Office, 1996).

The publication of the main body of this study, which was undertaken by criminologists at the University of Hull and completed some time ago, has been mysteriously delayed.

Privatization and the Prison Population

The impact that privatization might have on the overall level of the prison population was a real concern to those who opposed it. The argument simply put was that it would encourage the emergence of a penal-industrial complex driven by powerful and politically influential entrepreneurs whose best interests would be served by encouraging longer sentences and the greater use of imprisonment generally. For example, the evidence provided by Table 1 (below) and supplemented by Labor Research July (1993: 11–13) reveals there are powerful vested interests at work. Corporations like McAlpine, Shepherd and Tarmac have close links with the Conservative Party and are well placed to influence public policy. However, what Table 1 also reveals is that the private sector did very well out of the expansion of the penal system when it was entirely in public hands. In other words, to have any plausibility at all the argument should be that a penal-industrial complex, already powerful and in place, was significantly strengthened by the introduction of private prisons.

Having detailed these corporate interests at work we cannot entirely dismiss this line of argument. For example, the willingness of the private sector to meet the initial bill for building six new prisons announced in 1993, just at the time when the government was struggling to keep down its public borrowing requirement to meet the conditions of the Maastricht Treaty for monetary union, has arguably facilitated an expansion of the prison estate which will in its turn almost certainly lead to more people being sentenced to prison. However, it would be extremely naive to believe that sentencing policy is determined by such simple and direct relationships rather than by a wider set of more complex political interests, some of which we have already touched on, and other motivations which cannot be put down to the power and influence of a single lobby. For example, there is the determination of governments worldwide—as Nils Christie (1993) reminds us—to expand the use of prisons in their "war against drugs." Other factors, other interests are at work.

MANAGERIALISM

The introduction of privatization was accompanied by other significant changes to the administration and running of British prisons during the late 1980s and early 1990s. First, in an attempt to reduce "big government" the Conservatives introduced a policy called Next Steps under which government departments were to be hived off and given much more autonomy from central government in order to increase efficiency and make them more sensitive to

TABLE 1   Prison Building Programme: England and Wales
1985–1994

Main Prison	Date of Opening	Estimated Total Cost*	Construction
Wayland	January 1985	22,365	Carters of Norwich
Stocken	June 1985	17,182	Miller Construction
Thorn Cross	July 1985	13,014	Shepherd Construction
Full Stutton	September 1987	40,020	Monk Construction
Littehey	January 1988	34,002	Bovis Construction
Mount	March 1988	28,185	Wimpey Construction
Garth	July 1988	45,110	Tarmac
Swaleside	May 1990	33,539	Mowlem
Belmarsh	April 1991	161,273	Wimpey Construction
Moorland	July 1991	55,219	Higgs and Hill
Whitemoor	September 1991	54,100	Monk Construction
Brinsford	November 1991	45,563	Taylor Woodrow
Elmley	February 1992	82,782	Mowlem
Bullington	March 1992	64,339	Kier Construction
Wolds	April 1992	36,880	UK Detention Contractors (Consortium: Mowlem and Sir Robert McAlpine)
Holme House	May 1992	66,184	Sir Robert McAlpine
Woodhill	July 1992	117,753	Higgs and Hill
High Down	August 1992	91,058	Alfred McAlpine
Lancaster Farms	March 1993	73,150	AMEC
Blakenhurst	May 1993	80,432	Tarmac
Doncaster	April 1994	94,730	Shepherd Construction

*includes capital cost, contractor claims and property services agency's resource costs (£K.)

Taken from M. Ryan, 'Evaluating and Responding to Private Prisons in the United Kingdom' in P. Moyle, *Private Prisons and Police. Recent Australian Trends*, Pluto, Leichharde (1995).

consumer preferences. What this meant for the Prison Department
was that it was detached from the Home Office and given what is
termed "agency status." This put it at arm's length from the Home
Secretary who is still the Minister constitutionally responsible to
Parliament. The new Director General of the prison service was
thus expected to take increasing charge of day-to-day affairs on
operational matters, with the Minister answerable only on broad
matters of policy and sensitive issues like prison escapes (Home
Office, 1993: 6).

Second, the agency itself was to be slimmed down at the center.
Some of its many services, coordinating the assisted visits scheme
for example, were to be market tested and hived off to the private
sector. At the same time it was encouraged to decentralize its business by giving local and regional prison administrators and governors more control over health care budgets, even staffing. Finally, a
whole battery of management techniques borrowed from the private sector such as staff appraisal and performance-related pay
were to be introduced throughout the service.

To facilitate these changes a new Director of Prisons was recruited
from the private sector. Derek Lewis, a former television executive,
had no previous knowledge or experience of prisons. A once highly-
centralized state monopoly was thus to be transformed into a largely
decentralized and more flexible system in which competition between the public and the private sector—both answerable to the
Director General—would theoretically drive up standards and
improve conditions for prisoners. The market was coming to the
rescue.

The fragility of this model was demonstrated when the Director
General was sacked in October 1995 following the escape of several
high security prisoners. This drastic action showed that whatever
some commentators might claim about the fragmentation of the
Executive (Baggott, 1995: 87), the prison service at least was still
very much under political control (*The Observer*, October 22, 1995).
It also revealed that the "managerial revolution" had led to mountains of paperwork and the introduction of practices which were
quite unsuitable for running prisons. The government came under
direct fire even from its own supporters. One complained, for
example, that:

> Derek Lewis was conscientious, committed and clever. But he was
> deaf to prison alarm bells because he had no experience of listening

to them. Mr. Lewis knew nothing about prisons. That was even seen as an advantage. He was a manager with a business background. He had no time for the traditional idea of a disciplined service, of the psychological reality of prison life and the attitudes required of those expected to control it. He thought that as a chief executive he could affect the way in which prisons actually operated by showering governors with faxes and E-Mails...Mr. Lewis deserves his fate. But he also deserves sympathy as victim of that cult of managerialism that was developed throughout Whitehall but particularly in the Home Office in the 1980s. (*The Spectator*, 12 October 1995: 5).

This flirtation with managerialism does not entirely surprise us. Prisons are large, expensive institutions which even in the 19th century attracted the interest of entrepreneurs who were convinced that they could run them more efficiently than the state, even agreeing with Bentham that they might be run at a profit (Melossi and Pavarini, 1981). But as then, it is a fallacy to believe that the prison system can be understood and managed in such narrow terms, terms which eschew normative questions around increasingly repressive regimes and which deliberately perhaps put to one side the social and political context in which the present prison crisis has been generated. There are other agendas which managerialism simply cannot engage. It is to a consideration of some of these issues and agendas that we now turn.

THE EXPANDING PRISON

We began this chapter by pointing out that in 1996 the prison population reached unprecedented levels. There were 15,000 more people in prison on a daily basis than in 1993. Both the higher Crown Courts and the lower Magistrates Courts were sending proportionately more individuals to prison to the point where there had been a 50 percent increase in the use of custody by the former and a threefold increase by the latter (*The Guardian*, April 30, 1996). In June 1996, the new Director-General of the Service (who had replaced the sacked Derek Lewis) indicated that the system's capital budget would have to be doubled to 115M. This was to deal with a projected daily population figure of 60,000 which forecasters expected to see reached in the autumn of 1997. The relentless rise in the projected figures was exacerbated by the publication of the government's white paper *Protecting the Public* in April 1996. The paper contained a range of sentencing proposals which the Home Secretary, like his predecessor Leon Brittan twelve years earlier, had announced to party representatives at the Conservative's annual conference in October 1995. These proposals included: the abolition of early automatic release; the imposition of automatic life sentences on offenders aged 18 or over convicted of a serious crime for the second time; and the introduction of mandatory minimum sentences of seven years for drug dealers with two or more previous convictions and three years for burglars with two or more previous convictions for similar offenses. It was estimated that these proposals would cost between 375M and 435M while the prison population was expected to increase by 10,800 by 2010. This (typically underestimated) projection in turn would require 12 new prisons to be built, thus moving the number of institutions in England and Wales towards the 150 mark (National Association for the Care and Resettlement of Offenders, 1996: 1).

INTENSIFYING SECURITY AND PUNISHMENT

Howard was also at the center of a number of other policy developments which were immensely significant for the construction and direction of prison regimes. We wish to highlight three in particular.

First, in the aftermath of the escape by nine top security prisoners from Whitemoor Special Security Unit and Parkhurst dispersal prison, two inquiries were commissioned to investigate and report on how these events had occurred. These inquiries, which can be understood as part of what Foucault (1979: 234) called the "prolix technology of the prison," resulted in a major intensification in security across the prison system. This "[retreat] into a fortress mentality" (King, 1995: 66) has had a detrimental impact on the lives of prisoners to the point where pregnant women in labor have been chained and handcuffed in maternity wards. Other cases include that of a woman who was shackled at the funeral of her 10-day-old baby; an HIV-positive woman who was shackled for 24 hours a day and was compelled to empty her bowels and bladder while chained to a man on the other side of the lavatory door; and that of a seven-stone diabetic prisoner on remand for burglary who was also chained to an outside hospital bed and kept under 24-hour guard by prison officers (*The Guardian*, March 6, 1996; *The Guardian*, January 19, 1996; *The Guardian*, March 2, 1996).

Second, as we noted earlier, there has been a reassertion of the view that "prison works" and that regimes should be decent but austere. Howard asserted this argument at the Conservative Party Conference in October 1993 on top of a 27-point law and order package which amongst other things included imposing tougher restrictions on granting police bail and producing a review aimed at imposing harsher sentences in the community. This was followed by further disciplinary reforms in October 1993 and in May 1994 when the welfare role of the probation service was attacked and a greater disciplinary ethos was injected into the service including a proposal to employ increased numbers of former soldiers and police officers. At the same time the service's budget was cut and plans to build 40 new hostels were shelved while a number of the existing 112 hostels faced the possibility of closure.

Austerity has been reinforced by the Home Secretary's insistence that regimes should be based on incentive schemes which:

Under *Instruction to Governors 74/1995* ... become required in prisons in England and Wales. I G 74/95 states that the systematic introduction of 'earnable and losable privileges' will encourage 'responsible behavior,' 'hard work' and 'progress through the system' and will serve to create 'a more disciplined, better controlled and safer environment' for prisoners and staff. I G 74/95 requires establishments to introduce incentive schemes with 'basic,' 'standard' and 'enhanced' privilege levels, each reflecting the individual's pattern of behavior over a certain period of time. To qualify for privilege levels above the 'basic' ... prisoners are required to demonstrate 'good and responsible' behavior (Sparks, 1996: 7 emphasis on the original).

Once again, the impact on prisoners has been profound. Women in the newly opened Eastwood Park jail are confined for 22 hours each day in "battery hen" cells and have been denied access to a range of items including knitting needles and wool, alarm clocks, personal bedding, cardphones, showers and baths and the gymnasium. This means that on every day except Tuesdays and Thursdays basic regime prisoners "may spend the period from 5pm to 7am lying on their beds, their heads inches from their toilet bowls, gazing into the restricted space between cell walls." (*The Observer*, March 3, 1996). As result of these developments suicides, self-harm and assaults among women prisoners have risen (Ramsden, 1996: 8). This drive towards austerity has been further reinforced by attacks on those few spaces within institutions which have attempted to deal with the problems of offenders through psychotherapeutic and supportive regimes. While it is important to recognize the coercive power of the medical profession and the psychiatric state within British prisons (Sim, 1990), it is equally important to recognize that since the 1960s there have been a number of important innovations and developments which have provided "inmates with rehabilitative opportunities, without sliding inevitably and relentlessly into a state of tyranny which systematically denies any consideration of individual rights" (Genders and Player, 1995: 228). Faced with the onslaught of an austere law and order ideology these spaces have been increasingly restricted to the point where the internationally acclaimed Barlinnie Special Unit has been closed and those who have attempted to implement therapeutic regimes have resigned from the prison service. In his resignation letter to Michael Howard, Dr. Bob Johnson argued that:

> The harshness of your current prison policy has finally grounded my therapeutic endeavors at Parkhurst to a sickening halt... Against overwhelming expert evidence you maintain a bizarre attachment to "austerity", which bears especially hard on mentally ill offenders, who include the most unpredictable and dangerous of all...Now they have nowhere to go, and must face a degrading move every three months from prison to prison in solitary confinement for decades—I can no longer support such an inhumane, dangerous and expensive prison policy (cited in *The Guardian*, January 27, 1996).

In general, as Richard Sparks (1996: 9–10) has argued, these developments "consolidate under one banner a number of distinct political requirements" which include: emphasizing punishment, incapacitation and deterrence; organizing the prison internally through situational control and surveillance which is "much more congenial to the world-outlook of neo-liberalism than was the lingering welfarism implicit in the vocational ideologies...of many prison governors and some prison officers"; centralizing and monitoring standards so that staff experience more intensive control while simultaneously reducing "the tendency of the prisons to produce embarrassment in the form of escapes, headlines about coddling prisoners and so on." As Sparks concludes:

> Simultaneously, of course, the discourse of austerity offers to restore to the practice of punishment something of its traditional 'soul'... namely its amorous and unpleasant character—which are the tokens on the one hand of its supposed efficacy and on the other of its emotive satisfaction to its audiences...'Prison Works!' is also a populist

move... It claims to proffer solutions that seem plausible and intuitively appealing from the stand point of everyday 'crime-talk' whose presumptions are dominated by the tropes of 'system failure' and 'social breakdown.' As an electoral tactic 'Prison Works!' astutely diagnoses some of the anxieties of its audience, and seeks to turn dissatisfactions that are otherwise directly threatening to the prospects of an incumbent of a party that strongly self-identifies as "the party of law and order" to advantage (*Ibid*: 10).

The final element in the Home Secretary's austere trilogy has been built on fierce and sustained cutbacks in a range of areas inside penal institutions. These cutbacks are part of a 13 percent reduction in prison running costs which will be implemented between 1996 and 1999 and a 60 percent cut in capital spending. They will include: the axing of 3,000 jobs including 300 in the education service, the closure of industrial workshops, dispensing entirely with probation officers in particular prisons and a 40 percent reduction in simple security schemes. This last cut generated public and political controversy when it was revealed in July 1996 that the Home Secretary was in fact shelving a package of measures that would have cost 2 billion spread over four years and which was to include: bringing all prisons up to a minimum standard of security with strengthened perimeter fences and new closed circuit television systems; training prison officers for 14 days a year instead of the current five; replacing dormitory accommodations with cells; introducing electronic and magnetic locking systems; improving the searching of visitors; and building a new "supermax" prison to hold those labeled as the most dangerous in the system (*The Guardian*, July 4, 1996).

This latest controversy underlines what appears to be a contradiction in the Conservative party's prison project. On the one hand, the party has pursued a vision in which an austere prison system is integral to a broader law, order and welfare strategy which is designed to intervene into the social body and reinforce the Herculean pillars of discipline and punishment on which their monetarist and prudent social order rests. On the other hand the mantra that public expenditure and state intervention was imprudent and indeed subversive to this monetarist vision has meant that law and order institutions such as the police and prisons have been instructed to deliver their "services" in ways which are economical, effective and efficient (McLaughlin and Muncie, 1994). What does this apparent contradiction mean for the future of the prison system in England

and Wales as we move towards the end of the millennium? In the last section of this chapter we point to some issues which we think provide the key to answering the apparent contradiction described above.

THE STATE AND THE PRISONS

We began this chapter with a passage from Joseph Heller's novel, *Closing Time*. For many scholars that passage epitomizes the moment of the mid-1990s: an increase in the apparatus of law and order, coupled with draconian cut-backs in the welfare state, both of which are legitimated and sustained by a wider populist fear that the social order is collapsing and that those responsible for the collapse need to be confined, regulated and disciplined. In Western Europe in general, and England and Wales in particular, there is strong evidence to indicate that this process is occurring (Sim, et al., 1995). In the case of the latter the febrile law and order climate that dominates political and popular debate has meant that the penal system along with other sites of power such as the school, welfare and the family are increasingly regarded as:

> the sites where discipline is to be reasserted and imposed onto the bodies and into the minds of those identified as responsible for the apparent disintegration in moral values, community life and respect for the law. The presence, behavior and lifestyle of single parents (particularly women), young people, the homeless, scroungers, drug takers, illegal immigrants and the conventional criminal have been elided into one apocalyptic vision of chaos and breakdown, an unmanageable detritus out of control (Ryan and Sim, 1995: 124).

Furthermore, this moral construction builds on what Dario Melossi (1993: 273–4) has called a "vocabulary of punitive motives" held by the powerful which in turn is reinforced from below by what Richard Sparks (1996: 9) has called "populist punitiveness." Taken together both have a direct influence on the expanding rates of imprisonment.

Space does not allow us to explore the full nuances in the important arguments put forward by Melossi and Sparks but we would like to address what we see as an underlying unity behind certain apparent contradictions in the new order. To begin with, the debate on prisons has moved onto a terrain in which those who have worked within the system such as the former Director-General of Prisons, Derek Lewis, and the former Chief Inspector of Prisons, Judge Stephen Tumim, have become the voices of dissent to whom the mass media naturally incline for information and comment. However, while neither espouses a particularly harsh line in relation to punishment they are united on an ideological continuum which accepts the inevitability of the prison as a central institution in the apparatus of law and order. In a Gramscian sense these individuals can be understood as intellectuals whose "mode of being... [consists] in active participation in practical life as constructor, organizer, "permanent persuader" and not just simple orator... ." (Gramsci, 1971: 10). Despite differences between them they no less than the government legitimate the prison, leaving the spaces for other, more critical voices increasingly closed and restricted. It is also important to note that the apparent contradiction between the expansion in the prison system and the financial cutbacks ordered by the government to which we referred earlier, may not be as contradictory as first appears. In December 1995, the new head of the Prison Service, Richard Tilt, told prison governors that in order to deal with the cuts in the budget settlement for the service:

> we need to look at what the private sector is doing: the evidence so far suggests that private sector establishments are able to achieve similar levels of service for significantly less cost. That has been a critical component in ministers taking the view that the service can achieve further reductions in its costs. [The private sector generally provides] better value for money than comparable public sector establishments. We cannot ignore that gap and need to work at closing it (cited in *The Guardian*, December 20, 1995).

Again space does not permit us to engage in a full theoretical exploration of this issue. However, we would wish to argue that there are important parallels with the above statement and what is happening with the police in England and Wales where many of the organization's functions are being delegated to other groups and organizations under the general banner of crime prevention. Importantly, however, these "new" forms of governance do not necessarily parallel and run alongside of the "old" forms of state power but are dialectically interrelated with them (Coleman and Sim, 1996). A similar argument could be developed with regard to the prisons. The new managerialism that has emerged and the appearance of a private prison system should not be understood as

heralding the demise of prisons as we know them. There may well
be contradictions, contingencies and disjunctures in the government's strategy (as there are in all other areas of social policy) but it
is also important to recognize that the emerging public/private
prison network is being built on discourses, policies and practices
which ultimately unite rather than divide the new penal managers,
privatized prison workers and state servants from all levels of the
hierarchy in the traditional system. In taking this theoretical position in relation to these important penal changes we are not adopting either an instrumentalist, homogenized view of state power nor
reducing its institutional activities to the intrinsic logic of capital in
the Marxist sense or discipline in the Foucaldian sense. We are suggesting, however, that there is a need to develop what Bouventura
De Sousa Santos has called an "analytical strategy" for prisons and
to link prisons to the state. In making this theoretical connection it
is also important to note that bringing the state back into sociological analysis means recognizing that it may be operating in:

> a 'place' where it has never been before. Under current conditions
> the centrality of the state lies in the way the state organizes its own
> decentering... . The state may thus reproduce itself and indeed
> expand itself in forms which, by their novelty, appear as non-state
> political forms,...we are witnessing the explosion of the unity of
> state action and its law, and the consequent emergence of different
> modes of juridicity, each one politically anchored in a micro state. As
> a result the state itself becomes a configuration of micro states... (De
> Sousa Santos, 1992: 133–4).

In that sense private prisons (and the various other "new" forms of
private networks of control which are emerging in England and
Wales, for example CCTV cameras) can be analyzed as a novel form
of state power appearing in a non-state form.

The expanding penal system in England and Wales can thus be
understood in this theoretical and political context. Those individuals and groups caught in the penal net in the late 1990s are not very
different in their social characteristics from those who have been
the traditional objects of control and regulation: the unemployed,
the poor, the mentally ill, the unskilled, the homeless and poorly
housed and increasingly those drawn from the "ethnic minorities,"
particularly women. This is not to posit a deterministic relationship
between poverty and conventional crime nor is it to ignore the fact
that there are individuals in prison who pose a serious threat to the

safety of particular groups, for example those few men in England and Wales convicted of rape (Edwards, 1996). However, taking this position does mean recognizing that the expanding penal system in England and Wales will not be confining those in more powerful positions who engage in problematic and dangerous behavior. With some exceptions, that behavior still remains invisible and ignored. What is required is an analysis which recognizes the symbolic role of prisons in a society which is not only experiencing profound levels of insecurity but is deeply and increasingly divided along the fault lines of class, gender, race, sexuality and age. It is within this material context, which has been underpinned by the emergence and consolidation of an increasingly militarized, authoritarian state that prisons should be situated and responded to in the last decade of the 20th century.

CONCLUSION

The end of each millennium it seems thrusts prisons into the law and order spotlight. At the end of the 18th century John Howard's recommendations for change were important for moving the prisons onto a new ideological and material terrain (Ignatieff, 1978). At the end of the 19th century a similar process occurred with the Gladstone Committee (Garland, 1985). At the end of the 20th century Michael Howard has picked up the baton of reform in order to mold a prison system for the 21st century. Three different individuals covering two hundred years. And yet as Foucault recognized in *Discipline and Punish*, prison reformers are not very different from each other despite the cultural and historical distances between them. As he noted, prison is "always offered as its own remedy" when the institution is in crisis (Foucault, 1979: 268). In that sense Michael Howard's position may not necessarily be as extreme as various critics have alleged. He could be seen as not only building on the discourses and practices of those who have been Home Secretary since the Conservatives came to power in 1979 (Leon Brittan being an important example of this point) but he is also at the end of a much longer historical chain which links him to a broader set of deeply entrenched popular and official discourses which he has helped to sustain, develop and intensify. By offering the prison "as its own remedy" for alleviating the crisis inside he is plugging into this deeper historical tradition which in the words of

Giles Playfair is built on a "punitive obsession" (Playfair, 1971) with crime and punishment.

At this historical moment the future prospects for a critical and empowering reconstruction of prisons in England and Wales appear bleak. Opposition political parties are themselves increasingly standing on an ideological terrain which commits them not only to ensuring that the prison, alternatives to custody and community punishments should all be built on disciplined regulation rather than rehabilitation and reintegration, but that state welfare should also be built around targeted, monetarist efficiency rather than individual and collective need. At the same time, those at the sharp end of law and order policies in general and penal policies in particular may not endure them in silence for much longer. There is evidence that a serious "legitimacy deficit" (Sparks and Bottoms, 1995) is developing and that disturbances could erupt with potentially fatal consequences for those involved. If this occurs then perhaps this society will learn the lessons from its own primeval penal history and begin the search for an alternative set of discourses based around social justice and political inclusion rather than the atomized and brutal exclusions on which the current social order rests.

References

Baggott, R. (1995) *Pressure Groups Today*. Manchester: Manchester University Press.

Cavadino, M. and Dignan, J. (1992) *The Penal System; An Introduction*. London: Sage.

Christie, N. (1993) *Crime Control as Industry*. London: Routledge.

Coleman, R. and Sim, J. (1996) "From the Dockyards to the Disney Store: Surveillance, Risk and Security in Liverpool City Centre." Paper presented to the Law and Society Association Conference, University of Strathclyde, Glasgow, July.

De Sousa Santos, B. (1992) "State, Law and Community in the World System: An Introduction." *Social And Legal Studies*, 1, 2: 131–142.

Edwards, S. (1996) *Sex and Gender in the Legal Process*. London: Blackstone.

Fitzgerald, M. (1977) *Prisoners in Revolt*. Harmondsworth: Penguin.

Fitzgerald, M. and Sim, J. (1980) "Legitimating the Prison Crisis: A Critical Review of the May Report." *The Howard Journal*, X1X: 73–84.

Fitzgerald, M. and Sim, J. (1979) *British Prisons*. Oxford: Blackwell.

Foucault, M. (1979) *Discipline and Punish*. Harmondworth: Penguin.

Foucault, M. (1977) *Discipline and Punish*. London: Allen Lane.

Garland, D. (1985) *Punishment and Welfare*. Aldershot: Gower.

Genders, E. and Player, E. (1995) *Grendon: A Study of a Therapeutic Prison*. Clarendon: Oxford.

Gramsci, A. (1971) *Selections from Prison Notebooks*. London: Lawrence and Wishart.

Heller, J. (1995) *Closing Time*. London: Pocket Books.

Home Office. (1966) *Report of the Inquiry into Prison Escapes and Security*. London: HMSO.

Home Office. (1977) *The Length of Prison Sentences; Interim Report of the Advisory Council on the Penal System*. London: HMSO.

Home Office. (1979) *Report of the Committee of Inquiry into the United Kingdom Prison Services (Cmnd 7673)*. London: HMSO.

Home Office. (1984) *Criminal Justice: A Working Paper*. London: Home Office.

Home Office. (1993) *Framework Document, HM Prison Service*. London: HMSO.

Home Office. (1996) *Research Findings No. 32 Wolds Remand Prison— An Evaluation*. London: HMSO.

Home Office. (1996) *Projections of Long-Term Trends in the Prison Population to 2004*. Home Office Statistical Bulletin 4. London: Home Office.

Hudson, B. (1993) *Penal Policy and Social Justice*. Basingstoke: MacMillan.

Ignatieff, M. (1978) *A Just Measure of Pain*. Basingstoke: Macmillan.

King, R. and Morgan, R. (1976) *A Taste of Prison: Custodial Conditions for Trial and Remand Promises*. London: Routledge.

King, R. (1995) "Woodcock and After." *Prison Service Journal*, 102: 63–67. Labor Research July 1993: London.

Maguire, M., Morgan, R. and Reiner, R. (eds.) (1994) *The Oxford Handbook of Criminology*, Oxford: Clarendon Press.

Melossi, D. (1993) "Gazette of Morality and Social Whip: Punishment, Hegemony and the Case of the USA 1970–1992" *Social and Legal Studies*, 2, 3: 259–279.

McFadyean, M. and Renn, M. (1984) *Thatcher's Reign*. London: Chalto and Windus.

McLaughlin, E. and Muncie, J. (1994) "Managing the Criminal Justice System" in J. Clarke, A. Cochrane and E. McLaughlin (eds.) *Managing Social Policy*. London: Sage.

National Association for the Care and Resettlement of Offenders. (1995) *Criminal Justice Digest*, 86, London: Communications Department.

National Association for the Care and Resettlement of Offenders. (1995) *Criminal Justice Digest*, 88, London: Macro Communications Department.

Newburn, T. (1995) *Crime and Criminal Justice Policy*. London: Longman.

Playfair, G. (1971) *The Punitive Obsession*. London: Gollancz.

Prison Reform Trust. (1993) *Prison Report* Issue no. 25, Prison Reform Trust.

Prison Reform Trust. (1995a) *Prison Report* Issue no. 31, Prison Reform Trust.

Prison Reform Trust. (1995b) *Prison Report* Issue no. 32, Prison Reform Trust.

Prison Reform Trust. (1995c) *Blahenhurst Briefing*. Prison Reform Trust.

Ramsden, S. (1996) "Chainings: A Symptom of New Harsh Women's Prison Regime." *New Statesman and Society*, 19, January: 8.

Rutherford, A. (1986) *Prison and the Process of Justice*. London: Heinemann.

Ryan, M. (1983) *The Politics of Penal Reform*. London: Longman.

Ryan, M. and Sim, J. (1984) "Decoding Leon Brittan." *The Abolitionist*, 16, 4: 3–7.

Ryan, M. (1985b) "Some Arguments Against Private Prisons" in C. Martin (ed.) *Contracts to Punish: Private or Public?* London, ISTD.

Ryan, M. (1995) "Private Prisons in the United Kingdom; Radical Change and Opposition" in P. Moyle (ed.) (1994) *Private Prisons and Police; Recent Australian Trends*. Leichhardt: Pluto Press.

Ryan, M. and Sim, J. (1995) "The Penal System in England and Wales: Round Up the Usual Suspects" in V. Ruggiero, M. Ryan and J. Sim (eds.) *Western European Penal Systems: A Critical Anatomy*. London: Sage.

Ryan, M. and Ward, T. (1989) *Privatization and the Penal System: The American Experience and the Debate in Britain.* Milton Keynes: Open University Press.

Sim, J. (1987) "Working for the Clampdown: Prisons and Politics in England and Wales" In Scraton P. (ed) *Law, Order and The Authoritarian State* (Milton Keynes: Open University Press).

Sim, J. (1990) *Medical Power in Prisons* (Milton Keynes: Open University Press).

Sim, J. (1994) "Reforming the Penal Wasteland? A Critical Review of the Woolf Report" Player E. and M. Jenkins (eds), *Prisons After Woolf: Reform Through Riot* (London: Routledge).

Sim, J. (1991) "We are Not Animals, We Are Human Beings: Prisons, Protest, and Politics in England and Wales, 1969–1990" *Social Justice* 18, 3: 107–129.

Sim, J., Ruggiero, V. and Ryan, M. (1995) "Punishment in Europe: Perceptions and Commonalties" in Ruggiero V., Ryan, M. and Sim, J. (eds) *Western European Penal Systems: A Critical Anatomy* (London: Sage).

Sparks, J.R. and Bottoms, A.E. (1995) "Legitimacy and Order in Prisons" in *British Journal of Sociology* 46, 1: 45–62.

Sparks, R. (1996) "Penal Politics and Politics Proper: The New 'Austerity' and Contemporary English Political Culture," Paper Presented to the Law and Society Association Conference, University of Strathclyde, Glasgow, July.

State Research. (1982) "Crisis in the Prisons" State Research, 29: 100–103 (London: State Research).

Windlesham Lord. (1993) *Responses to Crime 2. Penal Policy in the Making* (Oxford, Clarendon Press).

Young, H. (1991) *One of Us* (Basingstoke: MacMillan).

Chapter SEVEN

The Country of Cesare Beccaria: The Myth of Rehabilitation in Italy

Vincenzo Ruggiero

This chapter is concerned with penal developments in Italy from the 1970s to the mid-1990s and addresses several themes. It critically examines the ideology of rehabilitation in Italy, notes important contradictions in Italian penal practice, law and judicial administration and, finally, it analyzes the institutional and material functions of imprisonment and the "carceral social zone" in Italy.

THE MYTH OF REHABILITATION

Every country nurtures national mythologies which allow the respective dominant cultures to feel at ease with their own inconsistencies. Think of the strong official rhetoric in France, which is based on the assumption that the country displays the ideal Republican division of power between the executive, the legislative and the judiciary. This mythology, which dates back to Montesquieu's time, keeps surviving even in the recurrent periods when the predominance of the executive power in the country has suggested that France is governed by principles of "neo-Bonapartism." Or, take the example of Britain, where a dominant cultural presumption is that the country is the beacon of parliamentary democracy and the rule of law. The strength of this myth persists despite the criticisms of constitutional reformers, who rightly stress that half the British parliament (the House of Lords) is not elected by voters. Judges are appointed not by a democratic and transparent system but by "higher" authorities. As for magistrates, who lack any professional legal training, "their principal occupations may well be that of butcher, baker and candle-maker" (Mansfield, 1993: 207).

In the official rhetoric, Italy is the country of Cesare Beccaria; that is, the country of rational, non-vindictive, rehabilitative punishment. It is the country where imprisonment does not rest on retributivist but on consequentialist ideals. In other words, punishment in Italy is allegedly justified solely by its contingent, instrumental contribution to the resocialization of offenders (for a discussion of retributivism and consequentialism, see Duff and Garland, 1994).

Every country, in turn, attempts to preserve its national myths by means of more or less convoluted rationalizations which aim to neutralize the shortfall between its official self-image and reality. Similar to those "techniques of neutralization" commonly used by conventional criminals, these rationalizations help perpetuate the respective national mythologies. The Italian prison system can be examined against this convoluted backdrop, and its features regarded as the reflection of an intricate web of such rationalizations.

In this chapter I would like to suggest that punishment in Italy is the outcome of a rationalizing process in which the official myth of rehabilitation remains intact though penal practices keep contradicting it. The discussion of successive prison legislations is aimed to highlight such contradictions. Here, rehabilitation is treated as a "manifest" or official function of the prison system which hides a "latent" or operative function. In the final discussion, a brief attempt is made to unveil aspects of this latent function. But before engaging with the analysis, trends of imprisonment should be summarized.

The Capricious Use of Imprisonment

In June 1995 there were 50,339 prisoners in Italian institutions. This figure represented a 1.7 percent decline when compared to that of December 1994 and an 8.8 percent decline when compared with the figure of June 1994. About half the prison population was on remand and 4.7 percent were women (ISTAT, 1995). This decline followed an opposite trend which characterized the prison population between 1990 and 1994, when there was an increase from 25,931 to 55,220, respectively the lowest and highest figures in the history of the country. This capricious use of imprisonment in the country has been accounted for elsewhere (Pavarini, 1994a; Ruggiero, 1995) and its analysis will not be rehearsed here. However, one aspect deserving attention regards the types of offenders experiencing such anomalistic changes. For the last decade prisoners serving sentences less than two years have amounted to more than 80 percent of the total prison population. While the number of prisoners serving longer sentences remained virtually unaltered, it is this section of the population in custody which accounted for the intermittent drastic shifts referred to above. Even between 1985 and 1990, when the number of homicides rose considerably, prisoners serving long-term sentences remained virtually constant. "On the other hand, the bulk of the prison population upon which the changing social, legislative and judicial moods had a significant impact was formed by short-term prisoners" (Ruggiero, 1995: 48).

Are We All Reformers?

The recent history of the Italian prison system is marked by the year 1975, when new legislation came to fruition. This prison legislation was implemented in a situation characterized by concern for growing crime rates and, at the same time, distrust in the deterrent effect of custody. Overcrowding and unrest in most institutions were among the contingent reasons which made the reformist stance widely acceptable. Change to the previous prison system was also encouraged by the national association of judges and the Constitutional Court, with both arguing that prisoners should be released as soon as their rehabilitation had been achieved, rather than after their entire sentence had been served (Bruti Liberati, 1987). This proposition, which may have been prompted by the necessity to ease the management of overcrowded and volatile

institutions, was also consistent with the enlightened principles put
forward by Beccaria. According to the national father of penal
reform, punishment per se is anathema, retribution is unacceptable
and the only justification for imprisonment is the rehabilitation of
offenders.

Judges, reform groups, scholars and jurists could hardly object to
the prevailing reformist mood. Whether advocates of "just deserts,"
supporters of the Enlightenment or avowed positivists, they all felt
comfortable with the principles inspiring the reform. Beccaria
(1970) was not fully aware of how the abolition of the death penalty
would result in the increase of incarceration; nevertheless he
regarded custody as "excessive," therefore as unjust, for a wide
range of offenses. For example, he claimed that minor property
offenses should only be punished with a fine, because theft was
usually the outcome of misery and despair, a mere means of subsis-
tence (Bonger, 1936; Melossi, 1990).

The new prison legislation in Italy was also consistent with utilitarian principles, which are also part of the legacy of the Enlightenment. Advocates of these principles favored reform because prison
did not fulfill its role as a molder of disciplined, productive citizens.
Moreover, because in the Italian context the "prison as factory" was
hardly, and never had been, a realistic feature, even the mundane
goal of making prisoners productive while serving a sentence could
not be achieved. Prison, it was believed, did not mend the material
damage caused by crime; on the contrary, it added to that damage
by causing recidivism.

Finally, arguments in support of the reform legislation also came
from the Italian positivist tradition. According to this tradition
"therapy" aimed at individual rehabilitation and prevention, that is
to say against recidivism, could often be more successful if carried
out outside the prison walls (Ferri, 1929; Sighele, 1911; Ellero, 1879).
Many neo-positivists would also argue that rehabilitation itself was
among the most important elements which could guarantee public
protection, as identified in the notion of "social defense."

Advocates of prison reform in Italy, therefore, did not need to
mobilize critical or radical ideals in support of their argument.
Drawing on traditional penology, most jurists, scholars and pressure groups endorsed the argument that custody had to be
reformed and only used as a last resort. The Italian constitution, in
turn, makes it very clear that imprisonment, although a last resort,
is not to be intended as punishment in itself, not as a vindictive

measure which makes up for the offense committed (Padovani, 1990). Pure retribution is unconstitutional: Custody must lead to rehabilitation. If it does not, it has no rationale or justification.

At Odds with International Trends

One specific feature of the recent history of Italian culture of punishment is immediately apparent. This is that, unlike in other Western countries, consequentialist (reformative, rehabilitative) ideas were never completely abandoned while retributivist ideas were never actually revived, at least not officially. It has been noted that the retributivist revival, commonly associated with the decline of rehabilitative ideals during the course of the 1970s, was due among other things to the perceived failure of alternative penal treatment of offenders and a widespread pessimism in relation to reformative penality (Duff and Garland, 1994; Bottoms and Preston, 1980; von Hirsch, 1985; Hudson 1987). Disillusionment was also caused by the intrinsic limitedness of rehabilitative programs, which could only target a minority of the offending population and therefore had no deterrent effect on non-apprehended criminals. In the USA the decline of rehabilitative penality resulted in the abandonment of open sentences geared to the treatment and resocialization of offenders, and an increasing revival of "just deserts" ideas, along with the development of a fixed tariff for the punishment of offenses.

In contrast, the Italian penal system taking shape in the 1970s introduced forms of differential treatment and some elements echoing indeterminate sentences. These will be briefly described later. What needs stressing here is how the official culture of punishment found it difficult to participate in the revival of retributivism, engaged as it was in the attempt to perpetuate the rehabilitative myth. The elements of flexibility and indeterminacy introduced in Italy were not deemed inconsistent with rehabilitation, even though in many cases they translated into harsher punishment. It should be noted that the official rejection of retribution in Italy gained particular strength during the post-war period, when the Constitution was drafted. The notion that punishment should pursue the rehabilitation of offenders was never officially discarded, not even in 1946, when the Italian prison institutions held thousands of "fascist delinquents" who, according to large sectors of the public opinion, would indeed have deserved some ruthless form of retribution (Neppi Modona, 1973).

Both the tradition of the Enlightenment and that of positivism, as briefly discussed above, emphasized the role of social re-education and individual therapy respectively, though the latter tradition may have endorsed longer sentences when those in custody showed no sign of benefiting from the "therapy" received. Nevertheless, both traditions found idealistic philosophies of punishment and retribution, identifiable with the thoughts of Kant and Hegel, unacceptable. According to Kant, for example, punishment should not perform any general deterrent function, nor should it be intended as a means for the resocialization of detainees (Kant, 1963; Eusebi, 1989; Gallo and Ruggiero, 1991). In his argument, punishment is not a tool but a goal, a view which contains a strong anti-utilitarian concept. People, Kant argues, cannot be "utilized"; human beings are not to be treated as a means for the achievement of secondary goals. Thus punishment is not a means for rehabilitation: The offenders are punished *because* they have committed a crime. Similarly, according to Hegel, offenders "have a right" to be punished, in that they are, with punishment, honored as rational beings (Hegel, 1949).

The official rejection of these philosophies did not result in a genuine rejection of retributivist practices. The Italian participation in the international punitive mood assumed specific traits which cannot be understood without bearing the myth of rehabilitation in mind. For example, just two months before the prison reform of 1975 was implemented, a new piece of legislation was introduced which increased police powers to stop, search, raid, detain and question suspects in the absence of legal representation (Bricola, 1975; Canosa, 1976; Rinaldi, 1987). This new legislation, known as *Legge Reale*, neutralized the effects of the decarceration process slowly initiated by the subsequent prison reform, and increased the number of individuals being processed through the criminal justice and prison systems. This explains the paradox whereby during the 1970s both decarceration and incarceration increased in the country (Ministero di Grazia e Giustizia, 1993). More prisoners were released for noncustodial treatment than ever before in the past, but at the same time more new prisoners were brought in. The most important aspect of this dynamic was that the new prisoners could not benefit from alternatives to custody because they were on remand. In other words, while forms of rehabilitation for sentenced prisoners were implemented through increased contacts with the external society, *de facto* retribution was inflicted upon remand prisoners through the denial of such contacts. Individuals never found guilty by the judiciary were being punished thanks to increased and harsher police activity. I shall return later to this specific aspect of the Italian prison system, when it will become clear that punishment is increasingly escaping the constitutional control of the judiciary. In the next sections, my concern is with the shifting of power in the penal system from the judiciary to the administrators.

Shifting Powers

The joint implementation of the prison and the law and order legislations described above allowed for the official myth of rehabilitation to be perpetuated. This amounted to a technique of neutralization of the type defined earlier, and consisted of a shift of power between some of the actors playing a role in the criminal justice process. In the example just provided the police, prison administrations and the judiciary were all affected by the shift caused by the new law and order legislation. In turn, the prison reform of 1975, and subsequent new legislation introduced in 1981 and 1986, determined a redistribution of power among the specific actors involved in the very process of punishment, namely the judiciary and prison administrations.

The legislation passed in 1975 constituted a rupture with the past for its emphasis on rehabilitative treatment both within and outside the prison institution. However, while the right to be treated outside the prison walls was legally established, little effort was made to equip outside rehabilitative agencies with the necessary means to perform their task (Neppi Modona, 1976). The legislation passed in 1981 and 1986 slightly improved this crucial aspect by clarifying the technical procedures governing rehabilitation in the community. The involvement of local authorities, for example, became central, a circumstance which contributed to the affirmation of an important principle. This is that offenders had to be regarded as needy individuals, as clients of the local welfare system like other vulnerable and needy individuals such as the homeless, the unemployed, children or single mothers. It is beyond the scope of this chapter to discuss in detail the norms and articles of successive prison legislation. It must suffice for me to summarize the spirit, along with the main provisions, of these legislative developments and their relationship with the official rhetoric centered on rehabilitation.

In Italy, alternatives to custody can completely divert offenders from the prison system on the one hand, and can be applied while offenders are already serving a sentence on the other. While the first types of alternatives are ruled by courts hearing specific cases and dealing with individual defendants, the second types are formally ruled by judges who are in charge of prison supervision (Padovani, 1990; Ruggiero, 1995). These judges base their decisions on reports drafted by prison governors and staff, who are required to conduct "scientific" observation of prisoners' behavior and entitled to single out those deserving non-custodial treatment. Therefore, all decisions related to probation (granted to serving prisoners), day release, permission to leave, house arrest and so on, are ultimately taken by prison personnel, who lack the training and expertise that "scientific" observation of behavior would actually require. But more crucially, these decisions are taken, as it were, by the wrong constitutional power, namely by the executive. Let us examine this point.

Although officially revolving around the constitutional concept of rehabilitation, prison reform raises important problems in relation to the redistribution of power which underlies it. First, the supervision of the prison regime, and all decisions regarding the treatment of prisoners and their resocialization, should be the prerogative of the judiciary. The interference of the prison administration in these matters can be regarded as illegitimate, the prison staff being employed by government, therefore by the executive power. Second, in differentiating between deserving and undeserving prisoners the new laws indirectly endorse a notion of dangerousness which designates the personality, life-style and potential behavior of prisoners who cannot be granted alternative treatment. These prisoners are therefore punished before they commit a crime, or rather because they can potentially commit a crime. This is at odds with the constitutional principle whereby only concrete illegal acts can be penalized: *nulla poena sine crime* (Ferrajoli, 1989). Finally, the current legislation paradoxically contributes to the deterioration of the prison condition of those who do not benefit from non-custodial measures. Because these measures are selective and strictly granted *ad hominem*, any bargaining power that the incarcerated prison population may have, as a whole, tends to decrease. As a consequence, prisoners who are not given alternative treatment (e.g., non-custodial sentences) may be seen as unworthy of any effort to improve their personal condition (whether in terms of rehabilitation or simple comfort) while in custody. This contravenes the principle of equal treatment of prisoners stipulated by the Italian constitution.

The shift of power caused by the successive prison legislations, from the judiciary to prison administrations, was accompanied by amendments to the criminal code which increased penalties for a number of offenses. In this way, for example, statutory sentences regarding some offenses would exceed the limit within which non-custodial punishment could be given, with the consequent reduction of the power of judges to divert offenders from the prison system (Ruggiero, 1995). Finally, the redistribution of power also involved other prison professionals such as social workers, psychologists and probation officers. These professionals, traditionally employed by local authorities, increasingly became absorbed within the staff of central government, particularly the Ministry of the Interior, which also presides over issues of law and order. The co-existence of these two types of prison professionals is a constant matter for dispute, with those employed by the Ministry of the Interior expressing frustration for the "military" apparatus and management under which they are required to operate (Ciardiello, 1995). Moreover, should not the judiciary, rather than the agencies presiding over law and order issues, be charged with the constitutional running of prison institutions?

Zero-Sum Legislations

The notion of dangerousness allows for the suspension of the rehabilitative creed. The Italian prison legislation uses this under-defined category in order to select offenders and, at the same time, to hide its own inconsistency. Dangerousness allows, in other words, for the adoption of another technique of neutralization. It has been noted that definitions of dangerousness are as problematic as predictions of recidivism. Decisions over the dangerousness of offenders and their likelihood to reoffend offer the same probability of success as do decisions taken by "tossing a coin" (Bandini, 1987). This is one of the reasons why the concept of dangerousness was abandoned when the psychiatric reform, resulting in the closure of mental homes, was introduced in Italy in 1976. However, within the prison context, this concept was translated into that of selective incapacitation which, according to Italian legislators, was not inconsistent with the rehabilitative spirit in which the prison reform was designed.

The relationship between incapacitation and crime rates is far from clear, in Italy as elsewhere (Haapanen, 1990; Zimring and

Hawkins, 1995). In fact, what seems to be clear in Italian penal policy is the paradox whereby campaigns against specific offenders deserving incapacitation turn into increased penalties for either those who are not the target of these campaigns or offenders in general (Pavarini, 1994a; Ruggiero, 1995). "Faith rather than measurement is now, as throughout penal history, the engine for current reliance on general incapacitation in penal policy" (Zimring and Hawkins, 1995: 74). However, it is the specific translation of the concept of incapacitation into that of "social defense" which seems to grant its acceptability in the Italian context. Social defense, in its turn, does not exclude an element, if vague, of rehabilitation, as will become clear in the discussion that follows.

Article 90 of the prison legislation introduced in 1975 became notorious in the eyes of most Italian reformers. With this article legislators had intended to warn that punishment in the community and other alternative measures were not to be regarded as part of an irreversible decarceration process. Article 90 denied what all other articles of the prison law seemed to affirm, as it stipulated that rehabilitative and resocializing treatment be interrupted when security concerns prevailed. Security became the key notion which could guarantee but at the same time suspend prisoners' rights. This one article of the law encapsulated the possibility of annulling the whole law of which it was a part along with its rehabilitative underpinning (Pavarini, 1994b). Article 90 could be invoked "in exceptionally serious circumstances related to order and security, when the rules of treatment must be partly or wholly suspended" (Pavarini, 1994b: 214). But these "exceptionally serious circumstances" came to be seen less as contingent than as permanent when political prisoners began to fill Italian institutions in the second half of the 1970s. Article 90 could only apply for a limited period of time, normally three months, but could be extended if prison administrations expressed persistent security concerns. The suspension of rehabilitative treatment regarded individual prison institutions rather than individual prisoners, and consisted of censorship on correspondence, high surveillance on visitors, the limitation of collective internal activities and the banning of all resocializing external activities.

It is against this background that high security prisons were established. The specific "emergency" that gave rise to these special institutions was, in the mid-1970s, the surge of armed forms of struggle from the Left. These forms of struggle were the continuation, if

extreme, of widespread social conflicts, with more than 200 clan-
destine armed groups operating in Italy during the 1970s (Curcio,
1993; Ruggiero, 1993; Moretti, 1994). Between the late 1970s and the
mid-1980s more than 20,000 "political offenders" were processed in
one way or another through the criminal justice system. The top
figure regarding political prisoners of the Left was reached in 1983,
when they accounted for about 4,000. The political activists who
were processed through the criminal justice system in Italy were
faced with an apparatus which, according to many commentators,
was reminiscent of the Holy Inquisition. Emergency laws, which
were introduced immediately after the prison legislation, were
based on a somewhat medieval "philosophy of suspicion." The
courts were less interested in establishing the judicial truth than
they were in condemning political beliefs and ascertaining indirect
rather than personal responsibilities. Arrests would be made on the
basis of the physical contiguity or the political similarity of those
arrested with those in prison. An example: Imprisonment could
easily become the institutional response to those who were too
deeply involved in prison reform campaigning, as the very choice
of this field of political activity came to be seen as suggestive of the
dangerousness of those involved.

"Social defense," a notion mobilized against the emergence of
political armed struggle, did not annul the rehabilitative element
included in the prison legislation. In the official rhetoric even political prisoners could be "rehabilitated," provided that they distanced
themselves from their past, or reported their associates to the
authorities (Ruggiero, 1993). In these cases, of course, there was no
longer need for society to "defend itself." Differential treatment and
flexibility became the rationalizations of a system falling short of its
own officially-stated principles. However, political prisoners only
represented one of the "emergencies" allowing for such rationalizations, as in years to come they were to be followed by drug traffickers and members of organized crime.

Social defense, dangerousness and differential treatment survived
throughout the 1980s and 1990s and within the different prison legislations. Currently, although some prison establishments are still
regarded, at least by prisoners, as high security institutions, the official definition of "security" does not apply to specific prison establishments, but rather to specific prisoners. In other words, prisoners
whose rehabilitative program has been halted bring their "special"
condition of imprisonment with them when transferred to other

institutions. On the other hand, each prison now includes a high security unit where the ideals of rehabilitation are suspended. Those held in such units are commonly those who have undergone disciplinary sanctions while serving a sentence, or have in some way threatened the smooth running of the institution and caused problems to order and security.

A piece of legislation introduced in 1986 abolished Article 90, though it stipulated that strict surveillance rather than rehabilitation be applied to: (a) those who jeopardize security and upset order in the institution; (b) those who, through threats and violence, hamper the rehabilitative activities of other prisoners; (c) those who establish a climate of subjugation among other prisoners. While these categories are vaguely defined and are subject to discretionary interpretation by prison governors, a final category of prisoners for whom rehabilitation programs are not deemed viable is instead very clearly identified. This category includes offenders who have shown little willingness to be "rehabilitated" while serving previous prison sentences, irrespective of the offense committed. Arguably, this category is designed to penalize inmates who have been particularly active in internal struggles for prisoners' rights or have been involved in disturbances.

The notion of dangerousness underpinning special or "particular" forms of surveillance is not based on the perceived likelihood that prisoners will reoffend. In other words, it is not embedded in the belief in individual deterrence: Dangerousness is referred to the behavior adopted within the prison institution, irrespective of recidivism (Pavarini, 1994b). Again, it should be noted that decisions regarding special or particular surveillance on prisoners are taken by prison administrations, who inform the relevant supervising judge from whom they invariably receive permission for their decisions. There is, however, a summary procedure, under emergency circumstances, whereby prison administrations are allowed to press ahead with special surveillance of prisoners, and advise judges afterwards. However, the definition of "emergency circumstances" is itself arbitrary, and therefore attracts widespread criticism.

Although these practices could be described as anti-constitutional forms of "punishment inflicted within punishment," they do not fail to find justification in the official rhetoric. It is stressed that if we want to safeguard the general principles of rehabilitation, we also have to identify specific cases in which rehabilitation is unlikely to work. In other words, the proper treatment of some depends on the ill-treatment of others, and the survival of constitutional forms of punishment requires the occasional denial of constitutional principles themselves. This argument echoes similar views aired by supporters of the death penalty in the USA, where taking the life of murderers is presented as the best way to demonstrate respect for human life. Nevertheless, it should be obvious by now that public debate over the possibility of reintroducing the death penalty, which in Italy was abolished with the defeat of fascism, would cause too much embarrassment and would require an overt rejection of the rehabilitative ideals that legislators could not afford.

That these ideals of rehabilitation belong to the national mythology became even more clear when new rules for the treatment of offenders allegedly involved in organized criminal activity were introduced. This new emergency legislation was geared to the nature of offenses rather than to the personality of offenders, and unlike the example provided above, it ruled the suspension of rehabilitative treatment on the basis of individual behavior outside rather than inside the prison institution. Introduced in 1991, the new rules identified specific categories of offenders who could not be rehabilitated except in extraordinary circumstances (Mosconi, 1991). Drug traffickers and extortionists were among the categories of offenders identified, in other words offenders who, in the official wisdom, are typically associated with the Mafia.

According to these rules, which are still in operation, non-custodial alternatives can be granted to alleged members of organized crime only after the police and customs issue favorable reports regarding them. These reports have to assess the dangerousness of offenders and ascertain whether or not they have severed contact with the organized criminal group with which they were previously associated. Again, this procedure is at odds with the constitutional division of powers, in that prison regimes become dependent on decisions made by enforcement agencies rather than by the judiciary.

The final blow to the rehabilitative myth was dealt by legislators when, within the emergency rules discussed above, the new category of "collaborator" was introduced. This category designates offenders who provide detailed information that can be used for the prosecution of members of organized crime, and also includes those who have committed serious offenses such as murder. These "repented" members of organized criminal groups (968 in 1994) have access to rehabilitation programs and non-custodial alternatives (La Stampa, September 6, 1995).

This is the most controversial piece of legislation introduced in Italy over the last 20 years, because it ends up only benefiting those who occupy the high ranks of organized crime, who are in a position to provide relevant information about their associates and the overall structure of the criminal groups of which they are a part. In contrast, so-called "soldiers" of criminal organizations, who are unable to provide such information and often ignore the identity of their "officers," are denied rehabilitative treatment. It should not sound surprising that even in the face of such an unjust piece of legislation, the official rhetoric still invokes Beccarian mythologies, as turncoats and "supergrasses" are publicly described as the epitome of successful rehabilitation.

The Drug Crisis

Before 1982 the use of illicit drugs was not criminalized, and only supply brought a prison sentence. Users were dealt with by administrative courts and encouraged to undergo some form of therapeutic rehabilitation outside the prison system. In 1982 all this changed, as users were no longer encouraged but obliged to undergo therapeutic treatment if they intended to avoid custodial punishment. Processed through the criminal justice system, they could be given house arrest or supervision in the community if they volunteered to attend therapeutic agencies or residential communities. In 1986 the therapeutic choice was dramatically reduced for "recidivists," in the sense that users convicted for the third time could no longer opt for therapy but would incur imprisonment (Solivetti, 1994).

The harsher legislation of 1986 reflected the international war on drugs led by the Bush administration, but was also the result of increasing public alarm over the involvement of organized crime in the production and trafficking of illicit substances (Ruggiero, 1992; Ruggiero and South, 1995). However, the social panic fed by traffickers resulted in more users and small dealers being incarcerated (Ruggiero, 1995). This caused a dramatic congestion of the prison system, with about 30 percent of the prison population being officially described as drug addicts. As for the therapeutic option offered to users charged with an offense, reality soon belied theory. First, users with short sentences may discard therapeutic communities, which they perceive as being as punitive as custody. Moreover, if they face relatively short sentences, they may not bother to apply for therapeutic treatment outside the prison system because by the time their application is processed their sentence may have been fully served. Second, those who predict that their drug using career will continue may calculate that it is unwise to blow the opportunity of non-custodial treatment, from which they can only benefit twice, and may prefer therefore to serve a custodial sentence, while saving therapy for the future. Third, those who are willing to accept rehabilitation in therapeutic communities may just find out that all places in such communities are taken.

As mentioned above, almost one-third of Italian prisoners are described as habitual drug users, while about 10% are HIV positive (Accattatis, 1995; Ruggiero, 1995). According to the prison legislation the "right to health" should be guaranteed in every institution, therefore harm reduction strategies adopted outside should also be available in prison. The debate over the distribution of syringes and condoms in prison is currently very heated, with officers opposing the former for "security" reasons (they fear that prisoners would attack them with blood-stained needles), and some prisoners rejecting the latter for fear of being labeled and consequently bullied as homosexuals (Maisto, 1995). That prisons are not the ideal place for individuals suffering from serious health problems was stipulated by the Italian High Court (Corte Costituzionale) in 1994, when it was established that all HIV-positive prisoners, both convicted and on remand, should be released (Maisto, 1995). Inevitably, sections of public opinion and the media reacted to this by arguing that gangs of HIV-positive criminals would soon roam the streets and perpetrate offenses which, statutorily, could not be prosecuted. Two "AIDS-gangs" are said to be already in operation in Turin, where perpetrators are stigmatized for wanting to live "high" the last years of their life by raiding banks (La Stampa, August 26, 1995; La Stampa, September 16, 1995).

The Extremes of Differential Treatment

In 1994, the prison population in Italy reached 55,000, a record figure in the recent history of the country, and a figure which is double the official capacity of all custodial institutions (Cascini, 1994). About 20 percent were non-nationals, with the majority of these being citizens of African countries (Ministero di Grazia e Giustizia, 1993). The rate of imprisonment of minorities is all the more striking when we consider that non-nationals only form about 2 percent of the total population.

Sections of Italian public opinion would associate immigrants with illegal drug trafficking and dealing, thus sharing a stereotype which is also prevalent in other European countries. That this is indeed a stereotype is shown by official statistics indicating that only 20 percent of non-nationals are serving a sentence for drug offenses. The high percentage of minorities in Italian prison institutions should be explained by looking at a number of cumulative disadvantages that they experience both within and outside the criminal justice process. For example, estimates suggest that half non-nationals are "illegal" immigrants, as they overstay after their visa has expired. Their "illegal" status renders them vulnerable both in the face of employers and in that of the police. If arrested, they have poor legal representation and end up being penalized more harshly than their Italian counterparts (Cottino et al., 1994). Once in prison, they find it harder to benefit from pre-release and other non-custodial forms of treatment. Day release for work, for example, is granted to those who can rely on networks of acquaintances, friends and relatives outside. Minority prisoners can hardly rely on such networks, and many may even ignore the existence of charitable organizations which could support their application for work outside.

Similar disadvantages are experienced by women prisoners, who form about 4 percent of the total prison population (Campelli et al., 1992). About 45 percent of them are serving sentences up to three years, and 75 percent are officially defined as drug addicts. Although the type of offense and the relatively short sentences would suggest that women are in a good position to be granted some forms of alternative punishment, the reality is that this is more difficult to obtain for women than it is for men. Explanations of this incongruence vary, and include suggestions that perhaps women, in particular women drug offenders, are more stigmatized than their male counterparts. It may also be the case that the lifestyle and social condition of women offenders is regarded as less "amenable" to rehabilitation, because the majority of women in prison are more economically disadvantaged than male prisoners, and because they often lack support from family members, partners, friends and agencies which could facilitate their rehabilitation in the community (Ruggiero, 1995).

Women and minorities occupy one of the extremes of differential prison treatment in Italy, a condition which they share with other vulnerable prisoners whose lifestyles makes them "untrustworthy."

Take the example of younger offenders, who are usually single and are therefore deemed more unreliable. Because it is assumed that they bear no responsibility for dependents and that theirs is an "irregular" and unpredictable conduct, "young first-time offenders may be treated worse than consummate recidivists" (Ruggiero, 1995: 63). An example of the other extreme of differential treatment, which indeed concerns "consummate recidivists," is provided by corrupt politicians who began to experience Italian prisons in the early 1990s. Most of these are released after a brief "taste" of imprisonment as their social dangerousness is deemed negligible. A new piece of legislation passed in August 1995 stipulated that for all offenses which bring sentences of less than four years, remand in custody could be reduced to one month. All politicians were released, amid sensational protests from other prisoners and their relatives, including clashes between the police and prisoners' wives in Naples (La Repubblica, August 4, 1995).

Ironically, this new legislation on remand permitting the release of corrupt politicians and businessmen was also the result of long-standing pressure from prison reform groups and prisoners' organizations. Given that almost half the prison population in Italy was on remand, it was suggested that entire sectors of the judicial process were in danger of disappearing. Let us explain why. The trial was no longer ascertaining guilt and determining sentences, because both processes were in fact carried out before the trial itself took place. The phenomenally high percentage of prisoners on remand indicated the enormous power wielded by investigative judges who, pending court hearing, could decide whether a defendant could be released and when. This practice of punishing defendants "in advance" ran parallel with the decline of the power of courts, which were often faced with cases already dealt with, and with defendants already "punished," by investigative judges. The final pronunciation of guilt and the determination of the appropriate penalty were becoming redundant: The trial itself no longer existed (Fassone, 1994).

INSTITUTIONAL AND MATERIAL FUNCTIONS OF IMPRISONMENT

The Italian prison system is characterized by a high degree of differentiation and flexibility, whereby elements of rehabilitation coexist with elements of retribution. I have tried to show how these two sets of elements are interconnected, and how the recourse to retribution for some is commonly justified as the price to pay if rehabilitation for others is to be pursued. This paradox is part of the effort made by official commentators to preserve an image of the prison system based on Beccarian principles. The prison system as described above is the result of an ideological reconciliation of punishment within a tradition in which the word punishment itself is officially banned. I have mentioned how the concept of dangerousness is utilized in such an ideological fashion and how it feeds the myth of rehabilitation even in the face of "special" forms of prison treatment. In the remaining part of this chapter I would like to develop the analysis of flexibility and the coexistence of rehabilitation and "special" treatment further. Leaving aside the official interpretations of punishment, this final discussion will focus on the its latent function. This analysis relates to the debate engaged in Italy during the course of the 1970s, when the first high security units for prisoners were established. The replacement of high security units with "special" surveillance and treatment does not make that debate obsolete, rather it makes it a useful starting point for the analysis of the current prison situation.

Broadly distinguishing critical approaches to the analysis of punishment, two extreme positions can be observed: the former emphasizes the *institutional function* of imprisonment, while the latter emphasizes its *material function*. The first is embedded in the notion of retribution and, in its extreme manifestations, presides over the destruction of bodies. The second pertains to the productive use of bodies. Of course, analyses adopting a mixed approach to punishment are numerous, but it may be important here to focus on these two extreme positions and regard them as ideal-typical. In order to locate this debate, reference must be made to two classics of the respective approaches: Rusche and Kirchheimer on the one hand, Michel Foucault on the other. According to Rusche and Kirchheimer, both individual and the general deterrence pertain to the *material* sphere of society and are addressed to the classes which are the potential clientele of the prison system. The treatment of offenders, in other words, is to be analyzed against the background of the productive process and the labor market. Therefore, during depressions and with a labor surplus, there is a lowering of salaries and a correspondent deterioration of prison conditions. Ideally, this surplus labor should be destroyed, as should other commodities whose availability on the market is excessive. Consequently, the prison population, which is a sector of the surplus labor force, can also be destroyed. Prison conditions become more severe because they must be less eligible than the worst possible condition outside (Rusche and Kirchheimer, 1939). Conversely, in periods when the commodity of labor is scarce, its reproduction becomes of crucial importance for the productive process, and as a consequence prison conditions will improve. Even offenders, in such circumstances, will be "persuaded" to become productive.

On the other hand, according to what I define as the institutional approach, typified by the work of Foucault, prison constitutes the emblem of the modern disciplinary universe; it is a metaphor which is less addressed to prisoners themselves than to society as a whole. Foucault's analysis of the Panopticon is widely known, but it is worth revisiting in order to locate his argument within what I have artificially characterized as an institutional approach. The major effect of the Panopticon, in Foucault's view, is "to induce in the inmate a state of conscious and permanent visibility that assures the automatic functioning of power" (1977: 201). Surveillance must be permanent in its effects, even though it can be discontinuous in its actions: Power should tend to make its own actual exercise unnecessary, while rendering itself independent of those who exercise it. Let us identify one aspect of Foucault's thinking that helps our analysis.

A two-way current is set up between dominators and dominated. That is, there exists an interaction between the two poles of the disciplinary universe, without which the mechanism itself could not function. This principle is already present in Bentham's architectural-institutional paradigm, in which a certain arrangement of space is expected to induce an internalization of power and norms: Self-discipline is expected to lead to the self-management of norms. Coercion, ideally, should be exercised by prisoners on themselves. This metaphor aims to describe and explore the "much wider (and more contemporary) theme of how domination is achieved and individuals are socially constructed in the modern world" (Garland, 1990: 134). To establish whether this is achieved by means of physical violence or by the manipulation of the mind is otiose, the focus of Foucault's argument being the subjects to whom this metaphor is directed rather than the more or less brutal forms of coercion addressed to them. To Foucault, the clientele of prison is not simply formed by citizens as productive beings, but by citizens as citizens, therefore as emotional, social, sexual beings who interact with the institutions, with one another and with their own "knowledge." These beings do not only occupy a position in the productive process, but also in the power diagram which holds society together.

When high security institutions were first created in the mid-1970s in Italy, many wondered where this "anomalous" form of punishment came from. How could diverse forms of treatment and unequal intensities of punishment coexist in the same prison system? And what was the purpose of such an overt bypassing of the constitutional principle of equal treatment of all offenders carried out by the very supporters of the constitution?

The analytical responses to these dilemmas covered a wide range of the political spectrum. According to some groups of political prisoners on the Left, the rationale of maximum security institutions was only accountable for in terms of political warfare. Prison performed a strictly *institutional function*. The new regime, in its most brutal manifestation, was prompted by purely military necessity— the state had to destroy its armed enemies. In this view, the existence of a military machinery of punishment within legality testified to a social war in progress (Collettivo Prigionieri Politici, 1978; 1983).

In the opinion of some moderate scholars, high security prisons, despite their outstanding destructive overtones, were to be interpreted in the context of a so-called period of emergency. When social unrest subsides, it was suggested, more congruent forms of punishment based on Beccarian principles would once again be adequately devised (Magistratura Democratica, 1979). Again, this interpretation emphasized the *institutional* aspects of imprisonment, and omitted the consideration of any relationship between punishment and the economic sphere.

According to some socialist commentators, on the other hand, the high security model represented a major tendency towards the development of unreformable prisons, a hard-core of "institutional abduction" (Pavarini, 1986). In their opinion, other forms of control were operating simultaneously, based on ethnic segregation, cultural and social isolation, which made "soft" forms of punishment redundant (Melossi, 1980). In this view all prisons were destined to become high security establishments, their *institutional function*, associated with the destruction of prisoners, being tendentially prevailing in all Western penal systems.

The much discussed concept of bifurcation also gained some attention in this debate. This concept was introduced in Italy when the political movements of the Left reached their peak (Melossi and Pavarini, 1977). In the Italian context, particularly harsh sentences were imposed either upon members of armed political groups or members of organized crime, while a relatively reduced severity, or even decarceration, was the response to other offenses. The persistence of the former types of offenders, however, allowed this apparent bifurcation to exist, though the very same prisoners could experience both harsh and lenient punishment depending on their "behavioral career" as prisoners. Contrary to the analysis of Bottoms (1977), it became clear that bifurcation did not describe a characteristic trait of the prison system vis-à-vis two different types of offenders, but rather a dual possibility faced by all offenders. I shall return to this point.

According to successive specifications, it is inappropriate to draw a neat line between harshness and leniency, with the first characterizing punishment for serious offenders and the second treatment of "ordinary" offenders. Trends observed in many European countries indicate that the latter are met with increasing degrees of severity, even though they are punished in the "community" (Hudson, 1993). Disciplinary aspects and the emphasis on surveillance are becoming inescapable traits of "alternative" penalties to the point that the very survival of non-custodial alternatives could be put in danger if these traits were to disappear (Ruggiero et al., 1995). However, this analysis also seems to center on purely *institutional aspects* of punishment, focused as it is on the intensity of pain delivered by the penal system, whether in closed or in open environments. In this analysis one cannot avoid detecting a very orthodox view of the state, whereby the central locus of control resides in paramilitary institutions such as the prison system and the police, with both devoted to the management and repression of the "working class." This argument fails to consider the segmentation, competition and the diverse forms of identity which are found within the "working class," and overlooks how these are constituted by many forms of internal, and even internalized, social control. Moreover, while implicitly evoking Marxism, this analysis leaves aside a central Marxist concept, namely that the strongest source of social control in our society is to be found in the wage relationship itself (van Krieken, 1991). The power of penal and social control outside the prison walls is not to be forgotten.

THE CARCERAL SOCIAL ZONE

I have mentioned that analyses of punishment which utilize a mixed approach—that is, analyses which emphasize both institutional and material functions—are numerous. I would like to pursue this further. *The contemporary prison system in Italy can be identified as a synthesis of both the institutional and the material function.* Although the former seems to be prevailing, the latter is far from having become redundant. The institutional function is undergoing a technical evolution and manifests itself in the metaphorical annihilation of those prisoners who are deemed impervious to treatment. The material function, in turn, is also undergoing wide modification. We can still employ the term "material" because it conjures up a notion of productivity, but suggest that it should not be assimilated to the notion of the workhouse nor with that of "prison as factory" of early capitalism. Prisoners' work and exploitation are mainly to be found beyond the prison walls, notably in those social areas where marginalized activities and precarious jobs intermingle with overtly illegal activities. We could term these areas the *carceral social zone* to which a variety of forms of control and punishment are addressed, including, when softer forms prove unsuccessful, the threat of maximum security confinement and the consequent physical and mental destruction. In such a system, the general and individual deterrent roles of punishment are not only directed to highly politicized prisoners or to serious offenders but to the marginalized, underemployed and unemployed populations which characterize contemporary societies. One should consider that the different degrees of severity which inform the prison system are organized in a continuum rather than set in a bifurcation. Lenient punishments, in other words, can evolve into increasingly harsh ones when prisoners refuse to conform. The rationale of leniency, therefore, cannot be understood if it is divorced from the existence of severity. It is the combination of the two, or rather the potential use of different degrees of leniency and harshness, which constitute the synthesis between institutional and material functions of imprisonment.

As for the material function of imprisonment itself, this is now addressed to the precarious labor force, namely that *carceral social zone* identified above which hosts the marginalized, the underemployed, the occasional workers, the petty criminals and all others whose lifestyle and economic activity straddle legality and illegality.

This section of the population is "trained" to remain and survive in the carceral social zone like its counterpart in the past centuries was "trained" to the discipline of industrialism. Prison discipline aims at lowering their social expectations, an aspect which leads us back to the notion of rehabilitation. Leaving aside Beccarian myths and the techniques of neutralization which attempt to revive them, prisoners are deemed rehabilitated when they accept to stay in that specific sector of the working class which inhabits the social carceral zone. To mobilize overarching definitions such as "the working class" is to miss an important distinction. Ironically, one is regarded as rehabilitated when one accepts to work in precarious activities, in underpaid jobs, and last but not least, by implication, in the criminal economy. Of course, to accept this analysis implies the consideration of crime as one of the other occupational options available to this specific sector of the working class (Ruggiero and South, 1995).

In conclusion, this interpretation is consistent with the existence, in Italy and elsewhere, of a large labor force involved in casual work and/or in illegal economic activities. This "criminal labor force," and the adjacent marginalized labor force, constitute the "repository" of the prison population, the human reserve upon which custody, with its diverse degrees of harshness and rehabilitive rhetoric, projects its shadow.

References

Accattatis, V. (1995) "Diritti o barbarie." *Il Manifesto Mese*, 3: 37–8.

Bandini, T. (1987) "La valutazione clinica della pericolosità social." *Questione Giustizia*, 3: 697–704.

Beccaria, C. (1970) *Dei delitti e delle pene*. Turin: Utet.

Bonger, W.A. (1936) *An Introduction to Criminology*. London: Methuen.

Bottoms, A. (1977) "Reflections on the Renaissance of Dangerousness." *Howard Journal*, 16: 70–97.

Bottoms, A. and Preston, R.H. (eds.) (1980) *The Coming Penal Crisis*. Edinburgh: Scottish Academic Press.

Bricola, F. (1975) "Politica criminale e politica penale dell'ordine pubblico." *La Questione Criminale*, 1: 221–88.

Bruti Liberati, E. (1987) "Dieci anni di riforma penitenziaria." *Questione Giustizia*, 3: 611–24.

Campelli, E., Faccioli, F., Giordano, V. and Pitch, T. (1992) *Donne in carcere*. Milan: Feltrinelli.

Canosa, R. (1976) "La polizia italiana nel sistema repressivo occidentale." *Quaderni Piacentini*, XV: 81–96.

Cascini, G. (1994) "Carcere e processo penale." *Questione Giustizia*, XIII: 536–46.

Ciardiello, P. (1995) "Operatori sociali penitenziari tra discrezionalità e diritti." *Tracce*, I: 27–8.

Collettivo Prigionieri Politici. (1978) *Speciale Asinara. La settimana rossa*. Catania: Anarchismo.

Collettivo Prigionieri Politici. (1983) *L'albero del peccato*. Paris: FRAP.

Cottino, A., Sarzotti, C. and Tibaldi, C. (1994) "Uguaglianza di fronte alla legge penale." *Dei Delitti e delle Pene*, IV: 121–62.

Curcio, R. (1993) *A viso aperto*. Milan: Mondadori.

Duff, A. and Garland, D. (eds.) (1994) *A Reader on Punishment*. Oxford: Oxford University Press.

Ellero, P. (1879) *La tirannide borghese*. Bologna: Archivio Giuridico.

Eusebi, L. (ed.) (1989) *La funzione della pena: il commiato da Kant e da Hegel*. Milan: Giuffré.

Fassone, E. (1994) "Il processo che non c'é," *Questione Giustizia*, XIII: 521–35.

Ferrajoli, L. (1989) *Diritto e ragione. Teoria del garantismo penale*. Rome-Bari: Laterza.

Ferri, E. (1929) *Sociologia criminale*. Turin: Utet.

Foucault, M. (1977) *Discipline and Punish*. London: Allen Lane.

Gallo, E. and Ruggiero, V. (1991) "The Immaterial Prison: Custody as a Factory for the Manufacture of Handicaps." *International Journal of the Sociology of Law*, 19: 273–91.

Garland, D. (1990) *Punishment and Modern Society*. Oxford: Oxford University Press.

Haapanen, R.A. (1990) *Selective Incapacitation and Serious Offenders*. New York: Springler-Verlag.

Hegel, F. (1949) *Filosofia del diritto*. Turin: Utet.

Hudson, B. (1987) *Justice Through Punishment*. Basingstoke: Macmillan.

Hudson, B. (1993) *Penal Policy and Social Justice*. Basingstoke: Macmillan.

ISTAT (Istituto Nazionale di Statistica). (1995) *Statistiche Giudiziarie.* Rome: Poligrafico dello Stato.

Kant, I. (1963) *Metafisica della morale.* Florence: Nuova Italia.

La Repubblica. (1995) "Niente pi manette facili." August 4.

La Stampa. (1995) "Banda dell'Aids, manette ai replicanti." August 26.

La Stampa. (1995) "Colpisce ancora la banda dell'Aids". September 16.

Magistratura Democratica. (1979) *Il carcere dopo le riforme.* Milan: Feltrinelli.

Maisto, F. (1995) "Le gabbie dell'inciviltà," *Il Manifesto Mese,* 3: 39–40.

Mansfield, M. (1993) *Presumed Guilty. The British Legal System Exposed.* London: Mandarin.

Melossi, D. (1980) "Oltre il Panopticon." *La Questione Criminale,* VI: 277–362.

Melossi, D. (1990) *The State of Social Control.* Cambridge: Polity.

Melossi, D. and Pavarini, M. (1977) *Carcere e fabbrica.* Bologna: Il Mulino.

Ministero di Grazia e Giustizia. (1993) *Libro Bianco. I dati essenziali del sistema penitenziario italiano in cifre.* Rome: Poligrafico dello Stato.

Moretti, M. (1994) *Brigate Rosse. Una storia italiana.* Milan: Anabasi.

Mosconi, G. (1991) "La controriforma carceraria." *Dei Delitti e delle Pene,* II: 141–52.

Neppi Modona, G. (1973) "Carcere e società civile," in Various Authors, *Storia d'Italia.* Turin: Einaudi.

Neppi Modona, G. (1976) "Appunti per una storia parlamentare della riforma penitenziaria." *La Questione Criminale,* II: 319–72.

Padovani, T. (1990) *Diritto Penale.* Milan: Giuffré.

Pavarini, M. (1986) "Fuori dalle mura del carcere: la dislocazione dell'ossessione correzionale." *Dei Delitti e delle Pene,* 2: 251–76.

Pavarini, M. (1994a) "The New Penology and Politics in Crisis: The Italian Case." *British Journal of Criminology,* (special issue), 34: 49–61.

Pavarini, M. (1994b) *Lo scambio penitenziario.* Bologna: Martina.

Rinaldi, S. (1987) "Ordine pubblico e criminalità nel dibattito della sinistra giuridica," *Dei Delitti e delle Pene,* 5: 61–119.

Ruggiero, V. (1992) *La roba. Economie e culture dell'eroina*. Parma: Pratiche.

Ruggiero, V. (1993) "Sentenced to Normality: The Italian Political Refugees in Paris," *Crime, Law & Social Change*, 19: 33–50.

Ruggiero, V. (1995) "Flexibility and Intermittent Emergency in the Italian Penal System," in V. Ruggiero, M. Ryan and J. Sim (eds.) *Western European Penal Systems*. London: Sage.

Ruggiero, V. and South, N. (1995) *Eurodrugs. Drug Use, Markets and Trafficking in Europe*. London: University College London Press.

Ruggiero, V., Ryan, M. and Sim, J. (eds.) (1995) *Western European Penal Systems*. London: Sage.

Rusche, G. and Kirchheimer, O. (1939) *Punishment and Social Structure*. New York: Russell & Russell.

Sighele, S. (1911). *La crisi dell'infanzia e la delinquenza dei minorenni*. Florence: Rinascita del Libro.

Solivetti, L. (1994) "Drug Diffusion and Social Change: The Illusion about a Formal Social Control." *Howard Journal*, 33: 41–61.

Van Krieken, R. (1991) "The Poverty of Social Control: Explaining Power in the Historical Sociology of the Welfare State." *The Sociological Review*, 39: 1–25.

von Hirsch, A. (1985) *Past or Future Crimes*. Manchester: Manchester University Press.

Zimring, F.E. and Hawkins, G. (1995) *Incapacitation: Penal Confinement and the Restraint of Crime*. New York: Oxford University Press.

Chapter
EIGHT

Germany: Ups and Downs in the Resort to Imprisonment— Strategic or Unplanned Outcomes?

Johannes Feest and
Hartmut-Michael Weber

The following analysis investigates the "ups" and "downs" of imprisonment in Germany as regards their main characteristics. Our understanding of ups and downs, however, is not limited to mere quantitative aspects of prison contraction and expansion. It covers also the corresponding institutional and ideological background. Therefore, it is concerned, too, with qualitative ups and downs as they are reflected in penal ideology, in prison leaves and prisoners' rights.

INSTITUTIONAL AND IDEOLOGICAL BACKGROUND

The German developments to be described here must be seen in the context of three main factors. Firstly, there is a specific institutional

233

division of labor between federal legislation and the several states' implementation which provides certain diversities. In the second place, ideological contradictions within penal philosophy and between penal and prison philosophy contributed both to a powerful judicial discretion and to a compromise of "rehabilitative" prison philosophy which coincided with an unwillingness of politicians and some prison administrations to implement the Prison Act of 1976. Last but not least, the context of German separation and unification plays an important role in understanding the most recent developments, ranging from the Western colonization of the East German prison policy up to changes at the political level, based on a crisis at the economic level.

Institutional Division of Labor

Federal Republic of Germany penal legislation (including legislation on prisons) is a matter for federal legislation. But, whatever the legislature decides is then implemented by state police forces, state prosecutors' offices, state courts and state prison administrations. While the police forces belong to the jurisdiction of the Interior Ministers, the administration of criminal justice (including the prison administration) is coordinated by the Ministers of Justice.

There are a few exceptions to this institutional arrangement: In the context of terrorism, drug trafficking and, more recently, "organized crime," the federal government has been building up competing police forces, mainly the Federal Criminal Investigation Office ("Bundeskriminalamt") and the Federal Border Police ("Bundesgrenzschutz"), and has strengthened the position of the Federal Prosecution Agency ("Bundesanwaltschaft").

But, in general, and for the large number of cases, it is still true that the federal government has nothing to do with the day-to-day running of police forces, prosecution agencies, criminal courts or prisons. As a consequence, one finds considerable differences between regional and local legal cultures. At the level of the prison system, the inability of the federal government to influence prison conditions has recently become a problem vis-à-vis the Council of Europe's prison inspectors (cf. Feest and Wolters, 1994).

Ideological Contradictions

There is a wide gap between the philosophy of punishment as laid down in the German Penal Code of 1871 and the philosophy of the Prison Act of 1976, which is supposed to govern prison administration. The traditional philosophy of punishment is based on the (non-utilitarian) compensation of the "guilt" of the offender (as performed in the offense) and has been modernized through amalgamations with utilitarian (preventative) purposes. Nevertheless, compensation of "guilt" (retribution, justice) can be seen as the predominant concept of punishment. The prevailing concept of the Prison Act, on the contrary, is the preventative rehabilitative idea. Given this gap, one could have foreseen opposing discourses about the rehabilitative idea, which is rather incompatible with the philosophy of guilt. Given, furthermore, the general crisis of utilitarian purposes of imprisonment and in particular huge lacks in the implementation of the Prison Act, we can imagine that rehabilitation came under much pressure in Germany.

However, the most important consequence of the "guilt"-amalgamations, on the one hand, and of the gap between penal and prison philosophy, on the other hand, is the huge and not calculable discretion of the judges. In turn, this discretion may also be responsible for the remarkable variations of German sentencing and imprisonment rates. Some words should be said with regard to this gap for a better understanding of recent prison policy.

Penal philosophy: "Guilt" and its amalgamations with preventative purposes According to the Penal Code of 1871 ("Strafgesetzbuch"), the sentence has to be commensurate with the "guilt" of the offender. This means that the sentence has to be an equivalent compensation for the amount of guilt the offender has demonstrated by committing the offense. The concept "compensation of guilt" can be seen as a modernized kind of "good old retribution." It has therefore been criticized and denounced by some reformers as an individualized projection of blame on the offender, which ignores and even hides the contribution of social structural forces. But over more than one century, the view has prevailed that individual guilt should be at the core of the criminal justice system. At the same time, guilt considerations have been increasingly combined with and superseded by preventative ideas. This development resulted inter alia in amendments of the Penal Code in 1975 saying that not only the "guilt" of the offender is the basis for meting out the sentence, but that the judge has also to take into account the effects of the punishment on the future life of the offender in the society (cf. Article 46 Penal Code). A brief analysis of the leading German doctrines with respect to punishment in general and sentencing in particular may be helpful to understand this development as well as its pitfalls.

The so-called "amalgamation doctrine of the goals of punishment" ("Vereinigungstheorie der Strafzwecke") serves as the main theoretical background for legitimizing imprisonment and supposes that not only the compensation of guilt shall be emphasized, but that also the other penal purposes, such as prevention, rehabilitation of the offender, expiation and retribution for the unlawful act, shall be recognized as aspects of a proper penal sanction. This doctrine was specifically reinforced for life imprisonment by a 1977 decision of the Federal Constitutional Court ("Bundesverfassungsgericht").[1] On the other hand, there are some objections to the possible impression that the doctrine means just a combination of all those purposes.

Firstly, in 1977 and in later decisions the Constitutional Court emphasized the principle of guilt, so much so that it has taken priority over the other purposes. Secondly, in 1992 the Constitutional Court made clear in another decision regarding life imprisonment that—as to the compensation of guilt—each lifer's term should be commuted into a determinate term. However, this was and still is a most difficult task for the courts which review the terms of the lifers because the Constitutional Court did not set an upper limit for life imprisonment. As an example, in 1993 a judicial panel ("Strafvollstreckungskammer am Landgericht") set a "guilt"-tariff of 50 years for a person who had already served 35 years and whose life expectation, because of cancer, was seen by doctors as not more than another five years.[2] Thirdly, the preventative term to be served for reasons of "dangerousness" (risk assessment) may still exceed the guilt-tariff. The Constitutional Court never withdrew its opinion that it would be in accord with the Constitution to keep "dangerous" lifers in prison until the end of their lives. Therefore, we can conclude that both the compensation of guilt and the protection of the public are the most decisive penal purposes.

The so-called "guilt range doctrine" ("Spielraumtheorie") argues that the judicial determination of guilt does not result in only one possible sentence, but provides preventative discretion between an upper and lower limit of guilt (retribution), i.e. within this "guilt range." This doctrine, although an amalgamation too, can be seen rather in contrast to the amalgamation doctrine because it provides discretion only *within* the limits of guilt. The amalgamation doctrine, on the other hand, provides preventative discretion *exceeding* the upper limit of guilt (in the case of life imprisonment).

The guilt range doctrine was criticized heavily because the courts define lower and upper limits on such a large scale that preventative purposes could gain importance rather arbitrarily (cf. Schünemann, 1987: 209). But the Federal Supreme Court ("Bundesgerichtshof") has used this doctrine since the 1950s to give the judges discretion in gauging sentences.[3]

This relatively strong traditional emphasis of German criminal law doctrine on making the punishment fit the crime is often thought to be very much in line with "neoclassical" thinking. On the other hand, the guilt range doctrine is heavily criticized by advocates of neoclassicism because it would not be in accord with justice and the principle of commensurability (between the seriousness of the offense and the severity of the sentence) if, only for reasons of prevention, an offender who committed a less serious offense was sentenced more harshly than an offender who committed a graver offense (cf. v. Hirsch/Jareborg, 1991: 23). The traditional German guilt doctrine is also different from the neoclassical approach insofar as German penal law traditionally provides very long sentences and German judges mete out rather long sentences, whereas from a neoclassical point of view the sentencing system should provide rather short, fair and calculable sentences.

Summarizing the typical features of the German penal ideology, we would like to draw attention to the point that the predominant concept of guilt serves as a powerful background for a penal system producing substantial scope for discretion of the judges and—last not but not least—widening this discretion through its amalgamations with preventative purposes.

Compensation of "guilt" and its contradiction to "resocializing" imprisonment The (West) German Prison Act of 1976 ("Strafvollzugsgesetz") is influenced by the Scandinavian and Dutch treatment philosophy of the 1960s. The idea of correction by rehabilitation is explicitly voiced as the "goal of imprisonment": "In the course of imprisonment, the prisoner shall be enabled to lead the future life in social responsibility and without reoffending (goal of imprisonment)" (Article 2 Prison Act). All prisons must, in theory, contribute to this normative purpose of "resocialization."

Only secondarily and, as many scholars claim, only through resocialization, the German Prison Act foresees that *protection of the
public* shall also be achieved by imprisonment. During the 1980s,
however, the penal purpose "compensation of guilt" began more
and more to impinge on and to compromise the rehabilitation idea.
This was pushed by at least some of the prison administrations and
facilitated by a ruling of the Constitutional Court in 1983.[4]

This ruling again showed the importance of the concept of guilt
in the light of an oscillating jurisdiction of the Constitutional Court.
As late as 1973, this court ruled that resocialization should get priority in the implementation of imprisonment and compensation of
guilt should be placed subordinate to resocialization. In 1977, the
court decided in accord with its ruling of 1973 that lifers also were
entitled to participate in resocialization. On the other hand, the
Constitutional Court ruled in 1983 that the prison administrators
were entitled to take into account the particular gravity of guilt as
shown in the offense if they decide on leaves of absence. It also held
that in cases of very high guilt, it would not violate the Constitution
to have a life sentence served for the remainder of the offenders'
life, i.e. until his death. Although these decisions concerned two
Nazi criminals serving life imprisonment for multiple murder, they
had an immediate impact on other lifers and even on prisoners
serving determinate sentences.

As we can see, the concept of guilt and the compensation of guilt
had an important impact on compromising resocialization as the
only normative goal of imprisonment. On the other hand, it cannot
be said that the compensation of guilt overruled resocialization.
Rather, it contributed to watering down a concept which was never
fully implemented.

*The prison act, its non-implementation and the discourses on the
rehabilitative idea* The Prison Act 1976 was widely seen as a
blueprint for a humane reform of imprisonment. But, in practice, it
turned out much earlier that the Finance Ministers were not about
to provide the necessary funds for implementing some of the rehabilitative provisions of the Prison Act. This non-implementation
happened although the Constitutional Court ruled that the state
was obliged to provide the prison system with the budget necessary to realize resocialization.[5] "Indeed, reform in the old Federal
Republic has remained an empty shell, if one thinks about remuneration for prisoners in relation to their work performance or

about their inclusion in general health and pension insurance schemes" (Dünkel, 1995: 96). But as we have already seen, the Act's rehabilitative goals were also compromised by the court-initiated introduction of guilt-considerations into the prison system. Additionally, there also have been other shortcomings which shall be explored later.

It seems useful at this point to distinguish among three reformist discourses with respect to the Prison Act. The first one, a positive reformist discourse (still rather popular among liberal politicians and academics), led to demands for proper implementation of the Prison Act. In this context it was argued that rehabilitation was an important organizing idea for "humanizing" prisons and for getting the required funds. The second one, a negative reformist one (mostly led by abolitionists), was aimed at delegitimizing both the idea and practice of rehabilitation. It criticized the coercive character of rehabilitation, the poor legal status of prisoners and the arbitrariness of the prison administrations' use of discretion. It argued for a reduction if not abolition of imprisonment.

Taking into account that Germany was and is one of the countries with the longest prison sentences in Europe, there was a third debate which cannot easily be classified in terms of either a positive or negative reformist discourse. It was a discussion of short and fair sentencing according to the "just deserts" approach (cf. v. Hirsch, 1976). Some abolitionists argued that such a shift in penal policy could be an interim step towards a complete renegation of prison sentences. Others saw the renaissance of proportionality thinking in Europe, however, as a "transatlantic misunderstanding" (Weigend, 1982). They assumed that the "nothing works-ism" of the United States was not applicable to most of the European countries and were afraid that a withdrawal from the rehabilitative idea would bring about a dehumanization of imprisonment. One could counterargue that shorter sentences would at least result in less grave detrimental effects of imprisonment.

German Separation and Unification

In what follows, we will deal primarily with the old Federal Republic of Germany. This is due to the fact that we still do not know much about the workings of prisons in the former German Democratic Republic. From what we do know, however, it seems, possible to distinguish between a police state approach to prisons on the one hand, and a welfare state approach on the other hand, working concurrently in the German Democratic Republic (Arnold, 1995).

It is easy to show that East German prisons were run on a police model. They belonged to the jurisdiction of the Interior Ministry (not taking into account a number of special prisons run by the Ministry of State Security, the infamous "Stasi"); the Prison Act (of 1977) was not to be given to prisoners; there was no possibility for prisoners to ask for court review of administrative decisions; internal regulations gave guards sweeping discretion to discipline prisoners. Furthermore, the material conditions in East German prisons were, in many respects (cell space, medical care, etc.) not in accordance with the Standard Minimum Rules of the United Nations.

It should not be overlooked, however, that there was also another side to this: Every prisoner in the GDR had the right to work and this not just on paper, but in actual practice. And while the wages of prisoners where only about 18 percent of those outside, this was and is quite above the international average. There was a separate Reintegration Act, which envisaged far-reaching government measures promoting resocialization (accommodation and job offers, etc.), and society at large was expected to assist in this task. While many of these great goals were watered-down in practice, it should not be forgotten that there were "citizens who tried honestly and devotedly, in work collectives, as members of local authorities or as volunteers, to make the resocialization approach work" (Arnold, 1995: 86).

Since October 3, 1990, the day of German unification, all East German prisons have come under the authority of the newly established States of Brandenburg, Mecklenburg-Vorpommern, Sachsen, Sachsen-Anhalt and Thüringen. The (West) German Prison Act is now the legal basis for all German prisons. Most German prisoners in all parts of Germany are now getting the same low wages and no social benefits. Only those chosen few, who have been accepted into a work furlough program, receive normal wages and benefits.

We would like to emphasize that—also as to penal theory and practice—the term "unification" may not characterize correctly what happened after October 3, 1990. The GDR acceded to the FRG like a new member to an old club and had to "forget" its specific features, even positive ones like remuneration of prisoners' labor or societal support as to their reintegration after release. Western representatives of the criminal justice system have argued the superiority of their system in comparison to the Eastern system, but forget both the shortcomings of the Western and possible advantages of the Eastern system.

TWENTY-FIVE YEARS OF CONTRADICTORY DEVELOPMENT

Looking back at about the last 25 years, there are many contradictory developments regarding German prisons. We will pick out three for closer inspection: prison contraction and expansion, prison leaves, and prisoners' rights.

Prison Contraction and Expansion

The West German prison population has always been among the highest in Europe since the Second World War. But there have been a number of significant ups and downs. For most of the 1960s, the imprisonment rate (number of prisoners per 100,000 of the population) was consistently above 100. In 1968 it was 100.4 (see Table 1, Column A). This rate was brought down to an all-time low of 75.5 in 1970, and 75.7 in 1971 as an effect of the Criminal Law Reform of 1969, which was promoted by the federal government (cf. Feest, 1982). This low was mostly due to the extremely low rate of sentenced prisoners in the same years (55.4 in 1970 and 51.0 in 1971, see Table 1, Column C).

The 1969 reform was mostly influenced by the resocialization idea. It was argued that short-term prison sentences should be avoided because they separated offenders from their usual social and economic conditions of living. Short-term imprisonment would counteract the rehabilitation effort. Therefore, the reform discouraged "short-term" prison sentences of less than six months. On the other hand, there was the idea that offenders who committed serious crimes were in need of more—and time consuming!—rehabilitation.

For a more detailed analysis, we should look first to the developments between 1970/71 (the year of the all-time low) and 1983, the year with the absolute peak of the general imprisonment rate (101.4, see Table 1, Column A). In accord with its above aims the reform resulted first in an impressive drop of the rates of persons sentenced to prison sentences, from 33.9 percent of all sentenced persons in 1968, to 15.5 percent in 1970 (16.0 in 1971), and remained rather constant until 1983 (17.8 percent, see Table 2, Column C).

TABLE 1 Prison Population, Rates Calculated from Average Numbers. "Old" Federal Republic of Germany (1968–1995), "New" States ("Länder") in Italics (1991–1995). Rates per 100,000 of Inhabitants

Year	A All Prisoners		B Remand Prisoners		C Sentenced Prisoners		D Others*	
1968	100.4		21.4		78.9		./.	
1969	87.9		19.2		68.6		./.	
1970	75.5		20.1		55.4		./.	
1971	75.7		22.0		51.0		2.7	
1972	82.8		24.5		55.3		3.0	
1973	84.7		25.1		56.5		3.1	
1974	85.1		25.4		56.9		2.9	
1975	84.3		24.5		56.8		3.0	
1976	85.2		23.4		58.8		2.9	
1977	87.4		23.3		61.2		2.8	
1978	88.8		22.2		63.8		2.8	
1979	88.9		22.3		63.8		2.8	
1980	90.9		23.6		64.5		2.8	
1981	93.3		24.8		65.7		2.8	
1982	99.5		26.6		70.1		2.8	
1983	101.4		25.0		73.6		2.8	
1984	99.7		22.6		74.4		2.6	
1985	95.4		20.6		72.4		2.4	
1986	88.0		19.0		66.7		2.3	
1987	84.1		18.9		62.8		2.4	
1988	83.5		19.2		61.9		2.5	
1989	82.3		19.6		60.3		2.3	
1990	80.1		21.0		56.7		2.4	
1991	76.9	*18.9*	22.5	*11.2*	51.9	*6.9*	2.5	*0.8*
1992	80.0	*27.3*	24.2	*14.1*	52.7	*11.8*	3.1	*1.4*
1993	87.1	*42.9*	27.7	*19.4*	54.4	*20.3*	5.0	*3.2*
1994	88.2	*54.0*	26.7	*21.9*	56.1	*28.2*	5.4	*3.9*

Calculated from unpublished statistics of the Federal Ministry of Justice ("Bundesjustizministerium"), Bonn. Since 1991, figures for the "old" Federal Republic include also the territory of former East Berlin. The rates for the New States (Former GDR) comprise all the five states for 1992, 1993 and 1994. For 1991 they cover only four states (without the State of Brandenburg, lack of data).
*Persons detained according to the Military Penal Code, non-German nationals detained for expulsion, persons serving secure preventative detention (as a 'measure', not as a punishment).

TABLE 2 Rates of Sentenced Persons and Rates of Persons Sentenced to Imprisonment. "Old" Federal Republic of Germany (1968–1993), Rates per 100,000 of Inhabitants

Year	A Total Persons Sentenced (All Sentences)	B Persons Sentenced to Imprisonment	C Persons Sentenced to Imprisonment in Percent of A	D Persons Sentenced to a Suspended Prison Sentence in Percent of B
1968	1084	368	33.9	36.1
1969	1016	279	27.5	47.0
1970	1046	162	15.5	53.1
1971	1091	175	16.0	54.3
1972	1120	182	16.3	56.0
1973	1128	181	16.0	58.6
1974	1127	195	17.3	60.0
1975	1075	178	16.6	60.7
1976	1137	189	16.6	61.9
1977	1179	195	16.5	63.6
1978	1205	202	16.8	63.9
1979	1172	198	16.9	64.6
1980	1190	200	16.8	65.0
1981	1212	208	17.2	65.4
1982	1253	224	17.9	64.3
1983	1278	228	17.8	64.9
1984	1231	223	18.1	65.0
1985	1180	213	18.1	65.3
1986	1155	205	17.7	67.3
1987	1131	202	17.9	67.8
1988	1144	201	17.6	68.2
1989	1119	190	17.0	67.4
1990	1105	183	166	67.8
1991	1078	177	16.4	67.2
1992	1091	178	16.3	68.0
1993	1157	189	16.3	68.8

Calculated from Statistisches Bundesamt (eds.): Strafverfolgung. Vollständiger Nachweis der einzelnen Straftaten.

Furthermore, the reform effected a remarkable rise of persons sentenced to suspended prison sentences as a percent of all persons sentenced to prison sentences: from 36.1 percent in 1968 to 53.1 percent in 1970 (54.3 in 1971), a trend which continued until 1983 (64.9 percent, see Table 2, Column D). Altogether these developments led rather soon to closing down many smaller prison establishments at the beginning of the 1970s. The all-time low of the general imprisonment rate in 1970, however, was very short lived. After this low there was a steady rise of this rate until the all-time high in 1983. This development needs to be explained.

It seems strange that the imprisonment rate of sentenced prisoners *increased* from 51.0 in 1971 to 73.6 in 1983 (cf. Table 1, Column C), while in the period 1971–1983 the rate of persons sentenced to prison sentences as a percent of all sentenced persons (cf. Table 2, Column C) was almost constant and the rate of persons sentenced to suspended prison sentences as a percent of all persons sentenced to prison sentences (cf. Column D) rose remarkably. This increase cannot have been caused by the rising rate of all persons sentenced to imprisonment (175 in 1971, 228 in 1983, cf. Table 2, Column B) because the rates of those sentenced to immediate imprisonment were constant (80 in 1971, 80 in 1983, calculated from Columns B and D). For an explanation of the rising imprisonment rate of sentenced prisoners it may be helpful to compare the length of immediate prison sentences. In 1971 there were 22,217 persons (45 percent of all persons who got unconditional prison sentences) who were sentenced to imprisonment of less than six months; in 1983 the number was 10,787 (21.6 percent). As to long sentences of more than two and up to five years, the number for 1971 was 3,715 (8 percent), while for 1983 it was 7,282 (14.6 percent). The numbers for the longest sentences of more than five years were 566 (1.2 percent) in 1971 and 1,636 (3.3 percent) in 1983.[6] Therefore, the increasing imprisonment rate of sentenced prisoners can be explained mainly by the rise of length of prison sentences.

As mentioned above, the emphasis on rehabilitation as the sole normative purpose of imprisonment may have contributed to this trend. Additionally, a second factor had a remarkable impact on this development. The former Opium Act ("Opiumgesetz") of 1933/34 was replaced in 1971 by the Stupefying Drugs Act ("Betäubungsmittelgesetz"), which augmented the maximum custodial sentence from three to ten years of imprisonment. Since this repressive legislation did not appear to work, an amendment in

1982 raised the maximum sentence to 15 years. There is also a third factor which contributed to the trend towards the peak of the general imprisonment rate in 1983: The remand imprisonment rate increased from 22.2 in 1978 to 25.0 per 100,000 inhabitants in 1983.

If we look at the figures from 1983 to 1993/1994 (Table 1) we can observe the following trends: a drop of the general imprisonment rate from 101.4 in 1983 to a low of 76.9 in 1991 and then again an increase up to 88.2 in 1994 (Column A); a drop of the remand rate to a low of 18.9 in 1987 followed by an increase up to an all-time high of 27.7 in 1993 and 26.7 in 1994 (Column B); a very remarkable drop of the imprisonment rate of sentenced prisoners from 73.6 in 1983 to a low of 51.9 in 1991, followed by a slight rise up to 56.0 in 1994 (Column C) and a constant figure of about 2.5–2.6 for "Others" (Column D) until 1991, which doubled to 5.4 in 1994 (all rates for the "old" FRG).

A first attempt to explain the development of the general imprisonment rate leads to the conclusion that it was caused mainly by the developments of all the other rates which were in line with the development of the imprisonment rate, in particular the rates of remand and—to a lower degree—sentenced prisoners. With regard to the category "Others" the increase from 3.1 in 1992 up to 5.4 in 1994 can be explained by the harsher practice of detaining asylum-seekers before their expulsion, a development which took place in the course of the introduction of Article 16a into the Basic Law ("Grundgesetz," i.e. the Constitution) in 1993. This amendment greately restricted the rights of asylum-seekers.

Interestingly, between 1983 and 1989, the time when the general imprisonment rate dropped about 18 percent within six years, there was no corresponding reduction in registered crime to account for this. Neither was there new reform legislation. It was therefore generally thought that the reduction was due this time to changes in prosecutorial and judicial behavior and to government-sponsored attempts to provide alternatives to imprisonment, especially for young offenders (Feest, 1991; Graham, 1990; Prowse et al., 1992; Rutherford, 1990). But why did the sentencing behavior of prosecutors and judges change so much? First, there were the criticisms of some organizations, in particular the German Bar Association ("Deutscher Anwalts-Verein," representing all practicing advocates) which were scandalized by the high remand imprisonment rate. Suspected persons were put too fast and too carelessly under remand and were held too long in prison. Second, non-custodial alternatives—particularly for young offenders—were organized: alternatives to remand, community services, training courses, reconciliation schemes, etc. Third, there was an abolitionist movement against prison building programs which was picked up by the Green Party. This interest led to the first public experts' hearing on imprisonment in the parliament of the State of Hesse and gained very much public interest.[7]

The decrease in imprisonment continued until 1991, and resulted in the lowest general imprisonment rate of 76.9 ("old" Federal Republic) since 1970 (75.5). On the other hand, we can identify the precursors of the later peak of 88.2 in 1994 in developments since 1989. If we look at the ups and downs of remand and sentenced prisoners' rates in Table 1 (Columns B and C), we observe that rises and drops of the remand rates always affected the sentencing rate with a certain time lag. This also happened between 1989 and 1994, when the rate of persons in remand increased from 19.6 to 26.7 (Column B), a rise of 36 percent within six years.

This development makes it necessary to look again at the background of remand. For many years remand imprisonment was challenged as violating the Basic Law as to requirements of the rule of law, both with regard to its insufficient legal framework and its implementation. However, there has been no remand imprisonment reform since the harsh critique at the beginning of the 1980s (which led to lower remand rates). The preconditions for remanding someone into custody are still rather vague and make it possible for covert reasons ("apokryphe Haftgründe") to play a very important role. "Judges are said to be tempted to impose custodial remands in the name of general prevention, short sharp shock, deterrence, crisis intervention, expediting cases, extorting pressure to secure admission of an offense and preparing the way for a suspended sentence. All these reasons are not constituents of the StPO ["Strafprozeßordnung," Code of Criminal Procedure] and should therefore be regarded as illegal" (Prowse et al., 1990: 16). Since remand imprisonment remained very open to judicial discretion, one need not be surprised that it was instrumentalized as societal crisis intervention in cases where other institutions failed or as a means to calm peoples' fear of crime in the course of the process of German unification (Dünkel, 1994). As Dünkel argued, the rise coincided with the fall of the iron curtain and a far-reaching amnesty of prisoners of the former GDR. At the same time there was a migration from the former GDR and from other Eastern

European States to the "old" FRG. Furthermore, the criminal justice system of the FRG was introduced in the new States—a process which needed some time. Therefore, the length of procedures and the duration of remand increased. Dünkel's research revealed, too, that persons of non-German nationality, suspected of petty offenses, became the new target group of remand policy. This policy serves also as a kind of precursor for the later expulsion of such persons (see the rises of "Others" in Table 1, Column D).

The imprisonment rates of the former GDR should be seen apart from those of the FRG. From our point of view it may not be appropriate to calculate common rates for the whole new territory of the "new" Federal Republic because such rates would distort the different developments. In the former GDR the very high prison populations (with a rate of about 200) were brought down by amnesties and by a virtual standstill of criminal justice in the first years after unification, so that in 1991 the overall imprisonment rate for that part of Germany was a mere 19 per 100,000 inhabitants (see Table 1, Column A). This is also the reason why the remand imprisonment rate was higher than the rate of sentenced prisoners in 1991 and 1992 (see Columns B and C).

At this point we should recall the *drop* of the imprisonment rate between 1983 and 1989, and remember that there was no corresponding drop in the crime figures or any important legislation; therefore, this decrease was due to a change of the behavior of the prosecutors and judges. This means that a substantial decrease in the imprisonment rate was possible without endangering public safety. Obviously, also, the *increase* of the imprisonment rate between 1991 and 1994 did not reflect only the development of police recorded crime: This cannot be the reason for such an escalation of the imprisonment rates. We suppose that again the prosecutors and judges changed their behavior: this time in accord with moral panics on the rise of crime in the course of the unification. Meanwhile, a number of articles on the development of crime figures since the unification have been published. Their authors agreed that the development was not as threatening as some officials liked to make the public believe (e.g. Boers, 1994; Lehne, 1994; Pfeiffer and Wetzels, 1994; Pfeiffer, 1995). Significantly, Pfeiffer and Wetzels demanded to set up a special experts' commission just to interpret recorded crime independently and against the interests of populist politicians.

We interpret these ups and downs as a complex mixture of strategical planning and unplanned outcomes. In keeping with the

Council of Europe's reductionist policies and in the context of scarce resources, the justice administrations were in a number of ways trying to make less use of imprisonment. But the reductions of the prison population achieved in this way are more than set off by other developments. In the first place, drug law enforcement has for the last 20 years steadily brought in more new prisoners with increasingly long sentences. Second, as already mentioned above, the issue of resocialization contributed to longer prison sentences. Third, imprisonment on remand became more and more preventative after the unification in 1990. In the fourth place, the criminal law and in particular remand imprisonment has become an important mechanism to deal with unwanted foreigners, particularly asylum-seekers (cf. Messner and Ruggiero 1995: 144). Finally, life imprisonment[8] and its equivalents ("Sicherungsverwahrung,"[9] "Einweisung in ein psychiatrisches Krankenhaus",[10] "mehrere nicht-gesamtstrafenfähige zeitliche Freiheitsstrafen"[11]) are keeping prison cells and other accommodations occupied over many years.

Summarizing all this, since the penal reform of 1969 the judiciary has acted increasingly independently, resisting the policy demands of the police. This policy intensified after 1981 and focused rather clearly on "polarization" between "good" and "bad" offenders: discharges in cases of petty crime, new alternatives to custody (e.g., community service orders, etc.) in cases of petty and minor crime and custodial sentences of increasing length as examples of control and punishment (cf. Cremer-Schäfer, 1987) for those who were seen either in need of resocialization or as a threat to public order, in particular violent offenders, drug offenders and non-German offenders.

If we relate these findings to the traditional German penal philosophy of guilt and its origins in non-preventative retribution we could conclude that in practice both the legislature and the courts believed increasingly that preventative purposes of the penal law would work and behaved according to their preventative belief. In particular, the increasing harshness against special target groups of offenders as well as the reasonably widened alternatives to custody—in short "polarization"—could be seen as indicators for a stronger preventative belief, irrespective of whether their effects on the prison population were foreseen or not. On the other hand, we could draw a rather different conclusion if we take into account the impact of moral panics on legislation, sentencing and imprisonment, whether generated by the mass media or the government itself. According to this view the above penal policy may have been directed to make the public believe that penal responses were appropriate to diminish public fear of crime—whether this policy were efficient or not. Anyway, the depicted developments must be viewed critically and cannot be told as a story of success.

Total Institutions and Prison Leaves

German prisons have been traditionally very total and military-type institutions. Until about 30 years ago, prisons operated under the "Irish system" ("Stufenvollzug"), in which prisoners started out in complete deprivation of all outside contacts, but could earn their way up to a certain number of letters or even visits per year. This changed in the 1970s. More open prison regimes were tried out in some of the German states. So were home leaves and work furloughs. The results were seen as positive: The large majority of prisoners who were allowed to be temporarily outside the prison did not commit new offenses and came back voluntarily. The Prison Act of 1976 sanctioned earlier practices by giving prison administrations discretion to send prisoners on home leaves for up to 21 days a year. The only criterion was the likelihood that the prisoner in question would not abscond or commit new offenses while on leave.

As a result, the number of home leaves, already considerable when the Prison Act came into force, increased substantially: "Between 1977 and 1988 the number of periods of home leave greatly increased from 243 to 654 per hundred prisoners and the number of short prison leave increased from 219 to 763 per hundred prisoners; even work release increased from 32 to 50 per 100 prisoners" (Dünkel and Rössner, 1991: 229). Almost every prisoner could at least dream of the possibility of spending some time outside prison before the end of the prison term. This contributed to a sharp reduction of prison breaks; it also led to a reduction of prisoners' swallowing all sorts of objects (nails, forks, spoons, even razor blades, etc.) in order to be at least temporarily out of the prison (i.e., in a hospital). Having "successfully" mastered home leaves became also something like a necessary precondition for early release.

Not every group of prisoners can, however, enjoy such "relaxations" of prison conditions. Internal administrative rules exclude "as a rule" any such relaxations for drug addicts and for foreigners who are likely to be extradited or expelled. These categories of

prisoners are seen by the administrators as constituting by definition a risk of absconding or reoffending. They are fast-growing
parts of the German prison population and feel treated unfairly in
relation to the rest of the prison population.

Long-term prisoners, especially lifers, find it very difficult to get
home leaves. The Prison Act itself envisages for lifers who are
accommodated in a closed prison a ten-year minimum incarceration period before home leave may be granted. On the other hand,
there is no minimum time to be served before the lifers' transfer to
an open prison. Furthermore, once accommodated in an open
establishment, even a lifer has no minimum term to serve before
leave of absence can be granted. However, we do not know about
such cases. But some states are reluctant to give leaves to prisoners
whose sentences are not drawing near. They claim that this is a consequence of the principle of guilt and/or necessary for general prevention. The courts have so far largely condoned this practice,
which is certainly not in accordance with the letter of the law (cf.
van Zyl Smit, 1988: 8). However, the huge differences between the
points of time for the first home leave or for the transfer to an open
prison establishment seem to us a symptomatic example for the
amount of discretion which the Prison Act concedes the prison
administration. Such discretion makes it possible to discipline lifers
extraordinarily.

There is also statistical evidence of differential implementation
across states of open imprisonment, relaxations (to work outside
prison, to stay outside prison for some hours per day) and leaves of
absence. In their documentation on imprisonment in Bavaria, the
Greens of the Bavarian Parliament (DIE GRÜNEN, 1991: 15) noted
that at the end of 1987 only 2.7 percent of the Bavarian adults sentenced were accommodated in open prison establishments, whereas
the respective percentage for the rest of the Republic was 13.4. As to
short-time stays outside prison in 1988 the average figure for
Bavaria was 2.2 per prisoner and year (leave of absence 2.8). These
figures were contrasted with an average of 8.0 for the rest of the
Republic and with a peak of 14.5 per prisoner per year for Lower
Saxony (leave of absence for the rest of the Republic 6.6, peak of 11.9
per prisoner for Bremen). It should be mentioned that this very insufficient implementation in Bavaria is ideological. As the Bavarian
Minister of Justice argued in Parliament, open imprisonment should
be granted not as a rule (as laid down in the Prison Act), but only as
an exception, and, furthermore, that all purposes of sentencing (not

just resocialization) should be regarded before granting relaxations of imprisonment (cf. Berghofer-Weichner, 1988).

But even those prisoners who benefit from the system of relaxations experience increasingly that home leaves and other relaxations of confinement have become the major disciplinary tool in the hands of the prison administrations. Regular disciplinary measures (from taking away certain internal privileges to solitary confinement of up to four weeks) are enumerated in the Prison Act and can only be inflicted following tightly regulated procedures (including the possibility of judicial review). In contrast to this, the withholding of prison leaves is rather decentralized, does not require much procedure and is regarded by many prisoners as an arbitrary exercise of administrative power.

Altogether these developments turn out to be contradictory: On the one hand, we find that there is a considerable increase in the number of relaxations (prison leaves, open regime, etc.); on the other hand, there is considerable regional disparity, and we see the exclusion of large groups of prisoners and the use of relaxations as a disciplinary tool.

Prisoners' Rights and Their Implementation

The idea that prisoners may have rights is relatively new in Germany. It was only in the early 1970s that the Constitutional Court did away with the time-honored doctrine of the so-called "special relation of domination" ("besonderes Gewaltverhältnis"), which had asserted that prisoners (like soldiers and civil servants) are part of the state and cannot therefore have rights against the state. The court announced that prisoners do have basic rights under the German constitution, and that these rights can be taken away only in the forms foreseen by the constitution (e.g., by legislation). This prompted the legislature to pass a Prison Act in 1976, the first one in German history.

The Prison Act grants prisoners, among other things, the right to seek court review whenever they feel that their rights as laid down in this Act have been violated. For this purpose, special judicial panels ("Strafvollstreckungskammern beim Landgericht") have been established near every major prison and their decisions can be appealed to the highest court of the respective state ("Oberlandesgericht"). In addition to reviewing prisoners' complaints, these courts also decide on whether a prisoner shall be released before the end of his or her sentence (i.e., in this respect they are the judicial equivalent of the Anglo-Saxon parole boards). This new system has led to widespread use of the courts by prisoners. Research has, however, demonstrated that the results of prisoners' rights litigation are mixed to say the least (for details cf. Feest, 1993). For further analysis it is useful to distinguish two types of litigations: conflicts about the interpretation of unclear norms, on the one hand, and questions about the individual application of (more or less clear) norms, on the other hand.

Since 1977 the courts have been helpful in clarifying some hitherto unclear points of law. This will continue to be necessary, since the Prison Act has a dynamic structure built in: A number of basic principles at the beginning of the Act allow for societal changes to be translated into prison rules. There are at least two problems with this function of the courts: Only individual, aggrieved prisoners can go to court, and at their own financial and personal risk. Since court proceedings may take many months, if not years, appeal requires prisoners with relatively long sentences. They must also have a good working knowledge of prison law and legal procedure. They need, finally, to be resistant to the adverse reactions they are likely to get from the prison staff. We have also to remember that the same courts which decide about prisoners' complaints also rule about their parole: in this latter situation some courts are known to hold litigiousness ("querulous behavior") against a prisoner.

Most prisoners who turn to the courts are, however, not primarily interested in the clarification of points of law. They have a conflict with the prison administration and want to have it resolved in their favor. Experience indicates that German courts are not very helpful in this respect. Most judges do not want to get involved in the nitty-gritty of prison life. They stay in their courthouses, never visit the prison and conduct their business in writing. Also, the Prison Act is not very helpful in these cases, since it gives the prison administration ample discretion in many of the most important conflicts. "Treatment" arguments are typically used against legal positions of prisoners. Even those prisoners who win their conflict in court may find that the prison administration has ways to avoid implementing the court decree. At the time when the Prison Act was dealt with by the parliament, most Members of Parliament believed that the prison governors would follow the law and respect court decisions in favor of the prisoner. They did not expect that prison governors as civil servants, and therefore especially obliged to implement the decision of a court, would resist court decisions. However, the research on refractory behavior of prison administration has been well known for a decade, and Parliament has not seen fit to amend the provisions although the Greens presented a proposal to Parliament to "fine" refractory prison governors.

The German history of acknowledging prisoners' rights in theory but not implementing them in practice makes clear a rather contradictory development which cannot be seen as just a story of success.

SUMMARY AND CONCLUSION: CONTRADICTIONS, INTENDED AND UNINTENDED CONSEQUENCES

In his thoughtful analysis, *Visions of Social Control* (1985), Stan Cohen suggested several models to explain changes in sentencing and imprisonment: progress, organizational convenience, ideological contradiction, professional interest and political economy. We think that some of these models may be helpful in explaining the changes and contradictions we described above. Our analysis started with a focus on the institutional and organizational characteristics of the prison system. We presented a short discourse on its contradictory ideological background, the German philosophy of "guilt" (retribution) and its "modern" amalgamations with preventative purposes. We then widened a bit the institutional background contradictions regarding unification and the consequent application of the western system of justice to the eastern part of Germany. Of course, the ideological contradictions were also transported from the West to the East. There followed a discussion of prison contraction and expansion. Prison leaves and prisoner rights also involved ideological contradictions.

Looking at the quantitative and qualitative "ups" and "downs" of German imprisonment, we wish to address the question of whether they are the result of governmental strategies, or an unplanned outcome, and what this might mean for the immediate future. We think that in particular Cohen's concepts of "progress,"[12] "organizational convenience"[13] and "political economy"[14] could contribute to an in-depth analysis. Some "progressive" attempts at reductionist criminal justice planning have been largely subverted by built-in contradictions as well as by unforeseen events. The same is true for attempts to render the prison institution less total. There were such plans, of course, and in some respects there was dissent about their proper implementation. There were also intended and unintended outcomes of the implementation of these plans.

The prevailing motives of the Penal Reform of 1969 were aimed at pushing back custodial sentences by reducing short-term sentences under six months, replacing custodial sentences with fines and widening the possibilities to suspend custodial sentences. These motives were "benevolent" and the reform was presented as "progress" typical of the 1960s. But, what should officials do with offenders who could not benefit from this progress? The answer was the introduction of the rehabilitative idea into the prison system, already some years before the Prison Act came into force. The Act promised rehabilitation, resocialization and reintegration, all fitting into the blueprint of "progress." However, at the end of the 1960s and the beginning of the 1970s there was no substantial discussion about the possible impact of the rehabilitative idea on longer custodial sentences and on the prison population. On the contrary, the penal reform of 1969 led to an all-time low of imprisonment rates. This situation promised that it was possible to realize a "correctional dream": to rehabilitate fewer prisoners more effectively. It was not foreseen that longer sentences for a more "efficient" rehabilitation would contribute to prison overcrowding.

Another, only partly unintended consequence followed from drug legislation. The two amendments of drug legislation in 1971 and 1982, both striving "progressively" for the protection of human health by augmenting the maximum sentences, did not work; instead, increasing imprisonment of drug addicts contributed to prison overcrowding. Much of this negative outcome could have been foreseen with regard to experiences with prohibition of alcohol and drugs in other countries. However, moral panics about drugs, created by the mass media and supported by many populist politicians, served as impediments for a rational change in drug policy.

We do not believe that the Constitutional Court was aware of the impact its decision in the very special cases of two lifers would have on other lifers and prisoners in general. Nor did the court anticipate that the Ministers of Justice of some states would deduce new purposes of imprisonment from this decision. Apparently, the existing ideological contradictions between traditional penal philosophy and "progressive" prison ideology contributed to the decision. The court may not have foreseen, either, that many prison administrations would exploit this decision to discipline prisoners ("organizational convenience"). This was possible because the court with the highest reputation was in favor of retribution and did not respect the letter of prison law, i.e., "resocialization" as the only normative goal of imprisonment.

Provisions of the Prison Act for granting leaves of absence and open imprisonment were also aimed at achieving humane rehabilitative purposes. They have been designed to make the prison less total and to reverse the mechanisms of adaptation to the artificial social world of the prison. But they resulted in just the opposite; that is, to discipline prisoners for their better functioning within the prison system. Nevertheless, one could have foreseen this development to some extent from the letter of the provisions which allowed huge discretion to the prison administration.

The non-implementation of prisoners' rights was neither planned nor expected. The legislature did not expect that prison governors would refuse to implement court decisions. However, even when the legislature was informed about such refractory behavior, the Parliament did not amend the law. Thus, we must conclude that the legislature agreed with this formerly unintended bad consequence, i.e., the low rank of prisoners' rights.

Many shortcomings of the Prison Act in practice could be explained through "organizational convenience"—an unwillingness of politicians to finance the costs of the Act (which may be interpreted also as a matter of political economy). In this context one should not forget that the introduction of a retributive concept such as "compensation of guilt" not only compromised the rehabilitative idea ("ideological contradictions"), but may have also contributed to legitimize ex post facto the non-implementation of expensive provisions of the Prison Act.

While reform efforts have fallen short, reform is still needed. The rise and fall of remand imprisonment rates demonstrates rather clearly the disadvantages of the highly vague criteria for remand. Therefore, it was possible that the judges used remand also for achieving illegal purposes which led to a first rise of remand rates. On the other hand, a scandalized public contributed to a drop of the rates. The second rise was related to the new economical crisis after the fall of the Berlin wall (accession of "poor" GDR to "rich" FRG), which resulted later in crisis management at the political level and led to a new authoritarian consensus which was clearly visible in the fundamental changes of German asylum laws in 1993. This all looks like a striking example for Cohen's concept of "political economy." However, on the level of the judiciary and the police, remand was used then to concentrate on the new target group after unification—non-German national offenders. These developments coincided with the rise of detention rates of non-Germans waiting for their expulsion, which in turn was the result of the new asylum laws. These changes can be interpreted as characteristic of a new authoritarian consensus on the political level. This must seem surprising in light of what we have said about the increased sensibility of judges and prosecutors concerning this question. It also runs counter to the declared policy of most justice departments to reduce remand imprisonment. But the Interior departments and their police administrations were able to define the situation with the help of a moral panic on the asylum question concerning alleged organized crime by foreigners. However, to some extent this development could have been foreseen.

Finally, there is a trend toward the polarization of sentence severity, both on the legislative and on the judicial levels. First, polarization may be seen as some kind of strategical planning on the political level aimed at coping with prison overcrowding and, second, motivated through benevolent motives to keep the "good" (or less "bad") out of the prison. On the other hand, this development was undermined by longer and longer sentences for the "bad," for those in need of resocialization, for special target groups, etc., which resulted again in very high imprisonment rates. This trend was partly caused by benevolent, partly by non-benevolent, motives. If this process of polarization cannot be stopped, Germany will face serious prison overcrowding.

Campaigns for public safety, based on fear of crime, were related to the target groups of the "bad" and were enlarged to "moral panics" (cf. Cohen, 1972; Cremer-Schäfer, 1995). In West Germany we saw such panics about "anarcho-terrorism" (mainly of the Red Army Faction), "violence" (as usual in particular of children and young persons) and "drug-trafficking" (in combination with "organized crime," too). Since the unification, "criminal foreigners and asylum-seekers" increasingly became the target groups of campaigns for public safety. The mass media emphasized more and more crimes which are ascribed to the "Russian Mafia," to "Rumanian Gangs" ("organized crime"), and to "terrorism" of Kurds who wish Germany to stop supporting the Turkish government in their war against them. Taking into account this development, we think that xenophobia will increase in the future and contribute to campaigns to protect the public from "criminal foreigners." Certainly this will lead to a further increase of the prison population. On the other hand, if this happens, the prospects for reducing attacks of the extreme Right on asylum-seekers will become worse.

As so often, penal law, criminalization and imprisonment divert attention from root causes. Particularly in times of economic crises—as after the German unification—this diverting function gains much importance. It makes the people believe that the state is caring for them. On the other hand, and taking into account also experiences from other countries, we do not believe that any long-term reduction of imprisonment will be possible as long as criminal law is used as the main instrument to "win" the "wars" against all such "target groups." On the contrary, moral panics, as the tools in the hands of the moral entrepreneurs, may augment peoples' fear of crime and enlarge social exclusion, particularly as a product of "(neo-)liberal" economic policy, which seems to have strengthened in the economic crisis following unification.

Notes

1. cf. *Entscheidungen des Bundesverfassungsgerichts*, Vol. 45: 187, 253.
2. The Court of Appeal ("Oberlandesgericht") reduced this term to 42 years. The Constitutional Court did not make objections against such long periods but criticized that the courts did not take into account the short time the prisoner had to live (Bundesverfassungsgericht, Beschluß vom 22. Mai 1995–2 BvR 671/95).
3. cf. *Entscheidungen des Bundesgerichtshofs in Strafsachen*, Vol. 7: 28, 32.
` 4. *Entscheidungen des Bundesverfassungsgerichts*, Vol. 64: 261.
5. cf. *Entscheidungen des Bundesverfassungsgerichts*, Vol. 40: 276, 284.
6. All figures from Statistisches Bundesamt Wiesbaden (eds.): *Strafverfolgung*. Vollständiger Nachweis der einzelnen Straftaten, Wiesbaden.
7. For more details on these background factors see Feest (1991: 137).
8. Since in 1982 parole of life imprisonment was introduced both the numbers of persons sentenced to life imprisonment and the terms to be served increased (Weber, 1993: 31).
9. Secure preventative detention ("measure," not regarded as punishment).
10. Hospital order with restrictions (forced accommodation in a psychiatric hospital; "measure," not a penal sentence).
11. Several determinate sentences which cannot be united to one single sentence. Sometimes such offenders serve longer terms than lifers.
12. "In response to the same combination of benevolent intentions and advances in knowledge which have always propelled correctional

change, a spirit of innovation and reform somehow gripped the social-control system in the 1960s. Old practices seemed outmoded in the light of the new ideas. The destructuring ideology appeared, offering not just novelty but a genuinely radical reversal of traditional assumptions. Diversion, deinstitutionalization, reintegration and the move to community all signaled a new era in deviancy control" (Cohen, 1985: 90).

13. "When reforms reach the existing system, they confront a series of powerful managerial, administrative and organizational imperatives. The reform impulse is resisted and blocked or (more frequently) it is welcomed, only to be absorbed and co-opted (for the wrong reasons) and in the process completely transformed, even in directions diametrically opposed to the original vision" (Cohen, 1985: 92).

14. "… a shift at the centre of the political economy (at national and international levels), causing crises, recession, and unemployment, is registered at the political level. A new authoritarian consensus emerges (or is engineered) about what must be done. In current electoral terms: Reaganism in the USA, Thatcherism in Britain, signs of right-wing populism in Canada. In broader political terms: the rise of the new right, neo-conservatism, the 'moving right show,' even 'friendly fascism'" (Cohen, 1985: 107/108).

References

Arnold, J. (1995) "Corrections in the German Democratic Republic: A Field for Research." *The British Journal of Criminology*, 35: 81–94.

Berghofer-Weichner, M. (1988) Bericht der Bayerischen Staatsministerin der Justiz Dr. Mathilde Berghofer-Weichner vor den Ausschüssen für Verfassungs-, Rechts- und Kommunalfragen und Eingaben und Beschwerden des Bayerischen Landtags am Mittwoch, 8. Juni 1988, 9.15 Uhr, zum Strafvollzugsgesetz. München.

Boers, K. (1994) "Kriminalität und Kriminalitätsfurcht im sozialen Umbruch." *Neue Kriminalpolitik*, 6 (No. 2, May): 27–31.

Cohen, S. (1972) *Folk Devils and Moral Panics: The Creation of the Mods and Rockers*. Oxford: Oxford University Press.

Cohen, S. (1985) *Visions of Social Control: Crime, Punishment and Classification*. Cambridge/Oxford: Polity Press/Blackwell.

Cremer-Schäfer, H. (1987) "Phasen der Kriminalisierungspolitik in der Bundesrepublik Deutschland seit 1953." In Forschungsberichte zum DFG-Projekt "Ökonomische, politische und Kriminalisierungsstrategien. Zur Geschichte der Kriminalnormgenese undanwendung." Kriminalisierungsphasen in der Bundesrepublik Deutschland, in Österreich, in England/Wales, in Schweden. Frankfurt a.M. (unpublished typescript).

Cremer-Schäfer, H. (1995) "Über den politischen Nutzen 'steigender Kriminalität'." In Schweizerische Arbeitsgruppe für Kriminologie (eds.) *Innere Sicherheit—Innere Unsicherheit? Kriminologische Aspekte*. Chur/Zürich (Rüegger): 131–151.

DIE GRÜNEN im Bayerischen Landtag (1991) *Knast in Bayern: Dokumentation der Parlamentsarbeit der GRÜNEN im Bayerischen Landtag zum Strafvollzug, 1987–1991*. München.

Dünkel, F. (1994) "Untersuchungshaft als Krisenmanagement? Daten und Fakten zur Praxis der Untersuchungshaft in den 90er Jahren." *Neue Kriminalpolitik*, 6 (No. 4, November): 20–29.

Dünkel, F. (1995) "Imprisonment in Transition. The Situation in the New States of the Federal Republic." *British Journal of Criminology*, 35: 95–112.

Dünkel, F. and Rössner, D. (1991) "Federal Republic of Germany," in D. van Zyl Smit and F. Dünkel (eds.) *Imprisonment Today and Tomorrow: International Perspective on Prisoner's Rights and Prison Conditions*. Deventer: Kluwer. pp. 203–248.

Feest, J. (1982) *Imprisonment and the Criminal Justice System in the Federal Republic of Germany*. Bremen.

Feest, J. (1991) "Reducing the prison population: Lessons from the West German experience?" in J. Muncie and R. Sparks (eds.) *Imprisonment. European Perspectives*. New York/London: Harvester Wheatsheat. pp. 131–145.

Feest, J. (1993) "Institutional Resistance against Prisoners' Rights." *The Howard Journal of Criminal Justice*, 32: 127–135.

Feest, J. and Wolters, C. (1994) *Verhütung von Folter und unmenschlicher oder erniedrigender Behandlung oder Strafe*. Bremen.

Graham, J. (1990) "Decarceration in the Federal Republic of Germany: How Practitioners are Succeeding Where Policy Makers Have Failed." *The British Journal of Criminology*, 30: 150–170.

Lehne, W. (1994) "Kriminalität ist nicht das Problem Nummer 1." *Frankfurter Rundschau* (Dokumentation), No. 34 (February 10): 12 and No. 35 (February 11): 12.

Messner, C. and Ruggiero, V. (1995): "Germany: the Penal System between Past and Future," in V. Ruggiero, M. Ryan and J. Sim (eds.) *Western European Penal Systems: A Critical Anatomy*. London/Thousand Oaks/New Delhi: Sage. pp. 128–148.

Pfeiffer, C. (1995) "Die im Dunkeln sieht man nicht. Die neuen Daten zur Kriminalität unter der Lupe eines Kriminologen: Warum werden immer mehr Jugendliche straffällig? Eine Kritik am konservativen Wertezerfall." DIE ZEIT, No. 30: 23.

Pfeiffer, C. and Wetzels, P. (1994) "'Die Explosion des Verbrechens?' Zu Mißbrauch und Fehlinterpretation der polizeilichen Kriminalstatistik." *Neue Kriminalpolitik*, 6 (No. 2, May): 32–39.

Prowse, R., Weber, H. and Wilson, C. (1990) "Reforming Remand Imprisonment: Comparing Britain and Germany." Working Paper presented to the European Group for the Study of Deviance and Social Control, Annual Conference, Haarlem, The Netherlands, September 4–7, 1990.

Prowse, R., Weber, H. and Wilson, C. (1992) "Rights and Prisons in Germany: Blueprint for Britain?" *International Journal of the Sociology of Law*, 20: 111–134.

Rutherford, A. (1990) "Putting Practice into Policy: Some Hopeful Lessons." Address to Reaffirming Rehabilitation Conference. National Center for Institutions and Alternatives, Alexandria, Virginia. Unpublished typescript.

Schünemann, B. (1987) "Plädoyer für eine neue Theorie der Strafzumessung," in A. Eser and K. Cornils (eds.) *Neuere Tendenzen in der Kriminalpolitik: Beiträge zu einem deutsch-skandinavischen Strafrechtskolloquium*. Freiburg: Max-Planck-Institut. pp. 209–238.

van Zyl Smit, D. (1988) "Leave of Absence for West German Prisoners: Legal Principle and Administrative Practice." *The British Journal of Criminology*, 28 (Winter 1988): 1–18.

von Hirsch, A. (1976) *Doing Justice. The Choice of Punishments*. New York: Hill and Wang.

von Hirsch, A. and Jareborg, N. (1991) *Strafmaß und Strafgerechtigkeit: Die deutsche Strafzumessungslehre und das Prinzip der Tatproportionalität*. Bonn: Forum-Verlag Godesberg.

Weber, H.-M. (1993) "Die lebenslange Freiheitsstrafe in der Bundesrepublik: Problemaufriß und Aktualität der Abschaffungsforderung," in Komitee für Grundrechte und Demokratie (eds.) *Lebenslange Freiheitsstrafe: Ihr geltendes Konzept, ihre Praxis, ihre Begründung.* Erste öffentliche Anhörung 14. bis 16. Mai 1993. Dokumentation, Köln (Komitee für Grundrechte und Demokratie): 21–56.

Weigend, T. (1982) "'Neoklassizismus' – ein transatlantisches Mißverständnis." *Zeitschrift für die gesamte Strafrechtswissenschaft*, 94: 801–814.

Chapter
NINE

Penal Practice and Social Theory in Poland Before and After the Events of 1989

Monika Płatek

June 1989 marks in Poland the end of an old and the beginning of a new era. The victory of the Trade Union "Solidarity" forces in the Polish Parliament and nomination of the first non-Communist Prime Minister was widely perceived as the end of the 50-year Communist regime in Poland and the beginning of the new, modern, democratic state. Poland was the first country in Central and Eastern Europe to achieve a post-communist government based on democratic legitimacy. The Communist regime attempted to use the criminal law and imprisonment to secure its domination. Widespread arrests and long terms of imprisonment, however, could not thwart the many waves of protest in 1956, 1968, 1970 and in June 1976. Repression only fueled anti-communist activities. Underground organizations of workers developed (one of them was KOR, The Committee of Workers' Defense) and "flying" universities become common despite authorities' efforts to stop them.[1] The more activists were sent to prison, the more anti-communist activities spread, culminating in the rise of an active political opposition within the "Solidarity" movement in August 1980. The Communist authorities answered with martial law in December of 1981 and an increase of criminalization and suppression soon followed.

By May of 1985 the Communist regime lost all vestiges of its authority, and the country fell deeper into economic crisis. The Communists tried once more to regain popular acceptance through the criminalization and penal repression of protesters.[2] This policy complicated the prison situation but did not bring the expected political effects. Ultimately, Communist authorities had to accept a political round table with the opposition, which led to free elections. As the result of the negotiation process, the first non-communist free government in post-war Poland was elected in 1989.

The revolutionary change was achieved without the shot of a single bullet, with no blood and no victims on either side. As is characteristic of most revolutions, this one evoked hope for changes almost in every area, including criminal justice and prison policy. Prison—as symbolic Bastille—has been associated with depravity and evil of the old regime, so there was a strong demand for the quick changes in the incarceration rate and in the penal regime (Moczydłowski, 1992). Prisoners themselves presented long lists of demands. Prisoner strikes were a sign of the changing times. There were hardly any political prisoners anymore, but all those imprisoned for criminal acts demanded revision of their cases, a decrease of imposed terms and the passing of amnesty law for activists. In 1989 prisoners also got the right to vote in national elections. Many "Solidarity" candidates elected to the Sejm (Lower Chamber of the Parliament) and the Senate (High Chamber of the Parliament) were supporting prisoners' strikes. Prisoners' demands meant that the prison staff lacked the ability to cope with a problem in a peaceful way. Prisoners' strikes were followed by prisons' staff strikes. Some strikes turned into riots. Several prisons were demolished; many others severely damaged. Seven prisoners lost their lives (four were shot while protesting on the Czarne Prison roof).

Changing the name of the system—from totalitarian to democratic—can be done easily, but the actual transformation is a time-consuming process. There is no guarantee of reaching the goal of justice for all. Poland after 1989 was in a particularly difficult situation as the country had no legal tradition or criminal procedure to follow. Only prosecutors and some of the Ministry of Interior functionaries went through the "verification" process. Communists were more formally than actually removed from power. Contacts, money, influence and business ownership stayed with old system functionaries. They themselves went into Parliament under the changed name, and until 1992 as the opposition. In the 1992 election they won majority places. In the 1995 presidential election a post-communist candidate won and become the president. The characteristic elements of Communism rule—such as state economic plans and state ownership of the main productive means; censorship; restricted movement; a ban on private initiatives in business, and centralized governmental power—all have been abolished, but it is the old nomenklatura that profit most from the present changes. They were well off before and became even better off after 1989. It is hard to decide if Poles could have solved the situation in 1989 differently. Poles are proud of having avoided a civil war in 1989, but the price for this was high.

To better understand the difficulties penal reformers are facing in so-called "post-communist" Poland, we must examine the prison system under the Soviet regime, where we find that prison served two main functions that it no longer serves.

THE STATE OF PRISONS BEFORE 1989

Prison as a Symbol of the Power of Communist Authority

Poland, with 40 million inhabitants, had before 1989 one of the highest rates of imprisonment in Europe—almost 300 per 100,000 inhabitants (Prison Conditions in Poland. An Update 1992). The average term of imprisonment was 22–27 months.[3] The Communist regime used the criminal law and imprisonment to secure its domination over the people (Kangaspunta, 1995: 49); these were the main tools to maintain order under the Communist regime, even though Poland had crime rates comparable to nations like Sweden, Great Britain or Germany—nations with much smaller prison populations (Messner, Rosenfeld, 1994: 2, 3–24; Kangaspunta, 1995: 147, 191, 65–66, 82; Kury, 1995: 12–16).[4]

Although not everything was perceived as bad in post-war Poland (there was access to work, educational opportunities, etc.), the communist system from the very beginning gained few advocates and believers. This is because Poland's Constitution heralded many civil rights (including freedom of speech and due process of law), but Polish authority hardly respected any of the constitutional statements (there was no freedom of expression, people were imprisoned without indictment for months). There were no procedures to claim the rights under the Constitution. Only seven percent of the Polish population graduated from the universities, yet one in eight adult males had spent at least six months in prison (Podemski, 1984: 6; Rocznik Statystyczny, 1995).[5]

The power of the old regime was based on ideology rather than on law. Communist ideology, treated seriously perhaps in Russia, was never treated with respect in Poland in the sense that very few people were eager to believe in communism and in the communist state. Yet the system of law reflected the communist idea. The law, according to the Communists, is not a tool to regulate relations among citizens and between citizen and the state authority, but a tool to overpower citizens by its authority. Andrei Vyshinsky, leading lawyer of the Soviet State already in 1938 described the special sense of the law: "The dictatorship of the proletariat is authority unlimited by any status whatever. But the dictatorship of the proletariat, creating its own laws, makes use of them, demands that they be observed, and punish breaches of them" (Vyshinsky, 1938: 48).

The distance between the promises of the authority and the reality in practice were easy to observe. There was less socialism than in Sweden, but much fear, injustice and poverty. Over the past 20 years there were several waves of protest,[6] and prison statistics indicate the way in which Polish Communist authorities tried to deal with a deteriorating political and economic situation. Comparing, for instance, the dates of major social protests with the number of inmates admitted to prison, we see that when protesters were brutally combated, prison statistics showed a sudden increase (See Table 1: 1970; 1971 after Dec. 1976; 1982, 1983, and 1985). When protesters managed to force the Communist authorities to accept some of their demands, we can observe a sudden drop in the number of prisoners, as in the years 1956, 1981, 1989. The jails and prisons filled with people who would not be perceived as criminals in the Western sense of the word; that is, people who plunder, rob and kill. In Poland, those sentenced to prison were sent there for being late to work for the third time, or for stealing milk or bottles of vodka (Utrat-Milecki, 1995: 93–108; Buchała, Szewczyk, 1995: 818). There were also many of those who fought against Nazi occupation as members of the Polish Underground Army and who survived the terror of World War II, only to be persecuted, tortured and

TABLE 1 Number of Inmates 1945–1992 (data
for Dec. 31) and in Jan. 1994

Year	Number of Inmates	Year	Number of Inmates
1945	24702	1970	82436
1946	61365	1971	102902
1947	56554	1972	115343
1948	77116	1973	124689
1949	92786	1974	81075
1950	98192	1975	96242
1951	93082	1976	97748
1952	87460	1977	85262
1953	84603	1978	97849
1954	89034	1979	106243
1955	80920	1980	99638
1956	35879	1981	74807
1957	61248	1982	79783
1958	70348	1983	85295
1959	92595	1984	76164
1960	98250	1985	110182
1961	98505	1986	99427
1962	95863	1987	91140
1963	105444	1988	67824
1964	71448	1989	40321
1965	80026	1990	50165
1966	94193	1991	58619
1967	97867	1992	61409
1968	98685	1993	61562
1969	64952	1994	63046

imprisoned by the Communist regime (Płatek, 1994). In addition to
helping consolidate state power as a symbol of the force of central
authority, the prison system under communist rule used excessive
criminalization and penalization as ways of trying to put the burden for existing socioeconomic crisis on "criminals." While serving

as a political tool, prison officially was supposed to be "resocializing" criminal offenders through a regime of work (Płatek, 1991: 73–76).

The Prison as an Economic Force

After World War II, Western countries got the Marshall plan and Eastern Europe got cheap prison labor. Behind the words of combating crime, prison served under the Communists as an important political and economic tool. In contrast to the Western countries, where prisons functioned as warehouses for labor-power that cannot be employed in the free market, prisons in Poland were a place to supply the economy with almost free manpower for the state economy. The Communist economy *symbolically*, at least, required extensive forced labor, of which the prison had a ready supply. Forced labor was meant as a deterrent to crime and protest, as labor discipline, and it was required to help fulfill economic plans. Prison labor became particularly important during the 1970s, when the percentage of gainfully employed prisoners reached nearly 100%.

By the 1980s, the 240 prison units in Poland under the Communist regime operated more than 60 independent production units, both industrial and agricultural. Prison enterprises were operating in the following production: furniture, metals, clothing, shoemaking, concrete, lithography and agriculture (The Penitentiary System in Poland, 1989). Many auxiliary workshops and supplementary forms of employment functioned in the prison system through contracts with factories. Prisoners not employed in workshops often carried on contract work in cells (Janiszewska-Talago, 1985: 59–70).[7]

Only about 30,000 people were working in prison-run enterprises, but almost all inmates were employed in some fashion. Some were hired for prison maintenance (kitchens, laundries, bakeries, office jobs, plumbing, electrical installation, rebuilding and building new parts of old prisons, fixing roofs, etc.). Prison maintenance work was perceived as non-productive because it brought no revenue to the state budget. The remainder (about the same number of inmates as those working at inside prison enterprises) worked outside the prison in the state-run enterprises, as contracted workers. They were mostly employed in construction, communication and in agriculture. Prisoners were paid less (or not paid at all) and they usually worked longer hours than free workers.

Prison enterprises were important on a national scale. The majority of enterprises normally had contracts with the key state enterprises. Cooperation and supply products constituted about 80 percent of their disposed-of produce, while the remaining 20 percent were market products. Prison production was part of the state's planned economy, as any other activity in the budget. As long as the most important point was to fulfill the budgetary plans, prison production played an important role. It was not necessarily profitable or cost effective, but it was in accordance with the plan. Prison enterprises were often the only ones to fulfill the plan on time. The state economy, however, did not reflect supply and demand of the market. It hardly took popular demand into consideration (Więziennictwo w Gospodarce Narodowej, 1985: 8–11).

In the mid-1980s, the prison production system started to crumble. It was the beginning of the end of the prison economic empire. The prison business had been prepared to fulfill budgetary plans, and could not adapt quickly to the mechanisms of the market economy, partially introduced already in 1987 by the Communist regime. Once the state enterprises got their freedom to choose the partner to cooperate with, the prisons started to lose contracts. Prisons were providing almost free manpower with all its negative consequences (low quality, workers not interested in the work, etc.). Prison production was not able to compete with other sectors of the Polish economy because it provided a cheap but unqualified labor force, no longer benefited from a tax deduction, and the costs of transport and necessary supervision made prisoner labor lose market competitiveness. With the number of contracts diminishing, overcrowding and idleness became serious problems—especially when the economy could barely garner enough money to feed prisoners. The need for reforms became clear even to the Communist prison administration, and some tentative steps toward reform were taken.

THE POLISH PRISON SYSTEM
AFTER THE FALL OF THE SOVIET SYSTEM

Promising Beginnings

The events of 1989 met a prison system ready for change because the situation had the sympathies of the newly elected officials (Moczydłowski, 1993). The Prime Minister, many new ministers and many Parliamentary members were among those who had spent some time in prison. They had personal knowledge of prison conditions and were sympathetic to the idea of the reform. The end of censorship allowed the public once again insight into prison conditions. The 1989 wave of strikes, revolts and various prison protests served as an additional argument to introduce reform (Płatek, 1995a: 89–105). Ironically, it seemed, the economic crisis would work well for prison reform since there was no longer an economic rationale for prison labor. And the political rationale—to help consolidate the state—should have been rendered obsolete as well.

Both of the new prison directors appointed in May of 1990 were university professors (a sociologist and a lawyer), and they quickly announced a new purpose of the prison: to "rehabilitate" through therapeutics. They had been advocating prison reform for years (Porowski, 1985: 155–175). They managed to open the prison to public control and to change the managerial style of work there (Sabbat-Swidlicka, 1992). The new style of work, as well as growing unemployment, brought highly qualified people to work in prison service. The atmosphere inside the prison greatly improved. Both prison staff and prisoners started to describe their relationships as relaxed and polite. And there have been some real gains in the penal sphere, such as creation of the Ombudsman Office. Established in 1987, the Ombudsman Office reports monitored human rights in the prisons. The atmosphere in prison became relaxed enough to encourage prison staff and prisoners to organize broadly different rehabilitation activities, such as Alcoholics Anonymous and "drug anonymous" groups, poetry contests, literature clubs, sport groups, alcohol and drug addiction education and crime victim compensation programs. These activities helped to change the image of the prison. During the first years after 1989, prison lost its alien character. Citizens got open access to prisons if they were interested in working there as volunteers or writing about them, or to carry out academic research.

These positive changes have been all the while accompanied by a slow but steady increase in the incarceration rate. Again new prison directors were appointed. The new directors are trying to continue the line of the reforms, but it is more difficult to advocate reform in 1996 than it was in 1989 (Wiezienia Interview, 1995). There is today less public discourse on prison conditions, more on the danger of crime, fewer programs for prisoners and more talk about getting tough on criminals. There is a looming crime "menace," which has replaced Communist ideological deviancy. "Enemies of the State" and prisoner labor exploitation have been replaced by simple "criminals," overcrowding and idleness. The new Polish authorities are failing to make imprisonment a tool of justice because convicts have lost public sympathy and there is popular support for repressive measures.

The deteriorating economic condition of Poland has merely provided a new rationale for oppression to replace the old one—from political deviancy to "crime," and the economic redundancy of prisoners under the free market helps ensure their inadequate treatment. As prisoners have lost their economic value, their prison conditions worsen. By the end of 1987, there were still over 90,000 people in prison (including pretrial jails, but excluding police jails). A 1988 amnesty helped to decrease the number to 67,000 (Gruszczyńska and Marczewski, 1995: 15–19). Radical political changes induced other changes in criminal policy. Detention was used less often, judges were more reluctant to impose imprisonment and conditional release was more frequently granted. At the end of 1989, there were 40,321 people behind bars (Kangaspunta, 1995: 28).[8] Many expected the new government to continue this decline, but soon after the number started to rise again (Andziak, 1995: 14). By July 1995, the number of inmates exceeded 66,000.[9] Radical changes in criminal justice seem to be in retreat.

This chapter concludes by focusing on three explanations for the stall in the current reform effort: (1) the general popularity of the "war on crime" in Poland, which is the immediate or proximate cause of stalled reform; (2) the frustration of criminological theory under Communism; and (3) Poland's culture and history of repression.

Crime Wave Spoils Early Reform

In its struggle to break away from the totalitarian past, Poland is facing among other problems a wave of crime accompanied by police ineffectiveness and a growing sense of insecurity among the people. The structure of crime has changed. Crime has become more violent, with greater gang organization. Bombing and gun battles are suddenly everyday news stories. In comparison with other post-communist countries and Western European countries, the level of traditional offenses and level of crime as such is still moderate. The number of homicides in 1994 in Poland, 1160, is still lower by about 300 than the respective figure for Moscow alone and, measured by homicides per 100,000 population, seven times lower than in Estonia, for instance (Jasinski, 1995: 8). However, 1160 homicides means twice as many as in the 1970s and 1980s, when the number oscillated around 500.

Each month over 1,000 new inmates are sent to prison, longer sentences are imposed and penal severity increases. Imprisonment of foreigners, mostly Russian and those from former Soviet Republics, have tripled in number since 1992. With the presidential election campaign, "getting tough" on prisoners is becoming more popular.[10] Prison furloughs, introduced in 1990 on a large scale, are now being curbed again. Emotion is beginning to play a more important role than "common sense" and empirical data (Checko, 1995: 11). The political changes of 1989 have brought not the expected improvement but a worsening of the living standard for the "Solidarity" working class and state employee workers. They are disappointed, and the old practice of blaming criminals for all failures is present again. For a possible solution, many are looking to countries perceived as successful—United States is the number one. For the disappointed and frightened, increasing severity in criminal policy is popular—especially when told that this is the approach taken by economically "successful" societies. This way, those who are fighting in Poland for an American standard of living are getting the American style of crime and criminal justice instead.

The "war on crime" in Poland is creating the same prisoner idleness and overcrowding that characterizes prisons in the United States. These conditions have put great pressure on the routine administration of prisons, encouraging administrative staff to cling to the regimentation of the paramilitary model that employs an armed and uniformed staff. Rehabilitation requires well-qualified specialists in the area of education and mental health (Porowski, 1995). But, another bureaucratic factor is at work supporting the old regimentation: Military service is better paid than civil service. According to present rules it is not possible to keep the paramilitary salary and change the job status into a civil one. Therefore, the draft of the new Law on Prison Service even strengthens paramilitary characteristics. And tradition, as well as the need to protect the country, in concert with police and military forces, are given as official reasons to hold a military character of the prison staff. Nearly all prison personnel—with the exception of a special category of prison staff like psychologist, doctor, nurse, etc.—are required to enforce military discipline (Art. 21 of the Law on Prison Staff from Dec. 10, 1959).

More than three decades of Polish penitentiary experience suggests that it is not possible to create a relaxed, educative environment within a system where the security and treatment roles are combined (Porowski, 1979). Therefore, one of the most important prerequisites to reform is the abandonment of the paramilitary character of the prison staff and its sole preoccupation with discipline.[11] This will require a legal guarantee to avoid prison overcrowding (Porowski, 1985; Moczydłowski and Rzepliński, 1990; Korecki, 1991). This is not a recommendation for public policy to build more prisons. The US experience shows that prisons are like highways—the more you build, the more overcrowded they become. It is rather a suggestion to adopt new policy requirements. The inability of political officials to solve social problems, on the one hand, and the absence of non-custodial penal alternatives, on the other hand, account for the current dismal prison situation. "Normalization" and "humanization" of the prison experience will remain hopeless ideals in this stalemate. As Zimbardo's social psychological experiments have shown, negative behavior in total institutions is an inevitable by-product of the way these institutions are constructed and operated; these hellholes have little or nothing to do with "bad actors," but require structural changes (Podgorecki, 1976: 180).

Criminological Theory and Practice

Russian influence in Poland after World War II was strong enough to impose throughout the 1950s the Russian "scientific" theory of crime. Durkheim's theory that crime is not only normal but a positive element of social life was deemed absurd, clearly discredited by events in the West (Fajst, 1995: 43–63). A theory of "relics" developed: After the Revolution crime in socialist societies became a "bourgeois hangover." Its main assumption is that crime is a phenomenon of capitalist values and social conditions and will disappear under socialism. Crime was a failure of the individual, certainly not the fault of the state. Criminals could be reformed, depending on their degree of capitalist "contamination." State officials determined how far the person was "contaminated" by capitalist ideology (Lernell, 1973). The seriously contaminated were eradicated, and the "slightly contaminated" could be rehabilitated through penal work and discipline (Heller, 1982: 38).

The Soviets attempted to impose the same interpretation on Polish criminology, especially between 1950–1955. The state's fierce animosity towards criminology had other than ideological reasons. Criminology is about asking questions. To ask a question is in a sense to create the reality. To ask the questions is to make people conscious of reality. To ask the questions is to get out of meaningless slogans, apply the forgotten words and search for data (Płatek, 1995b). Research on the youth problem was the one exception to this anti-intellectualism. Young people were officially given positive prognoses. This gave Poland the relative freedom to carry out some research, mostly after 1956 (Batawia, 1984). Criminology, both as a university subject and as a part of science, was accepted anew after the general political thaw of 1956. Over the last 40 years, there was generally no political interference into the syllabi of criminology courses. The "relics" theory was not treated seriously and Western criminology prevailed in the criminology programs. The Communist system has been often criticized by academics, and it was not necessary to be a Communist party member to work at the university. But at the same time, academics and the university were not perceived as dangerous forces to the Communist State. This is because criminologists, while freer than other occupations in Communist Polish society, were ignored in social practice.

So, the academic freedom of the post-war era was a squandered opportunity. A new criminal justice program was ready in 1989.[12] The effort of criminologists to work in cooperation with the Ministry of Justice and with the Prison Administration failed, however. Any ideas that differed from the official opinion were perceived as radical and dangerous. The academics working for prison reform and presenting contrary opinions were perceived as critical toward prison administration and were denied penitentiary research opportunities. The closer to 1989, the more open prison system research became (Płatek et al., 1991). In 1989 Poland was the site of the Fourth International Conference on Penal Abolition, where prison reform was discussed and a Scandinavian model rather than a Russian one was suggested as the natural choice by Polish academics and practitioners.

The politics of 1989 brought great opportunity to effect major changes in criminal justice practice. Almost 40 percent of old prison staff left the service (Gajdus, 1993: 32–43). In most cases, they were choosing to leave because they would not accept the new conditions. There were also staff members who were asked to leave because they were known as violent, aggressive and abusive. For years, people working in prison were placed at the bottom of the social prestige ladder. The work in prison was stable, well paid and very unpopular. With the post-1989 changes, the best college and university graduates are seeking positions in prison work. Of course, the first wave of unemployment helped recruit young and motivated university graduates, and prison reforms removed much of the stigma of prison work. The new prison policy and new attitude toward the correctional officer made this position really challenging for young, ambitious people who have initiative, new ideas and the ability to cooperate with others. Rehabilitation was stressed over punishment. Even people working 20 or more years in the system began to exercise their creativity to help change a dungeon into a place where inmates are taught responsibility and are helped to regain self-esteem.

But, for this to continue, not only must overcrowding be avoided, but structural changes are necessary. It is not enough to change the names and call the guard an educator. It is not enough to say that from now on, the guards are not to guard but to educate the prisoners. The everlasting tension between the security section (guards) and rehabilitation section (education) will not be avoided by mere cosmetics. For this actual reform is needed, and to reform the system one must have a clear vision of the goal of that system. Once established, officials must adjust the method to reach that goal. The new radical directors are gone, however. The Director General was replaced by L. Moderacki, someone with almost 20 years' experience in the prison service. He was very much in favor of the line set by his predecessor, Moczydłowski, but he too was fired because of internal differences. As of March 1996, the post of general Prison Director is not filled, and the new Prison Director has not been appointed yet.

Prison and Culture

Finally, some explanations for the failure of reform are to be found in Polish culture. Nothing is less adequate than the old and often repeated catchword that "prison reflects society," for it is only partially true and omits the fact that prison not only reflects but also shapes the society. Historical events of the last half century (including World War II occupation and the Communist regime) made people in Poland grow accustomed to severe punishment. To punish was a way to secure Communist power and to make society obey. When punishment does not work, the misguided use a lot of it hoping for an expected effect. It had to be constantly increased because, once people got used to one level of punishment, that became the new standard (Podgórecki, 1976(a): 622–633). The rough condition of "free" life blunts sensitivities and makes the public believe that long imprisonment is a "just" punishment. Added to this "brutalization" is the general disrespect for the "law" imposed by the Russians. Russia has a Hellenistic-Byzantine cultural tradition, whereas Poland has always drawn its heritage from the Latin-Western tradition. The Communist regime adopted from Russia a complete lack of an established consciousness of the need for the existence of law and the necessity of observing it (Lazari, 1995). For different reasons than in Russia, this specific attitude has been to a certain extent adopted also in Poland. For many, refusal to comply with the law of the Communist regime was as patriotic as not to obey the Nazis. This situation produced an almost "schizophrenic" attitude towards the law: On the one hand, people knew it did not protect them from the arbitrary power of the state. On the other hand, they were not protected from common crimes like theft, robbery, rape, murder, etc. Since they could not expect police to protect them, they at least hoped criminal law would punish criminals when they were apprehended.[13]

Council of Europe reporter Sir Geoffrey Finsberg's (1990) observation on the historical repression of the Polish people is apt:

> the history of Poland can be best described as phoenix-like after several ruthless attempts to obliterate it. Poland, after all, disappeared from the map between 1795 and 1918, partitioned between Prussia, Russia and Austria. But its proud and patriotic people always rose again. On the latest occasion the enemy was within and the genuine spirit of Poland was oppressed for some 40 years by an alien political creed. Despite a brutal regime which even encouraged the murder of a priest, the spirit of freedom was kept alive by the Church, and later, by an alliance between Solidarity and the Church (Finsberg, 1990: 3).

This somewhat exalted picture captures Poland's spirit of resistance. Poland has managed after World War II to avoid a fate of being just another republic of the Soviet Union. Poland survived as a separate State, yet its sovereignty between 1944 and 1989 was in many ways merely formal. This was also the case in regard to criminal justice policy and practice. The Communist system imposed upon Poland at the Yalta Conference by the Soviet Union, with Western powers' connivance, gave Russia the authority to control many aspects of Poland's political, economic and social life (Frankowski and Wasek, 1993: 143). The new regime made an effort to be perceived as a successor of the pre-war free Polish government and did not delegalize the old legislation, introducing several amendments instead. Shortly, the old names acquired new substance. The new Communist law drastically restricted the independence of the judiciary, and introduced severe decrees and austere punishments to make imprisonment a tool to govern and solve the current social problems (Płatek, 1994). The legacy of resistance may offer hope for the future, however.

CONCLUSION

Good intentions have not been enough to change the old habits of penal administration. There are four fundamental reasons for this: *First*, at the most immediate and practical level, greater effort should be given to harmonizing the goals of the Executive Code with the institutional means in the Prison Service Law. The Executive Code creates the idea of what imprisonment *should* be, but the law on Prison Service directs the *practice*. The Executive Code is about ideas; the Law on Prison Service drafts reality—it regulates most of the vital matters concerning prison officers: their status, rights, obligations, disciplinary procedure, financial benefits, etc. The new Law on Prison Service, passed in September 1996, reaffirms security and cost as paramount objectives; penal practice continues to contradict the ideology of the Executive Code, which proclaims resocialization a primary goal. *Second*, the prison system is just one link in the chain of social control. Its effectiveness depends on the role ascribed to it. And, in a democracy, the more modest that role, the better. *Third*, and most fundamental, the criminal justice system is only one part of revolutionary reform. The public's enthusiasm for prison reform and demand for change that began in 1989 lasted only a short while and was focused on political prisoners. After a short period of "Solidarity," prisons again became pretty isolated from the rest of society. Today, the level of sympathy and social interest is down as the economic condition of the country deteriorates. People are less interested in the welfare of prisoners because the prison condition reflects the average living standard of Polish citizens, which itself has declined. "Less eligibility" is an operative principle in Poland today, with many believing that prisoners have much better conditions than they deserve. Many are appalled to learn that the per-diem for prisoners is higher than for hospital patients.[14] *Fourth*, penal reform is predicated on greater understanding and communication among the three realms of penality: the realm experienced by those *in prison*, the one expressed in *law* and interpreted by judges, and the third as discussed by criminologists in the *academic literature*. Those very different realms rarely meet, largely because the actors of one realm almost never have the opportunity to witness, let alone experience, life in another realm.

Poland is still far from democracy, but we are now experiencing "survival of the fittest" capitalism. The old communist argument against penal reform gets fresh value: "Yesterday," officials were criticizing prison education ("Why should prisoners have access to high schools when noncriminal children do not always have that privilege?"). Today, work replaces education as the controversial issue. Many Poles, underemployed and unemployed, would like to see robbers and thieves at hard penal labor, building public highways, just like in the old days, *except that today* the public realizes that even unpaid work competes with their jobs!

Notes

1. Despite attempts at their suppression, so-called "flying universities" were very active. These were meetings, often in private apartments, never officially announced yet crowded with well-known intellectuals, academics, dissidents who were teaching free from official censorship and where officially inaccessible data were presented.

2. Ustawa z dnia 10 maja 1985 r. o szczególnej odpowiedzialnosci karnej (Dz.U. Nr 23, poz. 101). A May 10, 1995, law set penal repression in motion; people were jailed for petty crime. In many cases, judicial proceedings were simplified and expedited. Eighteen months of imprisonment for stealing a cigarette lighter, 24 months for illicit sale of vodka, were typical. In many cases the defendant's right to defense and the assumption of his innocence were considerably limited. Obligatory detention and unconditional imprisonment were introduced. Discretionary power of judges was considerably limited, changing the court into a kind of robot imposing imprisonment.

POLAND   279

3. Official statistics published in this article present data lower than the actual number of people behind bars because jails, juvenile offenders, and many of those sentenced to prison for misdemeanors were not included in the official statistics. They *are* in prison, however, and their presence contributed significantly to the constant problem of overcrowding. See Kangaspunta, 1995: 49. The prison data for 1986, 1988 and 1990 indicating the average length of prison sentences *actually served* in months are, respectively, 32.1, 32.4 and 30.9 months. Only the Ukraine among Eastern European countries has a longer average time-served, with more than 60 months.

4. Interpol (1987/1988) *International Crime Statistics*. Lyons, France: IPCO-Interpol General Secretariat. 3; Messner and Rosenfeld, 1994; Christie, 1993; Kangaspunta, 1995; Kury, 1995.

5. In 1995 there were 1,705,000 employed people with higher (University or Polytechnic) education, and 393,000 unemployed with high education. Source: Rocznik, 1995; Podemski, 1984.

6. The calendar shows the regularity of events before 1976: October 1956 brought worker demands for democratic changes; March 1968 brought intelligentsia demands to democratize social life, and in December 1970 workers again demonstrated against the Communist government, with considerable bloodshed, especially in Gdansk.

7. See also Prison Administration Reports on "Economic Effectiveness of The Prisoner Work": Efekty Ekonomiczne, 1979; Więziennictwo, 1985.

8. The numbers were lower only in 1945, with 24,702, and just after the workers' uprising of 1956, with 35,879. See Statistical Information, 1995; Kangaspunta, 1995: 28.

9. Statistical Information of Central Prison Administration, August 1995. Number of Inmates in 1995:

Total Number	65,848	66,004
Women	1,593	1,582
Detained–total	17,065	17,204
Women	593	589
Sentenced	48,133	48,229
Women	989	972
Sentenced for misdemeanors		
(up to 3 months)-total	650	571
Women	18	2

In 1987 there were 5,000 women (5–8 percent of the total prison population). This has declined; today it is not even 3% of the total (for example, in June of 1989 there were 1,726 women, or 2.9%, in jails, and 249 women or 0.4% in prison).

10. On November 5th, 1995, Poles were choosing for the second time their president. There were 18 candidates, but only one discussed solving the crime problem through social measures instead of punishing criminals more. But even he was in favor of "getting tough" on cases of all new crime such as terrorism, drugs and gangs.
The increase in the number of foreigners is as follows:
On Dec. 31, 1992, there were 468 foreigners in Polish prisons.
On Dec. 31, 1993, there were 1090 foreigners in Polish prisons.
On Dec. 31, 1994, there were 1139 foreigners in Polish prisons.
On July 31, 1995, there were 1339 foreigners in Polish prisons.
On August 31, 1995, there were 1431 foreigners in Polish prisons.
The numbers are still growing. Most of the foreigners come from Russia and other former Soviet Republics.

11. The paramilitary character of the prison sentence requires prison staff to be used also in cases of rebellion. Revolts are not frequent but it is hard to build a positive relation between people who can't expect mediation nor efforts to understand each other.

12. For years it was almost impossible to publish any of the material presented during the regular seminars. A book published after the conference on prisoners' work brought a ban on prison entry to several of the conference participants. See Holda, 1985; Walczak 1985; Szymanowski, 1987.

13. Forty-five percent of Polish society is of the opinion that punishment should protect society against the crime. Twenty-six percent believe punishment should stop others from committing crimes. Only six percent consider the punishment to be a tool of a resocialization, while 11 percent want punishment to be vengeance. Public Opinion Poll: Osrodek Badania Opinii Publicznej. Warszawa , lipiec 1995.

14. On September 4, 5 and 6, 1995, Polish television (Tv1) and radio (FM3) broadcast several discussion programs on how good work, health and living conditions of prisoners were, while conditions suffered by the unemployed, hospital patients and the lower working classes were described as appalling. Interestingly, no professional opinions were provided to refute these assertions.

References

Andziak, R. (1995) "Przepełnione cele." *Rzeczpospolita*, March 31, Nr 77.

Arendt, H. (1983) *Eichmann in Jerusalem, A report on the banality of Evil*. Harmondsworth: Penguin Books.

Batawia, S. (1984) *Wstęp do Nauki o Przestępcy*. Wrocław: Ossolineum.

Biuletyn Nr 315/IX kad., Kancelaria Sejmu, Biuro Prasowe. Warszawa: Komisja Administracji, Spraw Wewnętrznych i Wymiaru Sprawiedliwości, January 21, 1987.

Bramska, M. (1995) "Zatrudnienie," in J. Malec (ed.) *Stan i Węzłowe Problemy Polskiego Więziennictwa*. Warszawa: Biuro Rzecznika Praw Obywatelskich.

Braudel, F. (1982) *Civilization and Capitalism, 15th–18th Century*. London: Collins.

Buchała, K. and Szewczyk, M. (1995) "Wprowadzenie do Kodeksu Karnego (stan prawny na dzień 19 sierpnia 1995)," in *Kodeks Karny oraz Ustawa o Ochronie Obrotu Gospodarczego*. Kraków: Centrum Prawne. pp. 8–18.

Chećko, A. (1995) "Niskie Instynkty." *Polityką*, Nr 22: 11. (An interview with the newly appointed General Director of Prisons. Lech Moderacki).

Christie, N. (1981) *Limits to Pain*. Oslo: Universitetsforlaget.

Christie, N. (1993) *Crime Control as Industry. Towards Gulags, Western Style?* London: Routledge.

Efekty Ekonomiczne Zatrudnienia Skazanych w Latach 1973–1978 (kwiecień 1979) Ministerstwo Sprawiedliwości, Centralny Zarząd Zakładów Karnych. Wydział Ewidencji i Zatrudnienia, NE-187/79/Z.

Ehrlich, St. (1971) *Wstęp do Nauki o Państwie i Prawie*. Warszawa: Państwowe Wydawnictwo Naukowe.

Fajst, M. (1995) "Spór o Kryminologię w Okresie Stalinowskim". *Studia Iuridica*.

Finsberg, G. (1990) "Report on Poland's Application for Membership of the Council of Europe." Conseil De L'Europe. Parliamentary Assembly. 19 September 1990, Doc. 6289: 3.

Foucault, M. (1977) *Discipline and Punish: The Birth of the Prison*. Harmondsworth: Penguin Books.

Frankowski, S. and Wasek, A. (1993) "Evolution of the Polish Criminal Justice System after World War Two-an Overview." *European Journal of Crime, Criminal Law and Criminal Justice* Vol. 1, No. 2.

Gajdus, D. (ed.) (1989) *Wokół Reformy Więziennictwa*. Wrocław: Biblioteka WIP.

Gajdus, D. (1993) "Od Więzienia Będącego Narzędziem Sprawowania Władzy do Więzienia Służącego Rozwiązywaniu Problemów

Kontroli Społecznej." *Biuletyn Polskiego Towarzystwa Kryminologic-znego* im. Profesora Stanisława Batawii.

Gazeta Wyborcza. (1995) "Więzienia są dla Przestępców." An interview with newly nominated General Director of Prisons. Lech Moderacki, Gazeta Wyborcza, April, 15–17.

Gruszczyńska, B. and Marczewski M. (1995) "Recorded Crime and Penal Policy," in J. Jasiński and A. Siemaszko (eds.) *Crime Control in Poland*. Warszawa: Oficyna Naukowa.

Heller, M. (1982) *Świat Obozów Koncentracyjnych, Literatura Sowiecka*. Warszawa: Krąg.

Hołda, Z. et al. (eds.) (1985) *Praca Skazanych Odbywających Karę Pozbawienia Wolności*. Lublin: Uniwersytet Marii Curie-Skłodowskiej.

Hołda, Z. and Rzepliński A. (1991) "The Polish Prison System in Mid-course: Prisoners' Rights and Prison Conditions in Poland, On the Verge of Becoming Civilized," in D. van Zyl Smit and E.F. Dünkel (eds.) *Imprisonment Today and Tomorrow—International Perspectives on Prisoners' Rights and Prison Conditions*. Deventer: Kluwer.

Interpol. (1987/1988) *International Crime Statistics*. Lyons, France: IPCO-Interpol General Secretariat.

Janiszewska-Talago, E. (1985) "Wykonywanie Prawa i Obowiązku Pracy Skazanych w Zakładach Karnych," in T. Bojarski, Z. Hołda, J. Baranowski (eds). *Praca Skazanych Odbywających Karę Pozbawienia Wolności*. Lublin: Uniwersytet Marii Curie-Skłodowskiej.

Jasiński, J. (1995) "Crime Control in Poland. An Overview," in J. Jasiński, A. Siemaszko (eds.) *Crime Control in Poland*. Warszawa: Polish Ministry of Justice (Institute of Justice).

Jasiński, J. (ed.) (1989) *Problems of Social Maladjustment and Crime in Poland*. Wrocław: Ossolineum.

Kangaspunta, K. (1995) (ed.) *Crime and Criminal Justice in Europe and North America 1986–1990*. Helsinki: European Institute for Crime Prevention and Control. (Publication Series No. 25).

Kojder, A. (1995) Godność i Siła Prawa, Szkice Socjologiczno-prawne. Warszawa: Oficyna Naukowa.

Kolęda, K. (1995) *Złodzieje i Klawisze*. Warszawa: Polski Dom Wydawniczy.

Korecki, J. (1991) "Kształcenie Zawodowe Funkcjonariuszy Służby Więziennej w Polsce." Paper presented at a Seminar on Prison Staff organized by Central Prison Administration and Council of Europe, Kalisz; Unpublished.

Kury, H. (1995) "Fear of Crime in Postcommunist Societies," 51st International Criminology Seminar, Warsaw, September 12–16, 1996. Unpublished Paper.

Lazari, A. (ed.) (1995) *The Russian Mentality*. Lexicon, Katowice: Śląsk.

Lernell, L. (1973) *Zarys Kryminologii Ogólnej*. Warszawa: Państwowe Wydawnictwo Naukowe.

Messner, S.F. and Rosenfeld R. (1994) *Crime and the American Dream* Belmont, California: Wadsworth.

Moczydłowski, P. (1993) "Prison: From Communist System to Democracy; Transformation of the Polish Penitentiary System." Paper presented at the II International Symposium on the Future of Corrections. Popowo, Poland, October 4–8. Unpublished.

Moczydłowski, P. (1983) "Types of Penal Institution, Economic Organization, and Inmate Social Structure: Some Polish Examples," *International Journal of the Sociology of Law*, No. 11.

Moczydłowski, P. and Rzepliński, A. (1990) *Collective Protests in Penal Institutions*. Oslo: Universitet I Oslo.

Płakwicz, J. and Zielińska E. (1994) "Abortion in the New Europe: Poland," in B. Rolston and A. Eggert (eds.) *Abortion in the New Europe, a Comparative Handbook*. Westport: Greenwood Press.

Płatek, M. et al. (eds.) (1991) *Abolitionism in History*. Warszawa: Instytut Profilaktyki Społecznej i Resocjalizacji, Uniwersytet Warszawski.

Płatek, M. (1994) "Made in Prison." Paper presented at the Annual Meeting of Academy of Criminal Justice Sciences, March 8–12, 1994, Chicago, Illinois. Unpublished.

Płatek, M. (1995) "What it is Like for the Women? Crime and Criminology in Poland," in N.H. Rafter and F. Heidensohn (eds.) *International Feminist Perspectives in Criminology, Engendering a Discipline*. Buckingham: Open University Press.

Płatek, M. (1991) "The Służewiec Prison in Warsaw, Poland: A Penal Labor Center, or Half-Open Prison," in D. Whitfield (ed.)

The State of The Prisons—200 Years on. London and New York: Routledge.

Płatek, M. (1995) "Comparative Study on the Social Effects of Criminal Policy in the U.S., Norway, and Poland." *Studia Iuridica* XXX.

Płatek, M. (1995a) "Współczesne Zmiany w Więziennictwie Polskim," in M.P. Wędrychowski (ed.) *Prawa Jednostki, Prawo Karne.* Warszawa: Instytut Prawa Karnego, Uniwersytet Warszawski.

Podemski, S. (1984) "Koronny Swiadek." *Polityka*, No. 18.

Podgórecki, A. (1976) "Patologia Działania Instytucji," in A. Podgórecki (ed.) *Zagadnienia Patologii Społecznej.* Warszawa: Państwowe Wydawnictwo Naukowe, 1976.

Podgórecki, A. (1976a) "Zakończenie, Problematyka Patologii Społecznej-Próba Syntezy," in: *Zagadnienia Patologii Spolecznej.* Warszawa: Państwowe Wydawnictwo Naukowe.

Poklewski-Kozieł, K. (1995) "Ludzka Kara Smierci." *Polityka*, No. 36.

Porowski, M. (1979) "Administracja Penitencjarna-Zasady Organizacji i Kierowania." *Studia Kryminologiczne, Kryminalistyczne i Penitencjarne*, t. 9, Warszawa.

Porowski, M. (1985) "Karanie a Resocjalizacja." *Studia Kryminologiczne, Kryminalistyczne i Penitencjarne*, Vol. 16.

Porowski, M. (1987) "Służba Więzienna i Czynniki Decydujące o Prestiżu Zawodu." *Studia Kryminologiczne, Kryminalistyczne i Penitencjarne*, t. 18, Warszawa.

Porowski, M. (1995) "Uwagi do Projektu Ustawy o Służbie Więziennej." Ekspertyza nr 51 E-51, Lipiec 1995, Kancelaria Sejmu, Biuro Studiów i Ekspertyz.

"Prison Conditions in Poland. An Update" (1992) A Helsinki Watch Report, Washington, DC.

"Rocznik Statystyczny Pracy-1995 GUS." Główny Urząd Statystyczny 1995.

"Rozporządzenie Ministra Sprawiedliwości z dnia 2 maja 1989 r. w sprawie regulaminu wykonania kary pozbawienia wolności" (Dz.U. z dnia 29 maja 1989 r., Nr 31, poz. 166; z późniejszymi zmianami Dz.U. z 1991 r., Nr 3 poz. 14; z 1994 r., Nr 72, poz. 320.

Sabbat-Świdlicka, M. (1992) "Polish Prison Reform Focuses on Social Reintegration." *Social Issues*, 1(46), November 20, 1992.

Sharlet, R. and Beirner, P. (1984) "In the Search of Veshinsky: The Paradox of Law and Terror." *International Journal of the Sociology of Law*, 12.

Statystyka Sądowa. (1980, 1994) *Cz. II Prawomocne Osądzenia Osób Dorosłych*. Warszawa: Ministerstwo Sprawiedliwości, Departament Organizacji i Informatyki.

Szelhaus, S. (1969) *Młodociani Recydywiści, Społeczne Czynniki Procesu Wykolejenia*. Warszawa: Państwowe Wydawnictwo Naukowe.

Szymanowski, T. and Rzeplinski, A. (eds.) (1987) *Doswiadczenia i Perspektywy Systemu Penitencjarnego w Polsce*. Warszawa: Instytut Profilaktyki Społecznej i Resocjalizacji, Uniwersytet Warszawski.

The Ministry of Justice Statistical Information on Number of Inmates. (1995) *1945–1994*. Warszawa: Ministerstwo Sprawiedliwości.

Ustawa z dnia 10 grudnia 1959 o Służbie Więziennej (The Law on Prison Staff from Dec. 10, 1959) Dz. U. z dnia 31 maja 1984, ze zmianami. Dz. U. 84.29.149. Zm: Dz.U. 95.34.163.

Ustawa z dnia 10 maja 1985 r. o szczególnej odpowiedzialności karnej (Dz.U. Nr 23, poz. 101).

Ustawa z dnia 12 lipca 1995 r. o zmianie Kodeksu Karnego, Kodeksu Karnego Wykonawczego oraz o podwyższeniu dolnych i górnych granic grzywien i nawiązek w prawie karnym, Dz.U. Nr 95/1995 poz. 475.

Ustawa z dnia 23 lutego 1990 r., o zmianie Kodeksu Karnego Wykonawczego (Dz.U. Nr 14, poz. 85), z dnia 28 marca 1990. Draft and its reasons. unpublished typescript. Draft no. BL 200–1200/95.

Utrat-Milecki, J. (1995) "Więziennictwo w Polsce w Latach 1944–1956." *Studia Juridica* 27/1995. Prawo Karne w Okresie Stalinizmu.

Vyshinsky, A. (1938) *The Law of the Soviet State*. New York: MacMillan.

Walczak, S. (eds.) (1985) *Spory Wokół Reformy Więziennictwa*. Warszawa: Instytut Profilaktyki Społecznej i Resocjalizacji Uniwersytetu Warszawskiego.

"Więziennictwo w Gospodarce Narodowej w Okresie 40-lecia PRL." (1985) Warszawa: Ministerstwo Sprawiedliwości, Centralny Zarząd Zakładów Karnych.

III
East Asia, The Pacific, and South Africa

Chapter
TEN

Facing Difference: Relations, Change and the Prison Sector in Contemporary China[1]

Michael Dutton and Xu Zhangrun

Politically, the labor reform system of the CCP [Chinese Communist Party] is the same as its Soviet and Nazi counterparts. All use violence to suppress political dissidents. However, the labor reform system of the CCP differs from the other two in its conception and means of suppression—"mind reform through forced labor." ...In the PRC, labor reform camps are an economic enterprise. The product of the prisoners' labor are sold in domestic as well as foreign markets and have become an indispensable component of the national economy. (Wu, 1992: 5)

[China's] educational reform of criminals is one function of the People's democratic dictatorship and is undertaken to serve the socialist system and the economic base. It is inextricably linked to the great proletarian enterprise of liberating the whole of humankind and has the aim of transforming the vast majority of criminals into law abiding citizens of the socialist system and useful timber in socialist construction. Hence, there is a basic difference between this and the instruction教悔, education 教育, and rectification 矫正, of criminals within the bourgeois prison...

It must be said that bourgeois scholars in formulating the ideas of instruction 教悔, education 教育, and rectification 矫正 for criminals moved beyond the revanchist and intimidatory forms of slave and feudal society. Nevertheless, despite this, in advancing the content of these so-called theories of instruction 教悔, education 教育, and rectification 矫正 these theories carry in them traditional and old fashioned ideas such as, 'the prison is here to punish' (Li Kangtai, 1985: 42).

To tell the story of the Chinese prison system, one must constantly read between the lines. As these two quotations demonstrate, these lines are, all too often, battle lines drawn between scholars representing very different social and value systems. The ferocity of language deployed highlights the extent of difference between these two accounts, but consequently blinds us to what are more deeply shared assumptions about the system and its role. Thus, despite their almost diametric opposition to each other's readings, these two accounts both predicate their own prison stories upon a shared set of assumptions about, and shared readings of, the Chinese penal system.

Both, for example, ground their assessments on the centrality of labor production to the Chinese prison system although clearly they draw diametrically different readings as to what this means: For Hongda Harry Wu, the incorporation of prison production into the socialist plan in the 1950s led to the ruthless economic exploitation of prisoners for economic gain, while for Li Kangtai, it highlighted the proletarian nature of the educational program operative within the penal system (Li Kangtai, 1985: 35). "Dialectical materialists" says Li, "consider productive labor to be the most basic social practice... thought transformation, therefore, is inseparable from productive labor" (*ibid*.: 47). Indeed, mainland Chinese accounts of the incorporation of the economic production from the penal sector into the state economic plan point out that this illustrates the superiority of the socialist system, not its exploitative nature. According to these accounts, this incorporation ensures that penal labor is not discriminated against as it is in the Western penal system where labor is either reduced to menial and insignificant tasks or is deployed in economically insignificant fields (Liu Zhi, 1987: 49). The idea that labor can be reformative, therefore, is never really fully realized in the West.

Second, both Wu and Li also share a common belief in the centrality of "thought reform" in the Chinese penal system. Again, however, this leads to very different assessments. For Wu, following a long line of Western critics that leads all the way back to Lifton's classic psychological account of thought reform and "totalism" (Lifton, 1963), this means "brain-washing." In contrast, for all mainland Chinese scholars, it means living up to the old slogan of the Chinese Communist Party's Central Committee from 1955 that the system must reform the criminal as its first priority and carry out production as a secondary consideration [改造第一，生产第二] (Li Kangtai, 1993: 70–1).

Last, and from our perspective the most contentious point, is that both Wu and Li regard the Chinese penal system as a radical break with erstwhile forms. For Harry Wu the lineage of the Chinese system is traced back to Nazi Germany and the Soviet Gulag. For him, the Chinese system is a development, if not perfection, of some of the most inhumane trends noted in these two systems.[2] Nazi Germany had camps, but there was little interest in the development of long-term goals. The Soviet camps had long-term goals, but their methods were far from systematic or complete. Only the Chinese penal system introduced a systematic, complete and theorized program of thought reform and it is this which makes it even more inhumane than these earlier endeavors (Wu, 1992: 3). Li, too, highlights the uniqueness of the Chinese penal system which is again presented as an advance on, and radical break with, erstwhile forms. Again, however, this argument leads to very different ends from those of Harry Wu.

In dispatching Western penal systems, Li's argument is predicated upon a miniaturized Stalinist portrait of historical development. Socialism, he suggests, is an advance upon the capitalist mode of production. Therefore, it follows that the apparatus of the socialist state are, by definition, radically different from and superior to those of the exploiting class states (Li Kangtai, 1985: 42). Other Chinese scholars have pointed to the differences between their system and the Soviet one. Sun Xiaoli, for example, explains that while the Chinese were influenced by their "elder brother," it is quite wrong to regard the Chinese system as a mere replication of the Soviet penal system. Certainly, the Soviets sent "advisors" who were placed in important positions within the relevant Ministry[3] but they were few in number and, as one "old comrade" told Sun, their influence was restricted to offering advice on a few technical

matters such as "the system for guarding entrances" and so forth
(Sun Xiaoli, 1994: 18–19). Speaking to other "old comrades" confirmed this. It seems that the majority of Chinese penal cadres at
that time regarded the Soviet penal system as deficient in so far as it
paid too little attention to the role of labor in the program of
reforming criminals (interview,[4] 12/14/93). Thus, despite the fact
that both systems were guided by Marxism-Leninism, it was only
the Chinese who laid stress on the transformational role of labor. In
addition to this, Sun notes, there were "differences in national character" that set the Chinese system apart. Socialism, with Chinese
characteristics, resulted in a system that put far greater stress on
reformation and it was this more than anything that marked it out
from the Soviet system and demonstrated its superiority (Sun
Xiaoli, 1994: 20).

It is not the intention of this paper to adjudicate on this debate
between Wu and his jailors. Instead, we would like to start by dis-
puting the ground on which the last of these assertions was made.
That is to say, we would like to question the claim made in both
accounts that the Chinese penal system is a radical break with erstwhile forms. We do this by very briefly pointing to the link between
the Chinese reformative strategies of using labor and thought
reform and earlier Western and Soviet programs. In arguing that
links such as this are important, we are careful not to "bend the
stick" and argue that the Chinese system is simply a replica of former Western liberal reformist schemas. Instead, we suggest that the
strongly indigenous and traditional methods used in the Chinese
system do indeed set the system apart to some extent.

Following Sun's argument about the importance of Chinese culture in framing the response to crime and, in contrast to Li
Kangtai's reading, we would suggest that the Chinese prison system is much less a "socialist new thing" than an amalgam of traditional methods and values wed to a Marxist framework. In
reference to Harry Wu's work, we would suggest that the Chinese
system is much more closely tied to Western penal endeavors than
he would care to admit. We propose that the contemporary Chinese
penal system has drawn on a legacy which is both indigenous and
imported. While Dutton has dealt with the influence of Western
penology and Soviet theory on the Chinese prison system in great
detail (Dutton, 1992), far less has been written in English on the traditional indigenous technologies, methodologies and values that
have helped frame Chinese penal discourse. For that reason, we lay

greater stress on elucidating this component of our argument. Having discussed some of the influences that have helped frame the labor and thought reform programs within the prison, we will then move on to examine the problems these programs have encountered in the period of economic reform after 1978.

The labor and thought reform programs were crucial in framing the success of the Chinese penal system in the early period of the People's Republic, but they have proven less resilient in the period after 1978 when free market economic reforms robbed them of much of their moral resilience. These reforms radically reformulated the social landscape, producing a very different lifeworld to the one which predated the reform period. Modernization and economic liberalization ripped into the traditional social fabric and induced the classic symptoms of social dislocation: high labor mobility, rising unemployment, rapid inflation, rising rates of crime, rising recidivism rates and so forth.

This changing social landscape produced what Chinese police have described as the fourth and most serious crime wave in China's contemporary history (Dai Wendian, 1989: 4). This, in turn, has led to something of a crisis in policing and penal strategies. In spite of the huge social changes underway in China today, policing and penal strategies still seem to reflect the values and aspirations of pre-reform China.[5] Reforming the policing and prison system to cope with the new post-reform conditions has therefore been very much on the agenda in recent years. This, combined with a desire to outflank Western human rights groups and combat the claim that China's "reform through labor" prison system was simply "slave labor," culminated in a new law in December 1994 which replaced "reform through labor" laws with a new prison law. From this time onward China had a prison, not a reform-through-labor, system.

What we would suggest, however, is that the most significant changes to the system in recent years have not been in its change of name nor even the internal reforms this encouraged. Rather, the post-economic penal reforms, we believe, that are most significant are not even within the prison itself, but are the "carceral spread" one notes around it. In an attempt to remedy many of the newer problems facing law enforcement agencies, new institutions are emerging or older carceral ones are redefined or re-established. What we discover then, is an institutional "widening of the net." To understand the social dynamics that have resulted in these changing penal practices requires knowing more than the history of, and influences upon, the prison itself. It requires knowing a little about recent social history and social change within which penal practices are framed. It is in the last part of the essay that we will examine the social conditions that have led to prisons being "augmented" by other forms of detention.

This essay begins by tracing the various theoretical traditions that have fed into contemporary Chinese penal discourse. It then explores the social crisis that has forced a series of reforms to the system in recent years. What we conclude is that contemporary post-economic reform penal strategies are neither the complete and systematic "brainwashing" machine that Wu would have us believe, nor the perfected and advanced transforming mechanism of Li Kangtai's vision. Instead, we present a picture of an institution that is much more clearly buffeted by the winds of change. No longer part of an overall social enterprise, the Chinese penal sector now sits uneasily, and far less successfully, as simply one, albeit the largest and most important, of a panoply of strategies designed to combat crime.[6]

The various attempts to reform inmates through labor are increasingly rendered impotent in the face of fundamental changes to the social landscape. The various methods designed to imbue a self-less socialist work ethic among prisoners seem strangely arcane in a period when the dominant social ethos presents material accumulation as glorious. The penal regime reforms its transformational schemes, yet cannot shake off its attachment to a Marxist-inspired frame of reference. The penal and policing regimes reform their punitive strategies also, but they are strangely reminiscent of past solutions and bygone eras. Chinese penal strategies show a poverty of imagination that is perhaps best explained in the words of Marx himself, and it is therefore to Marx that we will turn in order to begin this genealogy of Chinese prison theory.

CHINESE PENAL DISCOURSE: LABOR REFORM

"The beginner who has learned a new language," says Marx, "always retranslates it into his mother tongue" (1977: 147). In China, the language of economic reform introduced in 1978 is the "new language," while the language of Marxism, which has been spoken since 1949, is the "mother tongue"—albeit one spoken with a strong

Chinese accent! These are the two "languages games" within which most of the changes in this sector have taken place. Every reform undertaken within the penal sector in recent years seems to be transcribed into the "mother tongue" of Marxism and, through this, into the paradigm of reform through labor.[7] The strength and resilience of this paradigm should not be underestimated, but it should be stressed that part of this strength comes from its pre-Marxist existence. This idea of reforming through labor clearly ties China back to a Soviet Marxist past, but it is a lineage that stretches back much further than this. It is a line of thinking in "positive penology" that stretches back beyond the Soviet era to early Western penal schemes that target the transformation of the criminal's soul through a disciplining of the body. Yet, as has been argued elsewhere, these "dreams of criminal conversion" that fueled the schemes of both Bentham and Howard were to be reborn in the unlikely setting of China under the Marx-inspired banner of "reform through labor" (Dutton, 1992: 291). In China, this idea of labor as educative was a Western import. Nevertheless, it was an idea appropriated long before the Chinese revolution and certainly predates the Soviet influence in China.

In the dying days of the 19th century, the last dynasty of China, in a desperate bid to modernize and "appear civilized," imported a whole range of new technologies and methods from Western countries.[8] One such idea was that of "reforming criminals through labor." While the Nationalist Party that subsequently ruled China until 1949 picked up on the idea of reforming criminal ideas,[9] it was only with the communists that "thought reform" and "labor reform" (as opposed to penal labor) were wed.

Contemporary mainland Chinese texts on economic activity within the penal sector make clear the high valuation Chinese Marxism places on the concept of labor as transformative. Indeed, in contemporary Chinese analysis, labor is said to have a two-fold effect involving both a transformation of raw inanimate materials and a cognitive transformation of the labor force (Wang Tai, 1987: Reform… 1989). The use of penal labor in contemporary China is therefore more than the recruitment of a slave labor force as Harry Wu suggests; it also includes a belief in the cognitive value of labor in bringing forth human transformation. Organized engagement in large-scale productive labor offers the prisoner the same organizational conditions that produced the proletarian. The inclusion of prison production in the state economic plan after 1956 was therefore more than a device to further exploit the hapless criminal. It was predicated, in part, on the belief that the move from handicraft production to large-scale manufacturing or farming would help bring forth a proletarian consciousness among the prison workforce.[10]

Yet Wu's argument that labor was enacted as a form of punishment should not be entirely discounted. The unconscious influence of traditional Chinese discourse has played a part in influencing the formation of contemporary penal discourse and radically undercut the high Marxist valuation of labor as transformative. As Sun Xiaoli points out, one of the things that separates Chinese Marxism from its previous forms was its strongly culturalist component and it is from this that we can see that the definition of labor in contemporary China is not always that which the Chinese Marxism texts would have us believe.

Shadowing the idea of labor as transformational is a far more arcane idea that penal labor is undertaken to punish. It is at this point one discovers that Wu's idea of labor as punishment, while never adequately theorized in his work, is nevertheless not totally without foundation. It is in the contradictory but dual way in which prison labor is read—consciously as transformational, unconsciously as punishment—that we can begin to understand the resilience of this particular discourse of reform through labor. It satisfies both revanchist and reformist constituencies; it is a form of coinage wherein both sides reinforce its value. This idea of labor as punishment, however, is the side of the coin that constantly remains face down. Once again, to even see its presence, let alone understand its significance, we must read between the lines. Once again, we must return to the question of language and focus on those aspects of the Chinese word that its translation into the English word *labor*, leaves out.

"When we learn to speak, we are learning to translate," writes Octavio Paz. He continues: "The child who asks his mother the meaning of a word is really asking her to translate the unfamiliar term into simple words he knows already" (Paz, 1992: 152). In explaining the task of a translator, Octavio Paz likens the process to child rearing. We are forced, he says, back to a "simple language." But as Paz goes on to note, even "simple words" are inadequate when it comes to cross cultural readings. Crossing cultures, he observes, still leaves an "inexorable foreignness" (Paz, 1992: 153) to the text, even in the best translation. At least part of the reason for this, we would suggest, is because a translation cannot carry the etymological trail that informs the meaning of the original word into the new language.

Translation obliterates the shadowy etymology which links words to their past meaning. This would not be a concern but for the fact that such past meanings are often still active in unconsciously framing the reception of words in the contemporary and making them intelligible. The etymology of Chinese words like "labor reform" are quite different from English usages and to fully appreciate the degree of difference and the "dual nature" of labor reform in Chinese penal discourse requires a return to the word.

There is a long (principally Confucian) tradition in China that separates mental and manual labor and this was largely a "sign" of class difference. This difference is well summed up in the traditional Chinese saying that "those who work with their heads rule while those who work with their hands are ruled" (劳心者治人，劳力者治于人). Liang Shuming has insisted that while traditional Confucian philosophy made this distinction, it placed no moral value on it. It was, he insists, simply the way things were. Indeed, he goes on to suggest, in a manner similar to contemporary Chinese readings of Marx, that Confucius held the laboring people in high esteem and people should be solicitious of them and recognize them as the creators of all wealth (Liang Shuming, 1986: 99–103). While this may well be true, it was an argument that did little to break down the long-held association between physical labor and punishment. Physical labor, in China, has traditionally been regarded as a form of enslavement and disgrace and this perspective is graphically illustrated in the penal vocabulary that operated in traditional times and which, interestingly enough, is still in use today. By returning to the traditional uses of contemporary words we are able to see the etymological trail that, we would suggest, still stalks contemporary usage.

The word for imprisonment in contemporary Chinese is *tuxing* [徒刑]. This is a compound made up of two separate characters *tu* [徒] and *xing* [刑]. In ancient Chinese, the character *tu* 徒 when combined with *xing* 刑 had a different meaning and the character *tu* 徒 was often substituted for the character *nu* 努 which had a similar pronunciation but a slightly different meaning. The character *nu* 努 meant "to engage in physical labor." Hence, the compound *tuxing* 徒刑 when read as *nuxing* 努刑, translated literally, and continues unconsciously to be read in this way in popular Chinese imaginings, as forced labor undertaken through penal servitude.

This popular traditional association between forced labor and penal servitude was further reinforced by similar associations made in the popular rhyming dictionary of traditional times, the *Ji Yun* 《集韵》. In this text, *tu* was explained as being in correspondence with the character *nu* 奴 which meant enslavement. Such was the power of this form of coupling that it even found its way into the classical legal codes. In the highly authoritative *Tang Dynasty Code and its Explanation* 《唐律疏议》 the character *tu* 徒 was again described as having the character and meaning of *nu* 奴 (*Tang Code*, "*Mingli-tuxing*"). Through this association with *nu*, the text asserts, the full implications of imprisonment become apparent: "Keeping criminals in conditions of enslavement and disgrace." Because China is a country where the past is revered, these understandings were not confined to the Tang Dynasty but were read into the legal codes of all subsequent dynasties. In this way, these values became part of the legal assumptions of each subsequent regime and part of the assumed cultural coordinates of the entire nation. They became part of that knowledge that, in another context, Paul Veyne once described as "the large zone of the unexpressed" which guides action but that is so deeply assumed it is never articulated or even consciously thought (Veyne, 1982: 191). Penal labor as punishment, therefore, became an unconscious, yet widely accepted notion long after the linguistic association between *tu* and *nu* died away. Moreover, it had become such an ingrained association that it was scarred onto the national mindset and no subsequent reformist agenda was able to fully erase it.

The history of post-1949 penal discourse stands as a testimony to this struggle for erasure. It is a history of a struggle over this word, yet the vapor trails of the past, despite the very best of Marxist intent, have never cleared enough to allow the "transformationist" agenda to be free of its ugly twin. The history of reform through labor reads like a constant battle between these two meanings. From the early accounts of prisons needing to produce to survive, through to more recent cases of labor being exploited for personal gain, the history of the prison in contemporary China reads like a "two line struggle" over this single word and its deeper meaning.

Even more generally, the battle lines seem drawn not only between mainland accounts and their rivals, but also within mainland China itself. While the government has always presented the laboring masses as heroic and worthy of emulation, the popular response was always stalking this high evaluation with the tactic of derision and this found expression in both verse and rhyme. The popular expression; "Why must I do this? I am not a prisoner" aptly sums up this common traditional sentiment that only prisoners should be forced to undertake the most arduous and dirty work for it is only they who should be subjected to penal labor and servitude. A similar etymological search through China's past reveals that the idea of "thought reform" is also not really a "socialist new thing."

CHINESE PENAL DISCOURSE: THOUGHT REFORM[11]

Long before the communists took power in China, the idea of thought reform was present in the moral discourses and "self-cultivating" practices of traditional discourse. Confucian pedagogy, for example, in developing codes for the correct comportment of the "gentleman-sage" (君子) was resplendent with principles and techniques that were designed to bring forth ethical improvement. These principles and practices were largely based on the Confucian principle of benevolence (仁 ren) as well as the idea of feeling, sentiment or emotion (情 qing). One discovers these ideas reappearing in prison vocabulary in the form of notions such as ganhua 感化.[12] This term has no direct English language equivalent, but could be translated as "helping people to change through [moral] persuasion" or "setting an example by which to transform people and help them to change." Ganhua is a word made up of two parts and it is the different meanings that are brought together in this compound that are explored in the classical Chinese text of Character Explanations 《说文解字》. In this volume, the term gan 感 is said to mean the production of feeling that is powerful enough to move the heart, whereas the term hua 化 is rendered as an action or actions on the part of a subject that brings forth change. Hence, the term ganhua combines the emotional state of bringing forth change with the practical action of a person actually inducing it.

   In classical times, it was the gentleman-sage of Confucian discourse who combined these two attributes. In the practices of self-cultivation these figures improved themselves, yet in undertaking such a course of self-improvement, they stood as a model for others to emulate. In the contemporary period and, within the prison, it is the cadre who occupies this particular role.[13] The prison cadre acts as moral guide and the inmates look to the cadre as a model upon which to build their own transformation. Through *ganhua*, correctional officers utilize the ethical and emotional ties they build up with the prisoner to bring forth a change in the inmate's life perspective.

Hence, the idea of reform within the prison operates on a twin register. *Ganhua* and the assumptions upon which it operates are quite separate from those which underpin the Chinese concept of labor. This Chinese concept of labor emanates from the wedding of a strongly authoritarian "Legalist" tradition with a more reformist but no less authoritarian Marxian one. The result is a highly ambivalent and often quite unstable notion that can swing from being a concept designed to transform to one being used solely to exploit and punish. For its part, "thought reform" is much less ambiguous. Based upon traditionally inspired technologies and unconscious cultural assumptions of the officials and inmates, this concept of *ganhua* actually builds on and into the cosmology of everyday life and simply works for its reconfiguration. This point is well summed up in the explanation of thought reform offered by the leading Chinese penal scholars Xu Juefei, Shu Hongkang, Shao Mingzhen and Yu Qisheng. They explain the process of thought reform as one of "replacement" and, in part, as being the transformation of criminal forms of brotherhood (*yiqi*) with socialist ones. They illustrate this in the following manner:

> Youthful offenders who have taken the wrong road often do so because they have failed to pay attention to the communist morality of self-cultivation... we must begin from the criminals' own situation, inspire and lead them to recognize that their own criminality emanates from their inability to learn communist morality and the morality of the public and that this, in turn, is directly related to the allure of the morality of the exploiting classes and produces the same sense of revulsion. Later, we can gradually lead them to distinguish between civilisation and barbarism, between criminal brotherhoods (*jianghu yiqi*) and comradely friendship, between desperadoes and heroes and between the morality of the exploiting classes and that of communism. (Xu Juefei et al., 1983: 135)

What is important to recognize about this prison "thought reform" process is how well it is in tune with the everyday cultural assumptions of daily life in China. Mayfair Yang, in her detailed study of social relations in China, believes that this idea of *ganhua*, along with the idea of *qing* or *renqing*—the emotional ties of affect and obligation—and brotherhood or *yiqi* form the basis of most

daily social interaction in China and are the pillars upon which contemporary ideas of networking (or *guanxi*), "face" (or *mianzi*), and
community are built (Yang, 1994: 119–123). It is these types of social
emotions that have established the basis for a Maussian type of
"gift like regime" of networks, friendships, communal ties and
"face" framing virtually all social and daily activity in China.[14] It is
into this form of "group consciousness" that the idea of *ganhua* can
have great play. It can be effective, however, only because of a radically different form of subjectivity that is operative in China and
which, by and large, is almost wholly absent from contemporary
Western society.

While individuality has a high valuation in Western culture
and law, it is the group that constitutes the crucial social unit in
China. Indeed the pictographic form of the character for benevolence (*ren* 仁) upon which notions such as *ganhua, renqing* and *yiqi*
rest, is itself split into two parts that combine to depict both the
character for "a person" 人 and the character for the number "two"
二 (Xu Zhangrun, 1991). In other words, benevolence begins picto-
graphically and often unconsciously from the care, concern and
importance of oneself to others and it is this that more or less frames
all the technologies for the construction of an ethical self in China.
Confucian patriarchal theory marks out the space where this concern
for others is both produced and perfected and that "space" was, in
traditional China, the family relation "from whence," it was claimed,
"all other virtues spring" (*The Classic...*, "zhushu"; 1980: 2545).

Socialist China may rely on other forms of "collectivity" to establish its own form of social and ethical discourse—and we can see
this in the way that the idea of labor under Marxist influence has
indeed travelled—but the continuing reliance upon the collective
nevertheless produces a need/desire to continue the reliance upon
modified forms of traditional social technology. Hence, despite, or
possibly because of its Confucian nature, the concept of *ganhua* still
has considerable purchase within contemporary Chinese socialism.
In the contemporary prison where the ideas of *ganhua* are said to be
used to instill proletarian values, it is the prison cadre and not the
gentleman-sage or father who acts as the model for emulation. The
cadre's "proletarian character" and high moral values are said to
"act" upon the inmates to reconfigure their "distorted" sense of
social collectivity.

The underlying idea of producing a form of socialist mutual-
ity through collective bonding is then pressed into the service of

forcing a re-evaluation of the criminals' life experiences. They are forced to confront their pasts and, through this, begin to empathize with their victim. Evoking shame is said to be the first act leading to rehabilitation and to the possibility of recovering a social sense of "face."[15] These techniques are still very much at the heart of the theory of thought reform in China and, as the above should demonstrate, it is too simplistic to dismiss such processes as "brainwashing."

At the same time, one begins to understand that such processes can only operate within a very specific cultural milieu. Yet this process, whereby criminals in China begin to empathize with their victims and through this, develop a sense of remorse, has, in recent years in the West, attracted a name and that name is "reintegrative shaming" (Braithwaite, 1989). The problem is, of course, that such "reintegrative shaming" strategies are, as the above argument makes clear, culturally specific and cannot be applied easily to societies without the collective customs and traditions that inform them. Moreover, these reintegrative strategies are wholly dependent upon the fact that the values they imbue and the technologies they deploy within the prison have a much wider social resonance. That these social resonances are now being called into question as a result of the 1978 Chinese economic reform program demonstrates that the problem of implementation is not only spatial contingency but also temporal contingency.

SOCIAL CHANGE AND PENAL REFORM

In China, temporal changes have brought forth a cultural sea-change that has led to a questioning of certain aspects of the "reform through labor" ideal. Reform through labor is no longer being reinforced by popular social practices but is, in many cases, running almost in opposite directions to them. As a result of economic reform, there has been a breakup of the collective vision of society. This breakup of the collective vision is not just the growing disbelief in Marxism, but has a structural and social expression also.[16] The structural and social manifestation of the breakup of the collective and collectivist vision are side-effects of the economic forces unleashed by the process of economic reform. Pre-reform China had a highly regimented and policed sense of community with strict prohibitions on internal migration reinforcing a traditional, highly sedentary and stable sense of moral community.

Centralized planning, a high level of state ownership of industry and an economy organized on the basis of a state plan reinforced this and also offered a space for prison rehabilitative programs to stretch beyond the prison and into the community. Local industries were not only ordered to make products for the plan, but they were also forced to take the employees they were allocated by the plan. This included taking former employees who had committed crimes back into their "bosom" after the completion of their prison terms. The inmates therefore returned to their (social, moral and economic) community and through "reintegrative shaming" and a highly coercive program of monitoring and surveillance, they were checked, monitored and finally "reintegrated."[17] The rehabilitative potential of *ganhua* and *renqing* therefore went beyond the penal regime and had a central place in post-penal transformational regimes of the work unit and the community. Post-reform China has robbed the prisons of these conditions.

First, there has been a massive growth in non-state sector enterprises and these are, by definition, exempt from the sets of commitments made during the era of socialist planning. After 1956, virtually all private sector enterprises were nationalized and campaigns in the 1970s against "bourgeois tails" mopped up those that were not. Economic reform set about to undo all this and by 1990, it had succeeded in reducing state ownership of industry to little over half (54.6% to be exact) of all enterprises, with this sector's production accounting for only 39.3% of all goods produced (Li Junren, 1992: 145–6). This new private sector was free to produce what it liked and hire whom it wanted and the well-documented social discrimination suffered by former inmates meant that they were not high on the list of possible employees (Li Junren, 1992: 134; Wang Wenyuan, 1993: 7). Second, even state sector enterprises have been buffeted by these cold hard economic winds of change. Economically, this was most dramatically reflected in the reorganization of enterprises away from planned goods produced through a state quota system and toward goods made for the market. Between 1979 and 1990, the state radically cut the number of industrial products produced under quota from 120 to just 60. It also cut the amount of state-designated materials and finances from 256 items to just 27. At the same time, the commerce department cut the number of products from 188 to just 24 (Li Junren, 1992: 144). This cutting of quotas was a way of cutting enterprises loose. If an enterprise no longer produced goods for the plan then its survival was not guaranteed but depended upon its profitability. Profitability, in turn, demanded an examination of *how* things were produced, not simply *what* was produced. So began a series of other reforms to give these enterprises more managerial "freedom" and, most importantly, maximize the conditions for profitability. Once these were experimented with successfully in non-plan producing state enterprises, even the enterprises producing for the plan were reorganized in this way. This liberalization process culminated in the passing of the enterprise law by the State Council in July 1992. This law gave the enterprise managers the right to hire and fire wage labor as they saw fit. In giving the manager this power, the state effectively offered managers in this sector the same "rights to manage" as existed in the private sector. Thus state sector industry, concerned with profit and efficiency and fearful of trouble or loss, now had the power to refuse prison requests for re-employment of ex-inmates (Guo Xiang and Xu Zhangrun, 1994: 44).

The passing of this law was but the final nail in the coffin of the old, post-penal rehabilitative strategy. Prisons no longer had the collective capacity to place criminals back into their own communities. Yet the dreams of an imagined rehabilitative community structure still haunted penal authorities. Thus, while prison officials speak of "reform" and in the language of the new, their dreams are of the past and how to recover it. Under this banner of "reform," the search for a post-plan rehabilitative strategy began. It took the form of a disparate range of experiments which shared little in common but their new language of reform and their old dreams of transformation. Part of the problem of reform for the prison was that it required a move beyond Marxist and Chinese traditions, yet the language and conceptual framework to enable this leap did not exist. The result, then, has been the production of a range of reform solutions and experiments that are still very much written in the mother tongue of Marxism or China's past and cannot adequately respond to the new situation China faces.

One example of this poverty of reconceptualization is found in one "reform" strategy being experimented with which attempts to establish a localized and privatized version of the employment conditions that existed under the plan. In a number of important trials, prison managements have started setting up their own local enterprises to employ ex-inmates and thereby give them an opportunity to reintegrate (Liu Chenggen, 1995). Such enterprises are only operating on a very limited scale and it is doubtful whether they will become a feature of the post-reform through labor scenario. The problem for them, of course, is that they must compete economically in the market place and there are some crucial factors that militate against their success. First, the quality of their ex-prisoner labor force is well below that of an ordinary workplace (Xu Juefei et al., 1983), yet in times of economic reform they must still compete on an open market. Second, these enterprises are "half-way houses" insofar as they train the ex-offenders and then encourage them to find employment elsewhere. Thus, even if the quality of the labor force were to improve, the very nature of these enterprises militates against maintaining a stable and well-trained labor force. Last, the problem of stigmatization, which is regarded as one of the crucial issues blocking rehabilitation (Wang Wenyuan, 1993: 7) and which led to the formation of these enterprises in the first place, did not disappear with the establishment of such enterprises, it simply pushed it one stage further away. Ex-inmates can find limited employment and training opportunities in such workshops and factories, but they must eventually leave and find employment elsewhere. Given that potential local employers generally know that these firms are centers for re-training ex-convicts, the problems of stigmatization appear once again, but this time, in relation to ex-employees of these particular companies.

The high financial costs involved in setting up these post-prison enterprises, coupled with the difficulty prison authorities have in placing ex-convicts in ordinary enterprises, has led the Justice Ministry to experiment with other post-release rehabilitative employment strategies. One such alternative strategy is to subsidize the former inmates' re-entry into society by sponsoring them as "individual traders." Indeed, the level of stigmatization suffered by ex-convicts in this "shaming" society can be gauged, to some extent, by the fact that "the vast majority of all recently released prisoners are going into business" for themselves (Guo Xiang and Xu Zhangrun, 1995: 45). Yet the high rates of bankruptcy in this sector, coupled with the fact that prison rehabilitative ideology suggests that it is the individual entrepreneurial ethos that has led to the decentering of socialist ethics and the rise in crime, make this rehabilitative strategy no less problematic than the first. Free traders are also highly mobile and this, in turn, undermines the ability of policing agencies to survey and monitor ex-convicts. Given that the re-integrative strategies turn, in part, on heavy surveillance, the necessary mobility of the ex-prisoner turned free trader is also a problem that this strategy faces.

In pre-reform China, an extremely low recidivism rate was achieved, in part, by the tight demographic policing of the population. In post-reform China, the conditions for this generalized tight demographic policing have evaporated.[18] Traders need to go to their supply sources and to markets, labor is needed in city construction, business people required fluidity and mobility and all these factors militate against the previous practice of tight demographic policing. The state, therefore, had to relax the tight demographic policing arrangements to allow the economy to develop. They did this but attempted to exempt certain types of people they were suspicious of, or wished to continue to monitor and control. This group, known within policing parlance as the focal population (*zhongdian renkou*), were the focus of special police attention and continued restriction. This focal population consisted of a range of different "suspicious characters," but one group definitely included in their number was "those who had been released from reform through labor units, reform through education institutions and criminal detention centres" (Yu Lei, 1987). For those within this focal population, special case files were opened and tight controls over movement from one jurisdiction to another put in place. Beginning in May 1982, the Ministry of Public Security placed great weight on the policing of this group of people, yet left the process of checking to individual police stations to determine. At the same time, however, they insisted that the handling of the focal population should be one key determinate in assessing the local police stations' overall performance (Deng Zhaoren et al., 1987: 3). The net result was highly contradictory. The police stations' performance assessment was based on the successful policing of this population, yet resources were scarce and stations understaffed. Moreover, conditions had so changed and police powers and abilities in this area so declined that the force was simply no longer able to institute tight demographic controls over even this small fraction of the population (interview, 1994).[19] The results were therefore mixed. Irrespective of the rate of success one thing was clear: This attempt at tight demographic policing of the focal population flew in the face of the Ministry of Justice's new rehabilitative strategies, which either sent the ex-criminals on the road as small-scale entrepreneurs, or sent them on the road in search of work.

The economic reform program has, therefore, eroded the structural bonds that tied communities together which, in turn, produced the space for *ganhua* to operate beyond the prison wall. It foreclosed upon the traditional reintegrative space that was once occupied by the ex-convict. At the same time, economic reform has brought forth such large-scale cultural change that even the internal operation of the prison's own rehabilitative program is made problematic. Economic reform introduced the idea of individual profit, and this not only made redundant many of the models and ideals propounded in the prison, but also led to an erosion of the high moral standing of the cadre. This has occurred, in part, because corruption within the penal sector has become, as one Chinese commentator recently noted, quite "commonplace" (Zhang Peitian, 1995). This fall from grace of the prison cadre seriously threatens the entire internal rehabilitative program for, as noted above, this program rests on the idea of *ganhua* which necessitates a cadre-model to emulate. It is for this reason that the whole issue of raising the quality of cadres in the prison sector has become so important in recent years (Zhu Hongde, 1993: 11).

In addition to the emergence of corruption within cadre ranks, economic reform has also introduced the profit motive within penal enterprises, and this gives new life and an economic motivation to the old, traditional revanchist view of labor.[20] As noted earlier in relation to public enterprises, economic reform has led to greater enterprise autonomy and corporate responsibility over profit and loss. Prison enterprises have not been exempted from this trend. They, too, have come under similar sorts of pressures to make themselves more economically viable. To promote economic efficiency, reform of penal enterprises and industry has been undertaken. There is now much greater managerial autonomy within the prison enterprises and a more generous remuneration of profit. These two factors reinforce a prevalent view that penal labor is the repayment of a social debt and not a mechanism of reform. Moreover, it increases the pressure to drive workers harder and, while this has been offset by the greater respect for prisoner rights that have emerged in post-reform China, this tendency is nevertheless all too apparent.[21] These new pressures emerge directly out of the economic rationalist logic that has been imposed on the prison sector. In the post-economic reform period, the prison sector receives only part of its running costs from the central government. The rest must be made up out of its own productive activity. This has proven to be quite difficult for both the prison factory and farm.[22] In relation to prison factories, the difficulties are four-fold: First, the state no longer provides the raw materials for production

and these must therefore be bought on the market at market prices.
Second, the number of prisoners far exceeds the demand for labor
within the prison enterprises leading to under-employment and
hidden subsidies ("Mao Zedong Thought..." 1994: 9). Third, because the prisoners' skill base is low and equipment antiquated, the
quality of goods produced is not good and it is difficult to find markets for prison-made products outside the state sector. Fourth, the
prison units are not ordinary productive units and incur a range of
additional costs for things such as inmate supervision, training and
so forth that other factories do not have to face and these must be
factored into the cost of the operations.

The problems are even greater if one turns to the prison farms.
Since the early 1950s, about half of all prisoners have been located
on prison farms, and while they therefore form a key component of
prison production, farms are even less viable than the prison factories. Because they have always operated under the principle of
avoiding competition with local people, prison farms were, from
their inception, established in areas that were very backward, poor,
remote or difficult to farm. This meant that most farms were established in more remote, backward and thinly populated provinces or
autonomous regions with the vast majority being in either Qinghai,
Xinjiang, Inner Mongolia or Guilin. This makes economically-viable
cultivation almost impossible as there are few people in these
regions, let alone markets or transportation facilities ("Mao Zedong
Thought..." 1994: 9–10). The net result is that they have contributed
greatly to the hardship of the prison sector. As economic reform
develops, the declining profitability of this sector becomes more
and more acute. Since 1990 in particular, the profits from prison
production have turned into losses and induced what one report
described as a period of "extreme economic hardship" within the
prison sector. In 1980, 18 provincial and city prison authorities reported profits in excess of 10 million *yuan*, and only five provinces and areas reported losses. By 1990, there were only three
provinces and cities recording profits in excess of 10 million and 23
provinces, cities and areas recording losses. Moreover, over half of
these loss-making authorities recorded losses in the "tens of millions." The net result has been a reversal of the order of the slogan
"reform first, production second" as prison enterprises try too make
themselves profitable again ("Mao Zedong Thought..." 1994: 8).

In essence, the problem the prisons currently face is that the cold
winds of economic reform have begun to steer the collectivist

"thought reform" strategies aground while simultaneously reinforcing certain aspects of the traditional revanchist notion of penal
labor. While this takes place behind prison walls, outside the prison,
the post-release rehabilitation programs have also run into problems that have led to the institution of piecemeal experimental
"reforms."

All these problems within the prison take place at a time of massive changes in the nature of crime, the "culture of crime" and the
profile of the criminal.[23] The rising recidivism rate[24] not only illustrates the problems facing the prison but, given the very close correlation between recidivism and crime rates in China, the problem
of crime more generally (Li Junren, 1992: 130). The case statistics
collected by the Public Security Ministry tell a tale of rapidly rising
crime with an average rise in cases of 32% between the years 1985
and 1991 and a 40% increase in violent criminal cases (Yu Lei, 1993:
45).[25] Those arrested are now quite a lot younger than in the past—
70–80% of those arrested in recent years have been between the
ages of 14–25 (Yu Lei, 1993: 45). They are also far more mobile.
Indeed, one discernable trend in recent years has been the enormous growth in mobile crime. These criminals are attracted to the
richer population centers and along the developed eastern coastal
regions and they now feature prominently in criminal statistics (Yu
Lei, 1993: 342–343). Furthermore, all criminal activities are tending
to be far more serious than in the past and this indicates an increasing likelihood of re-offense (*Research into*, 1992: 439–440).

While this problem is still far from serious by Western standards,
the changing cultural and economic landscape, coupled with the
inability of prison and policing authorities to halt the growth of
crime, has the authorities worried. They look with concern as they
see the revival in many of the crimes and misdemeanors that were
stamped out after the revolution and suggest that what is currently
being experienced is but a foretaste of things to come. As one, highly
influential text notes:

> In the 'fifties, our country eliminated such evil things as prostitution,
> the illegal drug industry, gambling, and the kidnapping and sale of
> women and children. In recent years, however, such crimes have
> come back from the dead and could even be said to be flourishing.
> Hence, we have undertaken to severely crack down on such things,
> to continuously attack them but even so, we have been unable to
> bring them to a halt. Part of the explanation for their resilience lies
> with the influence of foreign things, the allure of organised crime,

and the spread of illegal trading, smuggling and corruption. Another factor is the harmful influences the 'trading consciousness' has had among certain people. It has washed away their morality, made them spiritually empty and vulnerable and, in their search for the good things of life, led them to carry out degrading activities. This is an extremely serious social problem for if a society has these sorts of evil influences, then it will inevitably be from these seeds that crime and illegality will grow (Li Junren, 1992: 154).

The inability of the police and prisons to check this growth or turn it around has led to calls for the reform of these two sectors. Yet the reforms that have been instituted on both sides of the prison wall are not only piecemeal but also predicated on the logic and mindset of the pre-reform Maoist era. Again, it is language that betrays all.

Innovative policing strategies in the reform era reflect their Maoist past. One key new strategy of policing has been the revival of the Maoist "campaign," but this time to use the technology against target crimes. Another reform has been to call for a strengthening of the mass-line approach to policing (Dutton, 1996). Detention strategies, too, display a similar romance with the stable Maoist past of the 'fifties, and this is reflected in the resurrection of a range of institutions that have, in effect, seen a spreading of the carceral net. Like the police, the "penal remembrance" of the Mao era is not a clearly articulated and unified vision of how society should be (although it is unconsciously built on a recognition of this). Rather, it is an ad hoc and targeted series of responses to a number of problem crimes and misdemeanors. Just as police have targeted key areas (the eastern coastal regions and the cities) and suspect groups (the so-called "focal population") (Dutton and Li, 1993a), detention has "spread" to aid police work. Here, one finds that, along with the prison sector, a shadow economy of detention has developed to deal with some of these more troublesome problems now encountered in a country undergoing economic reform. The detention sector is neither as well regulated nor as well funded as the more developed and formal penal sector. In many respects, it is like the police response to targeted crimes: a "severe strike" that is ad hoc in nature and punitive in character. Moreover, it is built upon and reflects the thinking of a bygone era. Such practices emerge, in part, from the experiences of the immediate post-liberation period when vagrancy, prostitution and drug taking were a problem the communists inherited from the old regime and, in part, from the institutions set up to deal with political offenders in the 'fifties. From these two strands has developed a somewhat ramshackle collection of institutions, some under the Ministry of Justice, others under the Ministry of Public Security, that are concerned less with thought or labor reform than with controlling and punishing the felon. These institutions have emerged, not because of the omnipotence or despotism of the Chinese state, but rather because of the state's inability to effectively control things. This has led to something of a governmental panic and this is reflected in the series of ad hoc institutions that have emerged to deal with specific types of crime. It is to this "carceral spread" that we will now turn to for it is, to our mind, this sector that constitutes one of the most important and yet rarely discussed effects of economic reform on the penal sector.

CARCERAL SPREAD

Incarceration in China is divided into two forms: the detention sector and the prison sector. Unlike the prison sector, detention falls within the province of the Ministry of Public Security. Unlike Western lockups and watchhouses, however, Chinese detention centers can hold more than suspects. They can also hold convicts. Three types of detention centers exist. These are the *juyisuo* which are like local jails, the *jiuliusuo* which are like city versions of the *jiyisuo* and the *kanshousuo* which are like a watchhouse or lockup. There is a huge overlap in their responsibilities and all three tend to be used both as lockups and jails. Indeed, convicted criminals on minor offenses who are sentenced to two years or less of incarceration can actually end up doing their time in the *jiuyisuo* rather than the prison. Generally, however, such centers are used to detain those who have been charged but not yet convicted. Detention in the *jiuyisuo* runs from 15 days to half a year. In the *juliusuo*, suspects are generally held for no more than 15 days, while in the *kanshousuo* they can be held for up to ten days prior to charges being laid, and then three months if charged (Interviews, 1992; 1993). Apart from this form of short-term detention, there are also other forms of incarceration that lie outside the prison sector proper. These are for people who have committed no breach of the criminal code but whose actions or attitudes are in breach of certain administrative regulations. There is, then, a distinction between administrative and criminal detention.

In Chinese law, there are two types of detention. One is administrative detention, where the detainee receives labor education in a "reform through education" institution, while the other is criminal, and the prisoner undergoes labor reform within the prison sector proper. Since 1983, both the prison and the reform through education institutions have operated under the Ministry of Justice. The differences between the prison and reform through education are, in theory at least, quite significant. Actions that warrant detention for labor education are those which are regarded as insufficient to warrant a criminal charge being laid but serious enough to require "transformation."

Criminals have penalties imposed by the courts on the basis of the criminal code and sentences can range from between one year to life imprisonment. Generally, within the prison sector, those incarcerated for ten years or more, or those regarded as "sensitive prisoners" go to prison, while light offenders go to prison camps (*Encyclopedia*, 1993: 347).

In contrast, labor education is a non-criminal administrative sanction imposed by a reform-through-education management committee and while it leads to punishment, it does not result in a criminal record. The administrative regulations allow sentences of up to three years, with a possible fourth year extension. Sentences are imposed by a reform-through-education management committee that is made up of people from the local Party and government, the procuraturate and the police. The history of re-education through labor is different from reform through labor insofar as it emerged from a different set of needs and at a different time from the prison sector.

Basically, education through labor emerged as a device of the Maoist political campaign.[26] First muted in 1955 by the Party Central Committee in its "Instructions on Completely Wiping Out Hidden Counter-revolutionaries," reform through education formally came into existence in August 1957 with a State Council "Decision" on problems in reform through education (*Report*, 1991: 33). The main source of inspiration for this system came from Mao Zedong, who wanted a way to transform the ideological outlook of political opponents (Ladany, 1992: 115). It is therefore not surprising that the first uses to which reform through education was put were in relation to the rightists rounded up in the anti-rightist campaign of the late 'fifties. In the anti-rightist campaign of this time, large numbers of people, particularly intellectuals, were found to have "incorrect thoughts" that required attention. While they were political "deviants," their errors were regarded as being insufficient to warrant a charge of "counter-revolutionary criminal" being laid. The idea behind the reform-through-education system was to introduce a form of political re-education that would offer a non-stigmatizing space different from, but with the same aims as, the more draconian reform-through-labor system. So began reform through education.

Until 1983, reform through education was administered under the reform-through-labor system. Both of these were then transferred from the Ministry of Public Security to the Ministry of Justice and, after that, they slowly separated. From 1985 onwards, official sources insist they were completely separate, although other sources raise some doubts about this.[27] This separation allowed for different financial arrangements to be made between labor education and reform through labor. From this time onwards, internal conditions within reform through education began to improve. Unlike the prison sector, which must provide for some of its own costs, reform through education has its facilities fully provided by local authorities and the rest of its needs fully financed by the central government (Interview, Li Zenghui and Lu Jialun, 1993). Nevertheless, the reform-through-education units are a cause of concern given the less stringent demands over evidence required for one to be interned in this sector. Hence, reform through education has proven an increasingly useful device in the targeted, "flexible" campaign style of policing that has been the hallmark of the Chinese police since 1978.

With post-reform legal developments hardly keeping pace with the changing face of crime, administrative detention, including the reform-through-education system, has proven to be a convenient mechanism. The committees that have the power to sentence people to periods of detention are not independent of the police. Hence, incarceration in a reform-through-education institution can offer the police an "easy option" when dealing with many of the newer, more minor problems they face. Hence, while police "colonized" the Maoist political technology of the campaign and transformed it to cater for the new post-economic reform demands, penal authorities "colonized" reform through education and transformed it so that it, too, was better suited to the needs of the police. A system that began life dealing with minor political offenders shifted its target in post-economic reform China to the petty criminal. Inmates were no longer political deviants with "bad thoughts" but targeted "bad characters" caught in the sweep of the police campaign.

Administrative incarceration also offers the regime another advantage. Along with a range of other non-criminal forms of incarceration, reform through education has drawn much less Western attention than the significantly larger and better known reform-through-labor prison system. Incarceration of minor offenders in a reform-through-education institution, therefore, allows at least some of the negative consequences of economic reform, which are highly embarrassing to the regime, to remain less visible. Why are the negative consequences of economic reform so embarrassing? To understand this requires some understanding of traditional Chinese notions of face (面子) and law as well as an understanding of Chinese socialism.

Face, in China, as mentioned earlier, not only operates at an interpersonal level, but also plays a crucial role in framing all political discourse. "Face" always requires that the subject be regarded as dignified. Dignity rests with the appearance of being in control. A lack of control is, by definition, a loss of face. This conceptualization of governmental face is reinforced by the Legalist tradition in China. This traditional Legalist inheritance suggests that good government is strong government. Legalist theories of government posit the idea of a strong, strict state and suggest that the strength and endurance of good rule lies in its ability to force compliance. This traditional discourse feeds directly into contemporary socialist notions of the "people's dictatorship" and party rule. Face, in this context, becomes the ability of the state to ensure not only adherence to its rules and laws, but also to its dreams and imaginings. Crime not only disrupts the rules and laws of the state, but threatens its dreams also. This is because Chinese socialist theory posits the belief that socialism cannot spawn crime and must lead to its eventual eradication. The development of socialism should signal a declining rate of crime. The current rising crime rates gravely embarrasses the party and robs it of its socialist face.

Framing the problem in terms of socialist face helps to account for the rationale behind the crisis mentality that has enveloped government as police and prison strategies fail to halt the growth of crime and recidivism. It also helps us understand the way a form of political "utopianism," to use the words of Huang Jingping, Li Tianfu and Wang Zhemin, can reassert itself in this most pragmatic of spaces. Yet it is this form of "utopian pragmatism," we would argue, captured historically in the low crime rates of the '50s—and one should remember that on the very year that China declared itself socialist (1956) it had its lowest ever crime rate—and replicated in the belief that socialism eliminates the conditions that spawn crime, that has fuelled the popular and political demand for harsher, quicker and more effective measures against crime (Huang, Li and Wang, 1992: 6). It is against this benchmark that both police and penal authorities have been judged and found wanting. It is also because crime in China is thought of in such politically sensitive terms that it has become such an embarrassment to the regime and is dealt with behind closed doors, as quickly and expeditiously as possible. Crime in China is never "common crime" for it always has something of the stigma of class marking it out. Note, for example, the language used to describe new post-economic reform crimes by the former deputy Minister of Public Security, Yu Lei. He talked of crimes in China "increasingly displaying the characteristics of the Western advanced countries" (Yu Lei, 1993: 337). Police campaigns against crime then, are closer to the political campaigns of old than we might at first imagine. They are still political for, as crime increasingly appears Western, it is increasingly characterized as emanating from bourgeois Western thought. Moreover, this way of registering crime not only enables the crime to be read politically, but the action taken against it to be registered as political also. It introduces a kind of utopianism that warrants harshness of punishment in the name of the class struggle.

Such utopian pragmatism, we would argue, not only fuels the extensive desire to keep all materials related to this process of policing "classified" and out of the public (and particularly foreign) domain, but it also encourages abuses through the desire to deal with crime in one sharp, harsh blow. It is into this discursive space that reform through education, with its less stringent requirements of evidence and a procedure which allows for "fast track" incarceration, proves a useful adjunct to a police force committed to campaigns designed to "speedily and harshly" stamp out crime.[28] Indeed, the whole of the non-criminal administrative detention sector has become something of an incarcerating adjunct to the flexible police campaign style of targeting particular types of crime and criminals.

It was used in the 1983 "severe strike campaign" against street crime despite the fact that the criminal code had been modified to allow for easier arrests, prosecutions and incarcerations of targeted offenders. In the three and a half years (Aug. 83–Jan. 1987) that this campaign was run, some 1,647,000 counter-revolutionary and criminal cases were mounted, 1,772,000 criminals detained and 322,000 people were sent off for reform through education while 15,000 juveniles were sent off to juvenile detention centers (Yu Lei, 1992: 37). Reform through education was used even more extensively in the early days of the 1989 campaign against the "six evils" of prostitution, producing, selling and disseminating pornography, kidnapping of women and children, planting, gathering and trafficking in drugs, gambling, and defrauding people by superstitious means. By 1990, over 213,000 cases had been opened and 770,000 people charged. Of these, 6,129 were given criminal sentences, 5,650 were sentenced to reform through education and the remaining 536,000 were punished under the public security regulations of the administrative law (Dai Yisheng and Jiang Bo, 1990).

The flexibility of the campaign style of policing seems tied to a new way of using this more "flexible" penal space. Yet, while both policing and administrative detention are fuelled by a utopian desire to eliminate crime, their methods have actually resulted in dystopic abuse. One must be concerned by a penal regime that offers "flexibility" to the police which is based primarily upon a lack of strict legal regulations covering its operation. Yet this is precisely the advantage detention centers operating under the administrative regulations have. One has therefore found that when particularly troublesome forms of offense do emerge—for example the newly targeted areas of illegality such as prostitution or transient crime—they are dealt with by detention in centers operating under the administrative and not the criminal code. As a result, one finds that quite apart from the reform-through-education institutions, there are at least two other forms of detention that have been established or re-established in recent years which appear to be governed by no legislation other than the public security regulations within the administrative code. These two other institutions are the shelter and investigation centers and the "forced educational measures" taken against prostitutes.

SHELTER AND INVESTIGATION CENTERS (收容审查) AND THE "FORCED EDUCATIONAL MEASURES" TAKEN AGAINST PROSTITUTES

The shelter and investigation centers began life in the early '60s after the famine pushed large numbers of peasants into the cities despite the tight internal migration laws. These institutions were used specifically to offer short-term shelter and repatriation of peasants who had illegally entered the cities in breach of the internal immigration rules. They were set up on the basis of a 1961 internal document entitled: "Forced labor and investigative detention." In the period of economic reform, with greater internal mobility this basic document has been augmented with further, more elaborate sets of rules and regulations. On November 1, 1978, a document entitled "The Public Security Ministry notice concerning the rectification and strengthening of investigative detention work in relation to fleeing criminal elements" was put into effect. Later, further clarification and detail came from a National People's Congress (NPC) directive of February 2, 1980, entitled: "A notice from the NPC concerning two measures united into one to strengthen labor and investigative detention in labor education."

The reason for such legislative action in relation to shelter and investigation detention centers was because, for the police, these centers were proving particularly useful in the period of economic reform. First, as detention centers they were under police and not Ministry of Justice control. This meant the police had far more power and flexibility over their internal operation than they would have with reform through education. Second, their "flexibility" was guaranteed by the fact that they were not organized and run through formal laws but through police and Ministry regulations (Ministry of Public Security, 1988b). Last, because of their history, they were particularly well suited to dealing with one of the key target groups of the post-economic reform period, the transient criminal. After 1986, the severe strike campaign shifted its focus of attention to transient criminal activity and criminals on the run (流窜犯) and the shelter and investigation center took on a new augmented role: housing suspect transient criminals.[29]

The problem for the police in dealing with transients was obvious to all. The tight demographic policing of the past had given way to much freer movement under the impetus of economic reform. The tight internal migration laws had become something of a dead letter by the 1980s leading to huge numbers of peasants going into the cities in search of higher paid work. According to Public Security sources there are currently about 50 to 60 million people per day on the road in China and the figure doubles if one includes intra-provincial movement (Zhang Qingwu, 1994 interview).[30]

Even the most conservative accounts put the figure at 40 million with at least half heading into the cities' and accounting for
something like 15% of the total cities' permanent population (Xu
Hanmin, 1992: 136). But even with these conservative figures the
perilous nature of the situation for the policy is all too obvious. In
Beijing, for example, there are over 1,000,000 transients yet there are
only 50,000 beds in hotels and specially designated accommodations. Transients are therefore forced to accommodate themselves
either on the streets or illegally, thus increasing the difficulty of
policing and reinforcing a social panic which has increasingly seen
transients represented as an illiterate, semi-criminal population.
This popular rendition of the transient is reinforced by police-
supported research which not only highlights the connection drawn
between transiency and crime but goes on to argue that a substantial
proportion of city crime is now committed by transients (e.g., Yang
and Wang, 1989; Xu Miaofa, 1989; "The Basic Character...", 1989).
This research both justifies the harsh ad hoc policing and detention
measures taken and ensures popular support for such action.

Because of the large numbers detained in Shelter and Investigation
and because of the lack of a stable financial base for these institutions,
they were reputed to be the worst form of detention in China, even
by the Ministry of Public Security that ran them! (Ministry of Public
Security, 1985). But if conditions within the centers were a cause of
concern, so too were the flexible rules under which they operated. A
suspect was supposed to be detained for no more than three months
and, after this period, one was supposed to be released or the authorities were to ask for an extension. But the period of calculation of that
three months only began after the verification of the name and
address of the detainee (Ministry of Public Security, 1988a). One 1989
study from Hunan reported that something like 30% of the detainees
had been held for longer than the stipulated three-month period.
Indeed, the study indicated that some detainees had been held for
two-, three- and even five-year periods during which time nothing
had been done to solve their cases (Li Kangtai, et al., 1985). What one
discovers is that these centers were being used as an ad hoc and "flexible" form of prison for a new type of crime. Indeed, as one examines
the targets of police campaigns, one invariably finds that where there
is a target group, there is a harsh response built in part on this form of
ad hoc detention. Prostitution, for example, was another target crime
that has come to the attention of officials in recent years and been
dealt with in much the same way as transient crime.

With the launching of the six evils campaign in 1989, prostitutes fell into this category of a target population. The situation had become increasingly serious over the period of economic reform, especially in the larger eastern coastal cities. Indeed, it was suggested by one source that there were tens of thousands of prostitutes in the province of Guangdong alone (Interview, 10/17/93). Police response was quick and harsh. In 1981, police were advised to fully utilize the discretionary powers made available to them under the public security management punishment regulations and warn, fine or even administratively detain offenders (Ministry of Public Security, 3/10/1981, 1993: 420). In addition, police could even impose forced reparation on recalcitrants and demand that they undergo medical checks and treatment ("The National People's Congress... [9/4/91]", 1992: 163–5).

Building on these regulations was a 1983 document (number 23) issued by the Ministry of Public Security, the Party center and Women's Federation. This was entitled a "Report concerning the resolute outlawing of prostitution" ("The Opinion..." [8/7/1984], 1993: 414). In this document police were given regulatory cover for a series of calibrated punishments to be utilized in places where prostitution was rampant. By 1985, documents were already discussing the existence of a new form of detention known as "female education and fostering centers" 妇女教养所, which, it was claimed were "designed specifically to educate and raise females who are prostitutes or who have engaged in hoodlum activity" (Supreme Court, [9/16/85], 1992: 117). By 1987, many of these detention measures were of national significance. In that year, a notice was issued supplementing the "reform-through-education implementation methods," and this enabled the police to be more flexible in their response to re-offense. For prostitutes whose activities were regarded as insufficient to warrant criminal charges being laid, but who nevertheless continued to work after police warnings and punishment, detention for education was now the order of the day (Ministry of Public Security, [24/8/1987], 1993: 424). These harsher measures involved reviving institutions of detention and education that were once used to re-educate prostitutes soon after liberation. These institutions triumphantly ceased operation in 1956, when China proclaimed itself socialist and simultaneously proclaimed the elimination of prostitution (*Questions and Answers...* 1994: 80).[31]

The re-emergence of prostitution in the post-1978 period of economic reform was yet another "crime" that could be said to have caused Chinese socialism an immense loss of "face" by depriving it of some of its key moral claims. At the same time, the re-emergence of prostitution also offered older revolutionaries, suspicious of the new economic reforms, the chance to claim that the politics of the reform era had eroded the hard-won successes of earlier periods of "true" socialism. This politically charged and highly unfavorable comparison they drew with past "socialist" successes has fuelled the current movement for the revival of early reformative strategies.[32] Hence, one finds a return of the post-liberation "women's reform through education" centers in everything but name.

> **Question**: Why has it proven necessary to force prostitutes and street walkers to undertake concentrated education?
> **Answer**: Among the prostitutes and street walkers there are some who cause deep social harm and quite a few of them have sexually transmitted diseases. To get them to abandon their harmful life-style, quite a number of areas have had impressive results by adopting measures to force them to undergo educational transformation. On the basis of experience and [police] regulations, the police, in conjunction with related departments, can get them together and force them to undergo legal and moral education and productive labor and in this way make them turn over a new leaf. Prostitutes can be held in such places for six months to two years and this is a type of forcible administrative education measure. While undergoing education they can also have medical checks conducted and any sexually transmitted diseases cured ("Legal Weapons..." 13/9/91, [1993]: 413)

In 1949, the revolution glowed brightly. China had "turned red." In a perverse sort of way, this offered the policing authorities more leeway in dealing with prostitution for no one could doubt their determination to deal it "a final blow." A two-tier system of brothel closure was put into effect at that time. In places of political significance or where conditions allowed, brothels were immediately closed. The women, depending upon the extent of their culpability, were "rehoused and retrained" in women's production education and fostering institutes (妇女生产教养院) or prostitute retraining centers (妓女教养所). In places (Tianjin, Wuhan, Shanghai, etc.) where the material conditions did not permit this, the brothels remained open under a policy known as "first control and then prohibit," [寓禁于限]. This policy continued to be implemented until 1954, when the last brothel was closed and the remaining women sent for "re-education" (cf. *Questions and Answers...* . 1994: 80; Ma Weigang, 1993: 11).

In the contemporary period, all brothels are underground, and all police suspect. Stories of police corruption are legendary and older Party cadres' criticism, vehement. Police no longer have a residue of mass popular faith in their incorruptibility, nor do they have mass political support to help them "control" the problem. Nevertheless, the Party, conscious of its own slipping halo, demands of the police the impossible: Bring prostitution to a halt and revive socialist spiritual civilization. While internal corruption and the sheer scale of prostitution make the total eradication of the problem inconceivable, it has nevertheless forced police to take harsh measures and be seen to be acting. Pressed to act, the police have opened "detention education centers" 收容教育所 nationwide ("A Summary of the Minutes... ." 1989; 1992: 142). Unlike the immediate years after liberation, however, the police could not afford to wait until they had the physical resources to make them work effectively. Consequently, these centers were opened without the necessary financial support to make them viable. Particularly in the south, where prostitution is quite severe, accommodation is found for the interned in old, worn-out buildings desperately in need of repair (interview, 1993). Moreover, because these centers are run "without any clear legal basis," ("A Summary of the Minutes... ." 1989; 1992: 142), they are not subject to the same checks on them as the prisons or even the reform-through-education centers. Police, pressed for resources, intern women on the basis of little other than a letter from the woman's work unit or from her neighborhood committees, and women can be sent to these centers simply because they have contracted a venereal disease (interview, 1993).

Pragmatism, pressure and a fond remembrance of what things once were have fuelled the carceral spread in post-reform China. Nevertheless, as this spread envelopes the social, its failure to halt the drift away from socialist "spiritual civilization" becomes increasingly obvious. As various measures visibly fail to recapture the "glory days" when "over 11 million criminals were successfully reformed, including the successful transformation of Japanese war criminals, Nationalist war criminals, and all sorts of counter-revolutionary and common criminals" (Zhang Jinsang, 1993: 75), the authorities move from the warm embrace of persuasion and *ganhua* to the cold steely revanchist solutions offered within the tradition of classical Legalism. Legalism dreams the dreams of socialism. It too posits a centralized and strongly obedient society, yet it believes that only by following the rules of the prince can this state be achieved. It is these rules that now turn upon those who are socially marginal. Caught in this ever expanding but ever degenerating Legalist web are the subalterns: The gypsies, thieves, prostitutes and pimps that economic reform has enabled, if not encouraged. This, then, is the carceral spread and it is this that constitutes, to our mind, the key element in penal discourse in the post-reform era.

CONCLUSION

There is a character in traditional Chinese philosophy that can mean both reciprocity and yet, in another context, it can mean revenge. In both cases, it is a form of repayment of a debt. In many respects, the Chinese idea of "face" is similarly constituted. Face is something one is given through reciprocity and something one seeks revenge for if it is not given. Face makes the Chinese reintegrative strategy of *ganhua* possible, but face will also demand its revenge should this method falter. This is because what is at stake with reintegrative *ganhua* is not just the criminal's face, but also the face of the cadre, the police and the Party.

In the past, in those halcyon days of Chinese socialism, it was through working to re-establish a criminal's social face that the reformative strategies worked so effectively. Guards, police, Party and felon shared in this process of "giving and receiving face." For the felon "face" came with social reintegration while for the cadre, police and Party, face came in the form of an incontestable slogan: Only socialism can save your soul.

As the economic reform process erodes the conditions that enabled prisoner rehabilitation in the past, the bold claims of socialism's past seem ever more distant.[33] The higher crime and recidivism rates indicate a declining ability to restore the felon's social face and this, in turn, leads to a loss of face for the prison authorities and, ultimately, the Party. It is because of this that we can understand why, despite what are, by Western standards, very low crime and recidivism rates, the Party feels the urge to hide this new "ugly face" of Chinese socialism by making much of the information about crime and the penal sector "for their eyes only." Moreover, it is because of the loss of face that this "ugly face" induces, and the lack of response of those felons offered face and who do not respond appropriately, that one finds the reciprocity of past notions of *ganhua* being replaced with more draconian Legalist notions of revanchism.

There is a character in Chinese that aptly expresses the janus-faced message of this gift of face. This is the character *bao* 报. This character, under certain circumstances, can mean a gift offered in appreciation, while at other times, it can mean to extract revenge. This linguistic slip stands as a sign of a much deeper conceptual slippage that an incorrect response to the gift can bring. If the gift of face, of love, benevolence and support is spurned, then the face of the giver is lost and revenge sought. *Ganhua, renqing* or *yiqi*, can therefore turn the giver of love and support into the deliverer of retribution.

Here, then, is the secret of face-giving. Without this concept of (social) face, "reintegrative" strategies could not operate, yet with this concept, the surfaces of consideration extend beyond the inmate and envelope the guard, the police and most importantly, the Party. Reintegrative strategies that restored the criminal's "face" also enhanced the Party's. Tied into this web-like relation, prisoner and Party shared the enhancement to face that success would bring, but released a much more destructive impulse when the relation began to fail. It is for this reason that penal discourse in post-liberation China was never simply about *ganhua, renqing* or *yiqi* but has always been stalked by its authoritarian partner, namely, classical Legalism. Hence, one sees in the current climate a degeneration of the process to the point whereby Legalism is considered the only really viable option. Transients, prostitutes and other subalterns cannot be immediately reformed but must first be immobilized and controlled. The carceral spread attempts to still their movement but in so doing, threatens the movement essential for economic reform. This carceral spread, like the idea of face, is caught in the horns of a dilemma. It cannot conceive of success in its strategic field without inducing a massive defeat upon the economic reform process. To do this, however, would bring on the ultimate loss of face for the Party and as such, is inconceivable.

Notes

1. We would like to express our thanks to the Australian Research Council for help in funding this research. We would also like to thank Li Tianfu who helped research this paper.

2. It should be pointed out that Harry Wu's position is not commonly
   agreed to by other Western scholars. Even Western commentators in the
   height of the cold war have argued that the Chinese systems was more
   humane than the Soviet one. See Wint, 1960; Hinkle and Wolff, 1956.
3. Prisons were run by the Ministry of Justice for about a year after liberation. After that time, they were the preserve of the Ministry of Public
   Security which had within it, a "reform-through-labor" section. This
   changed in 1983 when the Ministry of Justice took responsibility for all
   reform-through-labor and reform-through-education institutions with
   the exception of one prison in Beijing, the Qingcheng prison, which is
   still run by the Ministry of Public Security. This is a prison where many
   of the more sensititve or important prisoners are held, including many
   of the state's more famous political activists.
4. This interview was with a senior official of the prison study association
   who had been a cadre in the prison sector in the 'fifties and had
   worked alongside the main Soviet advisors.
5. To this end, it is interesting to note that the Chinese police regard the
   contemporary post-economic crime rate as "abnormal." They suggest
   that the low crime rates of the early 1950s—a period when the glow of
   revolution was still fresh and the economy was centrally planned—are
   the norm and that the police should be working toward a return to
   these low rates (For more details see Dutton, 1996).
6. The number of prisoners in the "reform-through-labor" (or, as it is now
   called, the prison) sector is hotly disputed. Harry Wu suggests there are
   3 to 4 million prisoners in the labor camps alone (Wu, 1992: 11). These
   figures are substantially greater than the official figure. The 1992
   Australian Human Rights Delegation to China was told there were 1.2
   million inmates in prisons and camps and 150 thousand people in
   administrative detention (*Report of the Second...*, 1992: 21). Officials
   sources interviewed by us also suggested figures similar to those given
   to the Australian delegation. The prison population was said to be 1.3
   million with a further 170,000 inmates in the non-criminal reform
   through education sector (Interview with leading cadre at Ministry of
   Justice, Crime Prevention and Reform Through Labor Research
   Institute, Beijing, 10/17/93). For more details on the reform-through-
   education sector, see below.
7. The new "prison law" is a case in point. As noted earlier, this was the
   first time since the revolution that the term "reform through labor" was
   dropped and replaced by the more Westernized expression "the prison
   system." Nevertheless, despite the abandonment of the expression
   "reform through labor" as the overall name for the system this expression is constantly used throughout the new law and remains the guiding principle of the new prison system.
8. It is interesting to read this early adoption of the idea of reforming
   through labor alongside the recently introduced reformist "prison law."

This law, which was passed in 1994 by the National People's Congress, suggests that significant changes are underway within the system. Yet Chinese specialists in the area have insisted to us that while the expression "reform through labor" is no longer used to designate the system, its influence is still great. Moreover, one of the main reasons for changing the name is because of Western misunderstandings about the system (Yang Shiguang, Shao Mingzhen, Sun Xiaoli, Interviews).

9. The Nationalist government called their prisons *Ganhuayuan* or institutes of persuasion. The early penal practices of the CCP in the revolutionary base areas also used this expression. The first communist penal camps were set up in the revolutionary base areas from February 1932 on the recommendation of Liang Butai. These institutions were called institutions of labor persuasion or *laodong ganhua yuan*. See 'The Institutes of Labour Persuasion' in *Public Security Historical Materials*, volume 2, number 6, 1990, pp 30–32.

10. Michael Dutton has dealt with this at length elsewhere and tied it back to certain strands in Soviet Marxism. See Dutton, 1992.

11. This section extends arguments dealt with by Xu Zhangrun in his book (1991: 238–265) and also in work he has undertaken with Guo Xiang (1994: 38–48).

12. Indeed, it is worth mentioning that the State Council's 'White Book' on *Criminal Reform in China* devotes an entire chapter to the issue of *ganhua* (chapter five) (White Book, 1992: 16–18).

13. The term cadre was first used only in relation to active party workers but has subsequently been expanded to include virtually all government workers. Virtually anyone within the government who is not a manual worker is a cadre of some sort.

14. The term 'gift' is used here in the Maussian sense. See Marcel Mauss, *The Gift: The Form and Reason for Exchange in Archaic Societies*, [W.D. Halls trans.], Routledge, London, 1990. To understand the relevance of this concept in relation to Chinese culture see Mayfair Mei-hui Yang, *Gifts, Favors and Banquets: The Art of Social relationships in China*, Cornell University Press, Ithaca, 1994.

15. There is little time or space here to go into the intricate nature or importance of face in China. For more details see Kipnis, 1995.

16. On the growing disbelief in socialism and communism and how this effects crime see Li Junren, 1992: 153–154.

17. In post-economic reform China such practices were continued under the term "controlling the special population" (Yu Lei, 1987).

18. Along with this have gone the lower recidivism rates. Recidivism is defined as criminal reoffense within a three-year period of release. In an internal document put out to explain to cadres the publicly released "white book" on the Chinese reform-through-labor system and crime, Wang Mingdi reveals the extent of this rise. While the

"White Book" concentrates on the low recidivism rate of China in comparison to the West, Wang charts the rise in the rate in recent years (White Book, 1992: 2). Prior to the cultural revolution, recidivism rates were around 2–3%. During the cultural revolution (1966–76) they rose to 8–10% and currently stand between 6–8% (Wang Mingdi, 1993: 75). For more details see endnote 22.

19. This interview was undertaken with a leading member of the Public Security Ministry, research unit, in January 1994.

20. This emphasis on production at the expense of transformation within the prison system is identified by a number of scholars as a problem leading to a failure of the reform-through-labor program according to Cao Zidan (1993: 365).

21. It should be added here, however, that there are countervailing trends. The introduction of the new prison law, with its deemphasis on labor reform would suggest that labor is no longer the focus of rehabilitative attention and is increasingly seen as offering technical training for prisoners rather than spiritual and cognitive reformation. The increasingly Western view of law as a mechanism to ensure rights and responsibilities are recognized is also beginning to find a place in Chinese discourse, largely as an effect of the reform program.

22. Unless otherwise stated, the following points regarding prison factories and farms came from an interview with Li Zenghui and Lu Jialun of the Ministry of Justice, Crime Prevention and Reform Through Labour Research Institute, November 1, 1993.

23. Crime, according to official statistical accounts and commentaries, has changed dramatically in recent years. In the past, most criminal cases were said to be counter-revolutionary in nature and committed by people from "bad" (former ruling class) backgrounds. In the post-reform period, most cases are motivated by potential economic gain and are committed by young, working class or peasant males. While one should be wary of relying too heavily on such distinctions for they are, in part, an effect of the different taxonomies deployed and different policing strategies adopted, neither should one dismiss the distinction totally. This change is in part a reflection of the changing value systems that have accompanied the economic reform process. As Cao Zidan notes, there has indeed been an attitudinal sea-change in recent years and that is illustrated rather dramatically in the popular expression: "Being honest is for losers" (1993: 363). Clearly this is a long way from the socialist ethics the prison sector tries to imbute in inmates.

24. One should not exaggerate the extent of the problem which, by Western standards, is minuscule. On the basis of a five-year survey covering eight provinces, cities and autonomous regions (Shanghai, Tianjin, Shandong, Zhejiang, Guangdong, Hubei, Shanxi, Xinjiang) that was conducted between the years 1982 to 1986, the average recidivism rate was found to be 7%. A more detailed survey of adult

recidivism rates covering 27 provinces, cities and autonomous regions puts the rate at 5.19% but when you add to this "recidivism" in the non-criminal reform through education sector, this rises to 6.59% (Li Junren, 1992: 4). While this is remarkably low by Western standards, it masks the sharpness of the rise in recent years. As Wang Mingdi noted, comparing 1990 recidivism rates to those of 1987 reveals a rise of over 61% in such cases. (Wang Mingdi, 1993: 9). Moreover, an equally worrying trend is the rate of youth recidivism which acoounts for 20.54% of the cases according to Yu Shutong, (Quoted in 'Specialists... 1993: 9) and 30% and above according to Xu Hanmin (1992: 77).

25. Before 1978 the number of violent criminal cases ranged from a low of 180,000 cases in 1956 to 540,000 cases in 1977. On average, the figure hovered between 200 and 400,000 cases. This figure rose rapidly after economic reform was introduced in 1978. In 1979, there were 636,000 cases, while in 1989 there were over one million nine hundred thousand cases. The 'nineties have seen this trend continuing. In 1990 there were 2,216,997 cases while in 1991 nearly two million four hundred thousand cases (Yu Lei, 1992: 45,324).

26. Most of the information given here, unless otherwise stated, comes from an interview with Li Zenghui and Lu Jialun of the Ministry of Justice, Crime Prevention and Reform Through Labour Research Institute, November 1, 1993.

27. The seperation of the reform-through-labor and reform-through-education programs is debatable (see Ladany, 1992; Wu, 1992).

28. This was one of the key slogans of the 1983 "severe strike" campaign.

29. Largely as a result of Western pressure the system of Shelter and Investigation was abolished in early 1996. Despite this, the problem of transient crime remains and the abolition was also accompanied by legislation extending police powers of detention. Thus, while the centers have gone, the problem has not and the likelihood is that the police will simply use other detention centers under their control to house suspected transient criminals.

30. Interview with Zhang Qingwu, 1994 [Professor Zhang is the Director of the Population Research Institute, China's Public Security University, Beijing].

31. From the time of the Communist takeover in October 1949 through to the announcement of socialism in 1956, China was said to be in the new democratic stage. While prostitution was said to be eliminated it was not until 1964 that it was claimed that sexually transmitted diseases had been more or less eliminated in China. [See "State Council Notice..." (9/1/1986), 1993: 418].

32. Indeed, some of the notices even begin with a preamble to this effect. See the Ministry of Public Security [3/10/1981], 1993: 419.

33. It is noteworthy, in this regard, how old examples that are no longer relevant still feature prominently in government propoganda. In the

State Council's "White Paper" on penal reform the opening remarks feature the example of the successful reform of Japanese war criminals, former Nationalist officers and counter-revolutionaries (White Book, 1992: 2) but the rehabilitative "community" the prisons have faced since the early '80s are predominantly young people, from "families of the laboring classes" who are common not political criminals ("Mao Zedong Thought…", 1994: 5).

References*

Braithwaite, John. (1989) *Crime, Shame and Reintegration*. Melbourne: Cambridge University Press.

*————. "The Basic Character of Crime in Contemporary China" in Yu Lei (ed.) (1993) *Research into the Problem of Crime in China in the Contemporary Period* (Volume One 1989). China's Public Security Universtiy Press, pp. 40–55.

"当前我国刑事犯罪的基本特点", 俞雷 (主编), 《中国现阶段犯罪问题研究》 (第一卷)

Cao Zidan (ed.). (1993) *A Summary of Research on the Causes of Crime in China*. Beijing: China's Political Science and Law University Press.

曹子丹（主编），《中国犯罪原因研究综述》

————. (1980) *The Classic of Filial Piety in The Thirteen Classics*. China Publishing House. pp. 2545–2562.

《十三经注疏 · 孝经》

*Dai Wendian. (1989) "Some Reflections on Research into Current Problems of Crime in China" in Yu Lei [ed.] *Research on Crime in the Current Period in China*. (Volume One). China's Public Security University Press, pp. 1–11.

戴文殿，"对我国现阶段犯罪问题研究的一些思考" 俞雷 (主编), 《中国现阶段犯罪问题研究》(第一卷)

*Deng Zhaoren, Yang Weixin and Zhao Fengcan (eds.). (1987) *Questions and Answers to Help Understand the Professional Work of Rural and Urban Police Stations*. Beijing: Masses Press.

邓兆人，杨维新，赵逢灿 (编)，《城乡公安派出所业务知识问答》

Chinese texts marked with "" are those meant for internal circulation only. This means that circulation of them is restricted to personnel from within the Ministries of Public Security, Justice and the Procuraturate.

*Dai Yisheng and Jiang Bo. (1990) "Mobilise and Organise all Possible Social Forces to Strengthen Public Order." *People's Police*, Number 4: 4–9.

戴逸生，江波，"动员和组织各界社会力量加强社会治安"，《人民公安》

Dutton, Michael. (1992) *Policing and Punishment in China—From Patriarchy to 'The People.'* Melbourne: Cambridge University Press.

Dutton, Michael and Lee Tianfu. (1993) "Missing the Target? Policing Strategies in the Period of Economic Reform." *Crime and Delinquency*, 39: 3, July: 316–336.

Dutton, Michael. (1996) "Dreaming of Better Times: 'Repetition With a Difference' and Community Policing." *Positions*, Volume 3: 2, (Fall): 415–447.

*————. *Encyclopedia of Chinese Law on Reform Through Labour*, Shao Mingzhen, Wang Mingdi, Niu Qingshan (eds.) (1993) Beijing: China's People's Public Security Publishing House.

《中国劳改法学百科辞书》（主编：邵名正，王明迪，牛青山）

Guo Xiang and Xu Zhangrun. (1994) "The Theory and Practice of Criminal Re-education, Training, and Employment in China" [Trans. M. Dutton] in Sandy Cook and Bob Semmens (eds.) *International Forum on Education in Penal Systems, Conference Proceedings*. Melbourne: IFEPS.

Hinkle, L.E. and Wolff, H.G. (1956) "Communist Interrogation and Indoctrination of 'Enemies of the State.'" *American Medical Association Archives of Neurology and Psychology*, 76: 6 (December): 115–174.

*Huang Jingping, Li Tianfu and Wang Zhimin. (1988) "The Situation with Regard Public Security Management." *Police Research*, Number 4: 6–7.

黄京平，李田夫，王智民，"公安管理现状"《公安研究》

Kipnis, Andrew. (1995) "'Face': An Adaptable Discourse of Social Surfaces." *Positions*, 3: 1, (Spring): 119–148.

Ladany, Laslo. (1992) *Law and Legality in China: The Testament of a China-Watcher*. London: Hurst and Company.

Liang Shuming. (1986) *An Outline of Chinese Arts*. Sichuan, China: Ba Shu Press.

梁漱溟，《东方学术概观》

Lifton, Robert. (1963) *Thought Reform and the Psychology of Totalism*. New York: W.W. Norton and Company.

Liu Chenggen. (1995) "Promote Community Developments, Control Serious Cases of Repeat Offence." (Unpublished paper presented at the International Conference of Education, Training and Rehabilitation of Prisoners in Correctional Institutions, October 1995, Chengdu, Sichuan, China).

Liu Zhi. (1987) "Theorisation on the Status of China's Reform through Labour Legal Studies," in Zhao Mingdong, Xu Zhangrun and Zhu Ye (eds.) *Research Materials Outlining Reform through Labour Legal Studies*. Beijing: Central Broadcasting and Television University Press. pp. 45–52.

刘智，"论新中国劳动改造法学的地位"，周名东，许章润，朱叶；《劳动改造法学概论参考资料》

————— "Legal Weapons to Check and Prevent Prostitution and Customers—A Responsible Cadre from the National People's Congress Standing Committee working Committee on Law Answers Journalists' Questions (9/13/1991)," in Zhang Sihan (ed.) (1993) *Legal Materials on Cases from the Six Evils*. Beijing: Political Science and Law University Press. pp. 410–414.

"查禁卖淫嫖娼的法律武器"，《六害案件法律实务》（张泗汉 主编）.

Li Junren (ed.). (1992) *Research Into Recidivism in China*. Beijing: Law Publishing House.

李均仁（主编），《中国重新犯罪研究》

*Li Kangtai (ed.). (1985) *The Study of Reform Through Labour Education*. Beijing: Masses Press.

力康泰 （主编），《改造教育学》

Li Kangtai (ed.). (1993) *A Research Outling of the Legal Study of Reform Through Labour*. Beijing: China's People's University.

力康泰 （主编），《劳动改造法学研究综述》

Marx, Karl. (1977) "The Eighteenth Brumaire of Louis Bonaparte," in David Fernbach (ed.) (1973) *Surveys From Exile*. Middlesex: Penguin Books. pp. 143–249.

*——————— "Mao Zedong Thought on Carrying Out and Developing the Theory of Criminal Reform Through Labour," *Research into Crime and Reform*, 1994, Number 1: 4–12.

毛泽东思想关于劳动改造罪犯理论的继承与发展", 《犯罪与改造研究》

Ma Weigang (ed.). (1993) *The Prohibition on Prostitution and Drugs*. Beijing: Police Officer Educational Publishing House.

马维纲（编）《禁娼禁毒》

Mauss, Marcel. (1990) *The Gift: The Form and Research for Exchange in Archaic Societies*. [W.D. Halls, trans.] London: Routledge.

Ministry of Public Security. "A Notice From the Ministry of Public Security Concerning Resolutely Restratining Prostitution Activity," (3/10/81) in Zhang Sihan (ed.) (1993) *Legal Materials on Cases from the Six Evils*. Beijing: Political Science and Law University Press. pp. 419–422.

[*公安 部关于坚决制止卖淫活动的通知"《六害案件法律实务》(张泗汉 主编).]

Ministry of Public Security. "A Notice From the Ministry of Public Security and the Ministry of Justice Concerning the Question of the Investigative Detention and Labour Education of Prostitutes and Customers," (8/24/1987) in Zhang Sihan (ed.) (1993) *Legal Materials on Cases from the Six Evils*. Beijing: Political Science and Law University Press. pp. 424–425.

"公安部 司法部关于卖淫, 嫖宿人员收容劳动教养问题的通知", 《六害案件法律实务》(张泗汉 主编).]]

*Ministry of Public Security and the Ministry of Health. (2/14/84) (1985) "Ministry of Public security and the Ministry of Health Notice Concerning Prevention of Contagious Diseases Amongst Those Criminals Detained for Investigation," *Handbook on Preparatory Investigations and Watchhouse Work*, Volume 2, Beijing: Masses Press.

"公安部 卫生部 关于在押犯收审人员传染性疾病防治工作的通知"《预审, 看守工作手册》(第二卷)

*Ministry of Public Security. (1988a) "Ministry of Public Security Notice Concerning the Utilisation of Tight Control Proceedures Over the Detention and Investigation Centres" (1985) *Handbook* on *Preparatory Investigations and Watchhouse Work*, Volume 3, Beijing: Masses Press.

"公安部关于严格控制使用收容审查手段的通知"《预审，看守工作手册》(第三卷)

*Ministry of Public Security. (1988b) "Ministry of Public Security Notice on the Unsuitability of Openly Reporting on the Detention and Investigation Centres" (1987) *Handbook on Preparatory Investigations and Watchhouse Work*, Volume 3, Beijing: Masses Press.

"公安部关于不宜公开报导收容审查的通知"《预审，看守工作手册》，(第三卷)]

*————— "The National People's Congress Standing Committee Decision Concerning the Strict Prohibition on Prostitution (9/4/91)," in (1992), *A Collection of Rules, Regulations and Policies on the Comprehensive Handling of Social Order*. Beijing: Masses Press. pp. 163–5.

"全国人大常委会关于严禁卖淫嫖娼的决定"，《社会治安综合治理政策法规汇编》

————— "The Opinion of the Supreme People's Court, Supreme People's Procuraturate, The Ministry of Public Security Concerning the Handling of Cases of Prostitution, and Brothels" (8/7/1984) [document 19]," in Zhang Sihan (ed.) (1993) *Legal Materials on Cases from the Six Evils*. Beijing: Political Science and Law University Press. p. 414.

"最高人民法院，最高人民检察院，公安部关于卖淫，嫖宿暗娼案件应如何处理的意见"《六害案件法律实务》(张泗汉 主编).

Paz, Octavio. (1992) "Translation: Literature and Letters" in Rainer Schulte and John Biguenet (eds.) (1971/1992) *Theories of Translation*. Chicago, Illinois: University of Chicago Press. pp. 152–162.

*————— *Public Security Historical Materials*, Volume 2, Number 6, 1990.

《公安史资料》

*————— *Questions and Answers on Knowledge of Public Security History*. (1994) The Ministry of Public Security, Public Security

Historical Materials Collection Research Leadership Small Group Office, (ed.), Beijing: Masses Press.

《公安史知识问答 》

*————— *Reform Through Labour Economic Management*. (1989) Beijing: Masses Press.

《劳改经济管理 》

————— *Report of the Australian Human Rights Delegation to China* , July 14–26, 1991, (Draft Copy).

————— *Report of the Second Australian Human Rights Delegation to China* , November 8–20, 1992, Canberra: Australian Government Publishing Service.

————— *Research into Reform Through Labour in China*. (1992) Beijing: Social Sciences Literature Press.

《中国劳动改造 》

*————— "Specialists Discuss the Theoretical Questions Raised by the Special Character of Repeat Offenders in China" (1993) *Research Into Crime and Reform*, Number 2: 6–16.

"一部具有中国特色的重新犯罪研究的理论专著", 《犯罪与改造研究》

—— "State Council Notice on Resolutely Outlawing Prostitution and Preventing the Spread of Sexually Transmitted Diseases (9/1/1986)," in Zhang Sihan (ed.) (1993) *Legal Materials on Cases from the Six Evils*. Beijing: Political Science and Law University Press. pp. 418–9.

"国务院关于坚决取缔卖淫活动和制止性病蔓延的通知" 《六害案件法律实务》 (张泗汉 主编).

*————— "A Summary of the Minutes of the Meeting Concerning Researching the Attack on and Supression of Prostitution Activities" (State Council Document [1989] Number 18) in (1992), *A Collection of Rules, Regulations and Policies on the Comprehensive Handling of Social Order* Beijing: Masses Press, pp. 141–144.

"关于研究打击取缔卖淫嫖娼活动的会议纪要", 《社会治安综合治理政策法规汇编》

*Sun Xiaoli. (1993) *Laogai—The Chinese Prison System's Theory and Practices: History and Reality*. Beijing: China's Political Science and Law University Press.

孙晓霁, 《中国劳动改造制度的理论与实践—历史与现实》

*Supreme Court. "From the Supreme Court and Seven Other Departments on the Attack on Prostitution Activity and the Prevention of Sexually Transmitted Diseases" [16/9/85] in (1992), *A Collection of Rules, Regulations and Policies on the Comprehensive Handling of Social Order*. Beijing: Masses Press. pp. 117–119.

"最高人民法院等七个部门关于坚决打击取缔卖淫活动和防止性病蔓延的报告", 《社会治安综合治理政策法规汇编》

———— *The Tang Dynasty Code and its Explanation*. (1983) Beijing: China Publishers.

《唐律疏议》

Veyne, Paul. (1982) "The Inventory of Difference," *Economy and Society*, 11: 2 (May 1982): 171–198.

*Wang Mingdi (ed.). (1993) *Educational Materials for Professional Training on The White Book on Criminal Reform*. Beijing: Law Publishing House.

王明迪（编),《'中国改造罪犯的状况' 业务培训教材 》

Wang Tai. (1987) "A Brief Outline of the Theoretical Base Upon which Labour Reform is Founded" in Zhao Mingdong, Xu Zhangrun and Zhu Ye (eds.) *Research Materials Outlining Reform through Labour Legal Studies*. Beijing: Central Broadcasting and Television University Press. pp. 243–259.

王泰, "试论劳动改造的基本理论依据", 周名东, 许章润, 朱叶: 《劳动改造法学概论参考资料》

*Wang Wenyuan et al. (1993) "A Number of Specialist Theorists Discuss Researching the Special Character of Recidivism." *Research into Crime and Reform Through Labour*, Number 2: 6–16.

王文元等, "一部具有中国特色的重新犯罪研究的理论专著"《犯罪与改造研究》

Wint, Guy. (1960) *Common Sense about China*. London: Victor Gollancz.

Hongda Harry Wu. (1992) *Laogai: The Chinese Gulag*. [Trans. Ted Slingerland]. Bolder: Westview Press.

White Book of the State Council. (1992) *Criminal Reform in China*. Beijing: Law Press.

*Xu Juefei, Shu Hongkang, Shao Mingzhen and Yu Qisheng. (1983) *Reform Through Labour Study*. Beijing: Masses Press.

徐觉非, 舒鸿康, 邵名正, 于齐生, 《劳动改造学》

*Xu Hanmin. (1992) *Forty Years of People's Policing*. Beijing: Police Officer Educational Press.

徐汉民，《人民治安４０年》

Xu Miaofa. (1989) "Examining the Reform Tendencies Within the Household Registration System From the Perspective of the Transient Population." *Social Science*, February, Shanghai, pp. 37–40.

许妙发，"从人口流动看户籍管理体制改革趋势"《社会科学》

Xu Shen. (1934) *Character Explanations*. Beijing: China Publishing House.

许慎 《说文解字》

Xu Zhangrun. (1991) *Prison Study*. Beijing: Chinese People's Public Security University Press.

许章润，《监狱学》

*Yu Lei. (1987) *The Study of Public Security Administrative Management*. Beijing: China's Public Security University Press.

俞雷 (主编)，《治安行政管理学》

Yu Lei. (1992) *Contemporary Chinese Police Work*. Beijing: Contemporary China Publishing House.

俞雷 (主编)，《当代中国的公安工作》

*Yu Lei (ed.). (1993) *Research into the Problem of Crime in China in the Contemporary Period* (Summary Volume). Beijing: China's People's Public Security University Press.

俞雷 (主编)，《中国现阶段犯罪问题研究》(总卷)

*Yang Wenzhong and Wang Gongfan. (1989) "The Influence of the Floating Population Upon Social Order." *Police Research*, Number 2: 52–53.

杨文忠，王功藩，"流动人口对社会治安的影响"《公安研究》

Mayfair Mei-hui Yang. (1994) *Gifts, Favors and Banquets: The Art of Social Relationships in China*. Ithaca, New York: Cornell University Press.

*Zhang Jinsang. (1993) "Human Rights and the Special Character of China's Reform Through Education Work," in Wang Mingdi (ed.) *Educational Materials for Professional Training on 'The White*

Book on Criminal Reform'. Beijing: Law Publishing House. pp. 67–90.

张金桑，"人权与中国特色的劳改工作"，王明迪（编），《'中国改造罪犯的状况' 业务培训教材》

*Zhu Hongde. (1993) "Developing this Publication is Necessary to Raise the Standards of the Cadre." *Research into Crime and Reform*. Number 1.

朱洪德，"办好刊物是提高干警素质的需要"，《犯罪与改造研究》

Zhang Peitian. (1995) "The Corruption of Chinese Prison Staff and its Effects on Criminal Re-Education." Unpublished paper presented at the International Conference on Education, Training and Rehabilitation of Prisoners in Correctional Institutions, November, Tasmania, Australia.

Chapter
ELEVEN

The Japanese Experience: Effects of Decreasing Resort to Imprisonment

Elmer H. Johnson

In recent decades Japan and the United States have taken opposite courses in the resort to imprisonment as a major answer to the crime problem. The effects of a high and rapidly increasing imprisonment rate have received considerable attention in the United States. This paper takes advantage of the Japanese situation to take up a different but similar topic: What are the effects of a low and declining imprisonment rate?[1] The analysis begins by establishing that Japan *does* have a low imprisonment rate.

COMPARING THE JAPANESE AND AMERICAN RATES

Japan has trailed the United States since 1926 (when comparable data were first available) in the total number of convicted offenders in prisons, and that difference has consistently and sharply enlarged since World War II. The total population of Japan is about half the population of the United States; the effects of different-sized general population on differences in uses of the prisons are ruled out in Table 1 by imprisonment rates per 100,000 population.[2] Without any change in criminogenic factors and operations of the criminal justice system, an increase in the general population would generate a greater number of criminals and prisoners.

The Japanese rate dropped considerably in the 1940s when military mobilization removed many males from the community and aroused patriotic sentiments. During the socioeconomic chaos immediately after the war, the imprisonment rate peaked but dropped precipitously thereafter. The American rate rose rapidly until the nation entered World War II and then declined sharply. Until 1965, the post-war trend was modestly upward; the 1970s witnessed a decline before a sharp rise began that continues to the present day.

TABLE 1   Number and Rate Per 100,000 Population of Inmates Present at Year-End, Japan and U.S.

Selected Years	Japanese Prisoners		U.S. Prisoners		Ratio B/A(a)
	Number	Rate(A)	Number	Rate(B)	
1926	39,513	65.1	97,991	83	1.27
1930	41,188	63.9	129,453	104	1.63
1935	51,094	73.7	144,180	113	1.53
1940	38,599	53.7	173,706	131	2.44
1945	36,824	51.1	133,649	98	1.92
1950	80,589	96.9	166,123	109	1.12
1955	67,813	76.0	185,780	112	1.47
1960	61,100	65.4	212,953	117	1.79
1965	52,657	53.6	210,895	108	2.01
1970	39,724	38.3	196,429	96	2.51
1975	37,744	33.7	240,593	111	3.29
1980	41,835	35.7	315,974	138	3.86
1985	46,105	38.3	480,568	200	5.22
1990	39,892	32.3	739,980	292	9.04

Sources: Correction Bureau; Maguire, Pastore, and Flanagan, 1993: 608.

(a) The rates for each country are the number of prisoners (as counted on December 31 of the given year) divided by the number of persons in the country's total population that year and multiplied by 100. The ratio is computed by dividing the year's American rate by the Japanese rate.

The United States places greater reliance on imprisonment as a means of dealing with criminals, but the degree of greater reliance has varied over the years. The greater ratio in Table 1 the greater the superiority of the American rate over the Japanese rate. Until the end of World War II, the ratios reflected the erratic trend of greater American reliance. In 1950 the peaking of the Japanese prison population brought the Japanese imprisonment rate closest to the American rate. From then, the two rates progressively diverged from about one and a half times in 1955 to nine times in 1990.

Determinant sentencing policy in the United States has pushed prisons increasingly toward being instruments of toughness, according to Blumstein (1988: 237), and the demands of interest groups press judges to send more people to prisons and for longer terms. Most prosecutors and judges are elected and must compete for votes by promising to increase satisfaction of the demand. The prison population has grown at a rapid rate, prison sentences are longer and the prisoners are younger on average.

The rapid escalation of the prison population in the United States has aggravated the always formidable difficulties of prison administration. Overcrowding affects the physical and psychological well-being of inmates, as Porporino (1986: 227) points out, and appears to lead to more violence through destabilization of inmate social networks. Data derived from 19 prisons operated by the federal government of the United States show that assaults increased with overcrowding (Gaes and McGuire, 1985). Stastny and Tynauer (1982: 134–135) speak of the pluralization of prison subcultures as the "walls" became more permeable to developments in society at large. Fox (1982: 85) calls attention to shifts in prisoner values towards greater acceptance of interracial victimization, predatory violence and use of collective action for the resolution of problems. "Institutional programming is becoming more restricted in response to violence and the need to control it," Toch (1976: 44) warns, "to the point where we may be producing a malignant cyst of violence in places like readjustment centers."

On the other hand, reluctant use of imprisonment has enabled Japan to avoid the crisis of overburdened prisons and its effects. Prison environments are havens of tranquility and inmates are remarkably submissive to their keepers. Forced confinement inevitably will favor the development of distinctive inmate values, but Japanese inmates are far less inclined to mount subcultural opposition to the prison staff and its official goals. Those conditions, of course, are encouraged by the avoidance of crowded cells, but both the uncrowded prisons and the relative tranquility of their environments are also due to the Japanese culture and its expression in the administrative processing of suspects and defendants.

Structural Conditions for Leniency

Comparative criminology emphasizes the principle that criminal justice policy operates within the contours of sociocultural and legal systems varying among societies. Growth of prison populations, Joyce (1992: 358–359) concludes, stems primarily from public policy as reflected in criminal laws, law enforcement priorities and prosecution and judicial discretion.[3] Conversely, the search for a low-level and declining level of prison populations should consider those reflections of public policy. Behind the nature of laws, law enforcement priorities and the discretion of prosecutors and judges are the cultural values of the people, including the individuals who are criminal justice personnel.

In speaking of "Japan's sociocultural system," we expand the analysis to all influences exerted on groups and their members so that the multitude of behaviors fit together in maintaining the social order of Japan. In other words, social control touches every aspect of how the persistence of society is obtained. The "social" involves the patterned relationships among the members. The "cultural" refers to the set of standards followed in fitting the behaviors into the patterned relationships.

The social patterns and cultural standards of Japanese society and its members will be sketched below because of their vital importance in explaining Japan's reluctant use of penal incarceration. Second, the general sociocultural system underlies the willingness of the public and officials to avoid imprisonment of the repentant offender. Third, the sociocultural system has shaped the criteria applied in official decisions on who should be or should not be imprisoned.

The criteria are part of Japanese public policy and are implemented by officials who occupy positions within the structure of the procuracy and judiciary. Their offices encourage the procuracy and judiciary to grant leniency to the repentant offenders. "From the initial police interrogation to the final judicial hearing on sentence," Haley (1989: 495) summarizes, "the vast majority of those accused of criminal offenses confess, display repentance, negotiate for their victims' pardon and submit to the mercy of the authorities. In return they are treated with extraordinary leniency."

With the collapse of Tokugawa government and the threat of the political power of the West, the Meiji Restoration in 1868 began the modernization of Japan with only a fraction of the material and social–psychological resources required by this massive and profound movement. To manage the 27,000 prisoners who had been on the losing side in the Satsuma Rebellion in 1877, rice warehouses and stables were converted into inadequate places of confinement while the heavy expense of building prisons was assumed (Hiramatsu, 1973: 31–32; Beasley, 1990: 64, 71, 105). More to the central theme of this paper, the components of official leniency were established incidentally to the general movement for modernization. As will be explained below, incidental to meeting the crisis, the Meiji reformers introduced the principles of discretionary prosecution and suspension of prison sentences.

The priority during the Meiji Restoration was to ease the overwhelming demands on the public purse, and discretionary prosecution and suspension of sentences served that priority. Japan has continued to be noteworthy among industrial nations in its curtailment of the size of the national government and a preference to leave to the private sector many functions usually assumed by government (Pempel, 1982: 9, 20; Watanuki, 1986: 263–265). Miyazawa (1994: 91) sees a similar motivation in the persistence of discretionary prosecution and suspension of prison sentences: the preference for unsalaried volunteer probation officers, and the partial privatization of prison industry.

Unlike elected politically appointed justice officials in some other countries, public prosecutors and judges in Japan are careerists. By passing a national examination a candidate becomes eligible to take an even more difficult examination and gain entry to a two-year course conducted by the Legal Training and Research Institute of the Supreme Court. Four months are devoted to civil and criminal procedures, 16 months to field training and four months to final instruction on basic principles. Having survived a final examination after completion of training, the apprentice is qualified to be an assistant judge, prosecutor or lawyer. Full judges have had at least ten years experience in such roles (Abe, 1963: 156–160; Hattori, 1963: 133).

The Japanese tend to accept wide discretion in the interpretation of legal codes during processing of specific cases. Nakamura

(1964: 351) refers to the "disposition to lay a greater emphasis upon intuitive sensible concrete events, rather than upon universals." Similarly, Christopher (1983: 168) says: "The letter of the law in Japan can change drastically with little or no notice and no legislative action whatever. Judges can and do take advantage of the imprecision of their language to radically reinterpret the meaning of legal statutes."

Cultural Foundation for Leniency

In avoiding prison sentences whenever feasible, the decision-makers make a bet that structural and social–psychological factors in combination exceed penal confinement in capacity to terminate the criminality of many persons who appear before them. It is remarkable that the decision-makers are prepared to place the bet and, second, that so many of the defendants are worthy of the official leniency. Japanese values support the official leniency and also press the defendants to live up to the terms of leniency.

Broadly speaking, the Japanese stand at one extreme by being among societies that emphasize the subordination of self to the interests of the group, and Americans are at the other extreme by being among societies giving priority to the interests of individual members. The contrast exaggerates the distinctions between highly urbanized contemporary societies, but, for our purposes, the comparison focuses attention on the general tendency among the Japanese to accommodate themselves to the "realities" of their sociocultural environment. They are especially likely to adjust their personal strivings to the expectations of the group of which they are members and to find personal satisfaction in making a contribution to group accomplishments.

The word *giri* is basic to Japanese social-psychology and affords the opportunity for a brief summary statement. The term, Noda (1976: 175–178) notes, evokes too many ideas for a clear-cut definition but does convey several elements. Duty locates the individual in relationships with others according to the status of the respective parties; the feudal principles of a hierarchical order persist today. The person benefiting from the observance of duty cannot demand the other individual's observance but must wait for voluntary observance. *Giri* obligations are perpetual; they cannot be extinguished even when a duty has been performed. Although selfish gain may be involved, the relationships carry feelings of affection. The obligations are sanctioned simply by a sense of honor.

For further amplification of *giri*, Wagatsuma and Rosett (1986: 472–478) interpret the special meaning of apology to the Japanese. First, the individual wishes to maintain or restore a positive relationship with another person who has been harmed by the individual. (The public prosecutor and sentencing judge emphasize the offender's restitution and expressions of regret to the victim as a condition for leniency.) Second, the apology places the forgiven person in a limitless obligation to the forgiver. (The offender's desire to counter the effects of the offense is perpetual; pressure toward "rehabilitation" persists.) Third, the apology rests on a cultural faith in the deviants' capacity for self-correction and their commitment to harmonious relationships in the future. The principle of *giri* include the withholding of moral demands because the desired response of the offender must be voluntary.[4]

The high American crime rate, Lynch (1988: 181) believes, is partly the consequence of the tendency to legislate morality, including the criminalization of prostitution, drug use and other victimless crimes.[5] Here morality underlies the use of criminal sanctions as controls external to usual social relationships. The emphasis on morality in Japan probably is even greater than in the United States, but the Japanese morality operates to a greater extent within the regular contacts among group members. As explained above, Japanese morality places great pressure on the deviant, inclines the individual to abstain from law-breaking and encourages the deviant to abandon criminal ways. Members of the general public, and even the victims of criminals, are pressed morally to support the official reluctance to imprison the "worthy" offenders. The faith in the offender's potential for self-correction restrains any tendency to force compliance through penal incarceration. Instead, imprisonment is employed when the offender is deemed to be unworthy because of lack of repentance.

Principle of Discretionary Prosecutions

Japan has embraced the principle of discretionary prosecutions, George (1988: 265–266) says, since the establishment of its public procurator system. According to that principle the courts accept and adjudicate cases instituted by the public prosecutors, as opposed

to the principle of mandatory prosecution under which the prosecutor must pass on for trial every case involving a suspicion of guilt
and the court decides whether or not the evidence warrants formal
action.

At the turn of the century Japan was engaged in the turmoil of
moving from feudalism and developing the elements of a modern
society. The number of prisoners surged from about 32,000 in 1882
to 65,000 in 1885. Suspended prosecution emerged informally as an
immediate and practical solution, Nishikawa (1990: 3–4) says, without incorporation in the legal code. Public prosecutors seized opportunities to avoid prosecution of minor offenses, if reasonable
grounds existed, even when evidence was sufficient for conviction.
In 1905 the Law for Suspension of Execution of Sentence provided
formal recognition and authorization.

The present Code of Criminal Procedure offers general criteria
but leaves the concrete rationale to the prosecutors' discretion.
Article 248 says: "If after considering the character, age and situation of the offender, the gravity of the offense, the circumstances
under which the offense was committed, and the conditions subsequent to the offense, prosecution is deemed unnecessary, prosecution need not be instituted."

Suspensions of prosecution were a major disposition into the
1980s when referrals for formal trial became preeminent, and they
continue to hold a large share of cases (see Table 2). Shikita and
Tsuchiya (1990: 119, 133) attribute the decline in the use of suspended prosecution, a trend initiated in 1961, to increased prosecution of
assault, bodily injury and stimulant-drug offenses. Suspension of
prosecution is the major category of non-prosecution, but discretion
is not the sole basis. In 1991 suspensions were 78.8 percent of all
instances of non-prosecution. The remainder were justified by
insufficient evidence, 14.4 percent; lack of valid complaint, 2.5 percent; mental incapacity, 0.6 percent; and other reasons 3.8 percent
(Ministry of Justice, 1992: 96).

The principle of discretionary prosecution is found elsewhere.[6] It
enlarges the role of the public prosecutor in decision-making for the
sake of reducing the number of trials, but, as Satsumae (1977: 6–9)
acknowledges, the practice raises questions about the equality of
justice and the deterrent effect of law enforcement. However, he
insists: "The circle of public prosecutors justified the practice by as-
serting that the purpose of punishment was indeed not only to
deter the public by showing the authority of law, but also to make

TABLE 2 Prosecutors' Decisions for Violators of Penal Code
and Special Laws for Selected Years(a)

Number of Decisions	Total Pct.	Formal Trial	Summary Proceedings	Prosecution Suspended	Other Non-Prosecutions
			Percentage Distributions		
1931					
334,277	100.0	9.2	15.8	52.1	22.9
1941					
310,901	100.0	9.7	27.2	52.6	10.5
1951					
1,057,303	100.0	13.5	18.9	56.8	10.8
1961					
544,086	100.0	22.3	29.5	39.0	9.2
1971					
434,139	100.0	20.2	34.2	37.4	8.2
1981					
343,880	100.0	34.4	31.7	27.0	6.9
1988					
241,819	100.0	38.5	24.4	28.8	8.3

Adapted from Shikita and Tsuchiya (1990: Tables 22 and 24).

(a) These offenses were excluded: professional negligence and road traffic offenses.

the offender repent of his criminal conduct." Satsumae contends that even serious criminals are favorably impressed by "such generous dispositions" by the procuracy and judiciary and are moved to reform themselves, that "the practice is better able to reflect the individual circumstances in the case," and that the worthy offender is protected from stigmatizing publicity.

"In some countries judges do not consider whether or not the suspect has compensated the victim because, they say, the rich can buy their freedom but the poor can not," a former public prosecutor told me. "But we do not have any special mediation or reparation scheme. The most important advice of the defense counsel in Japan is to negotiate with the victim and his people for forgiveness and offer money as compensation. When the victim or his family write a statement that lenient treatment is acceptable, I, as the defendant's advisor, would take the piece of paper to the public prosecutor. If convinced by his own investigation that the victim is satisfied with the payment, the public prosecutor will take the statement into consideration. If the offender's past conduct has not been good or the amount of damage is too great to warrant suspension of prosecution, the case is highly likely to go to trial. The court will consider all those factors when passing sentence."

Suspending the Prison Sentences

The judge is authorized to suspend a sentence to prison under "extenuating circumstances." Article 25 of the Penal Code limits the leniency to persons sentenced to prison for no more than three years and, if previously imprisoned, had not been imprisoned again within five years after satisfaction of the previous prison sentence. In practice "extenuating circumstances," Kouhashi (1985: 3) says, include the following: The defendant has no or only a minimal criminal record or is young enough to change attitudes and life style. The victim excuses the offender, the victim and the defendant have agreed to terms for restitution and the offender exhibits readiness for rehabilitation. The offense was accidental, not deliberate.

Blameworthiness is measured in practice by deliberateness in planning, coldheartedness in execution of the criminal plan, inflicting excessive pain on the victim, repetition of offenses and other evidence of moral depravity. Favorable social and psychological factors are considered in evaluating the offender's capacity for positive behavior. Previous imprisonment is a negative factor contributing to the concentration of recidivists in Japanese prisons. Previous imprisonment, however, is no longer a barrier to suspension if at least five years had passed since the earlier penal confinement ended (Suzuki, 1979: 146–147).

The provision in the Japanese Penal Code for suspended sentences, Ancel (1971: 22–26, 36–40) reports, was modeled on the French-Belgian system. Alarmed by the increase of crime and recidivism, 19th-century France questioned the usefulness of imprisonment. Conditional suspension of prison sentences emerged in the Belgian law in 1888 and French law in 1891 when the Meiji reformers were examining European legal systems. In Belgium and France, the prison sentences were pronounced to intimidate the convicted offenders. Once intimidated by hearing his sentence to prison, the defendant capable of self-rehabilitation would be returned to the community without assistance or probationary supervision.

Over the decades the suspensions of prison sentences have attained greater proportions in Japan (see Table 3). As evidence of the approach's efficiency, revocations of the suspensions fluctuated around only 10 percent. The suspensions usually do not require probationary supervision because the judges tend to believe that official monitoring is excessive punishment of individuals capable of self-rehabilitation. Outcomes for 1990 indicate that the judges' expectations are usually justified by experience. For 30,101 persons granted suspensions of prison sentences without supervision in 1990, 2,503 were revoked (8.3 percent) for new offenses. For 4,774 granted suspensions with probationary supervision, 1,266 were revoked (26.5 percent) for new offenses. Another 188 individual revocations were due to previous offenses, violation of probation conditions and other reasons (Ministry of Justice, 1992: 102).

The rates of suspension vary among offenses because of differences in length of sentences as allowed by statutes. Crimes believed to pose greater threats to public security draw more sentences exceeding the three-year limit for suspensions. The Penal Code sets the limits; public beliefs, reflecting Japanese culture, influence the Penal Code and the courts' interpretations of "extenuating circumstances." The effects of those factors are illustrated by five major crimes: fraud, robbery, larceny, bodily injury and homicide.[7]

TABLE 3 Suspended Prison Sentences: Rates, Use of Probation, and Revocation Rates, 1931–1990

Year	Prison Sentences(A)	Suspensions (B)	Suspension Rate(C)	Pct Probation(D)	Failure Rate(E)
1931	35,219	4,817	13.7	—	10.5
1951	118,229	54,272	45.9	—	18.6
1961	83,249	43,142	51.8	18.7	13.6
1971	69,467	40,361	58.1	16.0	8.2
1981	76,219	44,269	58.1	18.6	14.3
1991	57,824	34,875	60.3	13.7	11.3

Sources: Shikita and Tsuchiya (1990: 165) and Ministry of Justice (1992: 99–102).

C: Suspension rate: B divided by A.

D: Percent Probation: number placed on probationary supervision divided by number of suspensions (B) multiplied by 100. Probation was introduced in 1949.

E: Failure rate: number of revocations divided by number of suspensions (B).

As defined in Japan, a record of previous sentences rules out suspensions for all five crimes; none of these crimes received suspensions when the convict had been imprisoned in the previous five years. "Extenuating circumstances" benefited only certain cases of fraud and bodily injury by granting new suspensions only for the two crimes in spite of a new crime during a suspension for a previous crime. Fraud is a property crime and bodily injury is among the crimes against persons, but both offenses include a great variety of situations, among which the motives and character of offenders sometimes justify leniency in the expectation of "rehabilitation."

Homicide and robbery, of course, are identified with extreme violence. Larceny is the most numerous offense and is especially likely to be referred for summary action and fines. The thieves sentenced to prison tend to be considered unworthy for leniency on grounds of "extenuating circumstances." The differences between property and violent crimes are narrowed when crimes against persons draw a prison sentence of three years or less. For the five crimes in that particular comparison, extenuating circumstances produce a high suspension rate for the few qualifying cases of homicide (all were "mercy killings") and robbery.

When the total number of crimes is considered, the rate of suspended prison sentences was 58.2 in 1990, a remarkably high general rate (Ministry of Justice, 1993: 16). As a whole, robbers (suspension rate of 15.8) and murderers (rate of 21.8) do benefit in some instances but to a more limited extent. In the cases of bodily injury (53.5 rate) and fraud (43.1 rate), the offenders in general do about as well as the cases discussed above. Larcenists in general (rate of only 28.1) are so varied in crime situations and personal characteristics that their suspension rates fall short of the discussed cases.

Only an Artifice of Low Crime Rate?

"Of course, fewer Japanese go to prison," a Dutch lawyer told me. "They are less likely than most people to commit crimes." He implied that the imprisonment rate, essentially and merely, mirrors the crime rate. He overlooked the fact that, even for persons convicted of crimes and sentenced to prison, a substantial share are immediately returned to the community.

The crime rates and imprisonment rates have diverged increasingly over the years since 1945 (see Table 4). Both sets of rates are accommodated to the increases in the general population of Japan.

TABLE 4   Crime Rates Compared With
Imprisonment Rates, 1926–1990

Years	Crime Rate(A)	Imprisonment Rate(B)	Ratio(C)
1926	1,171	65	18.01
1930	1,612	61	26.43
1935	2,183	72	30.32
1940	1,414	54	26.18
1945	984	68	14.47
1950	1,756	102	17.22
1955	1,608	74	21.73
1960	1,476	68	21.71
1965	1,367	54	25.31
1970	1,234	39	31.64
1975	1,103	34	32.44
1980	1,160	36	32.22
1985	1,328	38	34.95
1990	1,324	33	40.12

Source: Shikita and Tsuchiya (1990: 355, 371); Ministry of Justice
(1992: 54).

(A) Crime rate per 100,000 population, for penal code violations
other than traffic.

(B) Rate per 100,000 population for average daily prisoners present.

(C) Ratio: Crime rate (A) divided by imprisonment rate (B).

The divergence would be even greater if traffic arrests were included
in the crime rate; the erosion of traffic cases before imprisonment is
especially high. The crime rates have declined, but as the ratios
make clear, the imprisonment rates have dropped even more.

The two rates are related in other ways. The leniency of the procuracy and judiciary is favored by the public faith in the effectiveness
of law enforcement and the peculiar willingness of many Japanese
suspects to confess their misdeeds. From the perspective of Japanese
values, Van Wolferen (1989: 188–191) contends, "being picked up by
the police is, in any event, shameful, and there is comfort in convert-
ing an overwhelming sense of shame into an admission of guilt."

A cultural explanation does not take into account the workings of
the Japanese criminal justice system. By the leniency of their case

processing, the public prosecutors and judges encourage defendants to confess crimes without fear of subsequent stern punishments. Japan's low and declining imprisonment rate attests to credibility of the official encouragement.

The police emphasis on confessions leads to their preference for holding suspects in their own jails rather than sending them to the detention houses operated by the Correction Bureau. Article 1–3 of the Prison Law authorizes the police jail, but Article 203 of the Code of Criminal Procedure requires the police either to release the suspect within 48 hours, or to turn over to the public prosecutor the documents and evidence. When the public prosecutor believes that longer detention is necessary, Article 204 requires that, if prosecution has not been instituted, the public prosecutor request a judge for additional detention not exceeding 72 hours since the suspect was placed under restraints. Articles 206 and 208 permit the judges to extend detention for no more than 15 days when "unavoidable circumstances" exist or for crimes of insurrection foreign, aggression or concerning foreign relations.

The Japanese police argue that, because of the legal restraints on the length of detention, the immediate presence of the suspects in the police jail for interrogation is of great importance. In his empirical research of police procedures, Miyazawa (1992: 158) reports: "Among the detectives, there is an attitude that procuring confessions is primary in investigations and that other investigative activities must follow this." Furthermore, he notes (1992: 149) that "detention in the police jail is granted as long as the judge finds that there are no abuses of the suspect and no denial of the suspect's rights to defend himself." The possibility of forced confessions, however, has aroused concerns that abuses do occur, especially those expressed by the Joint Investigative Committee of three Tokyo Bar Associations (see McCormack and Sugimoto, 1986: 186–214).

Prison Capacity When Inmates are Few

Substantial growth in the number of prisoners raises questions about the sufficiency of prison capacity and how effectively and quickly the capacity can be increased. American experts have debated without a reliable conclusion whether or not the additional capacity has encouraged judges to sentence more offenders to prison (Blumstein, 1988: 258–261).

In spite of the long-term decline in the number of Japanese prisoners, the rated capacity of penal institutions (including detention facilities) has remained about the same and even increased modestly in the short term (see Table 5). All prisons and detention facilities (except prison jails) are under control of the Correction Bureau as a component of the Ministry of Justice in the national government. The total inmate population has declined sharply since 1950, with the percentage share of convicted prisoners hovering around 83 percent. Over the years, the number of inmates (including accused and untried defendants in detention centers) per 100,000 Japanese has dropped sharply and somewhat regularly.

In absolute numbers the trend for number of inmates present has been the opposite of the trend for rated capacity. The average usage dropped from 154.1 inmates per 100 spaces in 1950 to 70.4 inmates per 100 available sleeping spaces in 1992. The housing situation is

TABLE 5   Population of Untried and Convicted Persons: Prison Capacity and Utilization, 1946–1992

Year	Inmate Population(a)	Pct. Convicted	Imprisonment Rate(b)	Rated Capacity(c)	Average Usage(d)
1946	56,875	77.9	123.2	56,425	100.8
1950	103,170	82.6	198.3	66,941	154.1
1955	81,868	81.2	141.9	66,056	123.9
1960	75,821	83.5	118.9	56,955	133.1
1965	63,515	83.2	89.6	62,220	102.1
1970	49,209	83.2	63.7	63,581	77.4
1975	45,690	82.8	55.0	62,273	73.4
1980	50,596	83.3	57.7	61,522	82.2
1985	55,263	82.9	59.4	63,263	87.4
1990	48,243	85.3	48.8	63,613	75.8
1992	44,876	83.6	44.3	63,773	70.4

Source: Annual reports of Correction Bureau.

(a) Average daily population of detention centers and regular prisons.

(b) Number of inmates (in second column) per 100,000 population of all Japanese aged 16 and more years.

(c) The number of inmates for which the prisons and detention centers were designed to hold.

(d) The number of "beds" occupied on average divided by the number of available "beds." The American term is strange here in light of the Japanese use of futons.

noteworthy because obsolete prison buildings and public opposition to existing prisons in their neighborhoods provided reason for
abandonment of some sites. Urban growth has ended the previous
geographical isolation of many prisons; now they are surrounded
by private residences in suburban areas or by commercial establishments in metropolitan regions. A major program was undertaken in
the late 1980s to modernize the large prisons that had been constructed on the design of American and European prisons of the
1930s and 1940s. The cellblocks and workshops were poorly lit, and
sanitary facilities were introduced later in a provisional way.

Type of Crime and Length of Sentence

The diversionary decisions of the procuracy and judiciary may
change over time; our data permit examination of two relevant
variables: the crimes that sent convicted defendants to prison and
the length of the prison sentences imposed upon them. Changes in
the "menu" of crimes among prison admissions reflect differing
tendencies to break the law but also the enactment of new criminal
laws, modifications of old laws, revised law enforcement circumstances and new sentencing policies. The length of the sentences is
related to the perceived seriousness of the offense, and an increasing average length of sentence over time will contribute to an upsurge in the imprisonment rate.[8]

Among the crimes of prisoners admitted to prison over the
1970–1990 period, property crimes are most prevalent as expected
in an economically developed society. Larceny is numerically dominant, followed in turn by fraud, embezzlement, forgery, "intrusion
upon a habitat," arson and possession of stolen property. Larceny
has remained dominant in spite of the declining share of all property
crimes among all crimes from half of all crimes in 1970 to 38 percent
in 1990.

Violence is usually directed against other persons but what we
call "societal violence" has special meaning in Japan. Both violence
against persons and "societal violence" have declined over the
years. Violence against persons is predominately "bodily injury";
robbery and homicide are only a third of the number of bodily
injury offenses. Assault has minor importance, and kidnapping
is very infrequent. In "societal violence" the community is victim-
ized in the illicit economic gains of criminal syndicates known

as the *yakuza*, by death or injury resulting from the negligence in practicing a profession or occupation or by aggravated crimes with firearms and swords.

Traffic offenses punished by imprisonment stood third among the crime categories in 1970 and their share has also dropped over the years. Rape, indecent assault and pornography (a category of sex offenses) were of minor importance and consistently drew a smaller share of admissions over the years. Gambling and lottery plus prostitution were of least importance.

Drug offenses deserve special attention because, alone among the crime categories, they had a drastic increase from their less than one percent share in 1970. Laws against opium have existed since 1879, against narcotics since 1948 and against stimulant drugs (amphetamines) since 1951. The strong upsurge in prison admissions for drug offenses stemmed from violations of the Stimulant Drugs Control Law. During World War II drug abuse was limited to a few opium and cocaine addicts. During the post-war chaos, abuse of stimulant drugs became prevalent. One hypothesis is that the abuse spread suddenly because stimulant drugs produced for the military in wartime had leaked out to the public, and the arrests for drug offenses were dominated by violations of the Stimulant Drugs Control Law. Since 1985 the number of arrests each year have declined consistently (National Police Agency, 1992: 19–20).

A declining average length of sentence will reduce the number of prison inmates present in the long run, but, as Table 6 documents, this factor does not explain Japan's declining imprisonment rate. If a person were sentenced to three months of penal confinement, he probably would add to the prison population for only the year 1990. The person sentenced to five years and released on expiration of sentence would be present for the years 1990, 1991, 1992, 1993 and 1994. When admissions of persons with long sentences became more and more frequent over the years, that factor alone would raise the imprisonment rate, but Japan's imprisonment rate dropped *in spite* of the growth of the mean length of sentence from 17.52 months in 1970 to 20.93 in 1990. That trend is attributable to sentences that ranged in length from 12 months to 36 months. Sentences less than a year or more than five years have lost shares. Violence against persons and sex crimes drew the longest average sentences; the increased average length over time can be traced to property, societal violence and drug offenses.

TABLE 6 Length of Sentence for Males When Admitted to Prison
in Selected Years

Statistical Categories	1970	1975	1980	1985	1990
			Percentage Distributions		
Length of Sentence in Months					
Less than 6	16.7	18.9	16.8	11.3	9.6
6 to 12	36.3	34.7	34.5	29.9	23.7
12 to 24	28.5	27.3	29.3	38.0	40.9
24 to 36	9.5	10.2	10.8	11.7	15.1
36 to 60	6.1	6.3	6.4	6.4	8.1
60 Over	2.9	2.6	2.3	2.8	2.6
Total Pct	100.0	100.0	100.0	100.0	100.0
Mean Length	17.52	17.31	17.44	19.24	20.93
Mean Length of Sentence in Months by Crime Categories					
Property	16.7	17.1	18.4	19.4	21.7
Violence Against Persons	32.0	30.5	30.7	35.2	34.6
Societal Violence	11.8	13.2	14.5	17.0	19.4
Drugs	15.1	13.2	15.1	16.6	20.4
Traffic	7.6	6.9	6.9	7.0	7.7
Sex	30.1	31.8	31.8	32.3	34.3
Prostitution	8.2	8.9	11.1	13.7	14.4
Gambling	9.0	10.1	10.8	11.2	12.3

Source: Ministry of Justice, *Annual Reports of Statistics on Corrections*, Vol. 1, for given
years, Table 15 or 16.

Trends in Prisoners' Characteristics

Japan's low crime rate among developed and urbanized societies
helps explain the tendency to send relatively few offenders to
prison; both rates mirror the cultural emphasis on the average citizen's sense of duty and moral compliance. The structure and operations of the criminal justice system also reflect Japanese values when
the agencies extend leniency to a remarkable portion of those persons caught in their net. In diverting from imprisonment those
offenders who are deemed worthy of official leniency, the procuracy
and judiciary increase the average age of prison inmates, reduce the

number of persons exposed to incarceration for the first time and raise the proportional representation of the *yakuza* among prisoners.[9]

The official leniency previous to imprisonment is suggested by the history of the 8,060 males entering prison for the first time in 1990 (Ministry of Justice, 1991: 87). Of the 8,060 males 58.6 percent had received a suspended sentence after an earlier appearance before a court, usually for a crime other than the one for which they had recently been imprisoned. Also 13.2 percent had experienced an earlier referral to a juvenile training school.

For total male admissions the mean age consistently has exceeded 30 years and has risen from an average of 31.9 years in 1970 to 39.3 years in 1990 (see Table 7). The age categories differed greatly in the effect of time on their share of total male admissions. The younger

TABLE 7   Age of Men Entering Prisons in Selected Years

Statistical Categories	1970	1975	1980	1985	1990
	Percentage Distributions				
Age at Admission					
16 to 24	27.1	15.9	10.8	12.4	12.6
25 to 29	24.5	23.8	16.3	12.5	14.5
30 to 39	31.3	36.1	41.6	36.0	25.4
40 to 49	12.3	17.8	23.1	26.3	29.5
50 to 59	3.7	5.0	6.5	10.6	14.1
60 and Over	1.1	1.4	1.7	2.2	3.9
Total Pct.	100.0	100.0	100.0	100.0	100.0
Mean Ages	31.89	34.30	36.46	38.07	39.34
Age-Specific Rates by Age Categories					
16 to 24	76.1	52.5	40.8	48.1	31.8
25 to 29	137.4	112.4	98.5	95.7	77.4
30 to 39	95.6	104.7	114.4	109.6	65.4
40 to 49	49.1	58.9	77.7	92.2	65.3
50 to 59	22.0	27.2	29.7	43.9	39.3
60 and Over	5.5	6.1	7.1	8.9	9.1
Total Rate	67.8	63.7	64.7	67.1	45.3

Source: Ministry of Justice, *Annual Reports of Statistics on Corrections*, Vol. 1, for given years, Table 16 or 17.

group assumed smaller shares as the years unfolded; the percentage decline was 53.5 percent for age group 16–24 years, 40.8 percent
for age group 25–29 years and 18.8 percent for age group 30–39
years. The older groups took up the slack; their percentage increase
from 1970 to 1990 was 139.8 percent for age group 40–49 years,
281.1 percent for age group 50–59 years and 254.5 percent for age
group 60 years and more.

When possible the age of prisoners should be related to the ages
of all persons in the society who had been exposed to the chance of
being a law violator. Teenagers and young adults usually are more
likely than older persons to end up in prison, but, as age-specific
rates show, the relative chances of an age-cohort can change over
time. The age-specific rates in Table 7 were computed for each
given year by dividing the number of males entering prison in a
given age category (say, 16 to 24 years) by the number of Japanese
males of that age in Japanese society. The result is multiplied by
100,000 to give a rate per 100,000 Japanese males in the given age
group.

The total age-specific rate can drop even when the number of
persons admitted to prison is greater over the years. The number of
all Japanese males of that age group always is increasing, but the
rate of increase differs among the age groups. If the increase of
prison admissions of the age group falls short of the increase of that
age group in society, the age-specific rate in Table 7 will decline for
the rate for the previous year.

Measured by age-specific rates, the men in ages 25–29 years
within the Japanese population had the highest risk of being
imprisoned for all the years, but, unlike the ages above 29 years, the
ages 25–29 years had progressively lower rates as the years proceeded.

Only the most elderly group sustained increases in the age-
specific rates through 1990. The vulnerability of the aged inmates to
disease and incapacitation is an especially grave problem for the
Japanese prisons that put some two-thirds of the inmates to work in
industrial shops. Costs of medical care will grow rapidly, and there
will be great difficulties in placing incapacitated elderly inmates in
the community when they are released. Otherwise, the age groups,
especially those less than 40 years, experienced a sharp drop in age-
specific rates in 1990. The progressive increase in the number of all
Japanese males in those ages coincided that year with a definite
drop in prison admissions.

Previous imprisonment was among the criteria for denial of official leniency; the share of recidivists among males entering prison increased over the years. Table 8 documents two opposing trends: The percentage share of "first-termers" decreased from 47.4 percent in 1970 to 37.1 percent in 1990 and, concurrently, the percentage share of those in prison for at least the fourth time rose from 25.4 to 34.4 percent. The trends are summarized by the rise of the mean number of prison admissions for all males from 2.82 to 3.44. The trend for greater recidivism was intimately related to the trend for a more advanced average age of inmates entering prison. Leniency given "worthy" individuals delayed imposition of penal incarceration of

TABLE 8 Previous Exposure to Penal Incarceration of Men Entering Prison in Selected Years

Number of Admissions	1970	1975	1980	1985	1990
	Percentage Distribution				
1	47.4	42.5	40.9	38.9	37.1
2	16.8	17.9	18.2	18.3	16.7
3	10.4	11.5	12.3	12.4	11.8
4 more	25.4	28.1	28.6	30.4	34.4
Total Pct.	100.0	100.0	100.0	100.0	100.0
Mean Number Admissions	2.82	3.02	3.06	3.19	3.44
Mean Standardized by Age	2.82	2.65	2.47	2.43	2.48
Yakuza Males Only					
1	33.0	31.4	29.7	26.5	27.6
2	25.4	23.1	22.1	21.0	19.4
3	14.6	16.8	16.4	17.7	15.3
4 more	27.0	28.7	31.8	34.8	37.7
Total Pct.	100.0	100.0	100.0	100.0	100.0
Mean Number of Yakuza Admissions	2.89	2.98	3.12	3.34	3.45
Mean Number of Non-Yakuza Admissions	2.80	3.04	2.80	3.14	3.43

Source: Ministry of Justice, *Annual Reports of Statistics on Corrections*, Vol. 1, for given years, Tables 18 or 19, and 34 or 35.

defendants who were apprehended repetitively by the police, but, once sent to prison, those defendants were more likely to be returned.

To demonstrate the interaction between age of incoming inmates and repetitive imprisonment, the percentage distributions of the number of prison admissions were standardized to eliminate the effect of age. For each of the subsequent years, the total number of male admissions were redistributed according to the percentage distribution by age of all men entering prison in 1970. With all the years having identical percentage distributions by age, the estimated number of men in each age cell for the given year was multiplied by the actual rate of previous imprisonments for men of the age. The means, standardized by age, are presented in Table 8 and show that, with the age differences removed, the mean numbers of exposures to penal incarceration are reduced considerably and also decline over the years. In other words, by delaying the referral of serial offenders to prison, the procuracy and judiciary increased the average age of incoming prisoners. Their policy of leniency for the "worthy" defendants was reversed when a former prisoner was again apprehended. Then, the defendants previously sent to prison became increasingly represented among incoming inmates over the years.

The *yakuza* (the Mafia of Japan) have taken larger and larger shares of the prison population: 21 percent in 1975, 29.9 percent in 1985, 31.7 percent in 1989, and dropping slightly to 29.8 percent in 1991. They have been especially represented in Class B prisons which receive males evaluated as being psychologically committed to criminal values (having an "advanced criminal tendency") (Ministry of Justice, 1984: 120; 1988: 73; 1992: 70). In effect, the *yakuza* personify the kinds of offenders believed to have violated the values insulating most Japanese from engaging in criminal conduct.

The *yakuza* are especially unlikely to have entered the prison for the first time and that tendency has become stronger with the years (see Table 8). Also they have exceeded the non-*yakuza* males in the average number of exposures to penal incarceration.

As pursuers of illicit profits, the criminal organizations generate their own menu of crimes. Their imprisoned members have been especially involved in violence against persons and offenses lumped here as "societal violence": extortion, transgression of the law against violence, possession of "firearms and swords" (a centuries-old prohibition) and possession of explosives. Traffic in illicit drugs has drawn many of them to prison, but drug abusers also have that experience. Their share of these crimes is great and has increased considerably over the years. Although the number of admissions is small for violations of the law against prostitution and prohibited practices in gambling and lotteries, the *yakuza* are overrepresented among the men entering prison for those violations in their illicit enterprises. Sex, traffic and property offenses are more characteristic of the non-*yakuza*.

Effects on Prison Environment

The characteristics of prisoners, as shaped by the diversionary practices of prosecutors and judges, would appear to encourage violence within the prisons, but, in spite of the high level of recidivism and the heavy representation of the *yakuza* among inmates, the prisons are generally orderly. For all male adult prisons in 1990, the rule-violation rates per 100 inmates were: 0.27 for murder or serious bodily injury of an inmate, 0.03 for murder or serious bodily injury of a staff member, 7.56 for assault on an inmate and 0.81 for assault on a staff member. There were three escapes that year when the year-end population of inmates was 38,234 males (Ministry of Justice, 1991: Tables 3 and 83).

Parsimonious use of imprisonment and relatively short sentences contribute to the attitudes of inmates that are favorable to the noteworthy orderliness of Japanese prisons. Officials claim that most inmates agree that their sentences were appropriate. Prisoners have been socialized to the Japanese respect for persons in superior social positions Officer fraternization with inmates is prohibited in American prisons, but, in keeping with the Japanese conception of superior-subordinate relationships generally, the officers are expected to merge roles of moral educator and lay counselor with the primary role of security monitor. The competent and dedicated guard-force is maintained by the recruitment system of the National Personnel Authority and the Correction Bureau's program of in-service training that was established a century ago.

B-type prisons receive the inmates classified as having "advanced criminal tendencies" and whose activities are tightly scheduled and regulated closely by a set of formal rules. Intensive industrial work keeps two-thirds of the prisoners busy in a 40-hour week. Japanese prisons avoid the cancer of idleness of most inmates that encourages violence. Also the assemblage of inmates in a central dining hall has often led to riots in American prisons. After breakfast in the cells Japanese inmates are marched to workshops, have lunch there in separate dining rooms and are returned to the cells in the late afternoon for the evening meal in each cell.

The gangsters are dispersed among workshops and cells as a way of dampening potential intragang conflicts. Instead of the massive cell-blocks of some Western prisons, inmates are dispersed among sleeping rooms holding up to eight persons. Gang leaders and other inmates raising custodial problems are kept in one-person cells for appropriate work tasks. Positive rewards also induce compliant conduct. Task performance is among the criteria for promotion in the progressive stage system. The warden, not the inmate, initiates the application for parole.

CONCLUSION

The reluctant resort to imprisonment has been explained in this paper as an expression of Japanese values, generally and specifically, in the policies of the procuracy and judiciary. From that background discussion, the effects of Japan's low and declining imprisonment rate have been examined. The conclusions were as follows:

a) The low imprisonment rate and the low crime rate are interrelated but factors other than the crime rate *per se* influence the trends of the imprisonment rate;

b) The diversion of defendants and even convicted offenders from the prisons was explained by the combination of cultural values and policies that express those values. Prosecutors have lifetime appointments not dependent on the periodic approval of voters. They apply the principle of discretionary prosecutions to avoid referral for trial of selected defendants. Judges are authorized to apply similar leniency by suspending sentences to prison when the convicted offenders satisfy certain criteria;

c) The substantial growth in American prison populations has stimulated the growth of many new prisons, but the decreasing prison population in Japan has had little effect on available "bed-space";

d) In spite of the drop in total admissions over the 1970–1990 period, more persons have been imprisoned for drug offenses— partly an example of the Japanese criminalization of a victimless crime but also of *yakuza* trafficking in illicit drugs. With drug admissions removed, violent offenses and property crimes increased modestly, and sex and gambling crimes declined in importance;

e) Reduced average length of sentence was expected to contribute significantly to the reduced population of prisons, but the decline has occurred *in spite* of prolongation of the sentences for all crime categories. Sentences of 12 to 60 months have gained progressively larger shares of the total sentences as the years proceeded;

f) The public prosecutors and sentencing judges applied criteria in deciding which of the defendants should be accorded dispositions other than imprisonment. Their selective decision-making resulted, over the years, in raising the average age of persons entering prison, the average previous exposure to imprisonment and the proportional representation of the *yakuza* among the inmates;

g) Ironically, the Correction Bureau appears to be suffering the effects of diverting the most socially-worthy offenders from the prisons. Actually, these prisoners typically behave in an orderly manner—they too are subject to *giri*. The Bureau also deserves credit for administrative practices that have reduced chances of inmate disorder.

Notes

1. This paper stems from field research conducted in Japan through active collaboration of the Correction Bureau. The Takeuchi Foundation of Hitachi, Ltd. supported the 1988 research; a Fulbright Award was granted for 1990–1991. The project would not have been possible without the support of the Directors General: Minoru Shikita, Kazuko Kawakami, Kiyohiro Tobita and Norboru Matsuda. For this paper certain staff members were of special direct service: Ko Akatsuka, Koichi Watanabe and Kenji Teramura.

2. The published American imprisonment rates are derived from data on year-end population of prisons. For comparison, the Japanese rates were also based on that kind of data. Other tables in this paper use data on admissions to prison in keeping with the assumption that admissions are the best reflection of changes over time in the use of imprisonment. "Flow studies using annual admissions," Lynch (1988: 184) says, "are not affected by the accumulation of more serious offenders."

3. Langan (1991) studied changes between 1974 and 1986 in demographic data (race and age), crime and arrest rates for nine crime categories and the "imprisonment rate." He defined the imprisonment rate as the

number of prison sentences for every 100 arrests. He estimated that demographic changes accounted for 20 percent of the growth in prison populations, the changes in crime and arrest rates for only 9 percent and the war on drugs for only 8 percent. For higher imprisonment rates, the strongest determinant, Langan says, was the prosecutors obtaining more felony convictions in trials or judges giving more prison sentences.

4. Alcoholics Anonymous in the United States insists that the addictive drinker must realize actively that he has a problem and decide on his own to give up consumption of alcohol. Similarly, the Japanese values support extension of official leniency to the repentant offender on grounds that he is capable of self-correction.

5. To a modest extent, Japan has criminalized street prostitution (see Johnson, 1993) and drug use. Later in this paper, the increased imprisonment of drug offenders will be noted as a major trend.

6. See Johnson and Heijder (1983) for discussion of The Netherlands' application of the principle of discretionary prosecution; also see the chapter in this volume on The Netherlands by David Downes and his paper "The Origins and Consequences of Dutch Penal Policy Since 1945: A Preliminary Analysis," *British Journal of Criminology*, 22 (October 1982): 325–357.

7. The source of the data was the Japanese Supreme Court's *Annual Report of Judicial Statistics* for 1991.

8. This paper limits analyses to male inmates for the sake of concentrated attention in a limited space. As is common among prison systems, Japanese women prisoners are a small numerical minority (1,571 in 1992) compared with male prisoners (35,951 in 1992). Their percentage share of all prisoners present daily on average has increased from 1.44 in 1940 to 4.19 in 1992 because of the increased admission of prisoners of both sexes for violation of the Stimulant Drugs Control Law. The increase had relatively greater impact on the smaller population of women inmates. Opening the fifth women's prison—Iwakuni in the Hiroshima Correction Region—was necessary in 1989. For a fuller analysis, see Chapter 3 of my book: *Criminalization and Prisoners in Japan: Six Contrary Cohorts*, Carbondale: Southern Illinois University Press.

9. Non-Japanese in Japanese prisons constitute a type of prisoner attracting unprecedented attention in Europe. For example, Belgium has experienced an increase from 22 percent in 1983 to 34 percent in 1992 in the representation of foreigners in its prisons (Tournier and Barre, 1990). Arrivals in Japan of foreigners increased by 135 percent between 1980 and 1993 (National Police Agency, 1991: 15; Ministry of Justice, 1994: 16). Nevertheless, foreigners continue to equal less than 4 percent of all prisoners. Deportations have risen 10.3 times in a decade.

References

Abe, Hakaru. (1963) "Education of the Legal Profession in Japan." in Arthur Taylor Van Mehren (ed.) *Law in Japan: The Legal Order in a Changing Society*. Cambridge, Massachusetts: Harvard University Press. pp. 153–187.

Ancel, Marc. (1971) *Suspended Sentence*. London: Heinemann Educational Books.

Beasley, William G. (1990) *The Rise of Modern Japan*. Tokyo: Charles E. Tuttle.

Blumstein, Alfred. (1988) "Prison Populations: A System Out of Control?" in Michael Tonry and Norval Morris (eds.) *Crime and Justice: A Review of Research*, Vol. 10. Chicago: University of Chicago Press. pp. 231–266.

Christopher, Robert C. (1983) *The Japanese Mind: The Goliath Explained*. Tokyo: Charles E. Tuttle.

Fox, James G. (1972) *Organizational and Racial Conflict in Maximum Security Prisons*. Lexington, Massachusetts: Lexington Books.

Gaes, Gerald G., and McGuire, William J. (1985) "Prison Violence: The Contribution of Crowding Versus Other Determinants of Prison Assault Rates." *Journal of Research in Crime and Delinquency*. 22: 41–65.

George, B.J. (1988) "Discretionary Authority of Public Prosecutor in Japan." in John O. Haley (ed.) *Law and Society in Contemporary Japan: American Perspectives*. Dubuque, Iowa: Kendal-Hunt.

Haley, John O. (1989) "Confession, Repentance, and Absolution." in Martin Wright and Burt Galoway (eds.) *Mediation and Criminal Justice*. Newbury Park, California: Sage. pp. 195–211.

Hattori, Takaaki. (1963) "The Legal Profession in Japan: Its Historic Development and Present State," in *Law in Japan*, op.cit. pp. 111–149.

Hiramatsu, Yoshiro. (1973) "History of Penal Institutions in Japan," *Law in Japan*, 6: 1–48.

Johnson, Elmer H. (1997) *Criminalization and Prisoners in Japan: Six Contrary Coherts*. Carbondale: Southern Illinois University Press.

————. (1993) "Japan Reacts Against Street Prostitution: The Anti-Prostitution Law and Women's Guidance Homes." *International Journal of Comparative and Applied Criminal Justice*, 17: 29–41.

———— and Alfred Heijder. (1983) "The Dutch Deemphasize Imprison-ment: Sociocultural and Structural Explanations." *International Journal of Comparative and Applied Criminal Justice*, 7: 3–19.

Joyce, Nola M. (1992) "A View of the Future: The Effect of Policy in Prison Population Growth." *Crime and Delinquency*, 38: 357–368.

Kouhashi, Hiroshi. (1985) "Courts' Selection of Offenders to be Placed under Probationary Supervision." (Unpublished paper). Tokyo: United Nations Asia and Far East Institute for Prevention of Crime and Treatment of Offenders (UNAFEI).

Langan, Patrick. (1991) "America's Soaring Prison Population." *Science*, 251: 1568–1573.

Lynch, James P. (1988) "A Comparison of Prison Use in England, Canada, West Germany, and the United States: A Limited Test of the Punitive Hypothesis." *Journal of Criminal Law and Criminology*, 79: 180–217.

Maguire, Kathleen, Pastore, Ann L. and Flanagan, Timothy J. (1993) *Sourcebook of Criminal Justice Statistics—1992*. Washington, DC: Bureau of Justice Statistics, US Department of Justice.

McCormack, Gavan, and Sugimoto, Yoshio. (eds.) (1986) *Democracy in Contemporary Japan*. Armonk, New York: M.E. Sharpe.

Ministry of Justice (1984) *Summary of White Paper on Crime*. Tokyo: Research and Training Institute.

————. (1988) *Summary of White Paper on Crime*. Tokyo: Research and Training Institute.

————. (1991) *Annual Report of Statistics on Corrections for 1990*. Vol. 1. Tokyo: Correction Bureau.

————. (1992) *Summary of White Paper on Crime*. Tokyo: Research and Training Institute.

————. (1994) *Summary of White Paper on Crime*. Tokyo: Research and Training Institute.

Miyazawa, Setsuo. (1992) *Policing in Japan: A Study on Making Crime*. [Trans. Frank G. Bennett, Jr., with John O. Haley]. Albany: State University of New York Press.

————. (1994) "The Enigma of Japan as a Testing Ground for Cross-Cultural Criminolgical Studies." *International Annals of Criminology*, 32: 81–102.

Nakamura, Hajime. (1964) *Ways of Thinking of Eastern People: Asia, China, Tibet, Japan*. Philip P. Wiener (ed.) Honolulu, Hawaii: East-West Center Press.

National Police Agency. (1991) *White Paper on Police 1991 (Excerpt)*. Tokyo: Japan Times.

——. (1992) *White Paper on Police 1991 (Excerpt)*. Tokyo: Japan Times.

Nishikawa, Masakazu. (1990) "Adult Probation in Japan: A Case Study of Alternatives to Imprisonment." (Unpublished paper). Tokyo: UNAFEI.

Noda, Tosiyuki. (1976) *Introduction to Japanese Law*. [Trans. Anthony H. Angelo] Tokyo: University of Tokyo Press.

Pempel, T.J. (1982) *Party and Politics in Japan: Creative Conservatism*. Philadelphia: Temple University Press.

Porporino, Frank J. (1986) "Managing Violent Individuals in Correctional Settings." *Journal of Interpersonal Violence*, 1: 213–237.

Satsumae, Takeshi. (1977) "The Practice of Suspension of Prosecution." Lecture delivered at UNAFEI, Tokyo.

Shikita, Minoru, and Tsuchiya, Shinichi. (1990) *Crime and Criminal Policy in Japan from 1926 to 1988*. Tokyo: Japan Criminal Policy Society.

Stastny, Charles, and Trynauer, Gabrielle. (1982) *Who Rules the Joint? A Study of the Changing Political Culture of Maximum Security Prisons in America*. Lexington, Massachusetts: Lexington Books.

Suzuki, Yoshio. (1979) "Corrections in Japan." in Robert J. Wicks and H.H.A. Cooper (eds.) *International Corrections*. Lexington, Massachusetts: Lexington Books. pp. 141–161.

Toch, Hans. (1976) "A Psychological View of Prison Violence." in Albert K. Cohen, George F. Cole and Robert C. Bailey (eds.) *Prison Violence*. Lexington, Massachusetts: Lexington Books.

Tournier, Pierre and Barre, Marie Danielle. (1990) "Survey of Prison Systems in the Member States of Europe: Comparative Prison Demography." in *Prison Information Bulletin*, No. 15: 4–16.

Van Wolferen, Karel. (1989) *The Enigma of Japanese Power*. London: Macmillan.

Wagatsuma, Hiroshi, and Rosett, Arthur. (1986) "The Implications of Apology: Law and Culture in Japan and the United States." *Law and Society Review*, 20: 461–498.

Watanuki, Joji. (1986) "Is There a 'Japanese-Type Welfare Society'?" *International Sociology*, 1: 259–269.

Chapter
TWELVE

Penality and Imprisonment in Australia

David Brown

This chapter will proceed by way of first providing some basic information about Australian prison systems, which can be compared with other countries covered in this book. After outlining the historical trends in imprisonment rates, a contemporary picture will be briefly sketched out by way of data on current imprisonment rates, backgrounds of prisoners and other basic statistical and empirical information. Two key features of Australian imprisonment will be singled out: the considerable State by State variation, and the over-representation of Aboriginal people in prison. A very brief treatment of some current issues such as developments in privatization and sentencing directions follows. An overview will then be provided of trends in penal politics in recent decades against a backdrop of broader political developments and shifts in discourses of penality.

Over the last 30 years, the chief focus of this book, Australia like various other countries has seen a period of revolt, upheaval and "coming into sight" of prisons and prisoners in the 1960s and 1970s, followed by a period of backlash, "truth in sentencing," just deserts and selective incapacitation in the 1980s and 1990s. Finally, and most speculatively, I would like to come at Stan Cohen's "stories of change" (1987: 115–155) obliquely, by way of a brief examination of the lives of four people who have figured in different ways in the more recent history of Australian imprisonment. In a loose narrative around their lives and deaths the disparate stories might perhaps illustrate something of the diversity and national distinctiveness of penality and imprisonment in Australia, as well as serving to illustrate points of similarity in comparison with stories of change in countries described in other chapters.

A couple of other brief introductory points should be made before proceeding further. First, it will be noticed that already references have been made to penality and imprisonment. While the focus of this book is comparing prison systems, it is difficult to discuss imprisonment without at times talking more broadly about penality. This has the advantage, as Garland and Young point out, of signifying a "complex field of institutions, practices and relations rather than a singular type of social event" (Garland and Young, 1983: 14). The concept of penality is more attuned, for example, to drawing out the connections between imprisonment and colonial and neocolonial strategies of displacement, assimilation and forcible removal of the children of Aboriginal peoples in Australia, or of emphasizing the largely hidden rates of detention in local police lock-ups (cf. formal imprisonment).

Second, it will be noticed that reference has been made to Australian prison systems in the plural. This is not simply post-structuralist affectation, but an indication that there is no *Australian* prison system as such. Australia has a federal political system and imprisonment is a function that has been conducted by the states. There are Commonwealth (federal) criminal laws, indeed in increasing numbers in the drugs and fraud area, where they can be seen as relating to a head of federal power under the Constitution, such as the customs and excise power in relation to drugs. There is however, unlike the USA, no federal prison system. Defendants indicted under federal legislation are tried by state courts exercising commonwealth jurisdiction and if convicted are imprisoned in state-run prisons. There are thus not one but seven different prison systems in Australia, those of the States of New South Wales (NSW), Victoria (VIC), Queensland (QLD), South Australia (SA) Western Australia (WA), Tasmania (TAS), and the territory of the Northern Territory (NT), the Australian Capital Territory (ACT) having only a remand center, ACT prisoners being held in NSW prisons. This is of more than merely structural significance for one of the key features of Australian imprisonment is the significant difference in imprisonment rates across the states and territories.

HISTORICAL OVERVIEW OF PRISON RATES

Australian imprisonment rates (an aggregation of state and territory rates) were at their highest in the 1880s and 1890s, declining dramatically in the first two decades of the 20th century, after which time they have been reasonably stable, with some fluctuations in the 1960s and slight trends upward in the 1980s, especially in NSW. Mukherjee states that for every 100,000 persons aged 10 years or over in Australia there were 168 persons in prisons in the year 1900, dropping to 57 in 1941 and increasing to 78 in 1976 (Mukherjee, 1981: 97). Braithwaite notes the same pattern in relation to NSW and Victoria:

> overall, there is a fairly consistent and dramatic decline in imprisonment rates, beginning in the 1880s in NSW and the late 1850s in Victoria, which continues exactly until 1920 in both states. Since 1920 the picture has been one of stability in imprisonment rates rather than one of a consistent upwards or downwards trend (1980: 202).

Braithwaite discusses the Rusche and Kirchheimer (1939) thesis as amended by writers such as Jankovic (1977), Quinney (1977) and Scull (1977), who all sought in different ways to explain the persistence of imprisonment in conditions of monopoly capitalism, after Rusche and Kirchheimer had foreshadowed the disappearance of the economic importance of the house of correction with the rise of the factory system (1939: 6). All these theorists assert some fairly direct correspondence between economic change and penal developments. Quinney for example, argued that imprisonment is functional for monopoly capitalism in controlling the increasingly marginalized sector, particularly in periods of crisis. Scull argued that decarceration is functional for monopoly capitalism in terms of restricting the cost to the state of expensive imprisonment and developing more subtle, community-based forms of social control. Reviewing these arguments in the Australian context, Braithwaite argues that they are not necessarily inconsistent, and suggests following Rusche and Kirchheimer that the decline in imprisonment

rates between the late 19th and early 20th centuries may correspond with the "demise of serious labor shortages in Australia and
the concomitant destruction of the profitability of prison industry"
(1980: 203).

Garton attributes the decline in imprisonment rates in the 1920s
to the "more specialized role for the prison in the ensemble of state
incarceration institutions" (Garton, 1982: 103). He notes that "by
1920, prisons had become only one of a range of specialized institutions and therapies, which included reformatories, clinics, mental
hospitals, boarding out, social work, psychoanalysis, psychology
and psychiatry, for the policing of social life" (1982: 110).

In a more Foucauldian vein Garton questions the utility of reading penal developments as a manifestation of economic imperatives
and general notions of fiscal crisis. Recent Australian penal histori-
ography has generally seen penal developments as having complex
origins, as being influenced by a range of political factors, including
historically and culturally embedded popular sensibilities. The central concern of Australian historians of imprisonment has been the
convict period, and in particular questions of the class composition
and consciousness of the original convicts, the "incorrigibility" of
women convicts in particular, and the points of transition between
penal colony and democratic society (see: Hughes, 1987; Shaw, 1964;
Evans and Nichols, 1976; McQueen, 1970; Summers, 1975; Robinson,
1979; Hirst, 1983; Sturma, 1978; 1983; Neal, 1987; 1991; Oxley, 1991).

Garton argues that whatever its other virtues much of this histo-
riography has been more concerned with debates about "Australian
national character" and the "'true' nature of white Australia's
convict forebears." This has led to an "obsession with the moral
character of the convicts" played out around a series of moral
dichotomies: damned whore/good mother, petty thief/political
protester, rogue/worker forced to steal. He argues that "these
dichotomies, and the struggles over the relative size of each category, have diverted attention from the diversity of convict experience, the effects of policing practices in the construction of criminal
groups, the discursive constructions of the 'criminal class' and the
role of crime within the political economy of working class life"
(Garton, 1991: 79).

The themes of specificity, diversity and differentiation are use-
fully identified by Finnane as crucial to the development of a more
adequate, non-reductionist and non-functionalist history of imprisonment in Australia, particularly in the largely neglected period

between the ending of transportation and the 1960s. Following Garland (1990), Finnane points out that the "prison system is the precipitate of a mix of historical and social influences which leaves us with (physical) institutions and (social) regimes of disparate and often contradictory meaning and function" (Finnane, 1991: 108). He cites the examples of women's imprisonment, Aboriginal imprisonment, juvenile incarceration, imprisonment in specific segregation and punishment regimes, or prison farms, or in police lock-ups, to illustrate the diversity of histories, cultural meanings, material forms and political and ideological struggles around imprisonment. These forms of imprisonment are far from all of a piece and "while there may be a certain schematic unity which operates at a global level in a change of emphasis from discipline to welfare (and back again), it is not making a large claim to insist that local histories and jurisdictional differences as well as the differentiation of specific prisoner populations have produced variety" (1991: 116). Such an explanation runs somewhat against Marxist and abolitionist tendencies to find the meanings of imprisonment in various overarching functions of class repression, panopticism, social control or the "disciplinary society." It marks an increasing appreciation of the importance of seeing the institutions of punishment "as institutions for the expression of social values, sensibility and morality, rather than as instrumental means to a penological end" (Garland, 1990: 291). Such analysis provides a better basis for understanding historical and contemporary jurisdictional differences outlined later, and for engaging in local penal politics.

To update Braithwaite and Garton for the decade and a half since the 1980s, the imprisonment rate per 100,000 adult population was 89.9 in 1981–82 and 119.4 in March 1996, an upward trend of nearly 20%, mainly due to the significant increases recorded in NSW after the election of a law-and-order Liberal/National Party Coalition (conservative) government in 1988 (Walker, 1992: 3), and marked increases in Queensland in the mid-1990s.

CONTEMPORARY PICTURE: IMPRISONMENT RATES

In March 1996 there were 16,399 adult persons in custody in prisons in Australia, 15,614 males and 785 females. There were also 651 persons aged 10–17 years in juvenile corrective institutions. These are the figures for prisons and omit the large numbers of people held in police custody. There were 28,566 people held in police custody in the month of August 1988 and 25,654 in August 1992. The breakdown in numbers imprisoned in the different states is set out in Table 1 below for March 1996. Also included is the imprisonment *rate* per 100,000 of the adult population of that state.

One of the first things that strikes us about the figures in Table 1 is the considerable variation between states. The national imprisonment rate is 119.4 per 100,000 of adult population. The ACT, Tasmania and Victoria are below the national rate, and South Australia, Queensland, New South Wales, Western Australia and the Northern Territory above it. We can see, for example, that people in the NT are imprisoned at a rate of five and a half times that in Victoria. Does this mean that the crime rate in the Northern Territory is five and a half times, and in NSW nearly twice, that of Victoria?

The answer is, not necessarily. The relationship between imprisonment and crime rates in the various Australian states and territories is a complex one, its analysis compounded by methodological problems. While in general the high imprisoning states have been those with a higher Aboriginal population the disparities between NSW and Victoria are particularly difficult to explain, as both are populous (by Australian standards) states on the eastern seaboard with somewhat similar histories, yet NSW has long had nearly

TABLE 1   March 1996 Australian Prison Trends

State	Male	Female	Total	Rate per 100,000 gen. popl.
NSW	5871	329	6200	132.8
VIC	2285	122	2407	69.8
QLD	3170	125	3295	132.9
WA	2120	102	2222	170.6
SA	1404	85	1489	85
TAS	270	14	284	80.3
NT	463	7	470	388.2
ACT	116	7	123	34.8
TOTAL	15614	785	16399	119.4

Source: Australian Bureau of Statistics, *National Correctional Statistics: Prisons March Quarter 1996* (1996) pp. 3–4.

twice Victoria's imprisonment rate. One study put this down to differences in reception rates caused by more people coming before NSW courts (Babb, 1992). In a later study this was modified and it was claimed that the key factors were the existence of periodic detention in NSW and that state's greater use of imprisonment for fine default. When these two groups were controlled for, the differences were attributed to longer sentences served in NSW and a much greater reception rate (Gallagher, 1995: 3). The explanations are likely to be more complex than this and further work is needed here to elucidate state variation. Walker suggests that high crime rates do help to produce high imprisonment rates in the NT for certain sorts of offenses, but he also suggests that there is a very high "residual rate" for "discretionary imprisonment" which indicates that particular sentence preferences and policies also play an important part (Walker, 1991).

This is in keeping with international evidence which shows, for example, that in The Netherlands where they use imprisonment far less as a penal sanction than in other comparable countries, this is not due to lower crime rates, but is the consequence of specific social policy decisions. Nor are imprisonment rates a reflection of the size of the population, or level of industrialization. As we can see from the figures above, the two Australian territories with the smallest populations, have both the lowest (ACT) and highest (NT) imprisonment rates. Japan with a much larger population has an imprisonment rate of approximately one-third that of Australia (37.2 in 1994).

From this answer we can grasp one of the central understandings of the use of imprisonment as a penal sanction: Imprisonment rates are not mere end products of rates of crime, but effects of a whole range of social, political, legal and cultural factors, including kinds of behavior the legislature or the judiciary defines as criminal; the level of police funding and political and community pressure for certain sorts of policing; how the police define their priorities and exercise their considerable discretion; how evidence is gathered or constructed by police and presented to a court; what the rules of evidence and procedure allow; whether defendants are represented by lawyers; how prosecutors, magistrates and judges exercise their discretions; what the legislative sentencing structure provides; the range of available alternatives to imprisonment; sentencing practices and traditions among magistrates and judges in different states; the provision of remissions and parole; the portrayal of crime problems in the media; perceptions of community attitudes and expectations, and so on.

This understanding is important because it shows us that imprisonment rates are not natural, necessary or immutable. Neither are they infinitely modifiable at any particular point in time. But they are amenable to change. And changes in prevailing political, legal and social policy can produce changes in imprisonment rates. Such changes can be associated both with the political party in government and political party policy shifts. The two states which have shown the most significant shifts in their imprisonment rates over the last five to ten years have been NSW with a dramatically increasing rate after the election of a conservative Coalition government in 1988, and Queensland, with a significant decrease after the election of the Goss Australian Labor Party (ALP) State government in 1989, reversing to a marked increase in the second term of the government. Research by John Walker shows that "if we plot rates of imprisonment in Australia over the past fifty years, we find that coalition governments in the major states (NSW, Vic, Qld) and in federal power in Canberra ... are strongly associated with high prison populations while Labor governments are associated with lower rates (Walker, 1994: 21). It is this *political* context, of which the political party in power is only one crude measure, which is more closely associated with penal developments than economic measures of "fiscal crisis" or unemployment levels.

PRISON DEMOGRAPHICS

1. Offense Types

From 1982 onwards a National Prison Census has been conducted. The most recent available at the time of writing is for 1993 (Mukherjee and Dagger, 1995). The 1993 census shows that 9.4% of Australian prisoners at the time of the census were in prison for homicide. A further 10.9% were imprisoned for assault and 11.9% for sexual offenses. Therefore 3 out of every 10 prisoners are in prison for offenses against the person, or 4 out of 10 if robbery (12.7%) is classified as an offense against the person. Conversely over 30% of all prisoners were imprisoned for property offenses, or over 40% if robbery is classified as a property offense, with break and enter (14.1%) and other theft (7%) being the most common. Drug offenses accounted for 10.8% of prisoners. The remainder were imprisoned for public order, traffic and other offenses and failure to pay fines.

In terms of changes in selected offense-specific rates for imprisonment in Australia over the decade 1982–1993, imprisonment for homicide, robbery, break and enter and other theft have remained fairly stable while steady increases have occurred in imprisonment for sexual offenses, justice procedure (non-payment of fines), and drug trafficking.

In July 1993 1,833 or 11.5% of the total 15,866 prisoners were on remand, that is they were awaiting trial, and a further 827 or 5.2% were awaiting appeal. In terms of the time prisoners were expected to serve in prison the 1993 census reveals that 19.7% of prisoners were expected to serve less than 6 months imprisonment and a further 10.1% less than 12 months, 14.3% between 1–2 years, 22.9% 2–5 years, and 13.2% 5–10 years, with 8.2% of prisoners expected to serve over 10 years or life sentences.

By way of bald summary we can see from these figures that the tabloid media image of prisoners as predominantly violent offenders against the person is not quite correct. We also see that a significant proportion of prisoners are imprisoned on remand prior to being found guilty, despite the presumption of innocence. And we see that many prisoners are serving sentences of less than 12 months.

2. Prisoner Composition: Massive Aboriginal Over-Representation

In the same way that national prison rates obscure considerable state differences, so they obscure the significance of class, race, sex and age differentials. Prisoners are disproportionately male, young, unemployed and black. The sex imbalance (so often just taken for granted) is dramatic: 95.2% of Australian prisoners are male. Over 30% are less than 24 years of age, with a further 21.4% between 24–30; over 70% of those whose employment status was known (approximately 40% of the total) were unemployed at the time of their arrest and only 4% of those whose levels of educational achievement was known had completed secondary education; 56.5% of prisoners had been in prison previously; 15.2% of prisoners were of Aboriginal or Torres Strait Island descent, a 14.1-fold over-representation on a population basis. In Western Australia 31.4% of prisoners were Aboriginal (a 21.7-fold over-representation in population terms) as were 75.6% in the Northern Territory (a 10.8-fold

over-representation) and 15.9% in South Australia (a 20.3-fold over-
representation). The over-representation of Aborigines is one of the
distinguishing features of Australian imprisonment (*Australian
Prisoners 1993*, 1995: 46,24.). Indeed criminologists have referred to
Aborigines as the most imprisoned race in the world. The over-
representation by most serious charge is greatest in relation to
assaults, offensive behavior and other public order offenses (Walker
and McDonald, 1995: 3).

In 1993 the combined imprisonment rates per 100,000 population
by sex and Aboriginality were:

Aboriginal men:	2,749.3
non-Aboriginal men:	197.7
Aboriginal women:	152.2
non-Aboriginal women:	9.5

Expressed in terms of ratios Aboriginal men are imprisoned at 289
times the rate of non-Aboriginal women, 18 times the rate of Aboriginal women and 14 times the rate of non-Aboriginal men. Aboriginal women are imprisoned at 16 times the rate of non-Aboriginal
women, illustrating the centrality of race to the social construction
of Australian imprisonment rates.

The over-representation of Aborigines in police lock-ups is even
greater than that in prisons. A WA government inquiry found that
Aborigines make up 91.7% of prisoners in police lock-ups in that
state. In NSW a Bureau of Crime Statistics and Research Report
found that the statewide rate of police cell detentions for intoxica-
tion was 76% for Aborigines and 2.6% for non-Aborigines. The
national police custody surveys carried out in August 1988 and
1992 found that Aborigines comprised 28.6% and 28.8% of the
adults held in police custody in those months (McDonald, 1993: 9).
While the national custody rate fell by 10.2% between 1988 and
1992 the proportion of Aboriginal people in police custody
increased by 0.7%, an over-representation of 26 times.

3. Costs of Imprisonment

In 1993 the combined average prison occupancy rates (a measure of
overcrowding) were 100.5% for men and 86.4% for women. Two
States (NSW, NT) had over 100% occupancy rates for both men and
women (AIC, 1993). Overcrowding is endemic to the Australian
prison system despite a major prison building program in several

states in recent years (Harding, 1987; Weatherburn, 1988). Many of the new prisons have been built well away from the metropolitan centers of population, in areas remote from families, friends and visitors, forms of public transport and agencies of accountability. John Walker estimated in 1992 that adult corrective services cost $550 million annually (Walker, 1992). The cost of incarceration in NSW in 1993/94 was estimated at $34,000 to $50,000 per prisoner per year, depending on security classification. The cost per inmate per day was $139 for maximum security, $123 for medium security, and $94 for minimum security (NSW Department of Corrective Services, *1993–94 Annual Report*, 1994: 97). Despite the fact that at any one time there are nearly three times as many people under some form of community-based penal supervision as there are in prison and that the cost of imprisonment is around 20 times that of community-based alternatives, the prisons budget as a percentage of the total corrections budget is above 80% in all states and above 90% in some. Recurrent costs, that is running costs, take up most of the budget. But the capital cost of building new prisons is also considerable. The Australian Law Reform Commission in 1988 estimated the capital cost of a maximum security prison at $52 million at a cost per bed of $208,000.

In addition to the considerable financial costs of imprisonment there are numerous social costs. The most dramatic are perhaps the disproportionate number of deaths in prisons. According to the Muirhead *Royal Commission into Aboriginal Deaths in Custody*, 434 people died in police or prison custody in Australia between 1980 and 1988; 21% of these people were Aborigines. The majority of Aboriginal deaths in custody occurred in police custody, often only a few hours after arrest or detention for drunkenness or minor street offenses. A further 362 people died in custody in the five-year period after the Royal Commission to 1994, 16% of whom were Aborigines (Biles and McDonald, 1993; AIC, 1988–1996).

An Australian Institute of Criminology study found that prison suicide rates are five times higher than in the general population and prison homicide rates three times higher. A study by the NSW Probation and Parole Service found that the mortality rate of persons under parole supervision was six times that of the general population. Behind these bald figures of deaths lie multiple personal tragedies, tragedies which affect not only the prisoners themselves but also their families, friends and wider communities.

Imprisonment also entails the burden of social security payments for the families and dependents of those incarcerated. Prisoners and families suffer physical and emotional separation and economic hardship. There is the loss of ability and opportunity for prisoners to provide for families or to make recompense to victims. This in turn engenders a loss of pride, self-respect and sense of purpose. Imprisonment serves to stigmatize people (including prisoners' families) and to deepen exclusion from the labor market. Once released, those with a prison record find that jobs are harder to get and to keep. Human potential is wasted and the possibility of constructive, redemptive and responsible behavior is minimized in the authoritarian daily routines of the prison.

Some prisoners, particularly the young, the weak and the intellectually disabled, are subject to the risk of assault, rape and the possibility of contracting HIV/AIDS. Hard drug use is common in prisons. As a recent joint church report put it "gaols are frequently boring, brutal places where people learn more about crime than about acceptable and responsible behavior" (Combined Churches, 1988). Brutalization in prison by other prisoners or by prison officers can lead to individuals emerging from prison embittered. Upon release some subsequently commit far worse crimes than those for which they were originally imprisoned. There is a tendency, then, for current penal practices to reproduce and generate crime rather than serve the ends of crime prevention and community protection.

The Australian Law Reform Commission in 1988 concluded that prisons in all states except Tasmania suffered from severe overcrowding leading to increased stress for prisoners and staff and severe management problems, boredom and frustration stemming from the lack of useful activities, sexual and other assault, violence and intimidation, and dramatically increased drug use. The Commission found that the physical conditions, particularly in the many older prisons, were marked by isolation, conditions which subject prisoners to "sensory deprivation and/or climatic extremes," inadequate or inappropriate accommodation for the mentally ill, lack of space for educational, work and recreational activities, inadequate visiting facilities, a drastic shortage of drug and alcohol treatment programs, lack of civil rights for prisoners, and deficient medical care. The Commission argued that Australia was failing to meet internationally recognized standards in the treatment of prisoners (ALRC, 1988).

4. Women in Prison

The issue of women in prison has been marked by neglect, denial and trivialization. (For a comprehensive report on the state of women's imprisonment in NSW see: NSW Women in Prison Task Force, *Report* (1985); see also D. Brown et al. (1988); Hatty (1984); George and McCulloch (1988); Howe (1994); Hampton, 1994). The small number of women in prison has led to inadequacy in prison services and a neglect of the particular meanings of women's imprisonment. However, the number of women prisoners as a proportion of all prisoners is increasing slightly, from 3.9% in 1983 to 4.8% in 1996. Women prisoners present a similar profile to prisoners overall. That is they are predominantly young (half in their 20s), poorly educated, unemployed prior to imprisonment, with histories of drug addiction. They are commonly in prison for property offenses and nearly 60% were serving sentences of less than 12 months. Easteal (1992) identifies a range of issues affecting women's imprisonment:

* the high use of illegal drugs, both before entry to and while in, prison, with much of prison life revolving around drug searches;
* the high security classification of many women prisoners who cannot be said to present a danger to others;
* officer/prisoner relations marked by infantilization with a battery of petty controls, and punishments such as "naughty cards," "early to bed" etc;
* an informal inmate culture and hierarchy revolving around drug use and lesbianism;
* generally poor medical care and facilities and control exercised by access to medical care;
* poor counseling and other support services;
* limited access to methadone and drug withdrawal programs;
* high usage of prescription drugs;
* a high incidence of self-inflicted injuries and suicides and suicide attempts;
* limited access to useful work and educational programs;
* poor visiting conditions for children.

CURRENT ISSUES

1. Health Issues

Medical issues present particular problems in prisons, partly due to the fact that historically health issues have tended to be subordinated to disciplinary concerns and that facilities and services have been poor. A major NSW report, *Report of the NSW Prison Medical Service Review Committee* (1991), identified serious problems in a number of areas including the quality and quantity of psychiatric and dental services, HIV/AIDS and methadone counseling, health screening of prisoners, the high number of disciplinary transfers which disrupt medical treatment and significant problems in the structure, management and budgeting of the Prison Medical Service. An issue only recently receiving attention is that of the over-representation of people with an intellectual disability in the criminal justice system in general and in prison in particular, and the particular problems they face at various stages of the process. Estimates of the proportion of people with an intellectual disability in prison populations range from 1% to 40% (NSW LRC, 1994).

2. Penal Privatization

In Australia, Queensland was the first state to experiment with privatization following the recommendations of the Kennedy Report (1988). Borallon Correctional Center opened in January 1990, the first privately contract-managed prison in Australia following contractual arrangements between the Queensland Corrective Services Commission and Corrections Corporation of Australia (CCA), a consortium of Wormald Security Australia and John Holland Holdings together with Corrections Corporation of America. The Commission allocates $100 per day per prisoner. Borallon was followed in June 1992 by the Arthur Gorrie Correctional Center operated by Australasian Corrections Management. Assessments of the impact of privatization are difficult. Borallon has generally received a favorable press but there have been disturbances and upheavals at Arthur Gorrie. Moyle's research (1994) suggests that the private prisons are not necessarily proving any less costly in financial terms, although there are significant problems in calculating costs and in making direct cost comparisons, including access to full information. Indeed in 1994 Moyle, a leading Australian researcher on penal privatization who has been generally critical of privatization, was sued for defamation by CCA.

In NSW an exceedingly brief and thinly researched private consultant's report (Kleinwort Benson Australia Limited, *Report into Private Sector Involvement in the NSW Corrective Services System* (1989)) recommended that the Minister (Michael Yabsley) introduce privately-run prisons and remand centers, arguing that the operation would be more economic and efficient. The *Prisons (Contract Management) Act* 1990 was passed setting minimum standards, providing for the appointment of a monitoring officer and the establishment of a community advisory body. Junee prison, 360 kms south of Sydney, was opened in March 1993. It is operated by Australasian Correctional Management (ACM), a consortium of Wackenhut Corporation (USA) with Thiess Contractors and ADT security. The contract between ACM and the NSW government was made exempt from the *Freedom of Information Act* on the grounds of commercial security "and therefore the exact terms on which the government has delegated responsibility to ACM for the care and control of inmates are inaccessible to citizens of NSW" (Baldry, 1994: 135). Baldry points out that Wackenhut Corporation had been the subject of adverse findings in a US House of Representatives Report in 1992 including covert activities against critics of a trans-Alaska pipeline of which Wackenhut was the contracted security agent (*ibid*). In its first two years of operation Junee has had a number of serious disturbances, assaults, suicide and staff unrest. It is unpopular with prisoners and especially with prisoners families who are forced to travel long distances to maintain contact.

Victoria under the Kennett government has called for tenders to finance, design and construct three private prisons including one for women. Other Australian jurisdictions are considering the options and New Zealand is moving on tenders for two private prisons. Zdenkowski has described the whole process as "privatization of corrections by stealth," pointing to the "shallow research, desultory consultation and half-hearted media discussion which preceded the decision to privatize" (1994a: 11). As of 1994 8% of Australian prisoners were detained in private prisons. Harding estimates that by the year 2000 on current projections 16% of Australian prisoners will be housed in privately-run institutions.

3. Community Corrections

Community Corrections is a general term which is usually used to describe a range of non-custodial sentences or orders. The Australian Institute of Criminology in *Community Based Corrections Data: December 1991* reveals that there were 51,509 people under some form of supervision (mainly probation, parole, community service and/or attendance sentence orders) on December 1, 1991. The immediately striking feature is that this is roughly three times the number of people in Australian prisons on the same day. There is a tendency in both popular and specialist debates to posit a complete dichotomy between imprisonment and "freedom," so that release from imprisonment under some form of supervisory order such as parole or license is portrayed as "being free," on "early release," no longer subject to punishment. This privileging of imprisonment as the only "real" punishment has been the foundation of the "truth in sentencing" penal and sentencing debate, discussed briefly in the next section. It is of vital importance to contest this portrayal and to emphasize the connections between prison and non-custodial or post-prison orders. It should be stressed that all these orders are *sentences*, periods of supervision which are served in varied settings and under varied conditions, not the either/or of imprisonment or "freedom." Far more attention should be paid to the quality of the supervision and its accountability, rather than its location in a particular social agency or institution. The crucial question is, as Garland and Young point out: "not one of regulation versus non-regulation—penality is always the other side of social organization—but, rather, one of the specific nature of regulatory conditions" (1983: 33).

The second point to note is the considerable variation in comparative supervision rates among the different states, a point made above in relation to imprisonment rates. NSW had 17,650 of the Australian total number of persons under supervision, at a rate of 298.9 per 100,000 general population (Vic 164.9; Qld 408.8; WA 316.5; SA 329.7; Tas 343.4; NT 1220.6; ACT 171.8; Australian total rate 295.3 per 100,000 general population). As with imprisonment these rates do not necessarily correspond directly with crime rates in the various states, demonstrating again the social (and therefore alterable) nature of community corrections practices and patterns.

In political and strategic terms the proliferation of alternatives is often read as an expression of a declining punitiveness or a dispersal of social control. Many on the right, especially prominent radio talk-show hosts, lament the trend away from the overt infliction of physical pain. Some on the left read the proliferation of alternatives as an insidious extension of social control. It is the argument of this chapter that neither approach is helpful and that we need to look at the nature of specific regimes of punishment and subject them to political debate, not debate the propriety of a technical penology, nor perform a simplistic moral calculus (Hogg, 1988b). There is a tension between the retributive or expressive aspects of penality and the utilitarian desire to produce calculated effects such as deterrence. This tension is not entirely resolvable. The issues are complex, the processes, while socially constructed, cannot be deconstructed by an act of will.

4. Sentencing Debates: The Rise of Just Deserts and Selective Incapacitation

As in the USA and other countries just desert arguments enjoyed increased popularity in sentencing debates in Australia in the 1980s. Australian State sentencing structures broadly follow the British pattern of relatively high potential maximum penalties, broad ranging judicial discretion relatively unfettered by legislative direction and few minimum or mandatory penalties. The main sentencing options can be divided into unsupervised release, monetary penalties, supervised release and custodial orders. The Discussion Papers and Reports of the Australian Law Reform Commission in the late 1980s illustrate an Australian version of a modified just desert approach, with "primary emphasis on just deserts for the offender and reparation for the victim. Deterrence, rehabilitation and incapacitation should still be relevant but given a lesser priority" (ALRC, 1987: 17).

Other commentators were critical of the push for a "predominating rationale" for punishment (Brown, 1987; 1989). For if as Garland and Young (1983: 21) argue, the field of penality is a complex condensation of a whole series of relations which operate through the specific institutional site and are materially inscribed in its practices, then it seems doubtful that the selection of a just deserts rationale will solve much more than some legitimization concerns. "Confusion" and "incoherence" are products of assumptions about the necessity for a logical, unitary, rationalist sentencing practice. But if sentencing practices condense a complex and potentially contradictory and non-unitary set of relations, then elements of tension and contradiction cannot be so easily legislated out of existence. It is only if the rationalist assumption that "knowledge stands above and outside power relations and properly employed may bring about a correction of the distortions and inefficiencies they engender" (Hogg, 1983: 10) is adopted that the imposition of a logic from above can provide a model or mechanism for reform. By way of contrast, this chapter and a growing stream of Australian criminology over the last 15 years concur with Hogg's formulation of the task:

> If the system of criminal justice is a social construction then the way to proceed, if we are to change it, is not by imposing some logic upon it from above, which in turn serves to sustain and bolster it, but by dissecting and deconstructing it from below: to analyze the practices which constitute it as a field of power, their sources, effects, and the myriad networks of power and knowledge they enter (*Ibid*; see also Brown, 1987b; Brown and Hogg, 1992).

Legislative adoption of just deserts formulations has been varied (see Zdenkowski, 1994, for a review of recent sentencing developments). The NSW government's *Sentencing Act* 1989 used just deserts rhetoric in a general way as part of the argument for "truth in sentencing." This slogan was code for "certainty" and "finality" in sentencing, through the abolition of executive remissions on sentences and the fixing of a relation of 3/4 between imprisonment and parole. Otherwise no direction or guidance was given to sentencers. The effect of the *Sentencing Act* 1989 was to increase the length of prison sentences and contribute to the very significant increase in the NSW prison population of 50% between 1989 and 1995. In Victoria a lengthy period of sentencing review led to a more structured system with legislative guidance on sentencing and a graded penalty structure into 14 sentencing bands (for an excellent review see Freiberg, 1995).

The variable nature of Australian developments can be seen in two other tendencies. Australian John Braithwaite's influential *Crime, Shame and Reintegration* (1989) has served as a counter to just deserts (Braithwaite and Pettit, 1990) and has tied in with greater governmental attention to crime prevention issues and programs. Reintegrative shaming is the utilization of public, participatory shaming in order to resocialize the individual back into the collectivity rather than shaming through expulsion from the collectivity.

Braithwaite's ideas have been influential, especially in the juvenile arena where imprisonment rates have declined significantly over the last decade. The rate of juveniles in custody has dropped from 130 per 100,000 in 1981 to 65 in 1992 (Dagger and Mukherjee, 1994). Family group conferences which draw on reintegrative shaming are an emerging development, involving fact finding and guilt-determining processes as well as sentencing functions.

A further development has been the introduction in a number of states of preventive detention and indeterminate sentencing regimes as just deserts segues into selective incapacitation. This is another illustration of the political naiveté of demands that sentencing be organized around a single "predominating rationale." For selective incapacitation is clearly inconsistent with a thoroughgoing just deserts logic, and yet the political proponents of just deserts in the '80s are among the leading proponents of selective incapacitation today, despite the philosophical inconsistency involved. Both Victoria (1990) and NSW (1994) passed a *Community Protection Act* aimed at the detention of a single individual, and other states such as Queensland and Western Australia in 1992 legislated for indeterminate sentences for "dangerous offenders" and "serious repeat offenders" and "repeat violent offenders" respectively, the WA legislation aimed openly at Aboriginal juvenile car thieves.

A further emerging development of note is the rise of victim participation in the criminal justice system and the emergence of a more powerful victim lobby. Victim impact statements in the sentencing process and victim's rights to have their views heard on parole and release decisions have been promoted strongly and adopted in some states. While there is much to be gained from a genuine empowering of victims and the expansion of victims' services there are clearly a number of dangers in these developments. In particular victims' concerns and organizations have been pressed into service in punitive law and order programs in several states, involving attacks on due process protections accorded suspects and the urging of heavier penalties as a "solution" to crime. In this rhetoric there is little recognition that diminution of due process requirements for suspects may increase the likelihood of miscarriages of justice and thus further victimization. Families of prisoners have been a forgotten group politically, their punishment ignored by the prophets of just deserts and their domestic labor in caring and maintaining family ties taken for granted and exploited (Aungles, 1994).

PENAL DEVELOPMENTS SINCE 1960

By way of rather gross over-generalization, an overview of Australian penal trends from 1960 to the present might divide the period into two: a period of upheaval and reform in the 1960s and 1970s, and a period of reaction and increased punitiveness in the 1980s and 1990s. In the 1960s and 1970s the prison became increasingly visible as a site of political struggle. This increased visibility owed much to the upsurge of prison disturbances and prisoner militancy. Significant riots occurred in a number of prisons such as Bathurst in NSW in 1970 and 1974, the latter nearly razing the prison. Prison action groups espousing anarchist, neo-Marxist and abolitionist programs emerged. Prisoners became part of the wider discovery of new subjectivities, along with second wave feminism, Aborigines, psychiatric patients, environmentalists and many others. The election of the Whitlam ALP (Labor) government federally in 1972 under the "It's Time" slogan gave expression to the desire for change forged in a climate of mass opposition to the Vietnam war, the end of the White Australia immigration policy and an isolationist foreign policy.

Riots and assaults created the focus for governmental inquiries into the penal system, such as the Nagle Royal Commission in NSW in 1978. Such commissions did much to verify what the radicals had been saying: that prisons were brutal, counter-productive, stigmatizing and recidivist-producing in their effects. Governments spurred on by Royal Commission findings set about creating alternatives such as the community service order. At the same time among penal reformers, Stan Cohen's (1979) critique of community corrections as merely net-widening and extending social control out into the community in more subtle and sinister ways became widely accepted. A climate was created in which the prison was seen as having failed as an institution. Perpetually "in crisis," it did not fulfill its utilitarian functions, it did not protect the community from crime, it did not rehabilitate, it did not deter.

While there was considerable agreement over the failure of the prison, responses as to why this was so and what was to be done about were varied. Among prison movement activists, a strong abolitionist current emerged drawing on Marx, Mathiesen (1974) and the "new" criminology (Taylor, Walton and Young, 1973). In this stream, prisons were seen as fundamentally an instrument of class oppression, part of the repressive state apparatus of the capitalist state protecting the existing distribution of property and disciplining labor. The capitalist state was, like the prison system itself, to be opposed in general, while in the particular, a struggle was conducted against these "negative" reforms, to use Mathiesen's term, which would break down the power of the prison and open it up to democratic scrutiny and a phased abolition (for accounts of this period see Zdenkowski and Brown, 1982; Nagle, 1978; Tomasic and Dobinson, 1979; Findlay, 1982; Vinson, 1982; Anderson, 1989; Grant, 1992. And for a critique of abolitionism, see Brown and Hogg, 1985).

Foucault's influential work, *Discipline and Punish* (1977), which charted the historical emergence of new forms of normalizing and disciplinary power, was later grafted onto this basically class-struggle explanation, producing a more nuanced attention to the detail of specific disciplinary practices, the micro-physics of power embodied in the architectural forms, the file, the gaze and so on. It offered a less overtly functionalist account of the persistence of the prison. In Foucault's argument, the failure of the prison was rescued almost from the start by the utility of the prison in justifying the creation of police forces, the expansion of state coercive powers, the differentiation of "delinquent" from "respectable" poor and the neutralization of popular illegalities. In this account, penal reform became the very project of the prison: the reformed, humane and efficient prison constantly offered up as a solution to its own failure.

A different response emerged in the 1980s from populist politicians and those sections of the public convinced that any problems in the prison system really had their origins in the loss of discipline stemming from the processes of reform which followed in the wake of Royal Commissions like the Nagle Commission. The backlash against the reform period was led by Michael Yabsley, first as NSW Coalition (conservative) shadow minister for Corrections, then as Minister for Corrective Services in the Greiner government elected in 1988. To those like Michael Yabsley, Martinson's (1974) depressing message, or at least the widespread interpretation of it, that "nothing works," the failure of the rehabilitative ideal, high recidivism figures and so on, merely provided a platform for the argument that notions of failure were products of misconceived objectives: that the function of the prison is to punish and that this was the fundamental objective which had been obscured in the notion of prisoners' rights and the meddling social work practices of parole, prisoner's programs and "alternatives," what Yabsley called "the hogwash of sociological dictum" promoted by those he called "the small group of self-appointed society changers" (Yabsley, 1991: 75).

Declaring his chief desire to be remembered as "someone who has put the value back into punishment" (O'Neill, 1990) Yabsley led a savage attack on prison conditions, aiming quite literally to intensify the punitive force of the experience of imprisonment. Remissions on sentences were abolished, lengthening the time actually served, welfare and rehabilitation programs were cut, prisoners' property was confiscated, mechanisms of scrutiny and accountability were removed, parole was reduced, and a new *Sentencing Act 1989* was passed which had the clear effect of increasing sentence lengths. Both the numbers and the rate of imprisonment were increased significantly in NSW. (For a detailed account of the Yabsley years, see Brown, 1991a; and for a detailed analysis of the NSW license release scheme, its termination amid allegations of corruption in its administration, and the implications for penal reform, see Chan, 1992).

Although ostensibly at odds with the radical and abolitionist critiques of imprisonment, the intensification of penal discipline offered by Michael Yabsley and his many public supporters was able to build on the discursive ground prepared by them in two ways. First, as Hirst (1986) points out, constant talk of the failure of the prison to fulfill the utilitarian aims of deterrence and rehabilitation prepares the stage for those who argue that these aims are misconceived in any event, the function of the prison being to punish. Second, radical functionalist cynicism which sees penal reform as the very project of the (continuing) prison prepares the ground for a reassertion of the "less eligibility" principle in its various practical and rhetorical forms, portraying prisoners as an over-serviced and pampered group, living in "motel conditions" and lording it over their generic "victims" (Brown, 1991b).

The climate conducive to the rise of the new retributivism was also arguably fueled by liberal reformers who argued that there was a fundamental problem in the mix of sentencing objectives. The confusion of and contradiction between the various sentencing objectives highlighted the need to adopt a single "coherent," "predominating rationale" for imprisonment and sentencing and they looked to "just deserts" for that. Common, then, to many of these arguments coming from a variety of seemingly opposed political positions, is that punishment can and should be seen in terms of a single function, and that the prison is a singular and unitary institution.

There are a number of difficulties with this. First, as Paul Hirst points out, "means of punishment are artifacts of social organization, the products of definite institutional, technical and discursive conditions in the same way as other artifacts like technologies or built environments" (1986: 152). Second, that as such, they are not explicable in terms of some individual or singular "purpose," but by an ensemble of conditions under which such constructions or forms become possible. Third, as argued earlier following Finnane, it is important to acknowledge more clearly the diverse and differentiated nature of prisons and the experiences of imprisonment of Aborigines, juveniles, women, as being highly specific and often highly localized. Fourth, as Hirst notes, the action of a means of punishment is always "hypothetical" in relation to a specific individual, precisely because they suppose a " 'representative individual' as their object, involve definite forms of individuation" (*ibid*: 155). Fifth, far from being merely sites for the exercise of an exclusively negative power to punish—whether we interpret that in terms of class or race oppression, just deserts, deterrence, incapacitation, or whatever—prisons are also institutions for what Garland calls "the expression of social values, sensibility, and morality, rather than as an instrumental means to a penological end" (1990: 291).

STORIES OF CHANGE

There are, to paraphrase The Naked City, millions of stories in the history of Australian penality. Narratives woven around biographies have many and varied meanings, tell many different stories. Lives and deaths cannot be made to "stand for" fixed and unchanging messages or ideologies. Perhaps though, the following brief sketches of the lives and deaths of four Australians lived out in the realm of penality, may provide a glimpse of the recent history of Australian penal practice as illuminating or suggestive to readers in elucidating the themes of diversity and distinctiveness as the more orthodox empirical information set out earlier.

Malcolm Charles Smith: Neo-Colonialism: A Life and Death in Custody

Malcolm Charles Smith's story sketches some of the contemporary effects of deliberate policies conducted under the general rubric of colonialism and neo-colonialism. Lest the effects of such deliberate policies be consigned to some remote and unenlightened past, it bears remarking that conscious government policies of dispossession, forcible "resettlement," and the breaking up of families and communities by the systematic removal of children continued to prevail in many parts of Australia well into the 1960s. Aboriginal adults of today grew up under such policies which shaped their material conditions, their life chances and attitudes, just as the legacy of such policies shapes the lives of their children.

In April 1989 Commissioner J. H. Wootten of the Royal Commission into Aboriginal Deaths in Custody presented his *Report of the Inquiry into the Death of Malcolm Charles Smith* (1989), a story, in the Commissioner's words (at 1):

> of a life destroyed, not by the misconduct of police and prison officers, but in large measure by the regular operation of the system of self-righteous and racist destruction of Aboriginal families that went on under the name of protection or welfare well into the second half of this century.

Malcolm Smith died in custody in early 1983 several days after locking himself in a prison toilet and shoving the handle of an artist's paint brush into his left eye so that only the metal sheath and bristles were left protruding, in obedience to the biblical injunction: "If thine eye offend thee, pluck it out."

Malcolm Smith was taken from his family in 1965 when he was 11 years old. It was the policy of the child welfare authorities in NSW at this time, and had been the policy of its predecessors the Aborigines Protection Board and then the Aborigines Welfare Board since the 1880s, to remove Aboriginal children from their families whenever possible. One in six or seven Aboriginal children were taken in this way during the course of this century. Malcolm Smith was one of thousands. He did not see his family for another eight years. During this time he spent a combined total of only eight months outside some form of juvenile institutions. In the remaining nine years of his adult life he spent only a few more months outside prison. His final sentence and only serious offense was for the manslaughter of his sister's white boyfriend who he believed was abusing her. His distraught sister disowned him as a brother and members of his family gave evidence against him. He returned to prison, in the Commissioner's words "a changed man, obsessed with religion he little understood and carrying a bible he could not read. Burdened by guilt he became psychotic and embarked on a series of self-multilatory acts, culminating in his third fatal attempt."

Here then is one story of Australian penality, a story of the continuing legacy of colonialism and neo-colonialism, of the initial expulsion and expropriation of the indigenous people, of the penality of the church and mission settlement, of the role of church and welfare authorities in the displacement of Aboriginal peoples, of the assimilationist policies of removal of children and of the deep and continuing relevance of these events to Aboriginal people and all Australians today, especially given the massive Aboriginal over-representation in the prison population.

Ray Denning: Resistance/Repression

Ray Denning was a working-class lad with a career in juvenile detention centers behind him when he was convicted on charges of armed robbery. While in prison in 1978 he was convicted of a severe bashing of a prison officer during an abortive escape attempt. The officer later died. Denning denied involvement and claimed he had been verballed by police (had alleged confessional evidence implicating him fabricated by investigating police). He was classified as an "intractable," a "trouble-maker" in the prison system, and spent many years in effective solitary confinement in Grafton prison, notorious for the institutionalized bashing of intractable prisoners. Denning escaped in 1980, and during 19 months on the run he made a number of audio and video tapes which were delivered and played on radio and television. In these tapes he spoke of issues of fabrication of evidence (police verbals) in the criminal justice system, and of brutality in the prison system. He received widespread public support and became something of a folk hero among prisoners and their supporters.

Eventually captured, Denning was returned to prison in 1981. After a period of further militancy within the prison system he became a regular heroin user, common in NSW prisons at this time. In 1988 he escaped again and committed a series of armed robberies before being captured. Denning was facing return to a life sentence and an additional fixed period of many years. At this point he became an informer for police, going on the witness protection program, receiving favorable reports from authorities, sentence reductions and non-prosecution in return for information and giving evidence in several high profile crimes including the Hilton bombing case, some of it clearly false. Released early, Denning was dropped from the witness protection program and died soon afterward from a heroin overdose.

Denning's story might be read as a narrative around the themes resistance/repression, and rather speculatively linked to historical debates over the convict taint and the rogues or rebels dichotomy. Whether this story is seen as Rebel to Rogue, or Rogue to Rebel, will depend on one's standpoint. But more to the point, it suggests the inadequacies of such dichotomies and the blurred and ambiguous relationship between resistance and authority. Denning carved out a life within recent Australian penality and prisons, initially through a militant resistance and finally through incorporation and informing, including constructing evidence for reward as developments in the increased regulation of police confessional contexts displaced the production of alleged confessional evidence into the prison yard or cell, a privatization of police verbal. As with Vidoq, father of modern detectives, the dividing line between police/criminal is shown to be a blurred and ambiguous one, as is the relationship between authority and popular resistance in the history of Australian prisons, particularly in the convict period. Criminality is among other things a realm of information flows and exchange.

Violet Roberts: Domesticity, Violence and Penality

Violet Roberts and her son Bruce (aged 17) were convicted in 1976 in NSW of the murder of Violet's husband Eric Roberts. Violet was sentenced to life imprisonment and Bruce to 15 years' imprisonment. Eric Roberts had a 20-year history of drunken violence towards his wife and six children. Violet Roberts had left him on numerous occasions but was forced back through insufficient resources and concern for her children. In 1967 her husband was jailed for six months for a particularly severe assault on her. A few months after this Violet Roberts was admitted to a psychiatric institution for six months with a nervous breakdown. In the three months before the killing she attempted suicide three times. On a Saturday night Bruce Roberts shot his father as he slept, saying he couldn't stand seeing his mother and family bashed any more. Violet Roberts claimed she had fired the gun. Violet rang the police and both were charged with murder. At the trial Violet's defense was that she was suffering from diminished responsibility due to a depressive illness. The defense was supported by the Crown psychiatrist. Nevertheless the jury convicted both Violet and Bruce of murder, rejecting the diminished responsibility defense and Violet received the then-mandatory life sentence.

In 1980 a television program publicized the case along with other similar cases of homicide by women and children against a background of extreme domestic violence. In some of these cases juries had acquitted and in others non-custodial sentences had been awarded. A prison reform group, Women Behind Bars, took up the Roberts case, pressing for their release from prison on license. Eventually in response to the public campaign the government ordered the Roberts' release on license in August 1980, the Attorney General stating that a license was recommended because the Roberts had suffered a "serious miscarriage of justice." Upon release Violet Roberts moved away from the area she had lived in and some years later died in a fire probably caused by a cigarette setting fire to a mattress.

The Roberts' case highlights the issue of homicide as a response to repeated domestic violence. Along with other similar cases it led to significant reforms to the law of provocation in NSW and a shift in the case law more generally in Australia away from the requirement for a sudden response, which operated against women who killed when a husband was asleep or drunk. Debate continues over the appropriate standards of culpability in such contexts, the scope and relationship between defenses such as diminished responsibility, self-defense and provocation, and the status of a "battered woman's syndrome." The case illustrates the violent nature of the domesticity lived by many women and families, particularly in socio-economically marginalized communities, the difficulty of escaping from violence in the absence of wider support mechanisms and financial independence, and the fine line between killing and being killed. The connection between personal welfare and social and economic policy is often obscured in the legal arena as is the obvious fact that the resources for informally sanctioning and managing conflict are unequally distributed and that these inequalities are in turn associated with other social and economic inequalities.

Such cases also demonstrate the weakness in the liberal concept of penality as a bipolarity between punishment (or control/coercion) and freedom, each being understood in abstract general terms. "Freedom is conceived as the absence of external coercion and conversely, punishment hypothesizes its object in terms of the otherwise free and responsible individual for whom deprivation of freedom for a given time represents a punishment" (Hogg, 1988a: 79). Life experiences such as those of Violet Roberts call such assumptions strongly into question and highlight the dangers of subordinating an analysis of concrete penal practices and their effects to general and abstract propositions about punishment.

Ronald Ryan: The Politics of Punishment

Ronald Ryan was the last man hanged in Australia. Ryan was born in 1925. His childhood was a hard one; he was placed in care by welfare authorities, running away when he was 14 to work. He married at 23 and was a diligent and respected worker. At age 32 he was charged with false pretenses and over the next 10 years recorded a number of convictions for breaking and entering, receiving an eight-year prison term in 1964. In December 1965 he took part in an escape attempt, in the course of which a warder was shot and killed. Witnesses testified at the trial that Ryan had aimed and fired at warder Hodson a carbine seized in the escape. At the same time another warder in a tower also fired a shot, which he claimed was in the air. Tried for felony murder Ryan was convicted of murder. Appeals to the State Court of Criminal Appeal and the High Court were rejected. During the term of Premier Bolte's Liberal (conservative) State government 36 people convicted of murder had applied for and been granted a commutation of sentence to life imprisonment. According to an editorial in the *Age* newspaper of January 25, 1967, "some of the other 35 killed more than once; some acted with far more viciousness and cunning premeditation than that shown by Ryan." Stays of execution were granted as the case became a cause celebre in the lead-up to the Victoria state election. Ryan was hanged on February 3, 1967.

The Ryan case was arguably an important factor in the abolition of the death penality in all states and territories over the following two decades. Despite periodic calls for its reintroduction in the aftermath of particularly horrific murders, an abolitionist stance seems well entrenched among politicians of major parties and in broader public opinion. The case illustrates clearly the capriciousness of capital punishment, its use for cynical political ends (the reselection campaign of Victorian premier Henry Bolte). What ultimately determines who is executed is not the gravity of the acts involved or even whether the person actually committed them, but other cultural and political considerations. The case also illustrates the unacceptable irrevocability of capital punishment in the light of the proven fallibility of the criminal justice system and the dangers of miscarriages of justice. Innocent people can be and have been executed. There are considerable doubts about Ryan's guilt given the shot fired by the other warder, who later committed suicide (Hawkins, 1977). The case also illustrates the multitude of unintended effects of capital punishment. Subsequent interviews with the governor of the prison, prison staff, the prison chaplain, journalists who witnessed the hanging, legal and judicial figures, reveal the sad burden of guilt and taint they have carried since 1967.

CONCLUSION

The chapter has attempted to give an insight into Australian penality and imprisonment, with particular attention to the last 30 years. Evidence has been presented of the historical pattern of imprisonment rates, together with a snapshot of current prison rates and demographics. The two key features here are the significant state variations and the over-representation of Aboriginal prisoners. A brief sketch was presented of broad trends over the past 30 years from a period of upheaval, reform and alternatives in the 1960s and 1970s to one of increased punitiveness, just deserts and selective incapacitation in the 1980s and 1990s. However, this overview is overdrawn as state variations make a national picture misleading and as penal developments emerge against a context of local politics and sensibilities rather than global or national economic forces. Finally, four brief stories show the distinctive and diverse forms Australian penality can take, against the tendency to portray penal developments as marching to a single drum.

References

Anderson, T. (1989) *Inside Outlaws: A Prison Diary*. Sydney: Pluto Press.

Aungles, A. (1994) *The Prison and the Home*. Sydney: Federation Press.

Australian Bureau of Statistics. (1996) *National Correctional Statistics: Prisons March Quarter 1996*. Melbourne: ABS.

Australian Institute of Criminology (AIC). (1993) *Australian Prison Accommodation and Occupancy January–March 1993.* Canberra: AIC.

Australian Law Reform Commission. (1988) Report No. 44 *Sentencing.* Canberra: AGPS.

AIC. (1988–1996) *Deaths in Custody Australia* series. Canberra: AIC.

Australian Institute of Criminology. (1993) *Community Based Corrections Date*: December 1991. Canberra: AIC.

Australian Law Reform Commission. (1987) Discussion Paper: Sentencing: Procedure. Canberra: AGPS.

Babb, L. (1992) *Imprisonment Rates in NSW and Victoria: Explaining the Difference.* Crime and Justice Bulletin No. 4. Sydney: NSWBCSR.

Baldry, E. (1994) "USA Prison Privateers: Neo-colonialists in a Southern Land," in P. Moyle (ed.) *Private Prisons.* Sydney: Federation Press.

Biles, D. and McDonald, D. (1992) *Deaths in Custody Australia 1980–1989.* Canberra: AIC.

Braithwaite, J. (1980) "The Political Economy of Punishment," in E.L. Wheelwright and K. Buckley (eds.) *Essays in the Political Economy of Australian Capitalism* Vol. 5. Sydney: ANZ Books.

Braithwaite, J. (1989) *Crime, Shame and Reintegration.* Cambridge: Cambridge University Press.

Braithwaite, J. and Pettit, P. (1990) *Not Just Deserts: A Republican Theory of Criminal Justice.* Oxford: Clarendon Press.

Brown, D. (1987a) "The Politics of Reform," in G. Zdenkowski et al. (eds.) *The Criminal Injustice System.* Sydney: ALWG.

————. (1987b) "Some Preconditions for Sentencing and Penal Reform," in G. Wickham (ed.) *Social Theory and Legal Politics.* Sydney: Local Consumption.

————. (1989) "Returning to Sight: Contemporary Australian Penality." *Social Justice,* 16(3): 141–157.

————. (1991a) "The state of the prisons in NSW under the Greiner government: definitions of value." *Journal of Justice Studies,* 4: 27–60.

————. (1991b) "From purpose to pluralism, penology to politics, critique to policy," in National Center for Socio-Legal Studies, *Prisons, Prisoners and Politics: Australia and Abroad.* Melbourne: NCSLS.

Brown, D. et al. (1988) "Women in Prison: Task Force Reform," in M. Findlay and R. Hogg (eds.) *Understanding Crime and Criminal Justice.* Sydney: Law Book Co.

Brown, D. and Hogg, R. (1985) "Abolition Reconsidered: Issues and Problems." *Australian Journal of Law and Society*, 2: 56–93.

Chan, J. (1992) *Doing Less Time: Penal Reform in Crisis.* Sydney Institute of Criminology/Federation Press.

Cohen, S. (1979) "The Punitive City: Notes on the Dispersal of Social Control." *Contemporary Crises*, 3: 339–363.

Cohen, S. (1987) *Visions of Social Control.* Oxford: Polity Press.

Combined Churches. (1988) *Prison: The Last Resort.* Sydney: MSW Council for Social Services.

Dagger, D. and Mukherjee, S. (1994) *National Trends For Persons in Juvenile Corrective Institutions and Adult Prisons 1981 to 1992.* Canberra: AIC.

Easteal, P. (1992) "Women and Crime: Imprisonment Issues." *Trends and Issues* No. 35. Canberra: Australian Institute of Criminology.

Evans L. and Nicholls, P.A. (1976) *Convicts and Colonial Society 1788–1853.* Melbourne: Macmillan.

Findlay, M. (1982) *The State of the Prison.* Bathurst: Mitchellsearch.

Finnane, M. (1991) "After the Convicts: Towards a History of Imprisonment in Australia." *ANZJ of Criminology*, 24: 105–117.

Freiberg, A. (1995) "Sentencing Reform in Victoria: A Case Study" in C. Clarkson and R. Morgan (eds.) *The Politics of Sentencing Reform.* Oxford: Clarendon Press.

Foucault, M. (1978) *Discipline and Punish.* London: Penguin.

Gallagher, P. (1995) *Why does NSW have a higher imprisonment rate than Victoria?* Crime and Justice Bulletin No. 23. Sydney: NSWBCSR.

Garland, D. (1990) *Punishment and Modern Society.* Oxford: Oxford University Press.

Garland, D. and Young, P. (1983) (eds.) *The Power to Punish.* London: Heinemann.

Garton, S. (1982) "Bad or Mad? Developments in Incarceration in NSW 1880–1920," in Sydney Labor History Group (eds.) *What Rough Beast?* Sydney: Allen and Unwin.

Garton, S. (1988) "The State, Labor Markets and Incarceration: A Critique," in M. Findlay and R. Hogg (eds.) *Understanding Crime and Criminal Justice.* Sydney: Law Book Company.

Garton, S. (1991) "The Convict Origins Debate: Historians and the Problem of the 'Criminal Class'." *ANZJ of Criminology*, 24: 66–82.

George, A. and McCulloch, J. (1988) *Women and Imprisonment in Victoria*. Melbourne: Fitzroy Legal Service.

Grant, D. (1992) *Prisons: The Continuing Crisis in NSW.* Sydney: Federation Press.

Hampton, B. (1993) *Prisons and Women.* Sydney: NSW University Press.

Harding, R. (1987) "Prison Overcrowding: Correctional Policies and Political Constraints." *ANZJ of Criminology*, 20: 16.

Harding, R. (1992) *Private Prisons in Australia* AIC Trends and Issues No. 36. Canberra: AIC.

Hatty, S. (ed.) (1984) *Women in the Prison System.* Canberra: AIC.

Hawkins, G. (1977) *Beyond Reasonable Doubt.* Sydney: ABC Books.

Hirst, P. (1983) *Convict Society and Its Enemies.* Sydney: Allen and Unwin.

Hirst, J. (1986) *Law, Socialism and Democracy.* London: Collins.

Hogg, R. (1983) "Perspectives on the Criminal Justice System" in M. Findlay et al. (eds.) *Issues in Criminal Justice Administration.* Sydney: Allen and Unwin.

Hogg, R. (1988a) "Sentencing and Penal Politics: Current Developments in NSW." Proceedings of the Sydney Institute of Criminology, No. 78 Sentencing. Sydney: Sydney University Law School.

Hogg, R. (1988b) "Criminal Justice and Social Control: Contemporary Developments in Australia." *Journal of Studies in Justice*, 2: 89–122.

Howe, A. (1994) *Punish and Critique: Towards a Feminist Analysis of Penality.* London: Routledge.

Hughes, R. (1987) *The Fatal Shore.* Melbourne: Penguin.

Jankovic, I. (1980) "Labor Market and Imprisonment," in T. Platt and P. Takagi (eds.) *Punishment and Penal Discipline.* Berkeley: Crime and Social Justice Associates: pp. 93–104.

Kennedy, J. (1988) Commission of Review into Corrective Services in Queensland, Interim Report. Final Report. Brisbane: QGPS.

Martinson, R. (1974) "What Works? Questions and Answers about Prison Reform." *Public Interest*, 35: 22

Mathiesen, T. (1990) *Prison on Trial.* London: Sage.

Mathiesen, T. (1974) *The Politics of Abolition.* Oslo: Martin Robertson.

McDonald, D. (1993) *Deaths in Custody Australia: No. 2 National Police Custody Survey 1992: Preliminary Report.* Canberra: AIC.

McQueen, H. (1968) "Convicts and Rebels." *Labor History* 3–31.

McQueen, H. (1970) *The New Britannia.* Melbourne: Penguin.

McKillop, S. (ed.) (1991) *Keeping People Out of Prison.* Canberra: AIC.

Moyle, P. (ed.) (1994) *Private Prisons.* Sydney: Federation Press.

Mukherjee, S. (1981) *Crime Trends in Twentieth Century Australia.* Sydney: Allen and Unwin.

Mukherjee, S. and Dagger, D. (1995) *Australian Prisoners 1993.* Canberra: AIC

Nagle, J.F. (1978) *Report of the Royal Commission into NSW Prisons.* Sydney: NSWGPS.

Neal, D. (1987) "Free Society, Penal Colony, Salve Society, Prison?" *Historical Studies,* 22: 497–518.

Neal, D. (1991) *The Rule of Law in a Penal Colony.* Cambridge: Cambridge University Press.

NSW Law Reform Commission. (1994) Discussion Paper No. 35, *People With An Intellectual Disability and the Criminal Justice System.* Sydney: NSW Government Printer.

O'Neill, J. (1990) "The Punishment Salesman." *Independent Monthly* October.

Oxley, D. (1991) "Women Transported: Gendered Images and Realities." *ANZJ of Criminology,* 24: 83–98.

Quinney, R. (1977) *Class, State and Crime.* New York: David McKay.

Robinson, P. (1979) "The First Forty Years," in J. MacKinolty and H. Radi (eds.) *In Pursuit of Justice: Australian Women and the Law.* Sydney: Hale and Iremonger.

Robson, L.L. (1965) *The Convict Settlers of Australia.* Melbourne: Melbourne University Press:

Rusche, G. and Kirchheimer, O. (1939) *Punishment and Social Structure.* New York: Columbia University Press.

Scull, A. (1977) *Decarceration: Community Treatment and the Deviant.* Englewood Cliffs, New Jersey: Prentice Hall.

Shaw, A.G.L. (1964) *Convicts and Colonists.* London: Faber and Faber.

Sturma, M. (1978) "Eye of the Beholder: The Stereotype of Women Convicts 1788–1852." *Labor History,* 34: 3–10.

Sturma, M. (1983) *Vice in a Vicious Society*. St. Lucia: Queensland University Press.

Summers, A. (1975) *Damned Whores and Gods Police*. Melbourne: Penguin.

Taylor, I., Walton, P. and Young, J. (1973) *The New Criminology*. London: Routledge.

Tomasic, R. and Dobinson, I. (1979) *The Failure of Imprisonment*. Sydney: Allen and Unwin.

Vinson, A. (1982) *Wilful Obstruction*. Sydney: Methuen.

Walker, J. (1991) "Keeping People Out of Prison—Which Jurisdictions Do it Best?" in S. McKillop (ed.) *Keeping People Out of Prison*. Canberra: AIC.

Walker, J. (1992) *Derived Indicators of Imprisonment Trends by Jurisdiction 1981-82–1990-91*. Canberra: AIC.

————. (1992) *Estimates of the Costs of Crime in Australia*. Canberra: AIC.

————. (1994) "User-friendly Prisoner Forecasting," Jan/Feb *Criminology Australia* 21.

Walker, J. and McDonald, D. (1995) *The Over-representation of Indigenous People in Custody in Australia* AIC Trends and Issues No. 47: 3.

Weatherburn, D. (1988) "Note: Front-end versus Rear-end Solutions to Prison Overcrowding: A Reply to Professor Harding," *ANZJ of Criminology*, 21: 117.

Yabsley, M. (1991) "Punishment and Prisons." *Journal for Social Justice Studies*, 4: 67–72.

Zdenkowski, G. and Brown, D. (1982) *The Prison Struggle*. Melbourne: Penguin.

Zdenkowski, G. (1994) "Contemporary Sentencing Issues" in D. Chappell and P. Wilson (eds.) *The Australian Criminal Justice System: The Mid 1990s*. Sydney: Butterworths.

Zdenkowski, G. (1994a) "Foreword" in P. Moyle (ed.) (supra).

Chapter
THIRTEEN

Change and Continuity in South African Prisons

Dirk van Zyl Smit

The history of the South African prison system in the last 20 years is a history of both change and continuity. On the one hand, there is the history of a system which formed part of the state apparatus of a minority government which applied explicitly racial criteria. The prison system itself was governed by a highly restrictive legal regime which included explicitly racist elements. Change in this regard has been significant and on occasion has anticipated change in the national political structure.

On the other hand, the monolithic structure of the national prison system remains. It continues to imprison roughly the same number of people drawn from the same social groups as in the past and to hold them in conditions which in practice have not changed significantly. The key question is what impact the dynamics of change are likely to have on these, hitherto relatively unaltered, aspects of the penal system in the immediate future.

ELEMENTS IN THE REFORMIST STORY OF CHANGE

Law and Rights

Twenty years ago, on June 30, 1976, the South African prison system was rigidly segregated. The details of segregation were specified in the Prisons Act (1959) and the regulations made in terms of it. Black and white prisoners were not only to be kept separately but not within sight of one another (s. 23(1)(b) of the Prisons Act, 1959). White warders outranked blacks automatically (reg. 3(1) of the regulations made in terms of the Prisons Act, 1959), and a white prisoner could not be visited by a black minister of religion (reg. 108(2)(b) of the regulations made in terms of the Prisons Act, 1959). Only in the face of death were prisoners equal. All prisoners awaiting execution on death row were entitled to rations on the white scale (reg. 139(5) of the regulations made in terms of the Prisons Act, 1959).

Prison legislation expressly limited the rights of prisoners (s. 22 of the Prisons Act, 1959). The rights of security detainees were even further restricted (Mathews, 1986). Moreover, the system itself was protected by drastic restrictions on the freedom of the press to report on its actions (s. 44(1)(f) of the Prisons Act, 1959).

All this was legislated, but recourse to the courts was not entirely denied.[1] Although the courts applied the doctrine of parliamentary supremacy and could not strike down primary legislation, they continued to operate with a sophisticated jurisprudence which purported to recognize fundamental human rights and equality before the law.

One of the elements of the reformist story of change is therefore the use of the courts by imprisoned political activists. In this way they sought not only to publicize their cause generally but also to change the repressive conditions under which prisoners were detained. For many years they were unsuccessful. In the most notorious of the cases they brought, elementary human rights were denied. Thus, in 1964 in Rossouw v. Sachs the Appellate Division of the Supreme Court (then the court of final instance in South Africa) was prepared to deny reading and writing materials to a prisoner detained for purposes of interrogation. What next, Judge Ogilvie Thompson, soon to be appointed Chief Justice, asked rhetorically, champagne and cigars?

Similarly, in Goldberg v. Minister of Prisons (1979) a majority of the Appellate Division denied that prisoners had any rights, other than the most basic. It therefore refused to upset a ruling that political prisoners were not entitled to news of current events or of anything else of which the prison censors chose to deprive them. The rulings of these censors, which even the conservative majority of the Court found incomprehensible, were left unchallenged, for even arbitrary official authority was to remain unassailable.

But even in the dark days of these decisions endorsing official arbitrariness, elementary notions of fairness and justice were not entirely suppressed. The very fact that these cases were brought at all indicated that an alternative discourse was thought to be possible both in prison law and in the wider political framework. The former was signaled both by the strong academic condemnation of the decisions (Rudolph, 1979; van Wyk, van Niekerk, Nairn and Taitz, 1979) and, importantly, by the powerful dissent by Judge Corbett (the current Chief Justice) in Goldberg's case. The political aspect was overt. All important prison litigation was conducted by political prisoners and their pursual of this course allowed the legal assertion of prisoners' human rights to become an important factor in the debate about correctional reform. The turning point for the Appellate Division was a decision involving Mr. Nelson Mandela, then a political prisoner. Although he lost the case on the merits, the Appellate Division recognized that any basic right of a prisoner "survives incarceration except in so far as it is attenuated by legislation, either expressly or by necessary implication, and the necessary consequences of incarceration" (Mandela v. Minister of Prisons, 1983: 957G).

In 1993 the full imprimatur of judicial approval was finally given to the generous recognition of prisoners' rights in the decision of the Appellate Division in the case of Minister of Justice v. Hofmeyr. In one sense the case was an anachronism, for it involved allegations that correctional officials had not properly exercised their discretion on how a detainee should be treated but had allowed their judgment to be swayed by extraneous factors, in this case the views of the security police. By the time the case reached the Appellate Division the state of emergency under which Hofmeyr had been detained had long been lifted and the powers of the security police drastically curtailed. Under these circumstances the court had no difficulty in adopting a very wide definition of prisoners' rights and imposing a duty on correctional officials to apply appropriate procedures in limiting them.

These judicial developments are being consolidated. The so-called interim South African Constitution which was adopted in late 1993 and which came into operation after the first democratic elections in April 1994 contains an entrenched bill of rights. Among its clauses are fairly detailed provisions dealing with the rights of all persons who are detained (s. 25(1) of the Constitution of the Republic of South Africa, 1993). The new Constitution which was adopted by the Constitutional Assembly in May 1996 and which is currently being considered by the Constitutional Court contains a similar provision. The clause (clause 35(2) of the draft Constitution of the Republic of South Africa, 1996) has not been controversial. Its adoption reflects perhaps the extent to which many of the current members of government who had been incarcerated themselves entered into this legal, rights-based discourse about prisons.

Management

A second strand in the story of change is the role of the professional managers who have administered the South African prison system for the past two decades. The South African system is a single centralized bureaucracy, run, until very recently, on tight military lines. Because of the way in which it is structured it has been possible for the Commissioner who heads the system to exercise a great deal of control over the development of policy. The deformities of the South African prison system should not conceal the many ways which, even at its most repressive, it resembled the prison systems of other countries. The 1959 Prisons Act, which, although much amended, still forms the legal basis of the prison system, was modeled on the 1955 United Nations Standard Minimum Rules for the Treatment of Prisoners and the explicitly apartheid rules were grafted on to this base (van Zyl Smit, 1992). When pressure arose in the 1980s to remove the overt manifestations of so-called petty apartheid from prisons, they were simply repealed without any publicity. Nor was much control lost in the process. Formal seniority ceased to be racially based but for a considerable time there were few officers of color who outranked whites. At the more trivial level changes were even more subtle. The racial references were removed, for example, from the regulations governing the diets of prisoners on death row and replaced by a rule which laid down only that such prisoners would receive rations as determined by the Commissioner (amended reg. 139(5) of the regulations made in terms of the Prisons Act, 1959).

More complex strategies were involved in relation to the assertion of prisoners rights. Twenty years ago the public stance of the prison authorities was one of defiance. The removal of access to news and to study facilities from prisoners who defined themselves as political prisoners was also a symbolic exercise of power. When these prisoners sought unsuccessfully to assert their rights through the courts (in the action reported as Goldberg's case and discussed above) the political arm of government responded by amending the Prisons Act to make it even harder to bring such actions in the future—a move which was rightly condemned by human rights activists at the time (van Zyl Smit, 1987; 1992). The managerial response was more subtle. In practice, the ruling proposed by the minority judgment of Judge Corbett was quietly implemented and these prisoners were in fact again given access to news and permission to study.[2]

An even clearer illustration of progress to greater sophistication was the way in which the question of reporting on prison conditions in the media was handled. From the early '60s onwards reports appeared in the media condemning the conditions under which political prisoners and prisoners of color generally were held. The initial response was one of outright repression. In 1965 s. 44 of the Prisons Act (1959) was amended to make it an offense not only to publish "false information" about prisons or prisoners but also to place "an onus of proving that reasonable steps were taken to verify such information upon the accused" (s. 12 of the Prisons Amendment Act, 1965). The effect of this provision was that the state could compel anyone, including the press, to show that they had taken reasonable steps to verify their information. The provision was harshly applied by the courts and after a major newspaper was convicted for allegedly not taking such steps (S v. South African Associated Newspapers, 1970), effective newspaper coverage of prison conditions in South Africa ceased.

This blanket prohibition did not improve the image of the prisons. South African newspapers, which continued to be allowed some freedom of expression, hinted persistently that something was seriously wrong in South African prisons but that they could not report on it. Gradually the official policy, although not yet the legislation, changed. The first step was the publication in South Africa in 1984 of *The Confessions of an Albino Terrorist*, an autobiographical account by Breyten Breytenbach of his experiences as a prisoner serving a term following a conviction for terrorism. In the past such highly critical works by former political prisoners had invariably been suppressed. But Breytenbach was different, for in addition to being an ex-prisoner he was the greatest living poet writing in the Afrikaans language. After Breytenbach's detailed accounts of prison life it made little sense to continue to deny access to prisons.

In the same year the Prisons Service entered into an agreement with the Newspaper Press Union which represented the major South African newspapers. This agreement was of doubtful legality, for it purported to ensure that the newspapers could publish unedited accounts of prison life and escape prosecution on condition that they first submitted them to the prison authorities and also gave equal prominence to their response. In theory the prison authorities could not neutralize a penal provision by means of an agreement (Mihálik, 1989). In practice though, this pragmatic arrangement was effective and accounts of prison conditions, including serious allegations of maltreatment, began to appear in South African newspapers, accompanied routinely by denials from the authorities. The wall of censorship had effectively been breached and in 1992 the restrictive legislation was repealed (van Zyl Smit, 1992). By this time the prison authorities had developed a sophisticated media section. Although this initiative did not protect them against claims of abuse, the perception of a cover-up was largely dispelled.

Prison labor is another area in which there has been a long interaction between rights activists and the prison authorities. Historically productive prison labor, in the 19th century on the roads and in the mines and in the 20th century on the farms, has been a feature of South African prison life (van Zyl Smit, 1984). The battle surrounding this aspect cannot be documented fully here, except to record that the decline of the use of prison labor in commercial agriculture outside the prison has been dramatic. In the case of the so-called prison outstations,[3] it is possible to point to a specific catalyst. South Africa was warned that it was a contravention of the General Agreement on Tariffs and Trade to produce goods for export using forced labor and that the convict labor from the outstations was such labor (Corry, 1977: 157). As a direct result the outstations were closed down in mid-1988. At about the same time the practice of hiring out short-term prisoners to farmers was discontinued (van Zyl, 1996).

Patterns of labor use inside prison were more resistant to change. Accounts of conditions experienced by political prisoners in the 1960s and 1970s are replete with descriptions of stone breaking and other hard and relatively pointless manual labor being performed by prisoners under harsh conditions (for example, Mandela, 1994: 390). But such conditions were not restricted to political prisoners. As late as October 1984 the Swiss criminologist, Dr. Haesler, was shown prisoners who were breaking stones inside cages made of chicken wire at the maximum security Brandvlei prison in the Western Cape (Haesler, 1986). The cages were ostensibly to prevent prisoners from attacking one another with the heavy hammers they were using. Once the stones were small enough they were to be pushed through the gaps in the chicken wire. In this sphere too the authorities gradually bowed to pressure for those who emphasized rights and on March 24, 1992, stone crushing was formally abandoned (van Zyl, 1996).

New Players

The long battle for the recognition of prisoners' rights and the responses of an increasingly sophisticated prison management have been played out in very different circumstances in the 1990s. A key historical moment was undoubtedly President F.W. de Klerk's announcement on February 2, 1990, that various political organizations would be unbanned and that political prisoners would be released. In the same speech, although less widely heralded at the time, was the announcement that the death penalty would be reconsidered and that in the meantime there would be a moratorium on its implementation (*Cape Times*, February 3, 1990).

The release of political prisoners in the next four years eventually removed this group as a direct force for change in the prison system; but the process itself was extremely protracted and dogged by controversy. Much disputed was the question of who among the many thousands of sentenced prisoners should be regarded as political prisoners. At the overtly political level the initial attempt at applying a purely legal definition of political prisoners was compromised by further negotiations between the major parties (Keightley, 1993). The result was that some sentenced prisoners who did not meet the formal criteria were released simply because they had the support of one party and their release could be offset against the release of other (equally undeserving) prisoners supported by another party.

The release of political prisoners soon became embroiled in wider questions about the release of prisoners generally. The reality, which before 1990 was not widely discussed in the public media, was that the executive had long used its very wide powers to release prisoners before they had completed their full sentences. These essentially took two forms: administrative release by the prison authorities following the granting of remission or parole,[4] and the declaration of general amnesties by the State President, usually on official anniversaries, which would result in the mass release of prisoners and reduce the overall prison population to manageable levels for a while.

In 1991 both these powers were used under controversial circumstances. In that year the Prisons Act was amended significantly. As part of an attempt to reposition the Department both it and the act governing it were renamed with the words "Correctional Services" replacing "Prisons." The newly named Department of Correctional Services was to be responsible not only for prisons but also for correctional supervision, an extended community sentencing option for which the amended Correctional Services Act now provided. In order to enable it to implement the new system the Department was given additional powers to modify the sentences of offenders by placing those subject to certain prison terms on correctional supervision. At the same time their power to release sentenced prisoners was increased even further. Explicit provision was made for bursting, that is, for releasing prisoners if in the view of the Minister of Correctional Services the system was grossly overcrowded (s. 67 of the Correctional Services Act, 1959 as amended by s. 22 of the Correctional Services and Supervision Matters Amendment Act, 1991).

In mid-1991, ironically shortly before the new powers of release came into effect, a very large general amnesty was granted; some reports suggested that up to 57,000 sentenced prisoners, that is more than half the total number of sentenced prisoners, were set free (*Cape Times*, July 17, 1991). This number may have been exaggerated;[5] certainly the number of sentenced prisoners soon increased again. However, the perception was left with the public and with the remaining prisoners that releases were being manipulated, both to "solve" some of the problems relating to the question of which prisoners were political prisoners and generally to alleviate prison overcrowding.

The uncertainty surrounding release was a key factor in the increasing unrest among prisoners generally in the first half of the 1990s. In the past ordinary South African prisoners had been subservient and not widely politicized. Well-organized prison gangs had long existed and operated with extreme brutality, but their victims had usually been fellow prisoners. In the early 1990s, however, a prisoners' organization, SAPHOR (the South African Prisoners Human Rights Organization), emerged. It was headed by Golden Miles Bhudu, a charismatic leader with a flair for publicity.[6] Bhudu constantly reminded the public that he was a former common law prisoner. He spoke confidently on behalf of his former colleagues and emphasized that they too were victims of the social injustices of apartheid. He argued that their conditions should therefore be improved and most importantly they too should be considered for early release (Bhudu, 1995). It is not possible to determine what support Bhudu's organization had among prisoners. At least tacitly it could have been considerable and in the transitional period his voice could not be ignored.

Another new force which emerged in this period was the unionization of prison personnel. Its origins predated President de Klerk's speech of February 2, 1990, but only slightly. In late 1989 a dissident policeman, Gregory Rockman, had founded the POPCRU, the Police and Prison Officers Civil Rights Union. POPCRU rapidly became the focus for members of the prisons staff who supported the liberation movements. Notwithstanding the fact that these movements were being legalized and recognized as political parties, official reaction was initially very hostile. In 1990 the Prisons Act was amended to outlaw trade union activities by prison warders.[7] Warders who joined POPCRU were not only refused promotions but disciplined for infringing the Act.[8] Other problems abounded. The major national trade union federation was at first uncertain about whether it wished to recognize a union of security personnel. Moreover, there were tensions between the police and prison warder members, as to some extent their concerns differed and they had to deal with two different government departments. However, the sustained union activity and the changing overall political climate had its effect and gradually the principle of union membership by prison officers was accepted. The form that this acceptance and eventual formal recognition took was not what POPCRU activists had envisaged, for other unions entered the field as well. These were the PSA (the Public Service Association), the body which traditionally had looked after the interests of (mostly white) civil servants from all departments of government, and COUSA (the Correctional Officers Association of South Africa), a break-away group from POPCRU, which focused more narrowly on the interests of Black prison officers (*Cape Times*, March 8, 1996).

New Politics?

The run up to the first democratic elections in South Africa, which were to take place in April 1994, provided openings for the new players in South African penal politics to assert themselves. For POPCRU and its fellow unions the primary change was simply that, somewhat grudgingly, they were recognized and eventually allowed officially to represent their members in negotiations with the authorities. For SAPHOR the transitional phase presented more dramatic opportunities. The first issue that arose was whether prisoners would be allowed to vote. Initially, the legislation enacted after the negotiated settlement to govern the first democratic elections excluded many sentenced prisoners from voting. For the first time SAPHOR was able to mobilize prisoners around a specific issue on which it also had support from some of the major political parties.[9] SAPHOR grasped the opportunity, called on prisoners to embark on protests, what it called "rolling mass action," in prisons and at the same time organized demonstrations outside prisons (Bhudu, 1995). These resulted in outbreaks of violence in various prisons, but also in an important victory. The Electoral Act (1993) was amended in order to exclude from voting only prisoners convicted of murder, robbery with aggravating circumstances and rape.[10] In any event, it appears that when it came to voting the prison authorities did not attempt to apply even these limited restrictions and all prisoners who wished to do so were allowed to vote.

The victory of the African National Congress (ANC) in the elections brought the question of amnesty to the fore and again provided SAPHOR with an explosive issue. Precedents of the past and the public debates which had suggested that to some extent all inmates were political prisoners contributed to an enormous sense of expectation. In any case, President Mandela spoke of amnesty only in general terms in his inaugural address of May 10, 1994. A considerable delay followed during which Bhudu on behalf of SAPHOR made further calls for "rolling mass action" by prisoners. Some such action was undertaken and when a general amnesty which reduced all sentences by six months was eventually announced on June 10 it was rejected by SAPHOR and by many prisoners who rioted in protest. On June 27, 1994, a Judicial Commission chaired by Judge Kriegler was appointed to investigate unrest in prisons (Kriegler Commission, 1994). .

The installation of a Government of National Unity after the elections was a further important step towards the establishment of a new framework within which penal politics could take place. After some initial hesitation, the portfolio of Minister of Correctional Services was given to Mr. Sipo Mzimela, a member of the Inkatha Freedom Party, one of the minority parties in the government. At the same time the Parliamentary Portfolio Committee on correctional Services was to be chaired by a prominent Member of Parliament for the African National Congress, Mr. Carl Niehaus. From the beginning it became clear that the new Parliamentary Committee intended to play a far more active role in monitoring prisons and shaping policy. The potential for conflict on the reshaping of the prison system between the Minister, the Department of Correctional Services and the Parliamentary Committee was clearly inbuilt. To these had now to be added both the new players as well as more traditional welfare organizations such as the National Institute for Crime and the Rehabilitation of Offenders (NICRO) which had long sought to improve the lot of offenders by emphasizing their rights.

In January 1995 it was recognized that the existing structural arrangements might not be sufficient to cope with the diverse pressures for reform and, after a meeting called by Deputy President Mbeki and a conference on penal reform, it was decided to set up the Transformation Forum on Correctional Services. The Forum which met for the first time in May 1995 was to include "all stakeholders." These included representatives from the three unions, the Department of Correctional Services, various non-governmental organizations, including SAPHOR, and parliamentarians from the various parties represented in the Portfolio Committee. It was chaired by Carl Niehaus, the chair of the Parliamentary Portfolio Committee on Correctional Services.[11]

The combination of parties and personalities on the Transformation Forum did not make for smooth functioning. The fact that it was chaired by a high-profile politician gave a degree of party political color to its activities. At one stage the Minister of Correctional Services became so incensed by what he perceived as the obstructive tactics of the Forum that he instructed the Department to withdraw. Following intervention by President Mandela himself this dispute was eventually resolved and departmental representatives returned to the Forum but the Forum continued to function less than smoothly.

Actual Reforms?

Thus far the focus has been on process and institutions. But what has actually been changed in South Africa in the two years since the new government has been in power?

Only one substantive change, that relating to the detention of juveniles awaiting trial, has been embodied in correctional legislation. Its history reveals something of the difficulties of prison reform in the current context. The detention of juveniles in prison is of course a highly emotive issue and was one of the human rights abuses with which the liberation movements (with considerable justification) had taxed the previous regime (Britain and Minty, 1988). Section 29 of the Correctional Services Act, or the Prisons Act as it was previously called, had long provided that juveniles could only be detained in prison if this were "necessary" and no other suitable places of detention were available. However, considerable numbers of juveniles awaiting trial continued to be detained in prison and in late 1994 the Act was amended to make it procedurally far harder for juveniles to be held in prison (Sloth-Nielsen, 1995). Provision was made for the amendment to be brought into operation on a piecemeal basis. By proclamation it could be applied only to specific magisterial districts, thus allowing for the development of alternative secure facilities at so-called places of safety administered by the Department of Welfare.

Little or nothing appears to have been done to develop such alternative facilities and in May 1995 the amended Act was put into effect throughout the country by presidential proclamation. The motive appears to have been to use shock tactics to force the bureaucracy to act (Skelton, 1996). In any event, the effect was to unleash a public outcry that legislation had made it impossible for the state to detain juveniles accused of the most heinous offenses. The result was that in 1996 the Correctional Services Act was again amended to make it possible to detain juveniles (Sloth-Nielsen, 1996). Although the new amendment is supposed to apply only for a year and is hedged with qualifications designed to ensure that only juveniles accused of the most serious offenses are detained and then under better conditions than in the past, the practical effect appears to have been to reinstate the incarceration of juveniles in much the same form as it existed prior to the first attempted reform.

A similar pattern can be seen in relation to bail. The new constitution which came into effect in 1994 recognized the right of offenders to be granted bail unless their further detention was necessary in the interests of justice (s. 25(2) of the Constitution of the Republic of South Africa, 1993). Public perceptions that this right was being recognized too liberally led the new government to amend the Criminal Procedure Act in 1995 to make bail harder to obtain (Criminal Procedure Second Amendment Act, 1995). The unsurprising result has been a sudden increase in the number of persons being detained in prison while awaiting trial.

The trajectory of both these "reforms" can be explained as a response by the new government which, notwithstanding its broad commitment to human rights, has to deal with increasing populist public pressure to get tough on crime. This pressure has been increased by the abolition of the death penalty, a step which has enjoyed very little public support.

It is noteworthy that the death penalty was not abolished directly by legislative or constitutional enactment. Although the official position of the ANC was that it was opposed to the death sentence it agreed in the negotiations which preceded the elections of 1994 that the matter should not be dealt with in the interim constitution. The interim constitution provides only for general rights to life (s. 9), human dignity (s. 10) and protection from cruel, inhuman or degrading treatment or punishment (s. 11(2)). In 1995, in the landmark decision of S v. Makwanyane, the newly-created Constitutional Court unanimously interpreted these provisions as meaning that the death sentence is unconstitutional.[12] Although opposition parties attempted to have the issue revisited by seeking an explicit provision providing that the death penalty should be regarded as constitutional, the proposed final Constitution of 1996 is worded similarly to the interim constitution, so that this ruling of the Constitutional Court is highly unlikely to be overturned. The vehemence of the debates nevertheless revealed the extent of punitive public sentiment and may well have the effect that persons serving sentences of life imprisonment will in fact be detained for longer periods than had been the practice in the past.

In matters which relate to the internal prison regime rather than to the perceived use of prisons to control crime there has been more room for maneuvering. In this regard two actual reforms are worth mentioning: The first is the recognition of the need to treat with dignity prisoners who are HIV-positive or who are suffering from AIDS. A new policy which forbids involuntary testing of prisoners and which does not allow the segregation of those who are known to be HIV-positive on this ground alone is an indication that steps are not being taken against such prisoners upon grounds of prejudice alone. The steps that are being taken to educate prisoners about the dangers of HIV infection and to make condoms available to those prisoners who request them are part of the same policy (Department of Correctional Services, 1995a).[13]

Second, a major internal organizational change has been the abolition of military ranks and the removal of uniforms except for those staff members who have actual custodial roles. This demilitarization has been partial, in that ranks and insignia have been removed, but there has not been a fundamental restructuring and reorientation of the Department (Giffard, 1996). Nevertheless, the fact that even partial demilitarization took place and that it took place without any overt opposition from the personnel is an indication that the active cooperation of the unions through the Transformation Forum has the potential for allowing more fundamental restructuring of the Service.

Potential Reforms?

There are some further areas in which reform can be predicted with some confidence. The first of these is in the area of release policy. The Kriegler Commission found that matters relating to release were a major cause of the 1994 prison unrest. After the immediate dissatisfaction with the failure of the state to grant amnesty, the general release policy was a source of great dissatisfaction because it granted too much discretion to prison officials who were perceived by many prisoners to be biased. It referred this matter to a further statutory body, the National Advisory Council on Correctional Services. When the National Advisory Council came to investigate the matter it was faced not only with the initial views forcibly expressed by prisoners but also by strongly-expressed public disenchantment with any form of executive intervention resulting in the release of prisoners before they have served their full sentences. The published preliminary recommendations of the National Advisory

Council (NACOCS, 1996) are that all sentenced prisoners should serve at least half their sentences in prison, that the release of prisoners on parole be decided upon by reconstituted parole boards. The procedures of these boards would meet the requirements of due process appropriate to a decision where someone's liberty is at stake. The community would be strongly represented on the new parole boards, which would be independent of the Department. At the same time it recommended that executive intervention in prison sentences by way of amnesty or bursting provisions be curtailed.

If implemented, the effect of these recommendations, which in final form have been referred to the Minister of Correctional Services for consideration, would be paradoxical. On the one hand, they would contribute to correctional reform by emphasizing due process and transparency and by increasing community involvement in correctional decision making. From the point of view of the Department of Correctional Services they would have the advantage of not leaving them with the responsibility for justifying to the public decisions to release prisoners. On the other hand, the part of their sentences which offenders actually serve in prison would increase. The consequent growth in the overall prison population will reduce the ability of the system to introduce reforms which require increased expenditure per prisoner.

The second general area of potential reform is in the recognition of the human rights of prisoners.[14] Legislation to replace the Correctional Services Act with a new law which would follow closely the prescriptions of the Constitution in explicitly defining and protecting prisoners' rights is highly likely. Similarly, a judicial inspectorate will almost certainly be created in order to safeguard prisoners further against abuse. This may well be supplemented by some form of lay visitors scheme. It is also possible that internal reorganization of the prisons, with increased emphasis on unit management, will lead to better protection of prisoners.

Finally, the restructuring of the personnel of the Department will continue. Changes already made have led to the appointment of a number of senior officials from outside the Department who inevitably bring with them new ideas and new approaches. Combined with a policy of affirmative action, this is likely to change the racial composition of the staff and, in particular, of the top management, which hitherto has been largely white.

ELEMENTS OF CONTINUITY

The Statistical Picture

Reforms actual and potential should not distract attention from the statistical picture which shows that in some respects very little has changed. Twenty years ago, that is on June 30, 1976, the South African prison system housed 93,977 prisoners. Of these 78,838 were sentenced offenders and 14,993 were awaiting trial. The bulk of the small balance of 146 was made up by 62 judgment debtors and 69 security detainees, i.e., persons detained without trial in terms of the misnamed Suppression of Communism Act which was used to deal with the civil unrest which followed from the Soweto uprising earlier that month. (Neither of these provisions is still a basis for detention in South Africa). If one adds the miscellaneous category to the figures of awaiting trial prisoners one has the set of data contained in Table 1.[15]

It is fascinating to compare this table with the figures contained in Table 2, which are far more recent statistics: the average national daily prison populations for the month of June 1996.[16]

Focusing first on sentenced prisoners, it is noticeable that the number of sentenced white prisoners has declined in absolute

TABLE 1   Prisoners in Custody on 30 June 1976

	White	Black	Coloured	Asian	All Races
Unsentenced					
Male	493	11,209	2191	118	14,011
Female	25	915	183	5	1128
All Genders	618	12,123	2380	123	15,139
Sentenced					
Male	3403	53,731	16,129	390	73,653
Female	70	4309	786	20	5185
All Genders	3473	58,040	16,915	410	78,838
All Prisoners					
Male	3896	64,940	18,320	508	87,664
Female	95	5224	969	25	6313
All Genders	3991	66,164	19,289	533	93,977

Source: Department of Prisons, 1977.

TABLE 2   Daily Average Prison Population for June 1996

	White	Black	Coloured	Asian	All Races
Unsentenced					
Male	523	22,986	3622	108	27,238
Female	35	671	97	6	809
All Genders	557	23,657	3719	114	28,047
Sentenced					
Male	2867	62,294	21,203	409	86,774
Female	129	1536	387	12	2064
All Genders	2996	63,829	21,590	421	88,838
All Prisoners					
Male	3390	85,280	24,825	517	114,012
Female	164	2207	484	18	2873
All Genders	3554	87,486	25,309	536	116,885

Source: Personal Communication from the Department of Correctional Services, August 1996.

terms while the numbers for all other population groups has increased. However, these figures may be misleading as there has been a far greater increase in the black population than in the white population. Thus, the white rate of imprisonment in 1976 was 79 per 100,000 of population and that for blacks 350 per 100,000. By 1996 the rate for whites had declined to 57 per 100,000 while the rate for blacks had declined even more dramatically to 198 per 100,000.[17] Another noteworthy feature is that the number of sentenced female prisoners has more than halved from 5185 to 2064. While the number of sentenced male prisoners has increased by 15%, this increase is relatively small; smaller certainly than the growth in overall population of almost 37 percent over the same period. Indeed, the most prominent feature of the number of sentenced prisoners is that it has remained relatively static in absolute terms while declining in relation to the population as a whole.[18]

It cannot be said that the number of unsentenced prisoners has remained static. Notwithstanding the abolition of most provisions for detention without trial, it has increased by 46% in the past 20 years. Much of this increase has been relatively recent: From January 31, 1995, to May 31, 1996, there was an increase of 17.4% in the number of prisoners awaiting trial.[19] This increase can perhaps be attributed directly to the change in bail legislation, but the longer term increase is almost certainly a function of delays in processing cases through the courts.

One other statistical feature deserves comment. There has clearly been a significant decline in the number of offenders sentenced to terms of imprisonment in the past 20 years.[20] However, this decline has been offset by an increase in the length of sentences served, leading to the gradual growth in overall numbers of prisoners serving sentences of imprisonment. Table 3 gives an indication of the latter trend. To some extent these developments can be explained by the abolition of status offenses, such as laws which prohibited Africans from being in certain areas, but the trend has continued along after these offenses were removed from the statute book in the mid-1980s.

Conditions of Detention

Have there been significant changes in actual conditions under which prisoners are detained? This crucial question is very difficult to answer fully. Nevertheless, some attempt to do so must be made. One indicator of what prison conditions are like may be found in the amount of money which the state spends daily on each prisoner. Official estimates are that the average cost per day of imprisoning a prisoner has increased from R 12.27 in 1977 (Gordon, 1978: 115) to R 61.302[21] in 1995/96 (Department of Correctional Services, 1996: 28). However, in comparing these figures the rate of inflation has to be taken into account. Since 1977 the value of the rand has declined approximately ten fold. That means that in real terms the state is now spending slightly less than half of what it did per prisoner 19 years ago.

Another sphere in which some comparison with the past is possible is in the area of prison labor. As has been seen, one of the campaigns for change was to abolish degrading and commercially exploitative labor by prisoners. This was achieved, but the result has been that the number of sentenced prisoners who can be recorded as working in any way has declined dramatically: from 68% in 1972/3 (Corry, 1977) to just 25% in December 1995 (van Zyl, 1996). Closer analysis shows that almost all the job losses have been in the agricultural sector outside the prison. They have not been replaced to any significant degree either inside or outside the prison.

Table 3 Sentence Distribution of Prisoners Admitted During the Years 1984/85 to 1994 Expressed as Percentages

	84/85	85/86	86/87	87/88	88/89	90/91	91/92	92/93	1993	1994
1. Long-term prisoners (i.e. with sentences of 2 years and more)	9.78	12.62	13.80	13.51	13.65	15.22	18.13	19.94	20.86	26.34
2. Sentences of more than 6 months but less than 2 years	10.50	12.81	15.61	13.53	13.86	16.36	17.84	19.40	15.29	17.13
3. Sentences of 6 months and less	78.54	73.03	69.62	71.65	71.19	67.07	63.17	59.68	62.99	56.34
4. Other categories	1.18	1.54	0.97	1.31	1.30	1.35	0.86	0.98	0.86	0.19
	100%	100%	100%	100%	100%	100%	100%	100%	100%	100%

The statistics for 1986/87 differ from the statistics given in the Annual Report for 1986/87. The differences are ascribable to calculation errors. The 1991/92 period under review extends over 18 months as against the 12 months of the other periods of review.
Source: Department of Correctional Services, 1995.

The result is that while the abolition of racial segregation means that an elite of black prisoners now has access to jobs previously reserved for whites, prisoners overall are more likely to be idle.

Recent direct evidence on the quality of prison life is sparse but what there is suggests that prison gangs which have been a major factor in prison life continue to terrorize and exploit their fellow inmates (Africa Watch and Prison Project, 1994). Overcrowding remains acute in many prisons (Department of Correctional Services, 1996). Most worrying is the indication in a recent empirical study that there is a decline in control in at least some prisons. This is not making prison life less stressful but rather is making it more hazardous for individual prisoners than it was in the past (Dissel, 1996).

CONCLUSION

As this paper was being completed in August 1996 South Africa was experiencing a major panic about the escalation of crime. The matter was brought to a head by the public and televized lynching and murder of a well-known drug dealer in Cape Town by members of Pagad (People against Gangsterism and Drugs), a Moslem-led populist movement (*Cape Times*, August 5, 1996). A fortnight later a prominent German businessman was murdered in the course of having his car hijacked outside his Johannesburg home (*Die Burger*, August 20, 1996).

These events led to a flurry of activities with the three criminal justice ministries—Safety and Security (police), Justice and Correctional Services—vying to be seen to be introducing corrective measures. These would include both further restrictions on bail and a release policy, harsher than that proposed by the National Advisory Council on Correctional Services, which would allow courts to ensure that prisoners are not released on parole until they have served at least two-thirds of their sentences (*Die Burger*, August 23, 1996). It is clear that politically it will be extremely difficult for the government to persist with policies which allow the early release of prisoners. In the continued absence of an overall sentencing policy it is likely that the prison population will grow greatly in the short term and that the ratio of prisoners to the population may again reach the levels of 20 years ago. Strong hints have been given that there will be a major program of prison construction, possibly financed by the private sector. In the current climate of public concern about crime it may prove extremely difficult to consolidate in practice the recognition which has been granted in law to prisoners' rights in South Africa.

Notes

1. The South African courts in the 1970s adopted a relatively generous approach to the legal standing of prisoners to approach the courts and declined to follow the more restrictive English precedents of the time: see Hassim v. Officer Commanding, Prison Command, Robben Island (1973).
2. These facts were revealed recently when activists imprisoned in the late 1970s and early 1980s explained publicly to Judge Corbett that his interventions had been more successful than may have appeared from the pages of the law report.
3. Prison outstations were prisons built by farmers' associations and then handed to the prison authorities on condition that the contributing farmers were provided with convict labor on a pro-rata basis.
4. The latter was often a formality. For many years the majority of prisoners sentenced to terms of less than six months were released on parole on condition that they enter into prescribed contracts of employment— a scheme which lent itself to abuse (Corry, 1977).
5. The Kriegler Commission (1994: 72) recorded:

"The practice [of granting amnesties] continued during the period of political transition. On 10 December 1990 a six-month amnesty of seasonal goodwill resulted in 30,179 prisoners being released. Another six-month amnesty on 30 April 1991 and a one-third amnesty for first offenders on 1 July 1991 freed 25,467 and 9,237 prisoners respectively."

These figures are almost certainly more accurate than those contained in the media at the time, but it is easy to understand the perception of their cumulative effect.
6. In an interview Bhudu (1995) explained that he founded SAPHOR while he was imprisoned in 1988. Only after his release in mid-1991 did it begin to become active.
7. See s. 13B of the Prisons Act inserted by section 5 of the Prisons Amendment Act 1990. Ironically, the same amending Act also removed formal racially discriminatory provisions from the primary legislation.
8. Some of the many internal prosecutions are recorded in the law reports as the warders, like political prisoners before them, took recourse to the courts to expand their rights: Ciki v. Commissioner of Correctional

Services (1992); Dumbu v. Commissioner of Correctional Services (1992); Loggenberg v. Roberts (1992).

9. Particularly the African National Congress (ANC), the dominant liberation movement and the party that stood to gain most from the prisoner vote.

10. Persons convicted of attempts to commit these crimes could also be barred from voting. The Act could be changed by proclamation. The change was made by Proclamation 85 of April 25, 1994, that is on the day before the election.

11. An account of the history of the Forum as well as various of its reports have been published on the internet as part of the "Penal Lexicon": http://www/demon.co.uk/penlex/

12. By applying the same provisions the Constitutional court also outlawed corporal punishment as a sentence which could be imposed by a court on juveniles and by implication on adults as well: S v. Williams (1995). Corporal punishment as a sentence to be imposed on prisoners for disciplinary infringements had been abolished previously, in 1993, by an amendment to the Correctional Services Act (van Zyl Smit, 1994).

13. How the policy will be implemented remains to be seen. For a more skeptical view, see Achmat and Heywood, 1996.

14. The need for such a development was recognized by the official White Paper on the Policy of the Department of Correctional Services in the New South Africa (Department of Correctional Services, 1994a) and in the more radical Alternative White Paper on Correctional Services which was developed by the Penal Reform Lobby Group (1994), a coalition of NGOs, in response to the official document.

15. The terminology used in the tables and the text reflects South African government usage of the late apartheid era. In particular the term "colored" for people of mixed race origin should be seen in this context. It goes almost without saying that statistics of this kind remain important because of decisions based upon them. The figures in Table 1 were published in an official report while the most recent Annual Report of the Department of Correctional Services does not contain any racially segregated data. The figures contained in Table 2 were however, provided by the Department.

16. Figures for a single day, i.e. for June 30, 1996, were not available, but there is no reason to believe that average figures for the recent month of June 1996 should vary significantly from that of the single day sought.

17. According to estimates provided by the Department of Economics of the University of Stellenbosch the population of South Africa on June 30, 1976 was 26,566,600. (It comprised 4,357,000 whites, 2,485,000 coloreds, 785,100 Asians and 18,965,800 blacks). According to the same source the estimated population of South Africa as a whole on June

30, 1996 was 42,051,900 comprising, according to the same system of classification, 5,253,300 whites, 3,543,300 coloreds, 1,058,500 Asians and 32,196,800 blacks. In order to make comparisons the population of Transkei, 2,397,200 in 1976, should be deducted as in 1976 (but not in 1996). Transkei was regarded by the then-South African government as an independent state and its prisoners were not included in the South African statistics (For purposes of these calculations the population of Transkei has been assumed to have been totally black in 1976).

18. Sentenced prisoners comprised 326 per 100,000 of population on June 30, 1976 and 211 per 100,000 in June 1996. It should be noted that there currently are a sizable number of probationers, that is persons serving sentences of correctional supervision in the community. This sentencing option did not exist 20 years ago. On December 31, 1995, there were 12,214 probationers for whom the Department was responsible (Department of Correctional Services, 1996: 9). They have been left out of the comparative calculations, for it cannot be assumed that they are persons who would have been in prison two decades earlier. Similarly, parolees have not been considered as practices relating to conditional and unconditional release have varied greatly.

19. Information received telephonically from the Department of Correctional services on June 27, 1996.

20. It is very difficult to obtain figures to illustrate this claim fully. However, the 1975/76 Annual Report reveals that 273,393 sentenced prisoners were admitted in the 12 months covered by the Report (Department of Prisons, 1977). In the calendar year 1993, the last year for which such statistics were published, the equivalent figure was that 120,781 sentenced prisoners were admitted in a period of 12 months (Department of Correctional Services, 1994).

21. At the current (August 1996) exchange rate R 61.30 is US $13.47.

References

Achmat, Z. and Heywood, M. (1996) "'The weakest amongst us': Managing HIV in South African Prisons." *Imbizo*, 2: 11–18.

Africa Watch and Prison Project. (1994) *Prison Conditions in South Africa*. New York: Human Rights Watch.

Bhudu, G.M. (1995) "Interview with an Activist." *Imbizo*, 3/4: 34–46.

Breytenbach, B. (1984) *The Confessions of an Albino Terrorist*. Emmarentia: Taurus.

Brittain, V. and Minty, A.S. (1988) *Children of Resistance*. London: Kliptown Books.

Cape Times, February 3, 1990.

Cape Times, July 17, 1991.

Cape Times, March 8, 1996.

Cape Times, August 5, 1996.

Corry, T.M. (1977) *Prison Labor in South Africa*. Cape Town: NICRO.

Department of Correctional Services. (1994) *Annual Report for the Period 1 January 1993 to 31 December 1993*. Pretoria: Government Printer.

Department of Correctional Services. (1994a) *White Paper on the Policy of the Department of Correctional Services in the New South Africa*. Pretoria: Government Printer.

Department of Correctional Services. (1995) *Annual Report for the Period 1 January 1994 to 31 December 1994*. Pretoria: Government Printer.

Department of Correctional Services. (1995a) *Work Group Report: Health Care Services in South African Prisons*. Pretoria: Government Printer.

Department of Correctional Services. (1996) *Annual Report for the Period 1 January 1995 to 31 December 1995*. Pretoria: Government Printer.

Department of Prisons. (1977) *Report for the Period 1 July 1975 to 30 June 1976*. Pretoria: Government Printer.

Die Burger, August 20, 1996.

Die Burger, August 23, 1996.

Dissel, A. (1996) "South Africa's Prison Conditions: The Inmates Talk." *Imbizo*, 2: 4–10.

Giffard, C. (1996) "'Salute Culture' defies quick fix." *Democracy in Action*, 10(3): 19–20.

Gordon, L. et al. (eds.) (1978) *A Survey of Race Relations in South Africa 1977*. Johannesburg: South African Institute of Race Relations.

Haesler, W.T. (1986) "Sdafrikanischer Strafvollzug. Eindrucke einer Studienreise in September/October 1984." *Zeitschrift fr Strafvollzug und Strafflligenhilfe*, 35: 11–17.

Keightley, R. (1993) "Political Offenses and Indemnity in South Africa." *South African Journal on Human Rights*, 9: 334–357.

Kriegler Commission. (1995) *Report of the Commission of Inquiry into Unrest in Prisons* (constituted in terms of Proclamation R 125 of 1 July 1994 read with the Commissions Act 8 of 1947). Pretoria: Government Printer.

Mandela, N.R. (1994) *Long Walk to Freedom*. Randburg: MacDonald Purnell.

Mathews, A.S. (1986) *Freedom, State Security and the Rule of Law: Dilemmas of the Apartheid Society*. Cape Town: Juta.

Mihálik, J. (1989) "Restrictions on Prison Reporting: Protection of the Truth or a Licence for Distortion?" *South African Journal on Human Rights*, 5: 406–430.

NACOCS. (1996) Memorandum of 18 February 1996 on the Inquiry into the Release Policy of the Department of Correctional Services and the Disciplinary Structures for Prisoners. Pretoria: National Advisory Council on Correctional Services.

Penal Reform Lobby Group. (1995) *An Alternative White Paper on Correctional Services*. Mimeographed Report.

Rudolph, H. (1979) "Man's Inhumanity to Man Makes Countless Thousands Mourn: Do Prisoners Have Rights?" *South African Law Journal*, 96: 640–650.

Skelton, A. (1996) "Rethinking the Issue of Children in Prison." *Rights*, 1: 20–24.

Sloth-Nielsen, J. (1995). "Juvenile Justice Review 1994–1995." *South African Journal of Criminal Justice*, 8: 331–343.

Sloth-Nielsen, J. (1996) "Pre-trial Detention of Children Revisited: Amending S 29 of the Correctional Services Act." *South African Journal of Criminal Justice*, 9: 60–72.

van Wyk, D.H., van Niekerk, B., Nairn, R.G., and Taitz, J. (1979) "Four notes on Goldberg v. Minister of Prisons." *South African Journal of Criminal Law and Criminology*, 3: 52–79.

van Zyl, E. (1996) Letter, April 1996, with Appendices from the Deputy Commissioner of Correctional Services, E. van Zyl.

van Zyl Smit, D. (1984) "Public Policy and the Punishment of Crime in a Divided Society: A Historical Perspective on the South African Penal System." *Crime and Social Justice*, 21–22: 146–162.

van Zyl Smit, D. (1987) "'Normal' Prisoners in an 'Abnormal' Society? A Comparative Perspective on South African Prison Law and Practice." *Criminal Justice Ethics*, 6: 37–51.

van Zyl Smit, D. (1992) *South African Prison Law and Practice*. Durban: Butterworths.

van Zyl Smit, D. (1994) "Prisoners' Rights." *South African Human Rights Yearbook*, 5: 268–280.

Case Law

Ciki v. Commissioner of Correctional Services 1992 (2) SA 269 (E).

Dumbu v. Commissioner of Correctional Services 1992 (1) SA 58 (E).

Goldberg v. Minister of Prisons 1979 (1) SA 14 (A).

Hassim v. Officer Commanding, Prison Command, Robben Island 1973 (3) SA 462 (C).

Loggenberg v. Roberts 1992 (1) SA 393 (C).

Minister of Justice v. Hofmeyr 1993 (3) SA 131 (A).

Mandela v. Minister of Prisons 1983 (1) SA 938 (A).

Rossouw v. Sachs 1964 (2) SA 551 (A).

S v. Makwanyane 1995 (3) SA 391 (CC).

S v. South African Associated Newspapers 1970 (1) SA 469 (W).

S v. Williams 1995 (3) SA 332 (CC).

Statutes

Correctional Services Act (formerly Prisons Act) 8 of 1959.

Correctional Services and Supervision Matters Amendment Act 122 of 1991.

Criminal Procedure Act 51 of 1977.

Criminal Procedure Second Amendment Act 75 of 1995.

Constitution of the Republic of South Africa, Act 200 of 1993.

Constitution of the Republic of South Africa 1996 (Draft)

Electoral Act 202 of 1993.

Prisons Amendment Act 75 of 1965.

Prisons Amendment Act 92 of 1990.

Chapter
FOURTEEN

Conclusion: Imprisonment at the Millennium 2000— Its Variety and Patterns Throughout the World[1]

Robert P. Weiss

TOWARD A NEW WORLD (DIS)ORDER

It is not hyperbole to characterize the millennium 2000 as marking a "new world order." The primary force in this transformation is economic "globalization,"[2] and its guiding ideology is "neoliberalism."[3] Together, they have had a devastating impact on millions of workers throughout the world. Rapid advances in technology and increased international competition have over the last 20 years precipitated a massive migration of employment opportunities away from the advanced industrial nations of the West. The social effects of long-term wage stagnation and persistently high levels of unemployment have been aggravated by a neoliberal public policy of gutting New Deal social protections and shrinking the postwar Western European welfare state.

The majority of workers and peasants in the emerging-market nations are also suffering a drop in living standards while a propertied elite gets richer.[4] Economic liberalization in China, neoliberal economics in Latin America and laissez-faire capitalist "shock therapy" (Skidelsky, 1995: 142) administered to former Communist states have suddenly exposed tens of millions of workers to the harsh logic (or "illogic") of free market forces. Eastern Europeans are free of Communism, but millions are also unemployed, without health care, social security or safe streets. Millions of Chinese peasants have been liberated from their traditional dependence on land, and also from employment. A large reserve army of rural labor drives down Chinese labor costs and fuels the rapid growth of the urban capitalist economy, widening the inequality between city and countryside. The social contradictions of globalization have fueled social and political unrest throughout the world. The political reaction has been increasingly repressive, as leaders struggle to maintain a social order conducive to capitalist investment.

Comparing Prisons Systems is the first study to examine penal change on a worldwide basis in relation to recent social structural change. Nations from every continent except Antarctica are represented and, as expected, they exhibit a wide array of commonalities and differences. But the most encompassing factor determining penal policy across nations is globalization. Criminology and penology have not kept abreast of developments in the world's political economy. The source of this lacuna is obvious: The great diversity of nations—each with its distinctive cultural traditions, populations, regional tensions and economic systems—means a myriad of distinctive approaches to criminal justice.

Although the differences among the nations of this volume are great, comparative analysis reveals fundamental commonalities when penal trends—such as incarceration rates, prison admission rates, sentence lengths, prison conditions and prisoner rights—are compared to "common social, economic, or political denominators" (Vagg, 1993: 541–542) across a range of countries. A pattern of declining liberality and growing intolerance is unmistakably the most outstanding feature of world penal systems, and this repressive policy derives from a common overarching reality: Prisons throughout the world are expected to manage a rapidly increasing "surplus population."[5]

Inequality, Democracy, and Penal Repression

The U.N. reports that in 1995 a billion adults worldwide are either unemployed or underemployed (*New York Times*, November 26, 1996), and the fundamental transformation of work now underway will force tens of millions more into permanent unemployment. At the same time, nation-state competition places great pressure on national governments to reduce transfer payments in order to lower the corporate tax burden, further aggravating inequality. Growing income inequality undermines democracy by generating a spiral of repression and delegitimation (Robinson, 1995). As the condition of the working class declines and the general welfare deteriorates, political leaders seek to bolster legitimacy (and deter the surplus population from crime) by the centuries-old remedy of exploiting popular resentment against welfare "dependents" and "soft" prison conditions.[6]

The surplus population of the new world order creates niches in the informal economy, including the underground economy of prostitution, petty theft, local and international drug dealing and violence (Borón, 1996: 328). The research of Merva and Fowles (1996) reveals a strong correlation between growing wage inequality and violent crimes. But crime is not the whole of story of penal repression. Imprisonment rates vary independently of crime rates, most notably in our volume, for the US, Japan, Germany, Italy, The Netherlands and Poland before the fall of the Soviet Union (Greenberg, 1980: 201). Unemployment, not crime rates, has the most consistent relationship to incarceration in capitalist countries, as researchers have demonstrated in studies on a variety of industrial nations (Wallace, 1981; Greenberg, 1977; Sabol, 1989; Inverarity and McCarthy, 1988; Hale, 1989), *with the important exceptions* of Japan, The Netherlands and Poland before 1989.[7] Japan and The Netherlands have maintained low incarceration rates regardless of variation in unemployment rates, and the most outstanding social feature these two nations have in common is their low degree of inequality. And, in the case of The Netherlands, which has a much higher unemployment rate, a comprehensive welfare assistance program (transfer income) has helped counter increasing loss of labor income.

But, elsewhere in the industrial world, more coercive and exclusionary forms of social control are legitimated by heightened anxiety about crime. Amidst extreme inequality and high unemployment,

egregious examples of crime are used by the media and politicians
to exploit public insecurity and generate a severe "penal climate"
(Melossi, 1985). Rhetoric about drug mafias and illegal immigrants
helps deflect attention away from the social structure and its ruling
power arrangements. Moreover, in the developing world, chronic
social instability scares tourists and capital investors.[8] Managing
the specter and reality of crime will be a principal challenge con-
fronting rulers, both in "developed" and Third World nations. In
developing countries, the reconstruction of legal systems has played a
pivotal role in the process of establishing market economies. The
newly-liberated nations of Central and Eastern Europe began draft-
ing new constitutions and revamping their legal procedures even
before democratic elections. But, as the case of Poland reveals, legal
ideals formulated in revolutionary fervor have been severely taxed
by the subsequent crime wave and current popular law-and-order
reaction. In China, at "the local level, there is tremendous resentment of the small number of people who have become rich. This
has caused dramatic increases in crime and occasional riots"
(Overholt, 1996: 77). Recent economic reform in Latin America has
increased foreign investment and stimulated growth, most notably
in Chile, Argentina and Ecuador, but privatization and fiscal
restraint have caused much additional suffering—increased hunger,
disease, drug use and trafficking, criminal violence and the proliferation of shantytowns and street children. Latin American economic
reform has done little to mitigate the negative balance of payments
situation (Magdoff, 1992; Wysocki, 1996), the principal reason for
the neglect of social welfare, and so the future is being mortgaged
as well.

While the collapse of the apartheid regime in South Africa was
not a direct consequence of globalization, the new government's
success will largely hinge on developments in the political economy.
Primarily racist, Afrikaner economic policy neglected modern corporate business principles and left the nation's economy in a seriously disadvantaged position to compete on the world market
(Marcuse, 1995). The nation's low level of economic growth, high
unemployment (about 40%, as it is in US urban ghettos), tremendous inequality and rampant criminal violence threaten that
nation's future political stability and its move toward democracy.
Increasing inequality is antithetical to democratic processes.

The *advanced capitalist nations* have increased their reliance on
penal repression to help control a growing underclass left out of the

"Third Industrial Revolution" of numerical control and advanced computers (Rifkin, 1995: xvi; 60). United States policy over the last two decades is the world's outstanding example of repression over redistribution in advanced "democratic" industrial nations. The number of young men in state and federal prisons increased five-fold in the last 25 years, to mark the highest incarceration rate in the world after Russia. (The combined US jail and prison rate on December 31, 1995, was 600 per 100,000). This was also a period of widening income and wealth disparity (Holmes, 1996; Wolff, 1995). The watershed year was 1970, the year when the nation reached its apogee of equality (Fischer et al., 1996: 105), and, not coincidentally, a nadir of prison incarceration (96 per 100,000, the lowest rate since 1925). The gap between the rich and poor is wider today than at any time since the New Deal, when corporate liberalism replaced laissez-faire ideology.

Casualties from the informal economy in illegal drugs take the lion's share of new prison commitments, as the rates of other crimes have been in long-term stabilization or decline. Not only have prison commitments increased, but the quality of the penal experience has turned more severe. Prison regimes have divested themselves of all vestiges of rehabilitation. Stripped of such "luxuries" as drug treatment programs, higher education and meaningful industrial programs, state prisons have become a form of internal banishment for the "surplus population" of young African-American and Hispanic men, many of whom will never see legitimate gainful employment.

African Americans are disproportionately vulnerable to the global transformation of the labor market (Stewart, 1996). Together with young Hispanics, these minorities are "unruly groups" (Feely and Simon, 1992; Bourgois, 1995) targeted for management by intimidation. On the near horizon is a large crime-prone age-cohort with a nasty penchant for violence, and the latest proposed strategy is to imprison youthful offenders in less-costly adult facilities (Bennett, Dilulio and Walters, 1996), and reduce the minimum age of federal execution to 16.

This is a far cry from the origin of the penitentiary 200 years ago, when Revolutionary America served as a model for humane and progressive penal innovation. In Chapter 1, Dario Melossi and Mark Letierre chart the history of the penal system in the United States as a history of the inclusion and exclusion of select populations in the project of building a democracy. A brief examination of the liberal origins of the penitentiary will help our understanding of the current social transformation and its impact on punishment. The United States is our example because it serves as a world model, especially for emerging-market nations. The US government also exerts direct and indirect financial and diplomatic pressure on weaker reluctant nations. The penitentiary originated in the United States, and its evolution there is an instructive reminder of the crucial relation between democracy, punishment and changes in political economy.

The Great Transformation

Although the intellectual seeds of the penitentiary were European in origin (Hirsch, 1992), they lay dormant for centuries, finally germinating in the soil of the American political and industrial revolutions of the late 18th and early 19th centuries. The creation of a national economy, the beginnings of the factory system, technological development and, on the level of social relations, the new self-regulating market economy and the liberal state that promoted it, required a profoundly different relationship between individual and society than characterized colonial America. "When market conditions became the exclusive determinant of whether a man was paid well or badly, or whether or not he found employment at all, a decisive social transformation had taken place," concludes Stephen Thernstrom (1964), in his classic study of social mobility in a mid-19th century American city. By the second quarter of the 19th century—the so-called Jacksonian period—the proliferation of wage-earners in rapidly growing towns and cities began to displace, as mainstays of social order, the personal relationships and "family discipline" of the farm and cottage craft system.

Liberalism inspired new forms of social discipline to complement the working of the market economy. The "emergence of the penitentiary in the United States was a project *constitutive* of liberal democracy," observes Thomas Dumm (1987: 6) in his study of democracy and punishment. Self-rule "involved not only the establishment of representative government with an extensive suffrage, but also the establishment of institutions that would encourage the internalization of liberal democratic values, the creation of individuals who would learn how to rule their selves." Eastern State Penitentiary at Philadelphia was the centerpiece of this new order. Quaker merchants, professionals and philanthropists—the policy-making elite of the city—developed an expensive and dramatically new institution for the wayward in what they perceived as a free and economically fluid society. Penitentiary advocates sought to shape "a modest, self-interested" (Meranze, 1996: 14) citizen and diligent laborer.

There was a disagreement over just *how* to achieve this reclamation—manifested in the great debate over the Auburn and Pennsylvania models—but little question about the prospects for individual reform. The Auburn plan—based on manufacturing and factory training to prepare convicts for gainful employment—won out in the labor-hungry northern United States, while over the subsequent century 300 prisons in Northern Europe, Russia, China, Japan, South America and across the British Empire came to be based on the Pennsylvania System. Regardless of which version, "laboratories of virtue" (Meranze, 1996) or "ideal factories" (Melossi, 1987; Rusche and Kirchheimer, 1968; Ignatieff, 1978), they shared the common objective of reform through the inculcation of the habits of labor and good citizenship.

Without romanticizing the Jacksonian prison experience, the new Republic's carceral discipline *was* a measure of America's optimism about society and the perfectibility of humankind. In a nation where "everybody who wants work can find work, if the lowest social class consists of unskilled workers and not of wretched unemployed workers," argues Georg Rusche in his 1933 essay, "Labor Market and Penal Sanction" (Rusche, 1978: 4), "then punishment is required to make the unwilling work, and to teach other criminals that they have to content themselves with the income of an honest worker." Political leaders could still assume that there was enough property for everyone, even if the reality was that most of the upward mobility was within the working ranks.[9]

The new millennium stands in stark contrast. With an extensive labor surplus today, the foundation of penal liberalism is missing. Because prisoner welfare is entirely a matter of humanitarian sentiment, it is no surprise that the US is again in the forefront of penal developments—not as a liberal exemplar, but in the promotion of such retrograde slave punishments as striped uniforms, chain gangs and rock busting. This is a difference between a society mobilizing a labor force, and one trying to put one on ice. The cogent force behind unemployment in the industrialized countries is demonstrated by investor concern over its effect on inflation: News of a sharp drop in unemployment sends the US stock market into a tailspin (Gilpin, 1996; *New York Times*, June 9, 1996).

New Transformations

Championed by the UK (as "monetarism"), then the US and Australia, neoliberalism revives the "survival of the fittest" philosophy that had its heyday in the US from the late 19th century until the 1929 crash of the stock market. This "laissez-faire" economic doctrine abandons full-employment policy and opposes state welfare arrangements. It also invites the return of the inhumane prison conditions of the Great Depression in the United States. In the cogent words of Kari Polanyi Levitt (1995: 6–7), the reintroduction of the market society is again giving:

> ...priority of individual economic advancement over societal objectives of collective well-being and elemental social justice ... creating a culture of alienation manifested in the rise of crime, violence, xenophobia, and the general cheapening of human life. There is a pervasive sense of insecurity and fear in the West. In developing countries, the privileged elites have long lived behind protective walls, guarded by razor wire and fierce dogs. In the former socialist countries, a primitive form of robber capitalism is practiced in the streets of major cities.

While an interconnected global elite of incredible wealth and power is emerging, three billion of the world's people live on less than $2.00 a day. The social crisis is global, and the solution to the prison problem requires global action. By helping to establish the gross parameters of the crisis, the following review of the chapters in our volume is intended to provide a context with which to begin seeking a solution.

Variations to Globalizing Forces

The "global economy" finds different expression in each of the four continental regions of our reader. There is not only homogenization but differentiation between and within regions and nations, and a complex interaction between localism and globalism is unfolding. For instance, various bilateral agreements and regional trade blocs, such as the European Union (EU), the Asian-Pacific Economic Cooperation (APEC), Mercosur (Paraguay, Uruguay, Argentina and Brazil) and the North American Free Trade Agreement (NAFTA), which were formed to help mitigate some of the pains of international competition, tie together advanced industrialized nations with "emerging market" nations, as well as advanced capitalist nations with one another. These agreements directly and indirectly have an impact on penal strategies and policies of member nations. As we will argue in our conclusion, they have potential as vehicles for a more progressive penal policy.

Each emerging-market nation has its own distinctive political and economic history of imperialist oppression and resistance. Whether advanced or emerging-market, nations that are similar economically but culturally different sometimes take considerably different approaches to punishment. In this volume, the examples of Japan and the US, The Netherlands and the UK, Poland and Hungary, and Venezuela and Ecuador come to mind (see Graphs 1 and 2). Likewise, Australia, Canada and the US exhibit tremendous variation in incarceration rates within national borders (in the US, from 1650 per 100,000 in the District of Columbia, to 85 in North Dakota). Some socialist and capitalist nations have shared similar penal strategies and methods. Rich in detail, Comparing Prison Systems should help lay the groundwork for more sophisticated future social and cultural explanations for these patterns and variations.

We begin our discussion of Comparing Prison Systems with a focus on penal change and recent social structural developments in China, a nation across the globe from the penitentiary's origin. While culturally and politically as distinct from the United States as any society in the world, China and the US have a common history of utilizing labor in prisoner rehabilitation. This is a fundamental point of convergence, an examination of which can help shed light on social change and penal developments in both countries.

GLOBALIZATION AND PUNISHMENT IN EMERGING-MARKET NATIONS

Labor has been central to penal reform in *China* for over a century. Michael Dutton and Xu Zhangrun begin Chapter 10 with the argument that China's policy of "reform through labor" is not a "socialist new thing," as critic Harry Wu and Chinese officials alike assert; rather, it has indigenous and imported elements. It is neither "ruthless economic exploitation," nor merely liberating and transformational. "The Chinese system of reform through labor," the authors observe, "is, in many ways, a continuation of the dream of the early [Western] penal reform movement." The notion of labor as educative was borrowed from Western culture, imported in the late 19th century by China's last dynasty, along with a whole array of Western technologies, "in a desperate bid to modernize and appear 'civilized'..." (p. 295).

The Communist innovation was to wed "thought reform" to labor reform. Thought reform employs moral persuasion, principally through the influence of "prison cadres" who act as moral guides to help effect a "total transformation" of the malefactor. The notion of change through moral persuasion, or *ganhua*, is Confucian in origin, but has been neatly wedded with the Marxian notion of brotherhood and total social transformation. Criminals are encouraged to empathize with their victims, evoking a sense of shame as a vehicle of reintegration. Under the communist system, prison labor was also a vital component of this transformation. Prisoners worked at productive enterprises that contributed to the state plan and which prepared them for productive activity upon release.

Economic reforms initiated in 1978 changed China rapidly and profoundly in five major ways. First, the introduction of capitalist values of materialism and individualism contradict the collective customs and traditions upon which a "socialist ethic" or "reintegrative shaming" (Braithwaite, 1989) is based. Second, the increased geographic mobility required by free labor markets is eliminating locally-based informal social controls. Third, massive migration to the cities and growing unemployment generate a "problem population" of "floating elements" that become the objects of police attacks. This disciplinary process, Dutton and Xu argue, is reminiscent of Marx's description of the 16th-century "pincher movement" at the birth of capitalism in England, where Enclosure laws pressed landless peasants on the one side, and anti-vagrancy laws, on the other. Fourth, the internal regime of prisons has been drastically altered by economic reforms, especially those that have required prison industry to compete in the free market. Furthermore, former employers are no longer obligated to take back released prisoners. Finally, these market effects take place at a time of dramatic change in the nature and extent of crime, and an increase in recidivism. The introduction of capitalist markets has led to the reappearance of wealth, decentralization of authority and the disappearance of communist neighborhood committees, precipitating rising levels of violence, prostitution, armed robbery and drug trafficking.

As elsewhere among developing states, prosperity itself brings more crime and police corruption. Since China opened its borders and began decentralizing state power, the world drug trade has turned the mountains and rainforests of southwestern China into "a region of rampant crime, drug trafficking, gun running, prostitution and the spread of the AIDS virus" (Tyler, 1995a: A6). In Shanghai, cocaine and heroin are increasingly popular with those best able to afford drugs, young merchants and entrepreneurs. The generation in their 20s and 30s possesses more money but are alienated, "rootless and disenchanted with the post-Communist system" (Tyler, 1995a: A6). While the new Chinese bourgeois consume cocaine like Wall Street celebrants of the 1980s, unemployed peasants find economic opportunity in trafficking for local and global bourgeois drug needs.

These developments call for new and innovative approaches to crime control. But, "Chinese penal strategies show a poverty of imagination," Dutton and Xu argue (Chapter 10: 294). This is because the penal regime "cannot shake off its attachment to a Marxian inspired frame of reference." Unlike the Eastern and Central European political elite, the Chinese elite were deeply committed to communist values. Within the prison system, this has caused bizarre incongruities: "The various methods designed to imbue a selfless socialist work ethic among prisoners seem strangely archaic in a period when the dominant social ethos presents material accumulation as glorious" (p. 294). Various stop-gap supplements to imprisonment, spreading an ever-widening carceral net, suggest serious problems of human rights abuse that are largely ignored by Western human rights discussions.

***

The people of *Poland* had great hope for change after the 1989 fall of Communist domination, especially in the reform of criminal justice. Many of the new ministers and members of Parliament had served time in prison, and they were painfully aware of the role of the old prison system in political repression and labor exploitation. Several prison strikes, which gained widespread public sympathy, led to a general amnesty of prisoners in 1989. Reforms stopped, however, soon after the release of other political prisoners early in post-Communist period. Although prisons are no longer used to enforce political conformity, and the forced penal labor regime was quickly abolished, the reality today is that penal conditions have not improved and incarceration rates are climbing. Penal labor has not been replaced with meaningful work in prison, nor are there jobs upon release. Competitive conditions among free citizens are so bad that the Polish level of less eligibility cannot even tolerate uncompensated penal labor! Polish prisons today are overcrowded and regimented warehouses for the idle.

In Chapter 9, Monika Płatek offers four explanations for the stalled reform in Poland since 1989: a "crime wave"; the persistence of old elites in the new era; increasing inequality and unemployment; and Polish culture. A crime wave in the post-Communist period has been fueled by the capitalist "shock therapy" administered to Poland, which brought—along with the fastest economic growth in Europe—rising unemployment, growing inequality, retrenchment of public welfare and the breakup of central authority. A "buccaneer capitalism" has replaced Poland's planned economy, with an "opportunity to make a killing" atmosphere (Perlez, 1995) that blurs the line between theft and fraud on the one hand, and legitimate business activity on the other. Innumerable civil disputes and rampant street crime are effectively out of state control. The new police are well-meaning but sorely underfunded, and the courts creaky (Newman, 1991). Widespread disillusionment with an ineffective criminal justice system has motivated thousands to take law and order in their own hands (Perlez, 1995; 1996b).

Popular demands for law and order and increasing punitiveness recently found expression in a 30,000-strong student march protesting the murder of a university student; many carried placards calling for the death penalty (Perlez, 1995; 1996b). The principle of less eligibility is very strong in Poland today and, Płatek reports, there is great resentment over even basic creature amenities for prisoners. The new authorities are not politically disinclined, therefore, to return to the prison repression of the old order. Officials are also predisposed because, while there has been an almost complete turnover of low-level prison staff, middle and top government functionaries (apparatchiks) are still in place. While the Polish economy has changed dramatically since 1989, the polity remains basically unchanged from the late Communist period.

Discontent with economic developments helped to elect the current President, Aleksander Kwáśniewski, who is a former junior minister in the Communist government. His election was not so much an act of nostalgia for the old Communist order as it was an example of the persistence of post-Communist elites throughout Eastern Europe. Elite continuity was the key to the peaceful transition from Communist to post-Communist governments, theorize Higley, et al. (1996). The smooth transition of former members of the political and economic elites into the post-Communist system was predicated on their shallow commitment to Communism, as well as some deft maneuvering and clever bridgework during the long transition period to ensure involvement in joint state-private ventures and other institutional carryovers.

But the depth of Kwásniewski's commitment to neoliberalism or to genuine democracy must also be questionable. According to elite theories of power, smooth transitions (i.e., high continuity of elites) help budding democracies by limiting internecine conflict. But, if transitions are too smooth, opposition groups do not take hold and nations veer toward authoritarianism. High degrees of elite continuity "go hand-in-hand with post communist regimes that hide the substance of authoritarianism behind a veneer of democratic forms," argue Higley, et al. (1996: 138). "Beyond a relatively high threshold, in other words, the relationship between elite continuity and democratic progress becomes inverse."

Authoritarian methods now used on behalf of "law and order" in Poland help support a class system of increasing inequality. Polish officials claim to be looking Westward (Perlez, 1996a) for public policy models, which is bad enough, but there is also a great danger that some of the former Soviet-dominated states might be tempted to adopt the East Asian model of "new authoritarianism" (or "Asian authoritarianism"). Singapore, Taiwan, South Korea (and to a lesser extent, Malaysia and Indonesia) have produced astonishing economic growth, social order and general prosperity under charismatic authoritarians. Singapore's lack of political corruption, for instance, is attributed to Lee Kuan Yew's austere moral example. But Samuel P. Huntington (1996c: 12) warns:

> Yet while authoritarian rule may provide good government for a decade, or even a generation, it cannot provide—and throughout history never has provided—good government over a sustained period of time. It lacks the institutions of self reform.....

A big obstacle to Poland's quest for democracy is a lack of knowledge and experience in the basics of the rule of law and a long cultural history of authoritarian domination, Płatek points out. But, she also counter-argues that Poland has a long tradition of mass resistance movements that provide hope for democracy.

A comparison of Poland with Hungary over the next decade might be especially useful in measuring the impact of inequality on imprisonment. Hungary's economic stratification is among the least pronounced in the world (Crossette, 1996), and although both Poland and Hungary are today in the middle range of punitiveness as measured by incarceration rates (see Graph 1; Walmsley, 1995: 9),[10] Hungary does have the lower rate. On the other hand, Hungarian public opinion supports a high degree of *political intolerance*, even while favoring generous social welfare benefits (Higley, et al., 1996: 472). Although it has greater extremes of family income, Poland's growth rate has created the largest and has the most stable middle class of the former Soviet bloc nations, comprising an estimated 10–15% of the population (Perlez, 1996). Will this middle class grow and become a force for civil and political equality? Or will its insecurity support more repression?

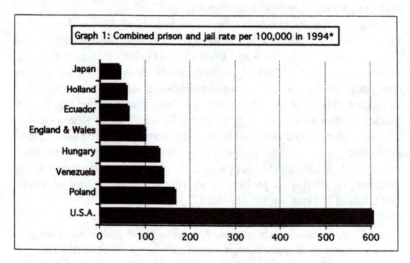

Graph 1 *Rate for convicted and pre-trial detention inmates per 100,000 general population.
Sources: US: US Department of Justice, Bureau of Justice Statistics Bulletin, "Prison and Jail Inmates, 1995"; Eastern Europe: Walmsley (1995: 9, 41); Andean Region: del Olmo, Chapter 4; The Netherlands, UK data for 1993: Human Development Report 1996: 190; Japan data for 1990: Christie (1993: 29).

***

Generalization about a region as large and culturally diverse as *Latin America* is difficult. But, aside from extraordinary inequality, one reality all Latin American nations share in common is a grim prison situation. Conditions are appalling by any international standard of humanity. In Chapter 5 on the Andean region, Rosa del Olmo argues that the central characteristic of Latin American prisons is the large number of "prisoners without sentence" (see Graph 2). Thousands of hapless suspects are held for years in idle and overcrowded prisons without benefit of trial, a practice that constitutes an international human rights issue. The constitutions of all Latin American governments, as those in the former Soviet Communist states, declare humane treatment and rehabilitation as guiding principles. But, there is a glaring gap between legal rights enshrined in constitutions and legal codes, and criminal justice in practice, which makes a

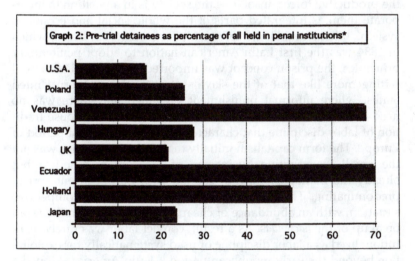

Graph 2 *European data for 1994; US 1995; Japan 1990; Ecuador and Venezuela, 1994.

Sources: US: US Department of Justice, Bureau of Justice Statistics Bulletin, "Prison and Jail Inmates, 1995"; Eastern Europe: Walmsley (1995: 9,41); Andean Region: del Olmo, Chapter 4; The Netherlands, UK data for 1993: Human Development Report 1996: 190; Japan data for 1990: Christie (1993: 29).

mockery of penology as a science. In Latin American prisons, "rehabilitation is not even a concept" (NACLA Report, 1996: 16).

"For five centuries," observes Eduardo Galeano (1989: 119), "Latin
American history has been a history of continued disjunction
between reality and words." The prison was a cultural importation
to Latin America, according to Galeano, imposed by the traditional
elite in a bout of cultural imitation. Colombia's Penal Code of 1837
stipulated incarceration as the principal measure of punishment,
part of the faithful reproduction of constitutional models of the
most "civilized" countries of the time. The trouble with this,
Galeano (p. 120) observes, was that "we had bourgeois constitutions without ever having a bourgeois revolution or a bourgeoisie."

Latin America did not have the social structural conditions associated with the penitentiary's origin in Europe and the United
States, according to Jesús Antonio Muñoz Gómez, who applies to
the case of Colombia the Rusche and Kirchheimer (1968) thesis that
"systems of punishment tend to correspond to the development of
the productive forces, insofar as the society is in a position to incorporate them as integrated parts of the whole social and economic
system" (Shank and Dod, 1987: xiv).[11] For instance, in Brazil, which
in 1834 was the first Latin American nation to adopt penitentiary
principles, the prison concept was imported into a social structural
setting more like that of the slave system of the southern United
States, where informal punishment prevailed and there was no
need for a penal science. There was certainly no workhouse tradition of labor discipline that characterized the mercantilist period of
Europe. The form capitalism initially took in Latin America was not
the small, competitive businesses of Jacksonian America, but
already the monopoly form of capital, with European enterprises
predominating. These early industries enjoyed a non-competitive
situation, with an abundance of cheap labor set free from the rapid
breakup of the *haciendas*. As a result, convict labor was rarely institutionalized as a labor discipline or used systematically for exploitation beyond the early republican period.[12] Latin America skipped a
stage instead and began where post-industrial nations have recently
arrived: disciplining a largely urban surplus population.

Because of their anachronistic introduction, prisons remained in
practice a secondary form of social control (after the Church and
the *encomienda*, a form of indentured servitude) until Latin
America's capitalist industrial "take off" of the 1930s, when
"import substitution" was the model adopted.[13] Rapid industrial

growth and urbanization ensued under populist regimes, most notably those of Juan Perón of Argentina and Getulio Vargas of Brazil, leaders who drew on urban working-class support. Employment in the large state sector and a primitive social safety net helped buffer the urban working class.

But import substitution was a model with numerous defects. Besides shoddy and overpriced products of protected state industries, extractive export industries had devastating consequences for the environment, poverty was not reduced and the income gap between city and countryside widened. Hyperinflation, the consequence of printing ever greater sums of money in an effort to appease everyone, dogged political leaders. Trade deficits soared, and debt crisis deepened, especially with the oil price increases of 1979 and the collapse of commodity prices in the early 1980s.

This economic tumult coincided with a decade (1972–82) of military rule, after which a new generation of civilian governments was forced to seek foreign loans from the International Monetary Fund (IMF) and the World Bank, contingent upon policies promoting greater free market orientation. Neoliberal economics in Latin America has been adopted with varying degrees of enthusiasm and commitment, with the stronger neoliberal regimes breaking their connection with labor. Urban masses are now asked to join the sacrifice long endured by the peasantry.

Neoliberalism has been advanced by a variety of political forms. *Peru's* "autocratic neoliberalism," however, is one of the most unusual and yet forceful today. Populism is a political form most economists previously thought was antithetical to neoliberalism (under the theory that capitalism and democracy are fraternal twins). But it turns out to be quite a comfortable fit in the case of Peru, a nation where the top fifth of the population receives over 60% of national income (Braun, 1995: 75). Perhaps the most telling statistic is that "85% of workers do not have full-time jobs" (Sims, 1996c). President Alberto K. Fujimori is the worst human rights offender in the region; Peru has a near-total absence of due process and lack of democratic accountability. The Fujimori type of rule is in the tradition of personalistic leaders, but with the twist that he campaigns against political parties, Congress and the judiciary rather than against the traditional oligarchy. Fujimori's "antipolitics politics"—supported by a coalition of urban middle class, traditional oligarchy and the military—first grew out of public frustration with deepening economic crises and governmental inability to deal with violence, particularly the Shining Path guerrilla movement. Popular disdain for Congress and the judiciary, and widespread cynicism of party politics, legitimized his military-backed *autogolpe* in April 1992, whereby he suspended the Constitution, dissolved Congress and purged the judiciary. This power grab was hugely popular, with a jump of public approval rating to 82% (Roberts, 1995: 98).

State repression is publicly justified as necessary in the war against "political terrorism," and "narcoterrorism," a distinction often conflated in practice. In the Andean nations and in Mexico, criminal justice under neoliberal rule involves not only trying to subdue a horde of destitute petty criminals, but front-line work fighting low-intensity wars and countering mass resistance in the forms of general strikes, riots, looting, demonstrations, protests, street violence and land takeovers. In 1989, for example, a public transport fare increase in Venezuela precipitated riots and looting that killed between 300 and 1500. The region's prisons are filled not only with common criminals, a category that is actually dwindling, but thousands of guerrillas, narcotics traffickers and corrupt politicians.

In Peru as elsewhere in Latin America, the US-sponsored counterinsurgency approach to the "drug war" is a major avenue of support for a repressive and technocratic state anchored in the military. In some nations, the drug war is used also as a cover for the more general fight against low-intensity conflict and political insurgency. The narcotics net catches many who are primarily political deviants, as US aid does not require a neat distinction. Mexico calls self-proclaimed guerrillas common highway bandits. And, in fairness, much like Eric Hobsbawm's (1965) "primitive rebels," the two groups are sometimes difficult to distinguish.

To the chagrin of national business leaders and foreign capitalists, *Ecuador* elected in early June 1996 President Abdalá Bucaram, a flamboyant charismatic known as El Loco (Schemo, 1996a). He waged a ferocious campaign against the "oligarchy" and rode on a backlash against neoliberal reforms that intensified unemployment, increased disease and brought a proliferation of street children and a breakdown in law and order. Even before Bucaram's election, the nation had been a reluctant neoliberal concerning the privatization of its highly protected industrial sector. And well-organized indigenous groups have successfully resisted foreign oil company drilling (Green, 1995: 223). Ecuador enjoys the lowest incarceration rate among those countries in Rosa del Olmo's Andean study, and its prisons have the least violence. But this relatively benign situation might not last much longer because, by January of 1997, Bucaram had reversed course and now embraces neoliberal reforms, including privatization, foreign debt restructuring and the elimination of legal guarantees of job security (Schemo, 1997).

Venezuela's growing poverty and violence has fueled increasing vigilantism (both civilian and police), the very negation of democracy. In Caracas, lynchings of muggers and petty thieves, averaging about one a week now, are broadly popular (Schemo, 1996a). The failure of police and judiciary throughout Latin America has intensified general political cynicism. Despite this lack of confidence, Venezuela managed to increase its incarceration rate dramatically, from 83.8 per 100,000 in 1980 to 147.4 in 1985, a period that included a severe recession. While the rate leveled off to 136.4 during the oil windfall of the US-Iraqi war, their rate remains well above the other Andean nations (see Table 1: 118). Professor del Olmo reports that "Venezuelan prisons are catastrophic, one of the worst [systems] in the American hemisphere, violating the Venezuelan State international obligations on human rights" (p. 132). On October 23, 1996, in one of the worst incidents, National Guardsmen, without provocation, set off a fire in a 12×12 foot cell at Caracas' La Planta jail that killed 25 inmates (*New York Times*, 1996; Schemo, 1996c).

Venezuela recently initiated an economic reform program based on a $1.4 billion dollar loan by the IMF to launch that country's market-oriented economy (Lewis, 1996). Those reforms could aggravate the crime situation even more. Following the example of Chile's recent "growth with equity" policy (Vergara, 1996), however, government officials are seeking "to protect the living standards of the country's two million poorest families from the impact of its austerity measures by giving them additional subsidies" (Lewis, 1996).

Meanwhile, as a means of economic survival, broad sectors of the Andean population are involved in the underground economy of drug production and distribution (del Olmo, 1993: 9). As the focus of the US war against cocaine in Latin America, *Colombia* has been under great pressure to eradicate coca crops and prosecute drug lords and corrupt government officials. But drug profits already have a firm grasp on politics through the twin evils of bribery and subversion. Peasants, who earn far more from coca than legitimate crops, are caught in the middle. Guerrillas of the Revolutionary

Armed Forces control much of the coca crop land, where they agitate for farmer rebellion against the crop eradication program (Schemo, 1996a). At the same time, the drug cartel is busy buying land and, with the help of the military, they have struck a deal whereby they "would help the politicians to cleanse these areas of sundry 'communists,' radicals, and campesino and union leaders" (Carrigan, 1996: 7) for carte blanche on the drug trade.

One thing is certain: Convicted, big-time criminals of all sorts are too powerful to be made to endure the fate of the majority in Latin American prisons. Colombia spends 54% of its prison budget on 1% of its prisoners, money which has built new maximum-security prisons to hold drug traffickers and guerrilla leaders in comfortable seclusion (*New York Times*, 1995). Meanwhile, the thousands of common criminals experience a "rough hewn" justice so deleterious to physical and psychological health as to constitute a war crime.

***

In Chapter 6, Michael Olivero focuses on the impact of the US drug war on penal conditions and criminal justice policy in **Mexico**. Severe economic recession, coupled with a burgeoning prison population, have greatly worsened prison conditions in recent decades. Overcrowding is in large measure a result of the drug war, especially in border prisons, where 90% of the commitments are for drug-related offenses, according to Olivero. US drug consumption, plus US federal drug policy to combat importation, have wreaked havoc on the Mexican prison system. Despite corruption, a burgeoning prison population and inadequate resources, Mexican prisons have positive features regarding prison life, especially in comparison to US prisons. They have a low level of violence and sexual exploitation is uncommon, due in large part, according to Olivero, to the minimal disjuncture between prison life and the free world. As in Colombia, the quality of prison life is scaled to the prisoners' personal budget for corruption. In a sense, Mexican prisons are in the forefront of the privatization movement with a form that at least has the virtue of replicating exactly the class structure of the outside, and without the dishonesty of the old "rehabilitation," nor the political histrionics of today's "less eligibility."

But, the law-and-order issue is broader than drugs. As elsewhere in the region, the lines between crime and insurrection are not always clear. "The degree of income disparity in Mexico is among the worst in the world, and is steadily growing more extreme," observes a *New York Times* (DePalma, 1996a) article on peasant protest. The bottom half of the Mexican population receives only 16% of national income, leaving an estimated 22 million in dire poverty. Living conditions have been harmed even more by the 73% peso devaluation between November of 1994 and February of 1995. The annual inflation rate is nearly 50%. The modernization of agriculture is forcing millions off the land and into cities already crowded with the unemployed and destitute. "Big gains in real wages and economic growth from 1963 to 1984 were wiped out as the previous two presidents followed their open-market policies," continues the *Times* article. Insurrections, train robberies, peasant occupations of luxury estates and guerrilla assaults on infrastructure indicate "a loss of respect for the rule of law and a frightening lack of Government control."

***

To summarize the Latin American situation: Despite the various privatization initiatives that have caused great pain, the region overall continues to lag behind the world's second tier of nations in competitive production. Peru has high rates of economic growth, but at great social cost. In order to survive, millions of the poor are enticed into the informal economy, where the manufacture and distribution of drugs is the most remunerative economic activity. There are other dangers to neoliberal policy. Liberalizing the economy and the polity at the same time creates many opportunities for corruption by politicians, preoccupied with campaign finances, who are auctioning off state-run financial institutions and industries. Liberalization works to "democratize" corruption, according to Eduardo Gamarra, political science professor at Florida Atlantic University (quoted in Moffett and Friedland, 1996: A7), "by opening the system to an aggressive bourgeois that had historically been deprived of political spoils." Mixing *privatization with politics* is not much different from the old *politics and bureaucracy*—perhaps just a different *style* of corruption. This state of affairs is quite favorable for capital at one level, but corruption and inefficiency have gone too far for the long-range interests of corporate capital. Embezzlement, bribery and corporate fraud flourish in a hothouse of billions in foreign investment dollars, venal politicians and an ethics-free bourgeois, making the region unsafe for international capital. *Wall Street Journal* reporters Moffett and Friedland (1996) observe:

> Unfortunately, Latin America's justice system has proved woefully inadequate to police this newly globalized economy... . Latin America is discovering that yoking a modern globalized economy into a creaky judicial system and regulatory apparatus is a blueprint for trouble.

This contradiction might be a blessing in disguise. "The transformation of the world economy in the last 30 years... [offers] little hope for long-term success in the new world order. Rather, neoliberalism is in danger of locking Latin America into a model of export-led growth based on raw materials and cheap labor, leading to growing impoverishment and irrelevance within the global economy," concludes Duncan Green (1995: 206).

***

South Africa recently underwent jolting social and economic change of the magnitude experienced by Eastern and Central Europe. But South Africa is distinctive in that, more than any other nation, its criminal justice system was involved directly in the national labor system: Convicts were forced to perform penal labor in agriculture and for mining companies, much like the convict lease system of the postbellum US South. South Africa's prison system was established during the late 19th-century colonial expansion, and it developed largely out of the enforcement of "pass laws" regulating the labor force in the diamond and gold mines.

The fall of apartheid in 1990 led many reformers to expect a sharp, clean break with the old penal conditions. But Dirk van Zyl Smit reports in Chapter 13 that, at best, South Africa can be characterized as a situation of *continuity and change*. While the explicitly racist features of the system have been removed, the "same monolithic structure" remains. South African prisons continue to incarcerate "roughly the same number of people drawn from the same social groups." Worse, with political prisoners gone, a direct force for change has been removed. As in Poland, the politics change, but the "key players in shaping national economic policy are the same individuals who held power before" (Marcuse, 1995: 46).[14]

The new political order has the same social categories of imprisoned, along with some new ones. The destitute have been joined by thousands of unemployed former resistance fighters in menacing cities, suburbs and countryside. As in Caracas and Warsaw, vigilantism is on the rise (Daley, 1995a; 1996b,c), especially against thieves and street-level drug dealers. With sanctions lifted, the global economy has opened South Africa to the international drug market, making addiction by the nouveau riche—young, white entrepreneurs—a growing problem (Daley, 1996a). Gangs, many of which are centered on the drug trade, have flourished since nonracial elections in 1994, and gang members have become targets for Muslim vigilante groups (Daley, 1996b).

The depressing penal scene in South Africa is the product of several factors that are at work in Eastern and Central Europe and Latin America: (1) street crime, (2) inequality, (3) domination by a proper-tied elite. The future for South Africa is problematic with more than 40% youth unemployment. The nation's current annual growth rate, at 2.8%, is insufficient to overcome high unemployment, especially among the largely uneducated and unskilled black labor force.

GLOBALIZATION AND PUNISHMENT AMONG THE ADVANCED CAPITALIST NATIONS

The Great Depression and World War II were watershed events in the history of punishment. The failure of the world economy based on the self-regulating market represented the "collapse of the 19th century," in Karl Polanyi's (1944) estimation. Defeat of the liberal economic order led directly to the New Deal, Stalinism and Fascism, Polanyi argued, as major political interventions in the market. The diversity of postwar penal and welfare systems reflected these political directions. Stalin continued his forced-labor system of the 1930s into the postwar period (Davies, 1995). After Stalin's death in 1953, there was some reduction of forced labor camps (Davies, 1995), supervised release was introduced and work teams and group responsibility was re-emphasized (from Bolshevik days) that "corresponded to the behavior and values of the broader society. An observer in 1965 commented on the effectiveness of the Soviet work system in measuring up to the standards of outside production" (O'Brien, 1995: 218). The Eastern and Central European Socialist bloc nations also retained the prison as the central penal feature, but introduced "resocialization" programs based on education and job training, and in Hungary a conditional release program. As a group, capitalist nations also exhibited a remarkable divergence in penal policy after the war.

After 1946, the capitalist world divided "between 'carcerating' countries (like the United States, England, Canada) and 'decarcerating' countries (like Italy, Japan and the Scandinavian countries)," Dario Melossi (1989: 4–5) observes in his comparative analysis of *Punishment and Social Structure*. The historical pattern of imprisonment rates in most European and North American countries *prior* to 1945 was cyclical; in Melossi's words, "cycles of punishing behavior" corresponded with business cycles.[15] That connection was moderated or broken in the postwar by nations maintaining the lowest levels of inequality—Japan and the Scandinavian countries, or, in the case of Italy, which had a strong state welfare provision.

Penal policies of England and Wales and *The Netherlands* provide a particularly valuable study in postwar contrasts between carcerating and incarcerating countries. Although England and Wales had a rate half that of The Netherlands in 1945, postwar incarceration rate trajectories moved in opposite directions. Additionally, both nations experienced a rise in the crime rate after 1955 (see Graph 1: 145). By 1975, "the prison population in the Netherlands had been halved, while England and Wales doubled, producing a ratio of 1:4 from rough parity" in 1952, writes David Downes (p. 144). Downes (1988) and Johnson and Heijder (1983) have examined various cultural explanations for "Dutch tolerance," but one social fact stands out: Inequality has been far greater in Britain (Fischer et al., 1996: 124–125). Using 1993 United Nations figures (Crossette, 1996: 21), the average per capita income of the poorest fifth of the population as a percentage of average per capita income for The Netherlands is 41%, for Britain, 23%. This supports the argument that nations with the least inequality are less inclined to generate a "vocabulary of punitive motive" (Melossi, 1989: 10) that encourages penal repression.

The 1950s and 1960s, a period of unprecedented general prosperity in Western industrial countries, was a time when income and wealth inequality decreased substantially (Wilterdink, 1995: 4). Workers were in a favorable bargaining situation because monopoly capital was able to grant generous wage-and-hour concessions and pass the added cost on to consumers (O'Connor, 1973: 23). Even in "carcerating" nations like the US, where imprisonment rates continued a modest climb in the 1950s and early 1960s, prison conditions moderated greatly, especially during the Great Society of President Lyndon B. Johnson. Civil rights legislation and the expanded welfare safety net of the late 1960s made prisoners more "eligible," facilitating the introduction of a prison reform movement, expanded rehabilitation programs and the flowering of a prisoners' rights movement, all while the nation sharply decarcerated.

But humane and sensible penal policy was short-lived, as a rapidly-rising crime rate collided with the world recession of the mid-1970s. This economic crisis was a major turning point in postwar penality.[16] In the United States and elsewhere except Japan, politicians clamored for increased punitiveness. The Netherlands' policy change is the most dramatic, as its incarceration rate has climbed steeply, from 22 per 100,000 in 1975 to a projected 78 in 1996 (see Chapter 5, Graph 2: 146). Downes points to rising rates and changing patterns of crime as causes for this growing intolerance, leading to "a new volatility in the politics of law and order." The Netherlands' low incarceration rate is, to a considerable extent, the product of the nation's tolerance of personal deviance, most notably its rejection of the "war on drugs" (Leuw, 1991). Importantly, the nation's relatively greater income equality has made politicians less tempted to follow the pattern of other Western nations in using deviants as scapegoats for economic hardship. But, inequality in the distribution of wealth and income increased significantly in The Netherlands between 1983 and 1991 (Wilterdink, 1995: 4). Political decisions since then are "buckling the shields" against ignorance and retribution as The Netherlands draws a harder line on drugs and cuts welfare, and as minority groups (many of which are immigrants from former Dutch colonies) "are disproportionately excluded from employment and effective citizenship...[and] are disproportionately involved in street crime." (p. 150).

The Dutch judiciary is holding out. Trends in sentencing are not becoming noticeably more punitive, according to Downes. But how much longer can The Netherlands remain tolerant, especially in its liberal drug policy? France (Newman, 1996) and Germany are the most vociferous European critics of the Dutch cultural attitude toward soft drug use, and they have been joined by EU diplomats in trying to get The Netherlands to crack down. Tightening up the formal and informal regulations governing the cannabis supply services of the Amsterdam "coffee-shops" is already underway.[17]

By imposing strict budgetary, debt and inflationary ceilings on member states, the EU is in other ways exerting considerable pressure on nations trying to meet the Maastricht criteria (Kamm and Rohwedder, 1996). Severe cutbacks in European welfare benefits and a curtailment of generous protective labor legislation have resulted. Hundreds of thousands of Germans (Cowell, 1996), Italians, Austrians, French and Spaniards have engaged in protest demonstrations, crippling strikes and job walkouts to protest this austerity.

In direct criminal justice terms, the EU has required contradictory policy decisions. On the one hand, the EU abides by the European Convention for the Protection of Human Rights and Fundamental Freedoms, which condemns racism and xenophobia, requires abolition of the death penalty and encourages the expansion of prisoner rights. On the other hand, fiscal austerity and the diminution of welfare state provisions are bound to increase penal repression. Furthermore, while the EU is committed to the removal of *internal* border and trade controls to facilitate movement of people, goods and capital investment, it is also strengthening the *external* borders of the EU region. This has resulted in a growing intolerance of illegal immigration, migrants seeking asylum and smuggling offenders. Such intolerance is also reflected in increased penal responses.

***

England and Wales are textbook examples of nations that choose increased punitiveness and legal repression as strategies to cope with economic crises. The 1974–75 recession brought labor disputes, a doubling of male unemployment by 1976, rising crime, increased prison disorder and political reaction. The New Right was given a political boost by a campaign against "moral decay" and "law and order." The Conservative administration of Margaret Thatcher matched Ronald Reagan's in generating a "populist punitiveness," in the words of Mick Ryan and Joe Sim (Chapter 6), marked by an increase in the proportionate use of imprisonment, deteriorating prison conditions and the militarization of the prison service, as well as greater emphasis on prisoner segregation. And even though England began a monumental prison-building program following the 1979 election of the Conservative administration, overcrowding has worsened.

Prison commitments have grown in England and Wales, from 45,817 in 1992 to nearly 54,000 by April of 1996. Three criminal justice factors are at work, according to Ryan and Sim: Courts have increased the number and length of custodial sentences, and time served has increased. This latest "tightening of the penal screw" is the flip side of the claim that "welfare doesn't work." The slogan "prisons work" has been Home Secretary Michael Howard's guiding rationale (echoed, incidentally, by right-wing populist US criminologist John DiIulio in numerous newspaper editorials).

Ryan and Sim also discuss privatization, one of the most interesting of recent penal developments in Britain. Following the example of the US, private corporations are now operating five high security prisons in the UK, and, as in the US (Weiss, 1987: 273), this privatization is helping neoconservatives achieve a dual and seemingly contradictory goal: shrinking of the state bureaucracy while increasing prison capacity, encouraging "managerialism" (see Introduction) and extending penal repression. A former "social expense" has been turned into "social capital" (O'Connor, 1973: 6–7). State expenditures are employed to directly increase private investment profits.

***

Germany represents yet another fascinating and in many ways unique story of change. In 1990, the Federal Republic of Germany (FRG) reunited with the German Democratic Republic (GDR), wedding an economically-backward Communist state with the Western European capitalist growth leader. Both nations shared as social objectives the welfare of workers; but worker productivity was bipolar. The economic impact of unification ($600 billion in subsides, incentives and aid to regions of former East Germany by 1996) staggered the former West Germany, one of the strongest economies in the world at the time. This absorption was especially challenging because West Germany, with about the highest labor costs in the world, was rapidly losing global market competitiveness just as the Germnies were reunited.

Over four million Germans are now unemployed. The Bonn government is preparing to reduce state-financed work projects greatly (Rohwedder, 1996) and to cut the welfare system dramatically in order to make the labor market more "flexible" and to prepare for the Maastricht criteria. Just when Germans need welfare support

the most, the government can least afford it. Under Chancellor
Helmut Kohl's 1997 spending plan, the nation will take cuts "equivalent to 2% of Germany's gross domestic product—which include
proposed cutbacks in pension eligibility, health benefits, and jobless
support" (Roth, 1996). Protests of 300,000 in June and 200,000 in
October of 1996 suggest the political difficulties ahead for austerity.
In Chapter 8, Johannes Feest and Harmut-Michael Weber observe
that social anxiety is being expressed not only in social protest but
in "moral panics on the rise of crime in the course of the unification." These fears are enhanced, no doubt, by knowledge of the far-
reaching amnesty of prisoners from the former GDR.

With an incarceration rate of over 100 per 100,000 by 1968, West
Germany already had been among nations with the highest rates in
postwar Europe. But West German incarceration rates have been
cyclical since then, starting with the steep fall to reach a nadir of
75.5 in 1970, reflecting the liberal penal wave among western capitalist welfare states. But, starting in 1971, the rate crept upward,
peaking at 101.4 in 1983. Again, this was followed by a cycle of
decline that pushed rates down to a 20-year trough of 78.5 in 1991.
This deflationary period was a product of prosecutorial and judicial
liberality rather than a declining crime rate, according to Feest and
Weber. This period was also the postwar heyday of the West
German economy, with an unprecedented strength of labor in terms
of union power and low unemployment.

But, since the 1990 reunification, imprisonment is once again on
an upswing. Feest and Weber have analyzed the imprisonment
rates of the former GDR separately from the old West Germany.
The rates for the former West Germany climbed upward by over 10
percentage points (in one of the steepest jumps since the 1940s, see
Table 1: 242). The authors point to a number of unplanned penal
outcomes resulting from new drug law enforcement, longer sentences in the attempt to achieve resocialization and increased
emphasis on prevention since reunification. But the rates for the
"New States" (the Former GDR) have skyrocketed from their very
low post-Communist rates, a trough that reflected widespread
amnesties and criminal justice paralysis attending the immediate
aftermath of governmental collapse.

Since German unification, all former East German prisons have
come under the authority of newly established states, with the
result, Feest and Weber point out (p. 240), of a decline in penal
treatment: "all parts of Germany are now getting the same low

wages and no social benefits" once characteristic only of the prisons of the former West Germany. Feest and Weber point out that the GDR took a dualistic approach to the penal function in the postwar period, making it simultaneously a police state and a welfare model. Western critics only spoke of the repressive function, particularly the special prisons run by the "Stasi," but prisons also followed a welfare approach. While East German prisons were militarized, and material conditions spare, prisoners did have the right to work and were paid above the international average. Moreover, there were genuine attempts by volunteers and local officials to resocialize released offenders.

Deteriorating prison conditions, along with the increase in the incarceration rate, suggest that Germany could be headed for a period of serious repression. According to Feest and Weber, the remand rates are rising, even if less spectacularly than for sentenced prisoners. This is largely a product of targeting a new group since unification: non-German nationals. Xenophobia is on the increase, with fears of "Russian mafias" and "Romanian gangs" bordering on a social panic. The slumping economy and increasing inequality, together with the pressure of international economic competition, do not augur well for a liberal penal regime.

***

Italy was a low incarceration rate nation in the years after World War II. And, during the turbulent 1970s, when its Western European neighbors were turning to more repressive policies, Italy embarked on a decarceration movement that further reduced the prison population. The rates declined after 1984, reaching a nadir of 45 per 100,000 in 1990, resting between Japan and Denmark at the low end of the incarceration continuum. The rate has since shot up, to 60 per 100,000 by 1993. Historically, as in The Netherlands, the legislature has been draconian while the judiciary "softened" the sanctions with lenient sentences. But, since the Reform act of 1981, discretion has gradually shifted away from the judiciary and increasingly has been granted to prison administrators, undermining the traditional flexibility and judicial leniency.

Although Italy has record unemployment (12% in April of 1996) and falling industrial production and retail sales, the Italian public has not demanded a "get tough" penal policy. But, neither does the public seem concerned about the atrocious prison conditions.

Overcrowding, suicide and medical neglect place Italian prisons within a Third World standard. A series of constitutional "emergencies" have allowed Italian officials to retain their ideological claim to Beccarian principles of rehabilitation and rational and proportionate sentencing, while cracking down on selected criminal groups. Since the early 1990s, Italian officials have imposed harsher penalties on minor offenders, especially drug users and foreign citizens (Bohlen, 1995). In Chapter 7, Vincenzo Ruggiero argues that, in addition to the *official or institutional function* of criminal justice, there is *a latent or operative function* of controlling the "dangerous population." No longer on the soft-side of the traditional "bifurcation" in sentencing, these "dangerous classes" join political criminals in being sent to special high-security prisons for long terms. And the judiciary, which historically mitigated much of the draconian legislation, has in recent years lost discretionary power in favor of prison administrators.

Italian prisons serve a symbolic function for potential malefactors. Ruggiero suggests a continuum of punishment, extending from within prison, to the work done by prisoners outside the prison walls, to the meager and precarious living conditions of the marginalized groups who are the principal source of offenders and prison populations. These groups—"the marginalized, the underemployed, the occasional workers, the petty criminals and all others whose lifestyle and economic activity straddle legality and illegality"—now occupy the "carceral social zone," according to Ruggiero, a prison within the community and the "human reserve" upon which custody will draw. "Prison discipline aims at lowering their social expectations," Ruggiero writes. Criminals are "rehabilitated" when they accept life in what he terms the carceral social zone.

***

Although US corporate capital developed a strong presence in post-war *Canada*, Ottawa managed in the 1950s and 60s to pattern its social and economic policies after the Western European nations of Germany and Sweden. Chernomas and Black (1996: 23) call Canada's political economy of the period "social or communitarian capitalism" because it "included a comprehensive social safety net, a major role for the state in the economy and a robust and progressive trade union movement." And, as elsewhere in the West, the conditions of imprisonment in Canada have been linked to the relative strength of organized labor. Although Canada's incarceration rate climbed steadily in the postwar period, it nevertheless always remained a fraction of the US rate. In January of 1992, Canada's combined jail and prison rate per 100,000 of population was 109, which is high for Europe (compare England and Wales at 97), but nothing like the US rate of 539.

The global capitalist crisis of the early 1970s led to the most dramatic changes in Canada's political economy and penal policy since World War II. Stagnation, inflation and social unrest led Canadian officials into fashioning "a miniature replica of the US form of individualistic capitalism" (Chernomas and Black, 1996: 23). Canadian penal policy has also begun to mimic US repressiveness. In Saskatchewan, the incarceration rate rose from 56.55 per 100,000 in 1975 to 84.87 by 1979 (Hylton, 1981: 19). In Chapter 2, Bob Gaucher and John Lowman discuss the "shift away from the policies of the liberal interventionist state" that intensified following the 1984 Conservative victory. The 1980s and 90s have seen climbing imprisonment rates, lengthier sentences and restrictions on parole.

But, Gaucher and Lowman hasten to point to the important Canadian provincial variations. Canada's penal policy is as variegated as those of Australia and the US. While Ontario gutted rehabilitation programs, for instance, British Columbia has resisted much of the neoconservative current. And, as it turns out, for good political reason: On October 26, 1996, tens of thousands of protesters took to Toronto's streets—shutting down subways, buses, and street cars—in resistance to fiscal cuts that damage the core of Canadian values (DePalma, 1996b). Moreover, Quebec remains liberal on penal policy and welfare provision. Canada, like its European sisters, maintains a "bifurcated" approach that has decarcerated less serious property offenses while getting tougher on serious crime. Unfortunately, Canada's drug policy takes the US hard line.

While abandoning rehabilitation in practice, Canada's penal management has "an important rights discourse" embedded in the rhetoric of its major policy document, the Correctional Service's *Mission Statement* (1989). According to Gaucher and Lowman, this gap in theory and practice can serve as a wedge for progressive change. Such an initiative, however, must deal with the growing "corporatization of corrections" which employs a "management approach" in response to the "accountability" movement in public affairs. As a rational, calculative approach, the new penology looks at traditional rehabilitation efforts as dubiously "cost effective."

***

Japan enjoys one of the world's lowest incarceration rates, neck and neck with The Netherlands, and it is one of the only nations with a declining incarceration rate over the entire period under study. Many observers point to Japan's low crime rate as an explanation for this penal prudence. Elmer H. Johnson points out in Chapter 11 that, while the crime rate has declined since 1945, the imprisonment rate has fallen more sharply. The low crime rate is only a partial explanation. Two central factors are more important than crime rates, Johnson argues: First, the overwhelming majority of suspects confess, repent and show willingness for self-correction. Second, authorities are lenient towards those who confess. Most such sentences are suspended or diverted to probation.

Japanese prisons are also notable for being orderly. Rapes, disturbances and escapes are rare. Johnson attributes this tranquility to the centrality of prison industry in their management strategy. Japanese prisoners are regimented, along the lines of the old Auburn prison factory regime—a model Japan drew on when it adopted the prison during its late 19th-century industrialization (Johnson, 1996). In contrast to China, Latin America or Northern Europe, Japan took to the Auburn system immediately, and in a big way. The Meiji rulers were attracted to the disciplinary potential of the assembly line system and its machine-determined division of labor (Johnson, 1996: 87). This penal method also proved fiscally prudent, and prisons soon became directly involved in economic development during the Meiji era.[18]

Japanese prison industry continues to thrive largely because prisons have strong links with the private industrial sector through subcontracting (with Japanese penal officials retaining control and supervision of production). In contrast to many western nations, there has been no systematic opposition to subcontracting in the private market from labor unions or the business sector. Japan's low unemployment rate and the nation's historic protection of the welfare of workers ("lifetime job security") have diminished political pressure to protect the free market. The most important factor of all, most observers agree, is the egalitarian distribution of wealth. Japan's inequality is the lowest in the world after Hungary and India, with The Netherlands (Crossett, 1996) not far behind (as measured in proportion of income going to the bottom 20 percent of the population).

Although there has been little political or popular support to "get tough" on crime, Japan's mix of cultural rigidity and rehabilitative tolerance regarding repentant offenders should be seriously tested by events of the next decade. Japan is already in a nasty recession. Official unemployment has climbed to 3.4% (*The Economist*, 1996a: 40, 106). Unemployment would be twice as high if calculated by European or US methods (conservative in themselves). Japan has virtually no welfare or government safety net (other than health care and day care): Shame, family obligation, low unemployment and income equality greatly reduce welfare state requirements (Kristof, 1995). But Japan is under great pressure from its western trading partners to ease trade barriers. Although Japan remains the most protected and regulated of major industrial nations, its workers are still uncompetitive. The majority of Japanese firms are now beginning to "downsize" their work forces, modify seniority-based pay systems and move production abroad. And illegal immigration has increased, putting added pressure on the job market. How much longer will imprisonment rates remain low as these pressures mount?

***

On January 18, 1788, the first fleet of convict ships in a long series of "living hells" arrived at Botany Bay, *Australia*. Over eight decades, the continent would serve as a penal colony for an eventual 135,000 British felons. After the last ship arrived in 1868, Australia began a pattern of incarceration similar to that of the Western European nations. According to David Brown in Chapter 12, Australia's rates rose rapidly during the late 19th century. But beginning in the 1880s, incarceration rates began a long and dramatic decline, reaching a low in 1920. Braithwaite (quoted in Brown, p. 370) has argued that this decline reflected the "demise of serious labor shortages in Australia and the concomitant destruction of the profitability of prison industry." From 1920 until the early 1980s imprisonment rates remained relatively stable, despite the Great Depression and the postwar period of tremendous immigration. During the 1960s and 70s, a period when incarceration rates were quite low (78 per 100,000 by 1976), Australia joined the worldwide political turmoil of student Vietnam War protest, struggles for civil rights and economic justice and prisoner activism. This insurgency had a direct impact on the politics of punishment, according to Brown. Australian penality entered a period of "upheaval and reform," fueled by a number of prison disturbances and a university-based abolitionist movement.

Beginning in 1974, Australia entered a long recession that by the mid-1980s left the commonwealth suffering its worst economic crisis (Linge, 1990: 33). Australia's politics drifted rightward, with political leaders enthusiastically embracing the neoliberal call for privatization. Social policies harshened: Welfare took deep cuts, and a new, tougher sentencing act was passed in 1989. Incarceration rates for adults increased, sentence remissions were abolished and parole was reduced. Unemployed Aboriginal men are now greatly over-represented in prison, 14 to 1 on average across territories. A substantial proportion of prisoners is committed for property offenses (30%) and drug offenses (11%). Overall, Australia's prison population is remarkably like the US prisoner profile: disproportionately young, unemployed, poorly educated, drug addicted and black, a growing number of whom are women.

Brown warns, however, against a reductionist interpretation of Australia's overall retreat from liberalism. Imprisonment rates among its territories are marvelously varied, just as they are among the states of the US and among the Canadian provinces. Australian territorial rates do not clearly break down on the basis of race or unemployment, Brown observes. New South Wales and Victoria, for instance, have many structural similarities (industrial, populous, with high unemployment rates), but vastly different imprisonment rates. And providing additional contrast, the Australian Capital Territory and the Northern Territory (see Table 1: 372) both have small populations, but polar rates.

The case of Australia again suggests the viability of alternative solutions, even *within* states, to the common problem of crime. In terms of structural-historical analysis, the identification of "alternative developmental tendencies" is the most important objective of a comparative study. According to Reinhard Bendix (1984), the great scholar of comparative uses of authority and the problem of legitimation, contrast with other societies is essential if the social investigator is to avoid reductionist tendencies, either materialist or idealist. As encouraging for human potential as are the exceptional instances found in our volume, however, we shall argue below that these alternative tendencies are evermore constrained by globalization.

SUMMARY AND CONCLUSION: TOWARD A GLOBAL PENOLOGY IN THE NEW MILLENNIUM

Comparing Prison Systems examines penal change since the mid 1970s in a variety of countries around the world. Our contributors document a dramatic worldwide increase in imprisonment rates, lengthening prison sentences and an increasing severity in penal regimes. In the West, this shift to retribution and social exclusion reverses a period, beginning after World War II, of "corrections" and rehabilitation ideology. Punishment moderated with increasing general economic prosperity, labor strength and growing economic equality and democratization.

"Globalization," in the form of heightened international competition and capital migration to cheaper labor markets, has brought chronic stagnation to western capitalist nations generally, and has increased inequality nearly everywhere. Together, these two developments, penal severity and growing inequality, represent a new social epoch. Neoliberal social and economic reforms, begun under Margaret Thatcher and Ronald Reagan and aimed primarily at enhancing national competitiveness, have hastened the dramatic increase in the concentration of global wealth and income (Wilterdink, 1995) worldwide. Meanwhile, in the name of "labor flexibility," conditions for the working classes are deteriorating: Western Europe suffers chronically high unemployment (especially among young workers), and the wages of North American workers have eroded seriously. While millions of displaced workers are swelling the ranks of a surplus population in the West, the impact of globalization is also widening the gap of prosperity between poor and rich countries. Because of this, the globalization process promises to be the major factor in the penal policy of developing countries in the new millennium.

Postwar capitalist growth began breaking down just when the power of the western military-industrial complex had exhausted the resources of the Soviet empire. The former communist states of Eastern and Central Europe were not introduced, therefore, to the postwar corporate liberal (US) and social democratic (Western European) versions of monopoly capitalism. Instead, neoliberal ideology guides emerging market societies in Eastern Europe, Latin America and in much of Asia, with predictable consequences. In the former Soviet bloc, "social inequality has increased in all cases. Whether by class, ethnicity, gender, or age, the Eastern European countries have become much more divided. Such inequality appears to be negatively correlated with both political and economic reform," conclude Centeno and Rands (1996: 370). In China as well, market economics has aggravated unemployment and dropped real income for about a third of families. Chinese leaders have recently eased up on the nation's austerity campaign, and continue unprofitable state-owned factories until they can create a safety net for laid-off workers (Smith, 1996). Elsewhere, however, political leaders are cutting social safety nets in preparation for aggressive new international competition in free markets.

Comparing Prison Systems provides some encouragement for the optimist, however. The most dramatic exceptions or "alternative realities" in our study are those nations with the most substantial income equality. For instance, countries with similar social structures that are experiencing comparable economic conditions—The Netherlands and England, Japan and the US (and states within the US, territories within Australia and provinces within Canada)—have chosen contrasting penal policy directions. The most apparent cultural difference among these nations is the extent to which they tolerate inequality (Wilkins and Pease, 1987).

There are also contrasting examples among developing countries. When Eastern Europe and Latin America are compared, we see that penal repression is much more severe in Latin America—even though Latin American nations experienced earlier transitions to democracy and market economics. As they imposed stringent austerity measures during the 1980s, most of the Latin American nations saw poverty increase and income inequality widen dramatically. Wealth and income in Latin American nations are much more concentrated than elsewhere in the world. Market transition in Eastern Europe, by contrast, has been supported by the region's history of social equity. Because "Eastern Europe retains one of the most generous social expenditure programs (as measured as percent of GDP) in the world," Centeno and Rands (1996: 381) argue, the "welfare state (even a frayed one) has made the market possible." Market growth does not require extensive inequality, in developing or developed industrial nations.[19] Political decisions are not based on economic reasoning alone, however. Culture, especially politics, plays an important part.

Latin America, South Africa and Eastern Europe have strong authoritarian legacies that must be overcome before a market economy or a democratic government can take strong hold. The many hardships required by adjustment to a free-market economy under-mine social cohesion. Moreover, given the continuity of elites in recent structural transformations, political leaders are no strangers to the exercise of repressive authority. What Paulo Sérgio Pinheiro (1996: 20) observes of Latin America, applies in lesser degree to other regions as well:

> This continuity suggests that, notwithstanding the political transi-tions to elected rule, the authoritarian regimes of the past and the new civilian democratic governments are barely differentiated expressions of the same system of domination by the same elites. Political democratization does not attack 'socially rooted authoritari-anism.'

While regimes employ the same tactics against assorted "criminals" under capitalist "democracy" that they employed under military rule to suppress political dissent, official violence, state-sponsored vigilantism, corruption and white-collar crime continue largely unpunished, delegitimating the state. Widespread injustice and cor-ruption contribute to pervasive political cynicism, further under-mining democracy.

To identify and describe universal problems is only one part of the comparative task; we must address the prospects for social change. How can fatalism be avoided? How can repressive legacies be overcome? What are the prospects for a progressive global penology in the new millennium, one which encourages judicious use of imprisonment and holds nations accountable to humane treatment? What are the material interests that might constrain reform ideas? Let us conclude by reviewing two approaches to change: intellectual mobilization for reform through human rights diplomacy, versus a change in macroeconomic policy.

Toward A Universal Standard of Penal Treatment?

The diplomatic approach Many policy-makers and human rights advocates are attempting to use the force of ideas and moral persuasion to foster improved treatment of prisoners. Ever since the American Revolution, American policy-makers have liked to believe that the US is a world leader in advancing human rights. The first penitentiary, which served for a century as a world model of penal reform, was an outgrowth of the Independence movement.

This was preceded in 1786 by Quaker penal law revision eliminating corporal punishment and greatly restricting the death penalty. An American, Enoch Cobb Wines, helped to organize the first international congress on prison reform, which met in London in 1872. At this congress, he was elected the first president of the International Penitentiary Commission. At the turn of the 20th century, the recently renamed American Prison Association (changed from National Prison Association in 1908), set out to promote reformatory ideology abroad. Buoyed by a period of moderate, though uneven prosperity and diminishing inequality, Progressive Era penal reformers advocated a spirit of "compassionateness," urging the Germans, for instance, to discard the old Auburn regime in favor of rehabilitation through education (McKelvey, 1977: 237).

More broadly, US foreign policy has always supported democracy, asserts Strobe Talbott (1996: 47), deputy Secretary of State. The reaffirmation of global democracy is the diplomatic priority of the Clinton administration. Measured by the cornerstones of free elections and the promotion of the "rule of law," Talbott points to many encouraging developments over the last 20 years. Since 1974, the percentage of countries ruled democratically has doubled; they include Cambodia, Eastern and Central Europe, the Philippines and the Latin American nations of Argentina, Brazil, Chile, Nicaragua and Guatemala. But these are shaky endeavors, with much backsliding and a great deal of political corruption that leaves the lower classes with very little political confidence (Carothers, 1997). In Hungary and Poland, under 30% of the respondents in a recent poll say that the ordinary person is better able to influence governmental decisions under the new system than under the communist regime (Hoffman, 1997). Furthermore, with the exception of the Philippines, which has one of the world's lowest incarceration rates, democratization has not translated into improved penal policy. Democracy may be a necessary, but it is not a sufficient guarantor of human rights and penal moderation.

Democracy and parochialism The belief in an emerging global culture based on western values is erroneous and dangerous, warns Samuel P. Huntington. In *The Clash of Civilizations and the Remaking of World Order* (1996b), Huntington reveals the follies of universalist ambitions, especially the effort to make the world "safe for democracy." Most fundamentally, universalism and democratization are at odds. "Democracy tends to make a society more parochial, not more cosmopolitan," Huntington (1996a: 39) argues. Ethnic, nationalist and religious appeals are the strongest in electoral politics. "The result is popular mobilization against Western elites and the West in general." Universalism requires imperialism, either military or cultural, Huntington continues. The West lacks the commitment and material resources to impose its will physically, and does not have the moral authority for cultural hegemony. Third World nations, for instance, denounce "human rights imperialism" as arrogant, especially when industrial nations are so obviously hypocritical (several western nations occupy places on the Amnesty International list of human rights violators), and guilty of double standards (as with US objections to prison labor in China but not in Japan). And the US policy toward China is not even consistent. The "Fortune 500 China lobby" has successfully reasserted dollar diplomacy, most recently in separating US trade policy from human rights violations regarding forced abortions, sterilization and engineered environmental disasters (Dreyfuss, 1996).

The US is more than hypocritical, inconsistent and selective in judging other nations. While politicians protest penal labor in China, Washington promotes a version of capitalism that forces "painful but necessary economic choices" (Talbott, 1996: 51) on nations that help drive its poorest citizens to prison in the first place. Yes, forced penal labor undercuts US labor bargaining; but, US corporations lead the world in industrial migration to cheaper labor markets. Business culture in general, and neoliberal economic philosophy and practice in particular, are much more universally influential than human rights rhetoric.[20] "By default, business enterprises are wielding political power in many important ways," according to Barnet and Cavanaugh (1994: 422). The "deglobalization of world politics is occurring even as the globalization of economic activities proceeds:

> ...as the world economy becomes more and more integrated, the processes of political disintegration are accelerating... . Bringing global economic institutions under the authority of political institutions is essential to protect the environment, human rights, and job possibilities around the world. Making both accountable to the people is essential if the new world order is to be democratic, and if it is not democratic it will enjoy neither legitimacy nor stability (Barnet and Cavanaugh, 1994: 421).

According to Huntington, the most likely configuration of transnational cooperation and influence will be *regional* and *cultural*.

"Global politics is being reconfigured along cultural lines," he continues, away from superpower alignments based on ideology. These "cultural communities" and their "spheres of influence" will be where any realistic hope for world penal improvement must begin, especially if they coincide with trade associations. Regional standards of penal treatment could be established, just as neoliberalism requires standards of economic behavior. Penal standards could be incorporated into regional trade pact membership requirements, just as the EU required Poland to abandon the death penalty for membership consideration (Perlez, 1996). Leading bloc nations could try to require a trade group or partner, as a condition of trade, to honor labor rights and humane penal treatment. But penal standards cannot be based on some abstract notion of humane treatment.

Material realities and uncertain prospects Penal reform must be grounded in employment opportunity and greater equality, which raise the general welfare. Otherwise, if the neoliberal version of the market economy continues its global ascendance and penal living standards are left to humanitarian sentiment, the "less eligibility principle" will prevail as an insurmountable obstacle to penal reform.[21] As Rusche and Kirchheimer (1968: 207) argued at the time of the Great Depression, only in a society that is "in a position to offer its members a certain measure of security and to guarantee a reasonable standard of living," can "the shift from a repressive penal policy to a progressive program…then be raised out of the sphere of humanitarianism to constructive activity."

Since the time of Rusche and Kirchheimer, however, providing a measure of security has become much more difficult. With globalization, individual nations are less able to act alone in maintaining a full employment policy through Keynesian methods. The full employment and comprehensive welfare policies, upon which penal reform was predicated, grew from a historical "context of clearly delineated, tightly organized, and highly competitive national states," whose fierce competition increased interdependency *within* states and promoted social cooperation and democratization, Wilterdink (1995: 11) observes. This was a time when capitalists depended on organized labor, "as did politicians on average citizens, and the higher on the less educated. This generated a rise of labor incomes relative to capital incomes, an expansion of transfer incomes, and a decrease of labor inequality."

The growing economic inequality that started in the 1970s is more than the product of a recessionary cycle, Wilterdink (1995: 8) contends. Instead, it "represents an important discontinuity, a 'structural' rupture in the development of western societies," whereby national class divisions are exacerbated as global economic interdependence increases. If this is the world's fate, our economies will continue to "breed hatred and apathy among the poor, anguish and resentment among the threatened middle classes, and indifference and contempt among the wealthy" (Wilterdink, 1995: 17)— infertile ground for global penal reform.

Notes

1. This chapter is not a comprehensive summary or overview of *Comparing Prison Systems*. Instead, it is an *interpretive* essay that highlights certain features of national penal histories, chosen to illustrate or support the theme of globalization. In the following discussion of the various national penal systems of our volume, the reader should assume that all interpretation of penal data is mine unless a contributor is expressly cited for specific attribution.

2. We borrow this succinct definition of "globalization" from Tanzer (1995: 1): "...globalization as commonly discussed refers to the explosive growth in the past twenty to twenty-five years of huge multinational corporations and vast pools of capital that have crossed national borders and penetrated everywhere. This globalization, in turn, is seen as largely the result of a parallel technological explosion in computerization, telecommunications, and rapid transportation."

3. "Neoliberalism," as defined by *The Concise Oxford Dictionary of Sociology* (Marshall, 1994: 352–53) is "a loosely knit body of ideas which became very influential during the 1980s and which were premised upon a (slight) rethinking and a (substantial) reassertion of classical liberalism..." This economic and political philosophy was first installed by Margaret Thatcher, then quickly adopted by the US. Closely associated with globalization, neoliberalism stresses free markets, laissez-faire economics and social-contract theory supported by the doctrines of free choice, rationality, economic individualism and limited government. Piven (1996) argues that neoliberalism is closer to the laissez-faire ideology of the late 19th century—"survival of the fittest"/Robber Baron capitalism—than to the classical liberalism that launched capitalism a century earlier.

4. "In 1970, the richest 20 percent of the world's population had an average income 32 times that of the poorest 20 percent; by 1991 that ratio

had almost doubled, to 61 times" (Tanzer, 1995: 12). See also Bradsher, 1995).

5. The "surplus population" can be defined as a pool of unemployed and underemployed labor. Karl Marx saw this "industrial reserve army" as an essential feature of capitalism that helps regulate wages. There are three strata of surplus population: a sediment of completely discouraged workers form the bottom stratum; at the top is an officially unemployed layer, and in between is an "invisible" stratum that does not show up in unemployment statistics because its occupants are not actively seeking work by reporting to unemployment offices. In the US, after a surge of women into the official labor force in the 1970s and 80s, female participation rates have reached a plateau, but over the last year the "invisible" category has seen an infusion of a million prime age men. Their willingness to work at low wage jobs "enable business to expand and hire more people without pushing up wages. So, the missing men may act as a buffer against the threat of wage-push inflation" (Wysocki, 1996). For an argument that recent changes in employment patterns—including the decline of male employment, flexible working, growing self-employment and "trainee" status—are making the very distinction between "un/employment" a questionable one, see: Walters (1996: 199).

6. The "less eligibility principle," first formulated by 18th-century English social writers, holds that the living condition of prisoners (and welfare recipients) should not be more "eligible" or desirable than the living situation of the lowest-paid free workers. This was a central concept in the work of Rusche and Kirchheimer (1968: 94), as the principle "is the leitmotiv of all prison administration down to the present time."

7. Greenberg (1980: 202) observes that Poland's postwar imprisonment rates alternated between crackdowns and general amnesties. This oscillation was the product of policy decisions, rather than responses to economic cycles. Today, however, imprisonment is increasing with increases in unemployment, as it did in the 1930s under the pre-Communist system.

8. In a recent *New York Times* (Tyler, 1996) article, for example, "Crime (and Punishment) Rages Anew in China," members of the Chinese business community and newspaper editors express concern that fear of crime and social instability will drive away foreign investors. On kidnapping of foreign business executives working in Mexico, see De Palma (1996), and on Mexico City's high and rising risk ranking by international risk analysts Kroll Associates, Inc., see Torres (1996).

9. America was never a land of equality, as colonial society had a wealthy elite. Jackson Turner Main (1973), in his classic study of the social structure during the Revolutionary period (circa 1765–1788), observes that class divisions existed but, except for a "permanent proletariat" of slaves and white indentured servants, class lines were fluid. Although

there was a pre-Revolutionary elite possessing vast wealth, early Americans enjoyed a substantial equality in comparison to today. As late as 1800, eighty percent of Americans owned their own means of production (Nettels, 1962). Nettels (1962: 263) describes economic activity in the United States, circa 1775–1815: "An outstanding feature of labor during this period was self-employment. Skilled artisans, shopkeepers, professional men, planters, proprietors of small businesses, merchants, traders, pioneers, and land owning farmers made up the majority of the free population." But, by 1828, "five years before Tocqueville visited the United States, the richest 4 percent of New Yorkers owned about 63 percent of all (corporate and noncorporate) wealth in New York City, and by 1845, its share had increased to about 81 percent" (Schwartz, 1995). What Tocqueville and Beaumont observed was not "the equality of conditions," but the widespread *perception* of opportunity based on some reality.

10. According to Walmsley (1995: 9), at the *low end* of rates per 100,000, from January 1, 1991, to January 1, 1994, were: Croatia, from 20 to 50; Bulgaria, from 80 to 95; in the *middle range*, are: Czech Republic, from 80 to 160; Hungary, 120 to 130; Poland, 130 to 160; Slovakia, 85 to 135. At the *high end* are: Russia, from 480 to 565; Latvia, 320 to 350; Estonia, 280 to 290; and Maldova, 255 to 280.

11. Ricardo D. Salvatore and Carlos Aguirre (1996: 3), in their superb and much-needed volume on the origin of the penitentiary in Latin America, point out that the adoption of the penitentiary across Latin America was an uneven process, extending over a century from first nation to last, and must be understood within the context of "the shifting ideological and sociopolitical environments from which they emerged." Our essay, of course, does not do justice to this complexity.

12. Penal labor exploitation characterized the colonial period, however. Ruth Pike (1983: 134–136) has examined the *presidios* of the Spanish Caribbean. Confinement at hard labor in the naval arsenals and other forms of penal servitude under colonialism in 19th-century Puerto Rico are analyzed by Kelvin A. Santiago-Valles in Chapter 5 of Salvatore and Aguirre (1996). Carlos Aguirre (1996: 54) discusses labor discipline as a central *purpose* of the 19th-century Lima Penitentiary. But, in a nation with few factories and where Indians were perceived by the elite as lazy and incapable of market behavior, the penitentiary remained more a symbol of modernization and a mechanism of the state's central authority than of labor discipline in the tradition of the European and North American models.

13. In the 1930s debt crisis an "import-substitution" model was introduced. This model of development is based on high tariffs protecting closed and regulated state monopolies, while exporting raw materials to gain foreign currency. This model reached its peak in the 1950s.

14. As an initiative to increase black participation in the economy, the National Empowerment Consortium, representing black business leaders and trade unions, has begun to purchase, at a discount, shares in formerly white-owned industries like the gold and diamond mining company, *Anglo American* (McNeil, 1966). But critics see this as a cooptative effort that enriches a few wealthy black individuals. See also Wells (1996).

15. The connection between recessions and rising imprisonment rates was not via the crime rate, most researchers agree. But there is dispute as to what extra-judicial criteria influence policy. Many Marxist social historians have asserted a directly economic function, through the labor market, mainly as a way to control a "problem population." Melossi argues against this reductionist and instrumentalist interpretation, and favors instead an essentially "symbolic, ideological role."

16. Since the mid-1970s recession, the job market has been in one long trough, no longer rising and falling with the economy. In the US alone, 43 million jobs have been lost since 1979. Job losses peaked in 1992 at 3.4 million jobs, and have remained the same since, with only 35% gaining new jobs at the same pay or better, and 25% having been reduced to part-time work, *despite record corporate profits* (*New York Times*, March 3, 1996).

17. Note, however, that The Netherlands' drug policy and practice are frequently misunderstood. See Ruggiero and South (1995: 31–33).

18. Critics in the US and UK, including Human Rights Watch, Amnesty International and the Japan Federation of Bar Associations (1992), complain that Japan's policy of forced labor for private enterprise and "draconian discipline and inhuman conditions" of industrial production, violate human rights. For their part, Japanese officials claim that their system of industrial labor is not punitive, but rather offers the "opportunity for 'self-purification'," (Johnson, 1996: 86), akin to the moral redemption of China's "thought reform." Self-discipline through work, they argue, is a cardinal value of Japanese society. In addition to issues of cultural interpretation (the reader is reminded of Dutton's point in the case of China), one can ask several questions concerning substantive differentiation in regard to the systems of other nations. While abusive treatment cannot be condoned anywhere, why select Japan particularly? What does it matter whether prisoners are forced to work for private companies directly, or for the state? For example, all able-bodied prisoners in Texas have, since the abolition of the convict lease in 1910, been compelled to work (mostly on cotton plantations) at no pay in support of a largely self-sufficient penal system (which in effect is a form of tax subsidization—corporate taxes are low, and Texas does not have individual income tax). Other critics of Japan's prison labor system argue that private production would be acceptable if it were based on "the consent of the prisoners

concerned and guarantees as to the payment of normal wages and social security" (Kaido, 1996). But, how does Japan's penal industry system differ in substance from the US government's Free Venture Program (Weiss, 1989) where, by sleight-of-hand, prisoners work for private industry at "competitive wages," only to see nearly all this deducted for taxes, victims's compensation and payment for "room and board"? And isn't truly "free consent" doubtful for prisoners who depend upon the mercy of authorities for early release, or when positive incentives for participation are so high as to make non-participation a punishment? Nonetheless, the question of how police authorities obtain such a high rate of confessions from detainees, and the issue of the legal provisions which enable lengthy detention, are also critically debated.

19. The high economic growth rates of the 1950s and 1960s in the industrialized world occurred during a period of low inequality, suggesting that "equality and growth are complimentary. The slowdown in growth that began in the 1970s was accompanied by rising inequality in both income and wealth," observes Wolff (1995: 63). Greider (1997) argues that greater equality makes good economic sense because high wages and full employment fuel consumption, the only solution to the problem of surplus or overcapacity.

20. "The fierceness of global competition in many industries at a time of prolonged global recession is producing a certain convergence in business cultures around the world," observe Barnet and Cavanaugh, (1994: 425).

21. Labor union objection to prison industry, which is especially strong during recessions, also contributes to less eligibility. Penal industry and skills training are the heart and soul of any rehabilitation or reformatory program, yet during the depressions of 1872, 1892, and the 1930s, unions successfully lobbied state legislatures and Congress to prohibit private contract labor (McKelvey, 1977: 128). Even though unions were weak in their contract bargaining power, politicians were accommodating because, in addition to business objection to unfair competition, such reforms were largely symbolic; prison labor did not seriously compete with free labor in the northern states.

References

Aguirre, Carlos. (1996) "The Lima Penitentiary and the Modernization of Criminal Justice in Nineteenth-Century Peru," in Ricardo D. Salvatore and Carlos Aguirre (eds.) *The Birth of the Penitentiary in Latin America*. Austin: University of Texas Press, 44–77.

Barnet, Richard and Cavanagh, John. (1994) *Global Dreams: Imperial Corporations and the New World Order.* New York: Simon & Schuster.

Bennett, W.J., Dilulio, J.D. and Walters, J.P. (1996) *Body Count: Moral Poverty and How to Win America's War Against Crime and Drugs.* New York: Simon & Schuster.

Bendix, Reinhard. (1984) *Force, Fate, and Freedom: On Historical Sociology.* Berkeley: University of California Press.

Bohlen, Celestine. (1995) "Bursting Population Overwhelms Italy's Prisons." *The New York Times,* February 28: A3.

Borón, Altilio A. (1996) "Governability and Democracy In Latin America." *Social Justice,* 23(1–2): 303–334.

Bourgois, Philippe. (1995) *In Search of Respect: Selling Crack in El Barrio.* Cambridge: Cambridge University Press.

Bradsher, Keith. (1995) "Gap in Wealth In U.S. Called Widest in West." *The New York Times,* April 17: A1.

Braithwaite, J. (1989) *Crime, Shame and Reintegration.* Cambridge: Cambridge University Press.

Braun, Denny. (1991) *The Rich Get Richer: The Rise of Income Inequality in the United States and the World.* Chicago: Nelson Hall Publishers.

Brent, Stephen R. (1996) "South Africa: Tough Road to Prosperity." *Foreign Affairs,* 75(2) (March/April): 113–124.

Carothers, Thomas. (1997) "Democracy Without Illusions." *Foreign Affairs,* 79(1): 85–99.

Carrigan, Ana. (1996) "An Unlikely Hero: Valdiviesco's Crusade Against Drug Corruption." *NACLA Report on the Americas,* XXX(1) (July/Aug): 6–10.

Centeno, Miguel Angel and Rands, Tania. (1996) "The World They Have Lost: An Assessment of Change in Eastern Europe." *Social Research,* 63(2) (Summer): 369–402.

Chernomas, R. and Black, E. (1996) "What Kind of Capitalism? The Revival of Class Struggle in Canada." *Monthly Review,* 48, 1: 23–34.

Chiricos, T.G. and DeLone, M.A. (1992) "Labor Surplus and Punishment: A Review and Assessment of Theory and Evidence." *Social Problems,* 39: 421–446.

Christie, Nils. (1993) *Crime Control as Industry.* London: Routledge.

Cowell, Alan. (1996) "Germans Stage Huge Protest On Budget Plan." *The New York Times*, June 9: 8A.

Crossette, Barbara. (1996) "U.N. Survey Finds World Rich-Poor Gap Widening." *The New York Times*, July 15: A3.

Daley, Suzanne. (1995a) "Blacks in South Africa Turn To Vigilantes as Crime Soars." *The New York Times*, November 27: A1.

—————. (1995b) "As Crime Soars, South African Whites Leave." *The New York Times*, December 12: A1.

—————. (1996a) "Apartheid's Fall Opens Door to Scourge of Cocaine." *The New York Times*, February 19: A3.

—————. (1996b) "Downtown's Denizens: Fear, and Fearless Vendors." *The New York Times*, August 21: A4.

—————. (1996c) "Drugs, Guns and Vigilante Justice in South Africa." *The New York Times*, September 20: A4.

—————. (1996d) "South African Constitution Is Approved by High Court." *The New York Times*, December 5: A11.

Davies, R.W. (1995) "Forced Labor Under Stalin: The Archive Revelations." *New Left Review*, 214: 62–85.

del Olmo, Rosa. (1993) "The Geopolitics of Narcotrafficking in Latin America." *Social Justice*, 20(3–4) (Fall-Winter): 1–23.

DePalma, Anthony. (1996a) "Income Gulf in Mexico Grows and So Do Protests." *The New York Times*, A3.

—————. (1996b) "Protesters Take to Streets to Defend Canada's Safety Net." *The New York Times*, October 26: 3.

Dillon, Sam "The Rebels' Call to Arms Echoes in Rural Mexico." *The New York Times*, September 19: A3.

Downes, David. (1988) *Contrasts in Tolerance: Post-war Penal Policy in The Netherlands and England and Wales*. Oxford: Clarendon Press.

Dreyfuss, Robert. (1996) "The New China Lobby." *The American Prospect*, 30 (Jan–Feb): 30–37.

Dumm, Thomas L. (1987) *Democracy and Punishment: Disciplinary Origins of the United States*. Madison: The University of Wisconsin Press.

Economist, The. (1996a) "Economic Indicators." June 8–14: 106.

—————. (1996b) "Poland: Grab that chance." July 13–19: 47–48.

Feely, M. and Simon, J. (1992) "The New Penology: Notes on the Emerging Strategy of Corrections and Its Implications." *Criminology*, 30(4) (November): 449–474.

Fischer, C.S., Hout, M. Jankowski, M.S., Lucas, S.R., Swindler, A. and Voss, K. (1996) *Inequality By Design*. Princeton: Princeton University Press.

Fowles, Richard and Merva, Mary. (1996) "Wage Inequality and Criminal Activity: An Extreme Bounds Analysis For The United States, 1975–1990." *Criminology*, 34(2): 163–182.

Galeano, E. (1989) "Democracy in Latin America: Best Is That Which Best Creates." *Social Justice*, 16, 1: 119–126.

Gilpin, K.N. (1996) "Market Takes Steepest Drop Since '91— The Dow Drops 171.24 After Jobs Surge." *The New York Times*, March 9: 1A.

Gómez, Jesús Antonio Muñoz. (1987) "Notes Toward a Historical Understanding Of the Colombian Penal System." *Social Justice*, 30: 60–77.

Green, Duncan. (1995) *Silent Revolution: The Rise of Market Economics in Latin America*. London: Cassell.

Greenberg, David F. (1977) "The Dynamics of Oscillatory Punishment Processes." *Journal of Criminal Law and Criminology*, 68: 643–51.

————. (1980) "Penal Sanctions in Poland: A Test of Alternative Models." *Social Problems*, 28, No. 2: 194–204.

Greider, William. (1997) *One World, Ready or Not: The Manic Logic of Global Capitalism*. New York: Simon & Schuster.

Grunhut, Max. (1948/1972) *Penal Reform: A Comparative Study*. Montclair, NJ: Patterson Smith.

Hagan, John; and Peterson, Ruth D. (eds.) (1995) *Crime and Inequality*. Stanford, California: Stanford University Press.

Hale, Chris. (1989) "Economy, punishment and imprisonment." *Contemporary Crises*, 13: 327–349.

Higley, John; Kullberg, Judith and Pakulski, Jan. (1996) "The Persistence of Postcommunist Elites." *Journal of Democracy*, 7(2) (April): 133–147.

Hirsch, Adam Jay. (1992) *The Rise of the Penitentiary: Prisons and Punishment in Early America*. New Haven, Connecticut: Yale University Press.

Hobsbawm, E. (1965) *Primitive Rebels*. New York: Bantam.

Hoffman, David. (1997) "How a Harsh History Stymies a Civil Society." *The Washington Post-National Weekly Edition*, 14(10) (Jan. 9): 17–18.

Holmes, Steven A. (1996) "Income Disparity Between Poorest and Richest Rises." *The New York Times*, June 20: 1A.

Huntington, S.P. (1996a) "The West Unique, Not Universal." *Foreign Affairs*, 75, 6: 28–46.

————. (1996b) *The Clash of Civilizations and the Remaking of World Order*. New York: Simon & Schuster.

————. (1996c) "Democracy For the Long Haul." *Journal of Democracy*, 7, 2: 3–13.

Hylton, John. (1981) "The Growth of Punishment: Imprisonment and Community Corrections in Canada." *Crime and Social Justice*, 15: 18–28, 35.

Ignatieff, Michael. (1978) *A Just Measure of Pain: The Penitentiary in the Industrial Revolution*. New York: Columbia University Press.

Inverarity, James and McCarthy, Daniel. (1988) "Punishment and Social Structure Revisited: Unemployment and Imprisonment in the United States, 1948–1984." *The Sociological Quarterly*, 29(2): 263–279.

Japan Federation of Bar Associations. (1992) *Prisons in Japan: The Human Rights Situation in Japanese Prisons*. Tokyo.

Johnson, Elmer H. (1996) *Japanese Corrections: Managing Convicted Offenders in an Orderly Society*. Carbondale, Illinois: Southern Illinois University Press.

Kaido, Yuichi. (1996) "Prison Labour in Japan." Unpublished Conference Paper.

Kamm, Thomas and Rohwedder, Cacilie. (1996) "Many Europeans Fear Cuts in Social Benefits In One-Currency Plan." *The Wall Street Journal*, July 30: 1A.

Kapstein, E.B. (1996) "Workers and the World Economy." *Foreign Affairs*, (May/June): 16–37.

Kristof, Nicholas D. (1995) "Japanese Say No to Crime: Tough Methods, at a Price." *The New York Times*, May 14: 1A.

Kwásniewski, Jersey and Watson, Margaret. (eds.) (1991) *Social Control and the Law in Poland*. New York: BERG.

Leuw, E. (1991) "Drugs and drug policy in the Netherlands," in Michael Tonry (ed.) *Crime and Justice*, 14 (1991).

Lewis, Paul. (1996) "Venezuela Gets Big I.M.F. Credit, Backing Market Reforms." *The New York Times*, July 13: 1.

Levitt, Kari Polanyi. (1995) "Toward Alternatives: Re-Reading The Great Transformation." *Monthly Review*, 47(2) (June): 1–16.

Linge, G.J.R. (1990) "The Australian Economy in Transition," in Roger Hayter and Peter D. Wilde (eds.) *Industrial Transformation and Challenge In Australia and Canada*. Ottawa: Carleton University Press, 33.

Magdoff, H. (1992) "Globalization: To What End?" New York: Monthly Review Press.

Main, Jackson Turner. (1973) *The Social Structure of Revolutionary America*. Princeton, New Jersey: Princeton University Press.

Marcuse, Peter. (1995) "Transitions in South Africa: To What?" *Monthly Review*, (November): 38–52.

Marshall, Gordon. (ed.) (1994) *The Concise Oxford Dictionary of Sociology*. Cambridge: Oxford University Press.

McKelvey, Blake. (1977) *American Prisons: A History of Good Intentions*. Montclair, New Jersey: Patterson Smith.

McNeil, Donald G. Jr. (1996) "Once Bitter Enemies, Now Business Partners: South African Blacks Buy Into Industry." *The New York Times*, September 24: D1.

Meese, Edwin III and Rostad, K.A. (1996) "Let Prison Inmates Earn Their Keep." *The Wall Street Journal*, May 14: A14.

Melossi, D. (1985) "Punishment and Social Action: Changing Vocabularies of Motives," in J. Lowman, R. Menzies and T. Palys (eds.) *Transcarceration: Essays in the Sociology of Social Control*. Aldershot, UK: Gower, 27–42.

————. (1989) "An introduction: Fifty years later, *Punishment and Social Structure* in comparative analysis." *Contemporary Crises* 13, 4: 311–326.

Melossi, Dario and Pavarini, M. (1981) *The Prison and the Factory: The Origins of the Penitentiary System*. Totowa, N.J.: Barnes and Noble.

Meranze, M. (1996) *Laboratories of Virtue: Punishment, Revolution, and Authority in Philadelphia, 1760–1835*. Chapel Hill: University of North Carolina Press.

Merva, M. and Fowles, R. (1992) *Effects of Diminished Economic Opportunity on Social Stress*. Washington, D.C.: Economic Policy Institute.

Moczydowski, Pawel. (1992) *The Hidden Life of Polish Prisons*. Bloomington, Indiana: Indiana University Press.

Moffett, Matt and Friedland, Jonathan. (1996) "A New Latin America Faces a Devil of Old: Rampant Corruption." *The Wall Street Journal*, July 1: 1A.

Morris, N. and Rothman, D.J. (eds.) *The Oxford History of the Prison*. New York: Oxford University Press.

NACLA *Report on The Americas*. "INJUSTICE FOR ALL: Crime and Impunity in Latin America." XXX(2) (Sept./Oct.).

National Institute of Justice. (Feb. 1996) "Alternative Sentences in Germany." *Research Preview*. Washington, DC: US Government Printing.

———. (1996) "Work in American Prisons: Joint Ventures with the Private Sector." *Program Focus*. Washington, DC: US Government Printing.

Nettles, C.P. (1962) *The Emergence of a National Economy: 1775–1815*. New York: Harper Torchbacks.

New York Times, The (1995) "In Colombia's Jails, Prisoners Get What They Pay For." May 28: 14A.

———. (1996) "The Downsizing of America." March 3: 27.

———. (1996) "Wall Street Jittery Over Jobs Report." June 9: D7.

———. (1996) "Venezuela Says Troops Set Off Fatal Prison Fire." October 24: A14.

———. (1996) "U.N. Reports a Billion Adults Not Fully Employed." October 26: 4A.

Newman, Barry. (1991) "Poland Has Plenty of One Thing: Crooks—Thefts, Communist Scams Thrive as Economy Shifts." *The Wall Street Journal*, April 9: A18.

———. (1996) "The Netherlands and Morocco Have Hash in Common, But World View Differs," *The Wall Street Journal*, April 23: 1A.

———. (1996) "Pining for Order: Russians Are of 2 Minds About New Freedoms And the New Poverty." *The Wall Street Journal*, May 31: 1A.

O'Brien, Patricia. (1982) *The Promise of Punishment: Prisons in Nineteenth-Century France*. Princeton, New Jersey: Princeton University Press.

———. (1995) "The Prison on the Continent—Europe, 1865–1965." Chapter 7 in *The Oxford History of the Prison*, in N. Morris and D.J. Rothman (eds.) New York: Oxford University Press, 199–225.

O'Connor, James. (1973) *The Fiscal Crisis of the State*. New York: St. Martin's Press.

O'Neil, Patrick H. (1996) "Revolution From Within: Institutional Analysis, Transitions from Authoritarianism, and the Case for Hungary." *World Politics*, 48 (July): 579–603.

Overholt, W.H. (1996) "China after Deng." *Foreign Affairs*, 75(3) (May/June): 63–78.

Parenti, Christian. (1996) "Making Prison Pay: Business Finds The Cheapest Labor of All." *The Nation*, 262(4) (January 29): 11–14.

Perlez, Jane. (1995) "Poles Dismayed at Unchecked Crime." *The New York Times*, June 19: A7.

————. (1996a) "Poland's New Leaders Are Gazing Intently Westward." *The New York Times*, April 6: 4.

————. (1996b) "Poland Finds New Support For Hanging" *The New York Times*, May 5: 4A.

Pike, Ruth. (1983) *Penal Servitude in Early Modern Spain*. Madison, Wisconsin: University of Wisconsin Press.

Pinheiro, Sérgio Paulo. (1996) "Democracies Without Citizenship." *NACLA Report of The Americas*, XXX(2) (Sept./Oct.): 17–23.

Piven, Francis Fox. (1995) "Is It Global Economics or Neo-Laissez-Faire?" *New Left Review*, Sept.–Oct., No. 213: 107–114.

Polanyi, K. (1944) *The Great Transformation*. New York: Farrar and Rinehart.

Rifkin, J. (1995) *The End of Work: The Decline of the Global Labor Force and the Dawn of the Post-Market Era*. New York: Putnam's Sons.

Robinson, Ian. (1995) "Globalization and Democracy." *Dissent* (Summer): 373–380.

Roberts, Kenneth M. (115) "Neoliberalism And The Transformation of Populism in Latin America: The Peruvian Case." *World Politics*, 48 (October): 82–116.

Rohwedder, Cacilie. (1996) "East Germans Dependent on Job Subsidy Find Bonn's Budget a Bitter Pill." *The Wall Street Journal*, September 24: A18.

Roth, T. (1996) "Europeans Are Moving to Overhaul Welfare." *The Wall Street Journal*, June 3: 1A.

Ruggiero, Vincenzo and South, Nigel. (1995) *Eurodrugs: Drug Use, Markets and Trafficking in Europe*. London: UCL Press.

Rusche, Georg. (1978) "Labor Market and Penal Sanction." *Crime and Social Justice*, 10: 2–8.

Rusche, Georg and Otto Kirchheimer. (1968) *Punishment and Social Structure*. New York: Russell & Russell.

Sabol, W.J. (1989) "The Dynamics of Unemployment and Imprisonment in England and Wales, 1946–1985." *Journal of Quantitative Criminology*, 5(2): 147–68.

Salvatore, Ricardo D. and Aguirre, Carlos. (eds.) (1996) *The Birth of the Penitentiary in Latin America: Essays on Criminology, Prison Reform, and Social Control, 1830–1940*. Austin: University of Texas Press.

Savelsberg, Joachim. (1995) "Crime, Inequality, and Justice in Eastern Europe: Anomie, Domination, and Revolutionary Change." Chapter 9 in J. Hagan and R.D. Peterson (eds.) *Crime and Inequality*. Stanford: Stanford University Press, 206–224.

Schemo, Diana Jean. (1996a) "Populist's Victory in Ecuador Worries the Elite." *The New York Times*, July 22: A5.

————. (1996b) "Oil Companies Buy an Army To Tame Colombia's Rebels." *The New York Times*, August 22: 1.

————. (1996c) "Jail Killings In Venezuela Reveal Fight For Power." *The New York Times*, October 27: 4.

————. (1997) "Ecuador Chief, the Populist, Is Anything but Popular." *The New York Times*, January 11: 4.

Schwartz, Benjamin. (1995) "American Inequality: Its History and Scary Future." *The New York Times*, December 19: 23.

Shank, Gregory and Dod, Suzie. (1987) "Overview of the Issue," in *Social Justice* Special Issue: Latin American Perspectives on Crime and Social Justice, No. 30, i–xxi.

Sims, Calvin. (1996a) "Prosperity in New Chile Nourishes Drug Trade." *The New York Times*, March 27: A9.

————. (1996b) "Blasts Propel Peru's Rebels From Defunct To Dangerous." *The New York Times*, Aug. 5: A6.

————. (1996c) "Peru's Economic Plan Brings Growth but Leaves Poor Behind." *The New York Times*, December 29: 6A.

Skidelsky, Robert. (1995) *The Road from Serfdom: The Economic and Political Consequences of the End of Communism*. Allen Lane: The Penguin Press.

Smith, Craig. (1996) "China Expects GDP To Expand 10.5% Over Coming Year." *The Wall Street Journal*, December 31: 4A.

Stewart, James B. (1996), *African Americans and Post-Industrial Labor Markets*. New Brunswick, New Jersey: Transaction Books.

Szelenyi, Szonja, Szelenyi, Ivan and Poster, Winifred R. (1996) "Interests and Symbols in Post-Communist Political Culture: The

Case of Hungary." *American Sociological Review*, 61 (June): 466–477.

Tanzer, Michael. (1995) "Globalizing the Economy: The Influence of the International Monetary Fund and the World Bank." *Monthly Review*, 47(4): 1–15.

Teeters, Negley K. (1944) *World Penal Systems*. Philadelphia: University of Pennsylvania Press.

————. (1946) *Penology From Panama to Cape Horn*. Philadelphia: University of Pennsylvania Press.

Thernstrom, Stephen. (1964) *Poverty and Progress: Social Mobility in a Nineteenth Century City*. Cambridge, Massachusetts: Harvard University Press.

Tyler, Patrick E. (1995a) "China Battles a Spreading Scourge of Illicit Drugs." *The New York Times*, November 15: A1.

————. (1995b) "Heroin Influx Ignites a Growing AIDS Epidemic in China." *The New York Times*, November 28: A3.

————. (1996b) "Crime (and Punishment) Rages Anew in China." *The New York Times*, July 11: A1.

United Nations Development Programme (UNDP). (1996) *Human Development Report 1996*. New York: Oxford University Press.

Vagg, J. (1993) "Context and Linkage: Research and 'International-ism' in Criminology." *British Journal of Criminology*, 33, 4: 541–553.

Vergara, Pilar. (1996) "The Pursuit of 'Growth with Equity': The Limits of Chile's Free-Market Social Reforms." in *NACLA Report on the Americas* (May–June), PeaceNet <peacenet-info@igc.apc.org>

Waldman, Peter. (1996) "The Philippines Shows Democracy Isn't Bar to Fast Growth in Asia." *The Wall Street Journal*, October 4: 1A.

Wallace, D. (1981) "The Political Economy of Incarceration Trends in Late U.S. Capitalism: 1971–1977." *Insurgent Sociologist*, 10: 59–66.

Walters, William. (1996) "The Demise of Unemployment?" *Politics & Society*, 24(3) (September): 197–219.

Walmsley, R. (1995) "Developments in the Prison Systems of Central and Eastern Europe." The European Institute for Crime Prevention and Control. Helsinki: HEUNI Paper No. 4.

Weiss, Robert P. (1987) "The Reappearance of the Ideal Factory: The Entrepreneur and Social Control in the Contemporary Prison," in John Lowman, Robert J. Menzies, and T.S. Palys (eds.) *Transcarceration: Essays in the Sociology of Social Control.* Aldershot, England: Gower.

————. (1987) "Humanitarianism, Labour Exploitation, or Social Control? A Critical Survey of Theory and Research on the Origin and Development of Prisons." *Social History*, 12: 331–350.

————. (1989) "Private Prisons and the State" in R. Matthews (ed.) *Privatizing Criminal Justice*. London: Sage.

————. (1995) "Prisoner Higher Education and the American Dream: The case of INSIGHT, INC," in Howard S. Davidson (ed.) *Schooling in a "Total Institution: Critical Perspectives on Prison Education.* Westport, Connecticut: Bergin & Garvey.

Wells, Ken. (1996) "South Africa's Economic Changes Begin To Bear Fruit, Deputy President Says." *The Wall Street Journal*, September 25: A18.

Wilkins, L.T. and K. Pease. (1987) "Public Demand for Punishment." *International Journal of Sociology and Social Policy*, 7(3): 16–29.

Wilterdink, Nico. (1995) "Increasing Income Inequality and Wealth Concentration in the Prosperous Societies of the West." *Studies in Comparative International Development*, (Fall) 30(3): 3–23.

Wilson, William J. (1996) *When Work Disappears: The World of the New Urban Poor.* New York: Knopf.

Wolff, Edward N. (1995) "How The Pie Is Sliced: America's Growing Concentration of Wealth." *American Prospect*, 22 (Summer): 58–64.

WuDunn, Sheryl. (1996) "Japan's Jails Are Regimented, But Safe." *The New York Times*, July 8: A3.

Wysocki, Jr., B. (1996) "Missing in Action: About a Million Men Have Left Work Force In the Past Year or So." *The Wall Street Journal*, June 12: 1A.

Young, W. and Brown, M. (1993) "Cross-national Comparisons of Imprisonment." In *Crime and Justice: A Review of Research*, M. Tonry (ed.). Vol. 17, 1–49.

INDEX